T0313845

THE OPEN SEA

FRONTISPIECE. Dog mosaic recently discovered at Alexandria. Copyright © Bibliotheca Alexandrina Antiquities Museum/Photo by Mohamed Aly

THE
OPEN
SEA

The Economic Life of the Ancient Mediterranean World from the Iron Age to the Rise of Rome

J. G. MANNING

PRINCETON UNIVERSITY PRESS
PRINCETON AND OXFORD

Published by Princeton University Press
41 William Street, Princeton, New Jersey 08540

In the United Kingdom: Princeton University Press
6 Oxford Street, Woodstock, Oxfordshire OX20 1TR

press.princeton.edu

Jacket illustrations courtesy of Adobe Stock (Juulijs)

Jacket design by Chris Ferrante

Library of Congress Control Number 2017954509
ISBN 978-0-691-15174-8

British Library Cataloging-in-Publication Data is available

This book has been composed in Garamond Premier Pro

Printed on acid-free paper. ∞

Printed in the United States of America

1 3 5 7 9 10 8 6 4 2

In memory
of
Karl W. Butzer
(1934–2016)
&
Mark Pagani
(1960–2016)

CONTENTS

ILLUSTRATIONS

MAPS

FIGURES

TABLES

PREFACE

A FEW YEARS AGO, I began to think about writing a "small book on a large subject," to quote one of the great economists of the 20th century.[1] The end result is larger and a little different than I had originally thought, but I have managed, I think, to write a reasonably sized volume on what is now a gigantic topic. It surveys, and I emphasize surveys, the major economic systems of the first-millennium BCE Mediterranean world from the beginning of the Iron Age down to the end of the Second Punic War (ca. 201 BCE), when a shift in political and military power marked the beginning of the process of Roman domination of the entire Mediterranean basin. I am taking on a larger scale of analysis, roughly eight hundred years of complex history, which is not the norm, and many historians might quibble about the lack of detail. For some topics such as household management I go even further back to illustrate some of the important structural continuities. The "meso-scale" that eight hundred years provide brings the many subspecialties of ancient history to the same table to ask: How can we understand the great changes seen throughout the Mediterranean world in these centuries? Moses Finley's influential book *The Ancient Economy* (1973), built a model for classical economies covering fifteen hundred years, from the beginning of Greek civilization to the end of the Roman Empire.

I, in contrast, do not tell a single story in these pages. Rather, I want to interweave several different stories that lead up to the unification of the Mediterranean under Rome. While Finley's temporal scale was about right, he left out altogether the early Iron Age expansion, western Asia, Egypt, and the Hellenistic period in general. The first millennium BCE was a transformational period in the economic history of the Mediterranean world. There was no "capitalist takeoff," as Finley would have been quick to assert.[2] But to view ancient economies from this perspective is to anticipate the Industrial Revolution. Instead what I am interested in here is the economic world before Rome, the achievements of these civilizations, how problems were solved, and the ways in which cross-cultural exchange deeply affected economic change.

I have two main aims. The first is to explore recent developments and trends in the study of first-millennium BCE Mediterranean economies. Secondly, while comprehensive coverage would be sheer folly, I hope that this book provides a broad account and an introduction to the material of the lived human experience in the Mediterranean basin in those centuries. I cannot hope to pursue all the themes or topics treated here as thoroughly as

I would like, and I place some emphasis on Egypt, the Near East, and the eastern half of the sea. Each of my chapters requires book-length treatment by a team of specialists. What I want to do instead is to give the reader a sense of how exciting the study of premodern economies is at the moment, and what I think will be some of the important ideas to pursue in the years ahead.

At the heart of this book is an effort to understand economic development during the first millennium BCE, a period of momentous political, economic, and social change in many parts of the world. I depart from most prior work on premodern economies by understanding Iron Age Mediterranean civilizations not as separate but as interconnected cultural entities within particular environmental and geographic niches. The economics literature that explains how and why institutions matter is now enormous. What premodern history contributes to it is to show how institutions are historically contingent and culturally determined. Climatic change and human adaptation to it, migration, demography, and cross-cultural exchange patterns were all important factors in moving societies, and in shifting political equilibriums. The cultural and temporal boundaries usually drawn between the civilizations of the ancient Near East and the classical world have been too sharply drawn at times This reification of the "classical," "ancient Near East," and "Egyptian" worlds has obscured cross-cultural exchange within what was the large region of western Asia/eastern Mediterranean, the "western core."[3]

The conflation of "ancient" with "classical civilization" ipso facto misses much in terms of longer-run development, interaction, and change. To be sure, the differential impacts of climate change, and the strong rainfall/irrigation gradient between core Mediterranean territories and the Nile and Tigris/Euphrates River valleys played important roles in developmental pathways. Yet a broader Iron Age perspective modifies our understanding of institutional change and also sets in better relief the achievements of the "Greco-Roman" world. Rome did end up dominating the Mediterranean by similar processes that led to the later European divergence because of its more rapid evolution in adaptive competitiveness and in military technology, something Herodotus also noted for the Greeks.[4] But we must view these competitive advantages within a longer "Iron Age economics" perspective. The "minidivergence" in the first millennium BCE can be explained by the combination of military and fiscal innovation of the Greeks and, later, the Romans. But there were other important factors, including resource endowments (e.g., silver, noted by Xenophon writing in the 4th century BCE as a "gift of divine providence" to the Greeks) and environmental differences (irrigation versus dry farming), that played a role.[5]

The competitive advantages imply two-way feedback mechanisms, and I argue throughout, therefore, that we must understand premodern societies as complex adaptive systems with positive and negative feedbacks. A consideration of the coevolution of "natural and human processes via an array of positive and negative feedback loops" is something that has up to now been almost entirely absent in the study of premodern economies.[6] We can see feedback mechanisms, for example, operate in the development of democratic institutions, in the scaling up of large empires, and in societal responses to climatic changes.[7] Periods of economic expansion were driven not purely by politics but by a combination of factors that include favorable climatic conditions, population growth, and institutions among which are legal institutions that protected property rights. Above all else, I argue for an evolutionary adaptive framework for understanding first-millennium BCE economies. This was a period when political and market integration grew stronger, and many important economic ideas (coinage, legal codes) spread far and wide.[8] Military power and empire building were crucial factors in political change, but many other things must be brought in to understand economic performance. One of my interests, then, is to highlight the constraints as well as the enabling conditions in premodern economies imposed both by institutions and by environments that account for differences in performance.

The study of premodern economies has become a very large and very exciting field in the last forty years, as my bibliography, concentrating in works in English and by no means comprehensive, attests.[9] But the discussion has been dominated by studies of the Greek and Roman imperial economies. Indeed quite often "ancient Mediterranean" stands in for "Roman," and all too often "ancient economy" is simply a cipher for the early European economy.[10] In recent years, however, studies of ancient Egyptian and ancient Near Eastern economies have been catching up and are producing different understandings of the relationship between the Near East, Egypt, and classical economies. We can see much more clearly now that cross-cultural exchange was a vital part of Mediterranean economies throughout the first millennium BCE. Global history has become popular. Comparisons with early Chinese history are becoming more common. So too is the study of long-distance trade and the origins of the silk roads traffic especially.[11] Work on New World societies can provide entirely new perspectives on Mediterranean economies. We need not focus, for example, just on price-setting markets. The Aztec economy, "without wage labor, private property, formal currencies, credit and lending institutions, and efficient forms of transportation," was "among the most sophisticated market systems ever to appear in the ancient world."[12]

That leads me to suggest that an open and interactive Mediterranean in which humans made connections, not only from point to point within the sea but also between the sea and a wide catchment in Eurasia, is the best framework for the first millennium BCE. It is this that made Eurasia the "most active" region in world history.[13] Open means not necessarily "connected" and not necessarily "fragmented," two key themes in recent work on the premodern Mediterranean as I discuss in chapter 3, but open in the sense of a historically contingent "shared" world, as Molly Greene has described the early modern Mediterranean.[14] Several forces drove cultural and economic exchange, and in the first millennium BCE we must treat the northern Mediterranean as politically and economically linked to western Asia, North Africa, and Egypt.

There is a second sense of the word "open" that I want to pursue in this book, and that is in the sense that future research in premodern economies will of necessity have to be more open, more permeable across many different academic enterprises. Not just in humanistic fields where the boundaries are mainly ancient languages, but embracing the full array of the social sciences, and the physical and biological sciences as well. Karl Butzer's plea for true interdisciplinary work between humanists and social, natural, and physical scientists should be the guiding principle, and I join Robert McCormick Adams in saying let "the boundaries dissolve."[15] By "interdisciplinary" I do not mean that classicists and Near Eastern scholars should have pleasant conversations with each other over coffee (although that is perfectly fine). Rather, I suggest that we should think about research the way biologists think about *convergence*.[16] Historians must pay much better attention to archaeology, and specialized teams should be built around solving particular problems. The study of ancient societies now requires not only philological and close reading skills, but wide reading in archaeological and scientific fields as well. Premodern historians should now read *Nature*, *Science*, and *Cell* as well as the standard historical and social science journals. Cultural evolutionary theory, genetics, paleobiology, and paleoclimatology are just four among a large number of scientific fields that will play important roles in understanding historical change in the premodern world.[17] Building more complex models of human behavior and identifying causal relationships in feedback loops demand that historians understand the potential contributions of the social, biological, and physical sciences. Not all historians will accept the idea that we should be aware of work in the biological or geophysical sciences, but if progress is going to made it is something that I believe we must do. The implication is that at least some of our work should be organized in flexible teams around answering questions and solving problems, rather than continuing to labor alone in our studies.

Since "history is a stimulus to the economic imagination," premodern economies provide rich and important information about how human societies were organized in the past and how problems were solved. Most importantly, the study of premodern economic behavior serves as a laboratory for understanding institutional change.[18] A broad and deep understanding of premodern economies is, therefore, an important, and an often ignored, part of understanding our own world. But history is nonlinear, and it was not a steady, progressive march from antiquity to the Industrial Revolution. What we can do with ancient material, though, is to understand historical processes over the long run. *All three* words in the phrase "the ancient economy" are problematic. There was no such thing as *the* ancient economy; the word *ancient* is too vague in terms of time and location, and the word *economy* carries with it many modern assumptions, and theory, that cannot simply be applied to phenomena of the ancient world not least because of the overlapping networks of social power that make it impossible to isolate economic behavior and institutions from religious, military, and political ones.[19] Indeed it is also not possible to isolate economic behavior as a separate sphere of human activity in the contemporary world either. Here ancient history might inform the contemporary world.

I bring several assumptions to this book. These include the following: (1) a broad study of ancient economic structures and institutions is important to the wider field of economic history; (2) we need not worry about Ranke's urge to tell "how it really was." Our main task should be to explain not only change over time but also persistence, or continuity, in institutions; (3) we must move well beyond ontological debates. To do that we need an evolutionary framework on larger timescales in which to understand short-term change; and (4) the heterogeneous and fragmentary nature of our sources demands a broad theoretical framework in which to understand change and continuity.[20] Explaining change is what historians do best, but this can be lost under the imposed burden of "legalistic" evidence collection, language specialization, and the tendency toward elegant prose narratives or unitary focus on narrow corpuses of material.[21] History matters; so does economic analysis, and so does culture. These need not nor should not be mutually exclusive, although cultural history, a dominant framework in classics, can obscure objective facts.[22] Evidence derived from many fields, including natural sciences, but also the core disciplines of philology, paleography, archaeology, and numismatics, must be sorted and analyzed together.

A somewhat unusual academic background informs my general approach to the premodern world. Three things have influenced me greatly. The first was a summer I spent in Kampsville, Illinois, while I was in high school. This very small river town was the hub of major regional excavations throughout the Illinois River valley, coordinated by the Center for American Archaeology and its summer school directed by Stuart Streuver and his team of "New Archeologists" (that was the preferred spelling at the time) who were rewriting the early history of indigenous populations in the Mississippi and Illinois River valleys.[23] You could feel their excitement every day. I still remember the small car ferry that took you across the Illinois River to this tiny town (population in 2010: 328) teeming with scientific inquiry, and to this day I get goose bumps every time I cross the Mississippi just to the north of that ferry and look at the mighty river, and the smoky vistas of green Illinois farmland stretching out as far as the eye can see.

I worked on a small seasonal occupation site dated to the Early Woodland Period, ca. 200 BCE (ironically the date that is a focus of my research and also the terminus for this book), and, at night, in the Soil Resistivity Survey lab. George Beadle gave a memorable lecture on the crop genetics of maize to a packed hall one hot and humid evening. I learned so much that summer about how science was contributing in various ways to reconstructing the past. I became a materialist that summer, something, I confess, that I have not shaken. I almost became a New World archaeologist but decided to pursue a childhood interest in Egyptology after college. I did my graduate training at the Oriental Institute in the University of Chicago. It was a rigorous degree, with emphasis on the historical linguistics of the Egyptian language and the reading of the various cursive scripts. It was an unabashedly traditional, formal, and long training. In my first week of graduate school I read Karl Butzer's *Early Hydraulic Civilization in Egypt*. It left an indelible impression on me. In fact I still remember the night on the fifth floor of the Regenstein Library when I first read it. My very first seminar at Chicago, in the spring and in considerable contrast to the language training, was offered by Arnaldo Momigliano (one of his last I think) and Lawrence Stager, entitled Economic and Religious Models of the Ancient World. The seminar was filled with advanced students and faculty, and, if I remember correctly, there were two of us first-year graduate students—who did not know exactly what we had signed up for!— taking the course for credit. I did not know what a "model" was, or how I was supposed to put together a coherent paper—how did I go from textual sources to a model? Or was it the other way around? The crowded seminar room was abuzz each week, energized with ideas, differing perspectives, and a few bitter disagreements. The course, as with Butzer's work, made an enormous impact on me, and in ways that I only much later understood.[24]

I gradually turned with a good deal of fascination to the later phases of Egypt's ancient history and to demotic Egyptian documentary papyri in particular. There was a strong future there, I thought, and they contained utterly fascinating data about individuals and families like nowhere else in the ancient world. After my fourth-year comprehensive PhD qualifying exams, which I somehow survived, I had an opportunity to go to Cambridge University arranged by John Ray, an extraordinary scholar of demotic Egyptian and a fellow at Selwyn College, and I jumped at it. I arrived two weeks after the death of Moses Finley. There I had the good fortune, indeed the privilege, of sitting in on seminars on the ancient economy by Keith Hopkins and Peter Garnsey, and on Greek law with Paul Cartledge. I worked with John Ray on demotic texts, and with Dorothy Thompson. With her I read through the first half of a large corpus of Ptolemaic Greek documents from the impressive *Urkunden der Ptolemäerzeit*, volume 1, at a time when she was working on what would become *Memphis under the Ptolemies*, now out in a second edition. I still have the notes I took. I also audited a wonderful course on the Greek of the book of Galatians at the Divinity School. I had the wondrous good fortune to meet an energetic group of advanced graduate students and young junior fellows. Talking to them regularly I soon realized, mainly sitting in a college pub after a stimulating seminar, that I was at the center of cutting-edge work in ancient history. The conversations were sophisticated, comparative, and broad. I discovered that first-millennium B C E Egypt could be similarly situated. My eyes were opened to a new world of possibilities that year.

The more I read, the more I was struck by the fact that Egypt had often been and still is left out of general discussions about ancient economies. But how, I wondered, could a civilization whose language was spoken for two-thirds of recorded human history and cast such a shadow over the eastern Mediterranean be left out? How could I bring the exciting later Egyptian material into dialogue with other regions? Linguistic boundaries tend to define academic disciplines in the humanities: classics, Egyptology, Assyriology, early China, and so on are each dedicated to one set of languages and scripts. This virtually guarantees that treatments of economic phenomena are written from endogenous points of view of textual and archaeological material, and from a particular place and time. It tends to produce narrow and truncated kinds of histories and can miss the larger forces of cross-cultural interaction, the impact of climatic change across larger geographic space, the diffusion of technological change, and so on.

I have had the benefit of superb colleagues at Stanford, from each of whom I have learned a good deal. There were very stimulating series of workshops, seminars, and conferences sponsored or cosponsored by Steve Haber's Social Science History Institute initiative in the 2000s. I sat in on more economics workshops and seminars than I can count and had the good fortune to audit a survey course on economic sociology taught by Mark Granovetter, and the History of American Law course taught by the doyen of that field, Lawrence Friedman at Stanford Law School. I got to know Douglass North very well, and Avner Greif, Barry Weingast and Gavin Wright too. My former ancient history colleagues Ian Morris, Josiah Ober, and Walter Scheidel have all shaped my work. I remain especially grateful to Morris. It was largely under his pen that we coauthored a short survey piece on the economic sociology of the ancient Mediterranean world that is the origin of some of my macro thinking about ancient history.[25] Ian and I hosted a meeting to which we invited not only specialists in various ancient societies but also social scientists, economists, economic historians, political scientists, and economic sociologists to respond to the specialized papers. We produced a small volume in 2005, paying homage to two of Moses Finley's books, wherein Morris and I tried to set out some sort of agenda, including the challenge of integrating, or at least discussing, the ancient Near East and Egypt in the context of broader treatments of "the ancient economy." I think we both had in the back of our minds the famous "City Invincible" meeting at Chicago in 1958 that brought such an impressively broad group of scholars around the table.[26] Morris's inspirational *Why the West Rules—for Now* (2010) is echoed throughout this book.

I moved to Yale in 2008, where I once again struck gold in the colleagues who surrounded me. My home base, as it were, is the very active economic history group, José Espin-Sanchez, Tim Guinnane, Naomi Lamoreaux, Noel Lenski, Francesca Trivellato, and the ancient history group, Noel Lenski, Andrew Johnston, and Jessica Lamont, wonderful colleagues all, and all of them were gracious enough at various points to offer suggestions or to read my work and critique what I had said, or had failed to say. I must also thank my friend and colleague Harvey Weiss, for teaching me much about paleoclimatology, and Ray Bradley at U Mass–Amherst, for being extraordinarily helpful in this regard as well. I list other friends and colleagues who have provided material or criticism of earlier drafts in the acknowledgments. I have also learned an enormous amount from my friend Peter Turchin at the University of Connecticut, over our monthly dinners and by having the pleasure of working with the Seshat global history project team, several of whom have also been generous with their comments.[27]

At one point a few years ago, I thought that the study of ancient economies had reached a peak; research and writing was slowing down, and not much interesting was happening. So I thought. Then I taught an undergraduate survey course at Yale. Collecting some recent work around a few themes dramatically changed my mind. Not only was there much going on in the field, but things were moving forward, and coevolving with other disciplines in very exciting ways. The literature was in fact exploding with new material, new ideas, and new approaches. I soon realized that I could easily write a book just summarizing summaries of "the ancient economy" that have appeared only in the last decade or so, let alone the last four decades.

What I want to do instead is to give the reader a sense of what is happening, and where at least some future work will go. There are two specific areas that will shape future work in important ways. The first will be more detailed work in explaining change with dynamic models. I think that evolutionary theories are very promising here. Secondly, and reflecting my own interest at the moment, there will be a better understanding of how climate and climatic change triggered societal responses and constrained premodern Mediterranean societies.

To paraphrase Frederick Jackson Turner, the great historian of the American frontier, not only does each generation of historians write their own histories, but there are now, as never before, an enormous variety of modes of historical writing, from microhistory to global history, now very much in vogue.[28] So too with economic theory; each generation, or each economic crisis at least, from Adam Smith up to today, seems also to create its own theories and interpretations. "Mega" or "deep" histories that seek evolutionary perspectives on human history and on human institutions are popular at the moment, from the point of view of not only longer-term history but global history as well, and even the history of the entire cosmos.[29] Microhistorical approaches, often not stated as such and with only a passing reference to the very large literature or the debates in the field, are common.[30] They are the natural by-product of the kinds of archival evidence that has come down to us from the ancient world.[31] But there is often no way of knowing if a particular case study is representative.

We live in a complex, messy world. But the premodern, or preindustrial, world was also complex, and in some ways even more complex than the modern world. It was certainly no less messy.[32] Even though there were far fewer humans on the planet, it was also a more fragile world. Considering this, it is all the more remarkable that political equilibriums could be established across enormous and complex territory for centuries at a time. Social scientists tend to build models of the world against which data can be tested, and the models recursively improved. Humanities-oriented historians tend to revel in the complexity of the society and the sources they study. The two don't often meet.[33]

It is the premise of this book that understanding and taking account of the historical and cultural developments of the early first millennium BCE are a fundamentally important part in understanding the increasing Mediterranean-wide economic integration of the Mediterranean world during the Hellenistic and Roman periods (i.e., after ca. 300 BCE). That is to say, the long economic development of Mediterranean civilizations was driven by cross-cultural exchange, by the experience of empire formation, by heterogeneous institutional responses seen in local legal traditions, and by the use of money and coinage, of credit instruments, and of banks. This persistence of institutions must be understood in conjunction, of course, with new cultural features brought about by the movement of people, by migration, war, climate change, and by new opportunity. We should no longer be motivated by debates about whether ancient economies were "primitive" or "modern," or by narrow considerations of classical economies as being defined, over fifteen hundred years, just by elite status behavior. That approach reinforces the idea that premodern societies were static. Long timescales are indeed a crucial aspect of studying change. But equally important are broader accounts of cross-cultural exchange patterns of both goods and ideas. Even more important, I think, is to consider how premodern societies interacted with the natural world. This requires a coupled human-natural systems approach, which I explore in chapter 5.

I divide the book into two parts. In part 1, "History and Theory," I begin in the introduction by looking back at the debate about the nature of "the ancient economy" as it coevolved with the field of economics. Here Moses Finley's *The Ancient Economy* looms large, but it stands at the endpoint of a long fruitless debate, and the bulk of current work operates within very different frameworks. In chapter 1, I highlight some of the important themes and new directions that studies of premodern economies are taking. Chapter 2, "Ancient Economies: Taking Stock from Phoenician Traders to the Rise of the Roman Empire," provides a historical survey of first-millennium BCE history and a brief overview of our sources for understanding economies of the Mediterranean. In chapter 3, "Time, Space, and Geography and Ancient Mediterranean Economies," I turn to one of the most difficult aspects of studying ancient economies, what I call time/space boundary identification problems. In part 2, "Environment and Institutions," I turn to an examination of key institutions in the economies of the Mediterranean and discuss the coupled dynamics between environment and economic institutions and the evolutionary forces that drove institutional change. Agriculture and labor, the topic of chapter 4, form the basis of all premodern economies, and a brief comparative study contained here shows that there were a wide variety of institutional solutions in the organization of agricultural production. In large part these solutions depended on the heterogeneous environmental endowments and climatic conditions of the Mediterranean basin. I explore these conditions further in chapter 5, "The Boundaries of Premodern Economies: Ecology, Climate, and Climate Change." Here I discuss the relationship between the physical boundaries of the Mediterranean world, climate and climate change and demography and their relationship to political economies of the ancient world, and the role of climate change as a forcing mechanism of social change. I consider the chapter to be experimental, using preliminary data and making some suggestions. The topic will not appeal greatly to many historians, but I would plead that we are only beginning to understand climate change and human responses in ancient history, and that there is a lot of work to be done. Paleoclimate data is difficult and diffuse. The analysis of changes on the ground caused by climatic change on several scales is challenging to say the least, and the use of paleoclimate data requires quite a lot of reading and thinking in a new area for historians. Chapter 6 explores individuals and households as economic actors. I also discuss, briefly, demography, and the relationship between them and the "state," which had a great variety of sizes and political institutional solutions. Chapter 7, "The Evolution of Economic Thought in the Ancient World: Money, Law, and Legal Institutions," explores how changes in the concept of money and the legal order evolved with increasing cross-cultural exchange patterns. Chapter 8, the last substantive chapter, "Growth, Innovation, Markets, and Trade," discusses the key areas of ancient economies that have been both central to their understanding and have been, and continue to be, controversial and much debated. Each chapter is meant to be freestanding. There is, then, some overlap in coverage between the chapters.

ACKNOWLEDGMENTS

ONE OF THE GREATEST pleasures of a book-writing project is to thank those who have helped in some way. By doing so, one is also reminded, if one needs to be reminded, of the great friends and selfless colleagues who have read, critiqued, sent along forthcoming work, prodded, cajoled, soothed, or otherwise gave advice. I am very grateful to Gojko Barjamovic, Peter Bedford, Manfred Bietak, John Brooke, Alain Bresson, Ari Bryen, Bruce Campbell, Willy Clarysse, John Collins, Mark Depauw, Paul Erdkamp, Christelle Fischer-Bovet, Tim Guinnane, Kyle Harper, Eric Hilt, Phil Hoffman, Dan Hoyer, Alexander Jones, Michael Jursa, Jessica Lamont, Naomi Lamoreaux, Noel Lenski, Colin Macaffrey, Andrew Monson, Juan Carlos Moreno García, Graham Oliver, Karen Radner, Jared Rubin, David Skelly, Dorothy Thompson, Gary Tomlinson, Dan Tompkins, Matt Toohey, Francesca Trevellato, Peter Turchin, Katelijn Vandorpe, Koen Verboven, and Harvey Weiss. Craig John (International Mountain Guides), Scott Tribby (Ranfone Training Systems), and Avi Szapiro (Roia Restaurant) kept my body and soul together. François Gerardin and Andy Hogan, my two senior and very fine graduate students, have provided remarkable assistance and support all along. I'm looking forward to seeing how their careers unfold in the coming years.

I owe a special debt to my friend Francis Ludlow at Trinity College Dublin. It was a fateful evening a couple of years ago, over a third glass of wine after a Climate/History group dinner, when I asked if he knew of any climate data that could help my understanding of the connection between Nile river flow and social unrest in the Ptolemaic period. When he got out his enormous laptop, heavy with global climate data of every kind, and showed me ice-core data that was about to be published, the trajectory of my research changed in an instant. He has been incredibly helpful and generous in many ways, including offering me his skill at data representation that you will see in this book. He has been instrumental especially in chapter 5, and in helping me build a great team of climatological expertise. We have worked closely now for more than two years on very exciting work that seeks to integrate climate and human archives. I am also grateful to our partners in this project, Bill Boos, Jennifer Marlon, Michael Sigl, Jim Stagge, Zan Stine, and Trude Storelvmo.

Joe McConnell of the Desert Research Institute in Reno warmly welcomed me for a week into his home and his ice core research lab in Reno, Nevada. Working in his lab and learning about how climate data from ice cores are generated, from preparing the ice cores in the cold room to seeing the output from the inductively coupled plasma mass spectrometers, was a truly remarkable experience. I am grateful also to Monica Arienzo and Roger Kreidberg for teaching me much about their work and the incredible facilities at DRI.

Invitations by Taco Terpstra to speak in the Economic History Workshop at Northwestern University, by Christelle Fischer-Bovet of USC, by John Haldon at Princeton, and by Greg Woolf to speak in the Ancient History Seminar at University College London jointly with Frank Ludlow allowed me to test very preliminary work, and I thank audiences in these places for rigorous questions and good suggestions.

Two anonymous reviewers, the unsung heroes of academic publishing, gave me a great deal to reconsider. Both improved the final results in very important ways, and I am grateful for the care they took in reading and in commenting on an earlier, incomplete manuscript. I am also grateful to BG for editorial assistance.

Finally, it is a pleasure to thank once again Rob Tempio at Princeton University Press for much sage advice and guidance. Emily Bakemeier of the provost's office, and Tamar Gendler, the dean of the faculty of arts and sciences, have both been extraordinary in their support since I arrived at Yale, and it has made a big difference in my work. I am constantly reminded, by the support of the administration, and by my colleagues and the superb students, what a joy and privilege it is to teach at this wonderful place.

I dedicate this book to two great scholars, Karl Butzer, whose work greatly influenced me as a young graduate student, and Mark Pagani, who warmly welcomed me into his paleoclimate world and supported my work at Yale in various ways. His untimely passing was a serious blow to both Yale and the paleoclimate community.

Skaftafellsjökull, Iceland

CHRONOLOGY

SOUTHWEST ASIA

Neo-Assyrian Empire	934–610 BCE
Neo-Babylonian Empire	625–539 BCE
Achaemenid Empire	550–330 BCE
Seleukid Empire	312–63 BCE

EGYPT

Third Intermediate Period	1069–664 BCE (politically fragmented)
Saite dynasty	664–525 BCE (centralized state)
Achaemenid imperial control	525–359 BCE (imperial province)
	404–343 BCE (local control)
Achaemenid imperial control	343–332 BCE (imperial province)
Ptolemaic dynasty	332–30 BCE (centralized state)

PHOENICIA

Expansion	ca. 1200–800 BCE
Achaemenid conquest	539 BCE

GREECE

Archaic	8th century BCE–480 BCE
Classical	480–323 BCE
Hellenistic	323–146 BCE
Roman conquest	146 BCE

PART I

History
&
Theory

History, Theory, and Institutions

APPROACHING THE ANCIENT ECONOMY

> I said at the beginning that I would not be giving economic history a narrow interpretation. I hope that I have carried out that promise. I have tried to exhibit economic history, in the way that the great eighteenth-century writers did, as part of a social evolution much more widely considered.
>
> —HICKS (1969:167)

OFF THE COAST OF the small Mediterranean island of Antikythera in the spring of 1900, the year in which Arthur Evans was beginning to excavate the palace of Knossos on Crete and the Boxer Rebellion raged in China, sponge divers came across an ancient shipwreck at about fifty-meter depth. The ship was apparently a ship of booty, perhaps bound for Rome. Among the items pulled from the wreck, dated ca. 60 BCE, were bronze statues, hundreds of other ancient objects, including storage jars, lamps, jewelry, and a small, mysterious lump of metal. The booty is now housed at the National Archaeological Museum in Athens. Excavations continue. Recently, human skeletal remains were found on the wreck, a very promising discovery since DNA analysis might reveal much.[1]

At first not much was made of the mysterious clump of metal. But over the years, and now with modern photographic, x-ray, and computed tomography techniques, this mysterious object has gradually begun to reveal its secrets. This "clump" turns out to be an astonishing mechanical calendar. It shows us the brilliance of both scientific knowledge and manufacturing capability of the ancient Mediterranean world. Probably dating to the 2d century BCE, it also demonstrates a keen knowledge of differential gears and incorporates many centuries of astronomical observation. The device was probably used to synchronize lunar and solar cycles in a nineteen-year cycle known as the metonic cycle. The accumulated knowledge of astronomical cycles culled from centuries of observations shows the influence of Babylonian astronomy. As we now know, it is a sophisticated timepiece, capturing the motion of the moon, sun, and five of the planets in "epicyclic motion through the zodiac, perhaps used on astrological calculations, extremely popular in the Hellenistic period."[2] The device continues to catch people unaware of the sophistication of the ancient world. There is nothing comparable in Europe until the 15th century.[3]

I begin with the Antikythera mechanism because it is a good proxy to think about the "ancient economy." It is also a good case study of the nature of ancient evidence. The machine is a single item and without context. Was it common or unique? Who owned it? Who invented it? The last question, I think it is safe to say, can be answered. This machine was not "invented." Rather, it was very likely the product of centuries of knowledge creation born of deep cross-cultural interaction in the Mediterranean. The machine itself appears modern, but its social context tells us that it belongs to a different world. And that is the key problem in trying to understand economic behavior and describing ancient economic phenomena.

The Antikythera mechanism (figure 1), as it is usually called, is a highly sophisticated, well-engineered machine. Of course Swiss watchmakers would now be able to produce a better and smaller version of this (in fact Hublot, who also sponsors current work on the underwater archaeological site where the machine was discovered, has done so, with a price tag of a cool $272,000), but this is a case of imitation being a sincere form of flattery.[4] It stands among the best evidence we have that the Mediterranean world of the late first millennium BCE was more advanced than once thought. The mechanism solved a particular problem in a spectacular way. But it was unproductive, that is, it was not used to increase labor productivity, or to improve overall economic conditions. It was deployed, perhaps, to calculate the timing of religious festivals, or as a teaching device, and as a prestige item to display knowledge and wealth.[5] We can hardly call this machine, or the stunning dog mosaic recently discovered at Alexandria (frontispiece), or for that matter the Great Pyramid at Giza, built more than two millennia before the mosaic, or the civilizations that produced these, "primitive." This presented a paradox to scholars such as Marx, who was aware of the cultural achievements of Greece but yet thought of its economy as underdeveloped.[6] Of course all these things were made for the elite, in the latter two cases two of the most powerful rulers in antiquity. A good deal of work on the ancient world, of course, concerns elite behavior, consumption, and tastes, and that is not insignificant given elites' role in driving change (as well as keeping inefficient institutions in place). What about nonelites? Studying farmers, the vast majority of all premodern populations, nomadic peoples, and merchants, has always been much more challenging. But they have left their mark, and we have gotten much better at seeing them.

Why does any of this matter? Because understanding the structure of premodern economic behavior is an important window into ancient life more broadly. But it is also one of the main sources of debate about what we can and cannot know about the ancient world. Indeed scholars looking at precisely the same evidence can conclude radically different things about

FIGURE 1. The Antikythera mechanism. Courtesy of the German Archaeological Institute, Athens. DAI-Neg.-No. Photographer 1 D-DAI-ATH-Emile 827. Photo by Émile Seraf.

what the evidence means for economic behavior or performance. To say that understanding the "ancient economy" has been a "battleground" for a century is an understatement.[7] The battle lines have been drawn in binary opposition: either/or, primitivism/modernism, substantivism/formalism, pessimists/optimists, use-value/exchange-value, status/contract, rational/irrational, *oikos/polis* (household/city), private/public, market/non-market, classical/Near Eastern, West/East, ancient/modern, sort of like us/not like us at all.

This kind of manichean framing, as I will argue below, is too simplistic, and to reduce historical investigation to opposed pairs in order to make arguments, usually directed to the other camp, and almost always to score points, makes little sense. In the end, classifying premodern economies as one type or another leads to "debates about nothing."[8] This conceptual poverty in both thought and language belies the ancient Mediterranean world's richness, complexity, diversity, and development over four thousand years. Neither third-millennium BCE Sumeria nor the Roman Empire of Hadrian can be characterized as a world of hunter-gatherers or of Silicon Valley venture capitalists. The very real problem is how best to describe ancient economies and their institutions. Sensitivity to language was something that Max Weber (1864–1920) already suggested was a problem in analyzing economic institutions of the premodern world, and we would do well to pay better attention to the language we use to describe the social realities of this world.[9] Modern categories like "market" and "private property," even seemingly obvious ones like "democracy" and "authoritarian rule," must be thought through very carefully in their ancient contexts because there was considerable change over time and important regional and cultural differences in what "market" or "private property" entailed.[10] The real challenge, in my view, is to find the right "analytic narrative," combining deep knowledge of the society with the explanatory power of theory at different scales of analysis. It is a field I call *analytical humanities*, and I believe that there are rich opportunities to further develop this approach.[11]

Cultural differences, as Joel Mokyr has elegantly shown in his study of the Industrial Revolution, as well as structural ones, must always be in the front of one's mind when comparing premodern to modern economies.[12] Nevertheless, the shifts in scale, the pulses in populations, and the technological changes of the ancient world show human creativity and ingenuity at every turn. But these differences, on the other hand, and the vocabulary used to describe them, have driven the fierce debates about the overall nature of "the ancient economy" as well as the nature of specific institutions. Being aware that the premodern Mediterranean was substantially different from our own world, we must also fight against the risk, to quote Barry Kemp, of "unnecessarily isolating the past and impoverishing the discussion." Ancient economic institutions were not "static entities devoid of mechanisms of adjustment to changing circumstances."[13]

My aim in this book is to set premodern Mediterranean economies in their social and environmental context. The first millennium BCE was a transformational period in the premodern history of the Mediterranean. Karl Jaspers developed a theory that some societies developed entire new ways of thinking about the relationships between politics, religion, and philosophy in this period. Throughout Eurasia after the Bronze Age collapse, between roughly 1000 and 200 BCE, large complex empires emerged at the same time as the "microstate" world of the Greek city-states came into being. Whether one follows Jaspers's "Axial Age" theory as he laid it out or not, the first millennium BCE was certainly a period of major global transformation of both political structures and economies.[14] Not all first-millennium Mediterranean societies appeared to show the Axial Age move toward more egalitarianism, but all major state-based societies underwent economic transformation.[15]

The literature on every subject that I touch on here is enormous, and getting larger every day. As I write this sentence, I am certain that another book, and several articles, have appeared on a subject relating to some aspect of economic life in the ancient Mediterranean world.[16] While this book lacks comprehensive coverage, I hope what it does is to give the reader a sense of how large, how dynamic, how rich and varied, and how deeply interesting the study of ancient economies has become since the appearance of an important review of Moses Finley's *The Ancient Economy*.[17] Unlike most recent studies, I also hope that there is value in discussing Near Eastern and Egyptian developments together with classical economies during the first millennium BCE. The origins of the classical economies, I argue, lie deep in a heterogeneous past connected by cross-cultural exchange patterns. By widening the discussion we can begin to develop new ideas about how the interconnectedness and the institutional heterogeneity of the premodern Mediterranean world shaped later economic history.

This book, then, proposes a different way of thinking about premodern or preindustrial economies. Movement and mobility, through cross-cultural exchange, through trade networks, through migration and resettlement and nomadic contact with settled populations, were important drivers of change. Just to give two examples, the Greek colonization of southern Italy (called Magna Graecia, "Greater Greece") was an important force in the economic development of Italy. Greek migration into Egypt beginning in the 7th century BCE changed the institutional basis of the Ptolemaic dynasty in the 3d century BCE. In other words, the classical economies existed alongside of others and interacted with them.[18] For Moses Finley the "ancient economy" was, *au fond*, static. The central role of social status within the classical Greek (Athenian) and Roman economies was sufficient to explain the core of economic life for fifteen hundred years. Without denying the importance of social status within all premodern economies, there is much that Finley's emphasis on status disregarded, not the least of which is the amount of social change and the huge variety of lifeways in and outside of the classical world.

"*The* ancient economy" was established as a subject of study in the 19th century. It was reaffirmed and enshrined by Finley, according to whom "the ancient economy" was a single entity, with unifying "Greco-Roman" characteristics. Much recent work has concentrated on regional and local economies, trying to understand how they fit into larger geographic and cultural frameworks of exchange.[19]

This scholarly trend, seeking out specific, contingent, and local stories, suits the kinds of evidence that we generally have from the premodern Mediterranean world. There has been a trend in recent years to speak in plural terms, of ancient *economies* in other words, and to focus on analytical units beneath the level of the state, on "super-regions," or microregions, with an emphasis on the heterogeneity of institutions.[20] A reemphasis has been placed on the political economy of ancient states, and the variety of state types that existed in the ancient world. Scholars of Egypt and the ancient Near East have begun to enter debates on how these places fit into premodern Mediterranean economic history.

This heterogeneity now raises important issues about physical and temporal boundaries as well as comparisons to other ancient societies. Scholars of the classical Mediterranean world have in the past monopolized "ancient history" and the study of the "ancient economy." There are, however, other claims to the "ancient" world that cover human civilization from ca. 3100 BCE to the rise of Islam in the 7th century CE by other cultures too. Perhaps a better break would be to study all "organic" economies, that is, all economies that use land as the "source of food" and "all of the material products of use to man" up to the 16th century Dutch republic, "the first modern economy."[21] Pride of place, in the study of ancient economies, and of ancient history more generally, has been classical Roman history, and therefore the Roman economy has been dominant here, if for no other reason than it is a much larger and better-documented field than Greek economies outside of Athens. The Roman evidence is less disputed and more abundant. But over the last decade or two, other fields (e.g., among which are Assyriology, Egyptology, biblical studies) have made significant contributions and, importantly, have demonstrated just how diverse ancient economies were.[22]

This short list of other disciplines covers a lot of ground in "premodern" history, but as I will suggest throughout this book, it is not only wider views that are changing the study of premodern economies, but scientific fields that offer us entirely new kinds of archives that will be especially important for understanding performance. In recent years the physical and biological sciences have made vital contributions in genetics, osteology, soil sciences, hydrology, climate change, remote sensing techniques, and many more fields. A generation or two ago the careful reading and interpretation of texts dominated most areas of ancient studies. But now, the rapid advance of science provides critical information related to historic change and demands that historians work within multidisciplinary teams across many fields that did not exist forty years ago.[23]

THE "ANCIENT ECONOMY"

In the preface to his highly influential *The Ancient Economy*, Moses Finley began:

> The title of this volume is precise. Although change and variation are constant preoccupations, and there are many chronological indications, it is not a book one would call an 'economic history'."[24]

This overlooked passage is, at first sight, as startling as it is telling. Why would a book about "the ancient economy" not be a part of economic history? Because Finley, the most influential scholar of classical economies in the second half of the 20th century, and many who came after him, thought that one could not write about the premodern world's economic history in the same manner as one could about the 17th century Dutch or the 19th century German economies. A barrier between premodern economies and economies of the last five hundred years was created both by conceptual and analytical concerns. Conceptually, it was argued, the ancient world, broadly defined, did not have a separate "economic sphere," no conception of the economic, and no vocabulary by which to understand it. Economic activity was "embedded" in other social activity; there was little technical innovation, no concept of investment, and no sustained real economic growth.[25]

Analytically, Finley insisted, economics could be of no help for understanding the premodern world. He was following in the footsteps of Weber cited in the epigraph to chapter 2. Markets were much thinner, states dominated activity, especially from the point of view of war and taxation, and the two were intimately connected in the premodern world. Since the majority of people were primary agricultural producers who lived on the margins of subsistence, the behavior of elites and their concerns about status, and nonmarket activity—euergetism, gift-giving, and the economic activity of private associations—were more important.[26] To be sure, there were unique cases, such as Greek city-states like Athens. But in general terms, Finley's focus on elite representation in literary texts, it was argued, was enough to capture how ancient, that is classical, economies worked. No amount of archaeological data, or evidence of private economic activity recovered in the papyri from Egypt, on cuneiform tablets from Babylonia, or in coin hoards from Spain, altered the picture very much. Finley's general model of the "ancient world" neatly explained what needed to be explained.

While the study of ancient history has been a shifting set of disciplines, economics has likewise undergone much change in its orientation. Critiques about the moral basis of capitalism, and the behavior of capital markets, have been a major part of economics especially in light of the economic events of 2008–9.[27] Economics itself has evolved considerably, not just in the wake of the most recent global financial crisis, but over the last "three or more decades" during which "key assumptions of perfect rationality, equilibrium, diminishing returns, and of independent agents always facing well-defined problems are somehow not trustworthy, too restrictive, somehow forced."[28] Living in the post-2008 world, assumptions about markets and market behavior, and the role governments should play in regulation, has created something of a major intellectual reaction, most stridently against Friedrich Hayek and Milton Friedman, but more broadly against what economics could and could not explain. This has brought Polanyi's work back into fashion at least in so far as it might force some reconsideration of his work and along with it a reemphasis on the origins and function of markets.

The reification of economies along timeless "national" boundaries, for example, "the ancient Greek economy," the "ancient Near Eastern" or the "ancient Egyptian," economy, and so on, fosters static description of evidence and can give the impression that certain kinds of institutions such as property rights or markets were unique to that place. The same tendency exists in the study of ancient legal systems. Fritz Pringsheim, for example, wrote a compelling and important study called *The Greek Law of Sale* (1950). But it covered nearly a millennium of Greek language-based legal documentation from across the Mediterranean, from Greek city-states to Ptolemaic and Roman Egypt.[29] Such a compilation of law obscures significant social, cultural, and economic change. Were there differences, for example, between contracts written in the Greek language and contracts that were written in the light of Greek law? The closest thing to real unity in the premodern Mediterranean world were the economies of the Persian and Roman Empires. Before then there are many boundary issues caused by a misalignment between geography and historical sources, for example describing the "Greek economy" with evidence limited to a few sites. I discuss these problems in the next two chapters.

Fifth/fourth-century BCE Athenian and the Roman imperial evidence generally, has dominated discussion, both about the use of economic theory and of the nature of premodern economies, almost exclusively. The economies of Egypt and of the ancient Near East have been treated in isolation and have rarely been part of larger discussions of understanding ancient economic behavior or development. Things have begun to change, but still contributions by economists to ancient economic studies, and discussions of the theory of Polanyi and others, have barely mentioned economic evidence outside of these classical economies. In general the classical economies of Greece and Rome have been treated together, while Mesopotamia and Egypt have been treated apart and separate from these.

MOSES I. FINLEY (1912–86)

Moses I. Finley, born Moses Finkelstein, was a child prodigy, matriculating at Syracuse University at the age of twelve.[30] He took an MA degree in public law at Columbia and then proceeded, remarkably, to study ancient history without prior knowledge of either Greek of Latin.[31] As a graduate student at Columbia, he was involved in Polanyi's research project there. He wrote for the *Zeitschrift für Sozialforschung* during the 1940s and for the *Encyclopedia of Social Sciences*. He was a contributor to the Columbia seminar, taught at CUNY 1934–42, and during WWII worked in relief efforts.[32] He then taught at Rutgers 1948–52, got caught up in the postwar communist hysteria led by Joseph McCarthy that led to his refusal to cooperate with the McCarren Committee. Ironically Karl Wittfogel, a former communist, who had left Germany and eventually became professor of Chinese history at the University of Washington (1947–66), had befriended Finley. Wittfogel (figure 2) is most famous for his anticommunist jeremiad *Oriental Despotism: A Study in Total Power* in 1957, a major comparative study of irrigation or "hydraulic" societies, but less well known is the more personal side of his politics. In 1951 he reported on Finley's sympathies to the McCarran Committee.[33] Ancient history can be a brutal, bare-

FIGURE 2. Karl Wittfogel (1896–1988).

knuckled world; it's an important reminder that political ideologies are difficult to separate from interpretive frameworks.

He was expelled from Rutgers and worked in Polanyi's seminar for a year before leaving for England and a fellowship at Cambridge University. Finley went on to serve Cambridge with great distinction, becoming the professor of ancient history from 1970 until 1979 and master of Darwin College from 1976 to 1982.[34] Like Polanyi, Finley's views about the proper framework for ancient history evolved. At first Eduard Meyer and Michael Rostovtzeff's approaches were admired, but he later preferred Weber, Hasebroek, and Polanyi as his guides, and a more generalized social theoretical framework.[35]

His work continues to receive a great deal of attention and is still widely read and admired. He had an unusual career, but then so did so many of the great scholars of antiquity in the 20th century.

Like many great scholars, Finley's thought evolved.[36] Finley's own internal contradictions, and indeed this can be extended to others, suggests that one of the problems in summarizing his thought has been overbroad characterizations for the purposes of locating one's own intellectual stance.[37] His first major work was a publication of his PhD thesis on the *horoi* inscriptions, "Studies in Land and Credit in Ancient Athens, 500–200 BC," 1952, which shows that he could do very careful philological work.[38] As a thesis it was typical of the genre, a careful, text-based analysis of one type of text. It presents a very different style than his later general writing and critiques.[39] He gained much knowledge in the social sciences through his work on the encyclopedia and by writing reviews for the *Zeitschrift*.[40] He revived the "great debate" while taking head on the traditional approach of text-based historians in the tradition of Eduard Meyer. Meyer indeed comes in for

FIGURE 3. Moses I. Finley (1912–86).

some fierce polemic, as do other historians in Finley's jeremiads.[41] Over time,
Finley came to see the weaknesses of
Polanyi's paradigm for ancient economies and made a return to Weber's
historical approach and to economic
anthropology.[42]

In the spring semester of 1972 Finley gave the Sather lectures, a presti-
gious annual event and one of the
highest honors in the classics profession, hosted by the Department of Classics at the University of California, Berkeley. It was the culmination of his
career. In them, Finley presented a summary of his ideas that he had developed over twenty years in various lectures and publications. The book
made from these lectures, *The Ancient Economy*, appeared one year later in
1973. It contained the following chapters: "The Ancients and Their Economy," "Order and "Status" "Masters and Slaves," "Landlords and Peasants,"
"Town and Country" and "The State and the Economy." A quick glance
at these headings signals that social relations were the key analytical tools. It
is a masterpiece of rhetorical power and constraint, although he does occasionally take on a critic with some choice riposte, most explicitly in the section "Further Thoughts," which he published in the second edition (1984).
There is very little theory on overt display, although Finley was a master of
social theory, and the book remains justly famous as one of the most important books ever written, in any language, on the ancient economy.[43] It was
the culmination of many years of work that summarized his pioneering
work in the use of historical social sciences in understanding economic behavior and in attempting to steer a new course away from the "primitive-
modern" framework.[44]

Finley's foreword to *The Ancient Economy* that I mentioned above is
rather striking and signals the core of his argument. How could a book
about the ancient economy *not* be about economic history? The answer lay
in Finley's ideology and his intellectual debts to Polanyi, partially, and to
Weber more fully.[45] And one can trace it directly back to what Bücher, in his
response to Meyer, thought was his own careful distinction between economic history and economic theory.[46] There were historical facts, mattering
less to Bücher, although indeed he really was trying to account for a good
stretch of recorded history, and then there was general theorizing about
stages of political economic development.

Finley was less concerned with explaining change over time, wanting instead
to "characterize the ancient economy."[47] He offered a general model, not a

full accounting of the evidence. History and prehistory should be carefully distinguished, European civilization had a unique trajectory, the ancient Near East and Egypt were structurally very different from classical Athens or imperial Rome. Social relations, hierarchical power structures, the role of the scribe in the ancient Near East were important distinctions; large temple and palace dominated redistributive economies were also very different from the classical world at least after ca. 1000 BCE, while the Bronze Age Minoan and Mycenaean place economies were rather similar to those of the ancient Near East and Egypt in fact. The important point was that Finley was working in a tradition that was concerned with constructing a fuller European history. Most problematic is the fact that Finley did not treat the Hellenistic period at all. Arguably this was a period of very important institutional change, but it was also a time when the center had shifted east, to the Ptolemaic and Seleukid states. Following in Max Weber's "ideal types" characterizations, Finley argued that the dominant patterns in the classical Mediterranean world were private property, private trade, light soils and rainfall, all in contrast to the organization of economies in the eastern Mediterranean and in Egypt. Finley chose his book title carefully; for him the classical economies of Greece and Rome were a unity.

Although Finley saw the ancient economy as a unity, he was concerned narrowly only with classical Greek and (primarily) the Roman imperial economies. These economies were organized so differently, they represented a "certain *quality* of economic and social relationships, an economic type," to quote Shaw, who rightly urged caution in attacking Finley's model merely by demonstrating that intensification is documented here or there in the Mediterranean.[48] But for Finley, there was no concept of economy in ancient thought, so one could not study any ancient economy the way one studied 18th or 19th century European economies. Finley defended his view by forcefully defining "economy" in chapter 1 of *The Ancient Economy* by quoting Erich Roll:

> If, then, we regard the economic system as an enormous conglomeration of interdependent markets, the central problem in economic enquiry becomes the explanation of the exchanging process, or, more particularly, the explanation of the formation of price."[49]

There were no price-setting markets; no state had an "economic policy"; there was nothing resembling "economic thought" or an "investment" concept in the ancient world. Land was acquired only by "windfall" purchase, not through markets. He described what he argued was characteristic of ancient societies, and that was sufficient. Anything else, certain market transactions for example, were too infrequent to bring them into any general treatment. Following Hasebroek and Weber, social status was the key, and wealth was the means to the ends of establishing and maintaining it; the values of ancient society were a brake against developing markets; slavery, and the division between citizen and noncitizen, limited opportunities to develop labor markets especially; the idea of "profit" was thus marginal in classical societies.[50] It was an agrarian world, with little innovation in that sector. Trimalchio, the fictional character from the 1st century CE *The Satyricon* by Petronius, stood proxy for the whole sector—an absentee landlord concerned not with "investment" or improvement of the land but only with the wealth generated from the land in order to display this wealth in elaborate dinner parties with friends.

Finley argued in the book that there was an absence of economic thought, and no "policy" of governments toward the "economy" in antiquity, even in the most important treatises that survive, Xenophon, *Oeconomicus*, and Pseudo-Aristotle, *Oikonomika*, two of the key texts concerned with household and estate management.[51] There was very little improvement in technology, no "capitalist mentality," "from the Homeric world to Justinian great wealth was landed wealth."[52] A different framework in classical antiquity is suggested by the fact that "modern" economic terms such as labor, capital, investment, demand, utility, and so on had no equivalent in Greek or Latin.[53] This is the essence of Finley's ancient economy. The debate, ever since Finley's arguments about what counted as "economic," centered on market exchange, and the formation of price, or market exchange as the main mode of integration. Here clearly is the heritage of Weber and Polanyi; for Finley (and others) no "market-centered analysis" was possible.

There was rapid reaction to *The Ancient Economy*. One review pointed out Finley's Weberian framework in seeking to contrast the ancient world's lack of an economic "takeoff" with early modern Europe's rational, profit-seeking, merchant dominating urban life.[54] Finley's focus on the status concerns of classical societies focused on how elite attitudes (Cicero's Rome) shaped the rest of society. Frederiksen saw this as an "extreme" position.[55] One of the main problems is that Finley wanted to characterize his "ancient economy" as static, unchanging, and as a stage in the categorical way of the German Historical School.[56] A simple snapshot of republican Rome or 5th century BCE Athens was enough to characterize it. But his emphasis on a few literary representations for the whole of the classical world can hardly be enough. We miss the actual behavior of elites that is increasingly better known now. Trade was downplayed by Finley, but trade networks obviously moved freely across status boundaries, and land could in fact be acquired by market purchase. It is well documented in Hellenistic Egypt for example, and Frederiksen already provided examples for Rome.[57] The Roman agrarian writers come in for particularly harsh comments by Finley, suggesting that they were utterly devoid of anything like sound economic advice. But Frederiksen reminds us that we should understand Columella and other writers in their particular social milieu. They provided advice only to a few entrepreneurs rather than to the whole of the Roman farming world.[58]

Frederiksen's brilliant review set the tone for much subsequent work, including what I think are two core ideas: (1) that analysis of "the ancient economy" must be located between the "static traditional economy" and a "fluid market economy" and (2), that in describing material evidence, archaeological, literary or otherwise, it is critical to use accurate language.[59] "Freedom," for example, a concept Finley denied existed in the Near East, is in fact a well-attested word in ancient Near Eastern languages and meant precisely what Finley thought was a concept that existed only in the classical world.[60] The use of the term "redistributive" to describe the entire economic organization of western Asia before Alexander the Great does not do justice to what was a far more sophisticated economic world.

A major historical gap, as already pointed out by Frederiksen and many others since, is the absence of the Hellenistic world after 400 BCE in Finley's account. This period of Mediterranean history, whether we call it the "Axial Age" or not, is arguably a turning point in the economic history of Eurasia. New institutions—increased market exchange, increased use of coinage, and technological improvements, including military technology—characterized the age.[61] Fourth-century BCE developments in the Greek world spread throughout the eastern Mediterranean and beyond it with Alexander. Without Hellenstic history we cannot understand Rome.

But how do we explain the changes, the increase in market exchange everywhere, the growth of urban centers like Alexandria, the thousands of private contracts recovered from the sands of Egypt and Iraq? Finley dismissed the contradiction between primitive economy and a modernizing politics at Athens.[62] The main problem was language, and an ideological stance that juxtaposed underdeveloped economic institutions with "modernizing" democratic political ones.

Moses Finley's *The Ancient Economy* was an intellectual watershed in the treatment of the nature of the "ancient economy."[63] His model, in many circles, was declared the victor.[64] But in fact it marked an *end point*. The "modernist" position has lived on and indeed has come roaring back despite the wishful thinking that it had died a "natural death" and had been buried in an unmarked grave.[65] The cycling between the two poles of primitivism and modernism lives on in part because Finley's own intellectual progression accepted some aspects of the modernist argument regarding the rise of the Greek polis as laid out by Weber. Anthropological perspectives were recognized as helpful but not wholly adequate because they could not account for the differences even between Greek cities let alone economic behavior across the whole of premodern Eurasia.[66]

The "great debate" about the nature of "the ancient economy" was interesting to early theorists, for a while, but is no longer productive. Moving forward, it is of little use other than to marshal the odd battalion or two of straw men. The problem of the simple opposition primitive/modern was already clear in Weber's work, and the boundaries became quite blurred in Finley's views of the ancient economy.[67] Narrow specializations, a lack of new information, and the insistence that political economic structural differences between societies was sufficient to explain the economic history of the premodern Mediterranean world kept the debate frozen like an insect in amber. Finley's treatment was brilliant, but it no longer represents what is happening in the very dynamic world of scholarship on ancient economies. So much has changed, and exciting new roads to understanding the past beckon. That is the subject of the following chapter.

CHAPTER 1

New Directions and Broader Contexts in the Study of Premodern Economies

For fifteen years or so cliometricians have been explaining to their colleagues in history the wonderful usefulness of economics. It is time they began explaining to their colleagues in economics the wonderful usefulness of history. Wonderfully useful it is, a storehouse of economic facts tested by skepticism, a collection of experiments straining the power of economics in every direction, a fount of economic ideas, a guide to policy, and a school for social scientists. It is no accident that some of the best minds in economics value it highly. What a pity, then, that the rest have drifted away. Does the past have useful economics? Of course it does.

—DONALD MCCLOSKEY (1976:455)

History writing in the global era can only be a collaborative form of inquiry, whether between types of approaches or between scholars from different parts of the globe. We are not just interconnected but also interdependent.

—L. HUNT (2014:151)

THE "DEBATE" ABOUT ANCIENT economies that I mentioned in the introduction, as it has usually been set up in opposed pairs, was largely a fruitless endeavor. Better, indeed, if such debates had fostered a deeper "knowledge of the social world."[1] Even though a dialogue of sorts between historians and social scientists has existed for a century, it has too often been a "dialogue of the deaf," to borrow the famous phrase of the French historian Fernand Braudel, entwined in post–World War II debates about postcolonialism, or a matter of simply talking past each other. Debates still rage over the use of general models, many ancient historians prefer social detail in any case, and etic/emic distinctions still occupy economic anthropologists.[2] It is telling to realize that neither Marx, nor Weber, nor Adam Smith would have worked within, or would have been happy working in, a single academic department.[3] Even though cutting-edge scholarship has moved beyond all the ideas summarized in the introduction, not everyone will agree on how far beyond them we have gone, or should go. And much scholarship in ancient history, as in the humanities more broadly, tends to lag considerably behind. That is

not always bad, but it creates severe dissonance between historians, economists, and economic historians about the terms of analysis, what is at stake
in the analysis, and how best to do the analysis.

The analysis of premodern economies as a whole, or individual aspects of
economic behavior, demands a variety of approaches and, I suggest here, new
paradigms.[4] Contemporary social theories, the sophisticated heirs of Formalism and Substantivism, are still divided about the unit of analysis, the
individual, the household or society.[5] Any close reading of current work in
these traditions will show that there are many things in common; in particular both are concerned with networks, with the concept of the "bounded
rationality" of human action, and an emphasis on institutions, including
social norms. New Institutional Economics (NIE) has been influential, and
general models have been built around rationality and market integration.[6]
Where the written evidence is at its thickest, such approaches have been
popular. Unsurprisingly, then, focus has been on the Hellenistic period and
the Roman Empire. For earlier periods of Egyptian, Near Eastern, and
Greek history, cultural and descriptive approaches remain popular. The further back in time, the more that archaeological theories prevail.

A NEW ROAD TO THE PAST?

We can trace the rise of mathematical and game theoretic models and the
concern for policy implications as economics became more about mathematical "engineering." That can be traced back to Augustin Cournot (1801–77).
But it was Paul Samuelson's work in the 1940s that marked an important
watershed in the history of economics. His work moved the field from a
"predominantly verbal-graphical exposition to systematic and thorough
mathematical treatment."[7] Economics and history, fellow travelers earlier in
the 20th century, parted ways. Economics has rarely dealt with premodern
economics since the 1920s while economic historians have followed divergent paths depending on tastes, training, and the questions asked of their
material.

When cliometrics, with its emphasis on quantified statistical data, arose,
sparked by the use of the computer analysis of data sets, another debate
emerged between economists and traditionally trained political historians
used to dealing with early modern English documents as the main evidence.[8]
The "debate" took place between two prominent men, Robert Fogel, famous
as the coauthor of the quantitative study of American slavery *Time on the
Cross* (with Stanley Engerman, 1974), and G. R. Elton, the political historian
of the Tudor revolution. The main points were captured in two papers that
they produced together, responding to each other's ideas, and published as

Which Road to the Past (1983). The book highlighted the differences between social scientific history that seeks general laws of human behavior and traditional narrative that puts stress on individual human agency. While disagreeing on methodology, the two very different type of historians agreed on much, to the surprise of some no doubt. Where they agreed, importantly, was on how to make good historical interpretation of evidence. In a way, the debate between these two scholars in the 1980s echoed a famous debate known as the "Methodenstreit" ("Debate on Methods") between Austrian and German economists in the 1880s on the use of historical information to build economic theory. And like that debate, we need not chose sides.

A recent treatment of Greco-Roman economic history has called for three items that demand more attention: (1) documentation of economic performance, (2) the clarification of structure and performance, and (3) the comparative analysis of why the "Greco-Roman economy" broke down.[9] I would add that we need an even wider view of the economic history of the premodern Mediterranean than the "Greco-Roman" framework provides: one that breaks with a purely Mediterranean European spatiotemporal configuration, and that examines cross-cultural exchange and utilizes as a framework evolutionary theory to understand institutional change and the dynamics of various facets of economic performance. Rather than seeking to compare premodern economic institutions to later European institutions, we should concentrate on the intercomparison of premodern economic institutions.

Increasingly, approaches now insist on dynamic modeling, and this is one of the most important trends in the study of ancient economies. Models of one kind or another have been around for more than a century as we have seen, but we have much better conceptual tools now, and many different types of models have been deployed.[10] Evolutionary theory, for example, offers a powerful toolkit with which to understand technological change.[11] Increasingly the concept of complexity has been understood as an underlying driver of institutional change, and the emerging field known as complexity economics may help to explain historical dynamics of the ancient world.[12] Above all else, there is now greater concern for fitting ancient economies within longer-term historical trends.

As I write this, the English-language version of Thomas Piketty's book on inequality continues to make a splash and foster debate in both academic and public arenas. Discussions of the implications of income inequality is probably the single hottest topic of global conversation.[13] Among the many virtues of Piketty's book, the most immediate one is the case that Piketty makes for the important role of history in understanding the modern world. In certain ways his book was surprising because it represented a return of

economics to an older mode, or at least a kind of corrective to what economics had emphasized. Piketty moved away from neoclassical analysis, especially as it was practiced in the United States during the second half of the
20th century, and "tool-based engineering" solutions and instead embraced
a historical narrative that coupled literary references, novels, and travel diaries with historical data.[14] But in what ways history matters has been the
subject of considerable, and sometimes acerbic, debate in recent years.[15] Piketty's work intended to expand Kuznets's study on US income inequality
from 1913 to 1948 by using data from the last two hundred years. Premodern
data provides an even wider, and necessary, view of long-run institutional
change, economic performance, and a host of other issues including the history of inequality.[16]

Ancient history writing, since Mommsen, has always been engaged in the
modern world and in contemporary debates. Preindustrial economies generally have often been compared to later development, and linked to long-term
economic history to show the contrast in performance. Taking into account
time, institutional change, and *geospatial variability* is crucial. But a quick
glance at Gregory Clark's often-reproduced graph (figure 4) might suggest
that not too much interesting happened anywhere before 1800 CE. The Malthusian trap appears to have prevented the entire premodern world, everywhere, from improving living standards and social development.[17]

The premodern world, in other words, from an economist's point of view,
was uninteresting, or at least unimportant, because there was no real change
in living standards and very little growth in income. Nothing much economic happened that was worth notice. The Malthusian trap pulled back all
temporary gains in income. There was no real growth, no increase in living
standards, population growth was slow at best, if not static, and there was
little technological change.[18] The human dependence on "natural forces"
reached "escape velocity" only with the Industrial Revolution.[19] But that
is looking at world history from the modern end, and it also ignores the important fact that data is far more fragmentary for the entire left-hand half of
the graph.[20] That attitude that ignores premodern economies, deeply engrained
in some circles of economic history, is changing, and ancient historical case
studies are beginning to be incorporated into larger historical arguments
about growth and about institutions and institutional change.[21] Let me be
clear. Malthusian forces were strong in the premodern world. But they were
not uniformly so. "Malthusian constraint" was not "inevitable," and certain
places and periods of time in the premodern world saw real growth.[22] The
cultural and intellectual gains, and the incremental improvements in technology in the premodern Mediterranean world, are all the more impressive
against the very real constraints of the premodern world.

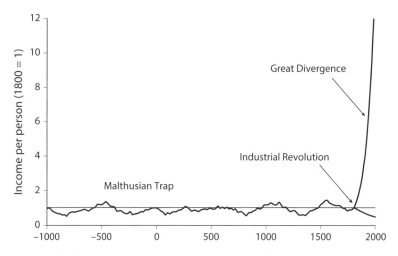

FIGURE 4. World economic history in one picture. From Clark (2007).

Assumptions about premodern economies has tended to prevent new understandings about their nature. By the early 1970s, the debate had been declared stale, or just about dead, with only occasional "post mortem spasms."[23] The "debate" was declared over in economic anthropology in the early 1970s, and in anthropology the "formalist/substantivist debate" was declared an "obstacle instead of inspiration."[24] A.H.M. Jones, in his collection of papers published between 1953 and 1970, devoted to the Roman economy, continued, in essence, a primitivist position.[25] This "debate" was framed in conceptual pairs and has been likened to a debate between a Buddhist monk and a Catholic priest about the nature of god.[26] Both sides were right, and both wrong in some measure. In large part, the theoretical discussions of ancient economies were always limited in range and in types of evidence. In broader surveys like Rostovtzeff's and Heichelheim's, theoretical orientations were altogether absent.

Twenty years after Moses Finley's landmark book was first published, several retrospective assessments were produced. In one, Morris reflected on the state of the study of the Athenian economy in a review of Edward Cohen's study of Athenian banking.[27] He was careful in distinguishing between primitivist/modernist and substantivist/formalist, and right to point out that conflating primitivist with substantivist positions leaves out the political agenda of the critique developed by Polanyi.[28] There have been many calls for changing the terms of the debate, for new approaches, for wider perspectives, and for the use of a fuller range of data.[29] Jongman's study of the economy of Pompeii, for example, was a major defense for the use of social scientific approaches to the study of the Roman economy, although such thoroughly social scientific, or neoclassical economic approaches to ancient economies are still rare among ancient historians.[30] In 1993 William Harris's wide-ranging state of the field of the Roman economy set an important agenda for describing and analyzing the Roman economy, and some cautionary guidelines, that have motivated, or provoked, Roman historians and economists for the last quarter century:

> For us, the point is to describe the nature and the dynamics of a system which was certainly not modern, but which is not for that reason to be thought of primitive, unsophisticated, crude, or small-scale.[31]

Andreau, writing in 1995, rightly questioned the "unity" of the ancient economy, suggesting instead that the emphasis should be on "detailed case studies," historical change, and comparison.[32] Morley suggests that a strong tendency in recent work has been to avoid the "great debate" altogether and instead to describe and to analyze an ancient society in its own terms, and, as one must, to describe economic behavior within a particular social context.[33]

Of course ancient trade cannot be studied as a modern economist would study international trade agreements. It must instead be analyzed in terms of social relationships and "social values" as well as trade flows.[34] John Davies has emphasized flow models, city typologies, theories of exchange, different genres of evidence, and heterogenous use of theories to frame or explain a particular body of evidence. He quite rightly insists that we need not focus only on a dominant type or pattern in what were complex social systems with an "extreme diversity of types of activity."[35] For the most part, though, debates about ancient economies have resolved themselves into two apparently new camps: the "optimists," in some cases even the exuberant, and the "pessimists."[36] But this division, traceable to Malthus and the various responses to his demographic theory, and the result of parametric framing of the evidence (the population of place X was between Y and Z), may keep us trapped in old debates.[37] Both "primitive" and modern" continue, however, to be refined and redefined as a means to locate an economy along a historical spectrum.

Richard Posner, for example, built a model of "primitive" or "archaic" society, including the societies reflected in Homer and the Old Testament, on the following assumptions: They had weak government (because of low literacy), the ascription of rights and duties was on the basis of family membership, gift-giving was the fundamental mode of exchange, there was strict liability for injuries, emphasis was on generosity and honor as ethical norms, and there was collective guilt in the community. All these are features of most primitive and archaic societies, and all derive ultimately from high information costs.[38] Social solidarity, cooperation, and insurance were key points, because there was no state to tax away surplus and redistribute to the hungry. He provided a score sheet of nonmarket and market-based exchange.[39] Clearly in Posner's survey of primitive and archaic societies there is economic behavior that can be analyzed in those terms. As with early systems of law, the structures of "archaic" societies were "rational responses" to conditions of uncertainty and high costs of information. This resulted in slow economic progress and slow population growth, a lack of privacy, and the prevention of wealth accumulation.

The so-called modernist position began to be developed at the same time as neoclassical economic theory, between 1875 and 1900.[40] Market-based analysis was usually viewed as the strongest, and clearest, expression of the "modernist" position.[41] Hellenistic economies, Rostovtzeff suggested, differed from modern economies only quantitatively, not qualitatively, despite Weber's views already clearly expressed in 1909 that ancient economies contrasted from modern ones both in quantity and in quality. Several scholars have recently advocated positions outside of the primitive-modern straightjacket, arguing that we ought instead to focus on "actual economic practices" in the ancient world.[42]

In more recent times a "modernist" position, reacting directly against Finley's views, is more often the orientation of scholars with a background in economics. This can be clearly seen in works by Edward Cohen, including *Athenian Economy and Society: A Banking Perspective*, Morris Silver's *Economic Structures of Antiquity*, Peter Temin's *The Roman Market Economy*, and Takashi Amemiya, *Economy and Economics of Ancient Greece*, just to give some recent examples in the English language.[43] But rather than criticizing this as simply more of the "modernist," neoclassical economics position, as some have, what has been emerging is a richer kind of economics.[44] The field has become a science of human behavior and is less focused on markets. Primitivism/modernism, substantivism/formalism can no longer describe the first millennium BCE. The substantivist position is "modern" in its assumption that in modern economies human behavior is fully rational and even "disembedded" from social relations.[45]

Ancient historians increasingly use the concepts of "modernity" and "modernizing" in other contexts. For the Greek historian Josiah Ober, to take a recent example, Thucydides was "modernizing," and indeed the 4th century BCE was a time of great social and economic change. So too for medievalists and paleontologists.[46] Modernity is not a specific time period indeed, as they argue, but a set of processes that existed in many places. If "modernity," then, is simply a break, a punctuation in time, a divide between this side and the other of a break, what is the relevance of studying premodern, or ancient, history? How is it connected in any way to "us"? How does history work, how much "contingency" can we allow? These questions are important aspects of explaining change over time of course. Giddens distinguished modernity from earlier epochs by its rapid change. This contrast between the rapid change of the last century from the slower, and uneven, change of antiquity is important. Even then, rates of change differed substantially across the ancient Mediterranean.

A notable feature in much of the earlier scholarship is the deep political engagement with the modern world. The field of ancient history is generally different today, less engaged politically with the modern world. Moses Finley, it appears, stood out among ancient historians of his generation, and most since, by stating that "value free and objective research" was an impossibility.[47] One senses now that a deeper engagement with the contemporary world is indeed reshaping scholarship in important ways.

Finley's book stood Janus-like looking back to the "great debate" that some had declared dead in that very same year, while synthesizing later developments in which his book was central. He summed up his views and advanced them by moving away from Polanyi's position while restating a modified substantivist position.[48] Morris was right to suggest that the debate, at least as it was couched so simplistically between "primitivist" and "modernist," "should really never have begun."[49] But it did sell a lot of books, and it occasionally packed a lecture room at an annual meeting. Finley's book was in a sense not only a monument in the study of the ancient economy, but also an endpoint of a long and often bitter debate that began in the middle of the 19th century.

The late 19th/early 20th century debate about the nature of ancient economy, though usually narrowly conceived, raised many issues. Among them was a boundary problem. Where should we draw the line between what counts as "economic" and the rest of society? Wilk and Cliggett illustrate the problem with the following story:

> Most people would have no problem calling it (scil. selling you a horse) an economic exchange if someone made a trade with you, giving you the horse in return for the right to cut some trees from your yard. But what if you got the horse in exchange for your sister's hand in marriage? Or if someone gave you the horse because he or she loved you? Or traded you a kiss for a promise? Where does the economic end and something else begin?[50]

If earlier theorists concentrated on markets and their impact on performance, modern economics has moved far beyond this narrow concern.

Economics is evolving extremely rapidly, embracing many new approaches; among the most important are behavioral economics, neuroeconomics, game theory, complexity theory, and cultural evolutionary theory, including multilevel selection theory, to explain institutional change.[51] Critiques of economics have accelerated after the 2008 crisis. But these tend to be focused on neoclassical analysis and on economic models applied to public policy. Increasingly, it is economic development and institutional change that must be explained.[52] Economics has moved far beyond analysis of markets.[53] For that, several fields are beginning to influence how we understand economic and institutional change over time. If anything, economic history has become more popular in the light of the financial crisis.[54]

It is fair to say that the interest among economists in history has been renewed since McCloskey's now classic paper pointed out the value of history to economics and to economists.[55] New trends include digital-data design and analysis, the use of GIS mapping technologies, a return to a deeper engagement with the role of culture in shaping societies, and an interest in the "Big Think" economic historical questions focused on explaining the wealth or poverty of nation-states, about income distribution, about the Industrial Revolution in Europe and "divergence," and the impact of colonialism on subsequent economic performance.[56]

Finley once suggested that "ideally, we should create a third discipline, the comparative study of literate, post-primitive (if I may), pre-capitalist, historical societies."[57] Note the struggle with categories and with language. Finley did not further develop this idea, but it was very much on the right track.[58] Indeed it is an echo of something Weber, at least privately, in notes written in the margin of a book by Menger, also felt, namely that economic theory could be developed for particular historical stages of human civilizations.[59]

It is a consensus now, especially when the ancient Near Eastern and Egyptian economies are brought into the discussion, that a simple stage theory from "primitive" to "modern" is too simplistic. The ancient Near East already in the third millennium BCE was far more sophisticated in its economic institutions than was thought. The economist Michael Hudson's group, International Scholars Conference on Ancient Near Eastern Economies, working in what is called "New Economic Archaeology," continue to analyze economies of the ancient Near East in the Polanyian tradition. Michael Mann's analysis of social power provides one way out of examining the nature of "embeddedness," the "four sources of social power" being to varying degrees in the premodern world overlapping and interested.[60] Economic power was never "disembedded" from the other sources of social power.

Disciplinary boundaries are being increasingly blurred across the academy. To understand and contextualize premodern economies, we need not only texts and philological analysis, but a large set of other disciplines in the social, physical, and biological sciences. What will be required in the years ahead is the creative joining of documentary evidence, including archaeological material, with more sophisticated contextualization. That will mean, too, that we must train students differently, and that we must work in teams.

There are three broad trends in recent work that are worth emphasizing.[61] All three emphasize the dynamics of social and institutional change. The three important trends are (1) the use of institutional and evolutionary theory, (2) the processing of new data, new texts, and new archaeological material, and (3) the integration of paleoclimate proxy data to understand the impact of human-natural systems feedbacks on economic performance on multiple scales.

Very often economic historians have tended to view the world through the lens of explaining real economic growth with the inflection point at the Industrial Revolution.[62] The role of markets has been a critical part of the story to be sure, but Mokyr's stress on the cultural context of early modern Europe, of the role of beliefs that laid the foundations for the revolution, is salutary.[63] In the preindustrial world, economic growth can be described by a flat line; after it, growth is a sharp rise up and to the right, producing the "hockey stick" of Clark's graph (and of world population since 10,000 BCE, figure 37). If sustained per capita, or real, economic growth is what matters, then history before 1800 teaches us little. Even at the height of the Roman Empire, with sophisticated legal and banking institutions, real growth amounted to no more than 0.1 percent per annum over the first two centuries CE.[64] But it seems to me that analyzing growth in a preindustrial, premodern context is less important than understanding institutional change generally.

There is more. Angus Maddison estimated that the per capita GDP in 14 CE, in 1990 US dollars, was, for the entire Roman Empire, $570.[65] But per capita GDP estimates like this do not tell us much. Even if you disagree with Maddison about the GDP per person estimates or the evenness of the distribution of wealth in the ancient world, there are good examples that show differences in income distribution in the ancient world; different political equilibriums produced different social structures and different economic outcomes.[66] There are other estimation problems as well, notably in population size and dynamics, despite a lot of good work on this in recent years.

World systems theory as developed by Immanuel Wallerstein, intended to explain the emergence of the modern capitalist system, has been transformed and applied by some scholars, notably Andre Gunder Frank and Christopher Chase-Dunn, among others, to premodern contexts, in particular in order to understand hegemonic power and "capital accumulation."[67] To be sure, linkages or connections between states in Eurasia were created by exchange networks, but equating a "world system" with interaction within a region without reference to scale or to quantification of "core" and "periphery" can be problematic depending on what one is analyzing.[68] Nevertheless, Shipley's work discussing the theory is useful in understanding what the new networks of trade and the "distance-related effects" were, and how to measure the "differential development at an interregional scale" for the late Bronze Age, and the Roman Empire.[69] The important relationship between Egypt and Rhodes comes to mind (see below). Hellenistic state formation, new centers of state (military) power, and the control of peripheral areas (e.g., contra Shipley 1993:283, Caria with respect to Egypt) certainly had implications for "core-periphery," if that is the proper way of thinking about the role of geography in this context, i.e., the extraction of resources over long distances.[70] Sherratt and Sherratt's new model of Bronze Age trade, not on the overall percentage of trade within an economy, but on the role of demand for high value goods, emphasizes the sophisticated societies of Bronze Age eastern Mediterranean and not merely their "agrarian" nature.

Another promising avenue of research is found in economic sociology, a branch of historical sociology, whose founding fathers were Durkheim and Weber, which has been "revived" since the 1980s with the work of Mark Granovetter among others.[71] The field is concerned with:

> The application of the frames of reference, variables, and explanatory models of sociology to that complex of activities which is concerned with the production, distribution, exchange, and consumption of scarce goods and services.[72]

Smelser and Swedberg add that social networks, gender, and cultural frameworks are all internalized to the field.[73] While both economics and sociology have traditionally concentrated work on modern nation-state market economies, both have strong historical components, and both rely, explicitly or not, on historical evidence for validation. Michael Mann's *Sources of Social Power* is an important study using premodern Mediterranean history as a beginning point for his theory of institutional change.[74] These approaches provide a valuable perspective on the function of economic institutions within specific historical and social contexts. While some scholarship has focused on deep historical development, most work using economic and sociological theory derives from the context of modern societies.[75]

The two most important economists behind NIE have been Ronald Coase ("Nature of the Firm," 1937; "The Problem of Social Costs," 1960, are foundational) and Oliver Williamson, although Douglass North (figure 5)

FIGURE 5. Douglass C.
North (1920–2015).

is often considered to be the founding father.[76] All three have won Nobel Prizes. Coase and Williamson focused on transaction costs, and one-off bargains. It is known as *New* Institutional Economics, in contrast to the *Old* Institutional Economics of Veblen and Commons.[77] NIE is used both in economic analysis and in economic history, and now in political science, contract theory, and a wide number of applications in legal and economic analysis. Transaction costs, property rights, methodological individualism and (bounded or perfect) "rational choice," and the cost of information are the core concepts of NIE analysis.[78] The aim has been to establish in historical time the connection between institutions and performance.[79]

North's work in New Institutional Economic History (NIEH), or Historical New Institutional Economics (HNIE), applies the basic concepts of NIE to explain comparative economic performance outcomes and "to establish a theory of the institutional structure of the state as a whole."[80] Much of the NIE, especially North's work, is concerned with explaining the rise and success of European civilization.[81] Good institutions lead to good economic outcomes. NIE approaches to economic historical analysis have been largely responsible in making ancient history fashionable again, or at least potentially an important source for understanding long-term changes in the structure and performance of economies and the relationship between economic and political institutions.

It should be stressed that NIE also has public policy aims, answering questions such as: why do some countries do better than others? The answer is: "institutions." The literature on this question is enormous, and continually growing. The structure and the performance of modern market, capitalist, nation-state economies, either on a national scale or a global one, bear little resemblance, if any, to ancient economies. The struggle is to find a sufficient theory of institutional change to be able to apply it to policy settings. Here there is great value not only generally for history, but also for premodern history especially.

"Institutions," in North's initial formulation, are the "rules of the game" in a society. They can be formal or informal, include both laws and norms, and are constraints on action as well as enablers of it. As such, the institutions of a society determine its economic performance. The historical path dependency of institutions, the tendency once in place for an institution to remain in place, is a notable feature of NIE analysis. Importantly, though, Ogilvie's historical analysis shows that institutions were not sticky because they were "efficient" but because they are designed to benefit elites.[82] Rules must be understood along with motivation or incentives to follow them.[83]

According to Ménard and Shirley, institutions:

> include (i) written rules and agreements that govern contractual relations and corporate governance, (ii) constitutions, laws and rules that govern politics, government, finance, and society more broadly, and (iii) unwritten codes of conduct, norms of behavior, and beliefs.
>
> Organizational arrangements are the different modes of governance that agents implement to support production and exchange. These include (i) markets, firms, and the various combinations of forms that economic actors develop to facilitate transactions and (ii) contractual agreements that provide a framework for organizing activities, as well as (iii) the behavioral traits that underlie the arrangements chosen.[84]

NIE analysis has been used to varying extents in the analysis of ancient economic behavior, and it has increased in the last ten years or so.[85] *The Cambridge Economic History of the Greco-Roman World* used NIE as the organizing principle as a means of integrating text and material culture into the same story with the aim of understanding economic performance.[86] Good work using NIE has been published on Roman agriculture and institutional change in ancient Greece, the latter especially attractive because it demonstrates the value of an ancient example for building out theory.[87] In this case it was democratic Athens and its mechanism design of democracy, albeit one differently configured than any modern example. Lyttkens lays out his NIE analysis of ancient Greece by highlighting key themes: "market relationships," indeed expanding market transactions, an increase in the use of coinage by the 5th century BCE, and taxation. Bresson in his new history of the Greek economy, building on his earlier work, also uses NIE as a framework.[88]

NIE can indeed sharpen the analysis of ancient economic institutions like markets and emporiums, credit and banking, contract enforcement, coinage, and the role of cities simply by forcing us to think harder about categories and definitions. Although NIE has rekindled some of the flame of old debates about the role of personal choice within institutional constraints, it is valuable to remind historians that economic thinking is important even if we need not always worry about the existence of price-setting markets. Robinson Crusoe made decisions without benefit of market transactions.[89] Decision making and mechanism design are two areas that we can study in some detail. How else to explain the mechanism design of Athenian finance of its ships known as the *trierarchy* other than through a game

theoretic approach to the information problem?[90] Not that the Greeks analyzed things in this way, but the concept of game theory was not unfamiliar.
They would have thought about it from the point of view of shifting risk and
the information problem onto individuals.[91] But the more important point
is that we now can analyze ancient institutions through game theory and
behavioral economics.[92]

The NIE approach is hardly universally accepted even within economics
or economic history. Much of the criticism of NIE comes in the form of a
general critique of neoclassical economic analysis. It turns people into cold,
rational, and calculating decision makers and leaves out a lot of the human
messiness of the real world. In a good recent example of the NIE approach,
Acemoglu and Robinson deemphasize culture, geography, disease, and climate, among other factors, to explain global inequality.[93] They offer instead
an elegant theory that explains that it is "political transformation" at "critical
junctions" alone that created "inclusive" political institutions that in turn
made some countries rich and others poor (i.e., created real growth). But they
argue that their "simple theory" explains "the main contours of economic
and political development around the world since the Neolithic Revolution."[94] On their reading, economic history in the long run tells us that only
institutions matter. It is a classic institutional argument; the enforcement of
property rights and investment in new technology creates better "inclusive"
institutions than do extractive institutions. Institutional arrangements do
indeed go a long way in explaining why nations, today, might fail, but it does
not fully explain success or failure in premodern economies. Very clearly, as
I discuss in more detail in chapter 5, environment, geography, and climate
change were critically important factors in comparative premodern economic performance.

NIE has been deeply criticized by, among others, Clark and Deirdre Mc-
Closkey.[95] For McCloskey, economics is not so much a science as a form of
rhetoric used to justify capitalism and market economies.[96] Instead, McCloskey, in a radically different model of Western divergence, has stressed values
and ideas that led to the institutional underpinnings of the Industrial Revolution. McCloskey is especially critical of NIE because, in her view, it merely
follows Samuelson's (neoclassical) economics too closely. It is too rational,
too bloodless and analytical; it leaves out much of what is going on in society
and does not take full account of culture, meaning, belief, political legiti-
mizing institutions, and religion (see further below, chapter 5).[97]

But New Institutional Economists themselves are well aware of these
shortcomings and the field continues to evolve rapidly.[98] If Polanyi was
wrong to miss market activity in antiquity, NIE-based scholars of antiquity
can be faulted for the opposite, of seeking, and finding, markets and transac-

tion costs everywhere. That is one key problem in Acemoglu and Robinson's analysis. There is an assumption of a market economy. In short, it is important to note that institutions do not come out of thin air; they derive from a particular culture at a particular place and time and established within a political equilibrium.[99]

Whether or not Acemoglu and Robinson's institutional argument can explain the modern world, it surely does not take full account of the historical development of the premodern world. Institutions evolved out of specific circumstances and cultural settings. The highly variable flood in Egypt, and what was probably endemic schistosomiasis among Egyptian farmers and elite alike, cannot simply be erased from the historical understanding of Egypt.[100] To be sure, historical change is contingent. But geography, climate variability, and short-term shock, drought, famine and disease, belief systems, and slavery, to name a few important things, were major factors in political equilibriums, in growth and decline of premodern economies, and in institutional change.[101] Institutions are of course critical, but they provide the direction of change, not the energy or the pace of change in the premodern world. It may be true that some regions—Hellenistic Greece, southern Italy in Roman times for example—may have performed much better in antiquity than in early modern times.[102] Volcanically perturbed periods, for example, the last three centuries BCE compared to the first two centuries CE (the "Roman Warm Period"), worked against societies in monsoon-dependent regions like Egypt and perhaps had wider impacts on interregional politics.[103]

By implication, if it were simply a matter of establishing the right set of institutions, for example, if ancient Egypt could only have democratized and created an "inclusive," or "open access" state, it would have performed better, or at least as well as Athens.[104] In fact substantial changes were introduced into Egypt from outside political powers on several occasions. Perhaps the clearest case is the shift from Persian to Ptolemaic to Roman governance. In Egypt, the fiscal regime was significantly altered, but these political changes probably did not alter growth trends or the distribution of income very much.[105]

This is not a problem but a challenge to economic historians, namely to turn an indifference curve into something like a real world of consumption preferences in an ancient Egyptian village or a Roman Italian town. Values and the role of culture have indeed become an important part of economic analysis and in fact signal a return to Weber. For ancient economies, we can see changing values even within the same families. The processes and the rate of change over the long run of human civilization have a different trajectory than North and colleagues' "natural" versus "open access" societies.[106] A good deal of scholarship is now being generated in response.[107] Climate and climate change and feedback loops have also not been part of NIE models of change over time. Here we see major differences between states in various parts of the Mediterranean.

Economic anthropology and historical sociology carry on the traditions of Weber, Durkheim, and Polanyi with their focus on "society."[108] Economic anthropology has had very little impact on the study of the "ancient economy" because "its place has been occupied . . . by Finley's method."[109] But that is a problem, since anthropologists provide us with rich information about a wide variety of societies that help us discern what is unique and what were widespread institutional solutions. The comparative anthropological framework that Goody's later work built takes us away from trying to find the origins of the European Industrial Revolution in ancient Greece and Rome and toward broader comparisons of economic institutions. Economic anthropology brings in much that has been ignored until recently, not the least of which is the feminist perspective that has become a major part of the field. Another strength is that these approaches, broadly speaking, contextualize and describe cultural totalities.[110] Granovetter's study was a serious critique about how to understand economic behavior within a social context.[111] Much of the criticism of neoclassical or NIE approaches have centered on the fact that this kind of analysis does not sufficiently take account of particular societies and their cultures; they separated economic behavior from the rest of society, in opposition to sociological, economic anthropological, and liberal humanist approaches by Weber, Polanyi, Finley, Oppenheim, and many others.[112] In one recent critique of NIE, Deirdre McCloskey eloquently pleaded for a broader economic history, one that could better explain the world.[113] And that has indeed also been a major trend in economic history. A renewed emphasis has been placed on cultural contexts, beliefs, and conceptions of the world, as drivers of change.[114] Economics has shifted emphasis away from markets to modeling behavior and information asymmetries. There has been, then, a wide array of approaches, from economic, anthropological, and world systems theory to economic sociology. There are two other fields that hold great promise and will, I believe, open up the study of ancient economies to a richer and more dynamic understanding of the premodern world.

EVOLUTIONARY THEORY

Perhaps the biggest change in economics since the 1950s has been in the use of sophisticated mathematical models and statistical techniques, game theory, and evolutionary theory particularly in the context of the coevolution of institutions and human behavior. Very little has been done with respect to premodern economies with this theory, but these new methods offer an extremely promising way forward.

If none of the earlier work fully explains institutional change over time, what is missing? Darwin. Yes, just when you think that mid-19th century social theory is far beyond usefulness, along returns Darwin's theory of evolution.[115] Evolutionary theory as the framework has now been established in several fields, including anthropology, sociology, economics, and history. Broadly termed cultural evolutionary theory, the field applies Darwinian theory to the evolutionary forces of change in cultural traits.[116] This powerful set of concepts allows us to move beyond stage theories or the dialectical history of Marx and begin to understand *Lamarckian* evolutionary processes, how learned behaviors and new ideas were taken up, and how older ones were replaced. The great variety of economics systems in the ancient world, and indeed in the modern, demonstrates the heterogeneity of "solutions to a common problem," namely how humans cooperated, and how societies "remain in existence for long."[117] Ultimately, evolutionary theory can help explain, by analogy with evolutionary biology, how past historical experience influences later developments. Evolutionary theory can also help us set a long-term framework by which we can understand discrete historical periods and particular questions.[118]

Evolutionary biology has given rise to evolutionary economics, a term first coined by Thorstein Veblen in 1898. Evolutionary theory is now a highly developed part of economics, and Hoffman effectively uses cultural evolutionary differences between Europe and the rest of the world to explain why Europe conquered the world.[119] Joel Mokyr's treatment of the Industrial Revolution also operationalizes the theory to explain the particular social and cultural circumstances of early modern Europe that gave birth to the modern economy.[120]

Culture and institutions coevolve and reinforce each other. As in the modern world, culture and institutions can explain the relative economic performance of premodern states.[121] Multilevel selection theory is a powerful set of tools to understand cultural and institutional evolution in the context of the processes involved in "imperial upsweeps." Cooperation at multiple levels of society led to institutional change, and, while multiple timescales should not replace microeconomic analysis, different scales allow us to see interconnections and interrelated levels of society. Premodern Mediterranean states offer a rich and diverse set of agricultural practices, beliefs, preferences, and values that led to different outcomes. Indeed they are a natural laboratory of cultural evolutionary forces that provide many examples for what Mokyr calls "useful knowledge," that is, improved ways of doing things, and in some cases locked in effects.[122]

Two important institutions that I treat later it the book, coinage and law codes, spread rapidly throughout Eurasia in the middle of the first millennium BCE. We are not always aware of the processes involved (borrowing, diffusion, independent invention), but evolutionary forces, the power of a good idea to catch on, perhaps, played a part in the development of Indian coinage within the state economy and in the spread of written law codes. It is conceivable that texts such as the *Arthashastra* (on which more below in chapter 2), were influenced by codified "best practice" rules of governance that are exemplified in Pseudo-Aristotle's *Oikonomika*. The Athenian Empire adopted some practices from the Persian Empire, the Ptolemies brought with them to Egypt Athenian fiscal practices, and the list could be enlarged.

Other examples of evolutionary forces could be given. Most important for the first millennium BCE is the formation of "mega empires" (territorial peaks of >1 million km^2): Neo-Assyrian, Achaemenid, Hellenistic, Mauryan, and Roman. The processes of forming large territorial empires requires large-scale cooperation through group selection.[123] Such cooperation by large numbers of people, in turn, presupposes "prosocial" norms and scaling up of defenses. Peter Turchin's theory suggests that "steppe frontiers" and "mutual feedback" mechanisms between agrarian empires and nomadic peoples drove empire formation. The Han and Achaemenid Empires are prime examples. But there were variants to the scaling up of territorial empires. In Europe, for example, empires tended to form on the periphery of other empires without reinforcing feedbacks from nomadic groups. Macedon and Rome are good examples.

Warfare was a major evolutionary force in the premodern world. In the first millennium BCE, military power was decisive in imperial state building and domination, and war was an important mode of acquisition as well. "Military revolutions," significantly, occurred on several occasions in the Greek world during the first millennium BCE and were the by-product of fierce interstate competition in the Greek world. The ability to adapt to changing circumstances, born out by warfare, was decisive in the 4th century Greek world, and, with the coming of Rome in the 2d century BCE.[124] War was a driving force in creating the large-scale societies of first-millennium BCE empires and, above all else, was strongly linked to their fiscal regimes.[125]

PALEOCLIMATOLOGY

Understanding in what ways environmental conditions and climate change, both on abrupt and longer timescales, had impacts on premodern economies is still a controversial topic in large part because the field is in its infancy and high resolution data are relatively recently available. Much of the proxy data has been focused on the last two thousand years (2K), and I hope that we will have much more high resolution data for the Iron and Bronze Ages soon. Pioneering work by archaeologists like Robert Braidwood in the 1930s and 1940s and Robert Adams in the 1960s and 1970s, and physical geographers like Karl Butzer, without the benefit of good climate proxy data, made good first steps in reconstructing the paleoenvironment of the Near East and Egypt with emphasis on state development in early civilizations and on scientific data.[126] For Greece, Michael Jameson's long-term environmental study of the countryside is a model of its kind.[127] The classic study of Braudel on the Mediterranean (see chapter 3), for example, devoted much of his study to the relationship between physical environment and historical processes. The physical environment of the sea allowed exchange on increasingly larger scale and not only united, at times, classical civilization but, over the course of millennia, brought in Egyptians and Near Eastern peoples, including the Phoenicians, who were the first movers to join the eastern and western part of the sea. Bringing in this wider world and greater time depth in which to understand the history of economies in this part of the world highlights the crucial role of cross-cultural exchange.

While climatic change has generally been recognized in earlier work as being an important consideration in the economic history of the premodern world, it was difficult to integrate climate proxy records with historical records because climate data was not chronologically precise enough to be useful for historical work. In the last few years, however, there has been a scientific revolution that has given us chronologically precise data and thereby a natural archive that we can use side by side with the traditional documentary evidence of texts and material culture. Chronologically precise climate proxy data, as I will show in chapter 5, now allow historians to correlate short-term climate shocks caused by volcanic eruptions with drought and political events. Having more refined climate data does not lessen the challenge in any way. Understanding the environmental and climatic constraints of early civilizations is an aspect of economic history that is still in its infancy, but there is much promise.[128]

These recent trends in the analytical frameworks—a better understanding of the role of institutions, evolutionary theory that helps us better compare institutional solutions, and a revolution in paleoclimatology that will give us improved understanding of human-natural system dynamics—are opening new possibilities of exciting research in premodern Mediterranean economies. Together they combine to offer us a means to construct coupled human-natural systems models.

Evolutionary theory in economics, understanding institutional change, cooperation, and social cohesion, raise a host of new and important questions. One important new framework is called *cliodynamics*, a new field of inquiry being developed by Peter Turchin and others. Using cultural evolutionary theory, multilevel selection theory, and quantitative modeling helps explain how human societies upscale from small "egalitarian" societies to "large scale hierarchical societies such as states and empires."[129] That is important since ancient Mediterranean economies moved from a large variety of states to a single empire.

Periodization should seek the best division of time in understanding change in the premodern Mediterranean. Normally, however, scholars divide up history by cultural phases as art historians do, and by languages. This produces archaic, classical, and Hellenistic Greece (which can be extended into Egypt as part of "the Hellenistic world" because of the Greek papyri), for example, or the Neo-Babylonian and Achaemenid Empires in the Near East. Although this can tell us some things, this kind of cultural periodization obscures at least as much as it reveals. The value of studying the premodern past, and especially the sophisticated economies of the ancient Mediterranean world, is the perspective it gives for long-run development of institutions—something usually missing from theoretical treatments in NIE and elsewhere.

Categories and disciplinary boundaries have been both a source of debate but also a serious barrier to real progress in the study of ancient economies. It is still all too rare for historians of one place and time to engage other fields or social theory. If theory is used, it is more often used passively "to reorient thinking, or borrow its vocabulary."[130] Yet the study of ancient economies has great potential to engage with and to extend, even occasionally improve, social theory, so much of it developed from studying modern national states. To better understand the pathways between early human society, ancient civilizations, and the contemporary world as a means to understand change is a richer and far more interesting thing to describe than to take a stance on either side of the great debate that I discussed. In other words, to say that the Greeks or the Babylonians were a lot like us, or not like us at all, simply does no justice to these ancient civilizations. A good and very promising example of the trend the field should move in is a recent volume on agrarian labor in the "archaic" Mediterranean, with papers on Egypt, Mesopotamia, the Levant, the Phoenician West, Greece (including Sparta), and early Rome.[131]

New types of data, new methods of analysis, quantitative modeling, and the use of various proxy data are becoming common. GIS mapping and high-resolution climate proxy data, to name just two areas where these are being deployed, are rapidly revolutionizing the study of antiquity (and beyond). Underwater archaeological techniques have given us some aspects of ancient Alexandria, and at least the beginnings of understanding trade flows from shipwrecks. The most exciting trend has come from the geophysical and biological sciences. Climate and ecology have been nearly completely ignored in the "great debate" between the early primitivisms and modernists. Sallares's book was pioneering, but science has advanced in astonishing ways since its publication.[132]

Work on ancient Near Eastern and Egyptian economies has finally begun to actively engage in general treatments of ancient economies. Near Eastern documents are now much more accessible to other scholars, both publication of archives, and their general economic context.[133] The onslaught of "handbooks," "companions," and encyclopedias provide the general reader with good accessible overviews of many aspects of ancient economies, above all the nature and extent of sources for each time and place. This has proven especially helpful for sources written in difficult languages. Temples in Egypt and the Near East are no longer seen as merely state redistribution centers, but places of private enterprise in their own right. And private economic activity itself is well documented throughout the first millennium BCE and beyond. We can, then, no longer ignore Egypt and the Near East as separate, very different types of economies that cannot be discussed alongside the classical world.

The *Hekanakhte* letters from Egypt that I discuss in chapter 6, and the Kanesh archives of Assyrian traders discussed briefly in chapter 8, are virtually unique and contemporary documents from the Middle Bronze Age, ca. 2000 BCE, and provide us with perhaps striking evidence for rational household behavior and for the private organization of long-distance trade in the search for profit long before the Iron Age revolution. They could not have been unique in the economic behavior documented.[134] A Western divide between women and men has tended to systematically exclude women from economic analysis.[135] Recent work highlights the role of women both within households and as individual economic actors as well.[136]

John Hicks once asked whether it was possible to build a theory of economic history. That dream may still be some way off, at least for now.[137] But we do have better building blocks now. We can build on Weber's and Finley's desire to develop a theory that is specific to time and place.[138] One important way forward, I suggest, is the use of evolutionary theory, to better understand the processes of human adaptation on multiple scales. The study of ancient economies adds both to a definition of "economic," which of course varied by culture, and to an evaluation of the nature of economics as a discipline. An examination of the wide range of societies that inhabited the Mediterranean world shows us that there were a variety of solutions to economic problems. As Barry Kemp suggested in his study of Egyptian history, the important question to ask of premodern societies is what kept them together for long periods of time?[139] Before we attempt an answer to that question, we need to have a brief look at Iron Age Mediterranean history and the kinds of economic sources that survived. The next chapter opens with one of the most intriguing people to have inhabited the Mediterranean, the Phoenicians. It was they who began to open up the entire Mediterranean to trade and other kinds of cross-cultural exchange at the dawn of the Iron Age. They mark a real turning point in the economic history of the sea. Before introducing them, I want to have a brief look at how time and change over time have been discussed by ancient historians.

CHAPTER 2

Ancient Economies

TAKING STOCK FROM PHOENICIAN TRADERS
TO THE RISE OF THE ROMAN EMPIRE

How, or on what conditions, can the historian know the past?
—COLLINGWOOD (1946:282)

Nothing could be more misleading, therefore, than to describe the
economic institutions of Antiquity in modern terms.
—M. WEBER (1909:45)

THE HISTORICAL EXPERIENCE IN the Near East and in Egypt followed a different developmental pathway than the classical world. In part this was because there was a longer state history in these regions. Another important consideration is that these regions had different climatic and material conditions, and different geographical constraints. Many of the important institutions that fostered economic performance—property, enforcement of contract, long-distance trade, city-states, and even arguably forms of democratic institutions—emerged in the third millennium BCE. Imperial states and kings dominated. From the Old Babylonian Empire of Hammurabi (ca. 1792–1750 BCE) to the Seleukid Empire (312–63 BCE), a succession of empires in western Asia built directly on previous cumulative imperial experience and institutional adjustments.[1] The rise and growth of the Achaemenid Empire in the 6th century BCE, the first "world empire," by military conquest was among the most important processes of the first millennium BCE. The origin of the Persians is obscure. Perhaps starting from scattered "pastoral groups," the Achaemenid Empire grew to become the largest empire before Rome, controlling more than five million square kilometers.[2]

Egypt had its own historical experience in state building along the Nile River, expanding southward into Nubia already by the middle of the third millennium BCE, and into the Levant during its middle Bronze Age empire, the largest of the second millennium BCE.[3] But in the Iron Age, and the dynamism that was increasingly in evidence in the Mediterranean, Egypt was a smaller player dominated politically by outsiders. The Saite dynasty, beginning ca. 650 BCE, consolidated political power, anticipating the subsequent development under Persian, Ptolemaic, and Roman control. The Saite period, during which political power was recentralized and a new administrative script (demotic) was gradually adopted throughout, is an important inflection point in Egyptian history.[4] Both the Achaemenid and Ptolemaic Empires built on this economic and cultural consolidation.

Various intensities of interaction occurred between the Near East, Egypt, and other parts of the Mediterranean world; and in some cases we have to insist on cultural differences. Egypt, as Herodotus later tells us for example, was far less receptive to outside ideas than the Greek world was. But while it has been common to draw East-West and North-South lines in the Mediterranean, such spatial and temporal boundary lines are, to say the minimum, problematic for ancient history.[5] To be sure, there were patterns of consumption, for example, that were defined by cultural preferences. It is the examination at the cultural and often the geopolitical boundaries where we can most clearly observe how cross-cultural exchange was a major driver not only of exchange itself but also of institutional change.[6] Bentley highlights three important topics that transcend cultural boundaries: migration, imperial expansion, and long-distance trade.[7] All three of these combined to bring about significant changes in the Mediterranean by the end of the 4th century BCE. I would add a fourth factor to the list, interstate competition. Greek cities in the Hellenistic period, for example, developed creative new finance strategies in response to the monopoly power (in grain supply) of the large territorial states like the Ptolemies and Seleukids.[8] Neither "classical," "Hellenistic," nor "Greco-Roman" therefore suffices to explain the economic history of the last three centuries BCE in the Mediterranean.

Karl Jaspers proposed a new way of looking at the first millennium BCE just after World War II.[9] The "Axial Age" (*Achsenzeit*) was conceived by him as a particular moment in Eurasian history, 800–200 BCE, with the "axis" centered around 500 BCE.[10] This "Axial Age" ushered in what he called a "new humanity, our humanity."[11] Yet only certain fortunate peoples (better to say a few ingenious thinkers) were selected: Chinese, Indians, Iranians, Jews, and Greeks.[12] Other scholars recently have focused on the two centuries 500–300 BCE, to understand the emergence, in China, India, and the eastern Mediterranean, of "personal transcendence," a new mode of thought that fostered greater prosocial behaviors.[13] Jaspers insisted on "universal parallelism," independent developments, without cross-cultural contact or "stimuli."[14] The rise and spread of coinage, markets, legal codes, written agreements, a tendency to disembed patrimonial power from state administration, and thinking about state fiscal structure are all features of the middle of the first millennium BCE (on these see further *infra*).[15] India and China experienced many of these same political and economic processes, and it may be true that social evolution followed general pathways of development.[16] Kautilya's *Arthashastra* (lit. the "science of wealth"), a remarkable treatise on revenues, good government, and statecraft, does compare well to Xenophon's *On the Revenues* (*Poroi*) and Pseudo-Aristotle's *Oikonomika*, which are also concerned with state revenues and best practices of governance.[17] These "Axial Age" thinkers did for fiscal sociology what others did for transcendental thought. Revenue and governance were inextricably connected. Whether these were truly independent developments or reflect cross-cultural borrowing is difficult to say with any certainty, but there were forces that already joined the Mediterranean to central and south Asia.

What drove the changes? Jaspers thought that the midmillennium changes were independent social evolutions that occurred in small, highly competitive states, not "in the centers of great empires."[18] Because Babylonia and Egypt ca. 500 BCE were contained within the Achaemenid Empire, they did not transform. Yet this does not account for affluent societies in the regions that Jaspers claimed were not "transformed." One recent study suggests that economic development, measured by an increase in energy capture, was the forcing mechanism behind the synchronous changes.[19] One cannot ignore the climate signals; the "subatlantic pattern," the current phase of the Holocene, began ca. 700–500 BCE (2760–2510 BP), bringing slightly cooler, wetter conditions.

In a sense, then, the cultural shifts in religious and philosophical practice were lagged, counterhegemonic, and secondary to economic and political transformation that began in the early Iron Age. Centralized, hierarchical empires were not innovative. In fact they were the opposite of that. Within them, the pressures were toward stability, consolidation, and integration. But this counterhegemonic emergence of political, economic, and religious reforms can arguably be placed, certainly in the Mediterranean context, in some measure, in the context of reactions to the Achaemenid Empire.[20] Around 500 BCE, the Achaemenid Empire reached peak territorial size, surpassed only by Rome in the early centuries CE (figure 11). The Axial Age philosophies were, then, as Morris rightly concludes, "more of a consequence than a cause of state restructuring."[21]

During the Bronze Age, in the eastern and western halves of the Mediterranean, there were great contrasts in material culture and social organization.[22] The Bronze Age was the age of the first empires in the Near East and Egypt, of large-scale trade networks across western Asia and the eastern Mediterranean, and the origin of what Broodbank has called the "pan-Mediterranean"

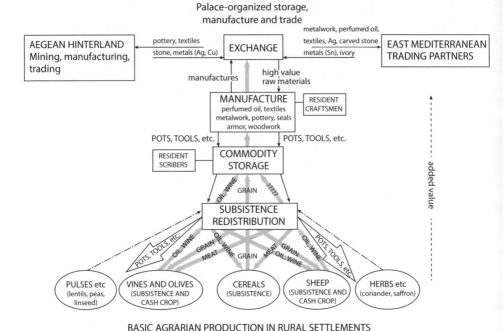

FIGURE 6. Model "palace economy" for Crete, mid-second millennium BCE. From A. Sherratt and Sherratt (1991).

Iron Age cultures of the first millennium BCE.[23] "Connectivity and mobility rose sharply in intensity and scale from the 3d to the 1st millennium BC."[24] There were "market shifts" based on demand for copper.[25] Importantly, there was territorial integration under the twin dynamic forces of empire formation and trade, at increasingly larger scales. An ever widening "interaction sphere" in Eurasia, between 1600 and 1200 BCE, joined Europe and South and East Asia together. These trends, and the shift from the Near East/Egypt to the Mediterranean as the "dominant area" of economic power, are critical to understanding first-millennium developments.[26]

The "palatial polity" was a dominant political form in the Aegean, in the Near East and Egypt, but it was hardly the only one (figure 6).[27] The old assumption that this form of economic organization—take, for example, the term *pr-c3*, "big house," standing in for the Egyptian king—was centralized, and "redistributive" *tout court*, is questionable.[28] Even the largest palace economies did not capture or control all economic activity in their region; there were larger-scale grain production and larger-scale economic "units," set within a hierarchy of larger urban centers and medium and small towns and villages. Palaces were the administrative centers of ever-larger economic systems of an urbanized eastern Mediterranean. Broodbank estimates that there were "forty to fifty principal producing, trading, and consuming centres" in the compact and densely populated eastern Mediterranean basin.[29] Intensive interaction between these "palace" centers produced a common economic culture through market exchange, and the standardization of goods.

The central role of the large institutions of the "palace" was similar in the Mycenaean world, Egypt, and the Near East. Indeed these so-called palace economies were public economies at scale. Over time more extensive coercive power became possible. Like the palaces of the Mycenaean world, temple estates in the Near East and in Egypt offered organizational capacity and scale to exploit labor and to extract taxes. They were not "redistributive" but distributive. Elsewhere, on Cyprus for example, families and family firms controlled trade.[30] The city-state of Ugarit is emblematic of the age.[31]

The second-millennium BCE "Copper Age" in the western Mediterranean and in Egypt reveals a different world until ca. 2000 BCE.[32] But the second millennium BCE was a period of "expanding networks" driven in large part by the exchange of metals.[33] The rate of social change varied from place to place; and a wide variety of political economies emerged.[34] Increasingly during the Bronze Age, from roughly 3000 to 1000 BCE, western Asia and the Mediterranean were growing more interconnected by trade and by diplomatic protocol.[35]

THE IRON AGE

Economic institutions in the Iron Age were substantially different from those in the Bronze Age. The beginning of the period is typically dated to ca. 1000 BCE, although no precise date is possible. Indeed it is better to view it as a slow transition with differential rates of change across the Mediterranean and western Asia. What is remarkable about the period are the substantial institutional changes.[36] Much remains obscure about the driving forces behind the changes, but a few things are clear. Threatening conditions forced change. Technological innovation created a new world, and a more intensive search for metal sources. States that emerged at the beginning of the Iron Age were larger, more coercive, and more extractive and were more rigidly bounded territories circumscribed by ethnicity and language.[37] Cities were bigger. These trends, also observed in China, were, in some ways, responses to the Bronze Age "crisis." At the same time small Phoenician city-states began to build a new world of long-distance trade, and pastoral nomads became part of a new "Afro-Eurasian world system."[38]

Iron smelting was in fact known by 13th/12th centuries BCE in Anatolia as a result of copper production on Cyprus.[39] The island was a key player in iron manufacture, in trade into the Greek world, and as a trading entrepôt throughout the millennium.[40] During the first millennium BCE, there was increasing homogeneity, and wider spheres of interaction. The process of "Mediterraneanization" in Morris's phrase, was "isomorphic," producing winners and losers (his example is first-millennium BCE Sicily); imperiogenesis, new military technology and organization, including navies, are the important processes that determined the winners and losers.[41] This was not only a world of iron technology, but also the age of silver, the main monetary standard until gold again rose to prominence in the Byzantine Empire.[42] The first millennium BCE was a period of remarkable expansion in the Near Eastern and Mediterranean worlds, and indeed elsewhere as well. Population grew by 74 percent between 400 and 200 BCE in China, India, and the Mediterranean; Ian Morris's "Social Development Index" almost doubled between 1000 and 100 BCE.[43] All this was pushed along by generally more favorable climatic conditions, but also, as a consequence of Eurasian steppe warrior expansion, Eurasia began to be exposed to plague.[44]

Another way of examining the Iron Age is through the lens of what has been called the "Axial Age" mentioned above.[45] Throughout the first millennium BCE, there was what Bellah has called an "evolution in capacity" of state power.[46] Smaller decentralized states, city-states (or microstates), in Phoenicia and in the Greek world emerged on the periphery of the old Bronze Age empires as the dominant socioeconomic organization. In the Greek world, at places like Sparta, Thebes, and Athens, cities arose where there had been Mycenaean centers.[47] There were cities elsewhere in the first millennium BCE that were equally significant in the Near East, and in the Egyptian Nile delta, but they were part of larger state systems.

The trading cities of Tyre, Sidon, Byblos, their wool and dye industries, and their nautical prowess were early movers in the new Iron Age (see further below in chapter 8). These cities were at the center of a massive Mediterranean-wide network, connected by harbors (maps 1 and 2). New regions of the Mediterranean were settled, concentrated in the south, the most significant being Carthage, which was founded as a colony in the 9th century BCE.[48] Among other things Phoenician traders were after were metal sources, more mollusks used in their purple dye industry, murex, and textiles.[49]

Iron-smelting technology required less energy inputs and used a metal that was more widely available. This less centrally controlled resource drove the emergence of the Iron Age.[50] It was a slow-moving shift in scale, hardly a

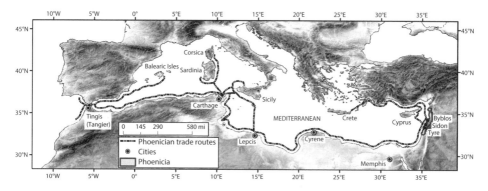

MAP 1. Phoenician trade networks.

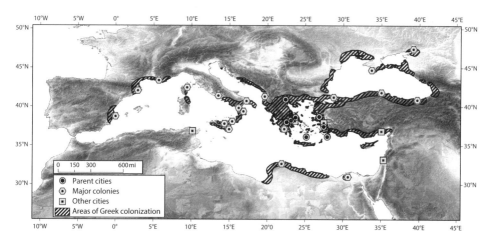

MAP 2. Greek colonization.

"single transformation."[51] The first use of the technology is documented ca. 1200 BCE. The Iron Age saw "the full realization of metals" and brought massive and important political and technological changes across the Mediterranean.[52] Iron was used in new rotary-power machines, in the digging of "deeper wells, waterproof cisterns, and dry farming on *wadi* beds." A shift from "large cities" to a more diffuse settlement pattern of "walled villages" was an important by-product of iron technology diffusion.[53] Transition to the adoption of iron has been linked to market forces by Warburton, and Liverani has noted that there was a "semantic shift" in the Iron Age economic mentality toward "profit/loss" calculations and from state administered trade to the "entrepreneurial" activity of Phoenician traders.[54] In the

Greek world there was a shift from "palace" to "polis."[55] Democratic institutions, notably at Athens, but elsewhere too, emerged.[56] Activities of states
increased dramatically. They were more extractive; there was a growth in
trade, in volume and intensity, and in urbanization.[57]

In 1000 BCE the Mediterranean world was called "prehistoric"; by 500
BCE it "formed a series of well differentiated zones within a world-system."[58]
There was a proliferation of writing, exemplified in the diffusion of law
codes, a change in military mobilization and technology, and an increase in
urbanization. This led to an increase in the rate of information flow, in consumption, and in innovation. All these represent an important "leap" in economic capacity during the first millennium BCE.[59]

After the collapse of Egypt's imperial New Kingdom ca. 1070 BCE, so
poetically signaled in the *Tale of Wenamun*, Egypt would not again be ruled,
with a couple of brief and notable exceptions, until the Egyptian revolution
brought Nasser to power in 1952. It had immediate consequences for eastern
Mediterranean history, in the Levant especially. Ironically, beginning
around 1200 BCE Egypt had been increasingly a Mediterranean, that is, a
delta, civilization. Broodbank has emphasized, in very broad terms, "mobility" as the key to change. It was something that the large territorial states of
the Bronze Age did not cope with especially well. The Hittite Empire in
Anatolia collapsed ca. 1200 BCE. Human mobility could undermine political authority and brought new networks and new modes of exchange. The
"peoples of the sea" known from Egyptian texts were the outcome of bigger
processes at the end of the Bronze Age. The rather more complex social and
economic world of the Bronze Age is revealed when the patina of centralized
state power is exposed as merely a thin veneer covered up by the anxiety of
centralized political control that the great kings wanted, but only partially
succeeded, to impose. It was the increasing complexity of the Mediterranean
world itself that the large Bronze Age states could not solve. Palace systems
broke down; merchants could not be controlled by kings; there was a general
collapse of central authority.[60]

Iron Age states were clearly different from their Bronze Age predecessors. Although some scholars have seen economic transformation, for
example, in land tenure and labor arrangements, in late Bronze Age "palace"
economies and in urban centers, the new states that emerged after 1000 BCE
had "more flexible, uncentralized and freelance trading practices."[61] The cost
of shipping by sea decreased, larger ships brought a significantly higher volume of trade, with more varied cargoes, and goods were exchanged in more
intensive market activity.[62] But metal mining and smelting was a driver of
the new age everywhere, including Italy, as was the much increased expansion in trade exemplified by Phoenicians moving into the far west end of the

Mediterranean in the 10th and 9th centuries, to Cyprus and Sardinia, and eventually to the mines in Spain.[63] Phoenicians improved the quality of iron by adding calcium.[64] Neo-Assyrian imperial demands, perhaps, were a force for Phoenician movement westward (map 1).[65] But there is more to the story than that. Phoenicians were entrepreneurs and filled in a gap in trading, with improved sailing skills, with improved naval architecture, and, it must be said, with a taste for risk, and no lack of courage, as is most dramatically attested in the claim that Phoenician sailors in the employ of the Egyptian Saite king Necho, so says Herodotus, circumnavigated Africa ca. 600 BCE.[66] Whether true or not, it says something about the age. Unfortunately we do not have a lot of direct information about how Phoenicians conducted trade. One treaty between Phoenician cities and Assyria does survive and suggests both strong political connections with the Neo-Assyrian Empire and a deep trading network:

> If a ship of Ba'al or of the people of Tyre is shipwrecked off the coast of the land of the Philistines or anywhere on the borders of Assyrian territory, everything that is on the ship belongs to Esarhaddon, king of Assyria, but one must not do any harm to any person on board ship, they should list their names and inform the king of Assyria.
>
> These are the ports of trade and the trade roads which Esarhaddon, king of Assyria, granted to his servant Ba'al; toward Acre, Dor, in the entire district of the Philistines, and in all the cities within Assyrian territory, on the seacoast, and in Byblos, across the Lebanon, all the cities in the mountains, all the cities of Esarhaddon, king of Assyria, which Esarhaddon, king of Assyria gave to Ba'al, to the people of Tyre, in their ships or all those who cross over, in the towns of Ba'al, his towns, his manors, his wharves, which . . . , to . . . , as many as lie in the outlying regions, as in the past . . . they . . . , nobody should harm their ships. Inland, in his district, in his manors . . .[67]

In the Near East, imperial states (Neo-Assyrian [934–610 BCE], Neo-Babylonian [625–539 BCE], Achaemenid [550–330 BCE], and Seleukid Empires [312–63 BCE]) were the dominant form of state throughout the first millennium BCE. Jursa suggests three main phases of ancient Near Eastern history: (1) the Neolithic revolution; (2) the "urban revolution" at the beginning of the Bronze Age, characterized by city-states, more specialized labor, and the so-called Uruk expansion ca. 4000–3200 BCE, an important, early instance of centralized state formation, perhaps even the first "world system"; and (3) the Bronze/early Iron Age transition, when the "regular" use of iron, domestication of the camel, innovation in writing systems, and new building techniques were introduced.[68] More intensive, productive farming produced a 24 percent increase in yield. Terraced fields, olive production, and deforestation led to year-round, as opposed to seasonal, production.[69] Intensification of year-round agriculture is shown in the increase in wells datable to the Bronze/Iron Age transition in Egypt and in Assyria, and the domestication of the camel allowed for increased long-distance trading.[70] Jursa observes: "the potential for structural change within an essentially stable technical, climatic and socio-economic framework was much greater" than in the Mediterranean.[71] The Babylonian imperial economy was focused on money-based (silver) wages and temple-based market exchange.[72] The 6th century Babylonian efflorescence was centered on the large urban area of Babylon itself, a rival in scale and in intellectual activity to the later Ptolemaic capital at Alexandria. Contemporary documentation offers us details of entrepreneurial activity, of private contracting, and of market transactions that reflect, if not long-term institutional history of the Near East, at least an alternative to classical Athens as a sole center of economic innovation in midmillennium.[73]

The emergence of Phoenician traders at the dawn of the first millennium BCE heralded a real turning point in the economic history of the Mediterranean, although one that is not as well documented as we would like.[74] Phoenician trade did not suddenly emerge, as far as the difficult evidence allows being certain, but rather should be understood as a continuation of the powerful trading cities of Byblos, Tyre, and Sidon, now given new energy and new direction to expand across the Mediterranean outside of Bronze Age imperial control.[75] To a certain extent too, Phoenician traders superseded Cypriote trading patterns in the central Mediterranean.[76] Phoenicians, or at least Phoenician-traded goods, are found far up the Nile as well, revealing the extent of their activity.[77]

The rather dramatic biblical text of the prophet Ezekiel against the perceived arrogance of Tyre tells us one reason Phoenician trading cities were stereotyped by later chroniclers—the competition to control trading networks and nodes had grown more intense by the early first millennium BCE.[78]

> " 'In the pride of your heart
>   you say, "I am a god;
> I sit on the throne of a god
>   in the heart of the seas."
> But you are a mere mortal and not a god,
>   though you think you are as wise as a god.
> Are you wiser than Daniel?
>   Is no secret hidden from you?

By your wisdom and understanding
   you have gained wealth for yourself
and amassed gold and silver
   in your treasuries.
By your great skill in trading
   you have increased your wealth,
and because of your wealth
   your heart has grown proud.
" 'Therefore this is what the Sovereign Lord says:
" 'Because you think you are wise,
   as wise as a god,
I am going to bring foreigners against you,
   the most ruthless of nations;
they will draw their swords against your beauty and wisdom
   and pierce your shining splendor.
They will bring you down to the pit,
   and you will die a violent death
   in the heart of the seas.
Will you then say, "I am a god,"
   in the presence of those who kill you?
You will be but a mortal, not a god,
   in the hands of those who slay you.
You will die the death of the uncircumcised
   at the hands of foreigners.
I have spoken, declares the Sovereign Lord.' "
The word of the Lord came to me: "Son of man, take up a lament
   concerning the king of Tyre and say to him: 'This is what the
   Sovereign Lord says:
" 'You were the seal of perfection,
   full of wisdom and perfect in beauty.
You were in Eden,
   the garden of God;
every precious stone adorned you:
   carnelian, chrysolite and emerald,
   topaz, onyx and jasper,
   lapis lazuli, turquoise and beryl.
Your settings and mountings were made of gold;
   on the day you were created they were prepared.
You were anointed as a guardian cherub,
   for so I ordained you.

You were on the holy mount of God;
   you walked among the fiery stones.
You were blameless in your ways
   from the day you were created
   till wickedness was found in you.
Through your widespread trade
   you were filled with violence,
   and you sinned.
So I drove you in disgrace from the mount of God,
   and I expelled you, guardian cherub,
   from among the fiery stones.
Your heart became proud
   on account of your beauty,
and you corrupted your wisdom
   because of your splendor.
So I threw you to the earth;
   I made a spectacle of you before kings.
By your many sins and dishonest trade
   you have desecrated your sanctuaries.
So I made a fire come out from you,
   and it consumed you,
and I reduced you to ashes on the ground
   in the sight of all who were watching.
All the nations who knew you
   are appalled at you;
you have come to a horrible end
   and will be no more.'" (Ezekiel 28:1–19)

The interaction between Phoenician traders and the early first-millennium BCE Greek world has received a huge amount of attention with little consensus about the role Phoenician contact played in the development of Greek civilization.[79] Homer does not present a kind image of the Phoenicians.[80] Yet Phoenician contact with the Greek world, and indeed Greek interaction with non-Greeks throughout our period, were of great importance in understanding the development of Greek institutions.[81] Nautical technological borrowing, and of course the alphabetic writing system, are two areas where Phoenician-Greek cross-cultural exchange had great consequences for Greece.[82] The emergence of the classical phase of Greek city-states and the rise of the Achaemenid Empire in midmillennium mark a key political transition in the Mediterranean. Achaemenid governance, too, had direct impacts on the later phases of Egypt's history, and impacts on the Greek world, through direct military conflict and through trade and the transmission of ideas of empire and material culture.[83] Expansion in early Iron Age Italy can traced both in the South, in the region called Magna Graecia, "Greater Greece," and in Etruria in the North. The Etruscans were not unlike the Phoenicians, with a strong naval presence and trade networks established as far as Marseille, acting as arbitrageurs between southern Italy and Rome.[84]

Egypt is frequently absent in the current vogue of macrohistorical narratives.[85] It is excluded, normally, because it was not considered to be a part of the Mediterranean world despite the Nile draining into it and despite extensive cultural contact between Egypt, the Aegean, and the Near East. Finley saw Egypt, and the Near East, as fundamentally differently organized so that it was not possible to speak in the same volume on the ancient economy along with the classical world. Far from being "immobile," however, Egypt was also transformed by the Iron Age trends that I have outlined.

At the beginning of the Iron Age, in the wake of the collapse of the New Kingdom Empire, Egypt was politically divided between Libyan rule in the delta, and theocratic control of much of the Nile valley by priests at the great Amun temple at Thebes. In the third millennium BCE, Egypt was oriented southward toward the first cataract of the river and the direction of Nile flow, and east out toward the Red Sea. So too North Africa was oriented east-west along the coast and southward.[86] The Ramesside imperial city at Qantir (Pi-Ramesses), "the first imperial entity to be based right on the edge of the basin itself," linked the Nile River up to the fifth cataract and Levantine coastal areas as well as other parts of the Mediterranean.[87] The site of Qantir was about six hundred hectares, with a population that may have reached eighty to one hundred thousand.[88] For a time at the end of the 8th century Nubians controlled the river valley. Assyrians invaded Egypt ca. 671 BCE. Political fragmentation and general political confusion was replaced by a new centralized state, based at Sais in the delta. The reconstitution of centralized political power under the Saite kings ca. 650 BCE brought with it the establishment of Naukratis as a major Greek trading enclave taxed by these kings, and also attracted Greek soldiers and Phoenician sailors into Egypt. But these 7th century developments can be traced back to the major commercial and political centers in the Egyptian Nile delta in Ramesside times ca. 1200 BCE. This Mediterranean-looking Egypt continued into the Saite period, with a Greek-staffed navy at the heart of a real Mediterranean power, but also, via the Nile and the Red Sea, with a reach deep into Africa. Achaemenid and later Ptolemaic control of Egypt built on Saite political recentralization and extended trade route connections that made Egypt a central point in long-distance trade routes that linked the Mediterranean to the Red Sea and to India.

By the early Iron Age, however, the delta, taking advantage of "new commercial circuits that were emerging in the Eastern Mediterranean and the Near East," followed a different economic path than the river valley.[89] In the early first millennium BCE, the Egyptian delta appears much more like the Near East, urbanized and connected to intensive trade networks in the Mediterranean.

Michael Mann, in his treatment of the emergence of Greek city-states in the early Iron Age, stresses three important characteristics: (1) technical innovations of the Iron Age, (2) and Greece's unique ecology and (3) location "astride maritime trading routes between semi barbarian plowing land and civilized empires of domination."[90] A shift from depositing precious items in graves to donating them to sanctuaries, with the possibility of "borrowing," seen in the 9th and 8th centuries BCE, was an important development in the public finance of city-states.[91] The small size of most Greek cities was a critical part of the development of democracy. Athens, as in so many things, was the outlier. The wide Greek cultural ecology was of one thousand city-states, historically unique, a "multipower actor civilization," with three competing, non-overlapping power networks: political, cultural identity, and the idea of the "unity of mankind."[92] In the 5th and 4th centuries BCE Athens was imperial, a "Greater Athenian state" in Morris's view (rather than "empire"), emphasizing the small size of the Athens's population and revenues compared to the Achaemenid Empire or the later empires of Rome and China.[93]

Homer's and Hesiod's poems, while still debated as sources for the early Iron Age, provide valuable information about social structure. Archaeology remains the key source for early Greece, and a careful new study suggests that the increased demand led to increased connection between Greece and the East.[94] Recently it has been strongly argued that there was sustained real growth in the Greek world. The starting point for this growth is the population collapse between 1200 and 1000 BCE. A recovery began around 800 BCE, and the population across the whole of Greece doubled during the 8th century. From 750 to 600 BCE, 2–3 percent of adult Greek males (twenty to forty thousand) left the Aegean for new homes for many different reasons. The percentage was even higher in trading cities like Corinth and Miletus.[95] It is no accident that Greek "colonies" were generally established in rich, rain-fed agrarian regions (map 2). This Greek expansion was of great consequence for the economic history of the Greek world and the vital role Greeks played through the Mediterranean in the second half of the first millennium BCE.[96] Greeks at the end of the Bronze Age settled western Anatolia, and cities such as Miletus on the Maeander River became large and very prosperous major centers of learning. Between 650 and 500 BCE the amount of territory that was integrated around the Mediterranean significantly increased.[97]

Bresson has emphasized the role of trade in Greek city-states very well.[98] The Greek city-state world began to rise at the same time as the Phoenician trading dominance began to decline in the wake of the Neo-Assyrian Empire's direct takeover of some Phoenician trade. Tyre revolted in 727 BCE, eventually to establish treaty relations with the Neo-Assyrian kings. It entered a tributary relationship with the Neo-Babylonian Empire and became a province after years of struggle.[99] The Achaemenid Empire, itself a Mediterranean power, gained control of the Phoenician coast.[100] The year 508–507 BCE marks the famous founding date of Athenian democracy, but there is an argument that democracy itself was "founded" earlier in other Greek cities.[101] The so-called democratic reforms were driven by several factors, and however we understand the processes of political change in the Greek world, it would be Athenian economic institutions that shaped later developments in the classical world.

FROM CLASSICAL TO HELLENISTIC TO ROMAN

As Greek, and especially Athenian commercial institutions influenced later economic developments from the 4th century BCE on, we see powers emerge on the periphery of the eastern Mediterranean: Carthage, Macedonia, and, finally, Rome. Alexander the Great would later leave his own mark on the great commercial city of Tyre during his seven-month-long siege. We do not know if that incident was related at all to his founding of what would become the greatest trading port of the Mediterranean, Alexandria, but it is tempting to think it played a role. The realignment of the political control of trade, and warfare as a productive economic activity, were never clearer than with Alexander's campaigns. The end of Tyre marked a symbolic end to the independent commercial city of the premodern Mediterranean. Two great Phoenician commercial centers, then, were destroyed by military conquest. Tyre, brutally destroyed by Alexander in 332 BCE, and Carthage, leveled by Rome in 146 BCE.

We tend to view these two events as turning points, one marking the beginning of the Hellenistic period, the other inaugurating the Roman Empire as the only remaining power of the Mediterranean. The "opening" up of the classical world to the "east" after Alexander the Great's spectacular conquest of the Achaemenid Empire at the end of the 4th century BCE marks a new phase of Mediterranean history. Its "modern" qualities have often been cited. But what seems "modern" to us about this world in fact are ancient features of our own. There are of course sound reasons to be wary of periodization in economic history, but few, I think, would still support Finley's dismissal of the Hellenistic period:

The term "Hellenistic" was invented by the great German historian J. G. Droysen in the 1830's to define the period in Greek history between the death of Alexander the Great in 323 and the death of Cleopatra in 30 BC. It has been accepted almost universally, and yet for the study of the ancient economy it is seriously misleading because in those three hundred years there were two basically distinct "Greek" societies in existence. On the one hand, the old Greek world, including the western Greeks, underwent no changes in the economy that require special consideration despite all the political and cultural changes that undoubtedly did occur. On the other hand, in the newly incorporated eastern regions—much of Asia Minor, Egypt, Syria, Mesopotamia—the fundamental social and economic system was not changed by the Macedonian conquerors, or by the Greek migrants who followed behind them, or by the Romans later on, as I have already indicated. There was therefore no "Hellenistic economy"; from the outset there were two, an ancient sector and an Oriental sector.[102]

As John Davies concluded, the paragraph is an "astonishing *aposiopesis*."[103] But it was not by accident or even neglect that Hellenistic period was left out of Finley's account. One can sympathize here with Finley that dividing the economic history of antiquity into neat periods of time, even if conveniently tied to the death of the two most famous persons of antiquity, does not explain very much by itself. For Finley, no important, observable change in the Mediterranean happened after 323 BCE that changed his historical view of premodern western history.

For Finley, nothing had changed in this post-Alexander world that was worth noting. But in fact there was a great deal of change driven by state reformations, by war, by urbanization, and by the increased use of coinage.

The main theme of Polybius, the great historian of the Hellenistic age, was *symploke*, literally a "stitching together," that is, the political and economic integration of the Mediterranean world, from the fragmentary states of the early Hellenistic period to the unifying forces of the Roman conquest of the basin during the 2d century BCE.[104] Indeed the Hellenistic period was interimperial, between the Achaemenid and the Roman Empires. In fact, though, as we have seen, the integration of the Mediterranean was a slower and much longer set of historical processes that had begun long before Rome was a hegemonic power.[105] We can understand this only in a bigger, and deeper, historical analysis.[106] The Phoenician trading cities opened up the entire Mediterranean to trade, to market, and to alphabetic writing; Greek colonization also expanded trade networks.[107] The real change in the Near East was political, the establishment of what might be called retrokingdoms in the old imperial cores. These were reformed parts of the Achaemenid

Empire now run by Alexander's successors cloaked in ancient kingship. As John Davies has reminded us in his essay, Polybius quite rightly stressed politics as the driving force of economic change in the Hellenistic period.[108]

In his recent study of world economic history, Angus Maddison began his account with the Roman Empire.[109] The Hellenistic period on its own received one-third of a page.[110] To be sure, quantifying the Roman imperial economy is further advanced, and more information is readily available for secondary analyses.[111] But it still comes as something of a surprise given Rostovtzeff's very accessible, if unquantified, data presented in his *Social and Economic History of the Hellenistic World*. Because the overarching narrative is less clear, the processes of new state formation are lost in the mists of time, and the most important city of the period (Alexandria) is nearly entirely absent for the purposes of economic history. Hellenistic economies can be dismissed as a kind of "little tradition," to borrow the famous concept from Robert Redfield, compared to the "great tradition" of the Roman imperial economy.[112] But this attitude tends to overwrite Hellenistic history with little regard to longer-run developments in the eastern Mediterranean ca. 400 BCE to ca. 200 BCE.

But does that mean that we should only count the 4th and 3d centuries, or just the 3d century BCE, as "Hellenistic," and the last two centuries BCE as Roman? "Hellenistic" is a term that all too frequently merely signals a pastiche, a loose conglomeration of ancient Greek and ancient Near Eastern institutions, rather than anything distinctive or new. The Hellenistic period marks a second wave of Greek expansion in the first millennium BCE, a "Post-Classical Expansion."[113] There has been much work on the eastern Mediterranean, but the western Mediterranean and the "Far East" are also worth our attention.[114] Once again the problems of Hellenistic/Roman historical boundaries are important for understanding institutional change. Scholars have often emphasized new economic institutions of the Hellenistic period such as coinage, but there was also considerable continuity in economic institutions.

The social, political, and economic history of Greek trade in the Mediterranean in the last four centuries BCE covers a much larger territory, both in terms of geography and in terms of economic institutions, and extends far beyond the traditional boundaries of classical Greek history. The many economic and legal reforms in 4th century BCE Athens are important in understanding Hellenistic economies. There are two other aspects that shaped Hellenistic economic institutions, the continuity of ancient Near Eastern patterns, and the growing political and trade connections between the Mediterranean and western Asia. This increasing interconnectedness, so famously noted by Polybius, was a major trend of the period. Andrew Wilson has provided an excellent example in his archaeological study of Euesperides in Cyrenaica (Libya). The strong connections, measured by quantifiable pottery remains, between Cyrenaica and further west in North Africa, and to Carthage are a "foreshadowing of the long-distance trade flows that are characteristic of the Roman world."[115]

The world of the kings did much to reshape the Mediterranean world before Roman conquest. Briant's work on the Achaemenid-Seleukid transition (the same holds for the Achaemenid-Ptolemaic transition in Egypt) suggests that much was changing before Alexander's arrival in the Near East:

> The predetermined, even overdetermined, periodization centered on the year 334, and approach the history of Alexander as part of a historical period that had its own dynamic, one that encompasses the entire half of the fourth century in an area spanning from the Indus to the Balkans.[116]

Thus the 4th and 3d centuries BCE form a bridge between the earlier history of the Near East and Egypt, the classical Greek world, and the mature Roman imperial economy of the first two centuries CE.

The rise of Macedon, and Alexander's campaigns against the Achaemenid Empire, is often understood as a major break in Mediterranean history between the classical and the Hellenistic periods. Certainly Mediterranean history after 400 BCE was a new phase of development and change. For Rostovtzeff it was enough to study a single person, Zenon, a Greek man, from Caria in Asia Minor, in the service of Apollonios, the finance manager of Ptolemy II, living in Finley's two worlds, "classical" and "oriental."[117] In that sense he *was* part of a new world. To understand what was new of course, one has to trace earlier economic activity, state and private, in the Near East and in Egypt. In both places the Achaemenid economy is essential. For Egypt, we have to understand the historical transitions not from the viewpoint of Greeks, but from the point of view of Egypt itself, and beginning with the 7th century BCE reforms of the Saite dynasty. For the Near East, the Neo-Assyrian and Neo-Babylonian Empires show the important continuities through the Achaemenid and Seleukid economies, and in Egypt between the Achaemenid and Ptolemaic regimes.[118] Large estates in Egypt run by Persian officials, for example, in many ways anticipate Zenon's work.

An interesting and important trend of the Hellenistic period in mainland Greece is the formation of groups of Greek cities, usually small, into "leagues," or "federations." This was not a new idea; cities had grouped themselves into leagues before, but not in the numbers that they did from the 4th century on. These leagues cooperated together in the issuance of coinage, in trade, in legal matters, and in mutual defense.[119] Creating larger internal markets, for example, connecting coastal towns to inland ones, and creating standard weights and measures, was an important driver of league formation and allowed Greek "dispersed authority" governance to continue.[120]

Ironically, and in part perhaps in reaction to Finley, work on economies of the Hellenistic period has exploded since the 1980s. Intensive work in papyrology, numismatics, and epigraphy, and, especially in archaeological excavations and surveys, has yielded new views of the period. Quantifiable data highlights expansion: the number of shipwrecks, silver production by proxy measure of lead in Greenland ice cores.[121] The role of cult, monetization, banking, private associations, the integration of archaeological material including intensive survey has shown excellent results for some parts of the Hellenistic world such as mainland Greece for example. The study of the Seleukid economy has been revived recently with several good studies appearing in the last twenty years.[122]

An assessment of what has gone on in Hellenistic economic history should begin with John Davies's programmatic piece published in 1984. Even in his own words, it was an updated Rostovtzeff, "already old-fashioned when it was published."[123] But it has set the agenda for a good deal of work on Hellenistic economies. In two sections of his essay, "The Degree of Economic Interplay," and "Change and Continuity," Davies characterized the period by setting economic trends within a much larger geographic framework, with very complex social forces that played out in many different ways across Eurasia, Africa, and the western Mediterranean. Davies accepts that a single "Hellenistic" economy, defined as a "continuous market-defined exchange of the whole range of goods and services throughout the eastern" Mediterranean, was probably not in existence, but he emphasized instead "segmental sets of activities."[124] "Regional" and local studies have been the trend, although defining what a "region" was is difficult, and there is a long way to go in understanding pottery typologies and how these can illuminate local/long-distance trade flows.[125] The new political economies of the Hellenistic kingdoms drove institutional change, new fiscality, including the introduction by the Ptolemies of coinage in their fiscal regime, even land reclamation, resettlement, founding of new settlements, new crops, and large-scale warfare. Large new urban centers like Alexandria also represent a significant change in scale.[126] All these were broad trends seen throughout the eastern Mediterranean, along with slave trade, and longer-distance trade in general into the Indian Ocean and Black Sea.

Since Davies's pioneering overview, three important volumes on Hellenistic economies have appeared. Together they provide a state of the field, emphasizing dynamism, regional interaction, flows, and change.[127] Davies's detailed agenda combines a diverse and wider range of evidence, along with trying to capture attitudes and behavior, in a more "realistic model."[128]

HETEROGENEOUS SOURCES, LUMPY EVIDENCE,
AND ECONOMIC HISTORY

There are two main caveats about sources for ancient economies. (1) It is fair to say that most human beings, and most economic transactions, are lost to us in the mists of time. (2) We tend to have the best evidence clumped in periods and places that we might call, following Jack Goldstone, "efflorescent," 6th century BCE Babylonia, 5–4th century Athens, Ptolemaic Egypt. In most cases the documents are circumscribed by location and time, for example, the sanctuary of Delos for Delian price series, and the Babylonian astronomical diaries. How then, can we write an economic history of antiquity? In two programmatic essays, Moses Finley discussed the nature and the problem of ancient sources for historical and economic analysis.[129] The "problems" are well known and are of a variety of kinds. Finley was concerned with evidence from the classical world, but his treatment applies equally well for the whole of the Iron Age Mediterranean world. The two basic kinds of sources, primary and secondary, must be carefully distinguished. Our primary sources, written texts and archaeological material, often present very different qualitative and quantitative kinds of evidence and can produce radically different conclusions. For the early Iron Age, our sources are, in the main, archaeological. For the classical world, the literary historical narratives, Herodotus, Thucydides, Polybius, Diodorus, have tended to be given priority because they naturally provide some kind of narrative of events. But they give far from complete coverage and have biases unique to them that are not always easy to evaluate. For Egypt and the Near East, the story is different. There we have no historical framing narratives, but, rather, an abundance of documentation, written for private or public purposes, and archaeological material. But for the first millennium BCE, once again, the archaeological work is very uneven. In every civilization that we are discussing here, the written evidence tends to provide information about the upper echelons of society. That is important to keep in mind when we are tempted to draw general conclusions about "typicality." The last forty years has seen spectacular growth in the publication of documents and in archaeological work above all.

Finley's fine-grained assessments about the very different ways in which sources have been used did not put an end to debates. There continue to be two main approaches to ancient sources. The first approach collects all available evidence and builds a picture, bottom up, of a certain aspect of economic behavior, say for example, the structure of land leases from Saite-period Egypt, or a study of pottery types from Cyprus. This method produces arguments from induction and/or fine-grained descriptions of the source. The second approach, represented by a much smaller number of people in ancient history, builds general interpretive models into which evidence is fitted. A model is declared useful if it takes account of the bulk of the evidence. This produces deductive arguments.[130] Finley's coda to his two fine essays remains important: "Documents themselves ask no questions, though they sometimes provide answers."[131]

Both approaches are valid, both are in fact necessary for studying premodern economies, and both present us with different kinds of problems, but without a question or a framework, they can lead us in all directions at once. Comparing, for example, 4th century Athens with 4th century Babylon would highlight that the type of evidence and the quality of it that survives from premodern Mediterranean societies differs in degree and in kind. We can for example, examine land tenure patterns and crop reports from a single village in the Fayyum in Egypt over the course of a decade. Yet for the same period, the end of the 2d century BCE, for most other places at the same time, even for other parts of Egypt, we do not have anything close to comparable village-level records.[132] The nature of literary sources and epigraphic material that have been used as the primary sources for reconstructing the classical Greek economy differs radically from the corpus of literary texts and temple inscriptions used to understand the pharaonic economy in Egypt. The former provides us with details of democratic institutions and individual action while for Egypt we tend to get the perspective of the king and a small circle of elite whose tombs survive. Even a seemingly straightforward category such as "the city" can be understood very differently in the classical world and in an Egyptian context.[133] Comparisons that do get done tend to be done by mix and match, taking for example the Athenian economy of the 4th century with New Kingdom economy of the 14th century BCE as proxies for "the Greek economy" and "the Egyptian economy." Such crude, chronologically invalid comparisons tend to reinforce sharp and artificial contrasts between "Europe" and "Asia" while ignoring change over time.[134]

When evidence from the ancient world *is* brought into more general discussion of long-run economic history, as in Maddison's or Acemoglu and Robinson's work dedicated to explaining why some countries are rich and others poor, it is almost always 4th century BCE Athenian (democratic) or the Roman (imperial) economic evidence that is discussed, and then almost always in a cursory fashion.[135] Happily Bresson's study, published in 2007 and 2008 and in a revised form in English in 2016, provides a detailed assessment of the Greek economy through the Hellenistic period. Rarely has Hellenistic period material, or ancient Near Eastern or Egyptian evidence, or sustained analyses outside of explaining growth in premodern economies, been brought into the discussion of longer-run economic development and performance. In part the problem is access to the dispersed academic output on ancient economies, written in many languages and scattered in hundreds of journals, conference volumes, monographs, and archaeological site reports. But in part too, a good deal of economic theory has been built on the thin scaffolding of modern nation-state experience in the last two hundred years, or even the last fifty. How developing countries can "get to Denmark," to use Fukuyama's phrase, is a more important question than what can the last five thousand years of historical experience tell us.[136] There may well be more value in comparing premodern economies to developing rather than developed ones. In any case, connecting the theory to historical development is still in its infancy, and the study of ancient economies can be a very important part.[137]

Egyptology and Assyriology have worked within "thick" descriptive narratives and cultural frameworks in the spirit of Clifford Geertz and Marshall Sahlins.[138] Why was Athens successful and, say, ancient Egypt was not? The answer typically lies in cultural differences. Egyptologists and Assyriologists are beginning to get involved in economic analysis, but it has been slow to come, and the history of these disciplines has tended to keep them isolated: the historical development of Egyptology in the 19th century tends to tether it to romantic ideas about an idealized past we have lost, connected to biblical archaeology, and captured by its own visual culture.[139] It is a comparatively small field, more prone to museology and cataloging than to social analysis. In 1979 it could still be said that the "economic history of ancient Egypt is still in its infancy."[140] Both Egyptology and Assyriology have also been slow to develop outside of a philological framework because decipherment of Egypt and cuneiform were accomplished only in the mid- to late 19th century. With respect to Greco-Roman Egypt, Greek papyrology has been ahead of demotic for the same reasons.[141]

Was there something particular about the classical world, and specifically classical Athens, the Roman republic, and the early empire, that was worth isolating? Yes, say many classicists. Democracy and law would be the first answers, closely followed by philosophy, the political experience of war and empire, the legacy of classical economies to later European development, and more recently, the fact that democratic, or "dispersed authority," political institutions may have created a wider distribution of income.[142] There is another reason for the emphasis on classical economies, but one that is increasingly difficult to defend, and that is the language barrier. Greek and Latin have never been "lost" languages; most texts are easily accessible and well translated. Classical scholars, and others interested in classical economies, have not faced a barrier to entry. Near Eastern and Egyptian scholars have hesitated to engage in part because of the difficulties of languages, and the nature of the documentation. Oppenheim's critique of Assyriology and its language barrier will provide a sense of what is still in some circles the dominant view among Assyriologists, and, by extension, among Egyptologists. Assyriology and Egyptology have tended to be isolated, reclusive disciplines that have avoided engaging with other fields.[143] Instead, the preference has been "textual" or philological approaches, as opposed to the "contextual" approaches of anthropologists and archaeologists.[144] The result has been terrible fragmentation, and assumptions that persist that Egypt and the Near East were essentially static or changeless over millennia. Those views no longer hold, but it might still come as news to scholars in adjacent fields.[145]

Michael Jursa and a team of scholars in Vienna (the Vienna Economic History of Babylonia project) have surveyed the first-millennium BCE Babylonian economy around key issues of geography, economic mentalities, agriculture, the use of money and growth.[146] This rich, detailed survey, the result of a decade of collaboration, focused on new sources and emphasized the nature, extent, and distribution of the evidence:

> In Assyriology, scepticism regarding "grand narratives" is common in general. Furthermore, the focus of research was usually more on structures in a synchronic perspective than on change of social structures and economic performance over time. What discussion there has been along these lines by historians working with textual data was focused on the impact that social structures had on the nature (not so much on the performance or the change over time) of the economy. As a result, the models and explanatory matrixes employed tend to be comparatively static and leave little room for structural change.[147]

Jursa has provided an important critique of Sherratt and Sherratt's palace economy model (figure 6) that has been used as a distinguishing characteristic between classical and Near Eastern economies. It is a major departure from earlier work in Assyriology.[148]

Ancient historians often bemoan their evidence nearly as much as they fetishize it. The more evidence, the less tendency there has been to theorize. Economic historians of later periods might be surprised by how much evidence we do in fact have even if, usually, we must emphasize qualitative over quantitative data, although not always. Indeed quantitative work in ancient history is gaining momentum. Any universalizing or comparative study of ancient economic structure of performance, as I try to do here, can easily founder on the qualitative differences in the kinds and amounts of evidence that survive in the various places covered. Much of our evidence is difficult to contextualize; falsifiable or testable hypotheses are difficult to construct. A glance at Weber's bibliographic essay written in 1909 is instructive for many reasons. The foundation of evidence with which he built his analysis of ancient society is, compared to our knowledge today, very flimsy indeed. Yet the broad sociological analysis is still well worth thinking about. The challenge remains for us to join together evidence and an analytical framework. Scholars tend to understand that temporal change brought more developed and complex economic institutions and, with them, more written documentation. That might be too much speculation, given how much written evidence we have lost, but it does explain the shape of the overall written evidence.[149] In the last forty years, much new evidence has been produced, better and much larger data sets makes new information more easily accessible, and many historical syntheses have made complex archaeological material and multilingual sources much more accessible to a wider audience.[150]

Yet the problem of disciplinary boundaries created by archaeologists, classicists, and scholars of the ancient Near East and Egypt persists.[151] Each of these disciplines works with different kinds of evidence and produces analyses at different social scales; the sources drive the approach and also drive the "stories" we tell.[152] Academic departments, another creation of the 19th century, are not set up to solve problems and in fact tend to obscure cross-cultural exchange over longer time horizons. I have argued elsewhere that retraining graduate students is a very real desideratum.[153] At the very least, studying the ancient economy in a broad context requires us to work more like the sciences in collaborative teams.

But premodern economic evidence is scattered and lumpy. Arguments, but also types of economic analysis, have been based on the nature of particular kinds of evidence that is impossible to generalize for "Greece," "Mesopotamia," or "Egypt."[154] Data is often conflated across these different analytical units, which makes it difficult to compare institutions across cultures and to draw general conclusions.[155] In some regions, cities, and towns are documented, sometimes fairly well; in other places like Egypt, rural areas and villages are often better known than urban centers; and Alexandria, ironically, is hardly documented at all by economic records. "Positivist fallacies," the assumption that the evidence that survives tells us significant things, are common.[156]

The study of price data goes back to the very beginning of the study of ancient economies, and efforts to collect references to commodity prices have been intense. Prices mentioned in the papyri from Egypt dated to the Hellenistic and Roman periods are well known but problematic. Sixty percent of grain prices from the Ptolemaic period, for example, are taken from penalty clauses in legal contracts and may not reflect actual market prices.[157] The two most valuable series of prices have come from Hellenistic Delos and Neo-Babylonian-Hellenistic Babylon.[158] New statistical techniques have been used for the latter series to take account of missing prices in the times series from 385 to 61 BCE.[159] The study of prices in Babylonia confirm that the region was a reasonably well integrated market that, like Egypt and the Nile, was aided by transportation on the Euphrates River.[160]

The opposite problem, analyzing in detail the sources that do survive, creates its own set of issues. Papyrologists focus, for example, on property rights and land tenure systems in Ptolemaic, Roman, and Byzantine Egypt because a high percentage of papyri concern that topic. The nature of the survival of papyri tends to privilege local records offices from the Fayyum and surrounding areas of Egypt, and private economic transactions (sales, leases, marriage agreements) from family archives from Upper Egypt. The political economies of democracy have occupied Greek historians because that is the kind of evidence that survives from Athens, and it is virtually unique. Rarely can we compare directly two different places with the same type of evidence. If we want to know something universal about the ancient Mediterranean, it gets even harder because we do not have very broad evidence across a wide territory for a long period. Even a brief cataloguing of the types and variety of the sources used in the analysis of ancient economies would indicate the mind-boggling variety of types and quality of it. The archaeology of settlements and of monuments differs significantly in various parts of the ancient world. Especially before the Hellenistic period, we often know very little about private exchange, and there is a tendency to study state or public economy. Types and quantity of evidence lead directly to the kinds of arguments that have been made about ancient economies.[161]

For example, some time ago, in studying the paucity of animal sales from the Ptolemaic compared to the Roman period, I suggested that the prevailing interpretation—that Ptolemaic centralized control of the economy inhibited such private sales, while Roman provincial administration enabled them—was probably not the correct interpretation.[162] The preservation of such ephemeral contracts in family archives was unnecessary. Rather, what we tend to have preserved in private documentation are texts that protected long-term property interests, hence land and house sales, and marriage agreements. On the other hand, the Roman papyri do not generally survive in private archival contexts, but, rather, in scattered archaeological contexts. Thus the kind of material we have preserved from these two periods of Egyptian history differs in number and in type. Arguments relying on a random distribution of material can be misleading.

Archaeological material is increasingly being used to discuss economic history but not without problems or fierce disagreements over interpretation.[163] It has long been recognized, even by Finley, who did not use archaeological material very much, that it has added important information about the extent, quantity, and quality of long-distance trade, and something about trade networks and economic growth.[164] But archaeological method-ologies differ radically in the Mediterranean; there are much better regional surveys in the Aegean, for example, than in Egypt, where work has, until quite recently, been dedicated to a handful of urban centers, temples, and tombs.[165] Overall, archaeological evidence, especially for settlement history, is extremely uneven for the first millennium BCE. Heather Baker concludes the following for Babylonia:

> For 1st millennium BC Babylonia there is barely a single excavated urban settlement for which the total area of occupation can be reliably esti-mated, at least within a historically meaningful timeframe.[166]

Major Hellenistic urban centers such as Ptolemais in southern Egypt or Seleukia-on-the-Tigris have gone virtually unsurveyed, at least so far. To be sure, politics are involved in site selection.[167] But one of the reasons that Ptole-mais has not been studied or even surveyed is that it is thought to have been a "purely" Greek city in Upper Egypt. Since Greek archaeologists tend not to excavate in Egypt, because it is not part of the national heritage of Greece, and Egyptian archaeologists have not cared too much about Greek culture in Egypt, the site has gone neglected. The modern demographic explosion in Egypt does not help. It is only recently that Ptolemaic Alexandria, among the most important urban centers in Mediterranean history, has received ad-equate attention. Overall, however, although the Nile valley is arguably one of the richest archaeological regions in the world, changes over time during the first millennium BCE, especially of settlements, remain very poorly understood.[168]

Rostovtzeff, in contrast to Finley, did stress archaeological material, al-though already by 1930 he declared that the increase in new archaeological material at the time was impossible to keep up with. What would he think now? New database projects, to some extent, help to solve this, but much remains unpublished. Archaeological and written sources do not always tell the same story at the same timescale, nor should we expect them to. In a real sense, it might seem easier (for papyrologists anyway) to write economic his-tory "as it really was" with evidence from the papyri, from the ground up, rather than from public inscriptions or literary texts. But this would be wrong. Features of the economies can be inferred on logical grounds with-out the need of positive evidence. The extent of the so-called invisible econ-omy at Athens must have been huge based on the wealth of aristocrats.[169]

Epigraphy, the study of inscriptions, has been the backbone of the study of classical economies for more than a century.[170] Epigraphic sources have been less exploited for Egypt, but the Edfu donation text is one of the most important texts for temple land holding in the Achaemenid to Ptolemaic period.[171] There are many other types of sources such as the famous trilingual decrees emanating from priestly synods in Ptolemaic Egypt, or inscriptions from the cities of Hellenistic Asia Minor that tell us a lot about the political relationship between elites and rulers. Inscriptions and papyri offer an important contrast, and some serious historical challenges to setting them into context. The private context of many papyri (letters, contracts) provides a different kind of evidence than the public nature of most Greek inscriptions. Both sources are biased but in different ways. The Greek papyri tend to come from more rural areas, the demotic papyri from temple-related contexts, and inscriptions tend to come from urban areas. Before the rise of the polis, Greek inscriptions that have survived have a different character "centered . . . on the individual and private concerns."[172] Classical inscriptions have been exploited for reconstructing the family and for inter alia demographic history, for land use and tenure arrangements, local political structures, public finance, and legal history.[173]

Numismatics has contributed considerably in recent years to the discussion of the relationship between money and coinage, how coins circulated and at what volume and velocity, and the impact coinage had on politics, on economic institutions like banking and markets, and on human behavior.[174] We can see the differential impacts of coinage in state fiscal systems, and how metal sources, above all silver, were connected to the geopolitics of the Mediterranean. Two main activities, trade and military finance, can trace the movement of money. Coinage, to a certain extent, aided both individual traders, who paid in small change as they traveled; larger-scale interregional transfers; and state collection of trade duties.[175] The issuance of very high-quality coins, well documented in Athens and widely imitated, and later the Greco-Bactrian coinage as well (figure 7), surely aided in the acceptance of coinage beyond the polities that issued them, but it is difficult to map circulation onto trade patterns directly.[176] In the mercenary world of Hellenistic states, paying for soldiers was an important reason to mint coinage. The movement of soldiers around the Mediterranean promoted circulation.

For Greece, literary sources, even early ones like Homer (ca. 750 BCE) and Hesiod (ca. 700 BCE), and poetic sources in general of course, are "always written from an aristocratic vantage point."[177] Nevertheless, the system of exchange in Homer, and Hesiod's observations in *Works and Days* on agriculture, are of some use in at least serving as a beginning point in Greek intellectual engagement with the world that would make spectacular advances in all fields of learning after 500 BCE. Despite the early literary

FIGURE 7. Greco-Bactrian silver coin of Demetrius I, ca. 200–180 BCE. Courtesy of the American Numismatic Society.

evidence, the debate about how much commodity exchange existed before the 6th century BCE, when the material evidence becomes clearer and more abundant, continues. Whatever the case there was an aristocratic "audience" for the poetry, and a negative attitude toward "commodity exchange."[178] The dismissal that Aristotle, or Xenophon, both geniuses of the 4th century BCE, may have thought "economically" but can hardly be representative of economic thought in their times is common.[179] Still, illiterates did not create the modern field of economics either, and there is much in both of these Greek authors that presage later thinking even in the realm of public policy. For classical economies, inscriptions and literary/philosophical treatments have generally provided the framework. Both Herodotus and Xenophon are important testimonies for the role of cross-cultural exchange in the Greek world. Polybius is an important (and no doubt underexploited) source for both the structure and scale of Hellenistic state economies, on settlements and migrations, on war and booty, and on the states as economic actors.[180]

Neo-Babylonian temple archives have provided an extraordinary wealth of information, but they come from a handful of places. Private archives such as the Egibi family archive suggest entrepreneurial trading activity in staple commodities side by side with institutional trade within regional networks.[181] Above all, the Neo-Babylonian archives are an especially rich source for economic historians and are beginning to be more fully exploited. Yet there is much more to do. Of the approximately one hundred thousand tablets in Western collections roughly eighteen thousand are now published. Jursa's team has transliterated another five thousand unpublished texts in a database. Catalogues exist of the most important collections, and therefore archives can be reconstructed.[182] The texts come from two major temples archives, and for private archival material of elite families, the majority of texts derive from five sites, Babylon, Borsippa, Nippur, Sippar, and Uruk.[183] Despite that, though, Babylonia in the mid-first millennium BCE is one of the best-documented places for economic activity in the whole of antiquity. The Babylonian astronomical diaries, amounting to roughly twelve hundred texts dating from the mid-7th century to 61 BCE, record the prices of six commodities, weather, and astronomical observations and are arguably the single most important dataset from antiquity.[184]

The Greek and demotic Egyptian papyri, often preserved in mummy cartonnage, are a unique source for economic history. They are attractive for many reasons, among which is that we can get some purchase on "nonelite" economic behavior.[185] The census documents from the Ptolemaic period are especially important for studying the structure of households, the range of professional occupations, and the role of the household census in the fiscal system.[186] Rostovtzeff already was prescient in warning: "It has become a habit among scholars to say that papyrological materials exclusively illustrates the economic life of Egypt and has no significance for the evolution of the rest of the ancient world."[187] Egypt has its peculiarities—its monsoon-driven ecology and its long, narrow shape being the most important—but, when we can compare, most of these peculiarities are common to Egypt and to other Hellenistic monarchies. Greek papyri survive from elsewhere, and these texts show that the structure and language of the texts bear close similarity to the Egyptian texts. The scattered survival of the texts, the bias toward Fayyum villages for the Greek papyri, the ancient sorting of texts that survive as recycled cartonnage in animal mummies (figure 8), and human mummy masks in family and official archives are some of the problems.[188] Figure 10 shows the number of dated texts; the peaks are attributable to large archives; for example, in 257 BCE the peak is the Zenon archive.[189] Some everyday economic transactions, leases, and animals sales were not written or do not survive in archives, which can be misleading in economic analysis.[190] Nevertheless the Zenon, Menches, Heroninus, and Apion archives are easily the best sources for a wide range of issues around land management and agriculture in the Hellenistic and Roman worlds.[191] The interesting class of funerary priests known as *choachytes* (lit. "water pourers") who maintained funerary libation offerings for the deceased have left us extensive information of the economic activity of a middling class in the Achaemenid and Ptolemaic periods in several large archives primarily coming from Memphis, Hawara in the Fayyum, and Thebes.[192]

How representative the archives were, however, for our understanding of economic behavior in the broader Hellenistic or Roman worlds remains problematic. For example, in his classic analysis of the Ptolemaic economy based on a small selection of texts from the Zenon archive, Rostovtzeff argued that the

FIGURE 8. Crocodile mummies from Tebtunis (Fayyum), Egypt, Ptolemaic period. Courtesy of the Egypt Exploration Society

texts stood proxy for an imagined new economic system imposed throughout Egypt and part of larger Hellenistic trends throughout the eastern Mediterranean, but this has been shown to be incorrect.[193] There were good reasons to use the Zenon archive: it is the largest archive from Ptolemaic Egypt, accounting for a good percentage of texts from the 3d century BCE (figure 10), documenting a large estate of a high official at Philadelphia near the Fayyum.

Ostraca (figure 9), small sherds of pottery or limestone, are also virtually unique to Egypt, at least in terms of quantity and the information they provide. Tens of thousands of these, written in Greek and demotic Egyptian, are in theory of great importance in measuring tax rates and agricultural production.[194] Most of them are tax receipts, and such texts provide evidence of local economic conditions, at least what was taxable, as well as social and scribal networks that were linked to institutions like banking.[195] But they remain extremely difficult as sources for the wider economy, because they often cannot be dated to specific years.

Papyrologists, like most scholars who work on Egyptian and Near Eastern material, tend to stick to the texts themselves and hesitate going beyond what the texts say. That leads to what can be narrow analyses of economic behavior

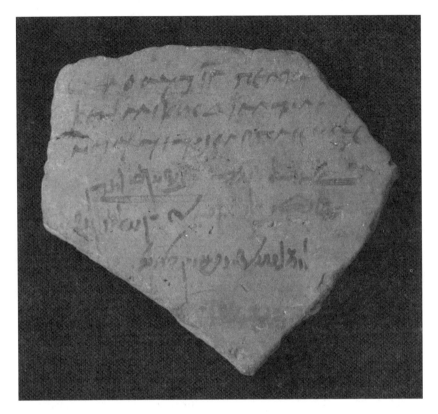

FIGURE 9. A Greek tax receipt ostracon, with demotic subscription. Copyright © Staatliche Museen zu Berlin—Ägyptisches Museum und Papyrussammlung, Scan: Berliner Papyrusdatenbank, P 4313.

and usually means analysis of archival material that comes from a single place, or at least a single cache of texts.[196] There are other kinds of texts that have received attention; among the more interesting are graffiti, common everywhere in the Mediterranean. Archaeological material increasingly is dominating discussions of institutional change and of economic performance.

Family and official archives from Ptolemaic and Roman Egypt provide unparalleled information of family structure and household economic activity. The database of archives in Leuven, Belgium, counts 502 archives dating from the Ptolemaic to the Byzantine period.[197] The information in them provide a variety of economic information on different scales, from individual household activity (property sale and lease, marriage agreements), to state business ranging from village land survey information and tax collection to the administration of temples and large agricultural estates. The papyri are an outstanding source for private law and the administration of justice.[198]

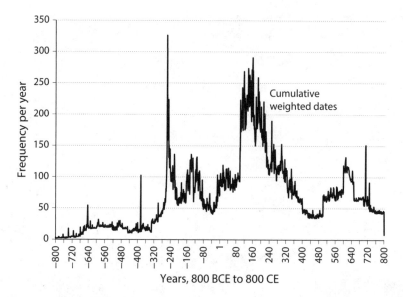

FIGURE 10. Totals of dated documentary texts from Egypt, 8th century BCE–8th century CE (n = 111,654), using the "weighted dates" method to show cumulative weights per year. From Van Beek and Depauw (2013).

Prosopography, that is, the assembly of information about individuals who are mentioned in the texts, has been a dominant method of working with papyri and ostraca, and a study of banking families at Thebes illustrates what can be done by such patient study.[199]

There is a good deal of evidence for ancient economies, but it is not easy to use, and much of it was ignored by general treatments of ancient economies. Rostovtzeff and Heichelheim established a path that is generally followed these days, with a focus on the collection of datable evidence, less attention or reference to economic theory per se. One of the features of scholarship in the last twenty years has been a much fuller account, place by place, and often archive by archive, of the ancient material. The use of evidence from the Hellenistic period now provides us with a much deeper body of material with which to build a richer economic history of the Mediterranean world of the first millennium BCE.

Although many have bemoaned the nature of premodern economic evidence, there is much that can be done quantitatively. It is true, of course, that it can hardly be compared to modern economic data. There are many gaps, many uncertainties; not the least is in the realm of demography, where our records allow only educated guesses of ancient populations. The best we can do here is to establish parameters, and to deploy comparative models.

Scholarship in the last forty years has proceeded apace, examining practically every detail of ancient economic structure and behavior. There are dozens of specialized studies of ceramics, amphorae transport vessels, and quantitative studies of coin hoards, coin circulation, prices, the distribution of land, and agricultural production in some regions. Intensive archaeological work, aided by the use of GIS and other technologies, and the ability to survey and excavate underwater, as the spectacular results at places like Alexandria have shown, have provided an overwhelming amount of new material and sheds light in some detail on certain places.[200] Generalizing from these results, however, remains difficult. We are still left, usually, with being more secure about saying something about a particular place than about the overall economy at the state level. Documentary evidence about towns and villages in Ptolemaic and Roman Egypt, often regarded as "parochial," have nevertheless been among the best places, along with Babylon, to reconstruct economic conditions of the land on local and regional scales and in some detail.

The quantification of data has been one of the most important trends of the last forty years, building on the earlier efforts of Heichelheim, Duncan-Jones, and others.[201] Archaeology is also playing a very large, indeed a central, role in the debates. Andrew Wilson, along with Alan Bowman at the Oxford Roman Economy Project on quantification of the Roman economy, is devoted to "the fundamentals of the Roman imperial economy and analyses all major economic activities (including agriculture, trade, commerce, and extraction), utilizing quantifiable bodies of archaeological and documentary evidence and placing them in the broader structural context of regional variation, distribution, size and nature of markets, supply and demand."[202] It is a project that can be imitated for earlier periods. As I will suggest in chapter 5, the integration of quantified climate proxy data will be an important aspect of all studies of premodern economies in the years ahead.

Surveying the evidence from which the economic history of the ancient world is built raises issues about our ability to draw general conclusions about institutional change. One of the important challenges here is to understand how the textual and archaeological evidence we have can be situated within temporal and spatial boundaries and long-term trends of first millennium history. That is the subject that I next want to survey.

CHAPTER 3

Bronze, Iron, and Silver

TIME, SPACE, AND GEOGRAPHY AND
ANCIENT MEDITERRANEAN ECONOMIES

> Throughout history, cross-cultural interactions also have influenced lives
> and fortunes across the boundary lines of societies and cultural regions.
> Indeed, they have often influenced ostensibly internal developments.
>
> —BENTLEY (1996:769–70)

> The Mediterranean has no unity but that created by the movements of
> men, the relationships they imply, and the routes they followed.
>
> —BRAUDEL (1995[1949]:276)

TIME/SPACE BOUNDARIES

Imagine if I were going to give you an exam, a pretty serious comprehensive
exam, in ancient history. I shall ask you to be able to summarize the history
of human civilization from the Neolithic revolution to Cleopatra. I am
mean, so I give you no study guide, and no bibliography to consult. What
would you do? Besides going to the library and asking a research librarian
for assistance, your first instinct might be to go on Amazon.com and start
searching for textbooks that would summarize the agricultural revolution,
the histories of early China, the Near East, Egypt, Greece, and so on. Or you
might do a search on Google.com and get summaries, some of them even
up-to-date. You might get some idea of history, of events, of the rise and fall
of dynasties, and so on. But if you put together the books, or the webpages,
in chronological order, would you be able to explain economic or social
change? It would be difficult. What appears to be a neat, cut-and-dried
march of funny names and places, a geographically and chronologically constrained series of events, and a seemingly endless series of wars belies the
messy nature of human history. Historical processes, rarely treated in ancient history textbooks or online, are more difficult to treat well and must be
explained in terms of temporal and geographical boundaries. In the next
couple of chapters I want to try to establish a framework for understanding
this messiness. I also want to examine some of the dynamic drivers of historical change by examining how time, space, and environment played roles.

One of my home departments at Yale, the History Department, categorizes me as being a member of the European history group, although my specialized work concentrates on Egypt and western Asia primarily. The reason for this is simple and an old one, and the same reason why Finley wrote about "the ancient economy" but was concerned only with Greece and Rome. Ancient history used to mean (it still does in many circles) classical history, a history of Greece and Rome, seeking an early European historical narrative. The history of Hellenistic states in Egypt and western and central Asia were left to specialists in other languages and cultures. But even then there are problems. In the case of the bilingual society of Ptolemaic Egypt, certain archives of Greek and demotic Egyptian papyri were published separately by specialists in Greek and Egyptian language, leaving the actual analysis of the complete archive for a later time.

Ancient historians tend to treat each phase of history as bounded, isolated polities. Each culture is usually defined by linguistic boundaries, for example, the Greek world, Greco-Roman civilization, ancient Egypt, and so on. As we saw in the previous chapter, there are different criteria to divide historical periods not by culture but by broader global trends as well. Superimposed on these cultural boundaries (and one could add other criteria such as religion), historians usually select a polity bounded by time and space, say 4th century Athens, or 6th century Babylonia, or, sometimes more broadly the Achaemenid Empire. Typically this kind of division is both conventional and dependent on specific evidence that can be deployed to examine economic behavior or a particular institution. But it is also a crude device for much of Mediterranean history. The Greek world, for example, was deeply connected to and interacted with Phoenician traders and, later, the Achaemenid Empire. We cannot understand Athens without taking account of the substantial number of slaves imported from the Achaemenid Empire.[1] It drew important lessons from both. Historians tend to treat the Achaemenid Empire and the eastern Hellenistic states (the Ptolemaic and Seleukid kingdoms) that succeeded as quite separate states. In fact there was essential continuity between them, and one can consider the Hellenistic successor states as "splinters" of the Achaemenid Empire while also recognizing certain changes in imperial rule.[2] There remains much work to do to distinguish, however, between institutional changes, whether Greek, Persian, or otherwise, and geographic or climatic constraints across political boundaries.

The new political boundaries of Iron Age states are an important consideration in economic performance. Imperial space allowed greater movement, of trade goods, people, and animals (as well as disease). Long-distance trade cut across political boundaries, and in some cases, the Phoenician trading cities being one, economic power extended far beyond political territory.

Disease, of course, had no political constraints. A change in ruler or even in dynasty was merely one type of superficial change; underlying societies moved at a different pace, and ethnic and cultural identities were complex. The heterogeneous attitudes that Jews had toward Greek culture in the Hellenistic period is one example. A soldier of Cretan descent living in the Ptolemaic military camp at Pathyris in Upper Egypt in the 2d century BCE is another example that illustrates the internested set of cultural boundaries and identities that could exist within a single family within what was the wider Greek *oikoumene* initiated by Alexander's conquests.[3]

Human agency is aided or constrained by geography and environment in several important ways. Steppe frontiers, what Marshall Sahlins called "ethnic borders," were regions of great historical momentum, "generating further advance" in societies.[4] New empires arose on frontier zones of intense competition between "metaethnic" groups. Metaethnic frontiers, an agglomeration of ethnic groups within a polity, generated greater internal social cohesion through competition, which yields greater cooperation, which in turn results in the ability of groups to expand. The internal cohesion within 4th century Macedon, and its conquest of the Greek and Achaemenid worlds, and the rise of Rome on the fringes of the Hellenistic world, for example, are good examples of the process.

Text-based historians face a different kind of selection problem than do archaeologists who work at a single site or a region. Moving from the evidence of one or two sites, or one archive of documents to analyze, for example, "the Ptolemaic economy" results in the same problem though, namely attempting to build a bridge from microhistorical evidence to broader claims about the economy of a premodern state. The definition of a region and thus of "interregional" interaction can be approached from several points of view, including political economy or the fiscal control of coinage, or by studying the flow commodities across space and time.[5] In recent years, social network analysis has been an important technique by which to understand the time and space of "region."[6]

Time/space boundaries of written archives and archaeological material are usually different, and combining them to explain performance, or rise and decline and so on, can become problematic.[7] The size and the political dominance of Athens would appear to be an exception, but we cannot leave out external relationships, especially with grain imports, and Athens can hardly stand for the entirety of the one thousand city-states of the Greek world. The same problem arises with Babylon in the Near East, exceptional in size and in documentation. Both Athens and Babylon, of course, had outsized roles culturally and as imperial centers. But the question arises to what extent Athenian or Babylonian institutions can stand in for all Greek or

Near Eastern cities. The standard political periodizations such as "Neo-Babylonian," "Achaemenid," "Classical," or "Hellenistic" are of limited value in analyzing long-term trends especially since they miss important shifts, as well as short-term changes either as a response to a crisis or shock, or a significant institutional change under the persuasion of a "cultural entrepreneur." Of course, such categories deemphasize continuity altogether.[8]

To draw a boundary around anything is "to define, analyze, and reconstruct it."[9] Understanding time/space boundary transitions is critically important for historical analysis and has often been acknowledged.[10] But the problems involved in specifying temporal and spatial boundaries and political transitions has not been sufficiently addressed by ancient historians. The concept of the "long" century or millennium (they are almost always long; "short" centuries rarely seem to occur) tacitly acknowledges the problem between temporally bounded time and heterogeneous rates of social change.[11] Here I survey some basic issues and how they have been treated in the past. In subsequent chapters I develop these ideas in the specific context of environmental, climatic, and institutional change. In the last twenty years, just about every conventional way of determining temporal and spatial boundaries in the premodern Mediterranean world has been challenged.

Historical geography involves clearly defining temporal-political boundaries around physical territory. This is challenging enough. Institutions don't stop or start, usually, in a moment in time. Geopolitical boundaries are even more difficult to define because such entities can be defined either by culture or by political control.[12] Modern Italy is easier than, for example, the Roman Empire, to delimit in any precise way, particularly to define time and space. Things were never static, but trying to establish time/space boundaries is an essential component of comparative analyses. One solution has been to work within well-defined regions, as Pomeranz has done in explaining the "Great Divergence" between Europe and China by a concentration on Lancashire, England, and the lower Yangzi delta in China.[13] Another solution to this basic problem has been proposed by the Seshat comparative historical database project, where two types of geographic unit are used to control historical data: (1) "Natural Geographic Areas" (NGAs), a fixed, bounded geographic area, one hundred kilometers by one hundred kilometers, and (2) "Free Form Areas" (FFAs) that define a territory that was encompassed by a political entity or some other defining characteristic, for example, a mining region.[14] For the purposes of coding and analysis, and the capturing of natural changes in the internal dynamics of a political system, the temporal boundaries of polities in the Seshat project, are two hundred to three hundred years. Social and trade networks that crossed cultural and geopolitical boundaries are becoming recognized as an important part of understanding not only small- and large-scale trade flows but a host of other kinds of exchange that drove institutional change across fixed temporal and spatial boundaries.

There are several types of change, and indeed several drivers of it, that are important: institutional change, environmental change, climate change, or changes in belief systems or mentalities, and so on. Most historians work on very short timescales of decades, perhaps a century. In many cases, ancient historians are bound by the temporal and geographic limits determined by the archives on which they work. Many important historical changes operate on millennial or even longer timescales. For some scholars like Horden and Purcell, about whom more below, there was no significant *change*, that is, no identifiable *trend*, in the Mediterranean, only *variability*. History was a random walk. But that leaves out, among other things, how different political economies played roles in the scaling up of city and state size, in war, and in responding to climate changes. States, in fact, were powerful forces for capturing, concentrating, dispersing, and focusing resources. The German historical school famously developed theories of change as linear stages.[15] This triumphalist, teleological, and Eurocentric approach is too crude to explain all the complexities of change.[16] Michael Mann's influential work has proposed what he called the IEMP (Ideological, Economic, Military, Political Power) model. In this model, which was inspired by Weber's analogy of railroad tracks along which society moved until "switched" onto a different track, every society comprises four overlapping networks of social power.[17] The collective action of humans within these overlapping power sources determined the direction and the rate of social change. Change itself was cyclical and nonlinear. Understanding the coupled dynamics between humans and climate change is even more of a challenge given the complexity of time and spatial scales in climatic change, which cannot be categorized as simply "long-term," but rather operating on several different timescales.[18]

In terms of spatial boundaries, other solutions to boundedness are possible. Many have been inspired by von Thünen's (1783–1850) work by studying a particular region. That is a more difficult boundary to define than, for example, river systems that provide a natural bounded system to analyze. Remarkably, though, this has not been carried through very often in the Mediterranean, for example, a history of the entire Nile River basin, as opposed to the Egyptian Nile, which has been well studied of course.[19] Recently, Peter Thonemann has provided an excellent history of the Maeander River valley in the long run, highlighting the links between human communities and a particular physical environment.[20] These links, between coasts, mountains, and rivers, between humans and their environment, and between state aims and human responses, are more complex to establish and varied considerably over time, but they are important.[21] The dynamism of climate and environment, the fluctuation of rainfall and river floods, soil erosion, earthquakes, and volcanic eruptions that suddenly changed conditions for short periods of time, the movement and interaction of people and animals through sometimes vast territory in longer temporal scales, is not easy to capture in historical analysis.

Finley used geography to define his "Greco-Roman world" with "common modes of behavior" "tied together" in a single climatic zone, the Mediterranean, from 1000 BCE to 500 CE.[22] This has stood for a long time for the territorial and temporal boundaries of "the ancient economy," although long-distance trade networks were also recognized as important. But the political boundaries of ancient states were not always well defined. Various studies of the "Greek" economy refer to Athens, Attica, the Athenian "empire," or the "Greater Athenian State" that includes polities that interacted with Athens.[23] Cross-cultural exchange patterns and empire building were important drivers in economic and territorial integration and in institutional change.[24] But it is no simple task to assess, for example, the impact of the Achaemenid Empire on territories that it either ruled or came into contact with it.

Egyptian and ancient Near Eastern civilizations were, seemingly, a world apart, part of the Asian and the African continents strictly speaking, whose inhabitants spoke and wrote Semitic and African languages. These civilizations were often treated as not a part of Europe, and therefore not a part of European history, cursed by their geographies and outside of the Mediterranean climate zone and, given the continuous experience of empire in these regions, often treated as "timeless." As we have seen, Egyptian and Near Eastern economies have been studied separately from classical economies. It was not uncommon in the 19th century to analyze institutions by language family, and so the emphasis was placed on Indo-European civilizations in studies such as Henry Maine's *Ancient Law* (below). Basic historical periodization was a mid-19th century European assumption of universal, linear "progress" from antiquity to modernity that occurred in stages "in progressive societies" as Maine argued. But not all societies proceeded accordingly. In large part this fundamental division goes back to Marx, who postulated a western European track and an "Asiatic" track, which was distinguished by the *Asiatic Mode of Production*, instantiated by the "hydraulic civilizations" that grew up in the river valleys of Egypt, Mesopotamia, and China.

In a good deal of work on premodern economies, Egypt and Near Eastern civilizations were often treated merely as prologue, or even as prehistory.[25] While Egypt and western Asia was the civilizational core of later Mediterranean developments, much of the analysis of "the ancient economy" has proceeded from the point of view of Europe, of democratic Athens, and the Roman Empire (and its legacy). Egyptian history, and the history of the ancient Near East, has hardly had the same historical treatment as classical economies in the scheme of historical developments. There are some good reasons for this. Perhaps the greatest challenge for historians of the Iron Age Near East is to assess historical change with the continual imperial overwriting of western Asia, which saw several imperial states governing the same territory. The Neo-Babylonian state took over much of the Assyrian Empire before it. The Achaemenid state was "Hellenized" by the Ptolemies and the Seleukids. Near Eastern states have often been shunted to the side in the historical social sciences because they were considered politically "despotic," and therefore were outside of the mainstream of western political and intellectual developments. It is a curious and indefensible intellectual gap because the first millennium BCE marks a major transition from Bronze Age civilizations centered in the great river valleys and the Aegean to an increasingly interconnected, pan-Mediterranean land-sea economic region.[26]

TRANSITIONS, SHIFTS, UPSWEEPS

Historians tend to work within cultural and physical geographies, rather than economic geographies, however they are defined. While there are good reasons to do this, it makes little sense in terms of the analysis of economic institutions over any sort of timescale that would allow an understanding of change over time. Better boundaries for economic history are shifts in scale and intensity, in larger states, larger urban centers, larger consumption of energy, and so on.

Bentley suggests three major shifts in the history of civilization:

Early Complex Societies, ca. 3500–2000 BCE
Ancient Civilizations, ca. 2000–500 BCE
Classical Societies, ca. 500 BCE–500 CE[27]

Another powerful way to periodize is to think in terms of complexity and state capacity.[28] "Upward" or "imperial upsweeps" began in the second millennium BCE when the first empires controlled more than one million square kilometers. A second phase of imperial state formation occurred in the first millennium BCE when the largest states reached five to ten million square kilometers. Improvements in military technology and "world religions" played the major roles in allowing states to control large territory and integrate large populations. Over the course of the first millennium BCE, we can observe the very obvious trend from multiple state actors to a single hegemon, Rome, by the 2d century BCE. Overall we observe an increase in territorial scale of the state, and a decrease in the number of state actors.

Turchin periodizes as follows:[29]

Chiefdoms, ca. 7500 BP/ca. 5500 BCE
First states and cities, ca. 5000 BP/ca. 3000 BCE
Megaempires, ca. 2500 BP/ca. 500 BCE

Brooke organizes premodern history through the lens of climate changes as follows:[30]

Agricultural Revolution
Mid-Holocene, Late Neolithic, and Urban-State Revolution
Agrarian Empires
    Bronze Age Expansion and Crisis, 3000–1000 BCE
    Preclassical Crisis and Age of Iron, 1200–300 BCE
    Global Antiquity, 500 BCE–542 CE
    Global Dark Ages and Middle Ages, 542–1350 CE

The first millennium can be periodized into two parts, the Iron Age "recovery" and the "classical optimum."[31] These were important periods of state building. I agree with those who argue that they had cumulative effects on later developments, and formed an essential part in the emergence of the modern world.[32] Much of southwest Asia was governed by imperial states, while Egypt cycled between political fragmentation, imperial provincial rule, and centralized control. In the first millennium BCE, we are concerned with the following spatiotemporal periodizations:

Southwest Asia
    Neo-Assyrian Empire, 934–610 BCE
    Neo-Babylonian Empire, 625–539 BCE
    Achaemenid Empire, 550–330 BCE
    Seleukid Empire, 312–63 BCE
Egypt
    Third Intermediate Period, 1069–664 BCE (politically fragmented)
    Saite dynasty, 664–525 BCE (centralized state)
    Achaemenid imperial control, 525–359 BCE (imperial province)
    404–343 BCE (local control)
    Achaemenid imperial control, 343–332 BCE (imperial province)
    Ptolemaic dynasty, 332–30 BCE (centralized state)
Phoenicia
    Expansion, ca. 1200–800 BCE
    Achaemenid conquest, 539 BCE

Greece
    Archaic, 8th century BCE–480 BCE
    Classical, 480–323 BCE
    Hellenistic, 323–146 BCE
    Roman conquest, 146 BCE

Ancient historians tend to look at a few places in time and space where the evidence is best. Archaeologists and text-based scholars will work on different places and historical periods. It is still commonplace for archaeologists and historians to divide up historical phases of Mediterranean by the dominant metals, that is, the Stone/Copper/Bronze/Iron Ages. "Victorian ladders of Progress" Barker called this kind of periodization, and in the Near East and Egypt, historians break periods down into ruling dynasties or kingdoms.[33] Dates are better than cultural boundaries, and yet both utterly obscure important change.[34]

Periodization, of course, also obscures the fact that changes of any kind, economic, climate, linguistic, or religious practice, did not happen at the same time uniformly across a given territory. The annual rhythm of the Nile flood in summer, or in the spring for the Euphrates, dictated different responses than rain-fed regions of the Mediterranean. The term "Hellenistic" normally describes a period of history in the Mediterranean from Alexander the Great to the death of Cleopatra. But if a driving force of this period was the spread or diffusion of Greeks and Greek institutions outside of mainland Greece and the Aegean, then it is reasonably clear that the "Hellenistic" period began at different times in different places. For example, in Egypt, one could argue that it was the Saite period when Greek settlement and cultural influence that marked an important cultural shift within Egypt. Greek cultural influence was far greater in Egypt, for example, than in the Near East before Alexander's arrival. In other words, the traditional political historical framework for analyzing economic history is insufficient for understanding institutional change and continuity.

Center or "core" regions and peripheries from which resources were extracted, taken from world systems theory, is often used as the framework. Cross-cultural exchange was arguably a powerful force from the very emergence of civilizations in the Near East, Egypt, and elsewhere.[35] Take Egypt as an example. Historians, and Egyptologists in particular, have been guilty of reifying a single, static, "coherent" entity called "ancient Egypt." But there never was a single coherent polity that we can label "Egypt," and Egyptian civilization was created by several different ethnic groups. The history of the delta, much better understood now than it was a quarter century ago, was a different world, much more a part of the Mediterranean in its urban character and in

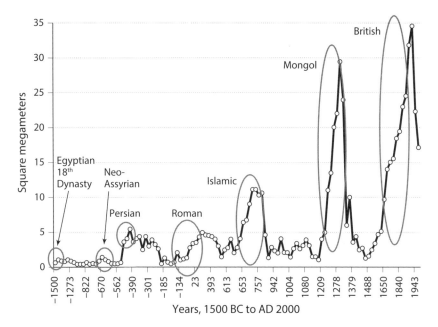

FIGURE 11. Imperial upsweeps. Chase-Dunn et al., http://irows.ucr.edu/papers/irows34 /irows34.htm. Based on Taagepera's (1978, 1979) growth-decline curves.

direct trade connections than the upper Nile valley that has given us so many royal monuments. And the Saite period was substantially different from the Old Kingdom despite the concerted efforts of Saite culture to claim political and cultural continuity with it.[36] Trade in the delta also brought the exchange of ideas; a new writing system known as demotic Egyptian developed here, perhaps under the pressure of recording large numbers of economic transactions, and later was diffused as the main writing system throughout Egypt. Moving beyond Egypt, the classic example of cross-cultural contact bringing change is the Phoenician contribution to alphabetic writing in Greece via, it has been cogently argued, Cyprus and mercenary activity there.[37] The Achaemenid Empire had profound effects on later economic developments in the Near East and Egypt but also on its rival Athens.

C. R. Chase-Dunn et al. divide their analysis into five major periods of imperial upsweeps in the "core" as follows:

1. Akkadian-Egyptian
2. West Asian-Mediterranean
3. Islamic
4. Mongol
5. Modern

The imperial upsweep curve (figure 11) provides a bit more nuance than the usual hockey stick growth curve, and also, importantly, some political context to economic expansion. In a sense though, Macedon and Rome, like Assyria and the Achaemenids before them, were "marcher states" on the periphery of older state systems.[38] Both arose on the periphery of larger states, on what Turchin calls "metaethnic frontiers."[39] It is worth pointing out that the durability of empires shows no significant increase over the long run.[40]

PERIODIZATION AND TIMESCALES

There have been a number of approaches to the basic problems of periodization and the meaningful capture of change over time. The core of the challenge is to identify what kind of change we are explaining and the location and vector of the change. Braudel famously divided historical time into three distinct scales, short term (events, individual human experience), medium term (political, social, economic history, agrarian and demographic cycles), and long term (*longue durée*, climate or "geohistory," civilizational scale).[41] The first, and the individual above all, was ignored, or at least downplayed by Braudel, in favor of longer-term forces of civilization and climate.

Spatiotemporal boundaries are often difficult to determine with any kind of precision. More recently, the idea of timelessness has been raised by Horden and Purcell's paradigm, but such an approach would only highlight different rates of change and would eliminate explanations of change over time altogether.[42]

The structure of time within a given political territory, while usually not theorized or operationalized in studies of premodern economies, is an important consideration. Dynamic cycles of political consolidation, or centralization alternating with breakdowns, events (wars, but also plagues, understandable in fixed time but with long-term effects), long-distance trade networks, migration, ecological and climate change (anthropogenic and natural), shifts in religious practice, the "expansionary forces" of imperial state formation, all these forces cut across spatial boundaries. All these must be taken into account in periodizing, and all these phenomena are most clearly seen in deep timescales.[43] Here there is a tension between historians who work with documents often dated to a specific month and year and geophysicists and geographers who work on much larger timescales.

Historical time is normally divided into "fixed units" of linear time that are determined by our ancient sources. Environment and geography, developed more fully in chapter five, played important roles in the frequency of cross-cultural interactions, and we might look to understand the dynamic exchange patterns that arose in the Aegean as an important contrast to exchange in what Broodbank calls "alluvium-focused empires."[44] With the rhythm of environmental changes we might expect differential rates of change.

History is about explaining *persistence* and *change* over *time*.[45] In human terms time can be reckoned in two ways. The first is linear or "cosmological" time, the passing of life day by day in succession. And second is "phenomenological" time, time experienced as verbal tense: past, present, and future.[46] The latter is important, for example, in the conceptualization of interest rates, which connects present to future time. It is important to note here that change, usually, proceeded slowly, almost imperceptibly, with "small innovations" and adjustments.[47] But institutional change, changes in norms and customs, and climate change can have an impact on several timescales.[48] The velocity of movement through territory, however, how long it took for information to reach point B from point A, how long it took to travel from one place to another, was a decisive factor in price-setting markets, or indeed the lack of them, in the premodern world.[49] Topography, land versus sea, and season mattered for speed of travel.

The effects of plague on human populations, and technological change, created "random" interactions with long-term timescales.[50] The importance of local time reckoning to communities is shown by the fact that conquering states overwrote or at least attempted to overwrite it. With imperial or dynastic time tied to religious rituals: the Ptolemies embedded their new dynasty within Egyptian dynastic history in the history of Egypt written by the 3d century BCE historian Manetho.[51] Ptolemy III attempted (unsuccessfully) to reform the Egyptian calendar by fixing the dynasty to cosmic time by establishing a dynastic festival at the added leap-year day at the beginning of the calendar year timed with the heliacal rising of Sirius.[52] The Seleukid kings dealt with historical time in a novel way, accumulatively counting the years of each king's reign "in a Seleukid era" a theft of time from the Babylonian calendar.[53]

Climate change can be measured over millennia and now with high-resolution proxy data, in decadal and in annual scales, but measuring the spatial impact of change, drought for example, is still extremely challenging.[54] The complex structure of time and timescale problematizes any kind of theory of causality, or any overarching grand theory of economic history.[55] Structural demographic change, technological change, fiscal and other kinds of institutional change, commodity prices trends, consumption preferences, to name just a few things, all move at different rates.[56] So much is emphasized by Broodbank, who provides a metanarrative of Mediterranean history that covers the Neolithic, during which diffusion of technology of agricultural production took millennia, to the Iron Age, when it took mere three months to travel from one end of the basin to the other.[57]

This shrinking, or "compression" of time/space induced massive institutional changes and innovation as well as reactions that reinforced local identities, which, for example, may have forced the thinking necessary for the creation of city-state political institutions.[58] The perception of time moving more rapidly in the first millennium BCE was real and is perhaps reflected in the technical advances in the instruments of time keeping that we see in the Hellenistic period and most audaciously seen in the Antikythera mechanism.[59] And it is equally important to stress coevolutionary processes and connections across the distinctive cultures of the basin. But we should stress that the rate of change in the premodern world did not come close to matching the rate of change in the modern world. For Anthony Giddens, the rate of change and time/space compression is a characteristic of "modernity."[60] It is an occasion for another hockey stick graph.

Yet historians still prefer coherent time/space units. In Greek history we periodize into three main phases: archaic, classical, and Hellenistic. Even with this straightforward division, new evidence and broader perspectives complicate the picture. Archaeological material, for example, has forced us to consider the 8th century BCE not as a "dark" age but as a "renaissance" but with at least certain places in the Greek world exhibiting strong cultural continuities with the past.[61] Place matters, and differential changes were often the result of local structural forces. It is arguable, for example, that the "Hellenistic" period began in Egypt in the 7th century BCE when Greeks first settled in Egypt, or with Athenian fiscal advice in the mid-4th century BCE, not with the Ptolemaic state in the later 4th century.[62] In other words, substantial social change was underway well in advance of Alexander. Political events, reinforced by our literary sources such as Polybius, were usually the markers of change. The Hellenistic period is problematic for a variety of reasons and tends to get absorbed by Roman history, but the eastern Mediterranean remained distinctive throughout the Roman Empire. Strict cultural/territorial boundaries miss longer-term trends and developments, which do not map onto the usual periodizations. World historians have stressed large-scale territorial connectivity, thinking in terms, for example, of an Afro-Eurasian world system that emerged in the Bronze Age.[63] Hicks understood the transformation from "custom" and "command" to "the rise of the market" "as a single process" up to the Industrial Revolution.[64] But it was a slow and gradual process and far from homogenous across the world. Phoenician and Greek city-states 750–550 BCE have been used as a watershed for the rise of the market.[65] It has been my argument here that this framing misses much of the earlier development of the economic history of the Mediterranean.

THE MEDITERRANEAN BASIN

Over the last forty years there have been many opinions about how to connect the "Mediterranean" to economic history. Opinions have been divided between seeing one single entity, many Mediterraneans, or no Mediterranean at all.[66] A basic climatological pattern would seem to be shared across most parts of the Mediterranean's lengthy coast: hot dry summers, cool wet winters, periodic cycles, high rainfall variability, and sudden catastrophic shocks (figure 12). The effective "unity" of the Mediterranean climatic zone, driven by such influences as the Atlantic westerlies, could technically include the "fertile crescent" and the Black Sea. But the ubiquity of the famous triad: olives, grain, and grapes, "probably established in Bronze Age Greece," has usually been used in culturally circumscribing the region.[67] This excludes Egypt and a good part of western Asia that are in different, "non-Mediterranean" climatic zones yet can be considered to be "connected" to the Mediterranean politically and/or economically.[68] The physical and climatological boundaries taken together are suggestive of a different "cartographic frontier."[69]

The Mediterranean is divided into two "subbasins," on either side of the Straight of Sicily; the eastern basin is twice as large as the western. The eastern Mediterranean-Levant region experiences "the most variable and extreme climatic conditions in the entire Mediterranean region" while the western half of the sea was moderated by proximity to the Atlantic Ocean.[70] There appears to have been an inverse precipitation relationship between east and west.[71] Beyond the cultural "triad," the flora of the Mediterranean region is one of the most diverse; some twenty-five thousand species have been documented.[72]

The topography and climate of the Mediterranean offers major contrasts to the great river valley civilizations. The Mediterranean climate has two basic regimes, a warm dry summer, with drought conditions, and wet winters driven primarily by Atlantic westerlies and cyclogenesis in the Mediterranean.[73] Dry (rain-fed) farming of the main cereal crops, wheat and barley, was the norm, and barley remained an important and more widely grown crop on account of its hardiness in poor soils and in drought conditions (figure 12). The complexity of landmass, mountains, "competing air masses," and the sea drove the regional variation, "strong horizontal and vertical climatic gradients," or "micro climates."[74] This climatic zone extends across the entire basin from the Alps to North Africa although there is a considerable climate gradient.[75] Greece has a very long coastline, twice as long as Italy at ninety-three hundred miles, and no settlement was more than sixty-eight miles from the coast.[76] The great ranges, the Atlas in Morocco, the Taurus in Anatolia,

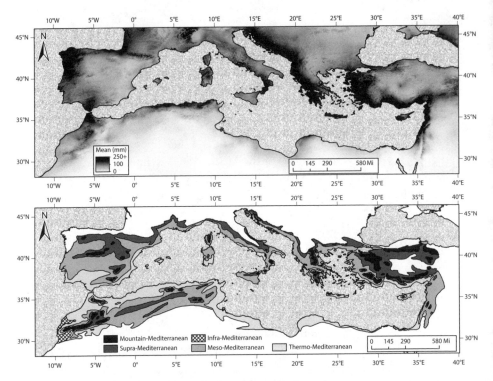

FIGURE 12. Unity or diversity? Rainfall amounts (top); Mediterranean vegetation types (bottom). The top panel shows the mean December rainfall at 30 arc-seconds resolution, 1950–2000, using the Worldclim v.4.0 data. The bottom panel indicates Bioclimate regions of the Mediterranean, indicating mean temperature of the coldest month, and indicative of vegetation types. Adapted from Quézel & Médail (2003).

the Pindos in central Greece, and smaller peaks in Macedonia, Crete, and elsewhere have different ecosystems.[77] Western Greece, for example, receives about twice as much rain as areas in the Aegean. This "hydrologic deficit" shaped the development of cities in the Aegean.[78] Rainfall patterns between western and eastern Greek mainland and the Aegean islands were strong, but cyclical changes in land use even in a single region are a reminder of how complex the interactions between human and geophysical forces were.[79] Mediterranean islands, Sicily, Cyprus, and Rhodes, like Malta later, were hubs, serving as cultural and economic crossroads between East and West, North and South. They served as the engines of cross-cultural exchange during the Iron Age and well beyond it.

The "Mediterranean" as a unit of historical analysis is, of course, a "construct," and largely built by those who are interested in seeing a holistic Mediterranean, that is to say in particular by Roman historians.[80] Finley's conception was different. For him, the Mediterranean was "static" because of high transportation, information, and transaction costs that served to limit exchange, and it was "cellular," because households were self-sufficient.[81] And to a certain extent it tracks the history of exchange in the region. There are earlier examples that suggest that a Mediterranean-wide trade network requires us to think across the entire sea in certain periods, but in other periods, across other physical boundaries.[82] The Bronze Age eastern Mediterranean linked Near Eastern states within a wider "trans-regional cultural system."[83] But one could go back to the early Holocene and the known exchange patterns that extended "from the Middle Euphrates to the Negev" generating trade flows from central Anatolia, the Mediterranean, and the Red Sea.[84] The control of metal resources was one powerful driver for establishing longer trade routes. The political control of rain fed regions was another. These regions became the location of Greek colonization and, later, of contested imperial space in the Hellenistic period. The long-run view of the Mediterranean basin does show a distinct pattern of agrarian intensification/disintensification around three iconic crops: vines, olives (both native to the region), and grains (barley and wheat), the famous "Mediterranean triad."

Braudel's study established the "unity" of the sea as "a complex of seas." For him a single Mediterranean provided the historical framework that allowed him to combine economic geography with different rates of change.[85] The Mediterranean basin is a complex region of the world, with much local variety in crop, soil, climatic conditions, and structural drivers: floods, volcanism, soil erosion, and so on. It is the only place on the planet where three continents are united by a single sea, in itself a powerful force for "connectivity" and exchange.[86]

Braudel's posthumously published work on the ancient Mediterranean traces the story of the sea from the Paleolithic.[87] His earlier framework was powerful, and even if most historians have moved beyond it, it still casts a shadow on studies of the Mediterranean world and serves as a model for studying other seas, even deserts, as well.[88]

Several large books have been published since 2000 that continue Braudel's tradition, in the main by reacting against it, but with major and important differences to Braudel's great study. Horden and Purcell's *The Corrupting Sea* (2000); Grove and Rackham's *The Nature of Mediterranean Europe: An Ecological History* (2001), Michael McCormick's *Origins of the European Economy* (2001), Christopher Wickham, *Framing the Early Middle Ages* (2005), David Abulafia, *The Great Sea* (2011), and finally, Cyprian Broodbank, *The Making of the Middle Sea* (2013).[89] None of these authors focused specifically on the first millennium BCE, but all provide context for the relationship between the physical environment and the economy, and especially trade.

In their important book, Horden and Purcell turned Braudel's work on its head. There was no single Mediterranean but, instead, fragmentation, uncertainty, and connectivity.[90] Horden and Purcell think of the Mediterranean framework as a "fuzzy set . . . loosely defined." Yet despite three thousand years of coverage, or perhaps because of it, many important places are missing in the model, including Egypt and southwest Asia. Horden and Purcell view the sea through the lens of "four definite places": the Biqa valley, south Etruria, Cyrenaica, and Melos. Although Egypt was not strictly speaking a part of the sea for Horden and Purcell, Egyptian evidence is occasionally used. To build a complete picture, of course, over three thousand years is not possible anywhere in the Mediterranean; neither the archaeological not the textual evidence allows that.

Within Mediterranean microregions, there was much uncertainty. High variability of rainfall, "topographical fragmentation," and social connectivity and mobility have characterized human history within the confines of the sea.[91] "Risk" within a specific microregion was a key driver of "connectivity" in the Mediterranean.[92] But risk, of course, of crop failure, and of drought, existed globally, and connectedness between human groups is a feature that is well documented in the Eurasian Upper Paleolithic as well as in historic times, and in river valleys as well along the coasts. Each society managed risk in different ways, and those differences matter.[93] Much of premodern Mediterranean history has focused on the eastern and central Mediterranean, but Horden and Purcell's work focused on interactions and mobility. Recent work on the Hellenistic period has stressed the inclusion of the entire sea, but as we have seen with the Phoenician expansion, we would do well to consider the entire sea from the beginning of the Iron Age.[94]

In 1985, Evans, Rueschemeyer, and Skocpol called for "bringing the state back in." Horden and Purcell suggested the opposite, that we should remove "state" as an analytical category, and cites likewise, and replace them with the concepts of "connectivity," "fluidity," micro-regions" and "continuities."[95] Long-distance trade is deemphasized, replaced by the small-scale, the more everyday rhythms of life. They blur the boundary between urban and rural, preferring a simple continuum. It is a major departure from Finley's paradigm, and is no doubt influenced by current trends in "globalization theory."[96] They emphasize networks, unbounded by the chronological and cultural constraints of Finley, and the distinctive characteristics of the "pan-Mediterranean" centrifugal forces.[97] But forces of centralization pull in the other direction too, toward new centralizations, and that is clearly seen in the history of empire in the premodern world.[98] This long-term perspective of Braudel; Horden and Purcell; Grove and Rackham; and Broodbank forces us out of our specialized fields to ask broader questions about what

Broodbank has called "emergent properties" or what I am calling time/space boundary identification.[99] These include the development of institutions, the evolution of states, and the impact of environment, climate, and climate change on humans.

Grove and Rackham stressed the dynamism of the Mediterranean, and the long-term impact of humans and of climate change on the land. Broodbank focused on its long-run history and the forces that shaped the region before the rise of classical Greece. Measuring human impacts on their environments is difficult; exaggerating collapse or degradation can be easy.[100] In his detailed study of land use patterns in Spain and southern Greece, for example, Butzer suggests that understanding the cause and effect of either anthropogenic or natural climatic change over the long term is difficult.[101] Complex feedback loops and human perceptions are both important considerations. I develop this a little further regarding Egypt to conclude this chapter.

One of the features of all these studies is the idea of the "connectedness" of the Mediterranean.[102] The growth in the "connectivity" in the basin is the major theme too of Broodbank's synthetic history. The Indian Ocean is certainly one such place, progressively connected to the Mediterranean economies by state expansion beginning in Hellenistic period and ending with the rise of Islam in the 7th century CE.[103]

The idea of "Mediterraneanization" or "Mediterraneanism," continues to be popular among classical historians.[104] The concept does capture the idea of interaction spheres or exchange systems with an emphasis on interregional cross-cultural exchange and movement. But it also leads us naturally to the necessity of contemplating a much larger catchment for ancient Mediterranean economies. Changes over time are important here. I see development from an eastern Mediterranean–western Asian core in the third millennium BCE to a wider Mediterranean in the first millennium BCE and finally a two-ocean world, Mediterranean–Indian Ocean by the end of the millennium. Work in the archaeology of India and around the Black Sea has been very revealing that both regions were intimately connected to the Hellenistic and Roman worlds. The Atlantic was opened up by Hellenistic explorers such as Pytheas, as was the east African coast and hinterlands. But "connectedness," by itself in the end, is too vague.[105] To paraphrase James McPherson's rather curt dismissal of Fogel and Engerman's railroad index, we should analyze not merely "connectivity," but how the Sea connected people and places, for what purposes, and in what quantity.[106]

There have been many words used to describe how the Mediterranean shaped human history: unified, connected, corrupting, fragmented, semi-closed, to name the main ones. And cultural boundary lines have been drawn between North and South, and to a certain extent between East and

West. What is special about the environment is the settlement density around the sea. Human mobility and political structures, trade, war, climate change, determined how and where there were connections. Mobility and information flow were important processes.

In reality, Iron Age civilizations in the Mediterranean were situated within a complex dynamic region that was integrated and dis-integrated over time. Polybius's view of Hellenistic period space beyond the Mediterranean serves as a justifiable guide.[107] In other words, a "Mediterranean" model works fairly well for classical history and for the development of Thalassocratic empires based in the basin from Athens in the 5th century BCE, to Carthage and ultimately Rome. Egypt was very much in and of the Mediterranean by the first millennium BCE:[108] the settlement at Naukratis, before that trade flow into Herakleion, the Saite dynasty's use of Greek mercenary soldiers, and above all the Ptolemaic and then Roman annexation of Egypt. Egypt became increasingly urbanized under the Ptolemies. Nome (i.e., district) capitals grew bigger. But one could also of course write Egyptian history from the point of view of the Nile River basin, an Afro-centric history of the Mediterranean, which would be a very different kind of history. The recent archaeological work in central Asia and India, and work on long-distance trade, increasingly suggests that we need a much bigger framework, one that includes the Indian Ocean, at least for Hellenistic and Roman history, and one that also includes central Asia. World historians and "world system" theorists argue that we should "globalize ancient history" following scholars such as Frank.[109]

Horden and Purcell saw earthquakes and volcanism as having only short-term impacts. But in fact volcanism in particular could have longer-lasting impacts on climate, and even local eruptions could impact things further afield.[110] Pliny the Younger's account of the eruption of Vesuvius in 79 CE provides a famous narrative of an eruption with dramatic local affects:

> My uncle was stationed at Misenum, in active command of the fleet. On 24 August, in the early afternoon, my mother drew his attention to a cloud of unusual size and appearance. He had been out in the sun, had taken a cold bath, and lunched while lying down, and was then working at his books. He called for his shoes and climbed up to a place which would give him the best view of the phenomenon. It was not clear at that distance from which mountain the cloud was rising (it was afterwards known to be Vesuvius); its general appearance can best be expressed as being like an umbrella pine, for it rose to a great height on a sort of trunk and then split off into branches, I imagine because it was thrust upwards

FIGURE 13. Mount Etna, 3,330 m (10,922 feet), May 2015.

by the first blast and then left unsupported as the pressure subsided, or else it was borne down by its own weight so that it spread out and gradually dispersed. In places it looked white, elsewhere blotched and dirty, according to the amount of soil and ashes it carried with it.[111]

Pliny's description has given the name to a particular style of explosive eruption, *Plinian*, that can transport sulphates into the stratosphere and thereby impact climate globally. Krakatoa (1883) and the Novarupta eruption in Alaska (1912) are recent examples of the type. The stratovolcano Mount Etna in Sicily (figure 13), the giant of the Mediterranean, unlike Vesuvius, has been active more frequently and continues to be active; its latest eruption, at the time of writing, occurred in May 2015.[112]

Fragmented coastal stretches gave rise to short-distance exchange patterns; there was considerable diversity in a relatively small, enclosed space.[113]

In summary, a strict Mediterranean framework for Iron Age Mediterranean history is not broad enough. For the first millennium BCE we need to include the Black Sea and Indian Ocean, and I would also add North Africa, and western and central Asia, a region of the world that was an important global motor since the Neolithic revolution.[114] Global climate drivers such as the Atlantic westerlies and volcanic forcing by explosive eruptions far from the Mediterranean itself, which I will highlight in chapter 5, suggest that a global framework offers a promising context for premodern Mediterranean economic history.

NORTH AFRICA/BLACK SEA/ASIA MINOR

Just as the Mediterranean has been described both by "connectivity" and "fragmentation," so too has North Africa, which was an increasingly important region in the first millennium BCE.[115] There are three distinct ecological zones here, Cyrenaica, the Maghrib, and Morocco, lying in between what Shaw describes as the "world's largest inland sea (i.e., the Mediterranean) . . . and the world's largest desert."[116] Shaw suggests that North Africa followed a different developmental path than other parts of the Mediterranean, having a distinctive pattern of trade and of urbanization. Carthage was connected to Etruria by the 7th century BCE, and Cyrenaica was also a key part of the Mediterranean zone, distinct from most of the rest of North Africa, and important in the trade flows with Carthage and other parts of western part of North Africa.[117] Trade flowed across the desert from Egypt in the East and from Fazzan in southern Libya to the coast. Herodotus writing in the 5th century BCE hinted at the existence of this trade.[118] Liverani has suggested that salt was exchanged for gold and slaves through an extended exchange network as far south as Ghana.

The Gebel Akhdar coastal plain in Cyrenaica (figure 14) contrasts with the surrounding Libyan desert and its neighbor to the East, Egypt, in having a Mediterranean climate. It was colonized by Greeks, most famously Cyrene, beginning in the late 7th century BCE, who were attracted to the rich rain-fed agricultural potential.[119] It later became a vital province of the Ptolemaic state at the end of the 4th century BCE. Ptolemy VIII bequeathed it to Rome in 155 BCE, and it was formally transferred in 96 BCE with the death of his son Apion. It became a Roman province in 75/4 BCE.[120]

Greek colonial expansion established emporiums on the Black Sea that linked this rich agrarian region to Athens from the late 5th century BCE onward, although the extent of grain trade is debated.[121] The Black Sea region was also an important source of slaves entering Mediterranean markets, and for timber as well.[122] Work on Central Asia and the Indian Ocean, in the Hellenistic and Roman periods, has grown exponentially in the last twenty or so years.[123] Trade, and the demand pull of trade discussed further in chapter 8, began to accelerate in the Mediterranean and Indian Ocean worlds in the Hellenistic and Roman periods, but the connections between the Indian Ocean, the Red Sea, the Mediterranean, and the overland routes are the heritage of successive empires in the Near East that date back to the second millennium BCE. Egypt's relationship with the Red Sea goes back at least as far as the third millennium BCE.[124] The "Indian Ocean system" joined the Mediterranean and the Indian Ocean, via Egypt and the Red Sea by late Ptolemaic times.[125] Trade diasporas, like Greek trade in the earlier

FIGURE 14. The Libyan desert and the Gebel Akdar plain.

Mediterranean, were an important aspect of the spread of culture and identity, and a force of standardization across a wide area.[126]

Just as Egypt and its river was a bridge that linked Africa and the Indian Ocean to the Mediterranean, Asia Minor served as a gateway between Asia and Europe.[127] It was a very busy frontier through which many important trade routes went. The invention of coinage in Lydia was no accident. Thonemann's transhistorical survey of the Maeander River valley in Asia Minor serves as an important contrast to the Nile River and is a very fine, recent example of historical geographic writing.[128] Human activity includes interventions, adjustments, responses, and at times even resistance to the environment created by the river. Its name is the origin of our word "to wonder randomly." The differences are clear; Maeander is 329 miles long, draining 10,000 square miles, and flowing east to west. Both rivers pass through great cultural diversity, joining cities and rural hinterlands, depositing fertile alluvium from winter rains, linking pastoral and agrarian modes of production, and had at least by the Hellenistic period major Greek cities. It joined Asia to Europe via the Mediterranean, just as the Nile served to join the African hinterlands to the sea. Beyond these basic similarities, a comparative examination of the Nile and Maeander River valleys shows vast and significant differences that shaped social structure, agrarian production, and economic life. Despite the climatic differences, though, both of these rivers were a vital part of Mediterranean history.

THE NILE

Herodotus's description of Egypt, written at some point in the mid-5th century BCE, occupies the whole of book 2 of his *Histories*. It is the first sustained narrative of ancient Egyptian society and history. It is also, along with the Joseph story in the book of Genesis, the earliest description of an Egypt profoundly shaped by its environment. "Egypt," in perhaps Herodotus's most famous line, "is the gift of the river."[129] While Herodotus was really referring to the fact that the delta was formed by alluvial deposition, it is more or less true, the oases and deserts notwithstanding, that Egypt was indeed a gift of the Nile.[130] The annual flood, divinized in the form of the god Hapy, and the quality of it was linked to the legitimacy of the ruler.

The Mediterranean status of Egypt has been much debated in recent years.[131] It does not easily fit the usual criteria for Mediterranean status that I have just sketched. One recent study has the Nile at the "the fuzzy edges" of the Mediterranean.[132] Egypt is situated between the Mediterranean and the Indian Ocean. Thus, like Spain and France, it had a "double sea exposure" linked by the Nile.[133] Among the few major rivers that drain into the Mediterranean, and the only major river that flows into it from Africa, it is among the longest rivers in the world, and, rather unusually for the world's rivers, it flows south to north for 4,132 miles (6,650 km) from equatorial Africa and the Ethiopian highlands to the Mediterranean, draining some 1,293,000 square miles, or approximately 10 percent of the African landmass (map 3). The annual flood was fed by summer rainfall in the equatorial plateau (mainly via the White Nile) and the Ethiopian highlands (mainly via the Blue Nile and the Atbara). Despite its enormous agricultural importance, its flood volume is comparatively small compared to the world's other great rivers.[134] Before the completion of the Aswan Low Dam in 1902, the annual flood or inundation characteristically began with rising waters first observed at the first cataract (at Aswan) as early as June. Waters peaked in late summer (August to September) and generally receded by October, when sowing of the main crops began.

In the economic history of Egypt, a direct causal link between the physical geography of Egypt and centralized state power has been axiomatic. To be sure, the origins of the ancient Egyptian state can be attributed to what Michael Mann has called the "social cage" created by the Nile river and the narrow cultivable flood plain flowing northward through an otherwise harsh desert environment.[135] That socioecological cage facilitated a ruler's ability to control a population, to monopolize communication along the river corridor, and to gain access to surplus production.[136]

The annual flood surge, a marvel to ancient geographers, was caused primarily by monsoonal rain in the Ethiopian highlands. Eighty-three percent of the flood surge seen in the Egyptian Nile is attributed to monsoonal rainfall in the Ethiopian highlands around Lake Tana, creating the Blue Nile, 13.8 percent from the Atbara River, and 13.3 percent from the Sobat River (map 3) (figure 29). Sixteen and a half percent of the water derives from the Great Lakes region, half of which is evaporated by the Sudd in modern Sudan.[137] Even recently, the unique features of the Nile dictate agricultural production: 95 percent of production is on irrigated land, and the sources of the water lie entirely beyond Egypt's borders.[138]

High agricultural productivity, in good years, was achieved by harnessing the flood through the management of a network of dikes, canals, and enclosures to maximize groundwater recharge and alluvial deposition along Egypt's roughly 745-mile (1,200 km) Nile valley. However, a major feature of the flood is its pronounced interannual variability. Ancient texts show that variability of the flood was always of interest to Egyptian society, with insufficient or excessive floodwater often coincident with famine and mortality. The variability of Nile flow (figure 15) and the spatial variability of water distribution on the land is the result of complex physical forces.[139] Precipitation drawn primarily from the Indian Ocean from the northward migration of the Intertropical Convergence Zone (ITCZ) in Northern Hemisphere summer (figure 16a), contributed most of the annual flood waters that reached Egypt (figure 16b). The El-Niño Southern Oscillation (ENSO) is responsible for 25 percent of the variability.[140] Important drivers of long-term variability of Blue Nile flow are the North Atlantic Oscillation (NAO), sea level pressure anomalies over the Arabian peninsula, and orbital, solar, and volcanic forcing.[141]

Annual flood levels recorded in pharaonic times, while far from complete, are sufficient to show the variability, which dictated regional agricultural productivity and taxation levels (figure 16).[142] That appears to be the case, for example, in Middle Egypt where the flood plain is wide but more susceptible to flood shocks since low floodwaters could not extend into the floodplain.

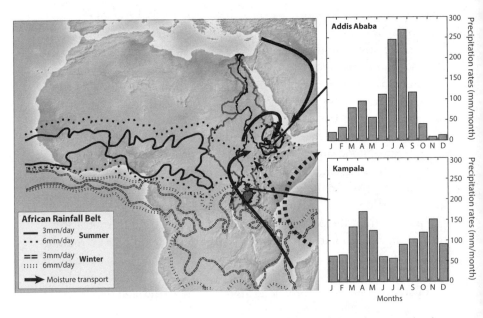

FIGURE 15. Moisture transport vectors of the annual flood of the Nile. From Blanchet, Contoux, and Leduc (2015). Thick lines indicate the 6 mm/day and dotted lines the 3 mm/day isohyets.

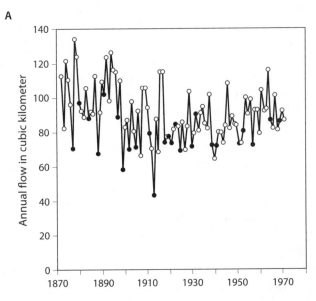

FIGURE 16. Annual fluctuations of the Nile for three different date ranges; note the low flows recorded after the Edjga, Lake, and Katmai eruptions, the last perhaps somewhat mediated by the low dam at Aswan, completed in 1902. Adapted from Oman et al. (2006).

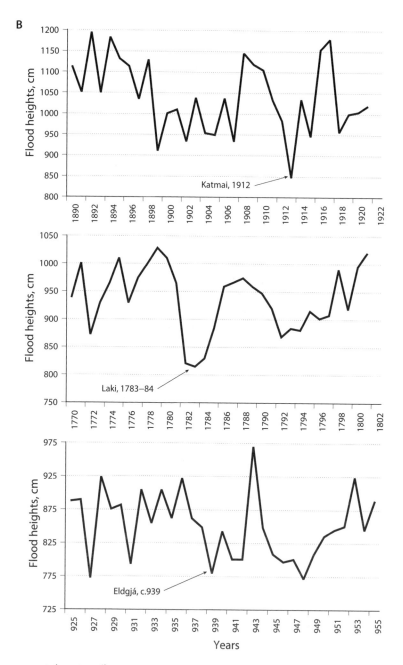

FIGURE 16. (continued)

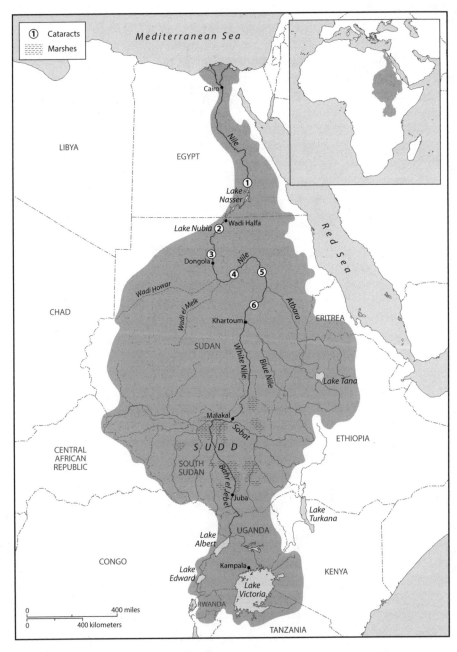

MAP 3. The Nile River basin drains 1,293,000 square miles, approximately 10 percent of the African landmass. From Macklin et al. (2015).

The area shows a cyclical pattern of settlement and depopulation.[143] The adjustment, or social resilience, to this variability was one of the most important drivers, if not *the* most important, of Egyptian history, and bad flooding was a factor in the decline of centralized political control and concomitant economic and demographic decline.[144]

Rivers raise the issue of boundaries in a particular way. The Nile, as with the Maeander in Asia Minor, never "corresponded to a single political, ethnic or cultural unit."[145] It is the delta that is the most important area for understanding the rich and deep history of exchange between Egypt and other parts of the Mediterranean world.[146] Egypt, by the Late Bronze Age, was part of a large network encompassing Cyprus and the Levantine coast as well, as the famous Uluburun shipwreck demonstrates.[147] The delta continued to be important throughout the first millennium BCE with trade contacts with the Near East.

There are several distinct eco-zones in Egypt. The major divisions are the river valley, the delta, the Fayyum depression, the western oases, and the deserts.[148] The delta was the main bridge between the Nile valley and the Mediterranean during the first millennium BCE and has twice the amount of potentially arable land as does the Nile valley.[149]

The Nile provided four main things:

(1) Water from the flood surge and rich alluvial soils
(2) Fish
(3) A superb "communication corridor"
(4) A rhythm to life, a unity of landscape and people, and a sense of
    stability and fertility used to great effect by the rulers and their
    unique visual cultural expression of political ideology

It was a natural transportation corridor flowing south to north, while prevailing winds from May to September, the Etesians, blew southward from the Aegean, which facilitated sailing upstream.[150]

It is no accident that an early, socially stratified state emerged in Egypt around 3000 BCE. The absence of political opposition at the local level in Egypt allowed the king to assert monopoly power over communications along the river as well as over raw materials (principally stone and metals used for tools), and the productivity of Egyptian soil produced large surpluses and allowed for "durable methods of taxation."[151] Flood recession agriculture yields high output per unit of labor but requires no direct royal involvement in the administration of water.

Everywhere there was irrigation there would follow highly centralized states, even in areas of plentiful rainfall like ancient Rome or Hawaii for example.[152] Irrigation was the *cause* of centralization and political rigidity. As

Butzer has cogently argued, however, such a theory overestimates vertical power structures and underestimates horizontal ones.[153] "The hang-up," Butzer concluded, "seems to be the tenacious assumption that early forms of intensification were a result of socio-hierarchical demands rather than cumulative, small-scale, local decision-making."[154]

The control of water was always managed at the local level and was centered around the natural flood basins because local conditions of land and water varied, and irrigation networks, and a local labor force required to maintain them, had to be managed locally.[155] Unlike Mesopotamia, the gradient of the river did not allow more extensive radial canalization except in the Fayyum, and therefore the basin irrigation system was essentially locally managed.[156] The lack of a central bureaucracy for irrigation, with no official titles linked to such centralized control, shows that control of water had always been decentralized:

> Its management defied centralization and was handled on a community basis. Unlike in the Karl Wittfogel model, irrigation never involved a managerial bureaucracy, nor did it become an instrument of authoritarian control.[157]

Similarly, the storage of grain was at least historically locally controlled by temples, although the emphasis on "royal granaries" and royal largesse under the Ptolemies in times of crisis might suggest some institutional shifts away from local management, a lack of evidence suggests some caution here.

Two types of irrigation of land can be distinguished.[158] The first, natural or "paleotechnic" irrigation, was characterized by the simple social response to the annual rhythm of flood and recession of the Nile by sowing land in the low-lying flood basins along the convex river valley. The annual flood replenished nutrients in the soil and, in good years, generated very high average yields. Careful attention to the timing of the water flowing into and out of the basins was required. This was a matter of local organization, but it was of course a concern to the king, and we see officials being instructed on such matters throughout Egyptian history. Improvement in this natural system led to the second type of irrigation, artificial irrigation. Improvements came in the building of feeder and drainage canals, and the building of transverse dikes to divide the natural basins of land into smaller production units. Such artificial irrigation of the fields is attested at the very beginning of unified Egyptian history (e.g., the so-called Scorpion Macehead, depicting the king clearing a canal ca. 3100 BCE, figure 17), and the clearly documented artificial canals used to build the pyramids in the Old Kingdom militates against arguments for the proposed "irrigation revolution" in Egypt during the First Intermediate Period (2160–2055 BCE).[159]

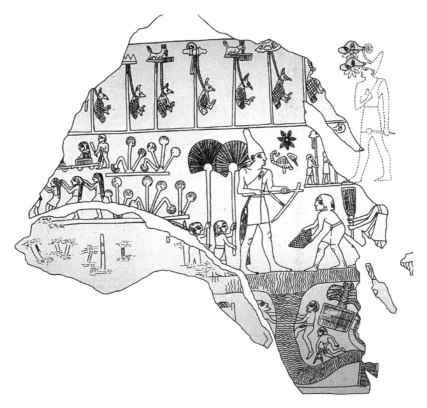

FIGURE 17. The Scorpion Macehead. Ashmolean Museum, Oxford University AN1896–1908. E3632.

Butzer has theorized two, not mutually exclusive, models for the development of artificial irrigation.[160] The first postulates that improvements in the natural flooding and recession of the river came as a response to environmental stress. Low floodwater prompted local farmers to cut sluices in the natural levees to allow for more water to come into the basins. This in turn may have led to more permanent structures of floodwater control, and the division of the land into small units. A second model is linked to the social stratification that is well documented from the early history of Egypt on. The hierarchic social organization of Egypt led to the working of land within family and other social groups and split holding of land that is dispersed geographically to reduce localized risk of crop failure. This method of exploitation in turn led to increased stability in productivity and a concomitant rise in population. The forced demand of a rising population produced greater pressure on the land that led to the need to expand the arable base, a need that also brought further development of irrigation networks. Both models presuppose a diffused, locally controlled response to the interannual variability of the river, and only limited intervention by the central state.

Mann suggests that once Egypt became a territorially centralized state it was "well-nigh continuous."[161] But centralizing dynasties alternating with phases of smaller polities is one of the most characteristic features of Egyptian history. The so-called intermediate periods between two centralized dynastic cycles is associated with demographic decline, a lack of central institutions, and thus political fragmentation and little monumental building. We must also note that the Egyptian Nile valley and delta was hardly uniformly settled. An important feature of settlement patterns in Egypt, especially in the middle of the river valley, is the alternation between new settlement and abandonment of sites because of the failure, at least in part, of the ability to control and sustain irrigation networks.

Once the Egyptian state was formed the pharaoh was at the center of state ideology and political power for as long as a central state existed. Egyptian governance has been categorized as "authoritarian." But this is too simplistic. The despotic nature of state ideology was probably a result of the local character of the Egyptian system, and the requirement of the king to be elevated above the diffuse, socially stratified local power structures.[162] Even the Ptolemies, whose intervention in Egypt in the late 4th century BCE has unique characteristics, maintained this pharaonic ideology. While much scholarship on Egyptian kingship has focused on this ideology, seen in the images and rituals of kingship depicted on temples throughout Egyptian history, the function of Egyptian kingship remained primarily fiscal.[163]

The case of Egypt, with its ancient tradition of powerful kings and a hierarchic bureaucracy, would appear to be an exception to Ernest Gellner's social model of an "agro-literate polity" that suggested that "laterally insulated communities of agricultural communities" was the norm.[164] But this natural tendency of political fragmentation and high costs was buffered by the strong "caging effect" of the river valley that achieved nearly a "unitary social system."[165] The bureaucracy was limited in its effectiveness, and the pharaoh relied on fostering the loyalty of the local elite, village notables, priests, and soldiers through a political system that sanctioned rent seeking by them in exchange for loyalty to the crown, and the requirement of mustering local labor when required. In fact the key to central power in Egypt was the ability of the king, through this elite, to muster local labor—for military campaigns (before a standing army was organized during the New Kingdom), canal clearance, expeditions to quarry stone—and, of course, to tax and redistribute agricultural production through the local temples. In periods of poor Nile flooding, however, the political structure linking villages, to district (nome) capitals, to the political center, in an "internested hierarchy" of population centers was often severed.[166] A "centralizing principal" expressed in phrases such as the "water of pharaoh" (i.e., "public canal") show the extent of royal ideology, but it does not measure royal intervention into local economies. The assignment of rights to land, especially new land, would also have been a royal prerogative, the normal mechanism of which was the gift of land to officials and to soldiers.

This political response, as in other irrigation societies, created a bottom-heavy or "feudal" social organization. The irrigation of fields was organized around the flood basins. The cleaning of canals, the protection of the dikes, the measurement of the flood, the lending of seed, the survey of the fields, and the payment of rent and tax from the land were all organized at the local level through local institutions (temples) yet with obvious great concern of the king and the organs of the central state. The "social cage" of the river did allow the central state to dominate the economy, in distribution and in trade, and the elites were synonymous with the "state." The state faced no internal rivals; there were no powerful city-states as in Mesopotamia to serve as counterweight to royal power.[167]

The Nile flood regime itself acted as the real despot, the main forcing mechanism created by the rich soil of the flood plain juxtaposed to the harsh desert environment on either side of it. The state, its institutions, and individual farmers had to respond and to adjust to the basic forces of the annual flood and its recession. The flood could not be altered, only contained, and the population was quite effectively "caged," and therefore easily taxed, in the river corridor.[168] The rural population was organized around a hierarchical village structure, complex social networks around land tenure and tax obligations, and a cohesive group solidarity focused on production in an irrigated environment.[169] The need to control a *diffuse* irrigated landscape led not to despotic kings who claimed ownership of the entire state and its apparatus, but to the development of bureaucracy and a "centralizing principal."[170] There never was any connection between irrigation and centralized state power outside of the concern for revenue.[171] The king could be a director, but it was the actors—the local elites and the growing bureaucracy—who were the players on the stage of a dynamic and variable ecosystem. The outcome could be rather different from the script.[172]

THE TIGRIS AND EUPHRATES

The Tigris and Euphrates Rivers, draining 158,302 square miles, is supplied by annual precipitation in the Taurus mountain range. The rivers were the main sources of water for Mesopotamia, and the key to the productivity of

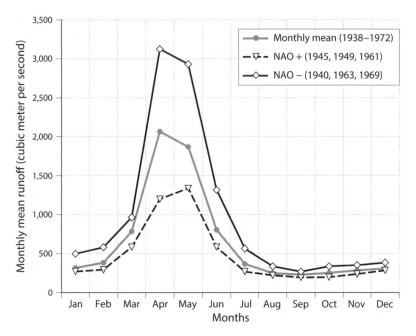

FIGURE 18. The North Atlantic influence on Euphrates flow. From Cullen, de Menocal, et al. (2000).

the Neo-Assyrian, Neo-Babylonian, Achaemenid, and Seleukid economies. Unlike the Nile River, which was mediated by desert and marsh and thus was a slow-moving flood, and exploited primarily by flood recession agriculture, the Tigris and Euphrates were supplied by Mediterranean westerly winter cyclones that produced a more dynamic flood. There were two components of variability. First, the seasonal rain runoff (December to March) and stream flow variability were driven primarily by the North Atlantic Oscillation (NAO) (figure 18).[173] Half of the stream flow was driven by the second phase, April to June snowmelt. The rivers required much more maintenance and control than did the Nile. The Euphrates "served as a marker to distinguish the Mediterranean zone from the Assyrian core," an ancient conception of the rivers as important boundary markers.[174]

The history of empires in western Asia shows an observable correlation between hydrologic variability and political stability.[175] The center of the Neo-Assyrian Empire was located in the desert steppe, a triangle between Nineveh, Ashur, and Arbela (figure 19). A "high degree of inter-annual variability" with frequent drought and multiyear dry periods are notable features.[176] During the first millennium BCE rainfall was high but more variable.[177] The pattern of rainfall in northern Mesopotamia was a con-

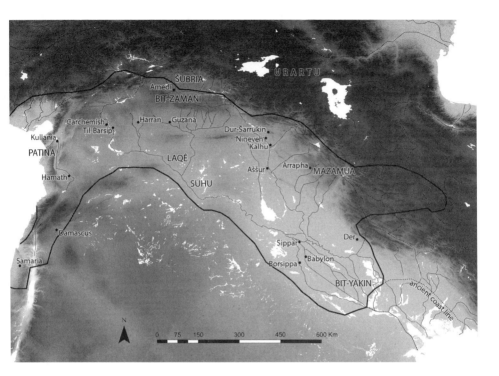

FIGURE 19. The Neo-Assyrian core. From Radner (2016).

straint in population density; Babylonia was potentially rich in agricultural resources and could support higher populations but, with no local sources of metal or timber, had to rely on imports.[178] Significantly, rainfall in the deserts supported nomadic populations, unlike Egypt. This had great historical significance for long-term historical dynamics in the Near East.[179]

Irrigation in southern Mesopotamia (Babylonia) was managed quite differently because radial canalization was possible, and more easily controlled centrally. Winter rains driven by westerly winds across the Mediterranean produce the rain and snowfall in the Anatolian and Iranian highlands where the sources the Euphrates and Tigris Rivers are located.[180] Western Asia is a far more diverse landscape than Egypt and is one reason for historical "divergences" between Egypt and the Near East.[181] The empires of the first millennium BCE experienced periods of intensification of irrigation networks, as well as periods of contraction tracking demographic shifts. It is the combination of the two rivers, whose beds constantly shifted, and the canal system, that makes up the basic physical grid that shaped social networks of communication and exchange in the Assyrian and Babylonian economy of the first millennium BCE.[182]

Changes in climate leading to episodic drought and salinization of the soil have been implicated in the rise and decline of the Near Eastern empires. Severe drought has occurred, for example, at 4.2 ka, setting set off massive migration, which arguably contributed to the sudden collapse of the Akkadian Empire (ka = kiloannus, or one thousand years; 4.2 ka = ca. 2200 BCE).[183] A major period of drought, lasting about two hundred years, began ca. 1200 BCE. In the mid-7th century BCE, population increase and severe drought was a factor in the decline the Neo-Assyrian Empire centered along the Upper Tigris River.[184] The causal links between climatic changes and political and economic institutions are complex. I will explore this further in chapter 5.

The first three chapters have established the basic contours of first-millennium BCE Mediterranean economic history. I have attempted to illustrate how the complexities of time-space boundary issues and periodization, and how geographic and climatic variability and cross-cultural exchange have shaped our understanding of premodern Mediterranean economies. I have argued that in order to better capture inter-and intraregional flows, we need a larger geography than the Mediterranean. The Indian Ocean, western Asia, and the Tigris, Euphrates, and Nile Rivers were all important factors in the first millennium BCE. In the second half of the book, to which I now turn, I explore the relationship between institutions and the environment. I suggested earlier that coupled natural-human system dynamics is an important framework to better understand premodern economic performance. I now turn to this framework in more detail. The next two chapters discuss the natural system. I begin with agriculture and labor, the basis of all premodern economies. I then move on to treat how the environment, climate, and climate change acted on various timescales as triggers to human responses. The last three chapters of the book take up human systems by looking at economic institutions in greater detail.

PART II

Environment
&
Institutions

CHAPTER 4

Agriculture and Labor

The civilizations of Antiquity, with their elaborate agricultures, provide a starting point. None of them, in the Middle East, Rome, China, Meso-America, in either prehistoric or early historic times, led to an industrial economy.

—E. JONES AND WOOLF (1969:1)

The oxen harvest the barley and emmer, the donkey eats it.

—*THE WISDOM OF ONCHSHESHONQY* 23, 21

AGRICULTURAL PRODUCTION AND DISTRIBUTION was at the heart of all premodern economies. Who owned the land, who worked it, and how labor was controlled are three key questions.[1] The variety of land-scapes, water source (rain fed or irrigation), the fertility of the soil, the types of crops, livestock and grazing practices, and the scale of agricultural units varied enormously around the Mediterranean. Premodern economies were "organic" economies; labor was done by humans and animals; "land was the source of food, also the source directly or indirectly of all the material products of use to man."[2] Every culture in the premodern world paid careful attention to the conditions of the soil, water, and crops. These conditions were a serious constraint on the production function, since in most places production was limited to one annual agrarian cycle.

The normative contrast between small holding in nuclear families in the Greek world and the large state-managed estates of western Asia and Egypt requires much modification. The distribution and tenure of land, state fiscal demands, the variability in environmental conditions, in labor organization and supply, in the productivity of the soil, in water sources, and interannual variability of inputs and yields should all be stressed. Changing political conditions, a trend toward commercialization, and an increase in market transactions from the 4th century BCE onward, at new, large urban centers, all appear to have had dramatic effects on agricultural production. Occasionally, we have a detailed picture of agriculture at important moments of economic change. Let me provide an illustration from the most famous archive of the Hellenistic period.

At the end of March 256 BCE, a man named Sosos, an agent of Zenon, sat down on a barge on the Nile, anxiously waiting instructions, with papyrus and *kalamos*-pen in hand, and wrote the following letter (figure 20):

> Sosos to Zenon greeting. I received your letter in which you asked me to put aside 100 artabs of the wheat, which we have on board and to sell the rest at the highest price we can get. Now as for reserving the corn, know that it is no longer possible. For not being aware that you would be wanting it, we sold the whole cargo of wheat in the harbor over against Aphroditopolis, through Ptolemaios the epistates serving under Archibiades, a total of 241 artabs at 7 artabs for each gold stater; and we gave the purchasers 3 artabs extra on every hundred to balance the incidental expenses. Charmos has brought me a message to give Pyrrhichos money for the purchase of hides at Herakleopolis. Know then that we have not so much money that we can give Pyrrhichos enough for that purpose. For out of the price of the corn Ptolemaios is still owing us 288 drachmai, about which I am bringing you a letter of guarantee to the effect that we are to receive them on the 10th of Mecheir, and I have 400 drachmai in hand. Be kind enough then to write and tell me where I am to obtain the money to give him and whether we are to send Styrax with him in order that we may keep an eye on the prices; for we know him to be reliable in such affairs. We have brought down also the lots of wine that were at Ptolemais. Send me word where I am to obtain corn for Ammonios the miller and how much I am to give him for the preparation of flour. We have also given Pyrrhichos 10 drachmai for travelling expenses. Farewell. Year 29, Mecheir 5.[3]

What does the letter tell us? A shipment of a large amount of wheat along with wine was sold at a high price, in cash, in a town across the river.[4] The wheat originated in the Fayyum, a region in Egypt that was reclaimed, resettled, and extensively exploited by the new Ptolemaic regime established in Alexandria some forty years earlier. Zenon, the addressee here, was apparently not yet the estate manager for Apollonios, the finance minister of King Ptolemy II; he would become so in a month or two, by the end of April or early May 256 BCE, and thus achieve immortality with the survival of his extensive archive of business activity.[5]

In this letter Zenon is acting on Apollonios's behalf in selling commodities in local markets. He had an apparently extensive personal network, an awareness of price gradients, and a deep knowledge of local markets and services. The letter comes from the largest archive of the Ptolemaic period, the Zenon archive, preserving roughly seventeen hundred useable documents that reveal an astonishing world of commerce on a large plantation run by

FIGURE 20. *P. Mich.* 1 28 (March 29, 256 BCE). Image digitally reproduced with the permission of the Papyrology Collection, University of Michigan Library.

Zenon on behalf of the finance minister. The texts document agricultural experimentation, a monetary economy, market transactions in coinage, letters of credit to purchase hides, an entrepreneurial spirit, but centrally managed from the center by the kings. It was an Egypt transformed by Greeks flowing into Egypt seeking opportunities afforded by the Ptolemaic kings. The papyri seemingly revealed a new economic order that impressed Rostovtzeff and many others. Rostovtzeff believed that the Zenon archive, and the agricultural economy represented in the texts, with an extensive economy in coin, agricultural experimentation, large scale farming on plantations, and tight centralized control of production, represented an "Egypt in miniature." Here we face a problem of interpretation. How typical were such market transactions? Similarly, the price data from the island of Delos in the Aegean was considered to be representative of the Hellenistic period's "universal price-setting market."[6]

In both cases caution is required. The estate of Apollonios was a special economic area, newly developed by the early Ptolemaic kings, and the Zenon archive covers only a generation. It may be true that Zenon was not particularly unique. But still, the middle of the 3d century BCE was a time of great economic activity in the Mediterranean, driven by large competing states formed in the wake of Alexander the Great's conquests, of the movement of Greeks to places like Egypt, of new settlements, new land, and more extensive trade across the eastern Mediterranean. Despite lingering images of an all-powerful, centrally controlled economy, Egyptian agricultural production during the Ptolemaic period was, as it had always been, a highly variable agrarian system; temples and large temple estates and privately held land remained an organizing principle in ancient areas in the Nile valley. The new state fiscal demands altered social relations, markets, and production. Free-threshing wheat, the preferred bread wheat of Greeks and sold by the Ptolemaic kings on Mediterranean markets, appears to have gained ground against the ancient emmer by the end of the 3d century BCE, part of a wider Mediterranean shift during the first millennium BCE from hulled to free-threshing grains (table 3).

We can presume, I think, that the transaction recorded in the papyrus, though large, was carried out privately on behalf of Zenon's boss, Apollonios. This kind of transaction was, probably, the way high offices worked. This large estate, roughly sixty-six hundred acres, was granted to Apollonios as a potential income stream. The land had to be developed and managed. Such land grants were an old feature of land tenure in Egypt, but the new Greek population that had come into Egypt in the early Ptolemaic period shaped economic networks and institutions, and even the crops and animals. Immigration and new settlement patterns, especially in the Fayyum, and the new city of Alexandria, forced changes in land tenure and in animal husbandry.

CHANGES IN THE LAND

Agricultural production occupied most people in most places and remained the main basis of wealth. Even in the "normal Greek *polis*," the estimate is that 80 percent of the "population was directly involved in agrarian production," but this estimate does not take account of changes and regional differences.[7] It has been estimated, for example, that in the region around Athens in the 4th century BCE, agriculture was not the main activity for the majority.[8]

Data is variable across the ancient world; in some places, as in late 2d century Kerkeosiris in the southern part of the Fayyum in Egypt, we know a lot about the entirety of land around the village for about a decade.[9] The use of comparative evidence has been a common tool—but there are dangers. In our inability to interview ancient farmers about what they were doing and how, it has been popular to use modern ethnographic studies as a proxy for ancient agricultural mentalities. If you have ever taken a cruise along the Nile River, you might be tempted, in looking at a farmer with his water buffalo plowing a small piece of land near the river, with ancient water-lifting machines still in use, to think that nothing much has changed; here, you might say to yourself, is ancient Egypt before my eyes. But this would be a seriously misleading understanding. Much in fact has changed—the type of crop, and seed, the absence of the annual flood of the river, and the village solidarity brought about by the ancient basin irrigation system; more importantly the mentality, the culture, the religious beliefs, and the relationship between the farmer and the market, and between rural populations and modern tourism.[10]

The same is true of the classical world, where it has been tempting, with popular ethnographic studies in rural areas of Greece, to understand a timeless "traditional" Mediterranean rural economy that might still reflect, in some measure, ancient life.[11] Used judiciously, though, careful ethnographic work such as Paul Halstead has done has preserved for us some important aspects of ancient agricultural life, not the least of which is the sheer determination and resilience to survive in what must often have been a struggle between the farmer, the environment, and, in most places at least, the tax man.[12] There has been a concerted effort in recent work to restore a balance between the polis and the countryside, to construct the totality of the Greek world and not just democratic institutions of some cities, with an emphasis on regional diversity.[13] Assumptions about a two-year bare fallow cycle in wheat and barley fields, and seasonal pasturage, may not always describe the situation. In antiquity, rural populations lived close to fields, and most farming was small scale, with cereal/pulse rotation. A scattered holding of land to reduce risk of crop failure in any one place was common. The integration of crop and livestock husbandry made manure more available, thus reinforcing intensive arable farming, although that picture cannot hold for the entire Mediterranean.

The ancient Mediterranean world was more diverse than the Mediterranean triad of wheat, olive oil, and grapes, although these crops were grown throughout. The production of barley, a hardy crop in dry and salty conditions, was also important, and the ratio between wheat and barley was regionally and annually variable.[14] Whether the land was watered by rainfall or irrigation determined much about social organization and labor on the land. Pastoralism went hand in hand with agriculture, although this is a less well-studied aspect of ancient agriculture given the more difficult evidence for it.[15] Political organization, territorial empire or city-state, rainfall or irrigation, made a great difference to land tenure rules and agricultural production.

TABLE 1. *Percentage Probability of Crop Failure in Larisa, Athens, and Odessa*

	One Year	Two Successive Years
Larisa		
wheat	28.5	8.1
barley	9.7	0.9
Athens		
wheat	28.0	7.8
barley	5.5	0.3
Odessa		
wheat	46.0	21.1
barley	15.6	2.4

SOURCE: Adapted from Peter K. Garnsey (1988:17).

A host of other issues must be understood. Among these are the political control of grain supply, especially flowing to large urban areas in the Hellenistic and Roman period, the balance between rural and the growing importance of urban areas during the first millennium BCE throughout the Mediterranean, and comparative and interannual yields. It is not possible to provide an overarching theory other than to say, as others have, that variability was a constant. Regional variation, change over time, political changes, availability of labor, crop type and crop changes, fallow patterns, and climate change drove variations in agricultural practices. Land-holding patterns and rules, and distribution of land were highly fluid in all the systems we are examining, and all systems balanced the needs of households with the requirements of the state for revenue, including the use of land grants tied to support the supply of soldiers. Ongoing advances in crop modeling offer a very promising way forward to break the deadlock we traditionally face in our patchy direct data on productivity, population, variability, and crop selection, including techniques for estimating carrying capacity independent of population.[16] Even in "normal" years, crops could fail locally. In one study of Mediterranean wheat and barley production in more recent times, wheat failed at a high rate (table 1). Under drought conditions in Egypt, the probability of failure, or significant decreases in production, must have been even higher.

Land is fixed in location, inelastic in supply, and heterogeneous in terms of soil quality, microclimatic conditions, and water inputs.[17] But the historical landscape throughout the Mediterranean was constantly changing, and substantial changes can best be seen in areas in which new populations came in and established new settlements and new agricultural land. Small-scale movements between intensification and abandonment could follow changes in the size and demographic structure of households, or "household life-cycles."[18] The role of the state, state fiscal and labor demands, the use of lease and labor contracts, and private land sales all show that social relations on the land changed considerably over the course of the first millennium BCE. Such was the case with the drainage and reclamation of land around Lake Copais during the late 4th century BCE and other parts of Greece.[19] In Egypt and the Near East, the role of temple and estates of land controlled by them is a constant feature of land tenure and land management. Population growth and movement also played an important role in social relations on the land, but we cannot follow it in any detail. Population movement in the first millennium affected the land directly by putting new land under cultivation. This is dramatically attested in Egypt, especially in the Fayyum, but everywhere Greeks began new settlements such as Sicily.[20]

The common claim that the kings owned all the land and were the prime movers of change, however, is an ideological one and should be better nuanced. Changes in the land were also motivated by local responses to conditions. Archaeological surveys in the Near East and in Egypt have given us a better idea of shifts in riverbeds and temporal changes in settlement patterns.[21] Paleoclimatological data combined with documentary records can now be integrated, and we can begin to quantify annual variability of the flood of the Nile and the Euphrates (see chapter 5). This will allow a more sophisticated understanding of human-environment interactions.

Displays of political power enacted by altering the landscape, to impose man-made structures and to change the land itself, were an ancient feature of the Mediterranean world. In the Fayyum, reclamation and settlement of new populations under Ptolemy II and III turned the region into a special area of royal power. Ptolemaic land reclamation in this location in the middle of the 3d century BCE was an impressive project, trebling the available arable land.[22] This ancient practice is paralleled in other parts of the Hellenistic world.[23]

The Ptolemaic case is a dramatic example of the sometimes intimate connection between ecological changes and ancient political economy. Grain production was the basis of dynastic wealth, tied to royal largesse, and correlated directly to military success. Over the course of the first millennium BCE, free-threshing wheat, the preferred bread grain for Greeks, displaced hulled grains such as emmer. The process of displacement involved a combination of natural change, demand, and imperial monocropping strategies (see below). Land reclamation for agriculture, and intensive canal building, has been documented for Hellenistic Mesopotamia, no doubt in large part

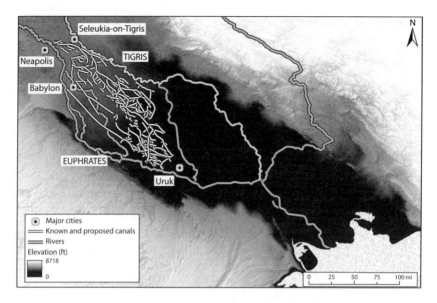

FIGURE 21. The irrigation networks reconstructed from archaeological survey (in white) by Adams (1981). Drawing by Frank Ludlow.

TABLE 2. *Comparison of Changes in Settlement Patterns in the Diyala and the Middle Euphrates Regions of the Near East*

	Lower Diyala		Central Euphrates	
Period	Estimated Hectares of Settlement	Estimated % Urban (10+ Hectares)	Estimated Hectares of Settlement	Estimated % Urban (10+ Hectares)
Ur III–Isin-Larsa	602	35	2,725	75
Neo-Babylonian– Achaemenian	134	7	1,769	51
Seleucid-Parthian	1,857	69	3,201	55
Sasanian	3,489	75	3,792	58

SOURCE: Adams (1981).

in response to the new Seleukid capital at Seleukia on the Tigris River. Robert Adams's survey work demonstrated that beginning in the Seleukid period, and extending into the Parthian, the Tigris gained in prominence, with the result that there was irrigation intensification and a shift in settlement patterns (figure 21 and table 2).

Attempts at reclaiming land were made around Lake Copais in central Boeotia, a natural basin that caught winter rainwater, in the late 4th century BCE, so too at Lake Ptechai in Eretria and elsewhere.[24] We do not know whether these projects were investments by wealthy Macedonians, as may have been the case with a certain Chairephanes, who in return for the reclamation at Eretria would have access to the new land to rent at a high price, or the result of demographic changes, or a combination of the two.[25]

EGYPT

Agriculture, arriving much later than in the Near East, is documented beginning in the fifth millennium BCE.[26] Production was characterized by flood recession agriculture, timed with water flowing into natural basins during the annual flood of the river. As in the Near East, by institutional holding through temples, land was given in exchange for state service, military or otherwise. Land was both worked by temple staff and leased out to others. Sharecropping was the standard form of tenure. This basic pattern lasted through Ptolemaic times. We rarely encounter individual famers directly in our sources (the *Hekanakhte* letters, discussed in chapter 6, are exceptional), but small- and medium-scale farming organized around households was probably closer to the norm. Although Hekanakhte's household size and his larger-than-average holdings may reflect his funerary-priest status, his letters must reflect a wider mentality in Bronze Age Egypt. Despite the ideology reflected on elite tomb paintings of large estates, small-scale subsistence family-based farming is usually hidden from view by the dominance of the state record generated by kings and elite in their tombs.[27] But landholding patterns also reflect the internested interests of individuals and state institutions; there was always institutional interest in grain-bearing land in the form of the harvest tax. There is little evidence for very large estates in private hands before the Roman period. Before then, temples were the major holders and managers of land portfolios. The state performed surveys of fields regularly. Emmer and barley in combination were the two main grain crops of ancient times.[28] A slow process of the evolution in the type of emmer may have made the contrast between the Egyptian preference for emmer wheat and the increased production of naked wheat less dramatic than is usually supposed.[29]

The rural history of Egypt has often been acknowledged but not carefully studied. Depictions of rural life, with local elites farming their fields in the "blessed west" appear in every textbook on ancient Egypt. Intensive regional surveys in recent years have really brought to light complex settlement patterns and agrarian strategies. The delta is much better known, and the environmental history of the Nile valley, the patterns of settled farming communities, rural social stratification, and the ways in which pastoral economies intersected with settled communities are now better understood.[30] As I suggested above, the Nile River and its annual flood, its interannual variability, and the social responses to it were the most important single factor in the economic history of Egypt until the construction of the high dam at Aswan was completed in 1970.

Temples became of major importance by the New Kingdom (ca. 1550–1069 BCE), controlling very large estates in land, and were "centers of patronage networks" and beneficiaries of military campaigns of the warrior kings of the New Kingdom.[31] Unsurprisingly the New Kingdom marks the height of the ancient population before the Ptolemaic period and was also a period of agricultural intensification. The use of the *shaduf*, the bucket and counterweighted pole irrigation machine, appears by the middle of the second millennium BCE.[32] Temples retained their holdings through the Ptolemaic period. Over the course of the first millennium BCE free-threshing wheat was introduced and intensified considerably under the Ptolemies. But the rich documentary sources from the period show that lentils, flax, fruit trees, principally date palm and primarily in the south, dôm palm production and viticulture remained important too. Wine making intensified under the Ptolemies, in part owing to cultural preference of Greeks and driven by the monetary economy. Privately controlled land existed in all historical periods, almost always with interlocking institutional (royal or temple) claims. State taxation of agricultural production is an early feature of the Egyptian state. The recording of land surveys, crop production, a biennial census of livestock, close monitoring of agricultural production, and flood levels are all features established by the Old Kingdom, ca. 2600 BCE. The processing and storage of grain, and distribution through temples to dependent temple personnel, are also ancient features of the Egyptian economy that carried over into the Ptolemaic period. Here there are hints of Polanyi's "redistribution" model that I mentioned in chapter 1 but only on a regional, not a state, level, and even then, this does not encapsulate the whole of economic activity.[33]

To be sure, temples, especially from the New Kingdom onward, became important economic institutions and part of the state economic system, managing large land portfolios and labor forces, but also operating business ventures. Agricultural land, organized in flood basins, always had institutional claims attached, even if the land also had private claims. This is above all the case for land in Upper Egypt. Land tenure conditions and rules were complex and developed considerably over the more than three millennia of ancient Egyptian history, and they were more complex than in Weber's description.[34] Production from the land provided the state with revenue and was the means of funding bureaucracy and, from the New Kingdom onward especially, military service. These observations are the result of extensive publication and some very fine analysis of Egyptian and Greek documents in the last century. It must be noted how good (and cautious) Weber's survey was, especially for the Hellenistic period. The demotic material, only very imperfectly known in Weber's day, provides extensive records of private holding, conveyance, sale, and lease of land and of wage labor. As always with the documentation, the state-centered bias of the documents can lead to an overestimation of centralized control, and the degree to which state activity "stifled" capitalist development can be debated.[35]

The *Hekanakhte* letters discussed briefly in chapter 6 open a window into the world of private household production and consumption that is rarely glimpsed before the Hellenistic period: interlocking land-holding patterns, scattered plots, tension between royal taxation demands, the considerable power held by temples, a range of soil conditions (that varied annually), and the tendency of land grants to become privately conveyable as "shares."[36] Maintaining land under cultivation was a perennial problem. By the late New Kingdom at the latest, ca. 1100 BCE, as the inflow of prisoners of war from the extensive military campaigns of New Kingdom kings stopped, and as Egypt was integrated into wider exchange networks in the eastern Mediterranean, there was an institutional shift within large temple estates away from centralized management and coerced labor toward the use of "free tenants" using land leases and wage labor.[37]

The conception of private ownership evolved from the right of access to the right to convey by private legal instrument. The Ptolemaic period land sales make this clear. "Private land" was held by a wide range of the social hierarchy in the first millennium BCE, and the large amount of documents that survive from the Ptolemaic period are probably only a reflection of archival survival from this period rather than a major change in land tenure arrangements under the Ptolemies.[38] A clearer picture of complex landholding patterns in Egypt begins to emerge with New Kingdom documents ca. 1500 BCE. Here we observe the complexities of economic power and land holding, with occasional tax exemptions granted, variable tax rates, and different strategies on royal and temple land. Perhaps under positive demographic growth and the population density in the narrow Upper Egyptian Nile valley, the amount of private land in Upper Egypt may have been higher than elsewhere. For this region, it has been estimated to be 72 percent of the agricultural land in the Ptolemaic period.[39]

In good flood years the yields on irrigated land in the Nile valley were high relative to other parts of the Mediterranean, about 1:10 for grain as a low estimate, 1:12–1:15 was "common."[40] By no means, however, could these yields be sustained year to year because of Nile flood variability. The price of land, as in the Near East, was generally low, roughly a year's production. The evidence is impressionistic, but it does suggest that labor was underutilized.[41]

Following the general trend in the first millennium BCE toward the use of written documents noted in the last chapter, the first land leases known date to the Saite period (ca. 670–525 BCE). They are almost always annual leases, a response to the annual variability of the Nile and the need for flexible tenure arrangements.[42] Written leases, however, were not required, and it was probably the case that unwritten leases of land were quite common.

Above all it is Ptolemaic and Roman Egypt that has provided us with the best documentary sources.[43] Historical studies of Ptolemaic and Roman Egypt have traditionally been heavily dependent on papyrological sources. And these sources tend to come from the Thebaid in Upper Egypt and the Fayyum. Even if one were aware of this bias, until twenty-five or so years ago, there was little alternative. Now, though, archaeological data as well as much improved methodologies and the use of new technologies such as satellite imaging techniques have provided much improved context for understanding the rich documentary sources.[44]

The balance between continuity and change is not easy to measure. Agricultural production and demographic development reached a peak in the Ptolemaic and early Roman period, probably not reached again before the early 19th century.[45] Without question, Egypt's Nile-driven agricultural yield could be exceptional, but the statement "at no time in the Ptolemaic or Roman periods, as far as we can see, did overall internal demand come close to matching or exceeding supply" must be qualified with "averages smoothed over the period."[46] And it is this interannual variability, a critical factor in understanding productivity, internal supply and distribution, and social response to crisis, which we are now in a better position to understand, although much work still remains to be done. As I will discuss in chapter 5, we now know a good deal about Nile variability, and its connection to fiscal pressures on local communities, social unrest, and, possibly, food shortages that suggests that even Egypt's productive soil could be diminished by Nile failure.

The private sale of land appears to be correlated with shocks to the Nile flood. The public auction was introduced from the Greek world by the early Ptolemaic period, and there is good evidence that land was bought and sold by this mechanism.[47] We do not know how extensive the practice was, but it was undoubtedly connected to other aspects of the Ptolemaic economy that introduced more market transactions. The surviving examples of the use of public auction suggest that this device was particularly used for land that had been abandoned during periods of severe social unrest or population dislocations.[48]

TABLE 3. *A Crop Report from the Fayyum, Egypt, January 235 BCE*

Crop	Arable under Production (in *arouras**)	Total of Arable (in %)
Wheat	135,315.5	74.6
Lentils	880.34	0.7
Beans	————	————
Barley	26,260	14.5
Olyra (emmer)	3,118.69	1.7
Grass	4,6121.5 +	2.5
Vetch (arakos)	10,109.5 +	5.6
Sesame	261	0.2
Castor	55	0.04
Poppy	100	0.06
(3 other crops)	201.5	0.10

SOURCE: *P. Petrie* III 75. Adopted from D. Thompson (1999b:129).

* 1 *aroura* = .66 acres

Large estates were an experimental feature particularly of the 3d century BCE. The Apollonios estate is by far the best known and is a good example, probably among the best for the Hellenistic period, that illustrates an adjustment between owners, in this case Ptolemy II, managers, and farmers who transformed the land through intensification and agricultural experimentation.[49] In the same period, the Seleukid kings were transforming the land around Seleukia on the Tigris River, and if we had more documents that survived from this region, we might see similar processes. The Ptolemaic Fayyum was a region of royal power. New crops, fruit trees, and new livestock were introduced, but this is a special kind of large estate of an important state official and very likely not representative of an "Egypt in miniature" as Rostovtzeff thought.[50] Zenon's work may well have been more typical of Greek mentality in the 3d century BCE.[51] New cultivars, and the intensification of vines, related to the new economy in coin, are a measure of Greek influence.[52] The massive shift to naked or free-threshing wheat crop (table 3), that appears to have displaced the hardier emmer, was another, and is among the most significant change in agricultural production in ancient Egyptian history.

In the partible inheritance system, each child of both sexes received an equal share of the family property.[53] Temples and the crown retained an interest in all productive farmland, but the system of granting land to state servants, officials, and soldiers was an ancient system; temples controlled large tracts of land in their own name and leased it out to others. Those who held land through state service treated the land as private property. The settling of soldiers on land grants in exchange for service, known as the kleruchy plot, was determined by rank. The land was subject to rent, and given as a lifetime grant. Gradually the land grants became conveyable to children, and by the late 2d century BCE the grants became private property, fully conveyable.

The debate over the existence of private property turns on the type of evidence used: state records like land surveys stress institutional control; private sale instruments from the Ptolemaic period especially, stress very clearly, and in great detail, exactly what private ownership of the land entailed. The bulk of land sales from the Ptolemaic period, where our evidence is best in the first millennium BCE, were for very small plots of land, although some larger plots acquired through the public auction are known.[54]

Private land holding is well documented in family archives, and written sales and leases, in Greek and in demotic Egyptian, provide a rich source for understanding varying conditions in land conditions, crops, and disputes over property rights. In the family dispute that I discuss in chapter 6, the sole focus of the dispute was the ownership of land roughly six American acres in size. Petetum, a priest in the local temple who had married twice and had a son and daughter by each marriage, was near death in 181 BCE. He divided his property between his two sons, who were half brothers, into 2/3 and 1/3 shares. The initial cause of the dispute was that the younger brother wanted to have the 1/3 share of the land fully in his control. He claims to have been defrauded in the joint leasing of the family land. He requested a real division of the land. The older brother made a deed of division to his younger half sibling, and the older brother's wife Chratianch, the plaintiff in the trial, confirmed this.[55]

Like the Fayyum, the delta was probably less densely settled than the river valley.[56] It was important for much of the first millennium BCE, with more than half of potentially arable land in Egypt, and has in the past not yielded much economic information. A recent study of the Mendesian nome in the eastern delta in the early Roman period on the basis of carbonized papyri and archaeological survey has revealed important new agricultural information for this region.[57] The regional variability, and the intricate nature of human relationships with the environment and to demands of the state, are set against the crucible of revolt and flight from the land. The key text, *P. Thmouis* 1, dated to 170/171 CE, documents a general crisis in the second half of the 2d century CE. Tax liability on much of the land, mainly private, was suspended because of a lack of water. Massive flight from the land (*anachoresis*) began "sometime before" 159 and ended 171 CE.[58]

Wheat dominated production in the delta, while barley was generally grown on marginal land. There was also land under vineyards, and pastureland was used for widespread cattle breeding. Overall an adaptive and diversified land use is apparent, specific to the environmental conditions of the eastern delta and its marshy zones. The interplay of longer-term environmental change, given the region's sensitivity to lower flood levels, human dislocation, state reaction, in the form of collective liability for local land taxes, and the shock of disease (a smallpox epidemic) combine to paint a stark picture of the region in the mid- to late 2d century CE. The most famous large-scale rural revolt in the Roman province of Egypt, the so-called *Boukoloi* (shepherd) uprising, broke out in 167 CE. The rebellion has generated much discussion, mainly on the basis of the literary texts that make mention of it, and has been well summarized recently.[59] *P. Thmouis* 1 is the only documentary evidence of the revolt. Blouin puts the text front and center, rightly, in the context of the "long term socio-hydrological pressures and Roman-period agro-fiscal dynamics" that have previously been treated cursorily.[60] In contrast to the literary treatment of the "shepherds" as evildoers from dangerous, marshy, liminal regions of Egypt, Blouin, rightly in my view, frames the discussion in environmental terms. Here, too, more can be said. These "shepherds," if that's what they were, appear very different to those called, for example, "herdsmen and servants of [the god] Horus" in Edfu in the 3d century BCE.[61] But that is simply to suggest a more complex typology of what and who herders were in Egypt, and the complexities too of land, man, and animal relationships in Egyptian agriculture.

ANCIENT NEAR EAST

Agriculture in the Near East presents an even more complex picture than Egypt, with a more diverse climate.[62] Agriculture arose here in the Neolithic, much earlier than in Egypt, and the main cereals, wheat and barley, were native.[63] Rain-fed or "dry" farming dominated northern Mesopotamia, while irrigation agriculture was dominant in the South. Babylonian texts are the main sources for agriculture practice during the first millennium BCE. Like Egypt, sharecropping arrangements were the norm in southern Mesopotamia. Barley and dates were the major crops. Wheat was produced in the northern rain-fed areas in winter production, and "owner-farmers" appear to have been the norm in this region, in contrast to the South.[64] Institutional control of production was more prevalent in irrigated areas, and family-based production obtained in the North.[65] Continuity of institutions was strong;

increasing urbanization during the first millennium BCE, imperial formation of Neo-Assyrian, Neo-Babylon, Achaemenid, and Seleukid states, and taxation and monetization brought change. Just around Babylon, four distinct
"eco-zones" can be distinguished: central alluvial plain with irrigation
canals, swampy areas, reed forests, exploited by hunters and fishermen; and
steppe lands, for grazing, and for settlements.[66]

Throughout the first millennium BCE intensification in irrigation and
date growing followed population increases.[67] For arable farming, the seeder
plough was used, "an ingenious implement allowing high returns on seed."[68]
Barley production dominated the Babylonian irrigated landscape, along
with intensive date palm production. The intensification in date production
in certain areas, and the switch from barley-based to date-based beer production and consumption, is a proxy measure of intensified land use and of
demographic expansion.[69] "Market gardening" is well attested in the larger
urban hinterlands associated with Babylon.

As in Egypt, internested landholding between the king, the temples,
elites, and small farmers was the standard pattern. The mix of large plots
exploited by temples and private landholders varied quite a lot. Landholding
was tied to state service. Temples held large estates in land, which at times
were located far from the temple center. Presumably this was a method of
reducing risk from local climatic fluctuations and perhaps also conflict.
Since temples were, in theory, permanent foundations, they also served as
stable structures in the management of local agrarian resources. Temple land
was worked by temple dependents and leased to private parties including
"entrepreneurs" who took on large holdings of land, attested from the 6th
century on. The Egibi family, for example, documented from the 6th to early
5th centuries BCE, owned a large amount of land, and the distribution of
agricultural commodities was a mainstay of the family business, as was the
development of date orchards around Babylon on a large scale.[70] Five generations of the family are documented for more than a century. While this archive of elite family trading activity is exceptional, the family was not
unique, and there are other archives of similar families, if not reflecting the
same scale of activity. The Egibis were members of an entrepreneurial class,
independent of the temples, living in urban centers, managing large estates
in land, marketing surplus production. Wunsch compares the trading activity
to the later *commenda* contracts of medieval Italy. A partnership formed and
credit extended to farmers for seed and animals, which was repaid at harvest. The harvest was collected, shipped, stored, and marketed, and the profit
was shared per the agreement. The crown collected fees for use of canals and
for storage.[71]

Altogether the new picture that is emerging from recent work on first-millennium BCE agriculture in the Near East shows that it was varied and flexible. Like Egypt, the agrarian economies here can hardly be described as simply centralized or redistributive in toto. The temple was and remained the key institution, along with the managerial nexus of complex social networks that connected the crown and elite to labor and production. Like Egypt, Babylonia shows similar changes in patterns of urbanization, agricultural intensification, a growing focus on cash crops, and monetization of the economy during the Hellenistic period.[72] Only sons inherited land, unlike Egypt, where all children in theory inherited.[73]

GREECE

Land holding was the basis of state service in Egypt and the Near East, and the basis of citizenship in Greek city-states. Agricultural production has been extensively studied in the Greek world, although many basic questions remain.[74] Dry farming dominated, which is a major contrast to the irrigated landscapes of Egypt and southern Mesopotamia. Rainfall patterns and risks varied widely across Greece and the Aegean islands. The distribution of land also varied widely. It is not easy to compare Greek agriculture to Near Eastern or Egyptian systems beyond generalities; there just are not comparable kinds of documentary evidence for Greece. There certainly was a good deal of crop yield variability.[75]

Literary sources are important for understanding the mentality of Greek farming. Hesiod's *Works and Days*, gives us a view from the small self-sufficient farmer, with the calendric rhythm of the agricultural year, and the use of seasonal labor at key times of the agricultural cycle, not unlike our Bronze Age Egyptian friend *Hekanakhte*. "Horizontal" social relations, as opposed to vertical power relations of social hierarchy or state demands, are stressed. He does not provide us with a detailed agricultural manual by any means, but we do gain a good sense of elite attitudes toward farming.[76] Xenophon's *Oeconomicus* is a similar source for the 4th century BCE.[77] Demosthenes gives us rich material for large estates and legal issues around property holdings as it was related to state service (*antidosis*).[78] Theophrastus, *On Plants*, is a good source for viticulture and the olive tree.

Archaeological surveys provide important information on regional land-holding patterns in the Greek world.[79] These regional patterns of agricultural production, land holding, and animal husbandry were a function of rainfall and topographic variation.[80] The distribution of land is the subject of intense debate and very different conclusions. Distribution was less equal in western and northern Greece, and more egalitarian in the South and in the Aegean.[81] Land around Athens was in the hands of a small wealthy elite, but in the 4th century the distribution across these citizen families was found by Morris to have been "comparatively even."[82] Inheritance was the main mode of acquisition of land. There was a tendency toward fragmentation of holdings caused by the partible inheritance systems.

After Alexander the Hellenistic kings shifted the political and economic equilibrium everywhere, and the effects can be seen in Greece. Field surveys have helped enormously here.[83] New foundations, gift estates, and population movements are documented, but, as elsewhere in the Hellenistic period, there was an increase in the concentration of land holding. There was growth in the size of estates of the wealthy, and new rules in Athens for citizen rights based on wealth.[84] There was also growth in the size of estates in Hellenistic Macedonia, and large estates were established in the Chersonsese (Crimea) in the Hellenistic period.[85] They were laid out in grids, reminiscent of the activity around Philadelphia that is so well documented in the Zenon archive with which I began this chapter.[86]

There was "considerable improvement" in the size of livestock.[87] Indeed the apparent overall improvement of livestock is one of the least appreciated technological achievements of antiquity. Alfalfa was possibly introduced by the Persian invasions and may have been related to improved nutrition and the size of livestock.[88]

Wheat, originally the preferred bread grain of the wealthy, and barley dominated agricultural production. Barley was favored even in Attica and in eastern Greece, because of its hardier nature. In western Greece and in the North, wheat production was preferred.[89] A two-year cycle of production and fallow was the norm. Overall in most places yields were low on grain-bearing land, perhaps between 1:3 and 1:7, although there are no hard figures from antiquity.[90] Olive cultivation was already known in Greece in the late Bronze Age in Cyprus and Crete and was widespread by the 7th century BCE.[91] Fruit tree orchards and vineyards were common.

Debates continue on the nature of animal husbandry in connection to agricultural land. Disagreements continue as well with respect to overall productivity, and hence of food supply.[92] One debate centers on the availability of manure from animals because of the practice of transhumance in many parts of Greece. Although compost was also used, the lack of manure may have constrained what would have otherwise been much higher productivity of the soil.[93] The debate is the result of the absence of hard evidence and the various interpretations of literary texts that we do have.

Land tenure arrangements were complex, consisting not simply of "family farms" but "reflect[ing] trade-offs between agrarian practicality, military need, and community authority."[94] One could directly farm the land, use a manager, or lease the land out.[95] Average productive units have been estimated to have been about 5 hectares or roughly 12.5 acres. There was a cultural preference for families as units, but military demands changed the dynamics, and the complexities of interlocking patterns of power over land resemble in some ways the Egyptian system. A community's possession of the land was under the care of a god, balancing personal and community interest in the land's productivity.[96] The system, also like Egypt, was a means of preventing real property becoming too fragmented through partible inheritance systems and from the exigencies of demography. The granting of land in exchange for military duties was replaced in many places by the rise of the professional mercenary soldier paid in coin.

Around Athens the risk of wheat failing was quite high, roughly a 28 percent chance of failure in a given year (table 1).[97] Here barley was preferred, and Athens famously relied on the importation of grain from outside of its region, from the Black Sea, North Africa, and Sicily, primarily, although quantifying the balance between internal production in Attica and the extent of imports from abroad remains a disputed endeavor.[98]

LABOR/SLAVERY

There were two sources of labor on agricultural land, animals and humans. I focus here on the latter. Human agricultural labor in all Mediterranean civilizations ranged from tenant farming to wage and slave labor. All these societies showed cultural preferences to avoid female labor in the fields, but we must leave the possibility open that they did so.[99] All premodern Mediterranean societies, including nomadic ones, had some form of slavery; the form and types of bound labor, and the location of slave labor within the productive sectors of premodern societies, varied widely.[100] In most cases, slaves originated from outside ethnic groups, and there were several modes of enslavement, war capture and kidnapping being prominent among them. In all Mediterranean systems, slaves are found in agricultural labor, mining, and other unskilled settings like factory work, and in the domestic context. Definitions of slavery, and the boundary between fully slave and dependent worker, can be difficult to discern, in part because of the lack of evidence and in part by the nature of our evidence that gives us several vantage points. Ancient categories with the exception of Roman law were fluid between the various kinds of dependent labor and slavery.[101] Slavery was increasingly formalized as shown in legal/property relations in Aristotle's discussion.[102] State concerns, and legal definitions, as opposed to literary characterizations, including cartoon versions of the "comic slave," vary. There have been many summaries of slavery in individual societies over the past twenty years, but no real advances driven by new material. Proxy measures by Scheidel and comparative work have elucidated and contextualized ancient slavery better. Economists have made important contributions about understanding the mechanisms of slavery such as manumission from a comparative point of view.[103] Dari-Mattiacci's recent study of slave manumission concludes concerning:

> the asymmetry of information between the slave and the master, which in turn determines whether manumission will be used by the master as an incentive for good performance.[104]

The availability of labor has been an important part of explanations for the origins of slavery. It is a highly contentious aspect of ancient economies not least because it is difficult to assess absolute numbers, and the categories are quite fluid ones especially in preclassical societies. Leaving aside the concept of "slave society," slavery is usually understood as being on one end of a spectrum of power relationships in a social hierarchy in all human societies.[105] Slavery was a widespread institution in Greek and the Roman worlds; it was defended and elaborated on philosophical grounds and taken for granted in literature. It was a major factor in Athenian democracy, found everywhere including in agricultural production.[106]

The Sumerians, already by the mid-third millennium BCE, had an abstract concept of labor, quantifiable into "work-days."[107] The same word came to mean "wage, hire, rent." So it became monetized. Slavery itself was not a major role in agrarian production in the ancient near east or Egypt. There, household slavery was more common. Foreigners were prisoners of war in both in the Near East and Egypt and are frequently documented as slaves.[108] The shortage of labor led to the necessity of force. Debt slavery, a "characteristic feature of ancient near eastern societies," was initially the main form of slavery in the Near East and in Egypt.[109] Manumission is rarely attested in sources from the Ancient Near East or Egypt.[110]

The theory of the "Asiatic mode of production" has often been invoked as an explanation for labor control. Irrigation systems generated managerial bureaucracies that in turn led to highly centralized political systems and widespread dependence. In fact there was a subtle interrelationship between environment, agricultural production, and state and household demands. An organized labor system in irrigation basins required cooperation on a large scale, and it is clearest in southern Mesopotamia and in Egypt. The rivers, in a very real sense, were the despots; the royal claims to control labor were secondary to the needs of farming in irrigated landscapes.

Seasonal labor obligations to the state were common both in the Near East and in Egypt from the third millennium BCE through the Roman period.[111] It was surely the earliest form of state taxation; it's easier to tax persons than agricultural production, which can be disguised or hidden. We must distinguish different types of bound labor: seasonal labor, wage labor, and permanent bound labor. Seasonal labor is commonly found in clearing irrigation canals, repairing dykes, and so on. Here again, the use of the word *corvée* itself tends to mislead, conjuring up the original use of corvée in more coercive systems like the 19th century labor requirements in Egypt under Mohammed Ali. The British abolished the institution in 1882, but even in 19th century Egypt, wage labor was also common in canal and dyke work.[112] Weber referred to all those who worked land as *"coloni,"* all labor including military service treated as an obligation to the state. I prefer to see it as public service obligation, a norm at village level, on free labor, seasonal, nonspecialized, imposed, or supervised, by state officials on the wider population. To be sure it is of a different nature than ad hoc seasonal labor.

Wage labor in parallel to corvée systems of labor obligations was common down through the Achaemenid and Seleukid periods in the Near East.[113] "Interest" on loans could be repaid with labor and is well represented already in the documents from Ur III ca. 2000 BCE. But wage labor could also be paid in silver as well as grain. Neo-Assyrian records document both nonspecialized (agrarian) and specialized (e.g., goldsmithing and the caravan trading) kinds of labor. The terms of labor contracts were between one month and one year in length and show the mobility of labor. The Neo-Babylonian record for slavery is more extensive.[114] Slaves were expensive, and ownership was restricted to the wealthy. Male slaves occupied a number of roles, from household service to agricultural and craft production to the management of property on behalf of their master. Privately owned slaves working as bakers are very commonly found. Privately owned slaves in Neo-Babylonia could be manumitted by contract. In some cases, the manumitted slave was obligated to remain in the service of the owner and upon death the slave was "dedicated" to a god and became a temple dependent (*sirku*) and, while remaining under its authority, was free to marry and own property.[115]

For Weber, the entire population of Egypt was "a tool of pharaonic power."[116] Actual slave labor in the agricultural production, however, was rare in Egypt in all periods. The word *bȝk* reveals the basic problem of nontechnical language; it meant both slave and "servant" or "worker" more broadly, as well as "tax." The title *bȝk* ("slave" or "servant") of a god can be compared to the *sirku* of Babylonia and the "sacred slaves" (*hierodouloi*) known elsewhere in the Hellenistic world. The root meaning was something like "obligation." The Egyptian language did not distinguish between slave and servant. It is unclear if *b3k* and *hierodouloi* are related terms, but in any case these were not slaves *stricto sensu*, but workers attached in service to temple estates. They are found in a variety of private contracts as parties to land sales.[117] We miss subtleties of normative coercive hierarchical relations, and we should not underestimate the coercive power of the "social cage" of the river itself.[118]

In both the Near East and Egypt in the first millennium BCE labor obligations evolved from subsistence wages to wages paid in money, usually silver. With respect to agrarian labor there was an evolution from the second to the first millennium BCE. Earlier, a wide range of bound agrarian workers on state land was typical. In first-millennium BCE texts, we find a "stratified peasantry," "free farmers," and the use of written labor contracts.[119] Here Weber's insights were impressive and remain valid:

> Thus we see that about the time of Bocchoris there first appear demotic contracts, in particular those connected with transfers of land. Commercial law seems to have changed, especially that relating to land, and a programme of secularization also was carried out.[120]

As elsewhere, Egyptian labor was "fluid," the boundary between state and private activity not strict, and most people in between free and unfree.[121]

More coerced forms of labor are documented on temple estates during the New Kingdom, and for large state construction projects. But the picture of cruel kings' slave labor used to build the pyramids of the Old Kingdom, still found in Herodotus's account of Egypt and perhaps coloring our understanding of Ptolemaic labor, belies a more complex system even in early Egypt. Lehner's recent analysis of the pyramid construction labor system, sparked by the superb archaeological work on the Giza plateau, shows fairly clearly that the system was highly complex, and workers ranged from fully free workers to workers who came from dependent staff from elite household and from temple estates, from specialized stone workers to captive labor.[122] A papyrus from Middle Kingdom Egypt preserves the record of a state bureau that kept careful track of state labor obligations, and punished severely those who fled such obligations by forcing those who had escaped labor obligation, or their dependents, into bound service on state land.[123] The state could conscript very large numbers of workers for state projects; quarrying work would have been unpleasant and often dangerous.[124] But we also know that such expeditions, organized by local recruiting of young men, could be motivated by pride, by pay, and by the promise of a feast afterward.[125]

Bound labor on land took on different dimensions, and a different scale, in New Kingdom Egypt, as prisoners of war poured into Egypt from military campaigns, and were forced onto agricultural estates and into quarries to work them. They were a "permanent presence" on the land, as were "condemned prisoners" and older soldiers.[126] Soldiers were granted land within temple estates. This continued into the first millennium BCE on temple estates.[127] The terms "free/private land" and "free/private persons" begin to appear in our sources, ca. 1000 BCE, concerning paying taxes to the state, at the same time that coerced labor disappears, probably the result of the diminishment, but not totally, of war captives by the late New Kingdom.[128] "Agricultural laborers" appear in sale contracts in first millennium BCE as being bought and sold. This seems to reflect a shift in agricultural production during the first millennium BCE away from institutional (i.e., temple) bound labor to the use of corvée labor and private laborers.[129] The status of those who were given land for state service, ranging from high-level military to craftsmen, herdsmen of sacred flocks, and so on, is debated. It is true that those who held land within temple estates in the Ptolemaic period have a status title translated either as "servant" of "slave of the god," but the title, common in private contracts from the Ptolemaic and early Roman periods, carries no more meaning than someone who was employed by the temple.[130]

Over the course of the first millennium BCE the Egyptian state moved from the taxation and control of labor to a system in which taxes in money grew in importance. The system reached new heights after 300 BCE. In Ptolemaic and Roman times corvée labor was treated as a tax reckoned as an amount of earth moved, with receipts issued. The tax was expressed as a royal claim on labor, but it had been entrenched for millennia as a norm.[131] The large reclamation project in the Fayyum used wage labor.[132] A papyrus contract details the reclamation, and the amount of labor involved, 51,600 work/days and the labor costs (figure 22).[133]

Most forms of labor outside of the household context were paid. Wage labor contracts are well known from the Egyptian papyri.[134] Many involve agricultural work, in land tenancy agreements, but some new contract forms appear, including contracts to do specific kinds of work within the so-called royal monopolies, called *paramonê* contracts. Slaves were generally not used in agricultural production, but mainly in households in Ptolemaic period.[135]

Foxhall has explored the nature of the dependency of tenants in classical antiquity.[136] The surrounding noncitizen rural populations formed the main source of labor in most parts of the Greek world.[137] There was a very wide variety of dependent labor forms in the Greek world and a highly fragmentary labor market.[138] Labor was in short supply; the resident alien (metic)

FIGURE 22. *P. Lille* 1 recto and verso. A schematic plan and a labor budget for new land development in the 3d century BCE Fayyum, Egypt, with calculations of labor costs in silver per unit of earth moved, showing the land, 10,000 *arouras*, divided into equal-sized plots, *perichomata*, of 250 *arouras*, and indicating canals and dikes. See D. Thompson (1999a:118–20) for a translation. Photo courtesy of the Institute of Papyrology at the Sorbonne.

system, wherein a person was tied to the city-state without citizenship but with certain basic rights, existed alongside slavery.

Sparta had its own system of slave laborers, the self-reproducing helot class.[139] In Crete and elsewhere, a similar class of slaves was called the *klarotai*, who were given certain rights.[140] By the 6th century BCE, slavery had become a dominant mode of labor at Athens, and by the 4th century BCE, slave numbers may have reached between eighty to one hundred thousand, or about 40 percent of the total Athenian population, with a "substantial portion" of those working in the silver mines.[141] Census records suggest that by the second half of that century slaves reached peak numbers, at the same time as the institution reached a peak in philosophical studies.[142] Wage labor and seasonal workers are also known but less well documented. Social status of these changed: *thetes* were propertyless casual laborers, and after democratic reforms at Athens they disappear; they had citizen status, which made coerced forms of labor, and the willingness of the *thetes* themselves less willing to be employed, problematic.[143]

Slavery in the Greek world, documented since Homeric times, occurred across a range of labor including agriculture, although the extent of the use of slaves, especially in the agrarian context, is still disputed.[144] Many of our sources are literary.[145] Nonetheless, we know the basic contours of Greek slavery, and it is very well documented for Athens. Chattel slavery, in which slaves were conceived as property bought and sold in slave markets, rose and expanded with the increased use of coinage and trade.[146] Slaves possessed a range of skills, from specialized soldiers and craftsmen, to those poor souls confined to the mines. Slave sources came primarily as a by-product of war, particularly women and children of the defeated side. But there is an argument that war was motivated, in part, by the capture of slaves as a part of war booty.[147] To be sure, captives sold into slavery were a by-product of war, and enslaving barbarians caused less anxiety.[148] The extent of slave breeding has probably been underestimated.[149] The shortage of labor required more coercive forms of labor. Democratic developments at Athens and some other cities drove the move toward slaves.[150] Ownership seems to have been widespread, and the relative price of slaves at Athens was low, the result of low transport costs and a steady supply.[151] Attitudes toward slavery changed during the Hellenistic period.

In Egypt, peasants had always been technically free; there was a long tradition of tenancy. Chattel slave labor on the land is rarely, if ever, encountered in Egypt. Local peasantry in Ptolemaic Egypt and the Seleukid kingdom were called *laoi* in Greek texts and probably represented varying degrees of dependence with respect to the land. They were legally free in Syria and protected by law from being sold in the future.[152] Of course freedom is a difficult concept in these cases since in practice rural populations were effectively tied to the land by practical circumstances; most people simply did not move around too far from the place of birth, traditionally bound within patronage networks, and often attached to temple estates.[153] But that left them vulnerable, especially to war, and to being taken into captivity and sold into slavery, in places where war occurred frequently. Egypt remained virtually unscathed by such activity. But it was not the norm in the Hellenistic world. This fact was further reinforced by the Ptolemaic fiscal system and its census that legally bound people and groups to a place. "Royal farmers" as they were called in Greek texts, farmed royal land on leases, with certain privileges and legal protections resulting from this status. "Sacred slaves" are also encountered.[154] Men with such titles were not slaves but rather persons attached to temple estates in the Near East and in Egypt and serving the estate in some capacity, from herdsmen and prostitutes to other kinds of specialized nonreligious functions. In Upper Egypt in the 3d century BCE they are found as herdsmen and buying and selling small plots of land by Egyptian sale contracts.[155]

The spread of Greek chattel slavery into the Hellenistic kingdoms was an important trend in the period, although it was already well established in places like Babylonia.[156] In other parts of the Hellenistic world, we encounter slaves in large factory settings (*ergasteria*), mainly, it appears, making military equipment in urban regions such as Pergamum and Miletos.[157] Greeks moving east to serve the new kings of the Hellenistic states, primarily as soldiers, brought the tradition of household slaves with them. And it is here, in the houses of Greek immigrants, where most of the household slavery existed.[158] It is difficult to know what world Egyptian wisdom literature sayings such as "Do not neglect to acquire a manservant and a maidservant when you are able" reflects.[159] We also move into documentary evidence and less literary material.[160] Slavery is documented on large estates in Egypt (Zenon papyri), working as weavers on the estates, but also as agents for the estate manager, in households. Manumission by testament was the "regular form of manumission."[161] House-born slaves had to be registered as part of the normal routine of household surveys.[162] They appear in the census returns.[163] Slave trade through various slave dealers, and some of the extant slave sales in the Greek papyri, provide a good amount of detail on the origins of slaves in Egypt: through sale at auctions, and state regulation of them. Slave markets probably grew in activity; Delos was the key node during the 2d century BCE with growing Roman demand in the wake of the crushing defeat of Carthage and Corinth.[164] Child exposure, especially of girls, was also a source of slaves, as was war, a near constant in the Hellenistic period, and, along with it, piracy. Debt slavery, an ancient institution, continued to some extent.

Agricultural production was the basis of household security and wealth. The taxation and the distribution of grain was a critical part of Iron Age Mediterranean politics as well, although fiscal structures of the first millennium BCE differed radically, as did land tenure and labor regimes. Another factor in the variability of agricultural regimes was climate and changes in climate that occurred on several scales. Paleoclimatology offers historians of premodern Mediterranean economies a new and growing natural archive of these changes. The challenge in the years ahead will be to integrate the documentation of human activity from texts and archaeology with these natural archives. It will not be an easy task, but this integration offers us an exciting new approach to ancient agriculture and to premodern economies more generally.

CHAPTER 5

The Boundaries of Premodern Economies

ECOLOGY, CLIMATE, AND CLIMATE CHANGE

When they found out that the whole of Greece relies on rainfall rather than its rivers, as Egypt does, to irrigate the land, they commented that the Greeks would one day have their high hopes dashed and would suffer the torments of starvation.

—HERODOTUS 2.13 TRANS. WATERFIELD (1998)

The most astonishing feature in the economic history of Asia was the equation between the monsoon winds and the limits of cereal cultivation. . . . The distribution of rainfall in the monsoon belts of Asia varied according to a pre-determined and observable pattern within the annual cycle.

—CHAUDHURI (1990:106)

THE ANCIENTS WERE KEEN observers of nature; that's clear in Egyptian poetry, in the flood myths of Mesopotamia, in biblical literature, and in writers like Theophrastus, who observed, among many other things, the human-caused climate changes in Thessaly.[1] The holistic vision of an interconnected natural world expressed by Alexander von Humboldt had a powerful impact on the 19th century imagination.[2] It was well known, thanks to Napoleon's scientists and later ethnographers, that Egyptian society based on flood recession agriculture had different features than regions relying on rain-fed agrarian production.[3] The Annalistes school of historians in France has devoted much attention to the relationship between climate and history.[4]

There is a long history of thinking about humans in the natural environment. But how exactly are they connected? Some of the new work that my colleagues and I are developing takes on the old subject of the connection between Nile flooding and the political history of Egypt. In our careful statistical analysis, we show that the correlation between explosive volcanic eruptions, which is linked to reduced precipitation in the Nile basin, and Nile flooding has a greater than 98 percent probability of being nonrandom.[5] Statistics, occasionally, can be damned lies, and probability is not causation. But the relationship is so very highly correlated as to suggest that there must be a strong connection. Similarly we have found that eight of the nine documented periods of social unrest occurred within a narrow window of these eruptions. Poor Nile flooding was not the only cause of unrest, and large volcanic eruptions were not the only cause of Nile variability. But these kind of climatic shocks can reveal structural weaknesses in society. The challenge for ancient historians is to build more complex social models. One of my hopes for future work is that we will be better able to link climate variability to impacts on agricultural production and water resources.[6]

Climate affected not only agriculture, but other areas of ancient life as well. While climate and climate change is important, then, understanding both climate reconstruction and climate change poses enormous challenges. Paleoclimatology and historical climatology are both relatively new fields. Both work with very complicated data, mathematical models, and some uncertainty in assessing spatial and temporal impacts of climatic change. What's more, for the premodern Mediterranean world, much of the climate data is new. The usual assumption that changes in climate regime drove social changes is certainly too simplistic. Rather, we should think about climate and climate change inputs as components of coupled human-natural system (figure 23).

Most earlier studies of premodern Mediterranean economies have acknowledged in one way or another the role of geography and climate, but there has not been extensive work on integrating climate and climate change data into a historical analysis of the ancient economy with respect to regional and transregional performance or growth.[7] Debates on the impact of climate change on economic performance have ranged from considering it insignificant on one end of the spectrum to it being the prime cause of socioeconomic distress and decline.[8] The great challenge for historians is to integrate very complex climate data, an understanding of the impacts of climate change, and human archival data assembled from texts and archaeological material.[9]

Much work remains, and there are many gaps in our knowledge. Our grasp of the demographic structure and disease pools of societies in the Mediterranean before 200 BCE, for example, remains far too imprecise at the moment, but recent studies of later historical periods demonstrate the great potential in integrating natural and human archives.[10]

A substantial amount of new paleoclimate proxy data has been made available in recent years. More precise data, with annual or decadal resolution, provides an opportunity for historians to engage in data on human scales. To be sure, climate change operated on several scales, from long-term warming/cooling trends and megadroughts that could last multiple decades to several centuries, superimposed on which are short-term shocks such as explosive volcanic eruptions that had impacts on an interannual (largely one-to-two-year) timescale. The spatial distribution of climate change, and hence its impacts, were uneven. Human responses to various kinds of climatic changes also depended on the society's resilience to shocks. At the end of this chapter I point out that climate drivers far beyond the Mediterranean, explosive eruptions by high north latitude volcanoes in particular, suppressed the Nile flood. Climate data allows us to develop a coupled human-natural system with feedbacks (figures 24 and 36).[11] In good years, Egypt, and its rulers, were rich in grain. But because of Egypt's dependence on the annual flood of the Nile, agricultural production could vary significantly on account of interannual variability driven by climate dynamics.

DETERMINISM AND CAUSALITY

The interaction of humans and animals within their ecological niches and their adaptation in response to changing conditions was interconnected. Much of the older literature was framed in terms of geographical or environmental determinism, "the assumption that nature has the power to forbid or encourage human activities."[12] But this monocausal model does not take into account human adaptive capacity. The extent to which environment and climate constrained individual or state behavior must be approached at several scales. The much improved climate proxy records from around the world have shown us that "environmental conditions" were always highly variable.[13] Rather than a linear or monocausal relationship, as crude deterministic models suggest, the relationship between humans and ecological conditions and climate shocks must be understood as a complex, coupled feedback system. Geographical constraints and climatic conditions played important roles in shaping the incentive structures of societies, in mobility, in trade routes, and in fiscal systems among other things.[14]

The use of "climate" in historical explanations of change is problematic because it can carry an assumption that environmental and climatic forces "determined" or constrained human fortunes. The so-called ecological fallacy was already a "standard concept" in sociology in the 1950s, and "fashionable" among some archaeologists in the 1960s.[15] Critics have rightly highlighted the problem of isolating the "environment" as a primary cause, when in fact the interaction between humans and their environment is highly complex. It is not just a matter of societal "collapse"; varying levels of human resilience is more often the story, and the impact of human activity on environments is now much better weighed against the natural forces of climate change.[16]

Another model, which has been called the "endogenous" model, was a by-product of initial instrumental record keeping in 19th century Europe and assumed that climate is a constant and not a driver of change.[17] That was more or less the conclusion in even a relatively recent study of ancient Greek agriculture: "We have to conclude that no methods are available to measure changes in climate and therefore accept, *a priori*, that climate is not likely to have changed radically."[18] But scientific advances now give us excellent methods to reconstruct ancient climates, climate variability, and human impacts on the environment. For example, paleoclimate work on the Mediterranean suggests that human action was less significant to soil erosion than plate tectonics and gradual climate change during the mid-Holocene (4000–3000 BCE).[19]

A model linking ecology to economy was proposed in Wittfogel's study of "oriental despotism." It was built on a long line of thought going back to Greek philosophy that drew strong distinctions between classical rainfall environments and the irrigated landscapes of Egypt, the Near East, India, and China. But it raised a fundamentally important question about the differences in economic performance between irrigation and rainfall-driven agrarian production. Scholars do tend to write about themselves in one fashion or another. Wittfogel, working in a Nazi concentration camp at Esterwegen in 1933, "experienced firsthand the despotic and murderous side of hydraulic engineering."[20] By the time his book was published in 1957, it had become a full-blown anticommunist attack. Its basic thesis was that the management of irrigation led to a radical growth in bureaucratic power that subordinated every other aspect of society and led to "total power" of the central state.

Irrigation has long been thought to be the basis of a highly centralized, despotic form of state.[21] Wittfogel's theory linking irrigation to politics, Karl Butzer mused, is a bit like Elvis, randomly appearing in unexpected places.[22] It is almost universally rejected as an overarching theory that explains agricultural production, including labor. If I were to assemble the literature on oriental despotism, the footnote would be as long as this book. This hydrological theory about Asian societies goes back to the 18th century and to the work of Montesquieu among others.[23] The model, to summarize, posits a causal connection between irrigation, managerial bureaucracy, and total power of the ruler. Many observers have associated irrigation landscapes with massive building projects and large coerced labor forces. Karl Marx's "Asiatic mode of production" and Max Weber's "hydraulic bureaucracy" posited a strong correlation between irrigation societies, social complexity, and centralized political power.

Oriental Despotism summarized much 19th century historical thinking about the political economy of early states, particularly Asian states, which were associated with irrigation agriculture. Its argument is complex, and Wittfogel's attempt to link water management to levels of technology, property rights, the structure of the state and social power was impressive. At its most basic level, the despotic model in Egypt was a "linear causality model," which linked environmental stress to irrigation; the need to control irrigation networks led to the formation of a hydraulic bureaucracy, which in turn led to centralized control of economic resources. The theory, while very interesting, is however overgeneralized and overextended. While highlighting the differences between East and West, it oversimplified the complexities of irrigated societies both from the point of view of intercomparison—Egypt, Mesopotamia, and China were all more or less the same in his treatment— and from the point of view of a particular society like Egypt, whose local social structure in relation to irrigation was more complex.

Wittfogel's theory also emphasized scale: despotic states were the result of large-scale irrigation works that required large managerial bureaucracies to maintain. Both of these are incorrect for ancient Egypt.[24] The causal relationship is more likely to have been in the opposite direction; that is, that locally managed irrigation schemes enabled elite appropriation of agricultural surplus.[25]

But, while Wittfogel's general theory fails to capture the full complexities in the connection between irrigation and politics, new work has broadened the debate even further by examining long-term pathways of economic development in different ecologies.[26] The difference between irrigated and rain-fed territory may indeed have been a decisive factor in state performance. Three types of states emerge in this work: transactional, insurance, and fragile. First, "high levels and broad distribution of human capital" lead to modern states; the second, "high levels, but narrow distribution of human capital" led to "moderate levels of economic development"; and finally the "fragile state" characterized by "low levels of investment in human capital" led to low levels of development and weak states. The gist of the theory is that "democracy and economic development were more likely" with "broad distributions of human capital, high levels of urbanization, well-developed systems of property and contract law."[27] The theory explains the world after 1750, but there are implications for the ancient world, and it highlights the important links between geography, climate, and economic performance while at the same time making an implicit contrast between the premodern world and modern global development.

A study of the relationship between environment and politics in specific locations is instructive because it highlights the fact that the polities we are concerned with in the first millennium BCE were complex adaptive systems. A "concatenation" of events, climate shock, war, disease, political crises, could lead to catastrophic societal effects or to positive resilient responses. The key is to examine societal "stress points," which is where paleoclimatology has

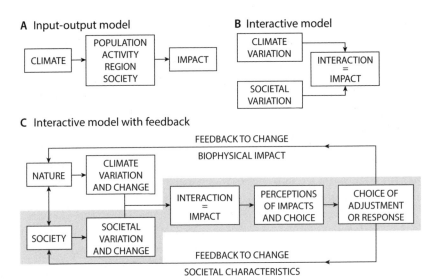

FIGURE 23. Various models, from a monocausal input-output model (a) to a coupled natural human system feedback model (c). From Hannaford (2014).

made such significant advances in our understanding of premodern societies.[28] The aim, then, is not to build a deterministic monocausal model leading from climate change or shocks to societal response but, rather, to understand the complexities of premodern societies by adding environmental constraints and shocks as an additional component to coupled human-natural system dynamics (figure 23).

Political and economic equilibriums are dependent on the link between agricultural production and taxation. Therefore environmental constraints and climate variability were crucial to political equilibriums in the premodern world. This is an important difference between the premodern and modern worlds.[29] The intense debate about how and the extent to which human societies adapted and adjusted to changing conditions is ongoing. The formation and decline of empires, the most important political phenomenon of the first-millennium BCE Mediterranean world, was, in part, driven by these imposed constraints and how the problem of mobilizing resources, and controlling territory, was solved. The movement of early civilizations was one from river valleys of Egypt and Mesopotamia to "the surroundings of a massively larger sea."[30]

Jared Diamond, a physiologist by training and now a professor of geography at UCLA, highlighted the role of environmental constraints. His 1997 book *Guns, Germs and Steel* attracted, and continues to attract, much attention. In it, an argument is laid out to explain how the interaction of geography, disease, and environmental constraints in the Eurasian core generated "positive feedback loops" that were important factors in explanations of historical economic performance. The book made an enormous impact, winning a Pulitzer Prize in 1998. While some critics charged that Diamond was simply revitalizing "geographical determinism," his thesis is far more intricate, combining factor endowments and geography with technological change and the role of disease to explain the trajectory of early civilizations.[31]

It was a salutary lesson for our jaded world that often forgets that our lives are still coupled to the natural world. We live in a globalized world; grocery stores are full of products from around the world as well as from local organic producers; hardware stores have everything one needs to build one's own house; YouTube provides instruction. Commodity, equity, and bond prices are joined into one continuous, dynamic, and integrated global market. We have, some say, achieved an existence outside of nature, insulated from shocks that might disrupt supplies of food and water, and in control of our own destiny. But that of course, is an illusion, and one limited to those living in a handful of lucky nations.

Indeed we are reminded from time to time that Mother Nature is still in charge, and those reminders seem to be more insistent at the moment. The massive Nepali earthquake in April 2015 (7.8 Mw, May 2015, with a major aftershock of 7.3 Mw), the destruction in Bangladesh caused by Cyclone Sidr in 2007, the current drought in western Asia, Hurricane Harvey, which is inundating south Texas as I am revising this manuscript, among many other phenomena, show us, or should show us, that humans are still exposed to natural forces, storms, earthquakes, environmental variability, and so on.[32] Even with increasingly good evidence of anthropogenic climate change, namely global warming trends caused, principally, by CO_2 emissions from human activity, the change can be denied in some quarters, or ignored. In part this ignorance is aided by the nature of the change. It is slow moving, differential in its global impact, and drives processes that are cumulative but nonlinear. Unlike an event such as an earthquake, flood, or a sudden drought, therefore, the ongoing nature of these changes is difficult to perceive.

Climate change, climate variability, and environmental constraints and topography can seem less dramatic than a major battle, but they were powerful forces in the premodern world.[33] It is critical, then, that studies of premodern economies begin to integrate this insight into analyses of economic institutions and of institutional change. The concept of bounded rationality should also extend to the physical constraints imposed on humans living in premodern societies by natural forces.[34] One of the most important trends in understanding premodern economies is the search for dynamic models.

The idea that ecology and the environment are coupled with human activity is of course an ancient one, going back, at least, to the Ionian geographers and early Chinese philosophy. Herodotus, at the very end of his *History* (book 9:122), indeed, with his last words about the Greco-Persian wars that had so shaped subsequent history in both Greece and the Near East, says this about how environment shaped human civilization:

> The proposal went something like this: "Since Zeus has given sovereignty to the Persians and to you, Cyrus, now that you have done away with Astyages, let's emigrate from the country we currently own, which is small and rugged, and take over somewhere better. There are plenty of countries on our borders, and plenty further away too, any one of which, in our hands, will make us even more remarkable to even more people."
>   . . . Cyrus was not impressed with the proposal. He told them to go ahead—but he also advised them to be prepared, in that case, to become subjects instead of rulers, on the grounds that soft lands tend to breed soft men. It is impossible, he said, for one and the same country to produce remarkable crops and good fighting men.[35]

That is a clear statement in the 5th century BCE of what we now refer to as environmental determinism. "Nature" determined "culture" in this monocausal understanding of the world.[36] It is an idea that goes back, as far as can be traced, to the Pre-Socratic philosophers of Ionia. There is a clear line from Plato's dialogues *Critias* and *Timaeus* and the famous story of Atlantis, to Aristotle's *Meteorologica* and to some of the observations of Gibbon on barbarians, that the connection between climate change and abrupt shocks were forces in human civilizations.[37] Consider, for example, the following passage from the Hippocratic corpus *Airs, Waters and Places*, part 2:

> And in particular, as the season and the year advances, he can tell what epidemic diseases will attack the city, either in summer or in winter, and what each individual will be in danger of experiencing from the change of regimen. For knowing the changes of the seasons, the risings and settings of the stars, how each of them takes place, he will be able to know beforehand what sort of a year is going to ensue.[38]

GEOGRAPHY/REGION

Location on the map is a critical part of understanding premodern economies. The environmental conditions, for example, of the Fayyum, southern Egypt, or northern and southern Mesopotamia and rain-fed regions such as the Greek mainland shaped their different political and historical trajectories.[39]

Shaw makes the point well: "The space in which social and economic systems were located and where they developed was . . . significant in itself."[40] The emergence and commercial success of Greek city-states, for example, can be attributed, in part, to a "historical conjunction of Iron Age innovations plus a unique ecological and geopolitical location astride maritime routes between semi-barbarian plowing land and civilized empires of domination."[41] The study of particular regions in the Mediterranean has been an especially productive field in recent years, although this unit of analysis remains problematic.[42] Reger defines region with three different boundary criteria: geography, ethnicity, and polity, using coinage as the marker of regional and interregional exchange patterns.[43] Networks, trade, and geography were intimately connected.[44] Already in the Bronze Age, by ca. 1800 BCE, the boundaries between what we tend to call classical or Aegean civilization and cultures in Asia Minor and central Asia were involved in "extensive interregional exchange" with the Aegean.[45]

Environment, climate, and climate change remain challenging to integrate in economic history, and the connection is often relegated to a casual, static description of major features such as mountains, rivers, amount of rainfall, and the like within the territory covered, in a "polite few paragraphs."[46] Shifts in settlement patterns, shifts in river beds, volcanism, changes in temperature, the spread of disease, and human adaptation to environmental conditions are among many other topics that add a dynamic component that is critical to any understanding of change over time.[47] But this is a subject that has changed dramatically in the last quarter century; a good deal of work has created a baseline of information about geography, climate, climate change, and environments that has been very important to the study of economies. William Cronon highlighted that it is "the natural ecosystems which provides the context" for human institutions, and yet it remains on "the margins of historical analysis."[48] While it is generally acknowledged as important, the way in which environment, climate, and climate change has shaped the economic history of the ancient world has yet to enter mainstream historical scholarship.[49] It is still the norm among historians that climate is an assumed but undefined influence and that climate and environment are thought to be more or less static on decadal or even centennial timescales.[50] Although environmental and economic history are two sides of the same coin, models that capture the dynamic role of climate and climatic change on multiple scales are still at an elementary stage for premodern economies.[51]

One of the regions of the Earth that has seen the greatest human impact on the landscape is the Mediterranean basin. Each region of the Mediterranean created unique conditions of climate, soil, crop, disease and disease vectors, transportation (e.g., location of harbors), and population density. Similarly land use and drainage, land management, reclamation, pastoralism, and grain harvest/grain prices differed significantly.[52] Historians have been slow to incorporate such understandings into narrative accounts. But environmental context is crucial for understanding, among other things, the growth of large urban areas. Finley's severe criticisms of Fraser's study of the city of Alexandria that it lacked a sense of urban dynamics was not altogether unfounded. More could surely be done on the impacts of Alexandrian "urbanization" on its rural hinterlands along the lines of Cronon's study of the impact of the growth of 19th century Chicago on its vast hinterlands.[53]

PALEOCLIMATOLOGY AND
ANCIENT ECONOMIES

The study of the coupled, nonlinear relationship between natural and human systems remains a controversial topic because the integration of quantified climate data into historical analysis is extraordinarily challenging, and many uncertainties remain in the climate record. In 1979, the eminent French historian Emmanuel Le Roy Ladurie published two influential pieces in English on the relationship between climate and history.[54] The first piece, "Writing the History of the Climate," pointed the way forward in just a few short pages, with little mention of paleoclimate proxy data. He called this kind of work *geohistory* and emphasized climate "fluctuations" that he identified in the advance and retreat of European glaciers.[55] But he also stressed the value of scientific data and mentioned tree rings, glaciology, and phenological studies of plant flowering as proxy measures of temperature variation. Much has changed, and dramatically so, since he wrote this piece.[56] While analysis of ice cores proxy records began in 1957–58, scientific advances in isotope analysis has been nothing short of spectacular since the 1980s.[57] Proxy data, and in particular annually and decadally resolved, have grown astronomically since the publication of Le Roy Ladurie's work (table 4).

The challenge lies not so much in the incompatibility of data sets now but, rather, as Izdebski and his colleagues point out, in the differences in research methods and how narratives are constructed by geophysical scientists, archaeologists, and historians.[58] The connection between climate reconstructions, climate variability and change, and the impact of climate change on past human societies has advanced remarkably since the pioneering studies of Le Roy Ladurie in the 1960s and 1970s.[59] Before the 1960s, historical climate work was largely qualitative.[60] In 1980 Jan DeVries could write confidently that "short term climate crises stand in relation to economic history as bank robberies do to the history of banking."[61] When he wrote those words he was right to point out that "climatological data" were "extremely limited."[62] Even with much better and more precisely dated climate records now, distinguishing between correlation and causality is challenging, and so too is our ability to weigh the balance between long-term impacts of climate change and short-term shocks. The tendency to oversimplify what are extremely complex physical and societal processes remains.[63] Both of these things mean that we need to develop sophisticated spatial and temporal models of climate-human systems. Nevertheless, recent advances in high-resolution paleoclimatology enable historians to compare historical and natural archives on the same timescale.

Ancient sources frequently provide us with references to climate conditions, strange climatic events like rivers freezing over, and even occasionally climate trends, in various parts of the Mediterranean world.[64] Climate history in the sense of the compilation of historic records of climatic conditions (flood heights, rain, glacier expansion/contraction, dates of harvest, grain price time series, and so on) is an old branch of history. Archaeologists have had an even longer record of interest in the reconstruction of climatic conditions at their excavation sites and in studying the connections between environment and civilization and in understanding climate impacts on human history.[65] A real advance came with the meeting sponsored by the *Journal of Interdisciplinary History* in 1979 that engaged in examining both methodology and in various types of proxy records (pollen, lake sediments) and the geophysical forces that contributed to climate change.[66] Climate science has progressed remarkably over the last forty years. Indeed the availability and sophistication of climate models and data has accelerated just in the last few years.[67] The reconstruction of past climates over the last two centuries has taken us from using instrumental records and glacial theory at the beginning of the 19th century to what is now a multidisciplinary scientific endeavor integrating branches of chemistry, physics, geology, archaeology, oceanography, computer science, and biology and highly sophisticated scientific instrumentation that can now measure the presence of isotopes in the parts per quadrillion (ppq).[68] This has created much deeper timescales and more refined data to examine the connections between climate and human history.

Historians have begun to use scientific data generated by climate science as a new and very rich kind of archive. This integration will surely be a major part of ancient history in the coming decade and well beyond. But even when we have good time series of grain prices, which exists for only a few places in antiquity, there are many factors, climate being just one, to consider when trying to explain price fluctuations. While the weighing of feedbacks between complex social dynamics, climate, demography, and the environment is

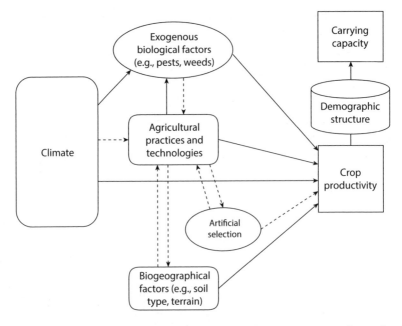

FIGURE 24. Factors determining crop productivity and carrying capacity of agricultural land. From Currie et al. (2015). Figure drawn by T. Currie.

at an early stage, the schema in figure 24 is a good model for thinking through the connection between climate and crop productivity, carrying capacity of the land, technology, human impacts on the land, and demography.[69]

Historians have often treated climate variability, like geography, as a "given," assumed in the background, but not a driving force of social change or of economic performance. Climate change could be more or less ignored as a historical driver of change because there was not a lot of specific data that could be correlated to events or social change.[70] But environment and climate are coming to be viewed not as a static backdrop to human agency but as interactive with it. Indeed climate variability, climate change, and disease are now being understood as critical forces in economic history, not least because climate change directly effects food production.[71] Demographic trends, migration, crop failure, and state fiscal capacity, among other issues, are now better understood within a framework of feedback responses to the environment, something that has been recognized by biologists, social scientists, and archaeologists, and, slowly now, by historians.[72] The problem is that "climate was both parameter and variable."[73] As figure 25 suggests,

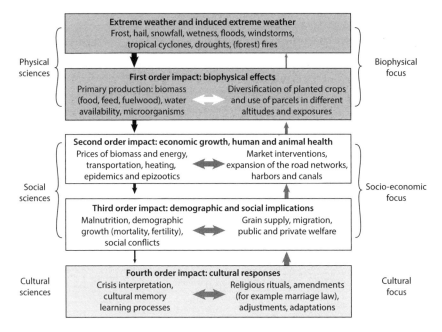

FIGURE 25. A model of climate variability, human responses, and the levels of intellectual engagement assessing impact. From Luterbacher and Pfister (2015).

several fields, and different kinds of evidence, must be integrated in order to understand the cascading impacts and the human responses to climate changes on various timescales. This is, by the way, a good way to think about teamwork in future historical climatology projects. We have only just begun to understand how we can quantify the heterogeneous impacts, spatially and temporally, of both short-term shocks like volcanic eruptions and long-term warming or cooling trends, and human responses.

In a recent study of the connection between climate change and human conflict, the authors observe that:

> climatic variables: temperature, rainfall, and water availability—these variables may be averaged over long or short observational periods.... Societies experience climatic variables in continuous time and respond to both short-lived and long-term changes, making the frequency of short-lived events a socially relevant feature of the climate.[74]

The serious challenge for historians is to build robust social models that reflect sufficient social complexity, and then to integrate environmental and climate data into those models to reflect as fully as possible coupled natural-human

TABLE 4. *Characteristics of Natural Archives*

Archive	Scale of Resolution	Potential Information
historical records	Day/hour	T, P, B, V, L, S
tree rings	annual/season	T, P, B, V, S
lake sediments	annual (varves) to 20 years	T, B, M, P, V, CW
corals	annual	CW, L, T, P
ice cores	annual/season	T, P, CA, B, V, M, S
pollen	30 years	T, P, B
speleothems	annual	CW, T, P, V, B
paleosols	century	T, P, B
loess	century	P, B, M
geomorphic features	century	T, P, V, L, P
marine sediments	century	T, CW, B, M, L, P, S

SOURCE: R. Bradley (2015:table 1.2).

NOTE: In column 3, T = temperature, P = precipitation, humidity, or water balance, C = chemical composition of air (CA) or water (CW), B = information on biomass or vegetation patterns, V = volcanic eruptions, M = geomagnetic field variations, L = sea level, S = solar activity.

system dynamics and to seek multicausal explanations for human responses and social change.

Paleoclimatology now offers an ever-increasing amount of high-resolution proxy data with which to reconstruct past climate variability and climate change. High-resolution climate proxy data such as ice core records and speleothems (figure 26) are now resolved at decadal and annual scales as opposed to the millennial and larger timescales that had made the use of data by historians unhelpful.[75] While there have been good studies of environmental conditions of the Near East and the Mediterranean for a long time, increasing interest and activity in climate and climate change and human responses is now being driven by more chronologically precise data and sophisticated modeling (figure 26).[76]

Historical records are themselves proving invaluable in conjunction with other natural archives for studies of past climate and human response.[77] The Babylonian astronomical diaries, and the commodity price series derived from them, provide perhaps the best record of climate and prices from the ancient Mediterranean. These texts record not only commodity prices but also weather observations and measurements of the Euphrates river flood. Egypt offers the earliest records of climate in the form of annual Nile flow measurements.[78]

High resolution paleoclimate records have the potential to produce a dynamic understanding of premodern economies, and with increasingly higher resolution data for specific regions and good archaeological surveys, we might begin to understand human responses at local and regional scales. Such data are beginning to be integrated into accounts of Roman and Byzantine history, and much has already been accomplished linking climate and historical records in these periods.[79] There remains much to do, and even more to do for classical history, the Hellenistic period, and the ancient Near East. One challenge is that the availability of high-resolution proxy data is not evenly distributed spatially.[80] Egypt, outside of the Fayyum depression and the delta, is one important place not especially well served with direct proxy data.[81] For the moment, most of the work has been done on top-down and on global scales.[82]

FIGURE 26. Living minerals. Cross-section of a speleothem showing annual "tree ring"–like growth rings. Photo by the author at the speleothem laboratory, Climate System Research Center, U Mass–Amherst, summer 2015.

CLIMATE VARIABILITY, CLIMATE FORCING, AND ABRUPT CLIMATE CHANGE

Several geophysical forces drive the global climate system. Variations in the tilt of the Earth with respect to the sun, and the shape of Earth's orbit (orbital forcing) are important long-term drivers of ice age cycles. Solar irradiance (insolation), the amount of solar radiation reaching the earth's surface, is the primary energy source that drives the earth-atmosphere system. While cycles of solar irradiance, as can be measured by sunspot activity and other parameters, are generally well characterized, the impact of such cycles of solar variability in driving climate change remains disputed (figure 27). Complex atmospheric and oceanic feedback mechanisms have been proposed to explain correlations between climatic changes and what are generally observed to be small changes (in absolute terms) in solar irradiance, as occur during the approximately eleven-year sunspot cycle. Perhaps most famously, a solar sunspot minimum (known as the Maunder minimum, 1645–1715 CE) has been associated with colder winters in Europe during the "Little Ice

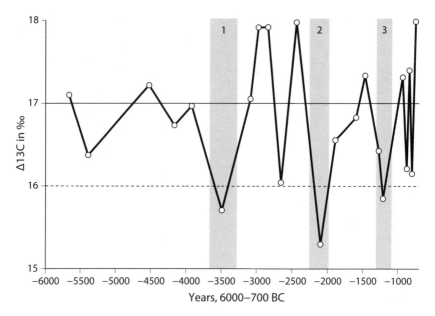

FIGURE 27. The pattern of drought variability in the ancient Near East. From Riehl et al. (2014). Below the thick gray line a higher probability of severe drought conditions, above the thin black line, more favorable conditions.

Age," and it is has been posited that more sustained reductions in solar irradiance as observed during "grand minima" like the Maunder minimum can lead to more pronounced impacts on climate.

The North Atlantic Oscillation (NAO), with a positive or negative phase, is important for northern hemisphere atmospheric circulation in (primarily) winter "with large impacts on temperature, precipitation and storm tracks."[83] This is important for climate variability in the northern Mediterranean. When the NAO is in a strongly positive mode, for example, North Atlantic storm tracks veer northward, leading to a reduction in the westerly winds that bring moist oceanic air into the Mediterranean region, contributing to a reduction in the winter rainfall essential for rain-fed agriculture.[84]

The second system, the El-Niño-Southern Oscillation (ENSO), also has two phases, warm (El-Niño) and cold (La-Niña) and drives changes in atmospheric circulation via sea surface temperature changes and is measured by air pressure differences in the western and eastern Pacific. ENSO is teleconnected, that is, closely related, to the African and Indian Ocean monsoon cycle that affects, among other things, Nile river flow.[85] Perhaps more dramatically, explosive volcanic eruptions have played an important role in short-term climatic shocks (see appendix). As I highlight below, such eruptions could have dramatic short-term impacts on the annual flood of the Nile (and on other rivers as well), which in turn forced social responses. Recent improvements in the accuracy and precision of ice-core-based chronologies of volcanic eruptions combined with historical data now allow us, for the first time, to observe a society in motion.

The Neolithic, or agricultural, revolution, perhaps more evolution than revolution, is arguably one of the most significant shifts in human history. It produced not only agriculture, but also the "secondary products revolution" that followed.[86] Settled communities, social hierarchy, states, taxes, and new diseases soon followed. This revolution was related to an abrupt, global shift in climate known as the Younger Dryas, the event that preceded the Holocene, the modern interglacial warm period.[87] Recent work might suggest a new paradigm for the transition to agriculture by drawing our attention to Central Asia.[88] Increasingly, information from this region is reshaping the story of early civilization and the major role of this part of the world in the spread of technology and long-distance trade, as well as disease.[89] Significant economic developments are associated with this warming trend. Although private property coevolved with the emergence of agriculture, by ca. 3100 BCE, agricultural intensification and surplus production in the early Holocene led to larger and more complex societies. The result was coercive, extractive institutions, the exchange of more things across longer distances, craft specializations, and cities.

Understanding climate change is a part of the story of growth, decline, connectivity, technological change, and long-distance trading patterns in Egypt, southern Mesopotamia, and the Indus River valley from 3100 to 1500 BCE.[90] An abrupt climate change event beginning at 4.2 ka (ka = kiloannus, i.e., ca. 2200 BCE), a three-century-long cooling and megadrought event, "has been linked to ocean-atmosphere circulation changes in the North Atlantic," although the climate dynamics of the event remain to be fully explained.[91] Its impact is documented by widespread drought in the eastern Mediterranean basin, and indeed with differential but widespread global effects.[92] It has been estimated that precipitation from the Atlantic westerlies was reduced by between 30 percent and 50 percent; the monsoon, important for Egypt, India, and East Asia, was also weakened.[93]

This abrupt climate change is documented by several climate proxies in the eastern Mediterranean ca. 2200 BCE and elsewhere (appendix, figure 43).[94] It is, of course, not a simple thing to connect abrupt changes in climate to institutional changes and other kinds of human response, in large part because of the spatial and temporal problems in assigning a causal connection between global shifts in climate regime and local and regional archaeological records. Yet a compilation of historic events is suggestive. The extensive

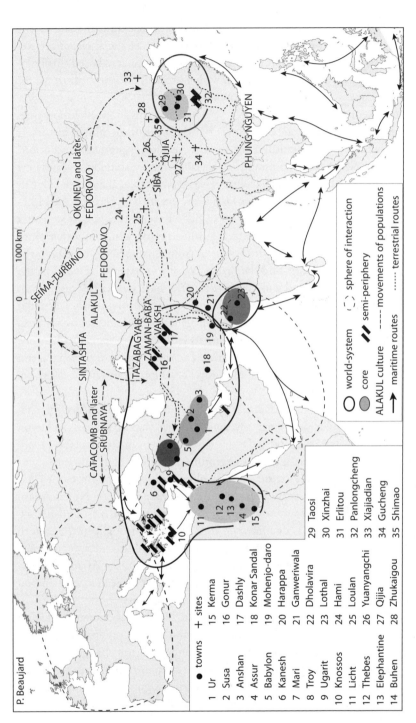

FIGURE 28. Eurasia and Africa end of third, early second millennium BCE. From Beaujard (2011:18, figure 3.9).

trading networks that had been established were disrupted; the rise of no-madic groups such as the "Amorites," in the Near East, and new political responses are attested. These include the rise of an administrative state, the Middle Kingdom in Egypt, the explosion of Minoan civilization on Crete, and an impressive uptick in urbanization across the eastern Mediterranean, Egypt, and the Near East. Mobility, port building, large-scale interregional trade, seaborne traffic (mostly in small vessels), alongside overland routes, and the rise of the "merchant," metal mining, smelting, and trading are char-acteristics of the eastern Mediterranean world in the second millennium BCE. So too is the increasing capacity of elites to organize and project mili-tary power across ever-wider territory. These forces are well documented in the first empires, New Kingdom Egypt, and the Hittite and Old Babylonian Empires in the Near East.[95] It is worth noting that the connections between state development and the control of trade routes were strong.

The Bronze Age "collapse" ca. 3.2 ka (beginning ca. 1200 BCE) was, like the 4.2 ka event, driven by a complex concatenation of endogenous, or "inter-nal," factors within Bronze Age states (demographic decline, productivity crises, migration, confiscatory fiscal regimes) as well as exogenous shocks.[96] There have been many explanations over the years, and the systemic collapse of the Bronze Age eastern Mediterranean interstate system remains to be fully understood.[97] The Hekla-3 eruption in Iceland, changes in technology, especially in military technology, and internal social disruptions have all been implicated in explanations for wide-scale disruptions at this time.[98] What emerges in recent work is that abrupt aridification, like the 4.2 ka event, led to large-scale drought lasting about three hundred years (ca. 1200–ca. 850 BCE) (appendix, figure 44) and likely contributed to pushing the re-gional system toward collapse.[99] Nile failures and food crises in Egypt and drought and/or food shortages in Anatolia, Israel, Syria, and Greece are documented, reflecting an impact on two different climate systems.[100] Like the 4.2 ka event, abrupt climate change at the 3.2 ka boundary is docu-mented in several places in the world, in East Africa, the Amazon basin, Ecuador, and the Caribbean/Bermuda region, suggesting a global event. It is also associated with a "longer crisis" documented by ice rafted debris in the North Atlantic, solar minima at 1450, 1000, and ca. 765 BCE (figure 45), and volcanic forcing all combined to produce a cooler, drier climate.[101] Solar minima have been posited to inaugurate periods of expansion and are also associated with endpoints of crises.[102]

States began to show signs of distress in 1200/1100 BCE throughout the eastern Mediterranean and western Asia. The effects of drought are widely documented, interregional links appear to have been severely disrupted, and there were large-scale migrations throughout the eastern Mediterranean.

The "sea peoples" of Egyptian inscriptions and "watchers of the sea" mentioned in Linear B texts from Pylos are indicative of migration and disruption and insecurity on several scales.[103] Beneath these large-scale migrations, there were also observable changes, notably with an increase in the activity of private merchants involved in small-scale exchange. This would be an important factor in the "emergence" of private trade on a larger scale in the Iron Age, although it should be stressed that there is increasing evidence that private trading was not much diminished between the Late Bronze and Early Iron Ages, and the "palace-economy models" have previously undervalued the role of private merchants in the Bronze Age.[104]

From roughly 700 BCE to 1400 CE the climate has been characterized by some as "optimal."[105] The period from the mid-4th century BCE to ca. 685 CE was climatically stable in the Mediterranean, situated in between two grand solar minima.[106] Grand minima (figure 45) are recorded at 1000 and ca. 765 BCE (the "Homeric minimum"). The minimum of ca. 765 BCE, "the largest of the past 3000 years," brought generally favorable agricultural conditions. It may have pushed demographic expansion and perhaps Greek "colonization," but others have concluded the opposite, and caution about links between broad climate changes and history is required.[107]

For the Nile, analysis of river sediments in Egypt and the Sudan allows the following basic chronology of river flow (table 5).[108] While there is a general consensus that the ENSO system plays a role in both the Nile flow and South Asian monsoons, with strong El Niño events and periods associated with droughts in India and low flow in the Nile, the Nile flow is complicated by East African topography and the possibility of phase shifts forced by changing conditions in the Atlantic.[109] The most recent analysis of Nile flow suggests that flow began to fall, and the floodplain contract, around 800 BCE, with low flow persisting through Ptolemaic and early Roman times, followed by a three-hundred-year expansion of the flood between 200 and 500 CE, the period when Egypt became an important sources of grain for the Roman Empire. More widely in the southeastern Mediterranean a positive NAO brought slightly more humid conditions, given the operation of a "Mediterranean Oscillation."[110]

What is called the "Roman Warm Period," or "Roman Climate Optimum," perhaps better referred to as the "Roman Warm Anomaly," reinforced after 1 CE by the "Roman Quiet Period" in explosive volcanic activity, corresponds to the expansion of the Celtic civilization in central Europe (La Tène culture) ca. 200 BCE, and the Roman Empire and the height of the *pax romana* ca. 200 BCE–150 CE.[111] But the impact of this warming trend, like earlier abrupt climate changes, was spatially and temporally heterogeneous.[112] A "quiet period" is documented in the volcanic signals detected in

TABLE 5. *Basic Chronology of Nile River Flow in the First Millennium* BCE

900 BCE, relatively high and rising water levels are recorded in Lake Victoria and Lake Tana, with increasing river flows in the Nile delta, and overbank flooding and floodplain sedimentation in the Nile valley.
Channel and floodplain contraction that may have started as early as 800 BCE and continued at least until 500 BCE, and diminishing lake levels and river flow. This culminated in a major hydroclimatic shift in the lower Nile at ca. 450 BCE reflected by falling water levels in Lake Faiyum and reduced river flow in the delta.
The Ptolemaic and early Roman periods show a reduced frequency of overbank floods, which is supported by a marked fall in water level in the lower Nile at Lake Faiyum and decreased river flow in the Nile delta during the second half of the first millennium BCE. There was however a period of exceptional flooding around 100 BCE.

SOURCE: Macklin et al. (2015).

the ice cores for the first two centuries CE (see the "Roman Quiet Period," figure 30) and, combined with a warming, wetter climate, probably contributed to the economic performance of the Roman empire at its height. And, while the impact of volcanic quiescence can hardly be described as an empire-wide phenomenon, this is perhaps a strong contribution to why the Roman agricultural writer Saserna (early 1st century BCE) suggested that "improved weather" made Roman soil more productive:

> Saserna, no mean authority on husbandry, seems to have given credence. For in that book on agriculture which he has left behind he concludes that the position of the heavens had changed from this evidence: that regions which formerly, because of the unremitting severity of winter, could not safeguard any shoot of the vine or the olive planted in them, now that the earlier coldness has abated and the weather is becoming more clement, produce olive harvests and the vintages of Bacchus in the greatest abundance. But whether this theory be true or false, we must leave it to the writings on astronomy.[113]

It may not have been the improved conditions of the land per se, but, perhaps, the improved climatic conditions during a less volcanically perturbed period that drove the observed increase in productivity.

As many climate proxies suggest, climate changes at 4.2 ka and 3.2 ka may have been a factor in social and economic change.[114] Climatic variability and the rate of change operate on several timescales, from low frequency, longer-term fluctuations and trends instantiated in solar output and glacier expansion/retraction cycles to high-frequency variability, and short-term "extreme" events. These variations could be either "periodic" or "nonperiodic" and have local, regional, and/or global effects.[115] Changes in temperature had more generalized effects than precipitation changes, which are inherently more spatially variable, and more strongly mediated by a given location's elevation, and other topographical characteristics. On a broader spatial scale, differing receipts of radiation and the "continentality" of a region were also important mediators of how any long-term climatic change would be expressed, and how these expressed changes would influence human societies. Long-term climatic changes lasting centuries arguably shaped the creation of the classical Mediterranean world.[116] Shorter-term changes having an impact of a year or two (and potentially longer when considered in terms of their cumulative impacts) are currently being intensively studied because of the availability of annual and decadally resolved data, both paleoclimatic and historical.

Solar and volcanic forcing have been recognized as important drivers of abrupt climate change on short timescales. Such relatively rapid changes have been associated with social unrest and violence. Shocks to the annual Nile flood forced by explosive volcanic eruptions were superimposed onto an already variable water supply and can be correlated with unrest, land abandonment, and other socioeconomic stresses and responses.[117] Changes in climatic conditions effect economic conditions, especially agricultural production, by causing changes in the expected mean climate state (temperature and water availability), which in turn effects production output, and causes secondary responses, at least in theory, in farming practices and in disease and pest outbreaks.[118] The best way to think about the connection between humans and climate is as a coupled human-natural system with cascading effects and feedback loops.[119]

VOLCANOES

The eruptions of Mount Etna in 44–42 BCE and Vesuvius in 79 CE, the latter destroying Pompeii and Herculaneum, are well known to ancient historians and are classic examples of the sometimes violent speed at which Mediterranean landscape change could occur.[120] While these eruptions certainly had local effects, large, explosive volcanic eruptions in other parts of the world had more important impacts on global climatic conditions.[121] We know, for example, that large volcanic eruptions were "teleconnected" to monsoonal rainfall, which is the source of the annual flood of the Nile. A massive tropical eruption in 44 BCE, the third largest in the last twenty-five

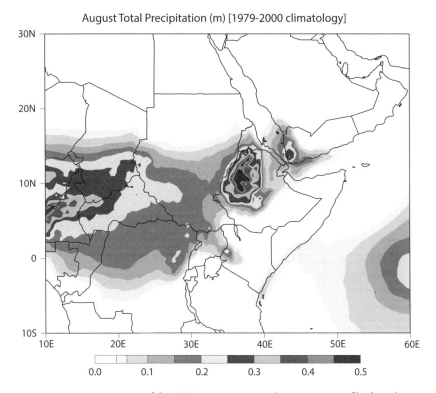

FIGURE 29. The migration of the ITCZ. Precipitation values are a mean of leading climate reanalysis models (CFSR, ERA-Interim, JRA-55, and MERRA). From Climate Reanalyzer (http://cci-reanalyzer.org), Climate Change Institute, University of Maine, USA. Image and data processing courtesy of Dr. Sean Birkel, Climate Change Institute, University of Maine.

hundred years, previously thought to have been the Etna eruption of 44–42 BCE, is likely to have had a serious impact on the Nile, and hence Egypt, but also impacted other places as well.[122] An eruption in 426 BCE, of unknown location, and the largest in the last twenty-five hundred years, must have had dramatic effects. The massive tsunami in the Malian Gulf reported by Thucydides and earthquakes that same year changed the course of the Peloponnesian War and may have been related.[123]

The basic mechanisms of volcanic climate forcing are well described and have been studied instrumentally and by satellite observations during the recent eruption of Mount Pinatubo (Philippines) in 1991.[124] Sulfate aerosols that are explosively injected into the stratosphere have short-term climatic effects, usually one to three years in length, by creating greater "optical depth" in the atmosphere, in which incoming shortwave solar radiation is scattered back to space, which in turn causes reduced surface temperatures and a suppression (on average) of the hydrological cycle. Sometimes these effects are global, depending on the size and location of the eruption.[125] "Large temperature anomalies" in some parts of the world can also trigger El Niño events in the tropical latitudes, and a growing literature exists that is unraveling the complex interrelationships between explosive volcanic eruptions and the subsequent occurrence or strengthening of El Niño events.[126] Certain historical periods, the Hellenistic period for one, were perturbed with both large eruptions not only occurring individually, but also in time with other eruptions, both large and small, and both tropical and extratopical in location. Such clusters have had longer-term impacts on agrarian production in Egypt, and other monsoon-dependent regions like the Blue Nile headwaters in Ethiopia, the main source of the Egyptian Nile summer flood (map 3) (figure 29).

The Tambora eruption of 1815, one of the largest eruptions ever recorded, has been well studied for its global climate impact and in the cultural responses observed in contemporary art and literature.[127] Likewise the impact of the Laki (Iceland) eruption in 1783–84 is also well documented in Ottoman records.[128] Its devastating effects on Egypt, perhaps compounded by several other eruptions around the same time, have been detailed in recent work: Nile flow was 18 percent below the mean, and plague, famine, low crop yields, widespread human and animal mortality, and banditry are well documented. Its effects were felt in Egypt into the 1790s.[129] An examination of the sequence of eruptions might suggest that clustered events (as in the second half of the 13th century, again around the year 1600—including the famous eruption of the Peruvian volcano, Huaynapunita, in 1600—and also in the first half of the 19th century) had a cumulative impact on Nile flow, and thus a longer-term impact on the river.[130]

VOLCANIC FORCING, SHORT-TERM SHOCKS, AND THE NILE

Many hypotheses have been advanced to explain the course of Ptolemaic Egypt's history, including its early success, later internal revolts, and interstate warfare, and its gradual decline in the face of rising Roman imperial ambitions and ultimate end with the defeat of Antony and Cleopatra against Rome at Actium in 31 BCE. The Ptolemaic state, of major importance to the history of the eastern Mediterranean after 300 BCE, was among the most powerful and long-lived of the Hellenistic states. Centered in Alexandria, it capitalized on Egypt's fertile alluvium to become a major commercial producer of wheat. The role of abrupt climatic shocks has been ignored in this story, which is a striking omission given that Egyptian fortunes were inextricably linked to the annual Nile flood.[131] From time to time ancient texts report food shortages, famine, Nile flood crises, and drought. But on the basis of the texts alone, it is difficult to observe a pattern.

Usually the impact of climate change on societies has been understood on century and millennial timescales. Occasionally though, with high-resolution data, we can observe effects and responses on shorter times scales. The Nile River provides an excellent laboratory to see these. The correlation between long-term changes in the interannual variability of the flood of the Nile River and stable, centralized governance has often received attention.[132] The decline in flood volume between Dynasties 1 and 2 (roughly estimated at ~30 percent); Dynasty 7–8 and the First Intermediate period, Dynasty 13 and the Second Intermediate Period, and Dynasty 20 and the early Third Intermediate Period has been noted. To be sure, other factors such as dynastic disputes, succession problems, institutional weakness, and external threats played their part in central state collapse. But it seems clear from the flood records that a correlation existed between centralized phases of Egyptian political history and optimal flooding of the river was correlated, and thus that the politically fragmented periods of Egyptian history are also associated to some extent with Nile flood deficiencies.

By the Ptolemaic period (305–30 BCE), the Egyptian population was well adapted to the diversity of ecological niches in Egypt, the Nile valley itself, the delta, the Fayyum, and the oases in the western desert. But the Ptolemaic kings substantially altered the environment in some regions (the Fayyum as I noted above) and increased the demand for free-threshing wheat. Fiscal rules were changed, a stricter bureaucratic control of taxation was imposed, and a greater emphasis was put on military mobilization. These basic changes in the political and economic institutions from the previous Persian provincial period must be understood against the environmental background about which we now have better insight.

Remarkably, understanding the effects of explosive eruptions requires turning first to data preserved in ice cores in Greenland and in the Antarctic. The redating of the sequence of volcanic eruptions identified in elevated sulfate levels in the ice is one of the most exciting developments in recent years.[133] We are now able to align the eruption sequence with historical records with greater accuracy, and identify the location of the volcanoes as either high north or south latitude or "tropical" (low latitude) as well as infer the scale of the eruption's injection of climate-altering sulfate into the stratosphere.

There were multiple explosive eruptions worldwide during the Ptolemaic period, of which the sixteen high-latitude Northern Hemispheric and eight tropical eruptions (figure 30) are likely to have induced the most deleterious reductions in the scale of the Nile summer flood. Four of these eruptions caused a greater reduction in solar radiation receipts than the estimated

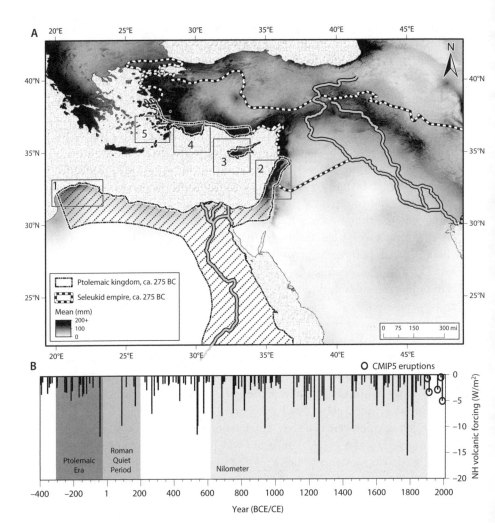

FIGURE 30. Political and environmental setting of the Hellenistic east Mediterranean, and volcanic forcing history. (a) Peak wet season rainfall (December mean, mm), 1950–2000 (worldclim.org), with boundaries of Ptolemaic (green line) and Seleukid (gray dashes) states, ca. 275 BCE. Key territories contested by these states are numbered (1, Cyrenaica; 2, "Koile," Syria; 3, Cyprus; 4, Lycia; 5, Caria), with indicative rectangles, centered on regions capable of rain-fed agriculture. Key urban power bases are indicated in Roman numerals (i, Babylon; ii, Antioch; iii, Seleukia; iv, Alexandria; v, Memphis; vi, Thebes). (b) Volcanic forcing 400 BCE to present. Courtesy of Francis Ludlow and Michael Sigl.

−6.5w/m² (i.e., watts per square meter) global radiative forcing of Pinatubo (Philippines, 1991), the largest climatically impactful 20th century eruption, while four others had a radiative forcing of at least −4.0 w/m². The period closed with the third largest eruption of the past twenty-five hundred years, with a radiative −23.2 w/m² in ca. 44 BCE. The impact of these eruptions registers in historical dust veil/aerosol haze observations from the Mediterranean and Near East, as well as growth reductions in temperature-sensitive Northern Hemisphere tree rings (figure 32), but absolutely dated annually resolved proxies to directly examine their climatic impact for Egypt are lacking.[134] Nor do annually resolved monsoon reconstructions extend to this period. Papyri do occasionally record local conditions of the flood, in letters, land leases, and other documents that were assembled by Bonneau.[135] We can rank the flood quality and test this against the volcanic record to examine how reliable these qualitative records of the ancient flood are.[136]

We are still in the early days in our understanding of the social impacts of the teleconnection between explosive eruptions and the perturbance of Nile flow. If the effects of Laki on Egypt are any guide, we may suggest that the sequence of eruptions that we observe in the Hellenistic period may have had impacts in four related areas: (1) agricultural production, (2) food supply, (3) social unrest, and (4) disease. It has been generally accepted that famine in the premodern Mediterranean was rare, but food shortage crises were common.[137] But we should be cautious. This conclusion is based on surviving evidence that tends to come from important political centers and not from regions most vulnerable to food supply shocks. Above all, grain supply shocks were a concern for every premodern Mediterranean state. Generally stable climate conditions obtained in the Mediterranean, even in Roman Egypt, but volcanic forcing could induce sudden shocks to vulnerable societies.[138] Not all such shocks produced food shortages of course, but in the case of an agricultural system, wholly dependent on irrigation, a failure of the river might well have had, at a minimum, psychological effects on the population, and comparable historical data suggest that shocks could well have catalyzed revolts.[139]

Urban centers, unsurprisingly, paid great attention to grain supplies. Regulations, for example, which restricted regional shipments other than to the relevant city, are well known from Athens, which had long depended on grain imports to sustain itself.[140] During the reign of Cleopatra, in time of severe Nile flood failure, famine, and disease outbreak, a royal decree was promulgated that prohibited shipping grain other than to the city on pain of death.[141] An inscription from Chersonesos in Crimea, dated ca. 300 BCE (based on paleography), concerns the regulation of grain transport and forbids the shipment of grain anywhere other than in Chersonesos itself in order to preserve the freedom of the city.[142] Farming strategies of mixing wheat and barley (maslin cropping) are documented in archaeological excavations, and the introduction of rye (perhaps in the 3d century BCE?) and migration are documented in the inscription, an unsurprising response to risk created by "climatic deterioration," that is, drought.[143] We do not know the cause of this drought, which appears to have been extensive. Nomadic peoples about 270 BCE overran the region and brought an end to Chersonesos. In other cases, however, we do know the cause of drought. Ancient papyri and inscriptions document repeated revolts in Ptolemaic Egypt (figure 31). The causes of these revolts have often been explained by "nationalist" sentiments among Egyptians resentful of Ptolemaic (i.e., Greek) rule, and/or pressures from state fiscal demands (e.g., to maintain military mobilization). But the new ice-core sequence shows that the eruptions occur closely in time with many revolt start dates (figure 31). More specifically, we see that eruptions occur within a conservative −3/+2 year window around eight of nine revolt start dates; that is, eruptions are dated to within the three years before revolts start dates up to two years following.[144]

Despite the small remaining uncertainties in the ice-core-based dating, the new volcanic sequence now provides an effectively definite timescale of these major natural events, random in their occurrence, but a now knowable instrument of economic change, unrest, famine, and, possibly, the spread of disease. Correlation does not mean causation, of course, and there is now more historical work to be done on Ptolemaic society, and the nature of these "revolts" themselves.

Combining the new ice core volcanic chronology, confirmed in its essentials by correlation with tree ring growth (figure 32), with detailed historical records sheds light on several further historical phenomena of the period: the function of imperial territory, war between the Ptolemies and Seleukids, the sequence of internal social unrest, and the impact of free-threshing wheat production, as well as resilient responses and possible mitigating factors including technological innovation. Ptolemaic external territory functioned as both defensive "fence," so Polybius tells us, around which Egypt could be protected, but also as economic zones of exploitation. This followed political and social patterns of Egyptian political history and took advantage of the political situation and the misadventures or distractions of the other successors of Alexander.[145] The imperial territories, and the Greek mainland, provided manpower and resources as well as markets for Egyptian grain.[146]

Failures of the Nile summer flood, volcanically forced or otherwise, may have motivated the Ptolemies to reduce their agricultural dependence on the Nile flood by maintaining control over rain-fed external territories in the contested Mediterranean (Cyrenaica, Turkey, and Syria) (figure 30). Ptolemy III

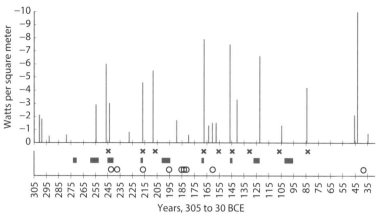

FIGURE 31. Volcanic forcing in W/m². This chart shows the reduction in solar radiation, along the y-axis, after eruptions. The Ptolemaic period (305–30 BCE) saw numerous explosive eruptions (16 high-latitude NH, 8 tropical. Four surpass the estimated −6.5 W/m² global forcing of Pinatubo (Philippines, 1991), the largest climatically effective 20th century eruption, while four others have forcing of at least −4.0 W/m² (Sigl et al. 2015). The period closes with the third-largest eruption of the past twenty-five hundred years at −23.2 W/m² in ca. 44 BCE (note, not shown to scale here). The periods of social unrest and the Syrian wars are plotted below. Courtesy of Francis Ludlow.

appears as an aggressor in the Third Syrian War, beginning 246 BCE at the height of Ptolemaic state power. This was started in the environmental context of a large tropical eruption dated 247 BCE with evidence of poor Nile flooding documented for 246 and 245 BCE. Despite a successful Mesopotamian campaign, Ptolemy III was forced to return to quell "domestic sedition" in ca. 245 BCE, and the war ultimately ceased in 241 BCE after a further eruption (high-latitude Northern Hemisphere) dated 244 BCE (figure 33).[147] We know from evidence in the Canopus Decree that in the case of a serious Nile shock, plausibly in the 240s BCE, Ptolemy III imported grain from external territories.[148] Although Cyrene was a major grain producer, we do not know if it was ever a direct source of grain for Egypt. The Canopus Decree informs us that grain imported to save Egypt from the Nile failure came from: "Syria, Phoenicia and Cyprus and many other places at great expense, [by which] they saved the inhabitants of Egypt."[149] It is remarkable, to say the least, that such a massive grain exporter in normal times was forced to import wheat during what must have been a major shock linked to poor Nile flooding. It is also remarkable that Ptolemy III claimed

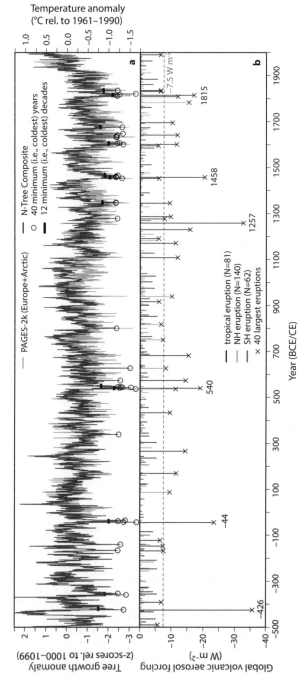

FIGURE 32. The new full volcanic reconstruction (below) with a composite tree ring series (above) for the last 2,500 years. From Sigl et al. (2015).

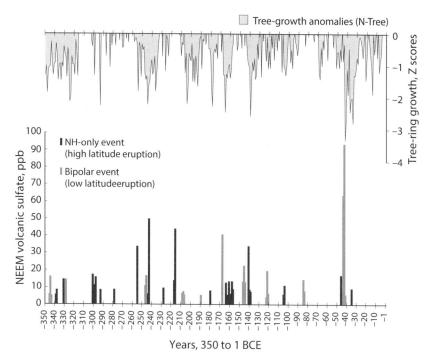

FIGURE 33. NEEM ice-core (Greenland) volcanic SO$_4$ deposition levels, 350 to 1 BCE, shaded according to whether deposition is bipolar (i.e., indicating low-latitude (tropical) or high-north latitude NH eruptions, respectively), with negative tree ring growth anomalies overlain (representing years of poor growth relative to 1000–1099 CE in the N-Tree composite of temperature-sensitive ring-width and density chronologies (Sigl et al. 2015). Courtesy of Francis Ludlow.

to have purchased the grain at great expense, which also must indicate something important about the relationships between Alexandria and its external possessions. In good years, the Nile valley was enormously productive. A decade after the shocks of the late 240s BCE, for example, Ptolemy III donated thirty thousand tons (one million *artabae*) of Egyptian grain to Rhodes after a devastating earthquake.[150] One important factor in societal and state resilience that is not well documented is grain storage. Without further work, the impact of each Nile flood shock on spatial variability of water flood availability is also poorly understood and likely varied considerably according to the changing topography of the Nile valley throughout Egypt. To be sure, not all Nile failures resulted in uniform catastrophe; some stresses may have been confined to select regions. A better understanding of this could be achieved through spatial modeling of flood heights accounting for local topographies.

FIGURE 34. *P. Edfu* 8. Courtesy of the Department of Papyrology, University of Warsaw.

One resilient response to a Nile flood crisis is documented in a famous Greek petition (figure 34), probably a draft and dated by many scholars roughly to the middle of the 3d century BCE. It therefore fits the context of a crisis in the 240s BCE. The text, requesting a royal audience and signaling the existence of some kind of new irrigation machine, was written by a man (probably a soldier given his name and title) living in Edfu, a major temple town in Upper Egypt. It mentions a Nile failure of three years' duration, and a new irrigation "machine" that could "save" Egypt from famine:

> To King Ptolemy, Greetings, from Philotas, the fire-signaller, one of the Kleruchs in Apollinopolis-the-Great. Given that now and for a long time, the inundation has become insufficient, I want, O King, to inform you of a certain machine the use of which does no damage and by means of which the country may be saved. Since during the last 3 years the river has not flooded, the dryness will produce a famine that . . . but if you wish, this will be a year of good flood.
>
> I ask you, O King, if it seems good to you, to order Ariston the strategos, to grant me 30 days' sustenance, and to send for me as quickly as possible to you or . . . a petition so that, if it pleases you, seed will grow immediately. Thanks to your decision, within 50 days there will immediately follow a plentiful harvest throughout the whole Thebaid. Farewell.[151]

We do not know specifically what the petitioner (was he one of Joel Mokyr's "cultural entrepreneurs"?) had discovered.[152] Was it a new invention or an "incremental" improvement of an already known machine? We know that the water-lifting device known as the *saqiya* is documented ca. 240 BCE, on the basis of its mention in Philo of Byzantium's *Pneumatics*. Michael Lewis has suggested that between 260 and 230 BCE many new water-lifting and ro-tary machines were invented in Alexandria, and agricultural development and expansion, especially in the Fayyum, may have driven innovation.[153] These inventions may be considered part of a wider "revolution" in techno-logical development.[154] While the petition is not precisely dated, its context as noted above would fit the mid-3d century BCE.[155] A large gift of grain to Egypt from Hieron II of Syracuse can perhaps also be placed in these years, "during a shortage of grain in Egypt" that would reinforce the suspicion that the 240s BCE was a period of Nile stress as suggested by the volcanic and tree ring proxy data (figure 33).[156]

Ptolemy VI waged a defensive war from 170 BCE (the Sixth Syrian War) but was overcome in 168 BCE with Egypt's invasion by the Seleukid king Antiochus IV. This occurred in the context of an immense tropical eruption dated 168 BCE, having the second-largest global forcing (-7.9 w/m^2) during the Ptolemaic period. In the mid-160s BCE, recorded in the famous archive of the dream interpreter Hor from Sakkara, we hear of abuses of the sacred Ibis cult by individuals and stolen food meant for the sacred animals.[157] A large delivery of clover for the sacred birds had apparently been misplaced (or stolen?). Internal unrest is documented from 168 to 164 BCE and a Nile failure recorded in 166 BCE.

Initially rich and powerful, particularly under Ptolemy II (283–246 BCE), Ptolemaic political power declined rapidly after 200 BCE. Polybius's story— how Rome within fifty-three years (220–167 BCE) took over the Mediterranean world—provides a partial sketch only. Polybius's theory of decline was in-formed by his views of Greek moral decline from the 4th century BCE, and the moral behavior of the Ptolemaic kings after Ptolemy III. At the same time, he does record demographic and climatic effects of decline without acknowledging them as factors.[158]

Success drew partly from Nile-driven high-yield wheat production (mainly *T. durum*) that increasingly replaced emmer, supplying urban Greeks and oth-ers in and beyond Egypt with their preferred grain.[159] This shift to naked wheat may have reduced agricultural diversity and increased the risk of adverse *portfo-lio effects* for wheat.[160] By contrast, the Seleukid Empire was more climatically diverse. Unfortunately, we cannot quantify annual grain production directly, although there is hope that grain harvest tax receipt ostraca might provide some insight. That is work yet to be done.

Free-threshing wheat might have proven costly with the return of frequent volcanically induced Nile failure imposed on the river's already high natural variability. Ice-core data reveal the period of initial Ptolemaic success as volcanically quiescent relative to later years, for which the dynamic role of volcanically induced Nile failure in the repeated revolts can be shown. Recent work has also shown that the connection between war cessation and disruptions of the Nile flood, clear in the 240s BCE but throughout the entire period, can be demonstrated.[161] The impact of eruptions was amplified by loss of Nile-independent agricultural territories post-195 BCE that had previously buffered the state during Nile failure, and the burden of ongoing military mobilization at notably greater cost than their Seleukid rival. There were state-level responses, including state grain distribution, and the settlement of more soldiers in the Nile valley after the great Theban revolt (starting ca. 207 BCE) was put down in the 180s BCE. Yet the volcanically active 160s BCE was a major turning point with two invasions of Egypt by Antiochus IV, 170–168 BCE. Following the great tropical eruption of 168 BCE, the Seleukid king faced his own challenges in the Maccabean revolt (167–160 BCE) in Jerusalem, and there was unrest in Egypt. While the dynasty officially ended with Cleopatra's defeat by Rome in the naval battle at Actium in 31 BCE, a little-recognized break came with the third-largest eruption of the past twenty-five hundred years in 44 BCE, compounding a high-latitude Northern Hemisphere eruption in 46 BCE. Nile failure, famine, and plague are recorded in our sources through the 40s BCE.[162]

The supposed "decline" of Hellenistic states in the eastern Mediterranean after 220 BCE might be explained, in part, by the differential impacts of ecological stress combined with and compounding dynastic instability, continuous war, tellingly described by Plutarch (*Life of Pyrrhus*, 12), and a fiscal regime that taxed agricultural production and at times could leave the population vulnerable. The Roman Quiet Period beginning around 200 BCE, combined with a stable period in solar activity, would have been beneficial for some parts of the Mediterranean. But this was not the case in Egypt. Its dependence on monsoonal rain left it vulnerable to the Nile shocks I have described. The "decline" of the Ptolemies is not the correct way to view the crises of the mid-2d century BCE. The scholarly literature on rebellion, riots, and other social conflict in the Hellenistic period is dominated almost exclusively by comparatively simple cultural or institutional explanations: overextraction of resources, ethnic resentment, nationalism, and/or weak, ineffectual kings.[163] Consider, for example, the conclusions of one Ptolemaic specialist in an overview of 1st century BCE Ptolemaic history:

After the end of the second century, the country seems to have returned to normality. There were setbacks—in 83 we still hear of disruption and depopulation, and the last ten years of Auletes' reign must have been particularly hard. But in fairness it must be said that his troubles were not (or not primarily) of his own making, and it is difficult to see how he could have defied the Roman superpower. Under Cleopatra, Egypt enjoyed peace and prosperity. In the administration there was the normal measure of incompetence and corruption but, on the whole, no oppression.[164]

But things were actually more complicated. The hitherto little-studied natural phenomenon, explosive volcanic eruptions that perturbed Nile river flow, provides a new window on societal responses to short-term climatic shocks. We can now begin to understand the links between shocks to the annual flood, panic, and in some cases famine and disease outbreaks. As for economic stress, unfortunately we have limited information on grain prices for the Ptolemaic period.[165] One indication of increased prices can, however, be observed in land tenancy agreements from the village of Tholthis dated 218–214 BCE where

> unusually high penalty prices [were observed] for unfulfilled rental payments in wheat and olyra (emmer). During most of the third century epitima (i.e. fines) were quite regularly set at 4 drachmas for the artaba of wheat and 2 drachmas for the artaba of olyra. In the Tholthis contracts, by contrast, they amount to 10 drachmas for wheat and 4 drachmas for olyra . . . penalty prices may not have been very sensitive to actual price fluctuation, but arguably they show prices of olyra to have doubled, while those of wheat had increased by 150 percent.[166]

The reign of Cleopatra can hardly be described as one of unadulterated "peace and prosperity." Even if we had no historical records at all, the size of the eruption in 44 BCE would indicate that Egypt should have experienced very bad times. The Ptolemaic period stands in strong contrast to the first two centuries of Roman rule in Egypt, when volcanism was more quiescent, the Nile was more stable, taxes on agricultural production were lower, and the wheat-growing land provided Rome with one of its most important breadbaskets.[167]

The Ptolemaic example that I have laid out here suggests that the deemphasis on the state and the insistence that there was very little "catastrophe" in Mediterranean ecology have underestimated the impact of shorter-term climatic shocks.[168] Clearly the economic and political performance of Egypt was fully dependent on the annual summer flood of the river, driven by

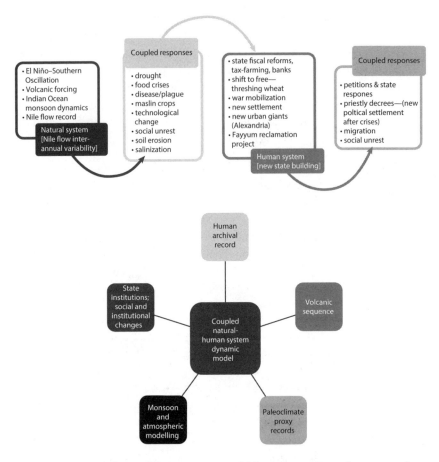

FIGURE 35. Coupled natural-human system model for Ptolemaic Egypt (320–30 BCE).

rainfall far distant in central and east Africa that in turn was dependent on monsoonal winds. Non-Mediterranean volcanic eruptions in Iceland, Alaska, Indonesia, Nicaragua, and elsewhere can be linked to reduction in Nile River water and thus, potentially at least, with socioeconomic stress. These were not *processes* but discrete *events*. It is true that Egypt generally recovered from these events. Indeed, I would stress the resilience of Ptolemaic Egypt but, at the same time, the frequency of social unrest.

Repeated shocks, even in an environment of high annual variability and therefore of "built-in" resilience to some extent, may have had a cumulative effect and a wider impact on the political economies in the Mediterranean, and, as a caveat, I would add that we know little yet on the history of disease in Egypt during the first millennium BCE.[169] More work is necessary to

FIGURE 36. The *saqiya*, introduced into Egypt and the Near East in the mid-3d century BCE, may have been a technological response to changing climatic conditions.

build a fully developed study of a complex society and how it coped with climatic change. The demand for free-threshing wheat by the kings and new large urban centers like Alexandria, high taxation of production, a rising population, decreasing the production of hardier emmer wheat from production, all may have combined to create greater risk.

The invention, or introduction, of water-lifting machines in the mid-3d century, including the *saqiya*, likely resulted from real crises, Nile failures that forced technical responses to "catastrophe," whether actual or feared. Technological innovation in response to water scarcity is one kind of reaction to climate change. But there were surely other types of responses that have not been studied in relation to climatic changes. An increase in military presence in Upper Egypt may have been one such state-level response; maslin crops that appear in some land surveys appear to be a local-level resilient response.[170]

Another such type of response lay in the realm of religious belief and social attitudes toward nature and to natural changes. The ancient association between the Nile and legitimate kingship, for example, can be clearly seen in prophetic texts written in the Ptolemaic period. *The Oracle of the Potter*, perhaps the most famous of the genre, expresses the direct link between poor Nile flooding and illegitmate rule that must be replaced by a "savior" king.[171] In fact the entire text can be read as a narrative of ecological disaster that would reflect, if the text can be dated to the later 2d century BCE, as I think it can, degraded environmental conditions brought about by a series of Nile failures, civil war, and a succession of political crises. Historical climate reconstructions demand that we understand ancient societies as complex adaptive systems. Repeated climate shocks forced adaptive responses to changes in background climate conditions. But the impact of climatic changes depended on the institutions that buffered society from such shocks.

What I have provided here is very much a first step in a longer process of combining historical and natural archives. As others have noted, we need more precise climate proxy records and many more regional studies of human-natural system dynamics.[172] Given the central importance of agriculture, and therefore water, to all premodern societies, the potential for much more refined models of ancient economies is the most exciting development in the study of these economies in the last forty years. In the last two chapters I have summarized agriculture, labor, and the environments in which the pagentry of first millennium BCE Mediterranean civilization played out. In the following chapter I turn to the third component of the model given in figure 24, demography, which is not only a factor in agricultural production, but is the basis for understanding a range of economic behaviors, from household consumption to trade, labor regimes, and war-fighting capacity.

CHAPTER 6

The Birth of "Economic Man"

DEMOGRAPHY, THE STATE,
THE HOUSEHOLD, AND THE INDIVIDUAL

The long path of historical research is (already) strewn with bones of
theories of the state.

—NORTH (1986:248)

Egyptians like Hekanakhte lived economics rather than thought it.
Having no word that we can translate as "profit" they could not strive for
it as an abstract measure of success in trading or making things. But this
did not hinder them from distinguishing a good from a bad price, and
should not hinder us from crediting them with an adequate business sense.

—KEMP (2006:323)

ACCORDING TO THE 2010 US Census, there were 116.7 million households, with an average of 2.58 people per household. The household remains
the basic unit for the modern census, and it has been the most important
economic unit for thousands of years. The modern nuclear family of 2.58
persons living under the same roof is a sharp contrast to premodern households, which were larger and were often composed of families and nonkin.
Max Weber drew a distinction between economic action that satisfied
"wants" from those that sought profit.[1] The household is the unit of production and reproduction for all premodern economies, and the main locus of
education and therefore of social reproduction. Premodern households are
often understood as isolated and self-sufficient, little was exchanged outside
of the household, and there was no noncoercive surplus production.[2] But
households always produced surplus if they could; there was simply no way
of predicting production in advance, and to produce just enough to subsist
would have been suicide.[3]

The household is a very important unit of analysis for premodern economies. Whether households were self-sufficient or not, household risk-
reduction strategies, behavior, food storage, land portfolio diversification
(i.e., scattered land holding), and diversity in crops grown, were key factors
in overall performance of economies at a state level.[4] Household structure
and behavior from a comparative point of view should focus on age at marriage,

inheritance patterns, and agricultural production, although none of these factors is well documented across the first-millennium Mediterranean to make systematic comparison a simple undertaking. Comparative work has been quite creative in deploying a wide variety of source types, myths, stories, texts, and archaeology as well as comparative and theoretical work to reconstruct what we know.[5] An evolution in household structure over time does not appear to have happened. Rather, what the evidence in toto suggests is that premodern Mediterranean households were adaptive to particular economic, environmental, and political conditions.[6]

Barry Kemp, in an important book on ancient Egypt, devoted a chapter to "the birth of economic man."[7] The chapter described documentation for New Kingdom Egypt (ca. 1300 BCE), but its picture is valid in some respects for much of the first millennium, and not just for Egypt. Private demand was tied to the "administered" sector of the economy. There are reasons for this to obtain in Egypt and in southern Mesopotamia for all premodern history, especially because both regions depended almost exclusively on agricultural production by irrigated water from the rivers. The "redistributive" systems that were established, tying households to state institutions through service in temples and shrines, is a visibly clear part of stable political equilibriums designed to meet the needs of state expenditure through taxing grain production as well as the needs of individuals who were buffered from shocks to food supply, in theory. It was a flexible and adaptive system because it had to be. In Egypt, as we have seen with the *choachyte* priests, household consumption in the form of a good house and a good burial were important parts of private consumption. We will encounter an individual, Hekanakhte, a funerary priest of a high official, shortly. In him, ca. 2000 BCE, one can see "economic man," writing letters home (although these may never have been read), making strategic decisions and household budgets, perhaps under the pressure of a coming famine.[8] After 300 BCE the Ptolemaic fiscal system, including the requirement to pay some taxes in coin, greater scrutiny over harvest tax payments, the presence of Greeks, and the creation of large urban centers, must have altered the ancient way of life to some extent, although it is not very easy to detect.

Like those in Egypt, Babylonian temples played major roles in economic life. Temple dependents of various kinds, from agricultural laborers, to bakers, brewers, and priests, served their local temple in exchange for maintenance. Like Egyptian temples also, Near Eastern temples were perpetual foundations, modeled on the concept of "household," serving as administrative centers that controlled and maintained agrarian lands and herds and employed full- and part-time labor. In large cities like Thebes in southern Egypt or those in Babylonia, these labor forces were large. Temples were important economic actors and have been the institution that some scholars have pointed to that distinguished a "redistributional" economy in Egypt and the Near East from a more market-based economy in the Greek world. But recent and fine-grained analysis of Near Eastern documents of the 6th century BCE shows that there was a good deal of private economic activity. Indeed temple economies were dependent on "outside" economic activity of traders and other private actors.[9] A similar situation was the case in Egypt at the same time, with entrepreneurial activity that linked individual profit motive with temple and royal economies.[10]

The Greeks theorized household structure. Here the Athenian evidence stands out: Aristotle, in his *Politics*, Xenophon's *Oeconomicus*, and Athenian law court speeches are key texts from the 4th century BCE. Pomeroy and Cox have analyzed Xenophon's text well. But these are idealized elite households. There we must reconstruct households and family structure primarily from private documentary texts, although some literary texts do provide insight into the cultural conceptions of family and inheritance.[11] The study of documents generated by the Ptolemaic census is invaluable.[12] The Ptolemies introduced a household census, but how often it occurred we do not know. The households identified in the census records were "tax-households." Willy Clarysse and Dorothy Thompson explain that these comprised "all those adults who lived together in an identifiable unit (not necessarily a whole house) both members of the immediate family and other non-kin residents, who might be either free or slave dependents of that family."[13] These records, among the more remarkable from the premodern Mediterranean world, allow us to compare Greek and Egyptian households side by side.[14]

DEMOGRAPHY

As I write this, the population of the United States as reported by the US Census Bureau (www.census.gov/popclock) is 320,597,250, a net gain of one person (births minus deaths) every fifteen seconds. The total human population of the planet in 9000 BCE was 7 million, 1.5 million *less* than the current population of New York City. It grew to 38 million by 3000 BCE (with an average annual growth rate .028 percent), to 252 million by 1 CE (growth rate of .063 percent), 477 million in 1500 CE (growth rate of .043 percent), and seven billion in 2011 CE (growth rate of .526 percent).[15] Human population is now doubling roughly every forty years. Both the scale of ancient populations and this rate of growth is a simple but important reminder of the differences between antiquity and the modern world. The long-term annual growth rates in the last two centuries BCE in the Roman world are posited to be 0.1 percent; Athens: 250,000–300,000 (with 20,000 adult

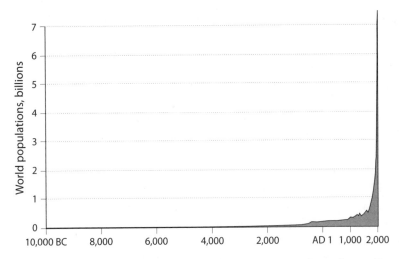

FIGURE 37. The growth in world population. Taken from Christian (2004:figure 8.2).

male citizens and a slave population of around 50,000).[16] Egypt at its height during the New Kingdom Empire amounted to perhaps three million, and perhaps a bit more than that in the Ptolemaic period.[17] The largest imperial polity before Rome, the Achaemenid Empire, was fifteen to twenty-five million.[18] The Mediterranean population under the Roman Empire at its peak reached sixty to seventy million. To serve as a contrast, it is worth noting that half of the growth in human population since 10,000 BCE has occurred in the last thirty years, with a fifteen-fold increase in annual energy consumption since 1900.[19]

At such a scale, from the contemporary perspective with population in the billions, nothing much appears before 1800, although the rise in population in the second half of the first millennium BCE is visible even at this scale (figure 37). The point is an important one. The premodern world was small compared to our own, and the demographic scale and dynamics were the most important constraint in aggregate demand and on the potential for real growth.

Demography, and we should include both human and animal populations and the ratio between them, is a key variable in ancient economies, and crucial for understanding demand, living standards, wages, and absolute economic performance, and, from a comparative point of view, social dynamics and institutional change as well.[20] Demographic change is important in calculating supply/demand issues for grain among other commodities, and for understanding the "cycling" of state expansion/contraction.[21] Yet overall numbers, life expectancy, and quality of life are all much debated at the moment in large part because of incomplete data sets and various methods of statistical analysis. High fertility/high mortality regimes would have been typical, and the average life expectancy at birth below thirty.[22] For the most part too, it is a subject that has been restricted to classical Greece and Rome, and Hellenistic and especially for Roman Egypt, where household census returns provide some quantifiable data.[23] Since we lack very reliable population figures for most places and time periods, the arguments are normally deductive. Estimates vary widely. A combination of model life tables and archaeological survey are the tools used, and funerary epitaphs and mummy tickets from Egypt provide some window onto seasonal mortality and morbidity.[24] Population density in most cases is even more problematic about which to reach conclusions. It is important, crucial even, to bear in mind that it is not just people that count, but animal populations too, in order to get the correct model of grain/fodder crops, although the latter has not been extensively studied yet. But both working animals such as the horse, camel, and donkey, and in Egypt the large numbers of sacred animals, consumed considerable amounts of fodder crops and therefore must be accounted for in agricultural production.

The historical demography of the premodern Mediterranean has received much attention in the last quarter century, providing various scenarios based on demographic modeling and the logic of population dynamics.[25] For Ptolemaic and Roman Egypt, the study of census returns has now provided a firmer basis for understanding household structure.[26] Estimates on the basis of these Ptolemaic household census returns are lower than have usually been suggested, with an estimate of 1.5 million for 250 BCE. Other estimates of the total population of Ptolemaic Egypt range between 4.5 and 8 million.[27] I prefer Hassan's estimates of 3.23 million as the best estimate for a population peak in the Ptolemaic period (figure 38).[28] Absolute size of states and of major cities continues to be debated. The total size of the Greek world, based on Mogens Herman Hansen's study, is now estimated between seven and nine million, with the Greek mainland in the late 4th century BCE amounting 3 to 3.5 million, roughly the same size as Egypt at the same time.[29] The Achaemenid Empire at its height contained between seventeen and thirty-five million.[30]

Life expectancy at birth (e_0) is generally understood in the context of model life tables and comparative estimates. Most studies suggest that e_0 in the premodern Mediterranean was between twenty and thirty years.[31] Upon reaching two years of age, life expectancy increased, but there was also a high infant (first year of life) mortality.[32] Population levels in early Roman Egypt were not reached again until the 19th century.[33]

Egyptian mummy tickets, or mummy labels as they are called, survive in the thousands through the 3d century CE. Written in Greek and/or demotic

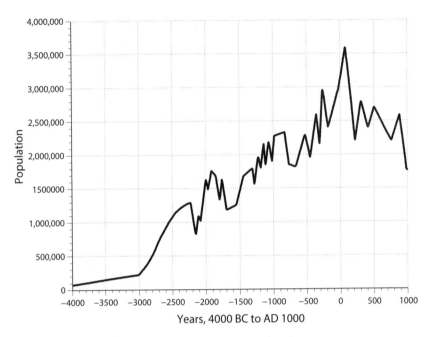

FIGURE 38. Population growth in Egypt, from Hassan (1994).

Egyptian this important corpus records not only the name of the now mummified person, but also, occasionally, professional titles and age at death.[34] The seasonal patterns of mortality and the disease regimes in Roman Egypt studied by Scheidel probably obtained for earlier periods.[35]

The coupling of human and animal demography to both the built and the natural environment is an important topic in economic history, and we have made great strides in the last few years in understanding this, although animal population studies continue to lag human studies. The gains have come from archaeological work, paleoepidemiology, paleopathology, and statistical and DNA analyses. The negative and positive impact of disease on economic performance has long been known, and ancient historians have made great progress recently in understanding morbidity, mortality, and disease in the ancient Mediterranean, although most work has been devoted to the Roman world.[36] Malaria, documented by the 8th century BCE, and schistosomiasis, documented in Egyptian mummies, would have been debilitating and a serious constraint on labor productivity and on economic growth.[37] Empires and human and animal mobility played a role in the spread of disease. The political formation and the increasing integration of larger territory by ca. 500 BCE converged "disease pools" in Eurasia.[38] Plague in the vague use of the term is documented at Athens in the early years of the Peloponnesian War, between 430 and 425 BCE, Ethiopian in origin, Thucydides informs us, although we do not know how widespread the outbreak actually was. Thucydides describes it in some detail.[39] It has now been identified as very likely either typhus or smallpox and is no doubt the best-known incidence in the first millennium BCE of disease outbreak. Its impact was significant, with a mortality rate approaching 25 percent.[40] In fact a series of plagues are documented from the 420s to the 360s BCE, although the Justinian plague (certainly *Yersinia pestis*) breaking out in 541 CE remains the first recorded pandemic.[41]

Military campaigns and trade were two drivers of such disease outbreaks; the growing size and density or urban settlement was another. Longer-term migratory movements and pandemics have been modeled and increasingly studied through DNA analysis, one of the most exciting developments for studying ancient economies. The causes of pandemic outbreaks are complex, and there is much ongoing work on this topic. Certainly climate change and drought played roles. Whether one can see a connection between plague outbreak in Egypt in the 40s BCE and the massive volcanic eruption in 44 BCE and Nile failures in the late 40s BCE remains to be fully studied. Among the more interesting results in DNA so far is the confirmation that the origin of the Etruscans in the Near East has been demonstrated by DNA analysis.[42] Such work, including the need to assess the longer-term impact of disease on first-millennium BCE populations, holds great promise for the future.

Unfortunately we have limited evidence for the demographic history of the Near East during the first millennium BCE.[43] Population growth in central Mesopotamia during the first half of the first millennium BCE is suggested by archaeological survey. The number and average size of settlements suggest an upward trend in population size and agrarian intensity, but much of our information remains based on a brief survey done by Adams in the late 1960s and 1970s.[44]

For the population of Greece, much work has been concentrated on Athens. Even with relatively good records there, almost everything remains disputed and uncertain.[45] Citizen numbers are generally derived from Thucydides (II.13.6–7); what we can say with certainty is that there was a "steep rise in citizen numbers since 508/7."[46] The number of noncitizen, metics, and slaves remains even more elusive, although this is a critical factor in understanding economic dynamics at Athens.[47] Immigration was an important element in growth in Athens, a combination of slave imports and others coming in through the deep trade connections in the Aegean and points further east. The famous citizenship law enacted by Pericles (451/1 BCE) reaffirmed earlier decisions on strict citizenship boundaries in the light of a

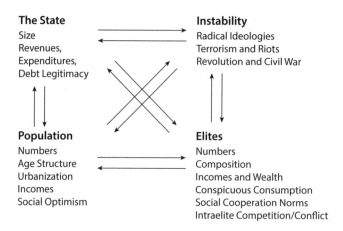

The State → **Instability**
Size
Revenues,
Expenditures,
Debt Legitimacy

Radical Ideologies
Terrorism and Riots
Revolution and Civil War

Population → **Elites**
Numbers
Age Structure
Urbanization
Incomes
Social Optimism

Numbers
Composition
Incomes and Wealth
Conspicuous Consumption
Social Cooperation Norms
Intraelite Competition/Conflict

FIGURE 39. The coupled demographic dynamics of structural demographic theory. From Turchin (2016).

growing population.[48] This population growth and political response had broad effects on economic behavior.[49]

STRUCTURAL-DEMOGRAPHIC THEORY

Structural-demographic theory combines the coupling of absolute population size and other demographic variables to the performance of the state, political stability, and intraelite competition within longer-term trends (figure 39). It provides a powerful tool for understanding internal conflict in societies, and more work on premodern material would be illuminating. Turchin and Nefedov have made a strong case that the integrative/disintegrative demographic trends in republican Rome and the Roman Empire are good examples of the nexus between intraelite competition and social instability.[50]

THE HOUSEHOLD

The household, Greek *oikos,* is the origin of course of the discipline of economics, and in many ways the foundation for studying premodern economies. The study of the household prior to 200 BCE in the Mediterranean world is dominated by evidence from ancient Greece, which theorized the household and has left us much evidence. In Xenophon, "household" meant both the nuclear family and the physical house itself and property belonging to the household.[51] Archaeological analyses of Greek houses promise to tell us more about household structure, the physical size of houses, the evolution of house design, and changes in living standards over time. But even in the

Greek world, we are limited by extensive evidence from particular sites like Athens and Olynthos.[52] Following earlier work that sought to define a Mediterranean-wide phenomenon that tracked the Mediterranean climate boundaries, there have been attempts to find a single pattern in Mediterranean household structure.

A recent study has emphasized the fluidity of household structure, and diversity within the Mediterranean, replacing influential earlier work that sought to define a Mediterranean "type" of household.[53] Evidence now suggests that even for the Roman period, the nuclear family was merely one type of what is best to consider a spectrum of household organizational solutions. Both women and children were important as "potential sources of labor and, in some legal regimes, substantial property owners."[54] What does seem to be common across the Mediterranean is, on the other hand, patrilineal descent, but that is not a fine enough distinction.[55] The location of the household across the diverse ecology of the Mediterranean world is another important consideration; urban household structure probably showed a significant divergence from rural ones.

The image of autarchic households, independent and self-sufficient, producing little surplus, and not exchanging in the market, is an image derived primarily from literary texts like Hesiod's *Works and Days*, Homer, and Aristotle (*Politics* 1.3.1256a1–1258b8) and is reinforced by more contemporary theorizing about premodern households.[56] Against the autarchic views of the ancient Greek household, new work in southern Attica, the region of Athens, shows the market activity here in the local "deme markets."[57] Lists of imported goods in Athenian comedy can be extended by archaeological material to suggest that after 600 BCE there was a wide circuit of bidirectional trade between the Aegean and the Levant that gave rise to a "consumer culture" in Greece.[58] Greeks did not distinguish *oikos* from business enterprise (*ergasterion*) for public projects, and "citizen, resident alien and slave workers often worked side-by-side, and were paid the same daily rates."[59] Certain industries in the Greek world such as textile production were commonly located within households. There is much that is still obscure about scale of production, the connection between household and market, and the distribution between domestic and imported textiles; the mix of slave, resident alien, and free citizen labor probably varied regionally and over time. The domestic economy in Greece, and no doubt elsewhere too, is best thought of in terms of a "plural" economic model.[60]

The Greek household, like Hekanakhte's and those of the well-documented families in the archives from Ptolemaic Egypt, was complex and fluid and often contained a nuclear family, extended members of the family, and nonfamily members.[61] Much of our information comes from legal texts concerned with the transmission of property within the family.[62] Indeed this emphasis on legal rules for marriage, property, and property disputes constitutes much of our evidence for Greek, Egyptian, and Near Eastern families. That means, of course, that we face the usual bias toward affluent households.

Private economic activity within households, both for household consumption and for sale outside of it, is less well studied, in large part because the archaeological documentation is diffuse. For wealthy households, their consumption of household goods and other items in the market can be studied in epigraphic evidence that records public auctions of confiscated property of those convicted of public unrest in 415 BCE.[63] Those were wealthy households. That is another serious constraint on our knowledge since almost everywhere it is impossible to derive a sense of household demand or consumption. As always, middling or lower levels of society remain difficult to study directly, but the presence of the market place (*agora*) in Greek towns, and lists of commodities mentioned in literary texts, do suggest widespread market purchases.[64] We might compare these to the list of women's property recorded in demotic Egyptian marriage contracts.[65] The lack of consistent information across first millennium BCE Mediterranean societies does not allow sustained comparison. But everywhere we have some information, and in the Near East, Egypt, and the classical world, we see that households were also centers of craft production, in agricultural processing, in textile weaving, and in small-scale manufacturing. In some cases, archaeological work does allow us the ability to study "household industries."[66]

In chapter 1 I mentioned that there is ongoing debate between which unit of analysis in historical economics is best, the individual, the household, or the society. The best way forward has been offered by John Davies, who suggests that we think in terms of a general, multilevel transactional model that captures all three levels:

1. Autarchic household transactions, storage
2. Interhousehold exchange, lend-and-return
3. Interhousehold via nonhousehold labor, slave or hired
4. Household—market transactions via various types of market exchange
5. Household and regional exchange
6. Market and "out of region" exchange.[67]

This basic flow model can be specified and scaled depending on size of territory, and the model can be complicated by moving beyond the focus on households by bringing in large land owners, temples and sanctuaries, business partnerships, the state, and so on. This kind of mapping of flows can be further specified for large territorial states and empires.

The debate about the nature of human rational decision making, and the best type and the role of states, has in fact been with us since at least the 5th century BCE when Herodotus began his inquiries into the origins of the Greco-Persian wars. In the 19th century, social theorists, looking to prove the correctness of their assumptions, turned to the preindustrial Mediterranean world and found what they were looking for. For Weber, like Bücher earlier, the self-sufficient household stood in contrast to the rise of the market. But as we will see, the history of premodern Mediterranean households is more complicated. The household stood not only as the basic social unit, but also in the Near East and in Egypt as a model for statewide structures as well. The entire Egyptian state was conceived of as the "household" of the king; temples were "houses" of the god.[68] It was, as in the Near East, not the only household, merely the largest. But the "oikos" model, the basis of the redistributive model for Near Eastern and Egyptian economies, has missed much economic activity by temples and by private households.[69]

To be certain, in Egypt and the Near East, palace economies taxed, stored, and (re)distributed agricultural surplus. Household surveys were the basis of state labor systems going back at least to the second millennium BCE, and these records provide some insight into household structure.[70] This "administrative" function of the state and larger temples acted as a buffer against the interannual variability of the grain harvest. It tends to be well documented, but it is clear that they did not control the whole of agricultural production.

The ideal type of peasant household, the subject of much theorizing in a Mediterranean context, is already called into question by an early, and surprisingly neglected, collection of letters sitting in a quiet, rather dark corner of the ancient Egyptian galleries at the Metropolitan Museum in New York. There three texts stand, lying behind glass sheets within a display case. Nearby there is a label explaining what these texts are.[71] The texts are known collectively as the Hekanakhte letters and provide astonishing details of the economic behavior and household strategies of a single middle Bronze Age "peasant" household (figure 40).[72] There are nothing like them again for another thousand years, and they are nearly contemporaneous with the Old Assyrian trading settlement at Kanesh. The letters have been compared to the Greek poet Hesiod's writing on household management.[73] These letters afford us a window onto an individual acting in his own self-interest on behalf of his household. They date to the Middle Kingdom, ca. 1950 BCE, and concern the management of land in middle Egypt, somewhere near the

FIGURE 40. Letter 1, Hekanakhte letters, Metropolitan Museum of Art.

Fayyum.[74] Almost as soon as the texts were uncovered during tomb excavations in western Thebes, Agatha Christie was inspired to write *Death Comes as the End*, using the ancient letters as the basis of her story. It's surprising then that the texts have not received much attention outside of the small circle of Egyptologists.

The letters were written (perhaps dictated) by a man named Hekanakhte and were meant to be delivered to his home. They were found in an official's tomb above Deir el-Bahari in western Thebes. Hekanakhte was a member of the "intermediate rural notable" class, a funerary priest of the vizier, the chief administrator of the state.[75] The household was substantial in size, nineteen persons in total including his mother, an aunt, married sons, a farmer and his three workers, and three female household slaves.[76] The economic strategies were remarkably intricate. The letters urge, and the sense of

TABLE 6. *The Household Income and Expenses of Hekanakhte*

Income			
Harvest @ 15 sacks/*aroura*	382.5	127.5	510
Expenses			
Grain tax @ 10%	38.25	12.75	51
Seed @ 1.5 sacks/*aroura*	38.25	12.75	51
Cattle tax	4	10.5	14.5
Year of food	25.8	90	115.8
Year of salary			136.2
TOTAL	242.5	126	368.5
(surplus)	(140)	(1.5)	(141.5)

SOURCE: J. Allen (2002:166).

NOTE: 1 *aroura* = .66 acre; 34 *arouras* sowed, 75 percent barley, 25 percent emmer wheat

urgency and focus do come through, the use of temporary wage labor, ownership of cattle, the leasing of land (with copper as the medium of exchange) in other villages if possible, and they acknowledge costs of land rental, and margins in budget making. Calculations were made in monetary terms using commodities as media of exchange, convertible between barley, textiles, and copper.

The agricultural details described in the letters are remarkable, and somewhat even surprising. Hekanakhte owned more than seventy *arouras* (roughly forty acres) that provided for his household and would have yielded much beyond that in good years. Twenty-three *arouras* were leased to others. Land was typically held by families in portfolios, a pattern that continued to be common in the first millennium BCE.[77] The main crops were barley and emmer, cloth was woven in the household and sold, and surplus grain was used for the purchase of other items. The letters also tell us that in years of poor Nile flooding, two bad years in a row we are told, even middling families risked starvation, and Hekanakhte uses this fear as motivation. The letters also tell us that in the region of middle Egypt at this period, half of the Nile valley floodplain was used as unimproved pasture or lay fallow (table 6).

Here we would appear to have an example of a pure *oikos* economy, the perfect unit of analysis for Aristotle, Rodbertus, Sahlins, and many economic theorists since. But the letters make clear that we do not have a self-sufficient "peasant" household conforming to Chayanov's "peasant mode of production," or Sahlins's domestic mode of production, feeding the family and nothing beyond, not least because a grain tax lurks here in the background to household production. There is no need for a "peasant mode of production" as a distinctive stage in the premodern agrarian world.[78]

Hekanakhte was an individual making rational decisions for his entire extended *household*, not just his *nuclear* family; but also, crucially, he leased out land, sold textiles, and collected on loans. Land was held in different parts of Egypt; the Thinite nome in the South, near Abydos, may have produced income related to his funerary priest duties. Household rations and salaries for work are distinguished. Hekanakhte could not have been a unique man, and if we had more such letters we could say with more certainty that the rational behavior exhibited in these remarkable letters was typical of Egyptian households. It is, perhaps, to be seen as an early glimpse of the family firm better attested in the middle of the first millennium BCE, and an important part in the history of the rise of the firm.[79]

These beautifully written letters show that rational budget-making decisions were made, as were decisions on crop type, on food allowances, on salaries for labor, and on leasing strategies. He knew what the crop yields and soil conditions were, and he was making money on leasing land and on selling textiles. It also provides a nice example of social reproduction, of the "vertical transmission" of knowledge from one generation to the next.[80] The letters are at once a snapshot of a self-sufficient household, idealized and moralized later by Greek authors, but also of the complex ways in which a household was connected to other households through land leasing, textile manufacturing, selling, and other activities.[81] We must remain cautious in drawing general conclusions; the nature of the Hekanakhte letters precludes reconstruction of the totality of his world.

The small archive of eight complete texts and five fragmentary texts presents us with important problems to consider, namely the unit of analysis in studying ancient economies. Ideally, of course, we should integrate individual behavior and household structure to regional economic patterns and state demands. But evidence does not usually allow for this. What makes this even more problematic is that the texts are unique for Egypt until much later, in the Greco-Roman period, at least in terms of economic documentation of household behavior. So were they unique or typical of Egyptian households of a certain level around 2000 BCE? Are they representative of households for all ancient Egyptian history? Certainly all the evidence suggests that Egyptian households, as with Greece and Near Eastern ones, were highly flexible in their composition and size, dependent on life cycles of the family, and that they were frequently tied in to larger extended families and patronage networks.[82]

Hekanakhte and his family lived in a small village world, no doubt typical of Egypt at the time.[83] His land portfolio was diverse, and he was well aware of hedging risks. This pattern of the small-scale family farm exploited by an extended family was probably typical throughout the premodern world even if it is not always so well documented. The context of Hekanakhte goes back deep into the Bronze Age, but I use it to bring up an important point. Generalized models or stage theories don't capture historical realities well enough and are often based on assumptions that collapse as soon as a document is provided. Hekanakhte lived in the middle of the Bronze Age, and the evidence for first-millennium BCE household behavior shows significant changes.

First-millennium BCE Egypt offers even better detail on individual economic activity from the family archives that survive. Property records preserved in the archive related to a family property dispute that I discuss in the next chapter give us a sense of the property holdings of a middling family, members of a priestly family of a small temple in Asyut in the 2d century BCE.[84] The property list details the ownership of shares of several storehouses, a house and outlying structures, shares of agricultural land (the object of dispute in the trial) and garden plots, and shares of priestly income from the local temple, as well as bread, oil, and other foodstuff as payments in kind, shares of priestly offices, and a one-twelfth share of a scribal office.[85] The property list is probably complete, and it allows us a glimpse at a middling priestly family's livelihood and income streams whose shares reflect the partible inheritance practices of Egypt.

The early economic structure of the Near East, like Egypt and other Bronze Age palace economies, was based on interlocking social hierarchies that linked individual households to temples and "service households" under the authority of the king. The second and early first millennium BCE was a period of political adjustments as well as shifts in territorial hegemony of empire. There were shifts from an *oikos* to a "tributary" economy; we find both "large institutional household managers," and land worked by individual farmers or "state elites."[86] The Near Eastern evidence provides a good picture of elite urban households.[87] In Neo-Assyrian slave sale records, a variety of household sizes are documented. Patrilineal descent patterns were characteristic of both lower- and higher-echelon households.[88] Studies tend to focus on onomastics, a close study of naming practices, and tracking family descent through these naming practices. The Neo-Babylonian evidence suggests early age of marriage for both males and females. Males on average were under 20 years of age at marriage, and women around 13 or 14. Getting a picture of household consumption patterns is difficult. Domestic archaeology has improved and offers promise; from what can be told so far, there was no "typical" household or house size.[89]

Finley saw the emergence of "entrepreneurs" in Greek lyric poetry ca. 650 BCE, a distinctly Greek literary form.[90] But in fact the emergence of entrepreneurs can be traced back to the beginning of the Iron Age and Phoenician traders. By mid-millennium, family "firms" are well documented in the Near East. The Neo-Babylonian period archives of the Egibi family, amounting to two thousand texts (apparently even larger when discovered, but much was lost by careless excavation practices), document five generations of family land holding and renting, money lending, and tax farming activity.[91] The Murashu family archive from the Early Achaemenid period documents three generations of a family in Nippur with similar business operations.[92]

THE ROLE OF STATES

The role of the state in premodern economies has been much debated, with opinions ranging from "insignificant" to "totalizing." William Harris has put the problem succinctly: "did the state have any autonomous existence, or was state-power a straightforward expression of the will of a dominant social class?"[93] Political economics and economic performance have been well studied in other contexts but have not received due attention for the ancient world. It is arguable that the continual process of state formation, and empire building, and the connection between the state and military mobilization (including technological improvements in weaponry and tactics), and between states, markets, and distribution, and incentives to move as we can observe in many parts of the Hellenistic world, was one of, if not *the*, strongest of forces in the economic history of the first-millennium BCE Mediterranean.[94] For some scholars, in contrast, neither states nor markets were particularly important considerations at all.[95] It is clear that we need better theory born out of careful case studies. As I have already suggested, Egypt cannot be simply identified as "despotic." Rather, even under the Ptolemies, it was a "fragmented" state, power being shared between kings, who pushed an ideology of centralization and strong control, and local elites, the priesthoods, cities, and the army. This had particular consequences for the development of markets.[96]

The variety in state size, and organization, capacity, duration, and type of governance is a notable feature of premodern Mediterranean states. States, however we define them, were important in premodern economies, as they are in modern ones.[97] States affected economic behavior in two essential ways. They (1) established a "cognitive framework" as part of the state-making process, in order to (2) extract revenue.[98] Certain things flow from the second, namely the state's role in public goods provision and "protection." The war-making capacity of premodern states was of major importance to their size and endurance as well as their extractive power, and war was a critical driver in economic change and in imperial performance in the first millennium BCE.[99] Revenue collection was of major concern of all first-millennium BCE states, and there were strong differences between the Greek world, with a preference for indirect taxation (although the *eisphora* tax on capital as an emergency measure was common), and Near Eastern states and Egypt, where direct taxation of people, transactions, and agricultural production was the norm.[100]

The war fighting capacity of premodern states was critical to economic performance and is clearly seen in the evolution of the first millennium BCE. War and warfare was oddly missing in Rostovtzeff's great work on the Hellenistic period, but it was crucially then that war, and the capacity to mobilize for war, occupied much of the state budgets, and therefore was a major object of the fiscal policy of the Hellenistic kingdoms.[101] War was a "mode of acquisition"; it was a "structural" part of premodern economies more broadly, a method of revenue extraction, a style of governance (rulers as war leaders); and the acquisitive aspect of war was something that Rome with respect to other Hellenistic actors benefitted enormously from.[102] Mercenaries were increasingly important in first-millennium BCE armies, especially in the Hellenistic world.

The first millennium BCE was a major transition in the nature of state power. Two broad theories of what states did exist.[103] Rational choice theory has been applied to ancient states in trying to understand how states are formed and how they endure. Revenue sources are a key consideration in understanding the behavior of rulers, the public goods they provided, bureaucratization, and the bargaining power of constituent groups.[104] Environmental constraints are also important, as we have discussed above; the "caging effects" of river valleys, nomadic groups within state territory, and military mobilization are also important considerations in durability.

The connection between irrigation agriculture and the structure of the state is a subject that has generated fierce debate about the organization and concentration of power in irrigation societies. Earlier scholarship on Asia and the Near East has often noted causal links between "hydraulic" agriculture and centralized power. Egypt is an excellent case study in how irrigation societies create intensive, cooperative local irrigation ecologies. In an important article, Eyre has sketched the intricate connections between irrigation and local society in Egyptian history.[105] He produces a composite image of Egypt from the Old Kingdom to the Ptolemaic period. Throughout Egyptian history, the central state placed an emphasis on order and on measuring the Nile flood, which was carefully monitored at Nilometers with a mark for the sign of life, an indication that sufficient floodwaters would be attained that year. Such bureaucratic orderliness, however, disguises the local complexities and variability of the irrigated landscape. Unlike irrigation after 1820 when a much larger system of interconnected basins was created, the ancient system was highly local and small scale in its operation. It required no management or coordination, and indeed very little coerced labor to maintain the system.[106] Even in the Ptolemaic period, a time in which it has been supposed there was a strong central state that intervened heavily in local economies, land management, and so on, there was a balance between state economic interest and local management. In the Fayyum, a region that had the most direct state presence, where the arable land was trebled and settled in the early Ptolemaic period, the local character of irrigation and agricultural production still prevailed.

Public goods provision, including law and legal institutions, as I will discuss below, has often been underappreciated, in particular in Near Eastern states and in Egypt. These were more than "fly trap economies," with revenue flowing only in one direction to rulers and elites.[107] That has often been the view of the Near Eastern empires. But it is now quite clear in the 6th century BCE Babylonian data and in early Ptolemaic Egypt, and probably under the Saite kings as well, that rulers were aligned with "political elites" in temples and urban centers in fostering commercial activities, and in establishing a legal order around property rights and market exchange.[108] These institutional adjustments coincided with rising populations and favorable climatic conditions.

The joining of "state and private enterprise," as Shaw pointed out, is "typical of development in the Mediterranean."[109] We will see this clearly in first-millennium BCE trade discussed in the next chapter, and with the Egibi and Marashu family business in Babylonian and Achaemenid Near East. In part this joining of public and private was a function of state fiscal structure. Fiscal sociology and the "New Fiscal History" has been a popular subject in several social science fields, and a recent volume highlights the important contribution premodern Mediterranean states can make to the literature.[110]

There are various assessments of what states are and what role they played in ancient economies. Finley thought that the state was "all." In Horden and Purcell's Mediterranean, in strong contrast, the state is entirely absent from their analysis. Yet states grew in size and complexity throughout the Iron Age, culminating of course with the Roman Empire. Iron Age states were of two basic kinds: territorial empires and "mercantile city states."[111] But city-states persist. City-states produce better rules for growth and were flexible and could be absorbed by empires while maintaining their internal cohesion.[112]

The role of states in exchange, control of territory, protection that lowered costs, building roads and ports, and overall well-being are a critical part of economic change. Imperial expansion during the first millennium BCE, in western Asia and in the Mediterranean, had multiple drivers, among them control of trade flow and, as we saw with Ptolemaic Egypt, control of a more diversified resource portfolio in their 3d century BCE imperial territory. As William Harris succinctly puts it for early Rome, the conquest of the entire Mediterranean had "the effect of making the Roman economy a huge affair spreading from the Atlantic to India."[113] But Rome did more than merely gain and protect an imperial space in which merchants moved freely and at long distances. Important were the creation of law, the consensual sale contract, for example (*emptio-venditio*), in guaranteeing and distributing food, and perhaps port building, as was clearly the case with 4th century Athens and Ptolemaic Alexandria

Alexander's conquest in the late 4th century BCE destroyed the old imperial framework of the 5th century, between Athens and Persia. New states were formed, older states, especially the Greek cities, made major adjustments in how they operated, and the institutional bases of societies around the Mediterranean world were altered. States competed fiercely with each other for resources. The immediate framework was the 4th century—the collapse of two dominant imperial frameworks, Athens and Persia, and the rise of Macedon on the Greek periphery. Political equilibriums were difficult to establish, the immediate concerns revolving around the creation of what Eisenstadt famously has termed "free-floating resources" bound up in a nexus of war-resources-coinage.[114] The new territorial monarchies that emerged and would dominate the scene were "radically" different from the ancient Greek concept of city-state.[115] Alexander did not merely open up the Achaemenid Empire to the Greek world. These new states had larger economies of scale. The level of military technology, the productivity of its resource base, and its administrative costs were factors that determined the relative size of each Hellenistic state.[116]

The spread of the Greek language among elites in the Near East and in Egypt created new identities and new social networks. How this mattered to economic development and performance is not easy to measure. In terms of economic institutions, much was old by the time Alexander reached Egypt and Mesopotamia. For Egypt, we would really need to begin in the 7th century BCE, the period of major state recentralization by the Saite kings, and have a different quality of evidence, to trace trends across seven centuries in order to measure effects of state building. For other parts of the Hellenistic world, political change happened at different rates. Geography, war, and luck, to name three variables, all played their part in state-building processes. As the new Hellenistic states emerged, they had profound effects not only in the public/royal sphere, but also in private economic activity through taxation demands and in the circulation of coinage.

The three Leviathans, the Antigonid, Seleukid, and Ptolemaic kingdoms, all continued imperial forms of state with a royal dynasty as the organizing political principle. On the Greek mainland (primarily) cities associated themselves into larger cooperative units (*koinon*, pl. *koina*) to fulfill some central needs, continuing Greek political habits. The nature of monarchy in the Ptolemaic and Seleukid systems differed substantially from the Antigonids in that the former two states were newer, personal regimes as opposed to the Macedonian tradition of "national kingship."[117] Beyond definitional issues there are estimation problems (secure population figures, certain annual revenue of the states), the physical geography and complex eco-zones that Hellenistic states incorporated, the degree of economic integration between the states, the interannual variability of water (of rainfall in the northern Mediterranean, of the annual flood of the rivers in Mesopotamia and in Egypt) and hence of production, the impact of the movement of population between regions (e.g., Celts/"Gauls" into the Hellenistic world, and internal colonization on new land as well as new population centers established by the kings), and the transference of population from one region to another.[118]

Statist views of the Ptolemaic economy in Egypt have been perhaps the strongest statement about the role of a strong state in reshaping an entire economy. The so-called *économie royale* was understood as the totality of economic activity.[119] But this is only a partial account, relying on state records to describe what was only the "public" or state economy.[120] The papyri taken as a whole present us with a very different world beyond state economic activities and remind us that everywhere in the Mediterranean, private economic activity was very often unrecorded, or has been lost to us.[121] Two institutions that have left us a great deal of information and that evolved considerably in the first millennium BCE everywhere, and both connected to states and to public economies, are law and money. I turn to examine these next.

CHAPTER 7

The Evolution of Economic Thought in the Ancient World

MONEY, LAW, AND LEGAL INSTITUTIONS

> How can we compare the economies of different cultures and at the same time recognize that each unique group of people defines the economy in a different way?
>
> —WILK AND CLIGGETT (2007:34)

> In many contexts, law is not central to the maintenance of social order.
>
> —ELLICKSON (1991:280)

THIS CHAPTER EXPLORES THE evolutionary processes that connected concepts of exchange and legal institutions to institutional change. The first millennium BCE offers rich sources for understanding major developments in economic thought that were tied to changes in political economy and the evolution of economic institutions. An examination of two key ones, money and law, demonstrates that the role of culture and states is important. These institutions functioned quite differently in the societies we are discussing, but in all cases the state played a critical role in cultural and economic change. Population movement was also a powerful force for change. Cultural differences in marriage, inheritance rules, the conception of private property, and legal institutions generally show heterogeneous variation across the Mediterranean world in the first millennium BCE. And yet Egyptian, Babylonian, and classical legal cultures all share some basic features that would militate against thinking in terms of an "East-West" divide.[1]

We can see this most clearly in the case of the Hellenistic period, when Greek and Jewish populations brought with them to their new home in Egypt their own legal traditions, which were maintained by the new state. But the formation of new political hegemonies in the Hellenistic period also reshaped legal and economic institutions. The concept of private property, and real property in particular, varying considerably, existed in all premodern Mediterranean societies. A distinguishing characteristic in the Near East and in Egypt was that land was tied to state service, and that private rights were embedded within a larger institutional framework with internested claims, and generally rights held by families. The private sale of land is documented in both, but the extent of market transactions, and the degree of disembeddedness of individuated rights in land, is debatable. Individualized private property in irrigated landscapes would not have been an optimal solution in any case.

This an important contrast between the Near East, Egypt, and the classical world, where the individual, as opposed to the kinship group, appears central in the 4th century BCE work of Xenophon, Plato, and Aristotle.[2] For the Greeks "economics," was literally household management as we have seen. The fundamental differences between household, or local, economic decisions, and state-level decisions, while perhaps first articulated by Greeks, existed in Egyptian and Near Eastern societies as well.

The analytical writing of Xenophon and Aristotle shows that many concepts that were developed in later writing and have become part of modern economics were present. These include the division of labor, marginal utility, market exchange, the properties of money, and optimum political equilibriums.[3] As has often been pointed out, this does not mean of course that economics as a field of analysis existed in antiquity or that abstract thought was applied to everyday human concerns.[4]

We have almost nothing beyond some general aphorisms from wisdom literature about Egyptian and Assyrian or Babylonian thought about their world, or any kind of systematic theorizing about law or economy. Temples and their priesthoods, as local managers of economic resources, may well have generated abstract thinking about what we may now think of as "economics," but it would have represented, as Kemp suggests, a "range of individual practices sanctified by tradition."[5] This tradition, it is important to point out, did not get picked up by European monks and others since the transmission capacity of Egyptian and Babylonian texts was lost until the 19th century. There is a good deal, however, that can be reconstructed about ancient Egyptian and Near Eastern cultural norms and beliefs about family life, exchange, and a wide range of issues that we would think of in economic terms and that they would think of simply in terms of daily life or problem solving. Hekanakhte, whom we encountered earlier, in calculating consumption budgets, in his decisions about land rental and the sale of a bull because prices had become higher, "lived economics rather than thought about it."[6] Literature was a common medium to convey common wisdom, no doubt collected from centuries of storytelling around the fire at night, not unlike Hesiod, *The Wisdom of Onchsheshonqy*, an Egyptian text written in the Ptolemaic period but with aphorisms, about 10 percent of which are concerned with agriculture, that probably were in circulation long before then.[7] Instruction literature had broad appeal and was a widely popular means of disseminating cultural norms and continued to be used by the Ptolemies in Egypt to instruct officials in their duties and expectations of office and as a way of signaling state aims about the public economy.[8]

MONEY AND COINAGE

The evolution of money and the growth in the use of coinage in economies across the Mediterranean during the first millennium BCE is one of the most important topics in the study of premodern economies. Significantly, this evolution is attested at the same time in other parts of the world as well.[9] Money, perhaps, the least understood aspect of premodern economies, is a very complex topic historically and theoretically, and it has been studied from a very wide variety of angles. Meikle has emphasized the role of money in the ancient world as the main prism through which to understand the differences between ancient and modern economies.[10] Recent work ranges from understanding "exchange value" and the origins of money and the sociology and cultural history of money to detailed quantified studies of coin hoards.[11] Perhaps most promising of all is to study it in the context of neuroeconomics, and to understand money as a "reinforcer," and part of the same neuromechanism of pleasure-seeking activity, and beyond then the normative understanding of money as "a general purpose exchange medium."[12] Money was a "foundation for the world's first large-scale societies of the ancient Near East during the third millennium BC."[13] There are the classic textbook definitions of money (medium of exchange, store of value, means of payment, and unit of account), but defining "moneyness," that is, what is functionally distinctive about money, has occupied economic theorists for a long time.[14] Seaford has suggested seven basic characteristics of money:

(1) It has value for the power to meet obligations
(2) It tends to be quantified
(3) It may provide a measure of value
(4) General acceptability
(5) Exclusive acceptability
(6) Fiduciarity
(7) The state may be involved in issuing money, controlling it, and guaranteeing it.[15]

In enumerating these characteristics Seaford's analysis highlighted the role of coinage in the Greek world and denied that silver had the proper characteristics of money in the first-millennium BCE Near East. But Jursa's very detailed study of the use of both silver and commodities in the exchange system of the Neo-Babylonian empire suggests that both here and in Egypt silver had the function of money by mid-millennium if not earlier, but silver had played a much more important role in Bronze Age economies of the Near East than in Egypt, no doubt because of the lack of silver sources within the latter.[16]

Money has been no less a complex subject for ancient historians; debates about the nature of money go back to the "Methodenstreit" in the historical social sciences in Germany. Money (and its connection to banks) has been a major point of contention in the debate over the existence of premodern capitalism.[17]

Money has a "dual nature"—it is both a physical thing and an abstraction. It serves individuals but can be appropriated by society at large; it is also an instrument of political power and a symbol of sovereignty.[18] Money is generally understood in economic theory as a medium of exchange: an exchangeable commodity, a symbol of such, or symbolic of a commodity standard.[19] But there is more to it. If we follow Herrmann-Pillath, it also has an emotional element. The theory of money in economics can be traced back to Aristotle's commodity theory, which was, essentially, an ethical argument about the proper use of money. Carl Menger sought the origins of money in commodity exchange.[20] Thus money also expresses "social relations," a "transferable debt" based on its basic role as a unit of account,[21] a medium of exchange, directly exchangeable but also "symbolic representation of a commodity standard."[22] But that leaves several basic questions open: "What is money? What does money do? How is it produced; how does it get into society; how is the value of money determined"?[23] Money is a promise, and it involves trust and originates not in exchange but in the idea of debt and in the concept of money of account.[24] An early form of money was *Wergeld*, an abstract determination of "worth" to compensate for injuries. States, in their war-fighting capacities, played an important role in the evolution of money and coinage and how it was regulated.[25]

The role of money in ancient economies has been another topic that has been intensely debated for a century.[26] For Finley, money played a minor role in ancient economies. Circulation of coinage was limited mainly to cities; it was mainly in the form of coinage; it did not affect supply or demand for commodities; it did not have a fiduciary aspect; it never signaled market prices, since coins were circulated within specific political territory, which made monetary exchange across political boundaries difficult.[27] But as von Reden suggests, the focus in recent years has been in the opposite direction. The study of the impacts of coinage and the monetization of Mediterranean economies, from the introduction of coinage into Greece, to the impacts of the much-increased use of coinage in the fiscal systems of Hellenistic states, has been extensive.[28] Technical studies of coinage, currency units, and the production and circulation of coinage have proliferated.[29]

The use of monies of account is well documented in Near Eastern and Egyptian texts. Precious metals were power and prestige symbols in royal and temple spheres since the third millennium BCE. One only has to glance at King Tut's golden mask to understand that gold in Egypt was a highly prized metal, and the pharaohs spent considerable energy, and the energy of slaves, to extract it from mines in the eastern deserts of Nubia, an Egyptian word derived from the word for gold. It is another example of metal sources playing a role in imperial expansion and trade. Even in Egypt, however, silver was a form of money along with gold in the second millennium BCE.[30] Grain, too, played a major role as a medium of exchange and a unit of account in both the Near East and Egypt. By the first millennium BCE, though, silver had become a kind of international standard of value for exchange, used as a commodity and as money. This had certain political effects; both Egypt and the Near Eastern states lacked sources of silver, for example; they had to trade for it, and this played a role in interstate exchange, and eventually in the Ptolemaic period the closed currency policy of the 3d century BCE, and, over time, its emphasis on bronze coins.[31]

The increased use of silver as money, in trade, as wages, and in taxation— "silverization" as van der Spek calls it[32]—was driven by state demand for taxes and by trade. This was part of a very wide trend in the Iron Age of new fiscal institutions, and these reforms seem to occur in the Near East, in Egypt, and in the Greek world during the 6th century BCE. But silver was already used in land sales dating to the third millennium BCE. Copper and barley were also used as fixed values against which other things were exchanged. There is important evidence that Near Eastern economies were effectively monetized from an early date:

> The hoards above mentioned proof [*sic*] that from the Early Bronze to the Iron Ages coils and fractioned coils are attested together with silver ingots of different types and scrap metal. All the evidence of bulks of silver discovered in the Near East seems to indicate that standardization of ingots, if present, was introduced for practical reasons, in order to make easier and speedy the weighing procedures, allowing the fractioning process and/or the transport. We can talk about silver used as money when it has a normal circulation in relation to a use as a means of payment, when it is adopted as standard of value or as accumulation of wealth. These "money functions" seem to be effectively attested in Mesopotamia already at the end of the ED period, confirmed by the silver analysis of the hoard contents.[33]

The 7th and 6th century BCE in the Mediterranean world was an important period for the history of money.[34] This was a transitional, I would say evolutionary, period between weighed metal money and the emergence and diffusion of coinage. Coinage was a transformative institution in economic history and a good example of what Arthur has called a "novel technology" that originated by "combining or integrating earlier technologies."[35] This was the period of interaction between the Near East and the Greek world, the Phoenicians playing a very important part in this "orientalizing" phase of early Greek history. The increasing pace of exchange that this monetary history suggests is paralleled, in Egypt, by the spread of the new demotic script during the 7th and 6th centuries BCE. This was a rapidly written script designed, in part at least, to record private agreements more quickly. The economic pace of exchange in the ancient world was picking up.

Jursa discusses the transformation of the Near East in the first millennium BCE.[36] His detailed survey of money, and especially the use of silver in the Neo-Babylonian Empire, covers both institutional and private sector economic activity, in the state fiscal system, and in slave and wage labor.[37] Silver wages demonstrate the "increasing monetarisation of temple economies."[38] The Neo-Babylonian economy was "binary," one of exchanges in kind, the other of silver.[39] Dates and wool were certainly still used as mediums of exchange, and silver was clearly used as a "money of account."[40] The old idea of a redistributive model to stand for the whole of ancient Near Eastern economic mode propounded by Polanyi and reinforced by Finley has been exploded by Jursa's detailed review of the Babylonian evidence. The succeeding Achaemenid Empire played an even stronger role in state intervention in terms of guaranteeing silver quality and in controlling interest rates.[41] Silver is also shown to have been used in everyday, "small value" exchanges, and, therefore, it circulated much more widely than had been previously thought. Monetary exchange between temples and other institutions was a characteristic feature of temple economies, and silver is well documented in private exchange as well.

Silver began to play a more important role in personal exchange in Egypt by the 6th century BCE. Temples were important, principally that of the god Ptah in Memphis, in setting standards of weight and in guaranteeing quality.[42] Studies of coin hoards in Egypt are important, especially the so-called mixed hoards consisting of both coins and broken pieces of silver. Such evidence proves that Egypt was "monetized," in the sense that there was a concept of money, in the form of weighed silver, guaranteed by a temple standard, long before the wider use of coined money in the Ptolemaic period.[43] The *degree* of "monetization," however, is very difficult to know on the basis of coin hoards and the mention of silver in a handful of documentary papyri. But private sales and loans, already known in the 8th century BCE, show that they were understood in terms of a price in weighed silver.[44] Mixed hoards begin to appear in the Egyptian record in the 6th century BCE.[45]

The process of the monetization of Mediterranean economies has been a major topic of analysis recently.[46] It has generally been understood in the context of the rise and spread in the use of coinage, but there is a longer history here that is worth exploring. Here the role of the state was crucial. In the case of Greece, it has been argued by some scholars that monetization had profound effects on social relations, disembedding family relations and allowing the state to regulate social relations, and the whole of Greek thought.[47] A similar process was already underway in the Hammurabi law code (see below). At Athens, the state's demands for tax payments, fines, and dues in coinage created circulation and thus a process of monetization.[48] This was also the intention in Ptolemaic Egypt where certain taxes were calculated and demanded in coin. How deeply monetization penetrated local, traditional society is debatable. Yet the Greek story is different. The shift from a precoinage world to one of coinage, stamped metal units of uniform size with some authorizing symbol guaranteeing wide acceptance, circulating with Greek city-states, was arguably a revolution, and a major turning point in the economic history of the wider Mediterranean world.[49] Coined money and the state coevolved, and this coevolution was also tied to the development of law (see below).

Understanding the relationship between uniform weighed metal and stamped coinage, the impact of impersonal exchange on social structure and on human thought, requires us to assign cause and effect in a rapidly changing first-millennium BCE world. Was coinage the cause of social transformation, or the result of it? It is not the evolution of markets that required the emergence of money, but precisely the opposite: "The evolutionary emergence of an artefact with the properties of early money made the emergence and growth of markets possible, which is exactly the shift towards derivative functions of money."[50]

Coinage was "invented" in Lydia, western Turkey, at some point in the 7th century BCE. The first evidence comes from the temple of Artemis at Ephesos. But the reasons behind the "invention" of coinage, and the impact of coinage on local economies, are still debated.[51] The location of the invention is important in two respects. Lydia lies in between the Near Eastern and Greek worlds. The earliest coinage was struck in electrum, a natural alloy of silver and gold native to this part of Anatolia. The location of Lydia and the medium of the earliest coinage combined to facilitate cross-cultural exchange:

The first genuine coins originating from Lydia, however, were made from electrum, an alloy of silver and gold. Thus, they could be interpreted

differently in the two societies, enabling cross-cultural exchange of signs
and goods. Further, in order to test the quality of coins, people applied
punches resulting into punchmark, firstly unintendedly. Once the coins
circulated, people discovered the possible use of the punchmarks as indi-
cators of origin. From this moment onwards, the custom of coining
emerged, with the incipient use of the punchmarks as signals. Hutter
speaks of an oscillation between the notions of "signed metal" and "metal
sign." Soon, the new coins were reintegrated into the political and the religious realm when local regents adopted the institution of minting.[52]

The nature of electrum itself, and the variable metal content, may also
have played a role in a standardized, state-guaranteed institution that
avoided the weighing and essaying of the metal for each transaction. It is the
famous Croesus (r. 560–547 BCE) who shaped the final stage in the development of early coinage by replacing electrum and weighed metal with silver
and gold coinage.[53] Secondly, the location of silver ore mines also played a
profoundly important role in developments. The (re)discovery of the Laurion silver mine in Attica in the late 6th century BCE certainly had profound effects not only in the military sphere (ship building) but also in the
overall economic life of Athens, and consequently in Athens's unique position within the Greek world.[54] Coinage became widely used in Sicily by the
mid-6th century BCE as well.[55]

Hoards of precious metal ingots and jewelry, including bags of metal
pieces of uniform weight, found in Cilicia, northern Mesopotamia, southern Syria, and elsewhere, raise questions about the "invention" of coinage in
Lydia in the 7th century BCE.[56] It was also invented independently in one,
or perhaps two, other places in world history, in China and in India, at
roughly the same time.[57] Reasons for this invention, and that is what it was,
a technical innovation, lay in exchange patterns between the Near East,
Egypt, and the Greek world, and the long tradition in the Near East of
weighed silver that may have necessitated the invention of a comparable institution in the Greek world.[58]

As we have seen elsewhere, cross-cultural exchange was an important
driver in innovation and diffusion. Weighed bullion was also a feature of the
archaic (and after) Greek economy.[59] The origins of coinage can be traced
much deeper into the past however, back to the Ancient Near East and
Egypt. The large-scale commercialization is well documented in temple
economies especially in agricultural production, and in small-scale trade.
Weighed fractional units of metal, so-called hacksilber, "cut" metal, and
standardized weighed silver is known in New Kingdom Egypt.[60] But actual
coinage in the Mediterranean, and in India and China as well, began to play

a more important role in state economies in the 4th century BCE. In the Achaemenid Empire there were no coins before the 4th century, but the first stamped silver under Darius I, the *sigloi*, functioned as a coin.[61] The first coins to appear in Egypt, tellingly, were the Athenian tetradrachms, known from the end of the 5th century BCE but very likely circulating earlier.[62]

Work on the ancient Near Eastern monetary system in recent years has produced arguments against the singular "invention" of Greek coinage.[63] Vargyas, for example, suggests that the monetized market economy of Babylonia in the 6th century BCE was developing at the same time as coinage was making an impact on the Greek world. Indeed "preweighed" silver placed in stamped bags, attested already in the early second millennium BCE, and the use of inscribed standardized weights were important parts in the development of coined money.[64] The debate about whether this is money or not boils down to how this is related to "general acceptability" and the extent of market transactions. The first Athenian coins appear at the same time, in the middle of the 6th century BCE, to aid in long-distance exchange according to Aristotle.[65] Coinage was also widely used in the Greek West (Italy and Sicily) by the mid-6th century BCE.[66]

It is no accident, as Jonathan Hall has observed, that this is the period of expansion of Greek trade through Naukratis in Egypt, and that the first use of coinage in the Greek world was the city of Aegina, an active player in this Egyptian port.[67] The circulation of silver is still problematic, but it was clearly an early form of money in the Greek world.

Athens prospered because of its local silver sources. Before then, weighed silver was used. A turning point came in 5th century Athens. The Greek polis played the key role in turning tokens into symbols of sovereignty. Money in 5th century Athens, and more so in the 4th century, became "flexible" and was used to make payments in many areas of public life, in naval finance, in jury payment, in public building, and in private economics transactions in rents, loans, land leasing, and dowries.[68] John Davies's study of "Athenian fiscal expertise," emphasized the mode of payments to and from the state. Such expertise was transferred to places like Egypt in the fourth century BCE. Among other things, coins allow numeracy, counting, and the calculation of transaction costs, which are embedded in the idea of coinage itself. State use of coinage served to pay for military, and public goods like city and harbor building, and as a marker of sovereignty.[69]

The role of lending and of banking before the Hellenistic period is still "contentious."[70] Stored bullion in temples, and in hoards, as in the Near East, constrained money supply. Coinage was especially important for Hellenistic and the Roman economies. Coinage facilitated trade, and the widespread usage of a general currency was recognized as an important element of political power.[71] The use of coined money expanded during the Hellenistic period, along with banking institutions.[72] The Ptolemies established banks in Egypt in the 3d century BCE, and there they had an important impact, particularly with respect to monetizing taxes.[73] In the Near East and to some extent in Egypt even after the introduction of coinage in the state fiscal system, coins were often still weighed as bullion rather than counted as individual units of money. In the end, coinage "never progressed beyond M1 (the amount of coin in circulation at any one time)."[74] Silver supply was a major constraint.

It is generally believed that the rise of credit-money in 15th century Europe is a distinguishing characteristic between the modern capitalist system and premodern, precapitalist economies.[75] In fact, though, credit-money, in the form of "recoverable debt," was "strategically important" in the Roman world. As Michael Hudson has stressed, the history of interest-bearing debt instruments as "general purpose money" extended deep into the Near Eastern past, and credit instruments in the form of mortgages and leases with prepaid rent lent in advance of the harvest well known in the Egyptian papyri are suggestive of a longer history of both debt and credit.[76]

LAW AND LEGAL INSTITUTIONS

Legal regimes and the laws that are generated by them shape, constrain, and move societies in various ways. The first millennium BCE was a period of massive changes in legal systems throughout the eastern Mediterranean. These changes paralleled political and economic developments and can be seen on two levels: (1) state equilibrium between elites and the rest of society that came in the form of public codification and (2) on the local level an increase in private order contracting. For the latter, there was a wide range of transactions, from state labor contracts and long-distance trade, to private agreements for sale, lease, and the like. A large number of documents from the ancient Near East and Egypt are legal in nature, involving contracts, disputes, petitions, and so on, and many of these are concerned with property rights and with the regulation of debt. We may see the evolution of law in the first millennium BCE as tied to the increased complexity in Iron Age economies and in trade and exchange in particular.

Law and legal regimes have rarely been brought into direct dialogue with respect to premodern economies, although they were intimately bound together, and it is an arguable strength of New Institutional Economics that law and economic performance can be linked.[77] The presumption seems to be that premodern states were too weak to enforce legal rules, but by the end of the period of this book's coverage, states had developed much stronger institutions, including registration of agreements, that improved enforcement. Whatever else Maine's work has done for the subsequent development of legal history, it established that the "evolutionary" (he used "progressive") relationship between law and society was intimate and important. His most famous statement, that "the movement of the progressive societies has hitherto been a movement *from Status to Contract*," established that connection, and it has been a fundamental part of the historical social sciences ever since.[78]

There was considerable evolution of legal institutions in the first millennium BCE. The major eastern Mediterranean traditions became more systematized, specialized, and logical.[79] In the Near Eastern and Egyptian traditions, legal "professionals," and scribes who drew up legal instruments, played a central role in this evolution. Writing per se did not drive the change. Rather the increased use of written legal instruments, observable in many places, and innovation in contract types, or at least the introduction of new clauses, was driven by underlying social changes, demographic expansion, and increased trade.[80]

Law played a key role in the development of the increasingly complex economies of the ancient world by regulating the distribution of wealth.[81] Writing in the 4th century BCE, Aristotle, in his *Nichomachean Ethics*, argued that money was bound to a community. Money or coinage, *nomisma*, deriving from the word for law, *nomos*, shows the nexus between authority, community, and social exchange. It worked on two levels: first, the state's relation to elites, in the form of public law codes that legitimized a social hierarchy; and secondly, on a local level, the connection between the state and private legal ordering. The role of private contract ordering in "mitigating conflict" would seem to be important and evolved with the increase in the use of written agreements in our period, but there is little way to confidently quantify it.[82]

Indeed the two-way coupling between the state, and economic and legal institutions is clear from the promulgation of the earliest law codes in the ancient Near East.[83] But informal legal norms and the "private ordering" of social relations were arguably more important for the bulk of premodern populations.[84] Social convention, unwritten contracts, informal arbitration in villages, all these of course are not well documented for the ancient world, but we should remember these "alternative institutions" as Dixit calls them, when we discuss the formal, written legal material.[85] *Personal*, rather than *impersonal*, exchange was the norm everywhere in the first millennium BCE (and before), and most transactions were private, small scale, local, and either undocumented or not preserved in private archives because the transactions were ephemeral, as I discussed previously in the case of animals sales in

Egypt. In the ancient Near East, too, there was no need for written documentation of sales of food or small manufactured goods.[86]

Weber, who had a thorough understanding of Roman law, paid a great deal of attention to the role of law in economies, with special concern of course for the rise of capitalism, a feature we have seen in most scholars who wrote about ancient economies in the 19th and early 20th centuries.[87] The Weberian view of law can be viewed now in terms of the "great divergence" or in terms of North and colleagues' distinction between "open access" and "natural states."[88] Law is used to bolster the view that it was uniquely the western legal tradition, beginning with mature Roman law (ca. 1st century BCE), that led to the rise of capitalism. Weber connected types of domination to legal systems. The path to capitalism had three essential requirements: (1) "advanced commercial contracts" that allowed "new economic relations" to be created,[89] (2) the legal concept of the modern corporation, and (3) a calculable legal order. Law must be predictable and administered by legal experts. Recently "non-Western" legal systems have been brought into the discussion of a more global and longer-term perspective on legal history and the heterogeneity of legal institutions across time and space, and this affords ancient historians an opportunity to engage in debates about both local legal cultures and the impact of colonial or quasicolonial transplantation of new regimes on ancient traditions. The interaction or coevolution of state politics and underlying cultural norms and beliefs certainly shaped legal institutions.[90]

But Weber also cared a great deal about historical developments.[91] He saw four stages in the historical development of law: (1) legal revelation through law prophets, (2) empirical creation and finding of law by legal honoratiores, (3) imposition of law by secular and theocratic power, and finally (4) modern law, elaborated by law and professionalized administration of justice by people who have been formally trained.[92] Thus while he examined a wide range of ancient legal systems, including some aspects of Mesopotamian law, because his main interest was the role of law in the evolution of modern capitalism, his attention was drawn to Roman and Jewish law. Roman law stood as the most important development, laying "the foundation for legal formalism in the West."[93]

Despite Weber's narrow concerns, at least from a premodern legal systems perspective, we cannot avoid studying ancient law in tandem with economies. An important trend to examine non-Western legal systems, going beyond the common/civil law dichotomy, is a heartening development in scholarship, and I would signal here that this should encourage a wider view of premodern legal systems.[94] The administration of law is an important part of the larger subject of studying the complex interaction between states and local actors in the organization and administration of law, and in the adjudication of private disputes. Yet, "the proper economic analysis of ancient institutions, especially the law, is still in its infancy."[95] How can we contextualize law in premodern Mediterranean societies before Roman law?

Premodern legal systems are, with the exception of mature Roman law as it was developed under the empire, generally treated as a separate sphere from economic evidence.[96] One of the major problems, which cannot be treated here, is to understand the relationship between Roman and pre-Roman legal systems. How much did Roman law absorb from the diverse legal practices it found in the eastern Mediterranean that had developed over many centuries? And how much did Roman law change local traditions?

Economic and legal rules have been understood as vitally linked since at least Aristotle in the middle of the 4th century BCE. Economic and legal institutions coevolved and were often so intertwined as to be impossible to distinguish. Legal institutions determined the distribution of wealth via property rights and the organization of economic activity.[97] It is no accident that legal and economic documents survive in large numbers in Mediterranean societies. The Greek and demotic Egyptian papyri offer the best and densest corpus of legal material of law on the ground as it were, and they document the manner in which people "negotiated daily life."[98] But there are rich sources elsewhere too.

PUBLIC LAW: CODIFICATION

Both Egyptian and ancient Near Eastern civilization had a long history of codified law, primarily instantiated by its famous law codes.[99] We should not get hung up with "code" as a comprehensive statement of legal rules for which the Code Napoléon is the model.[100] Egypt, for example, did not produce publicly promulgated inscriptions such as the Hammurabi code, as far as we know, but it did have an ancient tradition of codified, written collection of legal rules. The Near Eastern codes were particular to "Mesopotamian science."[101] All the more striking, then, is the appearance of legal codes in the middle of the first millennium BCE throughout the eastern Mediterranean. These codes, from very different places and times, show some structural similarities, namely the desire for order as existed in social hierarchies, for "cosmological order" as expressed in religious sacrifice, and in markets as expressed in the regulation of body mutilation and monetary penalties.[102] There appears to be a strong connection between states of various types and the encoding of legal rules. State order and legitimacy, at least the appearance of these, and sovereignty were important features of all premodern public law.

"Written public law" emerged, or reemerged, in the late 8th/early 7th century BCE. From the 7th to the 4th century BCE there was a diffusion of

law codes across the eastern Mediterranean world.[103] The law collection of
Hermopolis from Egypt, surviving in a 3d century BCE text, is among the
earliest. Fragments of laws survive from Dreros in 7th century BCE inscribed on the temple of Apollo Delphinios, at Tiryns in the Argolid, in the
city's marketplace (*agora*), at Rome, at Gortyn and elsewhere in Crete, in
Solon's published political and legal reforms at Athens in the early 6th century BCE (known as *axiones*), and in the Twelve Tables of Rome. The Gortyn
code is actually a series of enactments over two centuries from the 6th to the
4th centuries BCE. An emphasis on written publicly legible laws, associated
with the social and political changes throughout the eastern Mediterranean
during the "axial age" is discussed above. Written, public law went hand in
glove with the massive social and economic transformation in the middle of
the first millennium BCE under the pressure of increased urbanization.[104]
Regulating what the state would enforce within dominant political coali-
tions may have been the main purpose of such texts.[105]

In the Near East, a similar process occurred at the same time. From the 7th
century BCE, an "authoritative" function of law has been collected in Judah
and Samaria, that is, outside of imperial territory. Egypt has not produced
similar public law collections, but the law was reformed during the Saite reconsolidation in the 7th century BCE. There were other major modifications
in writing systems. Among the most important was the rise of demotic Egyptian, a cursive script and a stage of the Egyptian language that spread from the
delta throughout Egypt during the 6th and 5th centuries BCE. Texts rarely
provide evidence of institutional change, but in the case of demotic, we can
see, within a single household, the shift in script happening. A father wrote the
old hieraticform of Egyptian, his son adopted the new demotic script.[106] When
the Ptolemies reordered the Egyptian state toward their own ends, Egyptian
law for Egyptian communities continued, and there are several examples of
collections of legal procedures and contract boilerplate templates that survive
from the period. Demotic brought with it a major change in contract language, and also an increase in private contracting over the course of the first
millennium BCE.[107] The Ptolemies never produced a systematic "code" of law,
or a single court system that covered the entire population despite the regime's
modern reputation as a highly centralized system.

PRIVATE LAW: CONTRACTS AND
TRANSACTION COSTS

From the perspective of New Institutional Economics, the protection of private property rights and the enforcement of private contractual agreements
are the foundation for real economic growth.[108] To be sure, written private

agreements were well known in Egypt, the Near East, and the Greek world. The connection between private order contracting, state enforcement of these agreements, and economic growth is difficult to estimate in all cases. Increasingly, however, if we are tempted to generalize, private order contracting was effectively better organized and enforced. All attempts to reduce transaction costs in the premodern world were, in the main, unintentional, although some may have been effective, and the wider use of coinage may have been instrumental in transaction costs calculation.[109]

Transaction cost is a difficult issue, and the concept has generated two main approaches to the use of the concept and how it matters. One approach focuses on the role of the state, the role of agents, the functioning of markets and the cost of information. The other approach examines the costs of coming to a bargain, the cost of executing the bargain, and the costs of enforcing the bargain. Did ancient states foster legal rules that would create overall benefits to the society, or did they create rules that benefited only elites? Did law facilitate trade proper only with the mature Roman legal system?[110] This is not easy to determine in the case of Near Eastern legal traditions. To be sure, sale transactions were taxed. In Egypt, the traditional sale or transfer tax was reckoned at 10 percent. The Ptolemies continued to tax transactions, usually at 10 ten percent of the sale price, but also collected a tax to convert payments in bronze coinage to a silver equivalent.[111] The transactions were registered, which served to secure title to property.

The introduction of the public auction into Egypt, apparently a 4th century Greek institution, shows that the Ptolemies promoted greater access, at least in theory, to market transactions. But the institution was limited in its application as far as the evidence permits us to know. It did not appear, for example, to create a broad market in real estate. As in Greece, the auction was used to sell off land that had been confiscated by the state and not as a general mechanism for land sale, and it was also used to reward contracts in state-controlled industries. The rules for such public auctions were clearly written out and publicly posted before the event.[112]

Written contracts are well documented in Egypt and in the Near East, and they are the single most important source for understanding nonstate or private economic activity.[113] They show basic similarity in structure: an oral agreement before witnesses. Sales in both traditions, at their core, stated two things: reception of a satisfactory price, and a promise by the seller to guarantee title against future claims. Those that were written were "fully executed with only contingent obligations outstanding."[114] Of course we have no way of knowing how many purely oral agreements were transacted. The main contract types were: sale, hire, deposit, loan, pledge, suretyship, and partnership. Privately drawn-up agreements were very common in the

Egyptian papyri (*cheirographa*, or "handwritten agreements"), but, by the 2d century BCE, the state increasingly guaranteed agreements through registration and the use of notary scribes.[115] Greeks coming into Ptolemaic Egypt brought with them the "six-witness" or "double document contract."[116] This was a particular form of contract guaranteed by a private third party who held a copy of the written agreement. Gradually the Ptolemaic state encapsulated and guaranteed private contracts through registration offices.[117]

Fourth-century demotic Egyptian contracts, for example, compared to earlier written contracts, have much more detailed and specific boilerplate clauses. It is tempting to understand this change through the lens of evolutionary forces that were driven by an increase in the number of impersonal transactions. In the Ptolemaic period, ca. 200 BCE, the ancient form of contract that involved witnesses copying out the written agreement verbatim died out.[118] Greek notary scribes, documented in only a few areas, functioned as actual state notaries, negating the use of witnesses, and further streamlining some forms of contract.

As in Egypt, the importance of written contract grew from the second half of the 8th century BCE.[119] Babylonian law had two types of credit instrument: the promissory note and the partnership agreement.[120] The former, acknowledging debt, was very common. Partnership agreements were of two types, the "commenda" (*kharranu* contract) between an investor and an agent, and a "bilateral" partnership contract that allowed pooling of resources between partners. The latter was restricted generally to two or three persons, in order to establish a small business. This contract type was apparently widely used in the period.[121] Jursa is justifiably cautious about the impact of contracts on market integration and on growth. Sale tax on slave sales was collected; sales were registered in Achaemenid period, and probably for land sales as well.[122]

Changes in Neo-Babylonian contracts include improvements on the *kharranu* partnership contract in which "an investor, the capitalist, actively participates in the running of the company."[123] Neo-Babylonian scribes, as their Ptolemaic Egyptian counterparts, improved on old forms in adjusting to the needs of private parties. Demographic and urban expansion, increased specialization, and the increase in the use of silver, and later coins, and in market transactions drove changes in contract forms. In both Egypt and the Near East, there was far more "private initiative" than before.[124]

In Greece, each city-state had its own laws, but "the basic principles were essentially the same."[125] It is Athenian law that is by far the best documented of these.[126] Aristotle's *Politics* contextualizes law in Greek city-state society. Property was connected to "civic community" and tied to citizenship, with certain restrictions on the types of land one could own.[127] Contracts for sale, of which there were a variety of types, for example, sale in advance of delivery, are known from the early 5th century BCE; forward selling (of wine), to ensure the quality of the harvest, was secured.[128] Cadastral surveys of land and registration of contracts promoted private property rights.[129] Magistrates (*agoranomoi*) controlled law regulating activity in the marketplace and protected against fraud. Regulations were formalized in "market law" (*nomos agoranomikos*) documented at Athens and Rhodes, but these rules were broadly applied throughout the Greek world. Cities controlled market exchange, collecting a fee from merchants for the right to sell in the market and a sales tax for transactions. The *agora* reduced transaction costs by lowering the cost of information, guaranteeing quality and weights, and regulating "fair" prices. Costs of trials at Athens were low.[130] Auctions were used to optimize sale prices of confiscated property and to lease mines and other state property. "Leagues" (*koina*) became very popular in the Hellenistic period in mainland Greece and, among other things, coordinated legal rules and law courts between cities and issued coin in common.

The role of the state is well documented in first millennium BCE Egypt. Marketplaces were generally located in or near temple precincts. Temples were also the location of scribes who would draw up private written agreements. Egyptian contracting was conceived of as oral agreements established (not mandatory) in writing ex post. During the first millennium BCE, there was a shift. Although contracts were still conceived of as oral agreements, stressed by the verb "to say" ("Party A has said to Party B the following..."), the spread of the demotic Egyptian script from a local tradition to statewide during the 7th–6th centuries BCE in Egypt is a good illustration of the imposition of a writing system to increase institutional uniformity throughout the state. The demotic script itself, a very cursive form of hieroglyphic writing, apparently developed in the hothouse of Mediterranean exchange that was the Egyptian delta in the early first millennium BCE. It was the perfect Egyptian adaptation to economic change at least in part caused by the intensification of trade in the early Iron Age eastern Mediterranean.

There were other reforms seen not only in Egypt but also across the Mediterranean in the 4th and 3d centuries BCE. Special courts were created at Athens in the 4th century BCE to adjudicate disputes between foreign merchants. These courts were established as one means to attract trading into the Athenian port, very much an advantage when combined with the universal acceptance of Athenian coinage as Xenophon reminded Athenians.[131] New legal categories were created, the *dikai emporikai*, "commercial cases," to "avoid costly delays in dispute resolution and to place foreign traders on an equal footing with native Athenians in resolving contract disputes."[132] At Rome, the creation of the consensual sale contract (*emptio-venditio*) by around 200 BCE is noteworthy, as is the creation of several laws supportive of trade, including the *actiones adiecticiae qualitatis.*

PROPERTY RIGHTS

The role of property rights in economic performance, or growth, is another central tenant of NIE analysis. The conception of private property is one of the oldest human institutions, coevolving with the emergence of agriculture during the late Pleistocene.[133] Rights to property evolved in complex ways from the beginning of civilization through the formal Roman codes, and the great contrast seen between property rights regimes in the river valleys of Mesopotamia and Egypt is related to the important contrasts in environment that I highlighted in chapter 5. Conceptions of what constituted private ownership of property may not have differed that much between classical Greece and Ptolemaic Egypt, for example, but social relationships around property rights did.[134]

Local irrigation and production of crops in irrigation basins required a good deal of cooperation to maintain the irrigation canals, to manage the timing of water let onto fields, drainage, sowing, and so on.[135] Here is a great contrast to places like ancient Attica in Greece where individual family farms in dry farming were the norm.[136] As Eyre rightly stresses, such individual family farms were impossible in the Egyptian environment. It is the solidarity of the irrigation basin, of the village that was the key to agriculture in Egypt. Such a system is documented also in other places.[137] Family groups managed land portfolios, held individually in inherited "shares" that were dispersed geographically to reduce risk. Decisions regarding planting and working the land is made each year depending on local water and soil conditions. It was a flexible response to a chaotic environment but one that could produce impressive returns per unit of labor.[138]

Park's model is generally a good one for ancient Egypt. Gradually, temples and the king asserted managerial control over a good amount of land in periods of centralized control. Such control over flood basin land was very often managed by temple estates, large tracts of land that were nominally controlled by the temple domain but held privately, leased out, or worked by temple dependents in a complex local agricultural system. The system of property was complex. Individualized private property in the basins did not exist because it was not practicable in such a system. Rather, later legal documents describe a system of a "spectrum of rights" in land that was often held in families but could be privately leased or sold. The Egyptian system, rather like that discussed by Park, was also one consisting of an interested hierarchy of interests, rights, and obligations that connected the king and the temples (collecting taxes and rents) to local family/status groups responding to the flood.[139]

The common holding of property, essentially conveyable usufruct rights, rather than individualized private property, among kinship/status groups, as Park suggests for the Senegal basin, was not a matter of the cost of enclosure but, rather, owing to the fact that a hierarchical social system in a chaotic environment made annual reallocation of resources an efficient solution. Such a system would have been reinforced by the necessity of group cooperation in maintaining the irrigation canals, the timing of water into the basins, and so on.

In certain parts of Egypt with a higher density population, stronger private property rights, which are documented for Upper Egypt between Thebes and Aswan for example, may have prevailed.[140] The bridge to the central state was the local temple, at least in many areas that coordinated land tenure in its region, and in which the king played a ritual role of chief priest in the local cult.[141] Temples (I speak here about the major state temples as opposed to local shrines and smaller temples) held portfolios of land distributed throughout a large area and served as administrative and management (including the management of risk) centers. They were not, *stricto sensu,* "absentee landlords."[142] Temples provided employment and were the location of local festivals, the center of cult, symbolically the guarantor of stability and the social order, and conduit through which the king ruled. The hierarchical social system that evolved around flood recession agriculture and common property holdings, thus, would have created a major barrier to the formation of Athenian-style democracy. But the important point is that the Egyptian system of governance created an equilibrium often lasting many centuries.

With respect to property rights, there was a long tradition of contractual agreements in the ancient Near East and Egypt; a great percentage of private texts from both places were in fact concerned with this. Private sale, lease, and partnership agreements are an ancient form in the Near East, which have been compared to medieval *commmenda,* a type of contract, critical in medieval European economic growth, whose origins can be found in Old Assyrian trade agreements.[143] In one region in southern Egypt in the Ptolemaic period, it has been estimated that 72 percent of the agricultural land was in private hands, a situation that may have been a typical pattern for the river valley.[144]

Property rights in the Greek world were developed during the archaic period in city-states; property rights were restricted, in the sale of slaves and of land.[145] Greek city-states in the classical period had a well-developed conception of private property rights, although these rights varied per city. The registration and publicizing of sales of land were well developed.[146]

The increased rate of private exchange in the first millennium BCE drove an increased use of contract to buy and sell higher-value goods like land, houses, and animals. The early Ptolemaic legal manuals, which, based on some of the internal references, probably date back to earlier in the millennium, show us that private contracting was a normative part of the private law in first-millennium BCE Egypt.[147] Ptolemaic law was a new legal order established in Egypt over the course of the early 3d century BCE, from which emerged the development of parallel courts and a bureaucracy designed to administer disputes. It is generally assumed that Ptolemaic state building did not substantially change the underlying Egyptian legal system, but merely extended it by accommodating Greek language agreements and Greek courts.[148] But Alexander's conquest of Egypt and the subsequent formation of a new sovereign state and a bureaucracy based in Greek language did in fact shape Egyptian law and the organization of justice in new ways at the same time as the underlying local institutional structures and the use of demotic Egyptian continued. These changes are especially apparent in the relationship between the bureaucracy and the courts, but property registers may have been another institution carried over from, probably, Athenian experience.[149] Historic comparisons on the effects of invasion and institutional change, *mutatis mutandis*, could be offered—the Norman conquest of England comes immediately to mind.

Trial records of family disputes over land ownership dating to the middle of the 2d century BCE provides rich details of the interaction of the state and local legal institutions.[150] Three aspects of one dispute, from Asyut in Middle Egypt, are important in understanding the relationship between the Ptolemaic bureaucracy and local law. First, the local dispute over control of family land, and the subsequent complaint brought by the wife of one of the parties to the dispute, was initiated as a petition written in Egyptian (and presumably at some stage translated into Greek) and addressed to Ptolemaic officials. Both the *epistates* and the *stratêgos* were involved. Eventually the dispute was turned over by these Greek officials to the local Egyptian court to find the facts and adjudicate the dispute. This local court had an official representative of the state, the *eisagogeus*, present. Finally, the proceedings of the trial and the decision of the judges were recorded in full.

That text is in fact a copy of the trial proceeding, as is stated in the first line.[151] That implies that more than one copy was written. It documents both parties' oral responses to their written pleadings to Ptolemaic officials and marked, in theory, the resolution of the family dispute. That dispute went back to a division of family property by a dying man to his two sons by different wives. The plaintiff was the wife of oldest son, and the defendant was the younger son. The fact that we have before us a complete record of a

trial proceeding and the decision of the judges with their legal reasoning behind their judgment is important enough.[152] I will not be able to resolve here
whether such bureaucratic reporting of trial is a new feature of the Ptolemaic
bureaucracy or a continuation from earlier times.

The trial, the second occasion when an attempt at a legal resolution was
made, took place at Asyut in Middle Egypt, before the priest-judges of the
temple of Wepwawet, the local *laokritai* court as it was called in the Ptolemaic administration, under whose authority the final resolution (in theory)
of the dispute fell. The parties to the suit were associated with the temple,
and the land in dispute was located within the temple estate. Despite the
written petitions to Ptolemaic officials to have the dispute resolved by them,
the case was turned over to the local temple to decide. The trial occurred in
June 170 BCE, some sixteen years after the Ptolemies put down the most serious revolt against their rule in Egypt, the revolt in the Thebaid, 205–186
BCE, and just months before the first invasion of Egypt by Antiochus IV.[153]
In the aftermath of the great Theban revolt, the Ptolemaic bureaucratic system appears to have gained an even tighter control of the region. It was a
period when many scholars have thought that the Ptolemaic state was in full
decline, economically, culturally, and otherwise. And there is much to show
that in terms of international politics this was the case. And yet this trial
implies something else about state institutions. The response of the Ptolemaic officials, the orderliness of the trial itself, the precise citation of the
controlling law, and the introduction of supporting documentation of ownership show a well-functioning bureaucratic system. The text also highlights
the complexities of the bilingual system and also demonstrates that the Ptolemies protected private claims to land.

The trial presumably took place in front of the main temple gate, the traditional location of trials in Egyptian law.[154] The court was composed of
three priests and an "introducer" (*eisagogeus*), a Ptolemaic official who introduced the case before the judges and acted as an official representative of the
state.[155] The two parties appear before them, the plaintiff beginning with her
main claim, that all the land belongs to her and through her to her children.
To support his claim, she cited a passage from what is termed the "law of
year 21" concerning the rights of children of a first marriage to inherit. She
also claimed that her husband was forced to cede 1/3 of the land. Tefhape,
the defendant, then responded, at length, denying the claims and producing
documents proving his claim. The plaintiff then responded, and there was a
second response by the defendant, Tefhape.

The pleadings were then read out by a scribe in front of the parties. The
judges asked each party if they agree to what they have said. Then documents
were produced that supported each party's claims. The judges summarized

the main legal points of each argument, and quoted the "law of year 21," the same law cited by the plaintiff. Importantly, however, the judges cited a fuller version of the law, observing that the children of a first marriage have priority to the father's property *unless they have agreed to assigning shares to other siblings.* And that was what happened in our case. Chratianch's husband had agreed to the cession of 1/3 of the land to his half-brother, and she had, we learn, also agreed.[156] The judges found for the defendant on this basis and affirmed their decision with their signatures at the end of the document, along with the signature of the scribe of the judges, perhaps the author of the document itself.

Among the more noteworthy aspects of the technical details revealed in the Asyut trial is the complexity of the Ptolemaic legal system. That complexity was caused by two main factors. First, the bureaucratic system operated in two languages, Greek and demotic. Greek, or at least officials with Greek names, dominated state administrative offices (e.g., the *epistates*, the *stratêgoi*), while Egyptians, and the Egyptian language, dominated local temple administration.

In the family dispute, petitions that are preserved were written in demotic. These must have been translated for the Ptolemaic officials, at least those who were based in Ptolemais. That was also the reason, presumably, that priests of Anhour were involved with Ptolemaic officials in Ptolemais, a fact we learn because the losing party carried her appeal to them. Secondly, the variety of legal sources cited to support the case of each party was extensive. "The law of year 21," an apparent royal decree concerning Egyptian inheritance law, the "sixth law," "the eighth tablet," and so on, are cited by both parties.[157] Such citation of various laws appears highly technical and would probably be knowledge outside of the bounds of everyday life. The case turns on the fact that the defendant could produce notarized and witnessed documents that proved that the older brother agreed to the division by their father of family property between both brothers. Standing in parallel to the written Egyptian legal tradition and the local tribunal were Ptolemaic officials from Asyut as well as Ptolemais.

It is all this complexity that I think provides us with one of the most interesting historical facts coming from this archive. The judges asked Chratianch, the plaintiff: "Is there a man who speaks for you?" A man appears, with a non-Egyptian name, to answer a few technical points on behalf of the plaintiff. He was not a guardian (or a *kurios* in the Greek sense) because he would have been identified as such. Rather he is simply called a man, but it is difficult not to conclude that he was in fact functioning as an advocate on behalf of the woman. On the unrelated petition on the verso, a certain Tuot son of Petihor was specifically mentioned as an advocate for the priests of Isis at Aswan.

In a famous section on legal "Honoratiores," Max Weber sought to explain the emergence of advocates (as distinct from lawyers) in medieval French and English law.[158] There, out of the need for precision in the spoken word in the courts, "judgment finders" would be appointed by the court upon the request for one of the parties to "speak for" them in the case. We know very little about such advocates in pharaonic Egyptian trials.[159] But the context of Ptolemaic law, with its bilingual bureaucracy, an ancient system of complex written documents, a new bureaucratic system based in Greek language, with interconnected local, regional, and statewide levels, produced new institutional complexities.[160] Like Chinese law, Egyptian law never escaped bureaucratic control and thus "remained as an instrument of political and social control by the emperor or the imperial power hierarchy."[161] In both the Chinese and Egyptian cases, negative feedback loops between political economy, patrimonial bureaucracy, and economic institutions probably led to suboptimal economic outcomes. The overlapping property claims in land between institutions and individuals in both cases, in contrast to classical economies, affected market alienability of land and may have had important impacts on economic performance. That topic, performance or growth in premodern economies, has received an enormous amount of attention and is the subject of much current debate. That is the topic I discuss in the following chapter.

CHAPTER 8

Growth, Innovation, Markets, and Trade

Far from being peripheral events in the lives of ordinary people, markets
are much more likely to have been the same opportunities for excitement,
variety, and indulgence, that they were in Medieval and later times.

Market places were spaces for all kinds of business transactions, and a
reminder that exchanges (verbal and material) were not simply functional
exercises, but took place within a specific social and cultural setting.

—ARCHIBALD (2005:16)

King Solomon gave twenty towns in Galilee to Hiram king of Tyre, because
Hiram had supplied him with all the cedar and juniper and gold he wanted.

—I KINGS 9:11

I RAISE SEVERAL COMPLEX and interrelated issues in this chapter.[1] All
four have been fiercely debated for more than a century. They lay at the
heart of the nature of premodern economies. The final story on each of these
issues is yet to be written, in large part because our sources, with respect to
growth in particular, are almost entirely archaeological and subject to a wide
latitude of interpretation. Along with understanding shifts in trade and in
traded goods, we have, thus, to construct, site by site, what was produced,
what was traded, how items moved, and how the human condition changed
over time.

Trade is another topic of great concern and with a rich literature already.
The so-called orientalizing phase of Greek material cultural history (8th–
6th centuries BCE) is a cipher for the extensive contact between early Greek
civilization and the eastern Mediterranean basin.[2] Understanding markets
and transactions in markets is enormously complex. The existence of markets in the first millennium is beyond debate. More important work remains
in understanding how markets interacted with other modes of exchange,
and how institutions shaped and were shaped by markets and by demand.

GROWTH AND CONSTRAINTS ON GROWTH

The study of growth, or "economic performance," especially concerning
the classical world, has been a hot topic among ancient historians in recent

years.[3] But it is not a straightforward one. Conison provides a cautious context for studying growth:

> Economic growth occurs when there is a change in an economy's per capita output and income. At first glance, growth would seem to be well suited to historical analysis because it involves dynamic processes instead of statics. In practice, growth is surprisingly difficult to study, partly because data are generally lacking and partly because economists dispute the causes of economic growth.[4]

As we saw earlier (figure 4) Clark's graph suggested that the Malthusian trap kept the entire premodern world, everywhere at all times, from achieving real per capita growth. But the Mediterranean evidence suggests otherwise. There were in fact several sustained periods of growth in the Greek world, in the Roman Empire, and indeed, probably, although the empirical evidence is difficult, in Babylonia and in Egypt. But the basic living conditions we have already discussed, rising urban populations, protection of property rights, circulation of coinage, an increase in the number of better-functioning markets, and market transactions all suggest the possibility of positive prosperity cycles.[5]

While real economic growth is a central concern of modern government policies worldwide, it was neither a "policy" nor a "concern" of any premodern state. The concept of growing an economy, of making everyone in the society better off, was entirely absent in the premodern Mediterranean world. And all premodern economies were "organic"; humans, animals, wood, and water were the main energy sources, and tied to the annual agricultural cycle. Yet understanding growth in premodern economies has been a major activity recently.[6] At the moment, the classical Greek and Roman economies have received most of the attention. One recent estimate for growth in classical Greece suggests 0.15 percent and for the Roman Empire in the first two centuries CE, 0.1 percent per annum.[7] The best estimate at the moment for the Roman GDP per capita is that it amounted to roughly half of that achieved by early modern Europe.[8] This gives you a sense of scale and of the very real limits of growth in premodern, or "organic" economies. But much remains debated because of the problematic archaeological evidence and, for the Roman case, assumptions about slow technological improvement and a lack of human capital investment.

While considering growth, the types of growth, and the explanations for growth is an important aspect of understanding ancient economies, debates among modern theorists about the factors that lead to higher productivity and greater living standards also make conclusions about ancient growth tentative at best. Although the subject of growth has been declared an "intractable" one by some, for others attempting to measure growth has been pursued energetically.[9] Real per capita growth has been used as the major distinguishing factor between Europe after the Industrial Revolution and the rest of the world and all prior world history. The famous hockey stick after 1800 (figure 4) might suggest that the very low growth rates of the premodern world leave nothing to examine. Despite that fact, however, the topic has been popular in recent work on ancient economies, mainly with respect to Athens and the Roman imperial economy.[10] Because premodern growth was the result of particular social structure, geographical location, and environmental constraints, fiscal institutions, and so on. Much more quantitative studies and comparative studies of real wages, house sizes, and other proxy measures of real growth, have appeared, and these studies have provided much to think about.[11]

The importance of studying premodern growth is that it allows us to contextualize the long-run history of growth and contraction, under what sociocultural conditions these occurred, and what the differential impacts were of geography and environmental conditions. Many have viewed developments in the premodern world as an essential, "cumulative" part of understanding world economic growth in the last five hundred years.[12] John Brooke has recently and quite usefully summarized the debate about premodern growth, importantly bringing in climate change as a factor.[13] Schumpeterian-like exogenous shocks caused by climate change, as we saw in the case of the Nile River and the Ptolemies, could be a serious constraint.[14] We should not confuse "cumulative" with linear or sustained; rather, cyclical expansion/contraction with various periods of stability should be the basis of any long-term model, and real growth after 1500 CE was of a different kind.[15]

The causes or determinants of growth, or economic performance, are numerous, and economic historians weigh these in different ways.[16] Adam Smith emphasized trade; an increase in market access led to an increase in production. The Solow-Swan neoclassical model of growth, a core concept in economics, underscores the role of technical change in driving increases in per capita output. Connected to technological improvement is human capital (education), allowing sustained growth in productivity per worker. Technical change was real throughout the premodern Mediterranean, but for the most part it was small improvements rather than "major leaps" in technical know-how. Positive demographic change is correlated to the rate of technological change.[17] Other important factors include state fiscal systems that increased productivity, demographic growth, imperial expansion, and the trade-stimulating role of cities and towns and their growth during the first millennium BCE.[18]

Jack Goldstone has sought to develop new vocabulary to periodize growth and decline with the words "efflorescence" and "crisis." Understood as pulses or efflorescences, Bronze Age expansions exhibit "smithian" type growth according to Goldstone.[19] Turchin and Nefedov adopt this and analyze "secular cycles" of demographic and territorial expansion and decline driven by intraelite competition.[20]

New Institutional Economics places stabilizing or equilibrium-creating institutions at the center of a historical understanding long-term economic growth. Institutions shape conditions for growth. Law and protection of property rights are the "determinants of performance." But climate change and disease were also important forces for performance in the premodern world. Here the so-called climatic period known as the "Classical Optimum," between 400 BCE and 200 CE, may have been a global force for population growth. Notably, populations in the Mediterranean, India, China, and Europe grew 75 percent between 400 BCE and 200 CE.[21]

MEASURING GROWTH

There are two basic types of economic growth: intensive and extensive growth. Extensive, or aggregate, growth is measured by the increased output caused by a growing population, a more typical kind of growth in world history than the second kind.[22] Intensive growth is measured by the increase in per capita output and rising per capita incomes. It is this latter kind of growth that, in many economists' views, characterizes modern growth in the Western world.[23] E. L. Jones highlighted the conditions for an "optimality band" for "ancient" or premodern economic growth that combined freed-up factor markets and a "goldilocks" state, not too grasping or predatory, but not too weak so as to be able to protect property rights.

It remains the case, especially with crude guestimates of population, that "direct observations of economic growth have been more difficult to generate."[24] There have been two types of evidence used to quantify growth. The first, archaeological, has generated several proxy data sets, including shipwrecks, house sizes, meat consumption, human stature measured by osteological remains, coin production, levels of urbanization, and energy consumption.[25] The second kind of evidence has come from data derived from polar ice cores and lake sediments, that uses lead isotope analysis as a proxy for the industrial output of silver use.[26] Indirect observations are more common, as in the case for 6th century BCE Babylonia where an agglomeration of information exists around empire building, population and urban growth, labor specialization, and the intensification in agriculture especially in cash crops like dates from increased urban demand and an expansion in factor markets.[27]

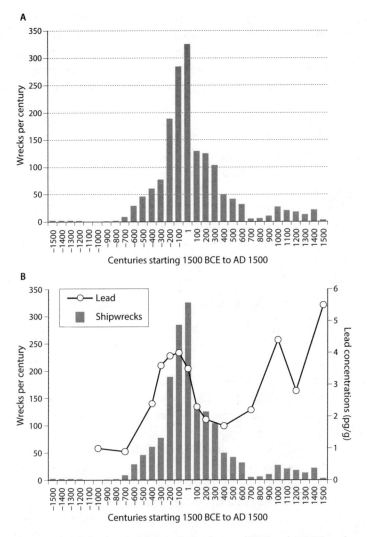

FIGURE 41. Updated shipwreck data by century (n = 1,646). From A. Wilson (2011:36). See also A. Wilson (2014). Lead isotope data taken from A. Wilson (2002:26). There is now new, high-resolution data from Greenland ice cores on lead isotope concentrations.

A. J. Parker's pioneering work on shipwrecks (n = 1,189) in the Mediter-ranean as a proxy measure of growth and decline in long-distance Mediterra-nean trade is one of the most widely reproduced datasets for Western an-tiquity (figure 41). It has been, and continues to be, updated and discussed.[28] The key problem with the data is that the wrecks can rarely be dated specifi-cally, and there is bias in archaeological selection. Among these are that found shipwrecks tend to be biased toward amphorae (as opposed to barrel containers common in medieval shipments) and marble cargo because of the nature of identifying these mounds on the ocean floor. Grain ships and "ships carrying perishable cargoes," because such cargoes do not protect the hull after sinking, have been vastly underestimated.[29] What's more, the known shipwrecks are biased to regions, the southern French coast for example, where it is simply easier to find wrecks. The North African coast (leaving aside the virtual blank that is the Indian Ocean), for example, has provided few wrecks, and the decline in the number of wrecks after the 2d century CE does not agree with the evidence of sea trade from "terrestrial sites."[30] Andrew Wilson's cautious remarks about shipwreck data, and other archaeological proxies used to chart growth, are important.

Growth in the Greek world has received a lot of attention in the last few years. In his new study of growth in the "Greek" world focused on population size and density, Ober argues that there was "dramatic" growth, seen in the increase in house sizes from the archaic to the classical period.[31] Ober suggests considerable expansion in a positive feedback loop after the Bronze Age collapse; egalitarian institutions, for male citizens, led to greater competition, which in turn led to innovation and drove down transaction costs, which in turn led to greater prosperity.[32] Democratic institutions encouraged demand and constant improvements in mass living standards. Dramatic demographic growth and high levels of urbanization encouraged specialization of labor and trade. He concludes that economic growth in Greece was comparable to a "modern pattern of a relatively egalitarian society with a broad middle class with a standard of living well above subsistence."[33]

The democratic transformation in Athens, its profound urban and egalitarian revolution between the 7th and 4th centuries BCE, is shown by marked increase in urbanization, improved diets, fostered by the use of fish farms, and large private houses.[34] By 700 BCE the largest cities reached ten thousand; by the 430s BCE the city of Athens had reached a peak size of forty thousand; and Syracuse in Sicily, another imperial center, also reached forty thousand in the 5th century.[35] Largely based on limited archaeological data, it has been generally concluded that the Athenian economy had a more even distribution of wealth than in other parts of mid-first-millennium BCE Mediterranean.[36] It was transformed "from the 'archaic' pattern of a poor population living near subsistence and dominated by a small elite, to a 'modern' pattern of a relatively egalitarian society with a broad middle class with a standard of living well above subsistence."[37]

These broad trends, with a slight downward turn in social equality, carried on into the Hellenistic period in many places, driven by larger volumes of trade. Recent work also suggests that it is not so much inequality per se but the visibility of wealth that had a social impact. Increasing the visibility of wealth may have decreased cooperation and wealth.[38] The diffusion of banks and the increased demand for credit in the Hellenistic period was accompanied by the innovation of entrepreneurial lenders.[39]

Just like much discussion about modern growth in the Western world, seeking real growth in the premodern world has been one of the main dividing lines between classical economies and those of the Near East and Egypt. The latter's "despotic" forms of governance, their bureaucracies, and the behavior of a small elite prevented growth. One of the problems that remains is that we simply do not have comparable archaeological evidence from the Near East or Egypt to be able to establish with certainty discrete periods of real growth.

But there was aggregate growth, and probably intensive growth as well, in many "nondemocratic" parts of the eastern Mediterranean in the first millennium BCE. This is clear in Egypt ca. 800–400 BCE, especially during the Saite period (650–525 BCE), coinciding with political recentralization of the state and a sharp increase in trading activity. Such growth has also been established for 6th century BCE Babylonia.[40] In the Greek world, between 800 and 300 BCE there has been estimated to have been a 50 percent increase in the standard of living as measured by the proxy of square footage of houses.[41] There remains considerable work to do in Egypt and the Near East in first-millennium BCE research to establish comparable archaeological data with which to compare growth elsewhere in the Mediterranean.[42] The rise of very large urban centers in the Hellenistic period are noted in Egypt (Alexandria, estimated to be as large as three hundred thousand by 200 BCE, and Ptolemais, eighty to one hundred thousand) and western Asia (Antioch, fifty thousand, Babylonia, maybe eighty thousand, Seleukia-on-the-Tigris, perhaps one hundred thousand). These functioned as the administrative centers of the centralized Ptolemaic and Seleukid empires.[43] Rome by 200 BCE, similarly the center of an expanding empire, reached a size of about two hundred thousand.[44]

Kron presents a very different picture of the economic performance of the Greek, primarily meaning Athens, and Roman worlds. Some now see a broader "middle class" in Greek and Roman society.[45] Wages were well above subsistence, and agricultural productivity was high.[46] Good diet-proxy evidence from skeletal remains has been used.[47] To be sure, there was growing inequality in the Hellenistic and Roman periods, and Greco-Roman incomes were probably unsurpassed in Europe until the 20th century. It seems clear that "many Athenians had some land and capital, running small businesses or farms rather than working for a wage, and skilled workers could earn much higher returns."[48] Houses were larger in Kron's sample, but admittedly it is a small sample.[49] He concludes that "the distribution of wealth at Athens is much more like that of a mid-20th century representative democracy and welfare state, with the American data from 1953–54 giving the closest fit to the Athenian distribution."

Kron is right to stress that the standard of living or well-being is a better measure of economic performance. But there remain barriers to using proxy evidence to measure these. Sample bias of osteological material, for example, and estimation of urban population in Italy are both problematic.[50] Likewise for the premodern Mediterranean, growth is best understood in comparison to other places and in relative terms. First-millennium expansion in Babylonia is well documented by an urban middle class, and by growth in population and in the number of settlements.[51] Economic activity in Hellenistic Babylonia is well documented by the Astronomical Diaries. The city was prosperous, and there was increased agricultural productivity, but these were certainly cyclical. Famine, war, and poor flooding often intervened.[52]

But there is not total agreement. The following quote from a recent overview is the clearest presentation of the case for, to phrase it in less euphemistic terms, long-term economic stagnation in the Near East:

> Several factors were decisive in letting economic growth remain at, or near, a level of zero per cent. Once basic technological breakthroughs in metallurgy, pottery and textile production, as well as in building and agricultural techniques and the organization of labour, had been achieved (fifth–fourth millennia BC), no further substantial developments that could have generated a significant quantitative productive output can be observed for the following periods of Mesopotamian history.[53]

Renger furthermore stressed the "limited" water supply that constrained irrigation potential along the Euphrates River and therefore limited the maximum area of land that could be cultivated. Limited energy sources (human and animal power) and natural resources were enough "to support the economic status quo" but were "not enough to sustain a measurable growth."

Many of the prosperity markers that Kron lists—social welfare investment, public infrastructure promoting health, and entertainment—may well have been present in Egypt and the Near East. Direct empirical data for real growth are difficult to come by. But there are many indirect indications of periods of prosperity. In some Assyrian royal inscriptions, for example, kings refer to the (alleged) prosperity reigning in their land, occasionally "proving" this claim by quoting favorable prices.[54] Jursa and his team have documented real growth in the "long sixth century" in Babylonia in great detail. They summarize:

> A growing urban population prompted agrarian change, stimulated the development of markets and money based exchange, and allowed increas-

ing economic specialisation and division of labour. This process brought about, and was in turn accelerated by, technological improvements and gains in efficiency in agriculture, and in the material and legal-institutional infrastructure of money-based exchange.[55]

On the basis of the available prices, the reign of Nebuchadnezzar and Nabonidus has been designated as a "golden age."[56] Archaeological survey has shown that there was an "acceleration" in urban growth in the Hellenistic and Parthian periods in Mesopotamia.[57] We do not know the amount of arable land in Hellenistic Babylonia, a comparatively slow process in the Hellenistic period, or intensification in agriculture and in settlement. There was more intense development in the Tigris region, especially around Seleukia-on-the-Tigris. The city of Babylon and its hinterland itself appears to have had a special status within the kingdom, an independent or quasi-independent status, "to some degree autonomous on a local level."[58] That Babylonia, however, was an important, if loosely integrated, part of the Seleukid kingdom is demonstrated by local Babylonian records of royal activity including visits to important temples in the area.[59]

For Egypt, real growth is also difficult to measure. If we could measure it, it would surely show a strong relationship to the production function; in other words, that patterns of expansion and contraction in economic output tracked the history of Nile flood volume. Archaeology is so far of some but limited value. I essentially believe that as in the Near East, E. L. Jones's view is correct, that states fostered intensive, but not extensive growth. There certainly was expansion during the first millennium, from the 8th to the 4th century. Greek traders and soldiers appear in Egypt for the first time in some numbers. Alexandria was perhaps the largest city in the 3d century BCE Mediterranean. Growth in trade grew (below), protected by a new navy, and enabled by a new canal between the Nile and the Red Sea and political reconsolidation of Egypt under the Saite kings after three centuries of fragmented political power and instability.[60] Demotic Egyptian, both a stage of the language and a distinct script, spread throughout Egypt. It took some time to be adopted in the South, as much as 150 years, and brought with it a new language of private contracting that would continue to develop through the Ptolemaic period.[61] There was renewed centralization of state fiscal institutions, and renewed attention paid to revenue from trade, throughout Egypt but notably at the new trading district at Naukratis, and revenue from persons as well.[62]

If the story in Herodotus is correct that king Amasis invented a new tax on the income of individuals, it antedates the *eisphora* tax at Athens known from 428 BCE onward and would have been substantially higher.[63] There is more to consider than high priestly families, always the wealthiest in Egypt;

the role of the military and military settlements, especially under the Ptolemies, but also a large professional class of scribes, and lower levels of priests. Death was big business in Egypt, and private demand and consumption, and tax payments collected by necropoleis where the tombs lay, generated by funerary activity was always an important part of economic activity.[64] Necropolis worker, mummifiers, tomb builders, craftsmen who made funerary goods, priests, dream interpreters, and others, constituted major business in urban areas.[65] Funerary priests, men and women, known as *choachytes*, and their funerary business activity, are the best documented, especially during the Ptolemaic period.[66] Tombs and the mummies they contained were private property, conveyable in shares to others as future income streams; partnerships between the priests were also formed. Such families, whose economic activities are well documented in family archives, were middling or even "middle class."[67]

While there was clearly expansion in Ptolemaic Egypt, the institutional structures probably prevented any kind of sustained real growth. There were technical improvements under the Ptolemies, some of the greatest minds of the 3d century Mediterranean world lived in Alexandria, and we hear about many inventions and ideas. How far these circulated, and whether these were applied to everyday problems, has been the subject of continuing debate.

Of all the subjects discussed in the literature on premodern economies, technological change is probably the one issue that has been transformed the most in the last forty years, and at the same time, much work remains. Moses Finley argued that there was very little technical innovation and therefore very little economic progress; there was no increase in either productivity or in "economic rationalism" as a result.[68] But now there is a growing consensus, on the basis of considerable archaeological evidence, that there was quite a lot of both technology "transfer," through cross-cultural exchange (the spread of iron in Ptolemaic Egypt for example), new demand, but also a lot of innovation.[69] Even the basic assumption drawn from Ricardo that there is a direct causal link between technical advance and growth has been questioned.[70] Nearly every technical category is represented: grain mills, olive presses, ceramics, glass, transportation, coin manufacture, animal husbandry, materials science, and mining/quarrying.[71] The late Hellenistic period (into the Roman), the period when the Antikythera mechanism was designed, would appear to be an intensive period of innovation, but clearly later manifestations were built on the scientific observations, the cataloguing of qualities of various wood as building material, and the scientific theory of Theophrastus (ca. 370–288/5 BCE) and others.[72] There was also considerable progress in observational sciences like astronomy and in medicine. It is not that there was no innovation. Rather, we should understand technological change as a mirror of the

problems that required solutions; the main goal was *phusis*, "balance" in society rather than making technical improvements to foster growth or efficiency.[73]

This is true even in a place like Egypt, which has often been considered
the place par excellence of technical stagnation. Technological improvements in irrigation methods were minimal and were introduced from outside of Egypt. The first improvement, the *shaduf*, a counterweighted pole
and bucket mechanism introduced from the Near East during the New
Kingdom (ca. 1350 BCE), allowed some lifting of water onto fields and gar-
dens, as did the animal-driven waterwheel known as the *saqiya* that is first
documented and was probably first used in Egypt in the 3d century BCE,
probably at a time of major crisis as I have suggested in chapter 5. These
mechanical lifting devices did not expand the arable land significantly until
the Roman period but were used instead in the intensive agrarian settings of
orchards and vineyards.[74] Central state intervention, experimentation, and
expansion of the arable land are well documented under the Ptolemies. It
was not until the 19th century CE, however, that the combination of a mercantilist government, massive new deep canal dredging, cash crops like cot-
ton and sugar cane, and barrage and weir technology allowed for large-scale
perennial irrigation.[75]

What is perhaps most intriguing about the Edfu petition discussed in
chapter 5 is that it is a private petition coming from a soldier living in southern Egypt. This invention, then, if that's what it was, came from an individual, not from someone sponsored by the royal library at Alexandria. There
was no "republic of letters" to which we can associate this man, and it is telling that the petitioner directly sought the patronage of the king.[76] But this
small papyrus letter may depict a world that is largely lost to us. Our attitude
toward innovation and growth in the premodern world has been deeply
shaped by our assumptions about both as they exist in our contemporary
world. Much of the work up to now has been dedicated to classical technology; we may have more to learn from careful study of Near Eastern and
Egyptian materials.

Lead isotope analysis in Greenland ice cores have long been used to show
the increase in silver production as a proxy measure of Roman growth.[77] Notably this continued a trend that began in the early Hellenistic period. As we
saw in chapter 5, the "Roman Quiet Period" probably reinforced and opti-
mized the institutional changes. The suppression of piracy and especially
the making of new rules in the field of what we could call commercial law
(like the so-called *actiones adiecticiae qualitatis*) are developments that pre-
cede the establishment of the *pax Augusta* of the first two centuries CE.
With the creation of the Roman imperial regime the most extreme forms of

predatory behavior disappeared. The fiscal system was reorganized on a new basis. The companies of tax-farmers were largely excluded from the collection of taxes, which was entrusted to the leaders of provincial communities.[78] On the other hand the establishment of peaceful conditions in a unified Mediterranean necessarily entailed a further reduction in transaction costs, with the diffusion of a "technology of measurement" and of common metrological systems, and above all with the creation of a unified monetary zone. The economic expansion of the Italian peninsula was also driven by the unification of the Mediterranean.

MARKETS AND EXCHANGE

We humans are a cooperative species; it is a major part of our success (so far). There can be no doubt that self-interest, reciprocity, and cooperation is a fundamental part of human nature, and was important as we evolved from hunter-gatherers.[79] In the absence of complete contracts, the role of trust-creating institutions, of morality and visible law, private associations and the like, would have been a critical part of exchange in the premodern world.[80] The tendency to "truck and barter," in Adam Smith's famous phrase, then, is indeed an ancient one and is documented even before the rise of civilization. We should, of course, include here altruism, charity, and what the Greeks called *euergetism* ("good-doing") as important aspects of premodern exchange patterns.[81]

If exchange is extremely ancient, the institution of "the market" is younger, but how much younger? The nature, the role, and the extent of transactions through markets have been one of the principal issues in understanding the evolution and development of premodern economies. Markets have been defined in many ways.[82] "Markets exist whenever two or more individuals are prepared to enter into an exchange transaction, regardless of time or place."[83] The existence or the extent of "price-setting market" transactions, on the other hand, has been the subject of debate. But the market mode of exchange actually incorporates "all effective demand," while actual price-setting markets in longer-distance impersonal exchange was more limited.[84]

Polanyi's three-part scheme of modes of exchange—reciprocity, redistribution, and markets—remains a good way of thinking about exchange modes in the premodern world. Similarly, three forms of economic coordination are generally recognized: markets, hierarchies, and networks.[85] Polanyi considered a "market economy" to be a purely modern nation-state phenomenon and therefore downplayed market exchange in the ancient world. The Kanesh trade network, for example, was an example of "market-less trading" organized through state-sponsored treaties and state-controlled agents.[86] But a recent, detailed analysis of the Kanesh trade that connected the core of the Assyrian empire to Kanesh, something like an eleven-hundred-kilometer journey, has shown that private merchants and market exchange were a fundamental part of this early exchange network.[87] The issue is hardly black and white. As we saw in the Hekanakhte letters in the last chapter, households were involved in some form of market transactions in the middle Bronze Age. Private traders are documented in the third millennium BCE, and redistribution through temples in the Near East and Egypt do not appear to have operated by Polanyian rules of "redistribution."[88] The famous Egyptian story of Wenamun, which I discuss in the next section, is a poetic proxy of the extensive commercial activity in the eastern Mediterranean at the dawn of the Iron Age, ca. 1075 BCE.

Indeed, market exchange arose gradually in early states.[89] The role that individuals played in moving from barter exchange to "fully realized commodity markets" has often been stressed.[90] But Schoenberger's analysis points to the interplay of people, institutions, and the state, and suggests that the emergence of markets was a complex social and political process. Hegemonic power can affect a wide commercial circuit of exchange, across localized regional exchange systems. States "integrated" markets and monetized taxation, which in turn stimulated market-based transactions. But markets were also a means for states to manage territory. Polanyi's concept of a "port of trade" meant state-administered trade, but it does not fully capture what the Greek *emporion* was.[91] Over time during the first millennium BCE, coinage was increasingly used in market exchange, aiding the mobilization of resources for states in the form of taxes.[92] Increased attention paid to cash crops like dates and wool in the first-millennium ancient Near East led to increased specialization.[93] The control of metal, and metals sources, and textiles are the important commodities in the story.[94]

Democracy and imperialism were drivers of monetization in Athens.[95] Paid jury duty and financing of the Athenian fleet were just two institutions that led to increased market exchange or "commercialization."[96] The fiscal policy of Hellenistic states such as the Ptolemies and Seleukids, their demand for taxes collected in coin to support war fighting, played a key part in monetizing exchange within their territories. Athenian institutions (apparently) like the public auction were introduced by the Ptolemies to Egypt in the 3d century BCE, along with banks, and were important parts of monetizing the fiscal system. Whether these extended the amount of market transactions generally is difficult to say. Our best evidence for the auction suggests that at least in some cases the new mechanism was used to award property to friends of the auction official rather than to the highest bidder.[97]

So how do we get from the "non-market" circulation of goods to exchange by "command" to Hicks's "rise of markets"?[98] The traditional view is that temples in the ancient Near East and Egypt were instruments of redistribution. But this has been overemphasized, and schematized to contrast with the rise of market economies in the Greek world. The Old Assyrian trade, and the later Phoenician trade patterns, shows us that long-distance trade market transactions without coinage based on contractual arrangements and private initiative date back almost to the beginning of civilization in the Near East.[99] In local contexts, there were specialized periodic markets in Egypt, for animals for example, and more regular markets for coffins and other funerary goods, an ancient and important part of private demand and consumption throughout ancient Egyptian history.[100] That is simply to say that much remained traditional in rural areas. The transformation, to use Hicks's term, was not from "non-market" to market. As we have seen, all three of Hicks's stages existed in the first millennium BCE. Rather, the growing use of silver coinage, increasingly integrated territory, and greater specialization in trade drove the economic transformation in the first-millennium BCE Mediterranean world.[101] The first two of these were political transformations, the third the result of an increase in scale. Totally free, "self-regulating" markets, we should remember, never existed in the premodern world. Instead they operated within both state structures and social custom.[102]

The understanding of how markets were connected to prices has advanced remarkably.[103] The best time series for market prices comes from Babylon beginning in the 6th century BCE and extending down to 61 BCE (figure 42). Market prices were recorded for six commodities—barley, dates, mustard (probably), watercress, sesame, and wool—in the context of astronomical and climatic observations including flood levels of the Euphrates.[104] New texts have been published with prices and without other kinds of information.[105] The texts do not record actual prices of commodities directly, but the purchasing power of silver in relation to the commodity; that is, they are generalized exchange values if you like, one shekel buys x amount of barley.[106] Jursa's conclusions about Babylonian markets is worth quoting at some length:

> The texts explicitly refer to the physical locations of buying and selling (e.g., *suqu* "street market," *kuru* "harbour district, commercial quarter," (some) city gates). There is much documentation for sale transactions of all kinds, from the most modest commodities to expensive real estate, and we have substantial price series for a whole range of commodities (staples, slaves, animals, real estate) which allow an analysis of price developments

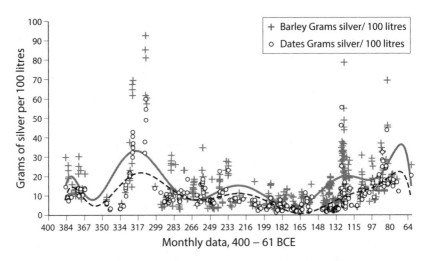

FIGURE 42. Monthly price data for two commodities, barley and dates, expressed in grams of silver per 100 liters of the commodity, 400–60 BCE, with tenth-order polynomial trend line (data: van der Spek et al. 2015). The solid line is a polynomial trend line for the monthly barley prices. The dashed line is a polynomial trend line for date prices. The price spikes between 320–300 and in the 120s BCE were periods of socioeconomic instability of un-known origin (warfare, drought, or a combination of factors). Courtesy of Frank Ludlow.

for the entire period under discussion. The data concern diverse goods de-pendent on quite different supply and demand structures and come from sources of different geographical and socio-economic origin. Seasonal vari-ations, short-term price crises for individual goods and generally the high volatility of prices preclude that we are dealing with administered prices. Nevertheless statistical analysis of the prices shows that they follow roughly the same long-term trend. This means that they reflect a single economic system, the monetised sector of the Babylonian economy, and that in this sector of the economy prices were determined primarily by the interplay of supply and demand—no other mechanism could have yielded a similar consistent result. . . . The volatility of commodity prices in Babylonia points to a low degree of market integration—much of the short term variation in prices must have been owed to problems of distribution rather than to ac-tual scarcity or oversupply throughout the country.[107]

It is generally agreed now that these commodity prices do reflect market ac-tivity, that markets existed from very early on in the Near East, and that the issue worth studying is the differential performance of markets and the fluc-tuation of prices over time and within "price regions" (figure 42).[108]

Jursa, noting Polanyi's influence even when it came to translating Babylonian vocabulary, has observed that the market place (*suqu*, lit. "street") was in fact associated with market exchange.[109] Supply/demand forces set prices; even temples were "market oriented." There was a good deal of private activity among priestly families in Babylonian archives; the basic model holds also for first-millennium BCE Egypt through the Ptolemaic period (and beyond indeed). Craft specialization among families, such as brewers, bakers, and scribes, were tied to temple stipends. Bleiberg uses a Polanyian framework for understanding interstate exchange patterns as customary "gifts" rather than as profit motivated in his study of Egypt.[110] But this can hardly describe the whole range of exchange patterns in pharaonic Egypt and certainly not for the first millennium BCE. Specialized funerary priests called *choachytes* ("water pourers"), for example, were organized into family businesses, with business rights passed down through families. They also made formal written agreements of association. Their property right to control particular tombs and the mummified bodies of people, as well as the income streams collected on the funerary rights, were bought, sold, leased, and donated by gift shares by private contract.[111] Much of this trading appears to have occurred within particular families, but we gain important insight into the cultural foundations of the private conveyance of particular property rights conceived as shares of income.

Market integration, the role of private merchants, and the role of states as regulators of trade flows have received much discussion in recent years. The old idea espoused by Hasebroek that elites in Greece, Rome, and elsewhere were not involved in trade or commerce because of aristocratic attitudes toward trading and traders, the social and political distance between the small group of elites and illiterate, poor foreign traders, has been generally abandoned.[112] It is a literary trope found everywhere (and in the modern world too), in part because traders were indeed often mobile outsiders. But this cultural attitude is belied by an ever-growing corpus of documentary and archaeological evidence of merchant activity. The Old Testament fantasizing about the fall of Tyre, that trading city par excellence of the ancient world, ultimately to meet a grim fate in actuality when Alexander the Great appeared in town in 332 BCE, can stand proxy for the attitude:

> I am against you, Tyre, and I will bring many nations against you, like the sea casting up its waves. They will destroy the walls of Tyre and pull down her towers; I will scrape away her rubble and make her a bare rock. Out in the sea she will become a place to spread fishnets, for I have spoken, declares the Sovereign Lord.[113]

Yet merchants and trading activity were intimately bound up with the political life of the Greek city, not least because of the taxation of trade.[114] The
slave trade into Athens has already been mentioned above. Foreign labor allowed larger-scale production, of fine pottery, of silver, and of weapons, three
very well documented commodities that were traded in volume through extensive market networks.[115] Roman traders and moneylenders played a major
role in the expansion of the Roman Empire.[116] Over the long run, the record
of first-millennium BCE trade suggests that there was an increase in the extent
of private trading for profit, as well as an increase in the volume of trade. But
private markets, in particular grain markets, cannot be the whole story. We
do not know much, and this is a major gap in our knowledge, about how
grain distribution worked in the city of Alexandria or, in times of crisis, in
other cities or in rural areas. In all likelihood, in my view, it was a combination of private and state institutions. To be sure, private grain merchants are
documented.[117] It is unclear in Cleopatra's famous edict at a time of severe
Nile crisis to whom the order to ship only to Alexandria was addressed:

> No one purchasing wheat or pulse from the nomes above Memphis shall
> carry it down to the low country or yet carry it up to the Thebaid on any
> pretext, though all may transport it to Alexandria free of question, on
> pain of being liable to death if detected.[118]

In terms of "integration," much continues to be debated. Finley famously
argued, more than once, against any suggestion of the existence of integrated,
or "interdependent," markets in antiquity, although it is often been argued
that Hellenistic and Roman economies can be characterized as such.[119] Temin
forcefully argued that the Roman economy was a market economy characterized by a "single integrated market."[120] Hopkins's "taxes and trade" model
connected taxation, markets, and coinage in the Roman Empire.[121] But there
are problems in drawing this conclusion so strongly; the data is too thin, demonstrated in part by Temin's use of Babylonian price data to support his conclusions about the nature of Rome's integrated market economy.[122]

The long-run view of market performance, defined as "the capacity of the
market to absorb unexpected supply or demand 'shocks' and measured by
price volatility," increased in the West, including Anatolia, between 500
BCE and 1500 CE, whereas prices appear to have been "remarkably stable in
Iraq and Egypt across in the same period."[123] Increasing market performance is explained by four factors: decreased risk in trade, change in consumption patterns, technological improvements, and better storage.[124] The
irrigated landscapes of southern Mesopotamia and Egypt did not improve
because it was not possible to change the basic constraints of irrigation and
the interannual variability of water. As we have observed, climate change

and climate variability had both global and local effects. At times of food crises in Ptolemaic Egypt, the kings opened up royal granaries or at least in one famous case, imported grain into Egypt. There is little evidence at this point that the Ptolemaic period shifted distribution to markets to smooth supply shocks as opposed the traditional state granary storage system well known from the New Kingdom.[125] Royal instructions and decrees about internal grain shipments show state concern for protecting food supplies to Alexandria but do not suggest that there were otherwise free markets between districts.[126]

The 4th century BCE, notably in Athens, was a particularly innovative period for "market enhancing institutions,"[127] notably the development of banking, the extension of credit to individuals and to cities by banks, and extending their role in tax farming in places such as 3d century BCE Egypt. The evidence collected from Hellenistic cities, and from important sanctuaries such as Apollo on the island of Delos, shows important financial innovation in this period, joining wealthy entrepreneurial individuals to sanctuaries and to cities in complex webs of lending and borrowing.[128] The entire trend was the outcome of several factors, among which were the development of banks, the development of the abstract concept of money as "a value-creating possession," and an increase in the demand for credit, seen also in Neo-Babylonian legal forms.[129] The role of the state in establishing standardized weights and measures, the issuance of coinage, the role of geography and distance effects, transportation costs, the location of permanent and seasonal marketplaces, and the impact of abrupt climate change must be part of any long-term model.[130]

After the Babylonian Astronomical Diaries, the next best corpus of price data comes from the island of Delos in the Hellenistic period.[131] Like the Babylonian texts, these too derive from a temple precinct, that of Apollo. In Reger's assessment the commodity prices that are recorded, for olive oil, pigs, grain, and wood, are "fair market prices," but it remains a difficult issue to sort out whether the prices actually reflect a regional economic system or a larger exchange circuit.[132]

TRADE

Trade is a word with many meanings in the literature.[133] I follow Harris's straightforward definition that trade is as an "exchange of goods in which a desire for profit is the motive of one party or both."[134] Long distance, cross-cultural trade, and by extension communication of information in general, played a very important role in innovation, and in political integration, but also had deleterious effects in the spread of disease to human and animal populations.[135] Cross-cultural exchange was a crucial aspect of Mediterranean trade even later, but for the first millennium BCE, and indeed going back to the origins of civilization, we must see the movement of trade flows across ever-increasing distances as a critical factor in state-formation processes.[136] Private merchants and state activity were intertwined at least since the Old Assyrian traders at Kültepe/Kanesh in the early second millennium BCE, and no doubt in the third millennium to some extent too.[137] Traders or merchants in the ancient Near East and Egypt, as far as they are documented, had statuses that attached them to a temple estate or the royal household. Grain trade and the supply of food to urban areas played an increasingly important role in state activity in trade.[138]

The debate about the role of long-distance trade has usually been framed in contrast with early modern economies.[139] No ancient city gave rise to a *merchant class, market,* and *capitalism.* The conjoining of these was important for Weber and Hasebroek, and it was Finley's main point in distinguishing ancient from early modern economies.[140] But that gets history back to front. Understanding the effects of trade in the premodern world is a matter of assessing the degree to which it had both smaller and larger effects.[141] Trading cities in the first millennium BCE played a major role in and prospered by the political integration of the Mediterranean. On a smaller scale, one might look to the rise of the Hittite empire in the center of the earlier Kanesh-Assyrian trade routes as an earlier example.

The role of long-distance trade before the early modern period in Europe has often been dismissed as negligible because it was in the hands of a small group of elites.[142] Bentley makes three important points about the role of long distance trade: (1) it was done by a small group of elites, (2) the prestige or high-value goods that they exchanged played a critical role in power hierarchies and (3) in cultural exchange and ultimately in institutional change.[143] As I have emphasized, Phoenician trading networks in the early first millennium BCE transformed Mediterranean trade. Mobile, elite Greeks in the 7th and 6th centuries traveled, traded, and returned home with new ideas.[144] Trade in luxury goods could expand into bulk trade and drove economic integration as it did in medieval Indian Ocean trade.[145] The power of regional integration can indeed by traced back to at least the Old Assyrian traders and the flow of good between Assyria and central Anatolia.

Identifying trade networks more specifically is now beginning to be studied by network analysis.[146] To be sure, trade was major driver of economic and cultural change, as well as political conflict, throughout the premodern world. Trade has been a central issue in Mediterranean history, and the most important mechanism of the integration and a force for the "unity" of the sea.[147] Earlier, Hasebroek, and indeed many other scholars, drew the strong contrast between medieval Italian and northern European merchants and their Greek predecessors and found the latter wanting. The medieval city-states were the "benchmark" against which premodern trade was assessed.[148] But even the Old Assyrian trading networks, for example, were family-based private traders, and these merchant families in the ancient Near East resembled a medieval city's trading activity on a smaller scale.[149]

Nautical technology, war, political discontinuity, urbanization in general, and the demand pull of a growing Athens in the 6th century BCE, and later of large new cities like Alexandria and Rome, shifted both trade flows and volumes. "Seaborne connectivity," the environment, networks, distance/time function, nautical architectural characteristics, are beginning to be modeled with GIS, and proving very useful in conceptualizing trade flows, distances, and costs.[150]

The scope of private enterprise has been doubted in some quarters, but it cannot be denied.[151] Warburton has forcefully argued that "international trade" played an important, even a dominant, role from the beginning of civilization in the ancient Near East.[152] But the shift from a "relatively centralized character of Bronze Age palatial trade" represented by the famous Uluburun shipwreck and its monetized cargo to "private mercantile enterprise" that arose in the eastern Mediterranean post–Bronze Age collapse marks an important economic transition.[153]

Phoenicians were the first movers in the Iron Age westward expansion in the Mediterranean in search of metal sources, and these traders created markets for high-value goods.[154] Emphasis was placed on southern and western sea routes, but overland trade routes into Anatolia, and south into the Arabian peninsula, were equally if not more important.[155] They are often compared to early modern mercantilist European cities, but mercantilism would be a misapplication of 17th and 18th century economic thought (of Adam Smith and others), and a misunderstanding of the Phoenicians, and their predecessor coastal cities in the Near East going back to the third millennium BCE.[156] Like in Greece, Phoenician cities were well located to take advantage of cross-cultural trade. They were the heirs of an exchange and a tributary network, as is well documented in the second millennium BCE, converting raw material to finished goods with a comparative advantage in nautical skill.[157] A "caravan trade," Rostovtzeff called it, replacing Old Assyrian land trading via donkey with ships by sea.[158] Metals and textiles were the main commodities in both cases. Independent commercial "firms" sitting astride vital trade routes between the Levantine coast and Egypt at Byblos and elsewhere, at the frontiers of the empires in the Near East, and in Egypt, have a long history providing raw materials like timber to Egypt, as middlemen, literally occupying the "middle ground," playing a careful game in the rise and fall of empire.[159]

In the famous Egyptian story *The Report of Wenamun*, an agent of the great Theban temple of Amun found himself in trouble and treated rather badly in Byblos. The story is usually taken as a signal of both the decline of Egyptian imperial power, and the rise of other powers in the Near East; in any case it shows us the contrast between city-based private merchant activities and the large bureaucratized trading activity of Egypt.[160] Tyre grew wealthy, specialized in the production of high-value finished goods, clothe, spices, and metal vessels among other things. The vital trade flows in which Phoenician cities were centered attracted the tribute-seeking, expanding Neo-Assyrian empire in the mid-9th century BCE; control and taxation of the major north-south, east-west trade routes that ran through Syria and the Levant made the region always attractive, for the same reason the Achaemenid and Hellenistic empires wanted to control it. Expansion westward across the Mediterranean "would have been the means by which the Phoenician cities could maintain themselves whilst maintaining their role within the Assyrian dominated regional economy."[161]

But there are other views about Phoenician expansion westward. Overpopulation of Tyre, for example, may have put pressure on that city to expand elsewhere. Being cut off from Anatolian trade routes perhaps provided another incentive to seek trade elsewhere.[162] Silver sources in Spain supplied the Neo-Assyrian Empire by the late 8th century BCE. Phoenician traders were highly mobile middlemen, linking demand for manufactured goods with raw material demand in a complex and sophisticated "western Asiatic trading system,"[163] far more decentralized than Bronze Age "palace economies." "Trading posts" were established; westward activity created, or reinforced, new networks that connected Spain to Cyprus, still a major source for copper, and Sardinia, Sicily, North Africa, and Italy. Phoenician traders converted "high-value, low bulk items ('luxuries') to standardised quantity production ('commodities'), whose mobility is made possible by interregional bullion flows ... (in) general exchangeability."[164]

Phoenician trading networks and organization set in motion subsequent trading patterns in the Mediterranean.[165] Copper, iron, and silver ore at Rio Tinto in Spain was an important aspect of Phoenician activity.[166] And of course Phoenician activity ranged from the far west in Spain, at Huelva, Cadiz by the 9th century BCE, if not earlier, to North Africa (Tunisia, Libya), Italy, Sardinia, Crete, and the Aegean Mediterranean.[167] The eastern and western Mediterranean was joined by Phoenician arbitrage in metals.[168] Merchant families arose, successors to the Old Assyrian trading families, and those in Ebla and Byblos, and to the Semitic group known as the Hyksos, who ruled Egypt for a century. Hyksos is an Egyptian word meaning "rulers of hill countries" (i.e., outsiders), which downplays the Hyksos' important trading prowess, and indeed reveals Egyptian chauvinism. Competition with other trading communities, namely Greeks, arose by the middle of 8th century BCE. One of the great Mediterranean cities, Carthage, was founded at some point probably by the late 9th century BCE century, once again for reasons that are still unclear.[169] Autonomous city-states and independent merchants historically created better initial conditions for growth.[170]

Traders are no less elusive in the first-millennium BCE trade in the Near East than elsewhere.[171] State activity is better documented, and in every Near Eastern empire there is some connection between empire formation, expansion, and the control of trade routes. We know more about state control of trade and the trading activity on the periphery of the Neo-Assyrian Empire, in the great commercial cities of Phoenicia, than we do about long-distance or local trade within the empire. For the Neo-Babylonian Empire, there is more discreet evidence about temple economic activity and the trading of family firms such as the Egibi. The apparent differences between these two states, and the balance between state control and private merchant families, is to some extent not easy to quantify, a function of the very different nature of the evidence that survives. The new empire supported temples and their economic activity and fostered a more integrated economic zone in Babylonia and organized around the Euphrates River.[172]

The Achaemenid Empire's famous road-building efforts, guarded and monitored and highly controlled, and requiring a use permit, might not have fostered long-distance trading, but it is indicative of traffic. Little is known about Achaemenid state involvement in trade.[173] Another great trading family, the Murashus, documented from their extensive archive, gives us the best evidence for Achaemenid period private trading activity, in the main in money lending and the leasing of agricultural land.[174]

The rise of the Greek city-state world was intimately tied to the Phoenician expansion and to competition for trade routes. Cross-cultural exchange can be found in the "orientalizing" material culture of early Greece and Etruria, but also in Etruscan exchange with Greeks in neighboring territory, and in wine exports to Marseille.[175] The emergence of trade in Greece in the early Iron Age was likely not so much a new type of trade but, rather, a "restructuring" of earlier trade flows based on a surge in demand led by population growth after Bronze Age collapse.[176]

The "Greek trader" appears in our sources at the end of the 7th century BCE.[177] A few of them we know by name.[178] They were neither illiterate nor poor as a group but in fact were a fundamental part of the polis. Bresson distinguishes two basic locations of trade, one, the *emporion*, for external trading by outsiders, and the other, the *agora*, for internal trade. At Naukratis during the 7th century BCE and in Athens's port at Pireaus built in the 5th century BCE, and elsewhere in the Greek world, incoming trade was monitored and taxed.[179] The importation of grain into Athens occupied a good deal of political attention.

In Hellenistic economies institutions that promoted trade while reducing costs and improving efficiency have received much attention.[180] The last four centuries were dramatic ones in Mediterranean history. It began with the defeat of Athens in the Peloponnesian War and the conquest of the Achaemenid Empire by Alexander, and it ended with Rome in a dominant political position. Much would change in these centuries. Even Polanyi himself saw an increase in markets in this period. Creative solutions to finance were found in Athens.[181] These were important factors in the historical development of Mediterranean trade and its expansion. Almost all studies of Hellenistic history emphasize increased intensity and scale of human activity: larger cities than ever before, the frequency of war, the volume of trade, the size of public buildings, the size of ships, and harbors, the mobility of people, and so on.[182]

The study of trade and the role of merchants is connected to almost every other aspect of Hellenistic economies: the movement of soldiers and other people (individually or in groups), war, the new political structures that established sovereignty over both ancient and new territorial space, the overlap of ancient trading patterns with new ones (connections between the Black Sea and Ptolemaic Egypt for example), money and credit, ethnicity, religious beliefs and their diffusion, artistic and architectural styles, and changes and fluctuations in both supply and a rising Athens in the 6th century BCE, and later, just to name a few areas where trade activity involved, and had consequences for, Hellenistic societies.[183] Without attempting to circumscribe "trade" around a particular set of issues or questions, we risk "losing one's way in the infinite," as one scholar once described the problem of analyzing ancient economies.[184] Importantly, the period from ca. 400 BCE on was one of *increasing* articulation of separate spheres of human action in economy, politics, and religion.[185] Keith Hopkins's overview of ancient trade and the fundamental questions that he asked about trade in the "classical world" are equally valid for Hellenistic trade.[186]

The Hellenistic and Roman Mediterranean, ca. 400 BCE–200 CE, was a part of a complex set of long-term processes of economic expansion, what Morris refers to as "Mediterraneanization," and there is little need to make a hard break between the "Hellenistic" and "Roman" in the 4th and early 3d century BCE.[187] Hellenistic trade and traders are essential in understanding the economic history of the Mediterranean, particularly in the realm of risk and the role of the state in supporting trade. The Hellenistic period may well have been a time of higher risk, and therefore of higher transportation costs, compared to the first two centuries CE. The highly competitive multistate ecology, and a nonintegrated "inner sea" (i.e., the Mediterranean), would have tended to cut against another Hellenistic trend, the lowering of transaction costs.[188] But the trading sphere of Hellenistic trade extends well beyond the Mediterranean basin and linked ancient trade routes of the Near East deep into Central and South Asia, for which there is increasing material evidence. As studies of "peripheral" areas such as the Red and Black Sea and Indian Ocean regions, for example, have increased in recent years, the overall appearance of Hellenistic trading appears even more complex. Clearly, we must include, however different was its ecology, the Indian Ocean and Red Sea trade in the context of "Hellenistic" trade. And we must credit the Ptolemies, and Greek traders in Egypt, with opening up this trade.[189]

The ability to quantify key data, shipwrecks, especially in assessing cargo volume and the ubiquitous amphorae, remains a key issue.[190] War and new state formation, interstate competition, piracy, and the drag of tax demands probably constrained trade. But states did attempt to lower transaction costs and foster trade; intercity agreements of the Greek world were even more extensive; tax exemptions were given. It is important to understand the balance between state-directed trade and private trade, which appears from the evidence to have increased over the course of the Hellenistic period and particularly in the last two centuries BCE. Here of course, the overlap between what counts as Hellenistic and what was Roman is significant.

One crucial area is political economy, that is, the relationships between the governance and the economic performance of Hellenistic states. Here the Mediterranean, Near Eastern, and Indian Ocean worlds before 200 BCE appear substantially different from the world of a unified Roman empire ca. 100 CE. The Hellenistic "republics," Rhodes and Rome, and their private merchants are often juxtaposed, in order to draw a contrast, to the Hellenistic kingdoms, particularly the Ptolemies and Seleukids, and their state-administered trade.[191] The former came to dominate Mediterranean trade, and underlying explanations have been readily forthcoming. This is not to deny the transformative effect of Roman power by the middle of the 2d century BCE. The data that have been frequently analyzed—the shipwrecks, the lead isotope analysis from Greenland ice cores, and meat consumption—all suggest that we are indeed in a new political framework after 200 BCE.[192]

In order to supply what is missing, however, one needs a deep historical understanding of hundreds of regions and local events and an understanding of both shifts and shocks to trade networks, and an idea of how regions were linked by the political power of the wide variety of states in the Hellenistic political ecology.[193] And that is how the study of Hellenistic trade has generally proceeded in recent years, with an emphasis on local or regional trade, for example, trade on Delos, or in the eastern desert of Egypt, or the role of merchant groups in Rhodes, and so on.

Much has been written about trade from the point of view of the institutional structure of ancient societies, and the extent of political control of trade versus the continuing pattern of long-distance trade that had been a part of the eastern Mediterranean world for millennia.[194] It is not so much a matter of arguing about the existence of markets as a mode of exchange, but rather how prominent a role markets played, and how new states, and new urban centers such as Alexandria, altered preexisting patterns. Polanyi's model, in which nonmarket exchange was dominant until the emergence of price-setting markets in the Greek world in the 4th century BCE and profit-motivated merchants in the Hellenistic period, has been compelling if only because in this case it tracks the increased density of our sources, and only serves to reinforce the important processes that opened up trade after 400 BCE. Geography and social networks have been important aspects in understanding the structure of trade. All these—markets, geography, social networks—and the new states that were formed after 323 BCE are important in considering how exchange patterns might have changed. Two broad theories have been advanced in recent years.

Thus, the questions about ancient trade asked by earlier generations remain to be answered.[195] The principal problems in the analysis of Hellenistic trade have come in the evaluation of the evidence of trade, how to strike the balance between private and state-driven exchange, how to connect "trade" to "market," and how to quantify trade (if we can at all), especially in the realm of the value and the volume of cargoes, the extent of long-distance trade, and, finally, the shift in trading patterns over time.[196] We cannot always distinguish between state-administered trade by the Hellenistic states through markets, and royal gifts of commodities such as grain or timber.[197] New fiscal institutions introduced by the Hellenistic kingdoms, new methods of taxation, and the use of coinage must have facilitated both long- and shorter-distance, interstate and internal trade, but precisely how we can quantify this remains elusive.

Another intractable problem has been and remains centered on the nature of the sources, which in general allow only partial answers to some of these questions. It is a particular annoyance that for the early Hellenistic period—a time in which the new port at Alexandria, with its enormous lighthouse guiding ships in, was literally the economic beacon of the Hellenistic world—our sources are so meager. It is that lumpiness, of course, that makes nearly every aspect of Hellenistic economies difficult to synthesize into anything that we might want to call "Hellenistic trade." But this is not the way forward. At a local level, we have many fascinating things that might be suggestive of private trading activity.

The papyri from Egypt, for example, provide much of interest about small, local traders. On a different level, the activities of Apollonios, the finance minister of Ptolemy II, mentioned below, and how his own trading activities, involving spices, incense, and slaves among other goods, through his personal network in Syria, has been the exception that proves the rule of a lack of small-scale activity caused by heavy tax demands.[198] But there are many examples of private traders. A man named Ptolemy, a religious recluse in the Serapeum at Saqqara outside of Memphis, for example, functioned as a kind of middleman, a "Hellenistic man of affairs."[199] In his textile operation centered in the Serapeum in Memphis, a temple to the popular Apis cult, he had an extensive personal network extending back to his home village in the Herakleopolite nome some eighty kilometers to the south.[200] This kind of trading, taking advantage of local networks, small-scale, short-distance selling at temples and between neighboring towns and villages, or during festivals, had been a feature of Mediterranean life everywhere from time immemorial. It was no doubt the main form of trading, and small-scale merchants and segmented trade, and consequently with higher transaction costs, were no doubt quite typical of the period if not always well documented.[201] Both men, it is worth remembering, were rather closer to the 11th century Jewish merchants of the Geniza documents, than to the majority of the farmers along the Nile, and constituted a small minority of those who profited from the institutional structures of Hellenistic society.[202]

None of these features of Hellenistic trade are likely to be known in any kind of detail, and in any case they do not appear to be anything especially new. Other kinds of sources, for example, inscriptions from Rhodes, might open for us a window into long-distance trade. To come up with a global picture that integrates long- and short-distance patterns of exchange, and that strikes a balance between the role of the state and the agency of individual actors, for any one period of Hellenistic history remains a challenge.[203]

If trade itself is well documented but problematic, the organization of trade and the role of traders and merchants is even more so. And yet understanding how trade was organized is without question a key to understanding ancient economies, particularly with respect to the differential role of market exchange over time. Since Hasebroek's study appeared almost a century ago (1928), most scholars have assumed that private traders played a marginal role in trade. They were, generally, noncitizens, illiterate outsiders who relied on loans simply to survive from one transaction to the next. Bresson has demonstrated that this view can no longer be sustained.[204] Private merchants were on the rise since archaic times; they played a crucial role in supplying Athens in the Hellenistic period and, importantly, assumed a great deal of risk that could, at times, provide them with considerable fortunes.[205]

For the Hellenistic period, and for the "ancient economy" as a whole, Finley went further, arguing that no ancient society could be characterized as having "an enormous conglomeration of interdependent markets."[206] Herodotus (1.152–53), Finley was quick to point out, described market exchange and its problems in the context of the Achaemenid Empire. But there were both institutional changes and continuities. Clearly there was an expansion of trading activity in the 4th century BCE, and a concomitant rise in piracy. Italian traders ("Tyrrhenians") mentioned frequently in our sources came to dominate trade networks with respect to Rhodes and elsewhere.[207] But Hellenistic merchants and traders moved within an ancient framework of well-established ports and harbors and within preexisting social networks. John Ma has emphasized what we might call Greek trade diasporas, which was certainly *one* constituent (and important) part of Hellenistic trade.[208] But there were also new states, and large new cities like Alexandria, as well as ancient patterns of exchange in all parts of the Mediterranean world, that lay underneath the political changes.

Rostovtzeff, in contrast, thought that trade was central to understanding Hellenistic economies, and it is still his general treatment of trade and traders that has been the foundation of most subsequent work. He divided the subject of Hellenistic trade by criteria of distance as well as by mode of transportation.[209] For the former, there was "internal" trade and "foreign" (i.e., interstate) trade. "Internal" trade meant trade between Hellenistic states, and foreign trade was concerned with trade between Hellenistic and non-Hellenistic states. Both of these were essentially long-distance exchange. One could also add internal exchange in the sense of intraregional trade as well, emphasized effectively recently.[210] It was no doubt the case that regional and intraregional trade outweighed long-distance seaborne trade in the period.[211]

If the substantive differences between Finley and Rostovtzeff have occasionally been exaggerated, the role of trade was one area where there was serious disagreement.[212] For Rostovtzeff, the Hellenistic period was precisely characterized by an increase in trading activity. Sea, land, and river were the three basic modes of transportation; the first was the most developed and the most important mode of transport. More ancient but continuing modes, land and river, continued of course to be important (e.g., trade on the Nile and in the eastern and western deserts, Near Eastern caravan routes).[213] The silk roads, overland and sea, are usually discussed in the context of Roman trade but were very much a Hellenistic phenomenon that got built out from old Achaemenid routes and extended, gradually, in the wake of Alexander's campaigns to connect the Greek core to the East.

Was this supposed increase the result of the creation of new Hellenistic states, or merely part of an overall trend in slow steady growth in surplus production over the course of the first millennium BCE?[214] Surely it was both, if we understand Hellenistic history within the larger context of a greater "transformation" of the Mediterranean world in the first millennium BCE.

Since the 1990s, archaeological work in Abukir Bay just to the east of Alexandria has uncovered the port of Thonis, also called Heracleion in Greek sources.[215] The city is mentioned in a Saite period text known as the Naukratis Stela (a second copy has been found now at the site) documenting the local temple of the goddess Neith collecting a tax on all trade, but the archaeological work has given us back the port itself, which had vanished by subsidence, probably caused by an earthquake in the 2d or 3d century CE.[216] Founded in the 8th century BCE, Thonis served as a port (*emporion*), and customs post, connected to the Greek trading colony at Naukratis further inland at least since Persian rule, by the end of the 6th century BCE.[217] A well-known 5th century BCE Aramaic document suggests that the Persian king collected trade levies at Thonis-Heracleion.[218] This new and very exciting work, still in its early phases, has already demonstrated the very clear and strong connections between Egypt and the Greek world from an early date and puts a new light on the later foundation of nearby Alexandria. About sixty shipwrecks have been found so far, 40 percent dated to the Ptolemaic period on preliminary analysis.[219] The work also suggests that Greek-Egyptain trade contact in the first millennium BCE grew in importance and was a transformative element in economic history that brought Egypt intimately closer into the Mediterranean world.

Connectivity between places was improved, driven by exploration, the wider use of coinage, and the building of new roads and new ports (state-driven activities), as well as new social networks established by new communities, or "trade diasporas." This expansion in volume, intensity, and connectivity was, however, Rostovtzeff argued, constrained by a prevailing mentality in Hellenistic states of self-sufficiency; the planned economy of the Ptolemies was a central point in much of his work on Hellenistic economies, although it is no longer a widely accepted concept. Trade was also constrained by the increasing political power of Rome and its magistrates who began to control Mediterranean trade in the 2d century BCE. Piracy, limited improvement in the technical aspects of sailing, political instability, and internal wars within the Hellenistic states, as well as particular events (e.g., the destruction of

Carthage and Corinth, the creation of Delos as a free port in 167 BCE) all contributed to the general constraints of Hellenistic trade that would be lifted, gradually and to a certain extent, by the imposition of Roman imperial control of the eastern Mediterranean.

For Rostovtzeff and all who have followed him, internal and external trade in the Hellenistic world was dominated by grain (specifically wheat) trade.[220] Supply and demand was irregular.[221] The grain trade certainly is still the best-documented aspect of long-distance interstate trade; the main sources were Egypt, Cyrene, Sicily, and the Black Sea region; and, broadly speaking, grain moved into Greek urban centers (Athens above all, the Aegean, and towns in Asia Minor as well).[222] The slave trade grew in importance, especially during the 2d century BCE.[223] The organization of trade was, and is still, not very well known. Rostovtzeff emphasized the centralized, state-controlled character of it, and in Ptolemaic Egypt above all other places he found much evidence. Rhodes, on the other hand, offers a view onto Greek polities in the period. Taken together, they offer us a range of evidence to understand the connections between political economies and trade as well as the role of private trading activity.

Egypt had been an important center of trading activity, connecting East Africa and the Red Sea, as well as trade coming from the East and southwest deserts in the oases, to the Mediterranean and the Near East, for many centuries before the Ptolemies established their regime. Herodotus already hints at the extensive trade routes, no doubt ancient, including those in the oases, crisscrossing Egypt in the 5th century BCE. Cleomenes of Naukratis's cornering of the Egyptian grain market to take advantage of a severe economic shock in Greece continues to get a good deal of press, most of it bad, and his fate seems well earned.[224] The earlier history of trade centered in the delta has been sketched, but there is more to do with respect to Greeks in other parts of Egypt in the first millennium BCE.[225] If the excavations at Tell el-Timai in the delta are anything like typical of Ptolemaic communities there, the shift from Egyptian to east Mediterranean tableware is a good indication that trading and consumption patterns reflected a cultural shift with the change in political power in the mid-4th century BCE.[226]

The documentation of Ptolemaic trade, and how it was taxed, has been well treated by Préaux, Rostovtzeff, and Fraser.[227] Ptolemaic evidence offers an important lens through which trade and traders in the Hellenistic world can be understood. Grain, papyrus, glass, and spices were among the important commodities moving from Egypt to external ports. Trade entering Egyptian ports was taxed at higher rates than elsewhere in the Hellenistic world. Given its location, the Ptolemies also took advantage of taxing the transit trade that moved through Egypt. Taxation is generally understood as Ptolemaic "protectionist" policy associated with the monopoly system and the Ptolemaic trading/currency zone.[228] A well-known document from the Zenon archive, for example, preserves a list of goods imported from Syria (some via Greek or Asia Minor ports) by Apollonios at Pelousion and shows that certain products were taxed at very high rates, up to 50 percent of the value of the cargo, rates much higher than other parts of the Hellenistic world.[229] A 10 percent tax was collected on imports in the Saite period text from Naukratis, and the Ptolemies continued to tax cargoes, at higher rates, ad valorem.[230] A parallel is suggested by an important papyrus dated to the period of Persian imperial control of Egypt, ca. 475 BCE. Therein, extensive information about cargoes loaded onto "Ionian" and Phoenician ships entering and leaving Egypt is documented. The Greek ships were the majority. Persian fiscal practice shows important differences from the preceding Saite period. The taxes on the ships and the men were collected under Persian rule at the port of Thonis (Heracleion) ad valorem just as in later Ptolemaic practice.[231] And while the Ptolemies clearly built on Persian foundations, the rise of Alexandria, certainly the "greatest trading city of the Mediterranean" in the period, altered trading patterns throughout the eastern Mediterranean.[232]

Internally, the development and extension of the road networks greatly facilitated trade coming from and moving through the eastern desert. The building of the two new deepwater ports at Alexandria itself played a great role in both the increased capacity of shipping moving in and out of Egypt and in security.[233] In terms of scale, compared to the Piraeus at Athens and to Roman ports, the Great Harbor (Portus Magnus) at Alexandria harbor was of average size.[234] The founding of many settlements along the Red Sea coast that supported trade as well as activities such as mining, the improved roads, and the increased presence of guards, however modest, in the eastern desert, and the erection of mile stones along the routes at road stations with cisterns, all attest to improved conditions for long-distance overland trading.[235] Other ports in the delta, Pelousion for example, remained important.[236] We should be careful not to overestimate the impact of all this; the provision of internal security, guards on ships and so on, also suggests problems with brigandage. Whatever the details, much of the early Ptolemaic activity in the desert appears to be state directed, but nevertheless it seems clear that early Ptolemaic activity improved conditions for trade.

The demand pull of and through Alexandria, a new city of some three hundred thousand in the middle of the 3d century BCE, would have been considerable, although as with so much else it is impossible to quantify.[237] Urban demand, along with state taxation along the network of tollgates on the Nile, kept prices, to the extent we know them, high in the city. Here again we are at some difficulty to assess the balance between private and state-driven mechanisms. To be sure, supply to places like Alexandria would have been driven by rent and tax demands of the Ptolemaic state, conducted largely through private ship owners.[238] But the channels of its distribution, for example, whether by market or by the state, is not well understood. The Ptolemaic state was certainly active in other aspects of long-distance trade, as the elephant-hunting activities show.

The display of exotica at the procession (*pompê*) in Alexandria in the reign of Ptolemy II celebrating the dynasty (*Ptolemaiea*) also suggests that many other luxury goods were arriving and moving through Egyptian ports to points north.[239] This would come into fuller development once the monsoonal trade winds were "discovered," and Egypt would become an important entrepôt for goods from India. We can begin to build out a more informed picture of the historical developments of Ptolemaic trade that led to what would become the enormous volume (and value) of Indian Ocean trade in the early Roman empire.

Fraser's overview quite rightly emphasized trade with the western Mediterranean as well.[240] Only traces of this trade have survived, but trade with Sicily and Carthage as well as Cyrenaica, a key part of Ptolemaic territory, may have been considerable. There was trade with Italy as well. This was presumably one of the reasons Ptolemy II had sent an embassy to Rome, the earliest known Ptolemaic contact with that city.[241]

Trade was an important source of revenue for the Ptolemaic state.[242] Quantifying how much revenue was raised by Ptolemaic control of trade remains highly problematic, and of course it is not a surprise that smuggling is documented.[243] Fraser, in his study of Ptolemaic Alexandria, argued that state taxation and control of long-distance trade constrained development. While the degree to which the Ptolemies were able to plan and tightly control the economy has to my mind been overestimated, to some extent this must surely be correct. Yet as in the Greek world, there were institutional changes that allowed for more trade, including a greater degree of protection for shipping. Increased urban demand, and tax incentives, as the declaration of Delos as a free port after 166 BCE reveals, is suggestive of the relationship between trading and state taxation.[244] On Delos and elsewhere, there is a notable expansion in commercial building space.[245] Ptolemaic trading activity, particularly involving the grain trade, was intimately connected to its external possessions. Cyprus, Crete, and above all Rhodes were the key regions for Ptolemaic trade. Grain was traded for among other things Rhodian wine. Other areas of the Ptolemaic empire were also important. Kos appears to have been a more important source of imports to Egypt than

Rhodes despite the overwhelming physical evidence for stamped Rhodian amphorae in Alexandria (and elsewhere in Egypt).

The island of Rhodes played a dominant role in Mediterranean trade in the Hellenistic period, aided by its political neutrality. Its special connection to Egypt formed a major part of the grain trade in the Hellenistic period.[246] The island was closely connected historically with trade to Egypt through Naukratis and the Phoenician coast. Already in the time of Cleomenes in the later 4th century BCE Rhodes functioned as a clearing-house for Egyptian grain exports.[247] Rhodes's excellent location, 325 nautical miles or three and a half days' travel from Alexandria, its year-round access, and its excellent harbors made it a natural entrepôt for the Ptolemaic grain trade.[248] It had a strong position politically and through its coinage to Ionia, the Cyclades islands, as well as to Caria.[249] But it was Rhodes's special relationship to Egypt, generally cordial in the period, that formed a powerful trading network linking the great port of Alexandria through Rhodes to Syria and Caria.[250] Rhodes had a strong navy and functioned as a "clearinghouse" as well as a major banking center. And perhaps the strongest force against Mediterranean piracy, although the effectiveness of this is debatable, Rhodes certainly gained from its reputation as a fighter of pirates.[251]

When Rome declared Delos a free port, Rhodian income from port duties was reduced by 85 percent, as was its ability to suppress piracy.[252] But its trade connections to places such as Knidos, Kos, and Chios continued, as did its increasing monopoly on trade from Alexandria at the end of 2d century BCE.[253] This appears to suggest that Rhodian wine-trading patterns in particular adjusted to the rise of Delos by focusing on eastern Mediterranean ports in general, and to Egypt in particular.[254] Problems remain about the interpretation of amphorae, caused by the circumstances of finds. Many collections of amphorae were not excavated in a controlled archaeological context, the ratio of stamped/unstamped are difficult to discern, the function of the stamps is debated, and there is no easy way to determine the scale of amphorae trade.[255]

There is now a good deal more material relating to Hellenistic trade and its physical and social configurations than even twenty years ago. This is due to the intensive archaeological work throughout the Mediterranean basin. But more material has not always led to new understandings of Hellenistic trade. If the rhetoric of Finley's *The Ancient Economy* is but a soft echo now, we must also say that at least some of Rostovtzeff's thundering certainties of progress, and capitalist tendencies, have also been muffled. Moreover, the traditional temporal boundaries of "Hellenistic," that is, the post-Alexander world, have been broadened considerably. The contexts of the new Hellenistic states are now set into the context of two important longer-term historical trends, namely the earlier expansion of the Greek world, westward into Magna Graecia, and eastward to the Black Sea and the eastern Mediterranean basin, and the Persian imperial economy.

Yet there are indications of growth, even in the periods of political instability in the 3d century BCE. If we can accept the fact that there was real growth beginning in the 3d century BCE, it was surely not due to Roman naval activity, but primarily to Hellenistic state activity in the eastern Mediterranean.[256] The increased intensity of trade and newly built harbors are two proxies. Unlike studies of Roman trade that emphasize seaborne trade in the Mediterranean, a consideration of Hellenistic trade would emphasize the decentralized nature of much Hellenistic trade, the extensive overland routes, many inherited from Achaemenid period trading patterns.[257] The major ancient overland routes would grow into what would become the main overland silk road network. The bulk of long-distance trade, in other words, from the point of view of the Ptolemies and Seleukids in particular, was differently configured than Roman trade centered on a politically unified Mediterranean. Both Hellenistic Leviathans built and extended overland routes, dotted with trading centers along the way, and competed against each other for control of trade flows through them. At the height of Seleukid political power in the early 3d century BCE, it straddled the major overland road from Antioch through Dura Europos and Seleukia out to central Asia. The early Ptolemies built and extended roads in the Egyptian eastern desert linked to a new port at Berenike in the Red Sea through which came war elephants, incense, cinnamon, and other spices. Sea routes were hardly ignored. Pytheas's adventures in the Atlantic at the very beginning of the period, and Ptolemaic exploration of the Red Sea and east Africa in the early 3d century BCE, are suggestive enough.[258]

Attempting to assess spatial-temporal boundaries of the trade in the Hellenistic period is a difficult issue. Should we focus on the movement of Greeks, on trading patterns and on technical improvements, or on political history, that is, on the new states created out of the Persian Empire in the late 4th century BCE? How should we consider the impact of Alexander the Great's campaigns? Classical scholars beginning with Droysen, following a tradition that extends back to Montesquieu, had a profound influence on later writers and have often emphasized a "great man" model of Alexander's impact as military conqueror and transformer of the Asian economy. Alexander revolutionized Mediterranean trade by, among other things, opening up the stagnant Near East; in Egypt by founding Alexandria; in Mesopotamia by removing the weirs set up for irrigation; and bringing peace to the Indus River valley.[259] The Hellenistic kings, in particularly the Ptolemies in

Egypt and the Seleukids in western Asia, extended Alexander's model. British India was often on the minds of French and British scholars in the early 20th century.[260] Briant cites the following passage of Wilcken that is worth considering here:

> The economic revolutions which have been described as brought about by Alexander's conquest of Asia and Egypt, and which confronted the Greek merchant and industrialist in the East, in process of time increasingly influenced the economic development of Greece itself; the whole foundation indeed of Greek trade in the Mediterranean was changed.[261]

The debate about Persian stagnation has been essentially closed by Briant's work.[262] Neither the Near East nor Egypt was stagnant. It is clear that focusing only on Alexander, or on specific periodization in which to understand economic change, leaves us a seriously flawed history of the period.

Confusion, or at least the disagreement, on what is meant by the term Hellenistic (does it describe political, geographic, or economic boundaries?) has caused certain things to be treated in both the Hellenistic and the Roman literature on trade. Indian Ocean trade for example, a phenomenon beginning in the 2d century BCE, has often been treated as part of Roman trade. It is of course properly both; the vantage point, whether from India, Rome, or Egypt, changes the scholarly emphasis. But it is Ptolemaic Egypt, and the institutional and infrastructural framework put in place by Ptolemy II and III, that led to the exploitation of the trade route initially, and supplied the port and harbor structure. And indeed there was a continuum from the Persian period, when roads were built, and Greek trade expanded in Egypt.

Not the least of the problems with the period is whether and how one can isolate things as distinctively Hellenistic, bearing in mind the continuities from earlier the Greek and Persian history carried into "Hellenistic" times, and the strong connections between 3d century BCE trade and trading networks and the rise of Roman domination of the eastern Mediterranean in the 2d century BCE.

Secondly, and far more important with respect to the role of trade in the economies of the Mediterranean in general, is the overall character of what we refer to as the Hellenistic period. It has been the subject of Manichean analysis that has been the bane of economic analyses of ancient economies: primitive or modern, substantive or formal, pessimistic or optimistic, market or barter, Greek or Near Eastern culture. The "downbeat position," of the Hellenistic period, to quote Paul Cartledge (1997:4n7), prominent in Peter Green's influential treatment of the period, has emphasized cultural and economic decline of the Greek world in the last three centuries BCE, and a distinct lack of success in planting Greek institutions in places such as Egypt. This is too facile a view of the period, and it emphasizes the wrong things. Greek culture had a strong and vital impact in the eastern Mediterranean for nearly a millennium. A simple narrative of decline is also insufficient for Hellenistic economic history. What most people think of as decline is the shift in the political economy of the Mediterranean from multiple, highly competitive polities to a single polity, the Roman Empire.

Several important conference volumes have attempted to delineate some of the most salient features of Hellenistic economies.[263] There were at least two distinct phases: (1) the 3d century, during which new states were formed; old states, particularly the city-states of Greece, adjusted to the new realities; and new institutional structures and new culture were created, and (2) the 2d and 1st centuries, when Rome came to play the dominant political and military role in Mediterranean economies. This second phase cannot be understood without the first. Beyond this simplified periodization looms, it must be said, Alexander himself. As elusive as he is in many ways, his campaigns, and perhaps his intentions as well, opened up a world that was, surely, already beginning to change. Rostovtzeff long ago deemphasized Alexander as a discoverer of some lost world of the Orient. Rather, what Alexander's campaigns did was to realign trading patterns and culture between the Greek and Persian worlds. Contact with India, the building of new cities, the formation of new "Leviathan" states in the eastern Mediterranean, the continuing effects of war, to name just a few features, shaped developments in the period. Shipley, echoing Rostovtzeff, suggests that we might look for:

> "global" distance-related effects attributable to the existence of a more or less homogenous, partly independent trade system stretching from southern Gaul to Afghanistan, producing—irrespective of any royal policy—a prosperous Greek "core."[264]

Recent scholarship, clearly building on the earlier work of Rostovtzeff, Préaux, Fraser, and others, has now well defined the chronological and institutional boundaries of the Hellenistic period. Beginning in the middle of the 4th century, and certainly with the added momentum brought by Alexander's campaigns, what sets the Hellenistic period in relief is the heterogeneity of institutional structures, the diversity of local traditions, and the intensification, integration, and reorganization of socioeconomic and legal structures; new political equilibriums were established once the diadochoi wars had been settled, between new state actors, principally seen in the "Leviathan" states of the Seleukids, Ptolemies, and Antigonids, and in private economic activity. To be sure, the new kings played a major role in state economies including trade. The small "international" elite of the Hellenistic world did move in the same cultural circles, distinct from the bulk of populations who continued to live in their more traditional local cultures, broadly speaking, a good example of Gellner's premodern state social structure.[265]

It seems to me, then, that there are two basic ways to think historically about Hellenistic trade. The first is to consider what, if anything, was particular or distinctive about this period of history. The second is to consider how the last three centuries BCE fit into the *longue durée* of Mediterranean trade. Both approaches, let's call them the medium- and the long-term approaches respectively, implicate institutions as the most important aspect in the analysis of ancient trade, and temporal and spatial boundaries as the main problem.

So to the issue of geography. Do we focus on the Mediterranean, as Roman historians of trade do, or do we include western Asia and the Indian Ocean? One of the issues, surely, in Hellenistic trade has been the processes by which Mediterranean trade became integrated into Near Eastern trading patterns, including Egypt. Here the Persian Empire stands as an important nexus in our understanding both of medium- and longer-term trading patterns and organization and intercultural exchange and its role in institutional change. Furthermore, it was Ptolemaic and Seleukid contact that opened the Indian Ocean trade to the Mediterranean. It seems reasonable, therefore, that Hellenistic trade is a two-ocean framework, the Mediterranean *and* the Indian Ocean. To be sure, in the Near East and in Egypt, trading patterns in the Persian period, and indeed before, initially continued largely unchanged by Hellenistic developments. But the new large cities, Alexandria, Carthage, and Antioch among the most important, affected demand and the administration of trade significantly. Measuring distance, "long-distance" trade, local trade, segmented trade, and so on, is important if possible since it helps understanding transportation costs, risk, and trade volume among other things.

It is difficult to produce a narrative of Hellenistic trade within the context of a broader framework of economic history. That was the genius of Rostovtzeff's treatment but also its main weakness. The documentary evidence by itself is lacunose and tends in any case to be better for the 2d and 1st centuries BCE. The current study of Hellenistic trade is a series of highly specialized, often not very well connected subdisciplines of ancient history: epigraphy, papyrology (for Egypt), numismatics, amphorae studies, underwater archaeology (shipwrecks), and survey and settlement archaeology, to name just the obvious ones. The publication of new material is ongoing, and large-scale archaeological projects in many regions promise much data.

To confront the issue of Hellenistic traders, we must overcome two negatives, namely the supposed negative ancient attitude toward traders, and negative evidence. These are difficult hurdles, and the problem is well known in Achaemenid period trade and in later periods as well.[266] Professional merchants and traders, those who made their living from trade, not unlike 9th century CE Carolingian, or Aztec merchants, do not appear in our sources as much as one would like. Indeed they are often "invisible."[267] What survives instead is lumpy and generally comes from the 2d and 1st centuries BCE. Still, Greek sources do distinguish between risk-taking *emporoi* and the less savory profit-motivated traders called *kapeloi*.[268] Traders often seem indeed to lurk behind the scenes disguised as other kinds of persons. What comes to the fore, rather, is trade administered by kings and warlords for their own revenue and prestige. Most were, surely, like their Roman period brethren, small-scale traders of modest means, operating within a small region. Ironically perhaps, pirates and brigands appear in our sources to be more visible than do merchants. At times, as a well-known passage in Diodorus suggests, the boundary between merchants and opportunist "pirates" was a thin line, and the label "pirate" was often used of one's enemies rather than as an objective occupation category.[269]

This is true in Greek and Latin as well as in Near Eastern sources. The negative, judgmental tone of literary attitudes toward merchants, and toward trading in general, are well known from classical sources, and it no doubt added to their seeming invisibility.[270] This dismissive stance—"don't trust a merchant, they will steal you blind"—is also documented in Hellenistic demotic Egyptian literary sources.[271] It was something "outsiders" engaged in, and the normative attitude toward them is not dissimilar to the view of pirates and brigands, and it says as much about prevailing attitudes of forces other than state regulation as it does about the merchants themselves. Their supposed absence in the historical record also says something telling about the way modern scholars categorize ancient economic actors. For example, the close association between pirates and the markets of the eastern Mediterranean has long been noted.

Social networks and associations have been an increasingly important topic in the study of ancient trade.[272] Associations are especially important in the context of understanding historical change in the postclassical Greek polis, but they have a longer history in Athens. They also have a history outside of the structure of the Greek polis or democracy. Concerning the growth of private associations, the highest density of evidence appears from the 2d century BCE onward, and their variety, modeled on the polis, in the Hellenistic period are of particular interest for the study of trade. No formal trading groups as such, or "companies" were recognized; such groups existed only in the short term to undertake particular transactions. While "national" or ethnic trade associations or guilds were well known and considered an important aspect of Hellenistic trade, the religious and social character of them (they were merely "club houses") was stressed by Rostovtzeff.[273]

State control of trade and state restriction was briefly mentioned by Rostovtzeff as one of the key problems in understanding Hellenistic trade on the macroeconomic level.[274] Such state control of trade was not absolute of course, but it does appear to be a characteristic feature.[275] Associations and how they operated show us at a local level an important aspect of private trade. Gabrielsen has argued convincingly that these social formations extended to civic institutions and realigned social structures within cities. In Aristotle's description, associations that had profit in mind (*chrematistikai*) were clearly involved in trade.[276] *Koina* or "national groups" of traders emerged. In Egypt, our documents begin to appear only in the later 2d century BCE, when trading intermediaries begin to be documented.[277] Rhodian *koina* are perhaps the best studied of the private Hellenistic associations, especially for the last two centuries BCE.[278] Certainly religion was "an indispensible framework."[279] But as Gabrielsen emphasizes well, the cult and "friendship" aspects of *koina* were just one aspect of these associations. Military (naval) functions, lending, and trade were all intimately bound up in *koina* as well.

Outside of Greek urban areas it is not as easy to see economic transformation caused by the apparent expansion of similar private associations, which had written rules and were also organized around religious cults.[280] The evidence for association members and trade is indirect, but it is not difficult to think that, like their counterparts in Athens, "faith," or at least common membership in an association, fostered trust. From that followed lowered transaction costs, in particular in enforcement costs, and, thus, an increase in exchange.[281] One Ptolemaic period demotic contract, for example, states that the agreement will be enforceable except in certain specified cases. A similar clause occurs in the written rules of association from Egypt, and so it is possible that the contracting party was a member of such an association.[282] One could easily compound the examples of exchange between persons of the same occupation whether they were members of formal associations or not.

That is still often the understanding of ancient associations but, as Ogilvie has recently demonstrated for medieval guilds, the emphasis on merely the social or religious aspects of private associations can mask economic behavior. Can we see them, as Ogilvie does, in a medieval European setting, as self-interested institutions of extraction that also benefitted state elites? These associations were certainly exclusive clubs, marked off by cult practice and burial rights, as well as clubhouse activities. They also received tax breaks and state protection. Taking Ogilvie's "conflict" approach to institutions, Hellenistic associations, benefitting particular closed groups, may not have produced overall gains in trading efficiency. Here we may see a contrast to Roman trading institutions as more "open access," and more efficient.

Reger has stressed the need of most Greek cities for imports and the dependence therefore on merchants and other state agents. That was especially true of the city of Athens that was particularly dependent on imports.[283] Some cities developed their own funds for regular purchases of grain. Merchants, *emporoi*, and *ekdocheis*, "forwarding" or "warehouse agents," are well documented, especially on the island of Delos, but are known from many other places.[284] Through public merchants or traders, *sitonai* and *elaionai*, public expenses for oil and grain purchases were organized and facilitated. These must have taken advantage of their own networks to facilitate trade and to obtain the commodity at an advantageous price. Purchase at a good price occasionally had side benefits for the merchant.[285]

Hellenistic traders and merchants were, to be sure, generally small-scale traders. Kings of course, were the largest merchants, dominant in the interstate grain trade, and so too were people like Apollonios, Ptolemy II's famous finance minister.[286] His social network and private trading activity was extensive.[287] It is enough to suggest that he was in fact a merchant albeit not a "professional" or full-time one; other affairs, too, occupied his days. But he would not have been unique. Nekhtnebef, son of Tefnakhte, a very wealthy Egyptian merchant from Naukratis, who must have died in the early Ptolemaic period, was not shy to claim vast wealth in his biography.[288]

The 2d century BCE Indian merchant, and his sources of capital, provides striking evidence of a private merchant and his networks outside of the Mediterranean.[289] His quite remarkable funerary stela found at Kandahar, written as an acrostic poem, tells us, among other things, that he had "accumulated a vast fortune" as a merchant, the result of years of adventure:

> having received money from others to "invest,"
> I left my country determined not to return there
> before having raised well high a heap of riches.

He had benefited from his well-connected family, from the power of the Mauryan and Greco-Indian Empires, and from the intense trade networks that transected central Asia.[290] Such a man, who left us this superb Greek grave stela, written in highly refined Greek, may have benefitted from both Mediterranean trade and trade in central Asia and India itself. We will have to guess on exactly how extensive his network was; it is not easy to locate the man precisely in either his home or in trading networks. But it is difficult to resist the temptation to link him to other great Hellenistic men who functioned in many spheres including the economic. Entrepreneurs like Apollonios from Egypt and Sophytos, then, stand as two rich examples, one for the middle 3d century BCE eastern Mediterranean, the other for 2d century BCE central Asia, of private traders and their networks that formed the basis of later developments. Many others, Protogenes of Olbia for example, could be listed.[291] They are only examples; they don't allow us to assess the role of private trader in the Hellenistic world, but these men would not have been alone.

Rhodian merchants, being very well documented, were, of course, an exception. By the last third of the 4th century BCE Rhodes was becoming a major center for merchants. If seaborne trade was of the greatest importance because of its lower relative costs, then we must consider Rhodes to be of the greatest importance in Hellenistic trade and a republican precursor to Rome.[292] Intercity agreements for privileged trading status with respect to duties (*ateleia*) of merchants of many ethnicities based in Rhodes were a feature of Mediterranean trade of the 3d century BCE and an important institution by which cities attracted trade into their port.[293] The bulk of the grain trade through Rhodes was in the hands of private merchants.[294]

The Hellenistic period, in many spheres, was an age of large things: the first "urban giants" of the Mediterranean, the Alexandrian Lighthouse, the Colossus of Rhodes, big altars, war elephants, and large ships.[295] Those ships were both man-o-war attack vessels and merchant ships. One such warship of Ptolemy IV was described by Plutarch in his *Life of Demetrius* 43:

> Until then nobody had ever seen a ship with fifteen or sixteen banks of oars, although it is true that at a later date Ptolemy Philopator built a vessel of forty banks of oars, which was four hundred and twenty feet long and seventy-two feet high to the top of her stern. She was manned by four hundred sailors who did not row and four thousand at the oars, and apart form these she could carry on her decks and gangways nearly three thousand soldiers. But this was only intended for show: she differed little from a stationary building, and since she was designed for exhibition rather than for use, she could only be moved with great difficulty and danger. But in the case of Demetrius' ships, their beauty did not at all detract from their fighting qualities, nor did the magnificence of their equipment make them any less operational: on the contrary their speed and their performance were even more remarkable than their size.[296]

If the *Syracusia* of Hieron, coming in at more than four thousand tons displacement by some estimates, was exceptional, it indicates in any case what the Hellenistic world was capable of.[297] If that ship is only an impressive example of the capability of Hellenistic naval architecture, the increasing size of more standard ships in the 4th century and Hellenistic world is impressive enough even by later standards.[298] The 4th century, with increased interstate competition, was an important inflection point in Mediterranean history against which the early Hellenistic period as normally conceived must be seen. Merchant ships were larger on average than before the Hellenistic period. Ships around one hundred tons would have been common, but large ships, over 130 tons, would not have been unusual.[299] The average size of cargo ships increased in the 3d century BCE, and once again late in the 1st century BCE.[300]

To be sure, political developments of the period, above all in the new Leviathans (the Ptolemies and Seleukids); the growth of large cities; a rise in population; the wider use of coinage: all were conducive to increase in demand and therefore of trade volume.[301] Even before the rise of the Hellenistic states in the eastern Mediterranean, very large volumes of grain entered Athens's port at the Pireaus.[302] That was not new. The Athenian population had been dependent on imported grain already by the middle of the 5th century BCE.[303]

In amphorae as in coinage production, relative production rather than absolute output is the cautious conclusion.[304] Nevertheless the circulation of coinage remains an important measurement of trade.[305] Some states, notably the Ptolemies, attempted to carve out territorial trading space by requiring a different weight coinage within the territory they controlled. This obviously added transaction costs to interstate trading. But no single currency in the Mediterranean emerged, and a variety of coins circulated even after Roman integration of the Mediterranean.

The study of Hellenistic trade has been dominated by shipwreck and ceramic studies. Stamped amphorae have been a major component of quantitative analysis of Mediterranean trade for well more than a century. They are, as John Davies wryly comments, both a "dream and a nightmare."[306] Both areas of research have profound impact on the understanding of both the volume and direction of trade and the relative influence of certain regions like Rhodes as an originating point and/or an intermediary for Mediterranean trade. Greater sophistication in the study of amphorae, their sizes and circulation, their contents, and the significance of the stamps on them, has been increasing since the frequently cited article by Empereur (1982). Furthermore, we now know that amphorae contained a variety of products, not just wine and oil; had different shapes and sizes for specific commodities; and at times were shipped empty.[307] All these raise the central question of how we can assess the value of cargoes and the flow of commodities.[308] Knowledge of ceramics has been considerably refined in recent years, but there is still some way to go in terms of sequencing, and of understanding the ranges of fabric types, and so on.

For shipwrecks, it has been generally conceded that shipwrecks are correlated to shipping volume, and that the distribution of shipwrecks follows a bell curve, rising steadily from ca. 600 BCE to 200 BCE, rapidly increasing from 200 BCE and peaking in the 1st century BCE, and with only a slight decrease in the 1st century CE, and a sharp decline beginning in the 3d century CE (figure 41).

Such a picture that connects shipwreck data as a proxy measure of shipping volume has been severely criticized. As in the study of stamped amphorae, reliable statistical analysis remains a problem in the study of shipwreck data. The increase in shipwrecks in the Hellenistic period has for a long time been taken as a proxy measure for the increase in the volume and the intensity of trade.[309] Yet beneath that broad characterization remain problems. In certain cases, debate remains about how to characterize the trade, especially in the western Mediterranean, as "Hellenistic" or as "Graeco-Italic."[310] There are problems with assessing exact size of cargoes, and assessment of perishable contents, particularly grain. Geographic holes remain in the data, especially for the eastern Mediterranean.[311]

Both shipwrecks and amphora handles present severe problems of quantification and, thus, of interpretation as well. In the case of amphorae, more publication is required, and even then, the contextualization of the stamped amphorae within the broader corpus of unstamped ones would remain a contested field. In the past it has been the stamped ones that have led to an overemphasis.[312] The drop in Rhodian amphorae numbers is usually mapped onto the political history of Rhodes and Polybius's report (30.31.12) of the Rhodian embassy to Rome and its supposed trading decline beginning in 166 BCE after Rome had declared Delos a free port. But significant doubts about Rhodes's decline have been raised.[313] We also need consistency in quantifying sherd counts in estimating the number of vessels at a site. Methods of doing so appear to be inconsistent.[314] Various theories have been propounded over the years to explain the purpose of stamping; Lawall argues that it is the product of amphorae—"efficacious organization of amphora workshops and agricultural production"—stressing the managerial control over the local production, in some areas, of jars, and their distribution through an agricultural production network.[315]

Much of the general work in building a model or a framework in which to understand ancient trade in the Mediterranean has been developed by Roman historians. Polybius is a major source, although his views, especially toward Roman action against piracy, are often overstated. The results have been increasingly more refined, but the conclusions drawn from them are generally well known among Roman historians. In a recent paper Scheidel has suggested, largely on the basis of later comparative evidence, that the principal driver in the scale of the volume of trade *in the Mediterranean* (my emphasis) was "imperial state formation.[316] Technical improvements were exogenous, and less important than the overall political framework of the Roman empire and its particular ability to reduce transaction costs, principally seen in the lowering of predatory behavior that had "knock on" effects on the cost of financing. Scheidel's model also suggests that Roman state power would have reduced uncertainties in the collection of tolls. All this lowered transportation costs; free trade grew under Roman monopolistic political power.

This is explicitly an institutional argument, supported by two key ideas: first, from the New Institutional Economics framework developed in North and Thomas (1973) that suggests overall lowered transactions costs (including the costs of bargaining) was the principal determinant in "scale and productivity of international trade;"[317] and second, that the political economic power of a state, not technological improvement, was the main driver in trade productivity.[318] In other words, changes in the stock of knowledge as well as technical changes in shipbuilding, design, and navigation, and so on were endogenous to the large shift in the political framework of the Mediterranean that allowed Rome to reduce predation on shipping, which in turn lowered transaction costs as well as the costs of financing.[319]

The internal institutional logic of the argument as well as the comparative evidence deployed by Scheidel are irrefutable, and I think that the evidence is fairly clear from the viewpoint of the Mediterranean in the first two centuries CE.[320] But the model, it seems to me, is too stark and is akin, to borrow from John Davies, to viewing history "from the wrong end."[321] Scheidel's "Roman period" model argues for change beginning at the end of the First Punic War in 241 BCE when Roman naval power had become the single dominant naval power of the Mediterranean. But change in trade volume is, as he himself says,[322] only "dimly perceptible." The year 241 BCE may mark a shift, but it does not mark a break. In one famous moment of economic shock in Egypt, ca. 238 BCE, Ptolemy III was able to import a large amount of grain "at great expense" to rescue a starving Egypt.[323] But most of the actual evidence of Roman imperial impact comes in the later 2d century and 1st centuries BCE, and indeed in the imperial period, that is, after 30 BCE. It hardly marks a break in trading patterns in the eastern Mediterranean, and it misses much historical development in the 4th and early 3d centuries.

Much of the institutional framework that Scheidel discusses, the lowering of predation and thus of risk, and the consequent reduction of transaction costs, as well as the increased aggregate demand of urban centers, was a trend that began in the 3d century BCE. Secondly, piracy, as measured by slave trade volume, fluctuated considerably even into the Roman imperial period, and the period before and after. Without question Roman dominance by the 2d century BCE represented a major shift in political and military power, and more gradually of economic power shifting to the west. But the connection between state power, piracy, and predatory behavior is not straightforward.[324] As Scheidel himself admits, the establishment of a

"Roman Mediterranean" was in fact a slow gradual process of change and did not alter preexisting trading patterns especially in the eastern Mediterranean.[325] Stamped amphorae evidence suggests that Rhodes reached the peak of its trading power between 200 and 175 BCE.[326]

Roman control of the Mediterranean was a shift, however significant it may have been, in the punctuated history of long-distance shipping in the Mediterranean. War could indeed interrupt the normal trade patterns. A famous example comes from Polybius's description of a Rhodian embassy to Rome in the summer of 169 BCE. Rhodes sought Roman permission to purchase grain from Sicily because its Egyptian supply had been temporarily cut off by Antiochus IV's invasion of Egypt.[327] Warfare and piracy were intimately connected to Hellenistic economies and, even more importantly, to their political economies. Piracy and brigandage were a part of Hellenistic trade and therefore should be considered an endogenous part of a model on Hellenistic trade.[328] Interstate conflict certainly would have impacted long-distance trade, but states, war, and the booty created from conflict was connected to piracy, and trade networks also took account of pirates and their activity.

It is interesting to note that Strabo, in commenting on the slave market on Delos, mentioned "pirates," but once they had entered the harbor and desired to sell their merchandise they became "merchants."[329] Piracy was simply another weapon in the continuing rivalries between the states, and there are many examples of pirates placing themselves in the service of one Hellenistic king or another.[330] The lack of rivals that Rome enjoyed once it had politically united the Mediterranean made a substantial difference. State protection of trade was a major force behind Rhodes's success and to some extent, at least as an excuse, for Roman expansion into the Hellenistic world during the First Illyrian War in 229 BCE. Political solutions to long-distance trade by treaties, *isopoliteia* treaties, and *asylia* decrees often involved institutions to better protect exchange between Greek cities.[331]

Archaeological survey work in Cilicia suggests that both the Ptolemies and the Seleukids built fortified towers and monitoring stations there.[332] Rhodes spent considerable effort fighting pirates, and even after Rome and Roman merchants had begun to dominate trade in the western Mediterranean, Rhodes still controlled the eastern Mediterranean and its important trade flows, particularly to Alexandria.

What is less clear, and this has implications for other aspects of Hellenistic history as well, is what the impact of Roman state formation and protection was in the expansion of Indian Ocean and Red Sea trade. For Scheidel these regions are configured as "outer trade," with higher risk but also higher reward.[333] The early Hellenistic period was a time of linking Indian Ocean and Mediterranean traffic for the first time. The Red Sea coast and the western

Arabian coast both received a good deal of attention by the Ptolemies and
Seleukids. The *Periplus* of course is well known in the context of Roman
trade in the Indian Ocean, but it was, as with the roads and ports, built on
Hellenistic development. Archaeological work in the Egyptian eastern desert confirms that the volume of trade coming from Red Sea ports as well as
state mining activity (gold, porphyry marble) substantially increased with
the Roman annexation of Egypt after 30 BCE.[334] Activities in the eastern
desert at Mons Claudianus map well onto the shipwreck data on large shipments of porphyry to Rome.

The Kingdom of Hagar benefitted from both Ptolemaic and Seleukid demand.[335] The use of coinage was an important medium between these states
and the Hagar kingdom. The aromatic trade was important in both kingdoms,
coming from Dhofar and shipped through Sumhuram (mod. Khor Rori), via a
series of intermediaries and consequent toll-collection points, to Gaza and to
Indian trade. Bahrain served as an important way station between India and
Egypt and western Asia. If the Muziris papyrus is any guide here, ships leaving
southern India must have attracted pirates like bears to honey.[336]

Scheidel's model should be usefully extended to Hellenistic trade, and it
would offer some contrast to Roman imperial history once the Mediterranean had been integrated into a single imperial space. The processes that
Scheidel has outlined—state formation, political and economic integration,
and the resulting political stability and reduction of war, the lowering of predation and the costs of transactions and of finance—can all be traced in the
Hellenistic evidence. War, and local crop failure, certainly affected demand
and supply on strategic commodities such as grain. The situation in early
Hellenistic Athens as described in the detailed study by Oliver illustrates
the effects of war but also the extensive shipment of grain into Attic ports.[337]
Disruption caused by war and competing generals, and problems of distributing grain even to cavalry are clear. Athens and its territory was dependent
both on gifts from external benefactors and on the Athenian *sitonai*.[338]

To be sure, there were attempts by states to lower transaction costs.
Rhodes and its control of piracy reduced predatory behavior. Tax exemptions were given to certain merchant groups.[339] Such exemptions, however
rare they were, are also documented in Egypt.[340] Tolls were generally also
low, as in the imperial period, but they were perhaps more unpredictable,
while private trade may have been taxed at high rates. We have less data from
the Hellenistic period to be certain. Evidence from shipwrecks suggest a different picture, one of small mixed cargoes, and cargoes that were split up
over several ships to reduce risk.[341] This picture of small cargoes would ac-
cord with Scheidel's model that posits an increase in the size of ships and a

higher trade volume resulting from lowered transaction costs and increased organizational efficiencies in shipping.[342]

Patterns of exchange in the Mediterranean between ca. 400 and 200 BCE can and should be analyzed in its own terms but also as a part of larger economic change in Eurasia. The legacy of Near Eastern trade, the movement and settlement of people, and the increasing interconnectedness of the Mediterranean with western Asia, in other words cross-cultural exchange, all shaped the period. Polybius's *symploke* was, importantly, an accelerating trend in the Mediterranean throughout the Iron Age. The nature and characteristics of Roman trade were a continuation and an extension of those of Hellenistic trade in the eastern Mediterranean. The Hellenistic period may well have been a time of comparatively higher risk, and therefore of higher transportation costs, compared to the first two centuries CE. It was also, compared to later Roman developments, a time of smaller, diverse cargoes. Equally important are the new trends of the period, an expansion of trade volume that came though the new cities in the eastern Mediterranean, facilitated by new roads and new entrepôts built on the Red Sea coast and elsewhere, and the new political structures of the Hellenistic monarchies. The lowered transaction cost environment stressed by Scheidel for Roman trade was the direct result of Hellenistic state building in the 3d century BCE. These features, new urban centers, new or newly extended trade routes, new ports, and the new political relationships established especially by the Hellenistic "Leviathans," for example, the Ptolemaic-Rhodian network, also shaped the behavior of traders and merchants of the period. The role of private traders and merchants has often been underestimated. They are best documented in the private associations of Rhodes, but this is probably merely a vestige of the survival of a particular type of document. In Egypt, and in places as far as Afghanistan, the image of the well-to-do merchant was probably just an indication of small-scale private trading throughout the Mediterranean and western Asia, fostered by the new political frameworks of the period, and by the increased circulation of coinage, among other things. The formation of the Roman imperial economy over the last two centuries BCE marks an endpoint of eight centuries of economic and political development, and the culmination of two millennia of complex trade and exchange networks. A single hegemon now governed the Mediterranean, a body of water called by the Romans *Mare Nostrum*, "our sea."

CHAPTER 9

Conclusions

To the pre-Enlightenment mind humans were not omnipotent and Nature was not invariably benign; first-hand experience, collective memory, and the Bible—most notably the Book of Revelation—all testified to the contrary. Modern economic historians may live in a less superstitious and more scientific and theoretically informed age, but on the power of humans relative to that of Nature our medieval and early modern forebears may have been the wiser. Moreover, they inhabited the world that we seek to understand. Certainly, with a mounting body of sound scientific evidence to draw upon, there has never been a better opportunity to explore the interrelationships between past environmental events and processes and the course of social and economic change. The time has therefore surely come to acknowledge that—alongside the class struggle, invisible hand of the market, creation and diffusion of technology and knowledge, and an array of human institutions (including many intended to mitigate and counteract the risks arising from environmental hazards)—"Nature" was an historical protagonist in its own right.

—BRUCE CAMPBELL (2010:310)

To the extent that we depend on prosthetic devices to keep ourselves and the biosphere alive, we will render everything fragile. To the extent that we banish the rest of life, we will impoverish our own species for all time. And if we should surrender our genetic nature to machine-aided ratiocination, and our ethics and art and our very meaning to a habit of careless discursion in the name of progress, imagining ourselves godlike and absolved from our ancient heritage, we will become nothing.

—E. O. WILSON (1998:298)

I HAVE ENDEAVORED TO survey in this book the long history of economic institutional development in the Mediterranean world from the rise of Phoenician traders, to the dawn of the new world created by the Roman empire. Understanding the highly developed Roman imperial economy must be informed by the historical experience of the many other civilizations that preceded it in the wider Mediterranean world. Roman political dominance beginning around 200 BCE marks an end point, not the beginning, of the slow process of economic integration through the sea, the major rivers, and the extensive and very ancient overland routes of western Asia, North Africa, and Europe. The Roman acheivements, built on Iron Age experience, rivaled anything else up to the 18th century CE in Europe in many categories. What I have presented here is an outline of key themes and a sketch of recent work in the developments of "Axial Age" economics.

The Achaemenid Empire looms large in this story. Although often in the background, it was the central player, at midmillennium, stretching from the Aegean into central Asia, its imperial institutions asserted over the largest land empire, controlling 5.5 km^2, in the West before Rome. This great empire is often forgotten about in the context of the first millennium BCE, but it had a profound impact on the second half of the millennium.

Much of the work by previous generations of scholars on the "ancient economy" has been static and descriptive, analyzing either the "classical" economy in a single framework, or particular regions or towns of the ancient Mediterranean. Work in the last forty years is moving dramatically beyond this framework, seeking dynamic models, emphasizing cross-cultural interaction and heterogeneity rather than a single line of development. In a very real way, the civilizations that grew up around the Mediterranean basin were like the gears of the Antikythera mechanism: some were small, others larger, each turning at different rates, but part of an interconnected whole. Decisive economic change was driven by political change.

I have suggested that there was no such thing as "the ancient economy." Rather we must understand developments on several levels, not just on the local or the "microregional" level but how households were connected to each other, how regions were connected to polities, and how polities in turn were connected to wider economic interaction spheres. But all the rich new material, new archives, much new archaeological material, and new osteological, genetic, and climate data suggest that a larger framework in which to understand premodern economies must be built. The great debate between "primitivists" and "modernists" that I mentioned at the beginning of this book has long ceased to be productive, or even interesting. It was narrowly framed around the origin of markets and the construction of antiquity as it related to later European history. In other words, it looked forward to later developments in Europe rather than backward to the historical experience of the wider eastern Mediterranean world.

New paradigms, using economic and social theory from a variety of social science perspectives, combined with human archives derived from written and archaeological material, and the new natural archives being generated by scientists in genetics, paleoclimatology, and a whole host of other disciplines offer us a new and very exciting window into the complexities of the premodern Mediterranean world. As in other historical fields at the moment, a variety of scales of analysis are not only possible, but also highly desirable.[1] The way forward, I believe, is to be as broad and open as possible in methods, in theory, and in the use of data.

One of the pieces of the new framework is, I suggest, to look beyond compartmentalized economic history, as in "the ancient economy," "the classical Greek economy," or "the Egyptian economy." Often scholars have proceeded in writing what are in effect "national" histories. One can of course still work within those kind of descriptive, political frameworks for some aspects of institutional history. After all the funerary business, and the mummification and burial of both humans and sacred animals, was a very important, and unique part of the Egyptian economy of the first millennium BCE. Beliefs matter in economic history, and Greek movement and Roman consolidation were major forces in the first millennium BCE. But we can miss other parts of the process of change if we exclude cross-cultural influences. We can hardly understand Greek commercial activity without reference to the role of Phoenician traders in the Mediterranean in the early Iron Age.

Rather than seeking to compare premodern economic institutions to later European institutions, we should concentrate on the intercomparison of premodern economies. One of the things that this will underscore is the ways in which culture, ecology, and geopolitical and political economy made enormous differences to what was a very heterogeneous world of lifeways in the first-millennium BCE Mediterranean. In part the desire to find a new framework is an outcome of contemporary concerns with the positive and negative effects of globalization.[2] But there are important reasons to understand premodern Mediterranean economic history within the context of more universal economic history. As we have seen, the great civilizations that I have surveyed here were intimately and strongly shaped by their environments and climate change patterns, both longer-term temperature shifts and droughts, and shorter-term shocks.

Jack Goody, in his *The Theft of History*, pointed out some of the obvious flaws in our current thinking about periodization and old categories of analysis in which we evaluate change. I have used the term "premodern" throughout the book, aware of the problems with the term. We tend to view history from the contemporary end of things, "retrospective" history Wootton has called it.[3] It is fine to read history backward as it were, to understand how we got where we are. But only if we accept that this assumes a linear transmission of success stories. In fact, though, historical processes are nonlinear. If we discuss only periods of success, we risk missing a great deal of developments, experiment, and the shear richness, and sometimes the failed experiments of the premodern world. And indeed we miss out on how important geography and climate were to premodern economies. This heterogeneity of solutions to the problem of social cohesion and the coupling of economic with natural forces provides, I think, a useful and important context for understanding our own circumstances.

Each first millennium BCE imperial polity we have encountered, to a certain degree, absorbed, transformed, and erased what had come before (what we have lost of Phoenician commercial institutions is one of the more important), and in the larger empires from the Achaemenid to the Roman, increasing homogenization and market integration occurred. We have lost much through imperial "theft," one empire replacing another, but we have also lost much through neglect. The great library at Alexandria was lost not by some conflagration caused by Roman or Islamic conquerors, but, probably, for the mundane reason that the practice of copying out manuscripts, an important part of textual transmission and preservation, stopped.[4] It is a lesson for our own age. Other vestiges of premodern Mediterranean economies remain. As I have suggested, when scholars remark on some feature mentioned in an ancient text as strikingly "modern," what they are pointing out is, in fact, an ancient feature of our own world.

To many economic historians, the Roman Empire, and the civilizations that preceded it, failed. They failed because they did not develop sustainable, "inclusive" political institutions. But this is to read against current success stories. The problems of modern Egypt lay in its ancient past, before the high dam at Aswan was built, but also in the 19th century colonial exploitation, not only because of its present narrow political elite, or because England had a revolution in 1688 and Egypt did not.[5] The high variability of water, and therefore of agricultural production, and periodic drought, famine, and disease, produced in the Near East and in Egypt large institutional structures centered around temples that created buffers to interannual risks. But neither the king nor these temples constituted the totality of the economic activity of southwest Asia or Egypt. This was not conducive to real growth, in our terms, to be sure, but, rather, to stability.

Explaining real growth, while a crucial part of modern economics, is not especially important for understanding premodern economies. Growth trends are more accurately described as "running in place" rather than "stagnation," and it reflects highly adaptive and resilient civilizations, with long periods of stability.[6] In Egypt and western Asia such political stability could endure for three to five hundred years at a stretch. That is what these civilizations wanted to create, political stability, and the results look reasonably impressive. We need not crudely compare the economic performance of two different states but ask, rather, how and why particular political equilibriums were achieved, and what cultural values and ideas were at stake. What emerges is not a single narrative of "the ancient economy" but indeed a multitude of such narratives, at different temporal and geographical scales.

Several things shaped the world of the first-millennium BCE Mediterranean. Radically different political economies emerged in the Greek world while new imperial states formed in western Asia. Egypt in the early Iron Age was a world of fragmented virtual city-states in the delta, and a theocratic state in the Nile valley, controlled by the great temple of Amun at Thebes. Political power was again centralized in the 7th century BCE as Egypt began to be connected to wider Mediterranean trade. Cross-cultural exchange and the trend toward increasing integration or connectivity were of great importance throughout the millennium. Iron and silver were important everywhere. The spread of coinage, important both for trade in for state fiscal systems, and new military technology undergirded the highly competitive world of Greek city-states and defined the age after Alexander. There was a rise in the use of writing, in legal codes and in private agreements. Environmental boundary conditions and climate changes at various scales and the human responses to them were crucial determinants of performance, but much work remains to be done in this area.

We in the contemporary world live in an age of "disenchantment." All of us are increasingly removed from nature, from the environment, and from each other by technological developments.[7] Almost all our daily needs can be met through Amazon.com, personal exchange transacted through the medium of the mobile phone. Those who lived in the premodern Mediterranean, and those who lived in other places in the world, lived in greater harmony with the natural world if not always with each other. Local environments shaped political economies and patterns of exchange. Climate change, both abrupt and slower-moving shifts, could have profound effects on grain production and distribution patterns, social unrest and war, but also on growth and expansion.

The shocks brought about by abrupt changes to the environment, drought or earthquakes for example, were well known to premodern populations. And they were more sensitive than we are today to climate changes because they were often better observers of nature. The *Oracle of the Potter* for example, a text written in Egypt probably in the late 2d century BCE, tells of catastrophic events and of things to come:

> The river [since it will not have] sufficient water, [will flood] but (only) a little so that scorched will be [the land], but unnatrually. [For] in the time of the Typhonians [people will say]: "Wretched Egypt, [you have been] maltreated by the [terrible] malefactors who have committed evil against you.
>
> And the sun will darken, as it will not be willing to observe the evils in Egypt. The earth will not respond to seeds. These will be part of its blight. [The] farmer will be dunned for taxes <for> wh<at> he did not plant. They will be fighting in Egypt because people will be in need of food. What one plants, [another] will reap and carry off.

When this happens, there will be [war and slaughter] which [will kill] brothers, and wives. For [these things will happen] when the great god Hephaistos will desire to return to the [city], and the Girdlewearers will kill each other as t[hey are Typhonians] . . . evil will be done. And he will pursue (them) on foot [to the] sea, [in] wrath and destroy many of them because [they are] impious. <the king> will come from Syria he who will be hateful to all men, . . . and from Ethiopia there will come. . . . He (together with some) of the unholy ones (will come) to Egypt, and he will settle [in the city which] later will be deserted.[8]

The sentiments expressed in this text (and there are many other such texts, including of course the book of Revelation) have usually been interpreted as purely theological manifestations of political oppression, as an anti-Greek (here called "Girdlewearers" and equated with the Egyptian mythic anti-hero Seth, here called the "Typhonians") "nationalist" tract against the Ptolemaic regime. But a better way to read the text is to take it in its historic context, the 2d century BCE (in fact other historical contexts could apply) and to read the text literally as a description of environmental and social distress caused by the continued fiscal demands in the light of Nile failure. Indeed one can even go a bit further without stretching credulity too much and say that the phrase *"The river [since it will not have] sufficient water, [will] flood] but (only) a little so that scorched will be [the land], but unnaturally . . . the sun will darken. . . . The earth will not respond to seeds"* is a perfect description of dust veils caused by the volcanic eruptions (in a similar way to the Babylonian Astronomical Diaries) and the subsequent impacts on the Nile flood and agriculture that I discussed in chapter 5. The prophecy was not anti-Greek directly but rather an ancient gloss on kingship that equated favorable environmental conditions with just kingship but also the reverse, that poor environmental conditions must indicate illegitimate kings. It is most interesting that the text also mentions taxation continuing after the poor flooding, and the invasion by the Syrian king (Antiochus IV) at the same moment, a time of Egyptian weakness.

If chronologically precise climate data are now being treated (as they should be) as an exciting new historical archive, we also have considerable new information from the traditional material of ancient history. Many more texts are being published more rapidly than before, and being digitized and made available in relational databases. Archaeological research projects throughout the Mediterranean basin, and now well beyond it, have achieved astonishing results in the last forty years showing the connections between the sea, western Asia, and Egypt. We are beginning to have a better appreciation that "antiquity" was a much bigger world now than was conceived of in the pioneering work of Bücher, Meyer, and others. What results, I hope, is a richer understanding of the lived human experience, what problems past societies faced, and how these problems were solved (or not). First-millennium BCE economies gave momentum to the Roman economy, which, like Roman law, absorbed the historical experiences of other, more ancient, civilizations.

We are not going to find modern kinds of economic growth, or lost manuscripts of Xenophon that suggest that he really was an immediate precursor of Adam Smith or Paul Samuelson. But the first-millennium BCE documentation shows us the variety of economic life of the premodern world, a long-run view of economic institutions that are still with us, and prompts an entirely new range of questions. It remains difficult to study "the ancient economy" in the aggregate, even if we focus on the Greek or the Ptolemaic economy alone. The ancient Mediterranean world was extremely diverse. I hope I have conveyed both some of the rich contours of the premodern Mediterranean, the interconnections, and long-term institutional developments. We have improved our methods for quantifying what is quantifiable. Much exciting research on very many fronts is underway, and to be certain I have not covered every aspect worth considering.

Values, attitudes, beliefs, and meaning were very different from our own. The development of charity, euergetism, gift-giving, the more ancient tradition of "feeding the hungry and clothing the naked" of elite Egyptian tomb biography tradition, all were important aspects of premodern economies that must be further integrated into our conceptions of premodern economic life.[9]

In the evidence from the premodern Mediterranean world, we see individual humans, ingenious, adventurous, risk taking, inventive, and we also see a variety of state forms and institutions, some of them perhaps better at creating wealth and well-being than others, but we also see the topic of every society protecting their own interests; we see legal concepts that are incredibly far sighted, even in some cases not far from our own views of justice, but we also see the ugliness of human behavior. In short, we can see real human beings, solving problems, making a living, surviving, and we also see them as war captives sold on slave markets and as temple prostitutes.

Much recent work has emphasized the contours of economic growth, well-being, and quality of life of first-millennium BCE populations, the distribution of wealth, the impact of war. As I have tried to signal throughout the book, understanding the impact of abrupt and slower-moving climate change is just beginning. I have indicated that high-resolution paleoclimate data is providing historians with a "natural archive" that gives us the possibility of developing more dynamic models of premodern economies. By combining scientific and humanistic disciplines toward the understanding of premodern economies, ancient historians may yet realize E. O. Wilson's "greatest enterprise of the mind."[10] That is not a bad goal.

Archaeology has been important, but in some areas, like the first millennium BCE, work remains remarkably underdeveloped. There are good projects underway, but we may well be very limited in what we will ever know. Current wars and political unrest around the world have made archaeological work in key areas of western and central Asia virtually impossible. But in Egypt, the delta, often silent in the past, has seen spectacular work at Tanis and elsewhere. The brilliant work by two French teams in the Alexandrian harbor has given us some remarkable new evidence for the important role Egypt played throughout the first millennium BCE in Mediterranean cross-cultural exchange patterns.

Rather than simple characterizations, future work will place more emphasis on explaining change over time, on complexity and diversity, on interaction between places, and on dynamic models. The impact of climate change on the ancient world in all its aspects offers us indeed the "new framework."[11] An understanding of climatological conditions in the ancient world shows us, among other things, that already in ancient times civilizations were globalized in the sense that they can be connected by the same events, monsoon failure leading to drought, even if they were not directly in contact. So far environmental constraints and climate change has not been fully integrated in any major economic theories in NIE, economic sociology, or anthropology, or anywhere else for that matter. It is a challenge for the next generation of scholars. Understanding highly resolved climate data provides us, for the first time, with the potential for dynamic models that link climate change to drought, food crises, price movements, migration, disease outbreaks, and even war.

Peter Brown's recent and magnificent tour de force study of the long, slow process of the "Christianization" of ancient ideas about wealth, poverty, community, and money that had emerged from the late Roman world can be traced back to 4th century BCE Athenian rhetoric on wealth coevolved with an increasingly wealthy and powerful new institution in the Mediterranean, the Christian church.[12] It is a reminder that beliefs and culture matter in explaining change, and that the early Christian world arose within the Roman imperial economy, which in turn had absorbed and reshaped an even earlier Mediterranean world forged in the ashes of the Bronze Age collapse.

New material and new ideas, combined with the new scientific data being generated every day by paleoclimatologists and other specialists, are opening up a new frontier, one which in an even stronger way reveals to us not a Manichean world of primitive or modern, but a rich tapestry of how human beings solved the problems they faced under very different constraints than our own. The possibilities of writing new kinds of economic histories of the premodern world, global in scope and more refined in social analysis, are more open than ever before. I hope especially that the young generation of scholars will take up the mantle. There is much to do, and much promise for new kinds of work in the years ahead.

I close with two thoughts that occupy me at present. The first is that studying ancient economies is important for a longer-term view of economic development and is a reminder of how earlier sophisticated human societies lived within nature. The ancients had an intuitive sense of "nature as protagonist" to quote Bruce Campbell's excellent study. Here is a great contrast between the premodern world and us. The ancients lived within the boundaries and constraints of the natural world that they not only observed with great care, but, as the Babylonian Astronomical Diaries show us, in considerable detail. In many cases the natural world was worshipped as manifestations of the divine and of the cosmic order. When things were out of balance, it was a sign of bad politics. We "moderns," on the other hand, are racing headlong away from the natural world. We have much to learn from our ancestors. If we do not learn from them we risk, to paraphrase E. O. Wilson, becoming nothing.

We stand, I believe, at the dawn of a new age of historical research, and ancient historians will be (or can be) major contributors to it. Science has advanced with incredible speed in the last quarter century and, for many problems, offers us new tools to allow more precision with dating, a better understanding of human and animal health and disease, and a more precise understanding of climate change on various scales and human response to it.

The "Roman Quiet Period" in the first two centuries CE, coincident with the *pax romana*, and a warming and stable climatic trend in much of the Mediterranean beginning ca. 200 BCE, may have reinforced the economic performance of the Roman empire. But the story of Antarctic and Greenlandic ice, and the records of volcanic eruptions deposited in them, tell us that the last two centuries BCE were neither a quiet period nor a good one for Egypt. Horden and Purcell, in their great book on the premodern history of the Mediterranean, made a distinction between history *in* the Mediterranean, analyzing politics, economy, and war, and history *of* the Mediterranean, concerned with how humans interacted with the natural environment of the sea.

What I have suggested in this book is that there can be no history *in* without history *of*.[13] Human society and the variable and fragmented environments in which humans lived around the Mediterranean were coupled, and their fates intertwined in the open sea.

Climate Data

EXPLOSIVE VOLCANISM IS A primary driver of abrupt climatic change and acts on interannual time scales mainly via direct radiative and indirect dynamical effects of sulfate aerosols injected into the stratosphere, where they may remain for up to three years.[1] Thus volcanic impacts on climate are generally short term but were a forcing mechanism of rainfall patterns especially in regions dependent on monsoonal rainfall.[2] While most studies on volcanic forcing focus on temperature, societies were often more vulnerable to abrupt precipitation change. These are harder to reconstruct and model, but recent studies have noted significant posteruption impacts on global and regional precipitation. Figure 47 illustrates the basic geophysical and geochemical processes caused by sulfate injection into the stratosphere. Figure 43 shows a stacked multiproxy record of the climate anomaly at 4.2 ka. Similarly, figure 44 is a multiproxy record for 3.2 ka, that is, around the time of the Bronze Age "collapse." The latter illustrates widespread precipitation changes in the eastern Mediterranean. Figures 45 and 46 are reconstructions of solar variabilty.[3]

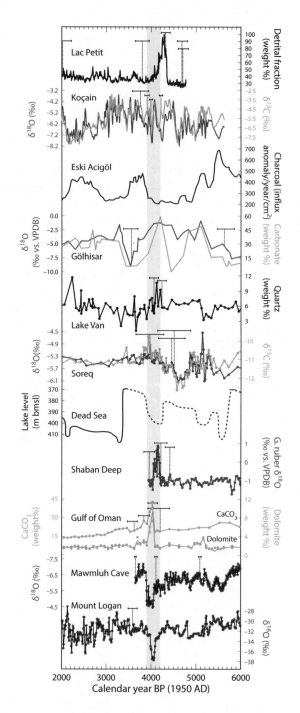

FIGURE 43. Stacked multiproxy record of the 4.2 ka climate anomaly. The gray vertical band covers three centuries of "collapse, abandonment, and habitat tracking in the eastern Mediterranean and west Asia synchronous with megadrought." From Weiss (2016:62). Courtesy of Mark Besonen and Harvey Weiss.

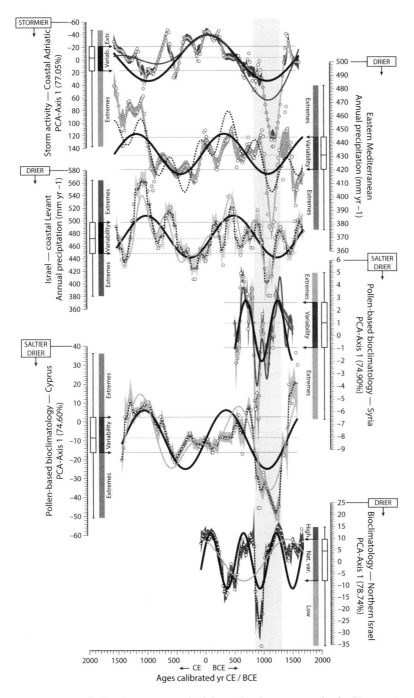

FIGURE 44. Stacked multiproxy record of the 3.2 ka climate anomaly, the "Bronze Age collapse," from Kaniewski, Guiot, and van Campo (2015).

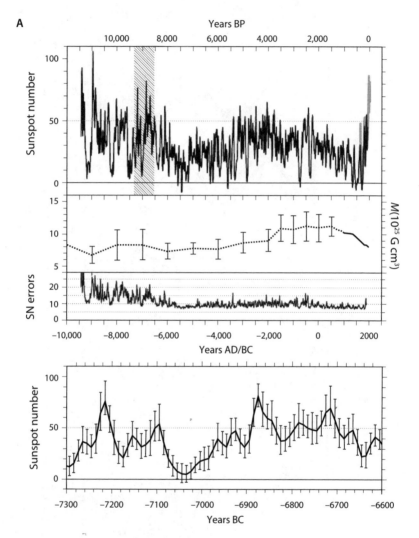

FIGURE 45. Solar activity measured by sunspot number (SN). (a) ten-year averaged SN reconstructed from Δ^{14}C data since 9500 BCE (blue curve) and ten-year averaged group sunspot number (GSN) obtained from telescopic observations since 1610 (red curve). From S. K. Solanki et al. (2004). Data at ftp://tp.ncdc.noaa.gov/pub/data/paleo/climate _forcing/solar_variability/solanki2004-ssn.txt.

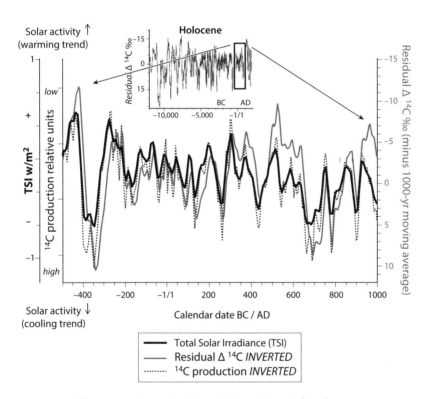

FIGURE 46. Changes in solar activity. From McCormick et al. (2012).

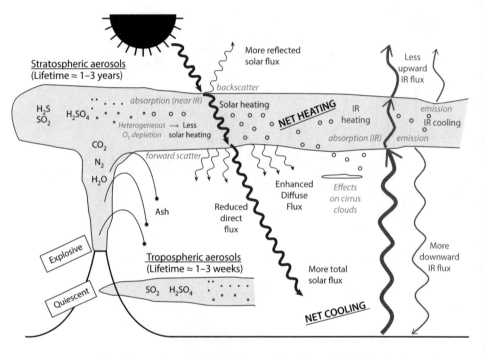

FIGURE 47. The climate impacts of volcanic eruptions. From Robock (2000:figure 1). Note that ocean-atmosphere feedbacks are not depicted here.

NOTES

PREFACE

1. Hicks (1969:1). A Nobel Prize winner in 1972, jointly with Kenneth Arrow, who passed away as I was writing the conclusions to this book (February 21, 2017). See "John R. Hicks—Prize Lecture: The Mainspring of Economic Growth." Nobelprize.org. Nobel Media AB 2014. Web. August 22, 2016. http://www.nobelprize.org/nobel_prizes/economic-sciences/laureates/1972/hicks-lecture.html.
2. Morris and Manning (2005b:14).
3. Broodbank (2013:595). On cultural contact as a force of change, see W. H. McNeill (1992). I follow Morris (2010) in his definition of the western core that includes western Asia and Egypt.
4. Morris, Saller, and Scheidel (2007:10). Cf. Goody (2006). On "lead in time," see Stiner et al. (2011). On the European divergence, see most recently Hoffman (2015).
5. Xen., *Ways and Means* 1.5.
6. Bruce Campbell (2010:309), treating preindustrial England but with global ramifications. This is something more easily seen in macrohistorical studies, as in Christian (2004), but as I discuss in chapter 5, high-resolution (i.e., chronologically precise) paleoclimate proxy data create possibilities for more detailed analysis of coupled human-natural feedbacks.
7. Below, chapter 5.
8. I agree with the comments of Morris (2003:45); and with Broodbank's (2013) emphasis on long-term development and interaction.
9. Between 1995 and 2009 there were sixteen conferences on the Greco-Roman economy, de Callataÿ (2014:5n1). And that of course does not include meetings on Egyptian or ancient Near Eastern economies, or the several general conferences that have taken place since 2009. For additional German bibliography, see von Reden (2015).
10. E.g., the very fine volume edited by W. Harris (2013a) on the Mediterranean environment, but almost entirely devoted to Roman topics.
11. Mair and Hickman (2014).
12. Hirth (2016:18).
13. E. Jones (1988:90). For a good survey of some of the themes I develop, see Demand (2011). A rich catalogue of material culture and some fine essays on Iron Age exchange patterns is available in Aruz, Graff, and Rakic (2014).
14. M. Greene (2000).
15. Butzer (2005); R. Adams (2012). For teamwork, Mike McCormick's group at Harvard serves as a wonderful example: http://sohp.fas.harvard.edu. The Seshat project is a good example of what can be accomplished by a global team: http://seshatdatabank.info.
16. See the report by the National Academy of Sciences: https://www.ncbi.nlm.nih.gov/books/NBK210155/. For me this is a more important concept than E. O. Wilson's "consilience" for the prospects of future work in premodern economies because I believe we need flexible teams organized around questions and historical problems.

NOTES TO PREFACE

17. See, for example, the collection of fine essays, mostly focused on Roman history, in W. Harris (2013a).
18. Donald McCloskey (1976:454); Spolaore and Wacziarg (2013).
19. Mann (1986).
20. A good introduction to social science methodology is Gerring (2012). Rightly also stressed by Jongman (2014a:169). For cultural evolutionary theory, see D. Wilson (2002); Bowles (2004); Richerson and Boyd (2005); Turchin (2013), and below. On Ranke, see the comments by Finley (1985:47–66).
21. See Haber (1999:310–11) comparing social science approaches to "traditional history."
22. Mokyr (2016). For a critique of cultural history, see Haber (1999).
23. Streuver and Holton (1979). http://www.caa-archeology.org/about-us/about/.
24. On Butzer's career, see the necrology by Mathewson (2017).
25. Morris and Manning (2005a).
26. The Chicago meeting was surely one of the most wide-ranging and impressive gatherings in the latter half of the 20th century of scholars concerned with ancient economies, although to my knowledge it has not been widely treated in the history of scholarship. Among the participants were a young Robert McCormick Adams, just barely two years out from his PhD (Near Eastern archaeology), William F. Albright (Near Eastern archaeology), John Wilson (Egyptology), William Edgerton (Egyptology), I. J. Gelb (Assyriology), Hans Güterbock (Hittitology), David Grene (classics), Mircea Eliade (religion), Leo Strauss (political philosophy), Karl Polanyi (economics, Columbia), Freidrich Hayek (the economist and fierce critic of Polanyi, listed as a member of the Committee on Social Thought at Chicago because of the tension between the Economics Department and the president of the university, Robert Maynard Hutchins), William H. McNeill (history), Brad Welles (ancient history, Yale), and Sol Tax (anthropology). For the full list of participants, see Kraeling and Adams (1960:xi–xiv). On the warm December days: https://weatherspark.com/history/30851/1958/Chicago-Illinois-United-States.
27. Turchin et al. (2015). http://seshatdatabank.info.
28. L. Hunt (2014); Stearns (2010).
29. Christian (2004); Shryock and Smail (2011).
30. Trivellato (2011). Cf. Hickey (2009) for microhistory and papyrology.
31. Hickey (2009) discussing writing history from the Egyptian papyri.
32. Morris (2013:18) discussing Tilly (1984:46–50).
33. Bagnall (1995) on the particular problems of establishing falsifiable hypotheses even with the comparative density of material offered by the documentary papyri from Egypt.

INTRODUCTION. HISTORY, THEORY, AND INSTITUTIONS: APPROACHING THE ANCIENT ECONOMY

1. http://www.nature.com/news/human-skeleton-found-on-famed-antikythera-ship wreck-1.20632. I thank Jessica Lamont for informing me of this recent discovery.
2. Hannah (2008:744). There has been much discussion and analysis of the device in the last twenty years. See the overview in Marchant (2009), and now the monographic study by Alexander Jones (2017). The website http://www.antikythera-mechanism.gr/project/overview provides an up-to-date bibliography as well.

3. Early Chinese mechanical clocks are treated by Needham et al. (1986).

4. http://www.hublot.com/en/news/mp-08-antikythera.

5. A nice overview and observations by several scholars working on it is found in Marchant (2006).

6. Nafissi (2000).

7. Hopkins (1983); Scheidel and von Reden (2002:2).

8. Kemp (2006:334).

9. Weber (1998[1909]); Searle (2010).

10. On the evolution of markets in the long run, see, e.g., van der Spek, van Leeuwen, and van Zanden (2015)

11. Bates et al. (1998).

12. Mokyr (2016).

13. Kemp (2006:303).

14. The Seshat project is currently investigating the Axial Age framework. Turchin et al. (2015). On Jaspers, see Miron (2012); and below. Cf. Graeber (2011:223–50).

15. Cf. Turchin et al. (2015:88).

16. I note in passing, by way of example, that three important books that have appeared or will appear in 2014–16 on the ancient Greek economy alone: Migeotte (2014); E. Harris, Lewis, Woolmer (2016) and Bresson (2016), the last an English translation of work published in French in 2007 and 2008.

17. Frederiksen (1975).

18. On early Italy, see Morel (2007).

19. See, for example, Morkot (2016) on Egyptian trade within an African context.

20. Horden and Purcell (2000:4). Reger (1994); Reger (2011); Archibald (2013:193–248) on the "super-region" of the northern Aegean; Horden and Purcell (2000).

21. Wrigley (2010:9). On "the first modern economy," see DeVries and van der Woude (1997).

22. I have been struck by Hirth's (2016) treatment of the Aztec economy as an "ancient economy." A comparison with the premodern Mediterranean would yield fascinating results.

23. See the essay by Izdebski et al. (2016) discussing the methodological issues in the integration of past climate change and historical analysis.

24. Finley (1999:9).

25. The concept of "embeddedness" in the ancient economy has received much comment. On its broad applicability to economic life, see Granovetter (1985); Granovetter (2005). See now the summary by Launaro (2016).

26. On private associations, see Gabrielsen (2007).

27. See Plender (2015). On critiques of capitalism, see the literature in Lipartito (2016).

28. Arthur (2015:ix).

29. Criticized by Finley (1951). See further Gagarin (1995), who rightly stressed the lack of evidence that prohibits certitude on the concept of "unity."

30. See the brief sketch of Finley's career by Shaw and Saller (1981).

31. Nafissi (2005:195).

32. Naiden (2014).

33. On "oriental despotism," see briefly below, chapter 6.

34. See the retrospective of Finley's career in the series of articles published in the special issue of *American Journal of Philology* 135/2 (Summer 2014). See also Shaw and Saller

(1981); Bresson (2003a and b); Walbank (2004); Nafissi (2005:191–283); Tompkins (2008); and Tompkins (2016) on Finley's background.

35. Nafissi (2005:206). For Meyer (1855–1930), see Calder and Demandt (1990).

36. For Rostovtzeff, see Austin (1986). For the evolution of Weber's thought, see Swedberg (1998:173–206). On Polanyi, see Granovetter (2004).

37. Nafissi (2005:267).

38. See the retrospective and critique by E. Harris (2013).

39. See Jew, Osborne, and Scott (2016).

40. Nafissi (2005:203).

41. On Meyer, see Finley (1985:53–55). Peter Fraser's *Ptolemaic Alexandria* (1972) received an especially harsh critique in the same volume, pp. 62–66, where it is pronounced a "pseudo-history" and an example of "anachronistic antiquarianism." Cf. Morris (2006). Finley was not wrong in his observation that Fraser lacked any kind of theoretical orientation to urbanization, being more concerned with cataloguing facts than with economic analysis of the ancient city. But the work remains the standard account of what was known about the city. Proper archaeological investigation of Alexandria has only begun in recent years when underwater work was possible, and this work has added substantial new information. See below.

42. On Weber's influence on Finley, see Morris (1999:xxxiiin10).

43. See Morris (1999) for fine context of the book.

44. Launaro (2016). See the valuable discussions and a series of critiques in *Annales: Histoire, Sciences Sociales* 50/5 (1995).

45. For an excellent analysis, see Nafissi (2005). I follow him closely here. See also Tompkins's (2008) review of Nafissi.

46. Nafissi (2005:49).

47. W. Harris (2011a:11); Frederiksen (1975:164).

48. Shaw (2001:431).

49. Finley (1999:22).

50. Finley used the concept of "status" in different ways, for which see Zurbach (2013: 960–61).

51. On Xenophon, see Pomeroy (1994).

52. Finley (1965b:29).

53. Finley (1999:21).

54. Frederiksen (1975).

55. Frederiksen (1975:165).

56. Frederiksen (1975:166).

57. Frederiksen (1975:168).

58. Frederiksen (1975:169).

59. Frederiksen (1975:171).

60. Von Dassow (2011). For the term *mar-banê* in Babylonian texts, see Jursa (2010:57). In Egyptian, the term is *nmh*, used to refer to either "a free person," or "unencumbered" land. See Moreno García (2016b:232–38). Cf. Goody (2006:58).

61. Russo (2004) provides a useful summary of Hellenistic science, including an assessment of what we have lost.

62. Nafissi (2005:277).

63. Good summaries of Finley and the impact of *The Ancient Economy* are given by Morris (1999), and Andreau (2002).

64. Morris (1994); Andreau (2002:33).

65. Millett (1991:9).
66. Nafissi (2005:232).
67. Nafissi (2005:227).

CHAPTER 1. NEW DIRECTIONS AND BROADER CONTEXTS IN THE STUDY OF PREMODERN ECONOMIES

1. Sewell (2005:1).
2. Bang (1998).
3. Sewell (2005:2).
4. Verboven (2015a) and Verboven (2015b) are good expositions on the uses of theory and models in studying ancient economies.
5. For an attempt to reconcile the two within historical materialism, arguing that historical specificity matters a great deal, see John Haldon (2015).
6. Rathbone (1991); Christesen (2003); Bresson (2016).
7. Ekelund and Hébert (2014:627). Good introductions to the history of economic thought can be found in Medema and Samuels (2013); Ekelund and Hébert (2014).
8. Polanyi (1944) and historians such as Braudel (1995[1949]) were early critics of the use of statistical analysis.
9. Scheidel et al. (2007:7).
10. See, for example, Bang's (2008) "bazaar economy" model for the Roman economy; the flow models for Greek city-states by J. Davies (2005). For the Near East, Jursa (2010:783–800) has proposed two basic models, the "commercialization" model and the "traditional" model. For ancient Egypt, Warburton's (1997) work has been informed by Keynes.
11. Mokyr (1991); Mokyr (2016); Bowles (2004); Beinhocker (2006).
12. See Arthur (2015). For the Roman economy, see Poblome (2015) and more broadly Verboven and Poblome (n.d.).For brief criticism of evolution and complexity, see Morris (2013:18–20).
13. Piketty (2014).
14. On the history of economics in the 20th century, see Morgan (2003).
15. L. Hunt (2014).
16. Scheidel (2017) argues that inequality has always accompanied prosperity and little can be done short of violent shocks to redistribute income.
17. Cf. Morris (2010:161, figures 3.3 and 3.7). See the important review of Clark by R. Allen (2008). For studies of demography, see below.
18. A quick thumbing through of Oleson (2008) on classical technology would dissuade the reader of the idea that the classical world was static in terms of technological change.
19. Shryock and Smail (2011:244).
20. As pointed out by A. Wilson (2014:149).
21. Keynes, for example, quoted in E. Jones (1988:53), thought there was "no progress in living standards until the sixteenth or seventeenth century." Stiner et al. (2011) provide a salutary perspective. On growth, see further below.
22. See the excellent overview by Erdkamp (2016).
23. Salisbury (1973). Frederiksen (1975:170, "a small and rather unimportant duel"); Posner (1980); Morris and Manning (2005b).
24. Wilk and Cliggett (2007:4).

25. A.H.M. Jones (1974).
26. Wilk and Cliggett (2007:13).
27. Morris (1994).
28. Morris (1994:354).
29. Andreau (1995); Parkins (1998); J. Davies (1998).
30. Jongman (1988). See the review by Frier (1991). On the limited attempts by ancient historians, see Morris (2002).
31. W. Harris (1993:15).
32. Andreau (1995).
33. Morley (2004:48–50).
34. Morley (2004:49) citing von Reden.
35. J. Davies (1998:241).
36. Cf. Hoffman (1996:196–97). Jongman (2013) combines primitive/pessimistic and modern/optimistic.
37. See Harper (2015) on Malthusian theory.
38. Posner (1980:8–10).
39. Posner (1980:18, table 1).
40. Meikle (1995/2002).
41. Meikle (1995/2002:236).
42. Saller (2005); Parkins (1998); Lyttkens (2013:8).
43. D. Jones (2014) has produced a kind of microeconomic tool kit designed for ancient historians to use in order to analyze a particular problem.
44. Meikle (1995/2002:249).
45. Lyttkens (2013:7).
46. Smail and Shryock (2013:714–15).
47. Finley (1965a), reviewing Oppenheim (1964), cited by Nafissi (2005:193). On the broader debate about historical objectivity in the American historical profession, see Novick (1988), but with little regard for ancient history.
48. Nafissi (2005:237).
49. Morris (1986:4).
50. Wilk and Cliggett (2007:33).
51. The literature is enormous. For an orientation, see the special issue of the *Journal of Economic Behavior and Organization* 90, supplement (June 2013). Sanfey (2007); Glimcher et al. (2008); Mokyr (2014) and (2016). For neuroeconomics, see Herrmann-Pillath (2009). On complexity economics, understanding economies as "complex adaptive systems," see Arthur (2015). For multilevel selection theory, see Bowles and Gintis (2011); Turchin (2013). The Seshat historical database project is aggregating a massive amount of historical data around cultural evolutionary ideas. See Turchin (2015b). See the survey by Turchin (2015a) on cultural evolutionary theory. On evolutionary economics, see Bowles and Gintis (2011). On behavioral economics, Thaler (2015) is superb.
52. See the editorial comments by Scheidel and von Reden (2002:234).
53. See, for example, a recent issue of *American Economic Review* 106/5 (May 2016), providing a window onto current thinking in economics. I thank Phil Hoffman for the reference.
54. Abramitzky (2015).
55. Lamoreaux (2015).
56. Abramitzky (2015:1246–47).

57. Finley (1975:119).

58. Nafissi (2005:235–83).

59. It pays, sometimes, to go through a scholar's unpublished notes and papers. In *Untersuchungen über die Methode der Socialwissenschaften* (1883), Carl Menger argued that "one should not attempt to develop an economic theory for each stage of economic development. In the margin of his copy, Weber wrote: "Why not?" The story is told by Swedberg (1998:196 and 294n101).

60. Mann (1986).

61. Von Reden (2015) provides an excellent account of the history and current state of the field for classical economies.

62. I am deeply in sympathy with Brooke's (2014:262) views.

63. Mokyr (2016).

64. Saller (2005). For growth see below.

65. Maddison (2007:54).

66. See the important review of Maddison by Clark (2009) and the problem of quantification and in particular on Maddison's probably low estimate of "subsistence" before 1820 CE. See also Lo Cascio and Malanima (2014), who suggest a much higher Roman GDP per capita, $800–1300, which approaches late medieval/early modern European estimates.

67. Frank and Gills (1996). For a survey of "center-periphery" analysis, and some of the issues involved in transposing world systems theory to premodern contexts, see Champion (1995).

68. On the operationalized theory, see, e.g., Christopher Chase-Dunn and Hall (1997).

69. Shipley (1993:274); Monroe (2011:93); Woolf (1990).

70. A good summary can be found in R. Smith (2009)

71. An excellent survey of the field in Smelser and Swedberg (2005:3–25). Cf. Morris (2002).

72. Smelser and Swedberg (2005:3).

73. On New Economic Sociology and its emphasis on social networks, see Granovetter (1990).

74. Mann (1986:73–340). For a critique of Mann's theories, see John Hall and Schroeder (2006).

75. Ian Morris and I laid out an agenda for the economic sociology of the ancient Mediterranean in Morris and Manning (2005a).

76. Ménard and Shirley (2014).

77. Veblen (1899); Commons (1934). On this original institutionalism, see Hodgson (2004). "New Institutional Economics" was coined by Williamson (1975:1). A good orientation to NIE in Eggertsson (1990); Furobotn and Richter (2005); Ménard and Shirley (2005). See Aoki (2001) for some fine-grained, worked examples of historical institutional analysis.

78. Furobotn and Richter (2005:34–40). On transaction costs in ancient economies, see Kehoe, Ratzan, and Yiftach (2015), and below. Silver (1995:39–77) is the strongest statement of the application of transaction cost analysis in ancient Near Eastern economies, but it has its limits. A very different framework for the economy of the Levant is Boer (2015).

79. Alston (2008).

80. Furobotn and Richter (2005:37). A good summary for ancient historians in Kehoe (2007b:1–52).

81. North and Thomas (1973); North (1981); North (1990); North (2005); North, Wallis, and Weingast (2009). For North's legacy, see Galiani and Sened (2014).
82. Ogilvie (2011).
83. Greif (2006).
84. Ménard and Shirley (2005:1).
85. For some historical application, and critique, see J. Manning (2003); Bang (2009); Maucourant (2012); Verboven (2015a). One example of its use for Rome is Kessler and Temin (2007), and for ancient Greece, Bresson (2016); E. Harris, Lewis, and Woolmer (2016).
86. Scheidel, Morris, and Saller (2007). Reviewed from the point of view of the use of NIE by Bang (2009).
87. Kehoe (2007b); Lyttkens (2013).
88. Bresson (2016); Bresson (2000). Cf. E. Harris (2001) commenting on Bresson (2000).
89. Deirdre McCloskey (1996:124–26).
90. Kaiser (2007). On the institution of the *trierarchy*, see Gabrielsen (1994).
91. Lyttkens (2013:25).
92. On the application of game theory and mathematical modeling to premodern trade, see Greif (2006). See also the important critique by Goldberg (2012).
93. Acemoglu and Robinson (2012). Cf. Acemoglu, Johnson, and Robinson (2001).
94. Acemoglu and Robinson (2012:429).
95. Clark (2007).
96. Deirdre McCloskey (2015).
97. For other critiques of NIE see Maucourant (2012); Verboven (2015a).
98. See already the excellent accounts of the field by Furobotn (1997); Hodgson (2004); Wallis (2014).
99. Greif and Mokyr (forthcoming).
100. Kloos and David (2002).
101. "Climate" does not appear in the index of Acemoglu and Robinson (2012). On criticism for leaving out climate and geography in particular, see inter alia Sachs (2012). See further below, chapter 5.
102. Kron (2004).
103. Further below, chapter 5.
104. Ober (2015a) for the institutional arguments explaining Greek prosperity.
105. Monson (2012).
106. North, Wallis, Weingast (2009, 2013). See Hough and Grier (2015).
107. E.g., Gelderblom (2013) on trade in the Low Countries.
108. Wilk and Cliggett (2007); Bourdieu (2005). The series of monographs sponsored by the Society for Economic Anthropology (SEA) is well worth consulting: *Research in Economic Anthropology*: http://econanthro.org/publications/research-in-economic-anthropology/.
109. Andreau (2002:34).
110. A classic in this mode is Veyne's (1976) study of euergetism as a form of gift giving in the Roman world.
111. Granovetter (1985).
112. For an early critique, see Fusfeld (1957).
113. Deirdre McCloskey (2010). For a response to McCloskey's critique, see Greif and Mokyr (forthcoming).

114. Culture and economic history is treated well by Sewell (2005). On religion, see Iyigun (2015). Cf. the very valuable studies of M. Greene (2000) and Trivellato (2009) on cross-cultural trade in the early modern Mediterranean. P. Brown (2012) offers a compelling syntheses of ideas of wealth in the early Christian world. And in general John Haldon (2015); Mokyr (2016).
115. On applications of evolutionary theory to other contexts, see Harms (2004). On caution using the theory, see Mokyr (2016:28–32).
116. D. Wilson (2002); Richerson and Boyd (2005); Richerson and Christiansen (2013); Turchin (2014). See also https://evolution-institute.org/project/society-for-the -study-of-cultural-evolution/.
117. Kemp (2006:334). On human cooperation, see Bowles and Gintis (2011, esp. 79–92).
118. Dawkins (1976) and Skyrms (1996) provide a good general discussion of some key concepts.
119. See for a very brief introduction, see Witt (2008). Hodgson (1993); Hodgson (2004); Mokyr (2016). Hoffman (2015).
120. Mokyr (2016), especially pp. 22–56.
121. Mokyr (2016:8) defines culture as: "a set of beliefs, values, preferences, capable of affecting behavior, that are socially (not genetically) transmitted and that are shared by some subset of society."
122. For cultural evolutionary theory applied to crop yields and long-term time horizons, see Galor and Özak (2016).
123. See Turchin (2009) for the model.
124. See the surveys by Raaflaub and Hamilton in Raaflaub and Rosenstein (1999).
125. Morris (2014); Monson and Scheidel (2015).
126. Braidwood (1963); R. Adams (1965); Butzer (1971); Butzer (1976).
127. Jameson (1994).
128. Bruce Campbell (2016) for medieval European history is a brilliant exposition of the integration of climate change data and disease with traditional historical analysis.
129. An excellent overview in Turchin (2010). On multilevel, or "group" selection, see D. Wilson (2006).
130. Sewell (2005:5).
131. Zurbach (2015).
132. Sallares (1991).
133. The latter exemplified by Jursa (2010).
134. On other Assyrian trading cities, see M. Larsen (2015:280).
135. Wilk and Cliggett (2007:17–18).
136. See Foxhall (1989) on Greek household. Egyptian papyri provide perhaps the very best source for women's economic activity. The literature here is quite large. A good orientation can be gained in Rowlandson (1998); Johnson (1998); Donker van Heel (2014) provides a readable account of one woman's life ca. 550 BCE in Egypt.
137. See the comments by Mokyr (2005).
138. See the remarks by Bresson (2016:14).
139. Kemp (2006:334).

CHAPTER 2. ANCIENT ECONOMIES: TAKING STOCK
FROM PHOENICIAN TRADERS TO THE RISE
OF THE ROMAN EMPIRE

1. Kuhrt (1995).
2. Kuhrt (2009); Kuhrt (2000); Kuhrt (1995:652–60). For Persian imperial history see Briant (2002); Wiesehöfer (2009). On the Iranian "semi-nomadic herdsmen" theory see Young (1988).
3. W. Adams (1984); S. Smith (1995).
4. See Agut-Labordère (2013).
5. See the overview in Morris and Manning (2005b).
6. See, e.g., Bentley (1993); Bentley (1996).
7. Bentley (1996:752).
8. Gabrielsen (2011).
9. Jaspers (1949/2010).
10. There is a growing literature on the meaning and importance of the "Axial Age." See Eisenstadt (1986); Bellah (2011:265–566); Turchin et al. (2015).
11. Jaspers (1949/2010:44).
12. Jaspers (1949/2010:51).
13. Baumard et al. (2015).
14. Jaspers (1949/2010:14).
15. See the analysis of Graeber (2011).
16. Morris (2010:73). See, e.g., briefly, Graeber (2011:232–37).
17. The dating of the composition of the text is debated. McClish and Olivelle (2012) date the original composition between 100 BCE and 100 CE. Thanawala (1997) suggests a 4th century BCE date. See also Rangarajan (1992); Basu and Sen (2008).
18. Bellah (2011:269).
19. Baumard et al. (2015).
20. See the brief comments by Bellah (2011:270–71). There is far more Achaemenid evidence for the empire than he appears to admit. For an excellent orientation to this evidence, see Kuhrt (2007).
21. Morris (2010:263).
22. An excellent overview of the Bronze Age, and the Bronze-Iron Age transition in the Mediterranean is provided by Broodbank (2013:345–505).
23. Broodbank (2013:348).
24. Broodbank (2013:599).
25. Warburton (2003:59–62).
26. A. Sherratt (2011:4).
27. Broodbank (2013:355).
28. But see Halstead (2011), essentially defending the Polanyian position on the Mycenaean economy. Nakassis (2013) is a sustained critique of the palace economy model. For the "palace" economy model in ancient Near Eastern economies, see Stein (1994).
29. Broodbank (2013:413).
30. Broodbank (2013:408).
31. Broodbank (2013:391–96) provides a good description.
32. O'Connor (1993:570). See the recent survey of the western Mediterranean by Broodbank (2013:416–25).

33. Broodbank (2013:441).
34. For a good overview of Bronze Age trade in the Mediterranean see Toby Wilkinson, Sherratt, and Bennet (2011). There is rich material, especially for trade during the late Bronze–early Iron age transition, in Waldbaum (1978); Duistermaat and Regulski (2011).
35. Beaujard (2011).
36. Demand (2011:220–55).
37. A. Sherratt and Sherratt (1993:362).
38. Beaujard (2010). On Mediterranean-China comparisons in the Iron Age, see Morris (2010:227–79).
39. Broodbank (2013:451).
40. On the Cyprus-Greek trade, see Popham (1994).
41. Morris (2003). Broodbank (2011:33).
42. Fantalkin (2006). Muhs (2015b) on the increased use of silver as the medium of exchange in first millennium BCE Egypt.
43. McEvedy and Jones (1978). Cf. Brooke (2014:322–23). Morris (2010:227).
44. Brooke (forthcoming).
45. Brooke (2014:323).
46. Bellah (2011:xiv).
47. Mann (1986:190–230) provides a good sketch of the power dynamics. On Greece, see Bresson (2016)
48. See below on the founding date.
49. Aubet (2001).
50. Iron smelting: Wertime (1982).
51. Goody (2012:88).
52. Brooke (2014:283, 305).
53. Liverani (2003:133). See Ö. Wikander (2000); M. Lewis (1997).
54. Warburton (2003:253–57); Liverani (2003:133).
55. Morris (2007).
56. See Lyttkens (2013) on the framework of Phoenician influence.
57. On the role of trade in early Iron Age Greece, see Tandy (1997).
58. A. Sherratt and Sherratt (1993); discussed by Bellah (2011:656n10).
59. On "leaps," see Stiner et al. (2011).
60. Brooke (2014:305, see the bibliography cited on p. 306n38).
61. Broodbank (2013:468). Nakassis (2013); Liverani (2005); Foster (1987).
62. Broodbank (2013:602–3).
63. Giardino (1992); Arruda (2009); Rouillard (2009). On Rome's expansion being connected to the control of iron and copper, see the comment by W. Harris (2003:283).
64. Docter (2002–3).
65. More on the Phoenician expansion below.
66. Hdt. 4:42. On the new ships, see van der Brugge and Kleber (2016:191).
67. Parpola and Watanabe (1988).
68. Jursa (2010:48). On the Uruk expansion, see Algazi (1993); Algaze (2008); Rothman (2001). On the use of camels, see Liverani (2003).
69. Liverani (2014:391).
70. Liverani (2014:392–95).
71. Jursa (2010:52).
72. Jursa (2005).

73. Jursa (2010:56).
74. The term Canaanite is better, "Phoenician" being the Greek word for these people. A good overview is given by Liverani (2014:420–33). For the archaeology of early Phoenician expansion, see C. Bell (2016), and van der Brugge and Kleber (2016). The work of Lorenzo Nigro at the Phoenician site of Motya in Sicily is both extraordinary and important. See inter alia Nigro (2013).
75. For cities in the ancient Near East involved in large-scale trade, see Van de Mieroop (1999).
76. S. Sherratt (2003).
77. Gubel (2009), discussing the site of Herakleopolis in Middle Egypt.
78. On the Greek creation of the Phoenician stereotype, see S. Sherratt (2010).
79. See the collection of studies in Babbi et al. (2015).
80. Iliad 23.741–44; Odyssey 14.288–89.
81. Gschnitzer (1988); Gschnitzer (1993). General consideration of Greek/non-Greek interaction are taken up by Vlassopoulos (2013).
82. Morris (2007:240). Theories abound for the connection between Phoenician and early Greek writing. For one recent analysis, see Papadopoulos (2016).
83. M. Miller (1997); Raaflaub (2009).
84. Morel (2007:492–95).
85. On its absence in Horden and Purcell (2000), see Bagnall (2005). But there are many recent examples where there is barely mention of Egypt.
86. Broodbank (2013:39–40).
87. Broodbank (2013:537).
88. Personal communication via e-mail from Professor Manfred Bietak, October 26, 2016.
89. Moreno García (2016a:7).
90. Mann (1986:223).
91. J. Davies (2004:498).
92. Mann (1986:226–27). Ober (2015a) stresses the nexus between dispersed, or in Mann's terms "diffused," political authority and economic growth.
93. Morris (2009).
94. Morris (2007:214–19) discusses the demographic estimate used here. For the compelling new study, with a thorough examination of the archaeological material, see C. Murray (2017).
95. Broodbank (2013:523), citing Morris (2007:219), who cites Scheidel (2003).
96. On Greek mobility and some of its causes, see Demand (1991); Garland (2014). On Greek colonization, see Tsetskhladze (2006); Tsetskhladze (2008).
97. See map 10.2 in Broodbank (2013:508–9).
98. Bresson (2000).
99. See the summary of events in the history of Tyre in the Neo-Assyrian and Neo-Babylonian periods by van der Brugge and Kleber (2016).
100. The origin of the Greek city-state is well treated by Zurbach (2013). On Persian control, see Elayi (2013).
101. E. Robinson (1997); E. Robinson (2011).
102. Finley (1999:183). See J. Davies (2001:17–19) for remarks on the basic problems of the term "Hellenistic" as a distinctive phase of economic history. See also Cartledge's (1997) useful overview of the period.
103. J. Davies (2001:12).

104. For economic matters contained in Polybius, see J. Davies (2013a).

105. Broodbank (2013:578).

106. This is well emphasized by Broodbank (2013), especially at pp. 578–79.

107. This is well stressed by Mann (1986:192).

108. J. Davis (2013a).

109. Maddison (2007:12). The Roman conquest of the Mediterranean is treated briefly by Maddison (2007:18–28). Part of this discussion derives originally from Manning (2015a).

110. The Hellenistic world gets a bit more press, one page, in R. Smith's survey (2009) of premodern trade, and a chapter in Abulafia, specifically on Alexandria (2011:chapter 6), to name just two recent treatments in English. Abulafia, regrettably, misses out on all the recent archaeological work at Alexandria, for which see http://www.franckgoddio.org/ and http://www.cealex.org/.

111. On quantifying the Roman economy, see Bowman and Wilson (2009), particularly part 4.

112. Redfield (1956). In an important volume on ancient trade, of the thirteen articles in Garnsey et al. (1983), five are dedicated to Greek trade, seven to Roman trade, and one, Dorothy Thompson's study of Nile grain trade, for the entire Hellenistic period.

113. On Greek colonization, see Tsetskhladze (2006); Tsetskhladze (2008).

114. Prag and Quinn (2013); Mairs (2014).

115. A. Wilson (2013:153).

116. Briant (2009:188).

117. The literature on the archive, still not fully studied, is large. For a good orientation, see Pestman (1981). See further below.

118. For the Achaemenid economy, see Briant (2002).

119. Mackil (2013); Funke and Haake (2013).

120. Polybius 2.37–10–11.

121. Shipwrecks: Gibbins (2001), and further below; silver production: de Callataÿ (2005).

122. Aperghis (2004); Chankowski and Duyrat (2004); Capdetrey (2007).

123. J. Davies (1984a); J. Davies (2001:15).

124. J. Davies (1984a:270).

125. Reger (1994); Archibald (2013). On pottery, see the remarks by A. Wilson (2013).

126. Results of the excavations in the Alexandrian harbors have been nothing short of spectacular. For updated results and literature resulting from the excavations, see http://www.franckgoddio.org/ and http://www.cealex.org/.

127. Archibald, Davies, Gabrielsen, and Oliver (2001); Archibald, Davies, and Gabrielsen (2005); and Archibald, Davies, and Gabrielsen (2011).

128. J. Davies (2001:17). Cf. Davies's own attempt at a "flow" model in J. Davies (1998); J. Davies (2005).

129. Finley (1985:7–46). A brief survey of sources for Greek history is given by Jonathan Hall (2014b:16–40).

130. See the remarks by Hopkins (2002:194–97), who refers to Collingwood's (1946:257–61) caustic critique of the "scissors-and-paste" method of collecting data. Finley (1985:61) called this the "Tell-All-You-Know" method and then proceeded by example to critique Fraser (1972).

131. Finley (1985:46). Cf. Verboven (2015b:9).

132. For this Fayyum archives, see Verhoogt (1998).

133. Scheidel (2013a:144).
134. Cf. the remarks of Finley (1985:29).
135. Maddison (2007); Acemoglu and Robinson (2012:158–75), a very cursory treatment of the Roman economy, based essentially on two sources, Finley (1999) and Bang (2008).
136. Fukuyama (2011:14).
137. Morley (2004:31).
138. Especially Sahlins (1976).
139. An overview of the early development of Egyptology as a discipline can be found in Moreno García (2009).
140. Janssen (1979:505).
141. Warburton (1997:81–130) summarizes earlier uses of theory in analyzing the ancient Egyptian economy and advocates the use of a Keynesian model for understanding Egypt. A good recent overview of the pharaonic Egyptian economy is Eyre (2014). Recent trends in the study of the ancient Egyptian economy are discussed by Moreno García (2014).
142. Ober (2015a).
143. Oppenheim (1960).
144. R. Adams (1960).
145. A brief overview of economic theory and ancient Near Eastern civilization is given by Van de Mieroop (2004).
146. Jursa (2010).
147. Jursa (2010:17).
148. A. Sherratt and Sherratt (1991). Jursa (2014a) provides a good basic overview of the Babylonian economy in the first millennium BCE. See also Leick (2009), especially the articles therein by Jursa (2009) on the first millennium BCE, and Kuhrt (2009) on the Persian Empire.
149. Bagnall (2011a) elegantly reviews some of the silences of our sources.
150. See, e.g., the Digital Archaeological Record project: http://core.tdar.org/.
151. Briefly sketched by Jonathan Hall (2014a:215–19).
152. Finley (1985); W. Harris (1993); Morris (2000).
153. J. Manning (2005). Cf. Morris (1994); Jonathan Hall (2014a and b).
154. Cf. J. Davies (1998:228) on the difficult problem of "harmonizing" different types of evidence.
155. See Hoyer and Manning (forthcoming).
156. On "positivist fallacies" in ancient history, see the astute remarks by Jonathan Hall (2014a).
157. Rathbone and von Reden (2015:166). See the earlier studies by Heichelheim (1930); Maresch (1996).
158. For Delos, see Reger (1994); Reger (2002). The important volume by van der Spek, van Leeuwen, and van Zanden (2015) collects a large amount of price data from the Mediterranean. For Babylonian prices 385–61 BCE, see http://www.iisg.nl/hpw /babylon.php. See further below.
159. Koopman and Hoogerheide (2015).
160. Jursa (2015:100).
161. E.g., Morris's (1994) review of E. Cohen (1992); Cartledge (2002a) on the problem of evidence, and the bias toward a small group of elite.
162. J. Manning (2002–3).

163. An excellent overview discussing the role of classical archaeology and ancient history in Morris (2004).
164. W. Harris (1993); Finley (1985:7). On Finley and archaeology, see Jonathan Hall (2014a:213–14); Gates-Foster (2016).
165. On regional survey methods, see Alcock and Cherry (2004).
166. H. Baker (2014).
167. Jonathan Hall (2014a:211).
168. Bard (2008).
169. Morris (2009:116).
170. J. Davies and Wilkes (2012), especially the piece therein by Bresson (2012a). A good basic introduction is Bodel (2001). For its importance in studying the economy of Hellenistic Greece, see Oliver (2007); Bresson (2012a). For Rome, see Salmeri (2012); Scheidel (2012). For Hellenistic Asia Minor, see J. Ma (2000).
171. J. Manning (2003).
172. Bodel (2001:11).
173. A good survey by Bresson (2012a).
174. Good introductions to the use of coinage as a historical source are Howgego (1995); Thonemann (2015) for Hellenistic coinage. On money and monetization, see von Reden (2010), and below. On the impact that the Laurion silver mines had on Athenian politics, see Davis (2014).
175. Howgego (1995:92–95).
176. Duyrat (2015), discussing coinage in Syria and Mesopotamia, 6th to 1st centuries BCE.
177. Morris (1986:5).
178. Morris (1986:6).
179. Finley (1999:17–18); Morley (1999) on literary evidence. Some general remarks by Ekelund and Hébert (2014:10–12).
180. On Polybius as a valuable source for Hellenistic economic behavior and institutions, see the insightful essay by J. Davies (2013a).
181. Jursa (2010) provides an excellent survey of the material. On the Egibi family, see Wunsch (2009); Wunsch (2010); and further below.
182. I am grateful for Michael Jursa's confirmation of the number of texts (personal communication via e-mail September 19, 2016). Cf. Jursa (2014c).
183. Jursa (2005:172). Cf. the remarks of Radner (2015:329) on the narrower focus, constrained by limited documentary material, of Neo-Assyrian texts of royal activity.
184. The texts themselves are published in a series of monographs by Abraham Sachs and Hermann Hunger. A good overview of the material is given by Rochberg-Halton (1991). Important secondary studies on markets and prices based on the diaries by Slotsky (1997); van der Spek and van Leeuwen (2014).
185. But see Bagnall (2011a) on the extent of papyrus and everyday writing in the Mediterranean world. A good introduction to papyrology is available in Bagnall (2009a). See in particular therein the article by Cuvigny (2009). For Greek papyri outside Egypt, see the survey by Gascou (2009).
186. Willy Clarysse and Thompson (2006).
187. Rostovtzeff (1930:203).
188. On papyrology and historical analysis, see Bagnall (1995). On cartonnage, see briefly Vandorpe, Clarysse, and Verreth (2015:23–28).
189. Van Beek and Depauw (2013:102).

190. For an example, see J. Manning (2002–3).
191. The literature on each archive is enormous. For an orientation to the Zenon archive, see Pestman (1981); Vandorpe, Clarysse, and Verreth (2015:447–55). For the 2d century BCE official archive of the village scribe Menches, see the studies by Crawford (1971); Verhoogt (1998); Vandorpe, Clarysse, and Verreth (2015:440–46). For the important 3d century CE Apion archive, see Rathbone (1991); Mazza (2001); Hickey (2012).
192. See further below.
193. Rostovtzeff (1922). On the special character of the Fayyum, see D. Thompson (1999b); in contrast to the river valley: J. Manning (2003). Finley (1985:34–36) was extraordinarily severe, not without some reason, about the use of papyrological archives for economic history and the propensity to let description of documentary detail stand for a "synthesis of economic history."
194. The range of documentation on ostraca is in fact quite wide. See Bagnall (2011a:117–37).
195. Muhs (2011).
196. Bagnall (1995).
197. http://www.trismegistos.org/arch/list_all.phpwww.trismegistos.org. See Vandorpe (2009), and Vandorpe, Clarysse, and Verreth (2015) on the complexities and problems of reconstructing and analyzing archives.
198. Keenan, Manning, and Yiftach-Firanko (2014).
199. Bogaert (1994); Muhs (2011).
200. For Pompeii, see Jongman (1988). On GIS techniques, applied to the study of Roman agriculture for example, see Goodchild (2013).
201. Heichelheim (1930); Duncan-Jones (1982); W. Harris (1993); Bowman and Wilson (2009); de Callataÿ (2014).
202. http://www.romaneconomy.ox.ac.uk.

CHAPTER 3. BRONZE, IRON, AND SILVER: TIME, SPACE, AND GEOGRAPHY AND ANCIENT MEDITERRANEAN ECONOMIES

1. D. Lewis (2016a).
2. Taagepera (1979). On continuity as well as change between Achaemenid and Seleukid Babylonia, for example, see Sherwin-White (1987). I return to this issue with respect to trade in chapter 8.
3. Vandorpe (2002).
4. Sahlins (1977:226). See Dodgshon (1998). On "metaethnic frontiers," see Turchin (2007).
5. Cf. the comments of J. Davies (1998:242).
6. Malkin (2011); Waerzeggers (2014); Taylor and Vlassopoulos (2015).
7. On timescales in archaeology, see Wandsnider (2004) and the literature cited there.
8. Mokyr (2016:59–69) on the role of such entrepreneurs in social change.
9. Braudel (1995[1949]:18).
10. Braudel (1995[1949]:168–275). See Morris and Manning (2005a:132–33) for some basic considerations.
11. As always, there are exceptions. See, for example, Osborne (1996a) on the "short" 6th century in Greece.
12. A. Baker (2003:180).

13. Pomeranz (2000).
14. Turchin et al. (2015); Currie et al. (2015).
15. See Shaw (2008) and his excellent comments.
16. Goody (2006:31).
17. Mann (1986:28–29).
18. McMichael (2011) has identified six different timescales of climate change for human history: "(1) influences on biological evolution (over millennia); (2) great transitions in human culture and ecology (at times of state-changes in climate); (3) long-term climatic changes (multicentury); (4) medium-term climatic changes (multidecade); (5) short-term climatic changes (multiyear); and (6) acute climatic/weather events."
19. On the French tradition, see, e.g., Brunhes (1920); Dion (1934).
20. Thonemann (2011).
21. W. Harris (2005:4).
22. Finley (1999:29–30).
23. Morris (2009).
24. Bentley (1993); Bentley (1996). For cross-cultural exchange in the early modern Mediterranean, see Trivellato (2009).
25. See, e.g., K. Bradley and Cartledge (2011), and Neal and Williamson (2014), to name just two recent publications.
26. Goody (2006).
27. Bentley (1996). Following Irwin and O'Rourke's (2014) definition of shift as "slow-moving, long-term changes in comparative advantage or shifts in the geopolitical equilibrium," in contrast to "shock" (a "sudden jolt" to the equilibrium caused by war, or some other political event, or sudden climate "reversals" that created poor irrigation conditions). I take the term "reversal" from Brooke (2014).
28. Christopher Chase-Dunn and Hill (2009); Turchin (2010); Inoue et al. (2015).
29. Turchin (2010).
30. Brooke (2014).
31. Cf. Brooke (forthcoming).
32. Brooke (2014:263).
33. Barker (2009:4).
34. Cf. Broodbank (2013:80).
35. Well stressed by Bentley (1996).
36. I very much agree with Broodbank's (2013:604) "subversive" encouragement to write a new Egyptian history that takes account of the many regions, what Butzer called "eco-zones," of Egypt, the valley, the Fayyum, the delta, the oases, and the deserts on both sides of the river valley.
37. Woodard (1997).
38. Inoue et al. (2015). Morris (2010:263–70).
39. See Bennett (2016) for a mathematical simulation of the theory.
40. Scheidel (2013b:30). On the concept of metaethnic frontiers, areas that saw intense competition between ethnic groups but fostered tighter social cohesion within them, see Turchin (2003).
41. See Bintliff (1991:6, fig. 1.2).
42. Morris (2003:42) rightly calls into question the idea of "timelessness."
43. Marcus (1998). On networks, see Malkin (2011). On "expansionary forces," see Chaudhuri (1990:41).
44. Broodbank (2013:537).

45. Chaudhuri (1990:92–148) is an excellent treatment of the issues. As an example, the continuities between late New Kingdom Egypt and the first three centuries of the first millennium BCE have been pointed out by Morkot (2016).
46. Ricoeur (1988).
47. Horden and Purcell (2000:261–62).
48. Lyttkens (2013:18); Williamson (2000).
49. Shaw (2001:439). On travel times in the Roman Mediterranean, see now the Orbis project at Stanford: http://orbis.stanford.edu/.
50. Chaudhuri (1990:101; 103).
51. Gozzoli (2006:191–225).
52. For a translation of the Canopus decree, see Austin (2006:471). For a full treatment of the text, see Pfeiffer (2004). For the "social construction" of time, see Hannah (2008) and the literature cited there, and Feeney (2008).
53. Kosmin (2014:100–3). On the "theft" of time, see Goody (2006:14–18).
54. Treated briefly below in chapter 4.
55. Chaudhuri (1990:107).
56. I give an example in chapter 5 of how paleoclimate proxy data can now show us the random but fixable timescales of events correlated with climate change with respect to the Nile.
57. Broodbank (2013:505). Cf. Morris (2000:257–306). There was a time lag in technological diffusion in the Near East already in Iron Age 1200–1000 BCE. A. Sherratt and Sherratt (1991), diffusion of technology was slower to move west (and south).
58. Emphasized well by Morris (2000) for the archaic Greek world.
59. Hannah (2008).
60. Giddens and Pierson (1998:94–117); Morris (2000).
61. Hall (2014b:321).
62. On Athenian advice, see J. Davies (2004).
63. E.g., Frank and Thompson (2005).
64. Hicks (1969:7).
65. Hicks (1969:39–40).
66. Morris and Manning (2005b:15–25).
67. Luterbacher et al. (2012:129); Bresson (2016:119–29).
68. Mediterranean climate is briefly summarized by Bar-Matthews (2012), on whom I rely here. For a thorough study of Mediterranean climate and historical proxy data, see Lionello (2012).
69. Chaudhuri (1990:23).
70. Bar-Matthews (2012:165).
71. S. Manning (2013).
72. Luterbacher et al. (2012:126).
73. For overviews of the Mediterranean climate system, see Bolle (2003); J. Hughes (2005). The Sicilian climate is briefly surveyed by De Angelis (2016). A comprehensive multidisciplinary guide to the ecology and geophysics of the Mediterranean basin is Goffredo and Dubinsky (2014).
74. Luterbacher et al. (2012:138).
75. Bolle (2003:9).
76. J. Hughes (2005:2).
77. J. R. McNeill (1992:68–103);
78. Bresson (2016:37).

79. Bresson (2016:31–70). Butzer's (2005) study of the Argolid is important.
80. W. Harris (2005:4).
81. Morris (2003).
82. For example, the "single zone" in the early Bronze Age metals trade discussed by Barjamovic (2008), citing inter alia Rahmstorf (2006).
83. Kemp (2006:33).
84. Wengrow (2006:22).
85. Braudel (1995[1949]). On Braudel as a historian, see Poloni-Simard (2003). On his concept of time, see Santamaria and Bailey (1984). Cf. Broodbank's (2013:597) conceptual map of the history of seafaring in the Mediterranean. Cf. P. Burke (1990:39).
86. Gras (1995).
87. Braudel (2001).
88. The Indian Ocean has also been analyzed in a Braudelian framework by Chaudhuri (1985); Chaudhuri (1990). See a recent assessment by Fusaro (2010). More "Mediterraneans," are discussed by Abulafia (2005). On Braudel's legacy, Shaw (2008) is excellent.
89. For a thought-provoking review of the first three, see Shaw (2008).
90. Horden and Purcell (2000). *Corrupting Sea* has evoked much reaction. See, e.g., W. Harris (2005). On "ruralization" of Mediterranean history, see the comments by W. Harris (2005:29–34). There are many good reviews, among them Keenan (2000); Shaw (2001); Algazi (2005).
91. Horden and Purcell (2000:175–203).
92. Horden and Purcell (2000:263).
93. On Upper Paleolithic connectivity, see briefly Stiner et al. (2011:248–50).
94. See Prag and Quinn (2013), and an article by Purcell therein.
95. Horden and Purcell (2000).
96. Morris (2003).
97. Broodbank (2011:28).
98. Cf. Morris (2003:44).
99. Broodbank (2013:22).
100. See Butzer (2005); Brooke (2014:272–75) and Harper (2015); Harper (2016) for the debate. W. Harris (2005:10); Broodbank (2013:71).
101. Butzer (2005).
102. Shaw (2001:422).
103. De Romanis and Maiuro (2015).
104. W. Harris (2005:2). Cf. Demand (2011).
105. Morris (2003:33). On Atlantic exploration, Roller (2006). For Africa, see Burstein (1995). Exploration under the Ptolemies is summarized in Préaux (1939:356–59).
106. McPherson (1988). On attempts to quantify "connectivity" in the Mediterranean, see Leidwanger (2013).
107. J. Davies (2013a:322).
108. Bagnall (2005).
109. See the arguments by Morris (2003) suggesting a global orientation for ancient history.
110. Sallares (2013:167–68) catalogues some events. See comments by W. Harris (2005:-34–35). For the effects of Vesuvius on the Campanian wine industry, and its impact on wine exports to India, for example, see Williams (2004).
111. Pliny, *Epistulae* VI.16.

112. Broodbank (2013:76). For Mount Etna data and the history of known eruptions, see: http://volcano.si.edu/volcano.cfm?vn=211060. Plutarch, in his *Life of Caesar* 69, 3, noted the volcanic dust veil of the eruption of 44 BCE, and local crop failure.

113. Broodbank's map illustrates this well and highlights especially how this affected the Aegean.

114. Spengler et al. (2016). Baumer (2012–16) is a magnificent introduction to central Asian history and culture. On disease vectors and the role of central Asian sources in the medieval period, see Bruce Campbell (2016:241–43).

115. Quinn (2013).

116. Quinn (2013:261), citing Shaw (2003:93).

117. A. Wilson (2013).

118. Quinn (2013:266–68); Hdt. 4.181–85. Liverani (2000) on the archaeology of the trade routes. On Fazzan, see Mattingly (2003); Mattingly (2007); Mattingly (2010).

119. On the grain production capacity of Cyrenaica, see Bresson (2011).

120. *SEG* IX 7. Trans. Austin (2006:text 289). Hölbl (2001:210).

121. Hind (1995–96); Braund (2007); Moreno (2007).

122. Slaves: Avram (2007); timber: Hannestad (2007).

123. Mairs (2014).

124. Surveys of Indian Ocean trade in Chaudhuri (1985); Chaudhuri (1990). On life cycles in the Indian Ocean, Chaudhuri (1990:382–87). Seland (2006); Seland (2008); Seland (2010). For Roman trade with India, see the useful bibliography collected by Andrew Wilson, http://oxrep.classics.ox.ac.uk/bibliographies/indoro man_trade_bibliography/.

125. On the role of the Red Sea and its economic connections to the Egyptian interior, see Schörle (2010). A more extensive overview of Red Sea trade in the Hellenistic and Roman period can be found in Sidebotham (2011).

126. Seland (2008:73).

127. Marek (2016).

128. Thonemann (2011).

129. Hdt. 2.5.

130. There was more rainfall in Egypt, North Africa, and Spain than today. See Reale and Dirmeyer (2000), and Reale and Shukla (2000).

131. Horden and Purcell (2000:45; 397). Bagnall (2005); Bresson (2005a).

132. Bagnall (2005:340).

133. I take the phrase "double sea exposure" from Fusaro (2010:3). The deep historic connections between the Mediterranean and Indian Ocean is explored by Pollard (2014).

134. Said (1993). The Moulouya, in Morocco, 520 km in length, drains today 53,500km².

135. Mann (1986).

136. For the basic "labor exploitation" model of state formation, see R. Allen (1997).

137. Butzer (1999).

138. Hvidt (1998:2).

139. Fraedrich et al. (1997).

140. Said (1993:125–26); Hassan (2007). See below on volcanic forcing.

141. Kondrashov, Feliks, and Ghil (2005); Berhane, Zaitchik, and Dezfuli (2014).

142. They have been discussed by B. Bell (1971); B. Bell (1975); Butzer (1984); Seidlmayer (2001). Bonneau (1971) provides subjective observations collected from Greek papyri from Ptolemaic to late Roman times. It is in need of updating.

143. Eyre (2004:161–62).

144. Butzer (1984); Hassan (1994); Seidlmayer (2001); Eyre (2004).
145. Thonemann (2011:19).
146. A survey of the evidence for an exchange network between Crete and the delta is well documented from the Old Kingdom. See Steel (2010).
147. Steel (2010:472–73).
148. Good recent survey of these regions in Toby Wilkinson (2007).
149. Bowman (2009:181). Delta settlements are discussed by Trampier (2014). Cf. Butzer (2002). See Blouin (2014) for the delta in the Roman period; further below.
150. Aristotle, *Met.* 361b35–362a2.
151. Totman (1993:15).
152. For Hawaii, the classic work is Earle (1978).
153. Cf. Steward (1955), reflecting Wittfogel's influence.
154. Butzer (1999:381–82).
155. Eyre (2000); Bonneau (1993).
156. Rathbone (1994:35). The average gradient of the Nile River in Egypt proper is virtually flat, dropping about 1 m in 10 km, or 1:10,000.
157. Butzer (1999:382). The essential local control, centered on officials in the villages, is well documented in Ptolemaic times and later. See Bonneau (1993).
158. Butzer (1999).
159. Schenkel (1978).
160. Butzer (2001).
161. Mann (1986:110).
162. Cf. Mann (1986:97–98; 161).
163. On Egyptian kingship, see O'Connor and Silverman (1995).
164. Gellner (1983:fig 1); cf. Morris and Manning (2005a:150).
165. Mann (1986:114).
166. Skinner quoted in E. Wilkinson (2000:5).
167. Ekholm and Friedman (1979).
168. Mann (1986).
169. For ancient Egypt, see Eyre (2004). Bali's social organization centered around irrigation are instructive. See Lansing (2006).
170. Chaudhuri (1990:261).
171. O'Leary (1989:252). Cf. Butzer (1976:110).
172. Eyre (2000).
173. H. Cullen et al. (2002).
174. Purcell (2012:375).
175. Weiss (2015).
176. A. Schneider and Adalı (2014:436).
177. Butzer (1995:136).
178. Wunsch (2010:42).
179. Butzer (1995:142).
180. For a short overview of climate and economic history of the ancient Near East see Jursa (2010:33–35).
181. Cf. Morris (2010:186).
182. Jursa (2010:63–99) with relevant literature cited.
183. H. Cullen et al. (2000).
184. A. Schneider and Adalı (2014).

CHAPTER 4. AGRICULTURE AND LABOR

1. The literature on premodern agrarian systems is enormous. We await the next comparative sociological study in the tradition of Weber (1998[1909]).
2. Wrigley (2010:9).
3. Translation by Edgar (1931:90).
4. The word translated here as "corn" means "wheat." One hundred artabs of wheat is a rather large amount. A person could live on ten artabs per year. See Pestman (1990:49). Interestingly, this standard word for grain measure in Egypt is a Persian loan word.
5. W. Clarysse and Vandorpe (1995:28).
6. Reger (2002:135). On the Delian prices, see below.
7. Gehrke (1986:18–19).
8. Bresson (2016:143).
9. Crawford (1971); Verhoogt (1998).
10. See, for example, the stunning critique of Critchfield (1978) by T. Mitchell (2002:-123–52).
11. Halstead (1987). Reprinted in Scheidel and von Reden (2002:53–70). See, e.g., Jameson (1992); Forbes (1992); Mattingly (1994:97–103). Cf. cautious remarks in Isager and Skydsgaard (1995:6).
12. Halstead (2014), an excellent study of the regional and cultural variability of traditional agricultural practices in the Mediterranean and their applicability to the premodern context.
13. Osborne (1987).
14. For Greece, see J. Davies (2007:342–43).
15. Keenan (1985) and Keenan (1989) are classic microhistorical studies of agrarian/pastoral tension in Byzantine and Roman Egypt respectively. For the Near East, Briant (1982) remains important. For general considerations, see Horden and Purcell (2000:-82–87).
16. My colleagues and I have laid out a basic agenda in Currie et al. (2015).
17. D. Jones (2014:440–71).
18. Horden and Purcell (2000:264).
19. Bresson (2016:165–66).
20. De Angelis (2016:166).
21. Jursa (2010:33); D. Thompson (2012:8).
22. D. Thompson (1999a).
23. Cf. Kosmin (2014:196–97).
24. Bresson (2016:165–66).
25. Kaye (2015).
26. General surveys of Egyptian agriculture and the land tenure system: Eyre (2014); Katary (2007); Katary (2013a). For a good historical overview of Egyptian agriculture from ancient to modern times, see Bowman and Rogan (1999).
27. Eyre (1994); Eyre (1999).
28. For a survey of food production and processing, see the relevant chapter in Nicholson and Shaw 2000:505–671).
29. Sallares (1991:368–72).
30. Moreno García (2007); Agut-Labordère (2011).
31. Moreno García (2014:248). See also Moreno García (2016b) for a historical overview of temples and land tenure through the Saite period.

32. Moreno García (2014:244).
33. On the organization of the New Kingdom economy, and the role of temples, see Haring (1997). Cf. Horden and Purcell's (2000) non-Polanyian and vaguer use of "redistribution" as a catchall term that encompasses both market and nonmarket transactions, and the apt remarks of Algazi (2005:231–32).
34. Weber (1998:105–33).
35. See Haring (1997) and his fine-grained analysis of one type of temple estate of the New Kingdom. Cf. Weber (1998:253).
36. Katary (2013b:721).
37. Moreno García (2016b:228–32).
38. Katary (2013b:750).
39. Monson (2012:82).
40. See below, chapter 5, on flood variability. The yield figures are standardly reported in many sources; inter alia Eyre (1995:183–84); Eyre (2014:293). Stating average yields is of course problematic. On efforts to model crop yields, see Currie et al. (2015).
41. Cf. the comments by Erdkamp (2016:10–11).
42. G. Hughes (1952); Donker van Heel (1995); Agut-Labordère (2013:1018–20); Moreno García (2015).
43. Surveyed J. Manning (2003); Monson (2012).
44. For a good orientation to the recent work on archaeology, see Bagnall (2001); Bagnall (2011b).
45. Hassan (1993); Monson (2012).
46. Bowman (2013:220–21).
47. J. Manning (1999).
48. Vandorpe (2015:108–9).
49. Horden and Purcell (2000:255).
50. New varieties of grape: *P. Cair. Zen* 1 59033 (257 BCE); Milesian sheep: *P. Cair. Zen* 2 59142 (256 BCE).
51. Bresson (2016:166–67).
52. On new crops, and the scale of viticulture, see D. Thompson (1999b:133–34).
53. On private property: Jasnow (2003:328–39); J. Manning (2003).
54. J. Manning (2003).
55. On the trial, see more above.
56. Monson (2012:37). Cf. Rathbone (1990).
57. Blouin (2013); Blouin (2014), on which this summary is based.
58. Blouin (2014:259–60).
59. Blouin (2014).
60. Blouin (2014:269).
61. On the 3d century BCE Edfu texts (*P. Hausw. Manning*), see J. Manning (2003).
62. I rely here on Jursa (2010:184–206). See also Fales and Postgate (1995).
63. Jas (2000).
64. See Mayshar, Moav, and Neeman (2014) comparing land tenure arrangements in Egypt and the Near East, distinguishing "transparent" from "opaque" land conditions (from the point of view of the state) that drove differences in political economies and in fiscal regimes.
65. Jursa (2013).

66. Jursa (2009:225).
67. The classic study is R. Adams (1981). See now the survey by M. Hudson and Levine (1999); Joannès (2002).
68. Jursa (2009:225). As high as 1:24 according to Jursa (2010:48).
69. Jursa (2009:225); Jursa (2010:171–84).
70. On the family and their archive, see the convenient summary by Wunsch (2009); more details in Wunsch (1999).
71. Wunsch (2009:238); Wunsch (2010).
72. Jursa (2009:233).
73. Oelsner, Wells, and Wunsch (2003). See below.
74. Introductions to Greek agriculture can be found in Isager and Skydsgaard (1992); Jameson (1992); Burford (1993); J. Davies (2007); Bresson (2016:142–74).
75. Bresson (2016:158).
76. Burford (1993:104).
77. Pomeroy (1994).
78. On Demosthenes, see Macdowell (2009). Cf. Bresson (2016:146).
79. Morris (1994:363–64).
80. Bresson (2016:135–38).
81. Bresson (2016:143).
82. Foxhall (2002); Morris (2009:120).
83. Alcock (2007).
84. Bresson (2016:149–50).
85. For Macedonia, see Margaritis (2016).
86. Burford (1993:113–14).
87. Bresson (2016:162–63).
88. Burford (1993:128); Kron (2015:164).
89. Bresson (2016:120).
90. Bresson (2016:168). Cf. J. Davies (2007:342n46).
91. Foxhall (2007:13); Forbes (1992).
92. Isager and Skydsgaard (1992:83–107); J. Davies (2007:346).
93. Burford (1993:122–24); Bresson (2016:121).
94. J. Davies (2007:349).
95. Burford (1993:167–81).
96. J. Davies (2007:350).
97. Bresson (2016:158).
98. J. Davies (2007:343); Oliver (2007).
99. Scheidel (1995); Scheidel (1996).
100. An overview of ancient Near Eastern and Bronze Age Aegean slavery in Steinkeller and Hudson (2015).
101. On Greek categories, see Vlassopoulos (2011).
102. Aristotle, *Pol.*, book 1.
103. For example, see Dari-Mattiacci (2013).
104. Dari-Mattiacci (2013:105).
105. Highly recommended as an introduction is O. Patterson (1982).
106. Jameson (1977–78); Cartledge (2002b); Jameson (2002).
107. Steinkeller (2015).
108. In the battle narratives of Thutmosis III, ca. 1450 BCE, for example. An important text from the Middle Kingdom in Egypt preserves a long list of Egyptian and "Asi-

atic" slaves, the latter in a domestic context. On the text, see Hayes (1955); Quirke (1990).

109. Westbrook (2001:334). Overviews of debt in Jasnow and Westbrook (2001); M. Hudson and Van de Mieroop (2002).

110. Snell (2011:15–17).

111. Steinkeller (2015:9–14).

112. Nathan Brown (1994); even in the Egypt of the 19th century under Mohammed Ali, however, wage labor was used to pay for canal and dyke work: Marsot (1984:151).

113. Radner (2015) on Neo-Assyrian wage labor.

114. Surveyed by Oelsner, Wells, and Wunsch (2003:926–33); Jursa (2010:232–40), on whom I rely here. Dandamaev (1984) remains a standard account.

115. Wunsch and Magdelene (2014).

116. Weber (1998:112). In Egypt, there have been several detailed studies of each period of Egyptian history. See Eyre (1987a); Eyre (1987b).

117. J. Manning (2003).

118. A review on the issue of degrees of coercive power in labor is treated by Goelet (2015).

119. Moreno García (2015).

120. Weber (1998:126).

121. Finley (1999:35–61). See the survey of pharaonic Egyptian labor by Cooney (2010).

122. Lehner (2015).

123. Quirke (1990:127–54).

124. Cooney (2010:166–68).

125. Lehner (2015); Hatnub graffito.

126. Moreno García (2015:20). See already Weber ((1998[1909]; 1998 ed.:118–33).

127. An important land survey text from the temple of Amun at Thebes text from the early first millennium BCE was published by Vleeming (1993).

128. Moreno García (2015).

129. Moreno García (2015).

130. J. Manning (1994).

131. On the tax, Muhs (2011:36); Blouin (2014:133–34).

132. D. Thompson (1999a) Cf. Pestman (1980).

133. D. Thompson (1999a:112).

134. A recent broad survey of wage labor contracts and contracts concerned with slavery in the papyri in Keenan, Manning, and Yiftach-Firanko (2014:401–69).

135. See the survey of Hellenistic slavery by D. Thompson (2011). Keenan, Manning, and Yiftach-Firanko (2014:442–69) surveys slavery as documented in Egyptian documentary papyri.

136. Foxhall (1990).

137. Burford (1993:183).

138. J. Davies (2007:352).

139. Cartledge (2011); on the helot population, see D. Lewis (2016a:326–27).

140. Plato, *Leg.* 6.776D–E.

141. D. Lewis (2016a:327); Rihill (2011:50).

142. Descat (2011:209).

143. Burford (1993:189–91).

144. Jameson (1992); Osborne (1995:32–34); E. Harris (2002). Good surveys of slavery in the Greek world by Garlan (1988); Burford (1993:208–22); Cartledge, Cohen, and Foxhall (2002); and K. Bradley and Cartledge (2011).

145. Surveyed by P. Hunt (2011).
146. See Zurbach (2013) summarizing the literature.
147. Braund (2011:119). On war booty, see Préaux (1978/1:366–70); Austin (1986).
148. Braund (2011:118).
149. Braund (2011:124).
150. Burford (1993:209).
151. D. Lewis (2016a:322).
152. D. Thompson (2011:198), citing *C.Ord.Ptol.* 22 (= *C. Ptol. Sklav.* 3.20–23).
153. Moreno García (2016b).
154. D. Thompson (2011:200–202).
155. J. Manning (2003).
156. D. Thompson (2011).
157. Descat (2011:210–11).
158. D. Thompson (2011:209–10).
159. *Wisdom of Onchsheshonqy* 7/17. A late Ptolemaic text but perhaps reflecting earlier traditions.
160. Keenan, Manning, and Yiftach-Firanko (2014:442–69) for a survey.
161. D. Thompson (2011:205).
162. See Keenan, Manning, and Yiftach-Firanko (2014:450–51).
163. Willy Clarysse and Thompson (2006).
164. Descat (2011:212–13).

CHAPTER 5. THE BOUNDARIES OF PREMODERN ECONOMIES: ECOLOGY, CLIMATE, AND CLIMATE CHANGE

1. *Plant Explanations* 5.14.2, cited by Bresson (2016:479n108). Cf. Hardy and Totelin (2016:177). Sections of this chapter derive originally from J. Manning (2010) and Manning et al. (2017).
2. See the wonderful biography of von Humboldt by Wulf (2015).
3. Cf. the classic anthropological study by Forde (1934).
4. Neville Brown (2001) provides a sketch of the history of the integration of climate and history.
5. See further below where I develop a case study of the volcanic impacts of the Nile during the Ptolemaic Egypt.
6. D'Alpoim Guedes et al. (2016).
7. S. White (2011) offers an excellent historical analysis of the "Little Ice Age" that links climatic change and drought to disease, social unrest, and famine in the Ottoman Empire during the 16th century.
8. Bruce Campbell (2016) is superb, and I rely here on his analysis.
9. Butzer (2012); Liu et al. (2007).
10. Bruce Campbell (2016). Harper (2017) on Rome is important.
11. Liu et al. (2007).
12. Lattimore (1979:35).
13. Bruce Campbell (2010:307).
14. Elis, Haber, and Horrillo (2017).
15. See Radkau (2008:28) with literature cited there.
16. Flohr et al. (2016). An extreme example of human-caused collapse theory in the premodern Mediterranean is J. Hughes (1994).

17. Lamb (1995:10–12); Brooke (2014:2). Cf. Bruce Campbell (2010).

18. Isager and Skydsgaard (1992:11)

19. Brooke (2014:275) with the cited literature.

20. Radkau (2008:91–93).

21. Wittfogel (1957). A quick Google Scholar search for "Oriental Despotism" yields more than twenty-six thousand items.

22. Butzer (1996).

23. Voltaire, *Essai sur les moeurs*, chapter 194. For treatments of the theory relative to the Near East, see Van de Mieroop (1999:112); Snell (1997:145–58); Dandamaev (1984:-70–76); Jursa (2010). See J. Manning (2010) for Egypt.

24. M.I.J. Davies (2009); J. Manning (2010).

25. Mayshar, Moav, and Neeman (2014).

26. Elis, Haber, and Horrillo (2017), with a good review of the economics literature.

27. Elis, Haber, and Horrillo (2017:5–6).

28. Butzer (1984:112); Butzer (2012).

29. Cf. Bresson (2016:27).

30. Broodbank (2013:607).

31. Huntington's work (1913); Huntington (1915) is foundational. See the review by J. R. McNeill (1997).

32. See, e.g., Hornborg et al. (2007).

33. See, for example, the study on "terrain ruggedness" that could constrain trade and growth or protect some communities from predation by Nunn and Puga (2012).

34. On the concept of bounded rationality, the idea, as opposed to "rational-agent" models of economic behavior, that humans make decisions based on information limited by cognitive ability, time constraints and incomplete information, see Kahneman (2003).

35. Trans. Waterfield (1998).

36. Horden and Purcell (2000:301).

37. *Decline and Fall* 3:30.

38. Trans. Francis Adams, the Internet Classics Archives, http://classics.mit.edu/Hippocrates/airwatpl.2.2.html.

39. Mayshar, Moav, and Neeman (2014).

40. Shaw (2001:434).

41. Mann (1986:223).

42. J. Davies (2001:44); Thonemann (2011). See the general remarks in A. Baker (2003:156–205).

43. Reger (2011).

44. Barjamovic (2008).

45. Barjamovic (2008:99).

46. Burke in E. Burke and Pomeranz (2009:xi).

47. See the overview in Martini and Chesworth (2010). For the Greek world, Sallares (1991); for Egypt, Butzer (1976); Hassan (1994); Scheidel (2001); for the Near East, see T. J. Wilkinson (2003); T. J. Wilkinson (2010). On disease: Sallares (2002); Sallares (2014).

48. Cronon (1983:vii).

49. Sallares (2007); Sallares (2009).

50. Emphasized well by Brooke (2014).

51. Pomeranz in E. Burke and Pomeranz (2009:8); Sallares (1991:33).

52. Carlsen et al. (1994).

53. Bowman and Wilson (2011). Morley's study of Rome (1996) is one useful approach. On the history of Chicago, see Cronon (1991).
54. See also his earlier monograph, Braudel (1971).
55. Le Roy Ladurie (1979:291).
56. Pioneering work has been published in the *Journal of Interdisciplinary History* since volume 10 (1980); Rotberg and Rabb (1981); D. Smith (1989).
57. On the history of ice core research, see Jouzel (2013), and the compelling account of Richard B. Alley (2000).
58. Izdebski et al. (2016).
59. See Braudel (1971); Braudel (1979).
60. Bryson and Padoch (1981:4).
61. DeVries (1980:603).
62. DeVries (1980:599).
63. Cf. Izdebski et al. (2016:6).
64. See the survey by Bresson (2014a).
65. R. Adams (1965); more recently Zettler (2003).
66. Published in Journal of Interdisciplinary History 10 (1980), and in Rotberg and Rabb (1981).
67. For a detailed use of paleoclimate records in deep history, see Brooke (2014). R. Bradley (2015) is an excellent introduction to paleoclimatology and the use of climate proxies and models. Izdebski et al. (2016) review the various modes of work (climate history, environmental history, and the historical reconstructions of climate).
68. Matthews et al. (2012:7–20). On ice core analysis techniques using inductively coupled plasma mass spectrometry, see McConnell et al. (2002).
69. Morris (2010) broadly uses climate change in his macrohistorical account of east-west divergence. For an exposition of the basic problems, see Petrie et al. (2017).
70. Bruce Campbell (2016:xvii).
71. Koepke and Baten (2005a and b); Malkin (2011:12); Broodbank (2013:43); Brooke (2014:1–13).
72. Schnaiberg (2005); Bruce Campbell (2010); S. White (2011); Petrie et. al. (2017). See the overview of some classical sources for climate by Bresson (2014a).
73. Harper (2015:562).
74. Hsiang and Burke (2014:41).
75. Cf. Rabb (1981:252).
76. R. Adams (1981); Butzer (1976); Butzer (1997); Butzer (2005); Butzer (2012). Garnsey (1988) using tree rings. On tree rings see also S. Manning (2013:136–45). R. Bradley (2015:4). A complete list of paleoclimate proxies, and their different timescale parameters is provided in R. Bradley (2015, table 1.1 and table 1.2).
77. See Brooke (2014:288–316) for a summary of long-term climate trends and history. He considers 3000–500 BCE to be a climatic optimum, but there was of course considerable local variability within this broad stretch of history.
78. The Palermo Stone is briefly summarized by Said (1993:134–35).
79. Reflected for example in McCormick et al. (2012); Brooke (2014); Harper (2017). See also W. Harris (2013a), again largely concerned with the Roman world; J. Haldon et al. (2014). See the bibliography for Roman and Byzantine climate studies in J. Haldon et al. (2014:119n9).

80. See the data sets and interactive map at: https://www.ncdc.noaa.gov/data-access/paleoclimatology-data/datasets. A large number of climate proxies for the Mediterranean over the last two thousand years were published by Luterbacher et al. (2012).

81. Marriner et al. (2012) on sediment core data from the delta.

82. Cf. Petrie et al. (2017).

83. Ortega et al. (2015:71).

84. Cullen and de Menocal (2000).

85. Kondrashov, Feliks, and Ghil (2005).

86. J. Diamond (1997); Barker (2009).

87. R. B. Alley et al. (1993).

88. Spengler et al. (2016) and the entire issue of *the Holocene* 26/10 (2016).

89. Rasmussen et al. (2015); Brooke (forthcoming).

90. On the climate anomaly at 4.2 ka, and the collapse of the Near East–Egypt interaction sphere, see Weiss (2015); Weiss (2016); Stanley et al. (2003). Beaujard (2011:20n212) leaves the reason why the Near East collapses, while the Indus River valley does not, open. The reason, in part perhaps, lays in the regional effects of climate change and the range of adaptive responses. The climate dynamics in the Near East is driven by Atlantic Ocean and the westerly air currents that flow across the Mediterranean; in India, as in Egypt, climate dynamics are dependent on the monsoon, although, perhaps crucially, there is winter rainfall in the Indus River valley as well. For the complexity of the Indus River valley, and adaptive responses, see Petrie et al. (2017). Egypt, on the other hand, and court culture, was dependent on exchange with the Near East. See also Butzer (1997) and Butzer (2012). Collapse is downplayed in his later treatment. On decline ca. 2000 BCE, see Potts (1997); Staubwasser and Weiss (2006). The model of Beaujard (2011:fig. 29) helps to visualize the trade links. A good general introduction to societal collapse is Tainter (1988).

91. Roland et al. (2014:11). See appendix.

92. Kaniewski, van Campo, and Weiss (2012); Weiss (2012); Weiss (2015). The debate on the nature of state collapse and resilience in this period continues, but it remains broadly resisted by historians.

93. Weiss (2016).

94. See Carter and Morris (2014).

95. See Carter and Morris (2014) for a good summary.

96. Liverani (2014:381–400) surveys the factors in Near Eastern societies. See also Höflmayer (2017). For the processes of the collapse of New Kingdom Egypt, see Butzer (2012). On the trade networks, see Dickinson (2006); Cline (2007); Tartaron (2013).

97. Some paleoclimate data is reviewed by Brooke (2014:302n30).

98. The timing of the Hekla-3 eruption is much debated. One theory, not broadly accepted, is that "earthquake storms" around the Mediterranean ca. 1275–1175 BCE, possibly correlated with volcanism, was a major factor in Bronze Age collapse. Brooke (2014:300), citing Nur (2000); Nur and Burgess (2008).

99. Kaniewski, Guiot, and van Campo (2015). Timescale is important in interpreting climate proxy data. Rohling et al. (2009) were more cautious with their data and worked within a millennial timescale, 1500–500 BCE.

100. Butzer (2012). On speleothem data at Alepotrypa cave in Greece, see Finné et al. (2014). For the serious famine reported in Hittite texts in the 13th century BCE, see Klengel (1974); the Great Karnak Inscription of King Merenptah of Egypt briefly mentions the sending of grain to the Hittite kingdom. For the passage, see Manassa

(2003:34). Drought is well documented now in lake core analyses, for which see Roberts et al. (2011).

101. Brooke (2014:301); Rohling et al. (2009); Kaniewski, Guiot, and van Campo (2015) review the paleoclimate records. On the solar minima/maxima activity, see Usokin et al. (2008). On the Hekla eruption, see the entry in the Smithsonian database: http://volcano.si.edu/volcano.cfm?vn=372070.

102. S. Manning (2013:132).

103. A summary in Demand (2011:193–219); Kaniewski, Guiot, and van Campo (2015). I thank Jessica Lamont for the Linear B reference.

104. S. Sherratt (2001); Routledge and McGeough (2009); Moreno García (2016b).

105. See Brooke (2014:300–16) for a summary of climate trends in the period.

106. S. Manning (2013:132–33).

107. S. Manning (2013:112–14).

108. Macklin et al. (2015).

109. Macklin et al. (2015); Hassan (2007).

110. Roberts (2012); Magny et al. (2013); Brooke (2016).

111. Harper (2017). The phrase "Roman Quiet Period" is from Michael Sigl.

112. McCormick et al. (2012:174). Different proxy records give slightly different periodizations. Pollen from Spain suggest the warm period there goes back to ca. 250 BCE for example. See Desprat et al. (2003). For the use of "anomaly," signaling a good deal of regional variation and dating uncertainty, see J. Haldon et al. (2014:121). See also Harper's (2017) summary of Roman climatic conditions; and Luterbacher et al. (2016).

113. Columella, *Rust.* 1.1.5. Cf. the remark by W. Harris (2007:513n5).

114. Halstead and O'Shea (1989).

115. R. Bradley (2015:13–54). For a detailed overview of the mechanisms of environmental change, see Matthews et al. (2012:361–535).

116. See Broodbank's brief comments (2013:41–44).

117. Butzer's excellent survey (1995) can now be significantly updated in many of its details.

118. Gornall et al. (2010).

119. Butzer (2012).

120. The following sections on volcanic forcing and the study of the impacts on the Nile reflects joint ongoing work with Bill Boos, Francis Ludlow, Jennifer Marlon, Michael Sigl, and Zan Stine that appeared in *Nature Communications* 8 (2017). I am grateful to all these scholars for being so generous with their time and knowledge. From each of them I continue to learn much.

121. There is a growing literature discussing the effects of explosive eruptions. See Robock (2000); Schmidt et al. (2015); LeGrande et al. (2015).

122. See, e.g., Ramsay and Licht (1997). Sigl et al. (2015) on the forcing of the 44 BCE eruption, perhaps to be identified now with Chiltepe in Nicaragua. Famine is reported in Chinese sources in 43–42 BCE. Ice core scientists can distinguish between eruptions in high north latitude and "tropical," or middle latitude, locations because the former are documented only in Greenland ice cores while midlatitude or "tropical" eruptions deposit sulfates both in Greenland and in the Antarctic.

123. Thucydides 3.89. Antonopoulos (1992). Thucydides 3.116 reports eruption activity on Mount Etna, perhaps in 425 BCE, that may have been unusual and may not have reached Greenland ice. It may be this event that generated the earthquake and tsunami. I thank Frank Ludlow for discussion on this point.

124. There is a growing literature on the mechanisms of volcanic forcing. R. Bradley (2015) and LeGrande et al. (2015) are good places to begin. For a good popular account, see Zeilinga de Boer and Sanders (2002).

125. R. Bradley (2015:50–54); Robock (2000).

126. R. Bradley (2015:50).

127. Brönnimann and Krämer (2016). See also the social response model by Luterbacher and Pfister (2015), and fig. 26.

128. Zeilinga de Boer and Sanders (2002:108–37); Mikhail (2015).

129. Mikhail (2015).

130. R. Bradley (2015:51); Kostick and Ludlow (2015). On eruption clusters, see the comment by Muscheler and Fischer (2012:458); Toohey, Krüger, Sigl, et al. (2016) and consult the database at http://www.volcano.si.edu.

131. Grainger (2010:411), for example, claimed that Egypt was "rich, populous and fundamentally stable" under the Ptolemies. The Hellenistic period is only briefly mentioned by Issar and Zohar (2010:206) as one of "favorable climatic conditions" that created "economic prosperity."

132. B. Bell (1971); B. Bell; (1975); Butzer (1984).

133. Sigl et al. (2015).

134. Sigl et al. (2015).

135. Bonneau (1971).

136. Recent work has tested this hypothesis and has shown it to be broadly reliable, J. Manning et al. (2017). We find that flood quality within −2/+3 years of eruptions (this window allows for ice-core and historical dating uncertainties, plus lagged or prolonged responses) ranks lower than expected randomly at 99.85 percent confidence (one-tailed p=0.0015, Monte Carlo equal means test. Consistent results are found for variant windows −1/+3, −0/+3, −2/+2, −1/+2, and −0/+2 (in all cases at >98.8 percent confidence, indicating Nile sensitivity to eruptions in this period.

137. Garnsey and Whittaker (1983); Garnsey (1988). On risk and response to variability, see Halstead and O'Shea (1989); Gallant (1991). For the Hellenistic world, see Rathbone (1983).

138. McCormick et al. (2012:174).

139. On the link between Ptolemaic revolts and explosive volcanic eruptions, see the preliminary study by Ludlow and Manning (2016). For comparison, see Bai and Kung (2011) and Jia (2014) for historical revolts in China linked to drought.

140. Dem. 34.37, 35.50–51, Aristotle *Oec.* 1348b–1349a. See Reger (2003:177) with the literature cited there.

141. See below.

142. *IOSPE* I^2 401. See Stolba (2005). For the text, see http://www.c-h-i.org/examples /ptm/gallery_cher_2008-old/cher_oath_index.html.

143. Stolba (2005:309).

144. We take the sequence of revolts form the study of Veïsse (2004) and use only dates that we think are start dates of unrest. This window allows for small uncertainties in ice-core-based eruption dates (e.g., from ice layer counting uncertainties and potential lags between the date of eruptions and the deposition of associated sulfate in the polar ice), potential delays between volcanically induced suppression of the Nile summer flood, and the onset of revolt, and potential uncertainties in the dating of revolt onset.

145. Polybius 5.34.2–9.

146. Buraselis (1993).
147. As described by the Roman historian Justin, *Epit.* 27.1.9; *FGrHist* IIB, 260 F43; Mc-Ging (1997:274).
148. *OGIS* 56, 17–18 (the Canopus Decree, 238 BCE). See Austin (2006:text 27).
149. Bresson (2011) on Cyrene's productivity. The Greek version of the decree (*OGIS* 56), lines 13–19. Trans. Austin (2006:471). For a full treatment of the text, see Pfeiffer (2004). On the locations of the "many other places," see Buraselis (2013:101).
150. Polybius 5.88–90, on which see Holleaux (1938:445–62).
151. *P. Edfu* 8; see Lukaszewicz (1999).
152. On the concept of "cultural entrepreneur," see above.
153. M. Lewis (1997:20–21). Cf. D. Wilson (2002:8). Whether the machine itself was "invented" in Alexandria or elsewhere in response to a specific crisis or for other reasons is unclear. See A. Wilson (2008); Oleson (2000).
154. Brooke (2014:284).
155. Lukaszewicz (1999:31–32).
156. *FGrH* III B, p. 606; Athen. V.206d–209e. All that is certain is that the gift occurred during Hieron II's reign (269–214 BCE), but the 240s BCE fits the circumstances neatly. Huß (2001:368) gives the broad time in which the gift occurred.
157. Ray (1976:136–46).
158. Bintliff (1991:25–26). Cf. J. Davies (2013a).
159. On urban demand for wheat, see Rathbone (1983:46).
160. Schindler et al. (2010).
161. J. Manning et al. (2017).
162. One final decree, in the style of a priestly decree but this time promulgated by a governor attempting to assuage the effects of drought and famine, came in 39 BCE. See Hölbl (2001:239); Burstein (1985:144–46).
163. On ancient rebellions, see Collins and Manning (2016). On the famous Maccabean revolt, see Honigman (2014). To my knowledge no one has raised the possibility of drought as an underlying factor of this revolt. I hope to do more work on this point.
164. Maehler (1983:8).
165. See Rathbone and von Reden (2015).
166. Von Reden (2007:70).
167. Erdkamp (2005:225–37); McCormick et al. (2012).
168. Horden and Purcell (2000:301–41). Cf. Broodbank (2013:64–65). See S. White (2011) for the impact of climatic changes on Ottoman social history.
169. For disease in Roman Egypt, see Scheidel (2001).
170. Mayerson (2002).
171. I provide a partial translation of the text in the conclusions.
172. S. Manning (2013:118).

CHAPTER 6. THE BIRTH OF "ECONOMIC MAN": DEMOGRAPHY, THE STATE, THE HOUSEHOLD, AND THE INDIVIDUAL

1. Swedberg (1998:31).
2. The peasant mode of production is stressed by Wickham (2005) in his study of early Medieval Europe.
3. Horden and Purcell (2000:272). Cf. Ps.-Aristotle, *Oikonomika* 2.2.17 on surplus grain.

4. See Garnsey (1988); Gallant (1991).

5. E.g., Goody (1976); Goody (1990). See now Huebner and Nathan (2017) for premodern Mediterranean patterns.

6. See Nathan's concluding chapter in Huebner and Nathan (2017).

7. Kemp (2006:302–35).

8. Ray (2002:25) on the letters perhaps remaining unopened.

9. Jursa (2010:769).

10. Agut-Labordère (2013:1009–26).

11. The Tale of Setne is one such text. It is preserved in P. Cairo 30646, which is generally dated to the early Ptolemaic period on the basis of the paleography. For the dating, see Vinson (2008:309). For an excellent new edition of the text, see Goldbrunner (2006). For an English translation, see Ritner in Simpson (2003:453–69), therein called "The Romance of Setna Khaemuas and the mummies." Published comments on the text are numerous. For an introduction to the literature, see Ritner in Simpson (2003:582–84). See also Quack (2005:32–35); Vinson (2011).

12. Willy Clarysse and Thompson (2006).

13. Willy Clarysse and Thompson (2006/2:230).

14. Cf. Pomeroy (1997:193–229).

15. Estimated global population growth rates, 9000 BCE–2030 CE providing century resolution population figures; tables II.1 and III.1A in Brooke (2014). Cf. Christian (2004:143).

16. Scheidel (2007:45).

17. Demography of Egypt: Kraus (2004); for the Ptolemaic period, Willy Clarysse and Thompson (2006). For Roman Egypt, see Bagnall and Frier (1994); Scheidel (2001).

18. Wiesehöfer (2009).

19. J. R. McNeill (2000:15). Cf. Christian (2004).

20. I rely here in this section on the summaries of Scheidel (2007); Scheidel (2013a). For ancient Greek demography, see Morris (2007); Bresson (2016:41–70). Animal husbandry has not been fully integrated into the economic history of the first millennium BCE.

21. Inoue et al. (2015).

22. Scheidel (2007:38).

23. Bagnall and Frier (1994).

24. M. H. Hansen (2006a) for 4th century Greece. On mummy tickets and Egyptian demography, see Arlt (2011). See Scheidel (2001) on seasonal mortality and morbidity in Egypt.

25. Parkin (1992); Scheidel (2007); Scheidel (2013a); De Ligt (2012) for Roman Italy; Bresson (2016) on the Greek world. A forthcoming handbook on demography in the Greco-Roman world has been announced.

26. Bagnall and Frier (1994); Scheidel (2001); Willy Clarysse and Thompson (2006).

27. Bowman (2009:181) with some of the literature cited. For other estimates, ranging from 1.8 to 6.16 million for the "Greco-Roman period," using different estimates of taxation rates, crop yields, and subsistence levels, see Hassan (1994:170).

28. Hassan (1994) provides a good overview of population dynamics in ancient Egyptian history. For the Roman period population, see Scheidel (2001).

29. M. H. Hansen (2006a).

30. These are the low and high estimates given by Wiesehöfer (2009:77).

31. Kron's (2012) estimate is exuberant. On model life tables, see Bagnall and Frier (1994). For a Roman model life table, see Frier (1982).
32. Around 30 percent. Scheidel (2013a:136).
33. The size of the Roman population, in particular the size of the population of the Roman Italy, has been debated for a very long time. The debate has been renewed in recent years, on archaeological grounds primarily. See Lo Cascio (1994); Kron (2005); Scheidel (2008).
34. See the important collection gathered by Vleeming (2011). Arlt (2011) treats the demographic information derived from them.
35. Scheidel (2001).
36. See the overview by Alfani and Murphy (2017).
37. On malaria, see Sallares (2002). On the seasonality mortality in Egypt of various causes, see Scheidel (2001). Schistosomiasis is discussed by Kloos and David (2002). In a recent and important study, Rasmussen et al. (2015) have found that a strain of the bacterium *Yersinia pestis*, less virulent than the related strain that caused bubonic plague, can now be documented back into the Bronze Age.
38. William H. McNeill (1976:77–147).
39. Strictly speaking, plague refers to a disease outbreak caused by *Yersinia pestis*, Alfani and Murphy (2017).
40. Thuc. 2.48–52. See the epidemiological summary by Littman (2009). On mass graves possibly associated with the outbreak, see Baziotopoulou-Valavani (2002).
41. Harper (2017).
42. Achilli et al. (2007).
43. Jursa (2010:36–48).
44. R. Adams (1981).
45. See the survey by J. Davies (1992).
46. J. Davies (1992:297).
47. See above on one recent estimate of slave numbers.
48. J. Davies (1992:299–300).
49. J. Davies (1992:302–5) outlines three areas: markets, capital accumulation (lending), and the public economy.
50. Turchin and Nefedov (2009).
51. On the complex range of meanings of *oikos*, see Cox (1998:132–35).
52. Nevett (1999); Ault and Nevett (2005). For Olynthos houses, see Nevett (1999:53–126); Cahill (2002). Morris (2005) makes use of excavations at Olynthos as proxy evidence for real economic growth in Greece over the course of the first millennium BCE.
53. Huebner and Nathan (2017).
54. Saller (2007:87).
55. Huebner and Nathan (2017).
56. Hall (2014b:262–68).
57. Foxhall (2007). Kakavogianni and Anetakis (2012).
58. Van Alfen (2016). For a list of commodities mentioned in Attic comedy, see D. Lewis (2016b)
59. J. Davies (2007:347).
60. J. Davies (2007:347–48).
61. Cox (1998:135).
62. Pomeroy (1997); C. Patterson (1998); Cox (1998).

63. E. Harris and D. Lewis (2016:19).
64. E. Harris and D. Lewis (2016:20–23).
65. Johnson (1998).
66. Cahill (2005). On weaving and textile manufacture, see Tsakirgis (2016). The archaeology of houses in Egypt is poor until the Roman period. See Huebner and Nathan (2017).
67. J. Davies (1998:246).
68. See the fine analysis of the "patrimonial model" in Lehner (2000).
69. Jursa (2005). On temple industries in Egypt, see for example the study of a Ptolemaic account of wine production in Edfu by Schentuleit (2006).
70. Tenney (2012).
71. Initial publication of the texts by James (1962). The rather long and detailed review by Baer (1963) is important.
72. J. Allen (2002). Ray (2002) provides some historical context.
73. Ray (2002:39).
74. J. Allen (2002:121–25) for discussion of the location of Hekanakhte's fields.
75. Eyre (1999:48). Eyre provides a good sketch of the archive; which has been republished with extensive commentary by J. Allen (2002).
76. On the household composition, see J. Allen (2002:107–17).
77. On the Egyptian household, see Eyre (2014).
78. See the comments by Scott (1998:164–68) with respect to Lenin's treatise *The Agrarian Question* on the productivity of peasant households.
79. Weber (1978:356–84).
80. On the important role of intergenerational transmission of culture, see Mokyr (2016:34–42).
81. Xenophon, *Oec.* 6.9–10.
82. Moreno García (2012).
83. For the village economy, see Eyre (1999).
84. Below, and see Manning (2003).
85. Manning (2003:203).
86. Renger (2009:190–91). See also Renger (2003).
87. Jursa (2010).
88. Galil (2007); Pearce (2014).
89. Rainville (2012).
90. Finley (1970b:101).
91. Wunsch (2010).
92. Stolper (1985); Stolper (2005). On the size of the Egibi archive, see Wunsch (2009:236).
93. W. Harris (2003:276).
94. Morris and Manning (2005a:149); Morris (2009:99).
95. Horden and Purcell (2000). Cf. Algazi (2005); Archibald (2013:98–105).
96. On the concept of the "fragmented" state, see Grafe (2012).
97. See the survey by Scheidel (2013b).
98. On cognitive frameworks, see Greif (2006). Tilly (1992) emphasized four activities: state making, war making, protection, and extraction. I subsume the first three under "state making."
99. The role of war in human society has become a very hot topic in the last decade, and the literature is now enormous. For a good survey of ancient war, see Raaflaub and

Rosenstein (1999); for the classical world, see Brian Campbell and Tritle (2013). More generally Morris (2014); Turchin (2015a).

100. On the complexities of Greek fiscal institutions, see Migeotte (2014). For Hellenistic sale taxes outside of Egypt, see Kaye (2015).

101. Fischer-Bovet (2014). On Hellenistic war and economy, see the seminal piece by Austin (1986). For war booty, Préaux (1978/2:366–70). Polybius is a good source for the sometimes impressive scale of the booty involved: e.g., Polybius 10.19.1–2.

102. J. Davies (2013a:327–30).

103. I rely here on Turchin (2010).

104. Blanton and Fargher (2008).

105. Eyre (2004).

106. Emphasized well by Eyre (2004).

107. E. Jones (1988:132).

108. Jursa (2014b).

109. Shaw (2001:441).

110. Monson and Scheidel (2015).

111. A. Sherratt and Sherratt (1991).

112. On the Greek city-state and economy, see Bresson (2016:96–117). Cf. Stasavage (2011).

113. W. Harris (2003:279).

114. Eisenstadt (1993).

115. Chamoux (2003:250).

116. On modeling state size, see, for example, Alesina and Spolaore (2003).

117. Ehrenberg (1969:141).

118. In general G. Cohen (1983). Gauls: Strobel (1996); Cunliffe (1997); S. Mitchell (2003). Settlement: Reger (2004); Mueller (2006). Population mobility in the Hellenistic world is summarized by Reger (2003).

119. Préaux (1939) codified the concept.

120. Cf. the remarks of J. Davies (1998:242).

121. Bagnall (2011a).

CHAPTER 7. THE EVOLUTION OF ECONOMIC THOUGHT IN THE ANCIENT WORLD: MONEY, LAW, AND LEGAL INSTITUTIONS

1. D. Ma and Luiten van Zanden (2011a:15).

2. On Aristotle, see Polanyi (1957a, b, and c) and Finley's response (1970a and b); Meikle (1995/2002); Bresson (2000:109–30). Some basic orientation may be found in Medema and Samuels (2013:4–17). See also G. Miller (2010) for a selection of studies on the economic analysis of ancient law.

3. Ekelund and Hébert (2014:9–19).

4. Meikle (1995/2002). For a good basic literature on ancient economic thought, see Ekelund and Hébert (2014:40–45). Oddly missing therein, as in other accounts, is the Indian tradition exemplified by the writing of Kautilya, on whom see above.

5. Kemp (2006:306).

6. Kemp (2006:323).

7. Ritner (2003:498).

8. Crawford (1978).

9. On early Chinese money, for example, see Horesh (2014).

10. Meikle (1995/2002).

11. I rely here in this first section on Ingham (2004). For a good overview of money from the point of view of economic sociology, see Carruthers (2005).

12. Herrmann-Pillath (2009).

13. Ingham (2004:3).

14. Stiglitz (1993:880–83).

15. Seaford (2004:17–19).

16. See the brief comments by Howgego (1995:13) on the role of silver in Near Eastern exchange.

17. Ingham (2004:107–33).

18. Carruthers (2005:359).

19. Ingham (2004:6).

20. Menger (1909).

21. Ingham (2004:12).

22. Ingham (2004:6).

23. Ingham (2004:34).

24. Ingham (2004:89–106). Cf. Graeber (2011).

25. Ingham (2004). Ingham's "military-coinage complex" is an important concept. Graeber (2011:229) adds slavery, thus "military-coinage-slavery complex."

26. Surveyed by von Reden (2002); von Reden (2010).

27. See von Reden (2010:9–10) and the literature cited therein summarizing Finley's position.

28. Shipton (2000); Meadows and Shipton (2001); Schaps (2004); von Reden (2007); W. Harris (2008).

29. Metcalf (2012).

30. Kemp (2006:315–16).

31. Neo-Assyrian Empire after its conquest of Carchemish, where silver mines were located, and activity in Spain. Postgate (1979:218) and Frankenstein (1979:287) on silver supply in the Neo-Assyrian Empire.

32. Van der Spek (2011).

33. Peyronel (2010:934).

34. Cf. remarks by von Reden (2010:23).

35. Arthur (2015:xvii).

36. Jursa (2005).

37. Jursa (2010).

38. Jursa (2005:175).

39. Jursa (2010:473).

40. Jursa (2010:474).

41. Jursa (2010:773–74).

42. Vargyas (2010).

43. Vargyas (2010:169). For the detailed argument on the nature of the phrase "silver, X *deben* of the treasury of Ptah, of refined (silver)" that refers to weighed silver mentioned in pre-Ptolemaic Egyptian private transactions, as opposed to earlier views that suggested the phrase implied "stamped bars," see Vleeming (1991:87–89).

44. Malinine (1953:3–14), treating P. Louvre E. 3228b, dated to 703 BCE.

45. M. Thompson et al. (1973).

46. Some of the issues are surveyed by von Reden (2010:18–64).

47. Seaford (2004:204).
48. Peacock (2006:643–44).
49. Kurke (1999); Schaps (2004); Peacock (2006).
50. Herrmann-Pillath (2009:22).
51. See Bresson (2006); Bresson (2009). Seaford (2004:318–37) lays out an argument against weighed metal as money in the Near East and in Egypt but misses out on much important evidence from the first millennium BCE, a period in which all Mediterranean societies underwent transformation, albeit in different ways. Jursa (2010) offers a detailed and important counterargument.
52. Herrmann-Pillath (2009).
53. Kroll (2008:18–21).
54. Davis (2014).
55. De Angelis (2016:263–66).
56. Le Rider (2001); Balmuth (2001).
57. India: Dhavalikar (1975). Schaps (2004:222–35) surveys the early history of coin types in all three places.
58. See Balmuth (2001), for recent advances in the study of early hoards in the Near East, and for arguments about Near Eastern–Greek interaction and the invention of coinage.
59. Kroll (2008).
60. Balmuth (2001). On the commercialization of agriculture in Egypt and the Near East, and the use of silver in private transactions going back to the 3d millennium BCE, see Moreno García (2016a:12–13).
61. Vargyas (1999).
62. Müller-Wollermann (2016:282).
63. Embodied in the works of Schaps (2004) and Seaford (2004).
64. Vargyas (2000). Cf. A. M. Hudson (2004). A. Sherratt and Sherratt (1993), on 8th century BCE inscribed weight units from North Syria.
65. *Politics* 1.3.13–14.
66. Rutter (2012).
67. Jonathan Hall (2014b:279).
68. Von Reden (2010:40); Kallet-Marx (1993); Shipton (2000).
69. J. Davies (2004).
70. J. Davies (2007:355).
71. Polybius 6.49–7–10, discussing Spartan strategy after the Peloponnesian War.
72. Gabrielsen (2005).
73. Von Reden (2007).
74. J. Davies (2103b:445).
75. Andreau (1977); Ingham (2004:107–33); W. Harris (2008).
76. W. Harris (2006); M. Hudson (2002:15). On the Near East, the literature and debates about the nature of debt and credit is extensive. See Westbrook and Jasnow (2001); Van de Mieroop (2002); Van de Mieroop (2005); von Reden (2010:102–10).
77. Henry Maine's (1861) famous treatise on ancient law, now largely forgotten but still well worth reading, despite all its well-known and much-discussed flaws, was an early demonstration of the connection between law and "progress" in premodern societies. For an appraisal of Maine's work and its influence, see Cocks (1988); A. Diamond (1991). See Frier and Kehoe (2007) on the law and economics approach to ancient economies.

78. Maine (1861:170); Shils (1991).

79. Swedberg (1998:90).

80. On the increase in writing itself driving the change in Egypt, see Muhs (2016).

81. Frier and Kehoe (2007).

82. Williamson (2002).

83. Whitman (1995); Powell (1996); Le Rider (2001).

84. Dixit (2004) on a good analysis of "alternative modes of governance."

85. See, for example, Dixit (2004).

86. Jursa (2008).

87. Trubek (1972).

88. Pomeranz (2000); Morris (2010).

89. Swedberg (1998:100).

90. D. Ma and Luiten van Zanden (2011b).

91. Weber's work on law is conveniently collected in Rheinstein (1964). A beautiful exposition of Weber on law and economics may be found in Swedberg (1998:82–107).

92. Swedberg (1998:89).

93. Swedberg (1998:99).

94. See D. Ma and Luiten van Zanden (2011b).

95. Kehoe, Ratzan, and Yiftach (2015:4).

96. For a good example of the law and economics approach to Roman law, see Frier and Kehoe (2007).

97. Frier and Kehoe (2007:113).

98. Keenan, Manning, and Yiftach-Firanko (2014). I borrow the term "negotiating daily life" from V. Hansen (1995).

99. Roth (1997); Westbrook (2003a) and Kitchen and Lawrence (2012) provide basic introductions to the Near Eastern law codes.

100. Lindgren (1995:150n3).

101. Westbrook (2003a:17).

102. Whitman (1995).

103. Knoppers and Harvey (2007). Kitchen and Lawrence (2012) is a good collections of Near Eastern and Egyptian material.

104. Knoppers and Harvey (2007:128).

105. North, Wallis, and Weingast (2009:47). Cf. Osborne (1996a:187).

106. Donker van Heel (1994). Muhs (2015a).

107. Well summarized recently by Moreno García (2015). See Menu (1988) on the evolution of demotic sale contracts.

108. North (2005).

109. Transaction costs analysis is another central issue in NIE, and only recently applied to ancient law. See Kehoe, Ratzan, and Yiftach (2015). It is the central theme of Silver's (1995) analysis of ancient Near Eastern economies and the development of markets.

110. On Roman commercial law, see the summary by Johnston (1999).

111. Vandorpe (2015:107–8).

112. J. Manning (1999).

113. Details are laid out in Westbrook (2003b).

114. Westbrook (2003a:64).

115. Rowlandson (2014:244).

116. Yiftach-Firanko in Keenan, Manning, and Yiftach-Firanko (2014:35–41).

117. Yiftach-Firanko (2009).
118. J. Manning (2015a and b).
119. Oelsner, Wells, and Wunsch (2003).
120. Jursa (2010:789–90).
121. The Babylonian term means literally "path, road." See Wunsch (2010:58n37).
122. Jursa (2008:609).
123. Jursa (2008:619).
124. Jursa (2008:627).
125. Bresson (2016:230). On Greek law and on transaction costs, I rely on Todd (1993); Thür (2015); Bresson (2016). On the "unity" of Greek law, see Gagarin (2005).
126. Thür (2015).
127. Bresson (2016:231).
128. Bresson (2016:232) citing Aristotle, *Rhetoric* 1.15.9 and 210–22.
129. Bresson (2016:227).
130. Thür (2015:36–43).
131. Xen., *Ways and Means* 3.1.
132. Ober (2015b:57). See further Lanni (2006:149–74).
133. Bowles and Choi (2013).
134. E. Harris (2016) usefully lays out the ten basic rights that define private property.
135. Said (1993:188–207).
136. The situation on the Greek mainland is in fact more complicated. Large estates were worked by dependent labor in Sparta; in Crete and Thessaly large private estates were worked by slaves; and small family farms were found, most commonly in Attica. See the important analysis of Greek agricultural labor in Jameson (1992).
137. See Park's (1992) analysis of the Middle Senegal river flood recession agricultural system in western Africa.
138. Park (1992:93).
139. Park (1992:96); J. Manning (1995); Monson (2012).
140. J. Manning (2003); Monson (2012).
141. The system I describe is based largely on documents from Upper Egypt. Other areas of Egypt are less well documented, but we would be wrong to conclude that tenure rules were uniform.
142. Mayshar, Moav, and Neeman (2014:22).
143. Lopez (1976); Van Bavel (2010). On the Near Eastern contracts, see M. Larsen (2015).
144. Monson (2012:82). For a recent overview of Ptolemaic Egyptian land tenure, see Vandorpe (2015).
145. Zurbach (2009), for Spartan law, see Hodkinson (2000).
146. E. Harris (2016).
147. Lippert (2004); Keenan, Manning, and Yiftach-Firanko (2014); Muhs (2016:179).
148. See, e.g., Allam (2008).
149. The classic account of the Ptolemaic court system is Wolff (1962). For Ptolemaic property registration see Yiftach-Firanko (2014).
150. A new study by Baetens and Depauw (2015) offers good analysis, and some differences from my own interpretation. The Erbstreit archive dating to the 2d century BCE from Pathyris offers comparably rich material for a legal dispute, and a series of trials, over inherited land. See Vandorpe and Waebens (2009:114–22).
151. *P. Brit. Mus.* 10591 recto. It is not certain why we have a copy. Was it issued to the winning party or to an advocate at their request? Some 3d century BCE Greek pro-

ceedings of trials from Krokodilopolis (Fayyum) were recorded in two copies. See Modrzejewski (2011:123n39).

152. For earlier records of trials, see Modrzejewski (2011:123–28).

153. Veïsse (2004).

154. On "justice at the (temple) gate," see most recently the survey in J. Manning (2011).

155. The official has a Greek name, but by no means is it clear in 2d century BCE context that this official was ethnically Greek. The Greek word for the institution tells us, however, that the person is functioning within the Ptolemaic state system in an official capacity. Whether this function has an ancient precedent in Egypt is debatable. For the argument in favor, see Allam (2008). To be certain, however, the role of the *eisagogeus* in Greek law was to introduce into court particular cases having to do with marketplace transactions, and they could also adjudicate cases involving small amounts of money themselves. See Bresson (2016:247–48).

156. Pestman (1961:135).

157. Cf. Diod. Sic. I.75.6.

158. On the distinction, see Rheinstein (1964:198n3). Weber (Rheinstein 1964:199) elaborates as follows: "Originally, the advocate stood before the court next to the party litigating. His position was thus quite different from that of the attorney (*avoué, Anwalt, procurator, solicitor*), who assumed the technical tasks of preparing the case and obtaining the evidence." To be sure we know very little about the training, whether this was an exclusive function or merely part of a broader administrative function, or whether these the advocates who appear in the papyri were paid.

159. That advocates were involved in Ptolemaic trials is certain. The clearest example comes from a well-known 2d century BCE Greek papyrus, *UPZ* II 162 (= *P. Tor. Choach.* 12; Thebes, 117 BCE). For a translation, see Bagnall and Derow (2004: text 132).

160. The famous trial of Mes, dating to ca. 1250 BCE, involving disputed land ownership and stressing written evidence, bears some resemblance to the Asyut trial, but there are sufficient differences between the two trials in terms of structure and procedure, and between the two document themselves, one recorded in a tomb, the other on papyrus, with more than one thousand years separating them, to warrant caution in comparing them directly. On earlier Egyptian law and trials, see Eyre (2004).

161. D. Ma and Luiten van Zanden (2011a:7).

CHAPTER 8. GROWTH, INNOVATION, MARKETS, AND TRADE

1. The section on trade is a revised and expanded version of J. Manning (2015a) appearing in a volume published by the Association of Ancient Historians and skillfully edited by Timothy Howe.

2. Gunter (2014) provides a good recent assessment of this "orientalizing" phase of Greek art, suggesting that the term does not sufficiently account for the depth of the contact between Greece and eastern Mediterranean civilizations or the impact of Near Eastern culture and ideas on Greece.

3. A good place to begin for the theoretical issues involved is D. Jones (2014:535–67). Cf. Morris and Manning (2005a:141–42). For ancient growth in the wider historical context see E. Jones (1988:53–72). For Roman growth and the use of quantifiable

data, see Bowman and Wilson (2009); de Callataÿ (2014). Growth in the Greek world is explored in a series of papers in E. Harris, Lewis, and Woolmer (2016).

4. Conison (2013:2269).

5. I follow Erdkamp (2016) here. Although he is speaking about the Roman Empire, the trends he describes are in place in other parts of the Mediterranean world by the second half of the first millennium BCE. See, for example, Jursa (2014a) on the "commercialization" model for Babylonia in the 6th century, with demographic expansion driving market growth and intensification of agriculture.

6. Temin (2013) summarizes the theory of growth, and Roman growth, especially, very well. Cf. Erdkamp (2016).

7. Greek growth is discussed by Ober (2015a:81–100); Bresson (2016:199–22); Roman growth is treated succinctly by Saller (2005).

8. Saller (2005); Temin (2013); Kehoe (2015).

9. Archibald and Davies (2011:2).

10. A good place to begin for the theoretical issues involved is D. Jones (2014:535–67). For ancient growth in the wider historical context, see E. Jones (1988:53–72).

11. Bowman and Wilson (2009) for Rome.

12. Brooke (2014:263) with literature cited there.

13. Brooke (2014:261–87); but see also the critique by Harper (2015).

14. Brooke (2014:318).

15. Acemoglu and Robinson (2012); Lo Cascio and Malanima (2014:248).

16. Aghion and Howitt (2009).

17. Scheidel (2007:52–55).

18. Yoffee (2015).

19. Goldstone (2002); cf. Brooke (2014:318).

20. Turchin and Nefedov (2009).

21. Brooke (2014:323).

22. E. Jones (1988).

23. Mokyr (2016).

24. D. Jones (2014:559).

25. Lo Cascio (2009). Bowman and Wilson (2009). On energy, see in general E. Burke (2009); Wrigley (2010). Smil's (1994:236) chart of per capita energy consumption in world history is instructive, as is Christian (2004:141) on per capita energy consumption of early human societies to the present. Energy is also treated by Bresson (2016:71–95).

26. A brief survey is provided by de Callataÿ (2005).

27. Jursa (2014b).

28. A. Parker (1992); A. Wilson (2009); A. Wilson (2011a); A. Wilson (2014). A. Wilson (2009:227) reports that 1,356 shipwrecks in the Mediterranean and Black Sea datable before 1500 are known.

29. A. Wilson (2009:219–20).

30. A. Wilson (2014:150).

31. Ober (2014); Ober (2015a). Cf. Morris (2007:226–30).

32. Morris (2005); Ober (2015a). Vlassopoulos is less optimistic in his review of Ober: http://bmcr.brynmawr.edu/2016/2016-03-04.html.

33. Kron (forthcoming).

34. Morris (2007).

35. Morris (2006).

36. J. Davies (1971). Developed by Ober (2015a).
37. Kron (forthcoming).
38. Nishi et al. (2015).
39. Gabrielsen (2005).
40. Jursa (2014a); Jursa (2014b).
41. Morris (2005).
42. J. Manning (2005).
43. The population of Alexandria has been extensively discussed and debated. See inter alia Scheidel (2004). Ptolemais has never been properly surveyed, so this is a rough guess based on Strabo's description (17.1.42) in the 1st century BCE, who states that it was not less than Memphis in size. For Memphis, see D. Thompson (2012:x), who speculates that sixty thousand is a maximum for the late Ptolemaic period. On Babylon and Seleukia-on-the-Tigris in the Hellenistic period, see van der Spek (2008). The size of Antioch was estimated by Aperghis (2004:94).
44. Rosenstein (2012:260). On the process or urbanization, see Morris (2006:31).
45. Kron (2014). Roman urban middle classes are discussed by Mayer (2012).
46. Slightly less optimistic views expressed by R. Allen (2009).
47. Jongman (2007:607–9); Kron (2014). On measuring stature, see Koepke and Baten (2005b), suggesting that medieval Europeans were taller than Romans.
48. Kron (2016:363).
49. On Greek house sizes, see Morris (2005).
50. Komlos and Bauer (2004); Pilkington (2013). See also Bodenhorn, Guinnane, and Mroz (2014). De Ligt (2012), with an excellent summary of the debate on Italian urbanism.
51. Jursa (2014a); Jursa (2010:800).
52. Van der Spek (2005).
53. Renger (2009:194).
54. Radner (1999:157).
55. Jursa (2010:799).
56. G. Müller (1995–96:165).
57. Van der Spek (2008:39). Cf. fig. 22 above.
58. Boiy (2004:216).
59. Boiy (2004). On the integration of Babylonia, see van der Spek and Mandemakers (2003:532); van der Spek and van Leeuwen (2014).
60. Agut-Labordère (2013) provides an excellent sketch of Saite political reforms and administrative structure.
61. Agut-Labordère (2013:980); Donker van Heel (2012).
62. For the administration and collection of trade revenue, see Agut-Labordère (2013: 1002–6).
63. Agut-Labordère (2013:1006–9).
64. Kemp (2006:308–18).
65. D. Thompson (2012:144–76) is an excellent account of the necropolis activities in Ptolemaic Memphis.
66. For an archive of *choachytes* from 2d century BCE Thebes, see Pestman (1993). Martin (2009) publishes a *choachyte* archive from Ptolemaic Memphis. See the summary for Saite period *choachytes* by Agut-Labordère (2013:1020–25). Donker van Heel (2014) is excellent in discussing the activities of *choachytes* and an important female *choachyte* archive from the Persian period.

67. Agut-Labordère (2013:1025).
68. Finley (1965b); reprinted in Shaw and Saller (1981).
69. K. Greene (2000); K. Greene (2008).
70. See Grantham (1999).
71. H. Schneider (2007). Overviews in Oleson (2008); Irby (2016). On animal husbandry, see Kron (2008b).
72. Cooper (2008:226).
73. Lucas (2012).
74. Cf. Butzer (1976:41–51); Eyre (1994).
75. Marsot (1984:137–61).
76. Cf. Finley (1965b:41), discussing the Roman emperor Tiberius's executing rather than rewarding the inventor of unbreakable glass. Mokyr (2016) emphasizes the scientific network known as the "republic of letters" in 16th and 17th century Europe as an important pretext for the Industrial Revolution.
77. See Kehoe (2007a:546–48).
78. Scheidel (2015).
79. Bowles and Gintis (2011).
80. Bowles and Gintis (2011:200).
81. Domingo Gygax (2016), stressing the reciprocal nature of public benefaction in Greek cities.
82. Archibald (2013); Chankowski and Karvonis (2012). Hirth (2016) provides an excellent perspective on markets from the point of view of the Aztec economy.
83. Gravelle and Rees (1992:3) cited by van der Spek, van Leeuwen, and van Zanden (2015:3).
84. J. Davies (2013b:443). Cf. Finley (1999:22); Warburton (2003).
85. J. Manning (2011); J. Davies (2013b).
86. Polanyi (1957b).
87. M. Larsen (2015).
88. Beaujard (2011:17).
89. See the brief introduction to the history of premodern trade by R. Smith (2009).
90. Schoenberger (2008:665).
91. The term encompasses two related concepts, a type of settlement and an institution. Archibald (2002); Möller (2000); Möller (2005); Bresson (2002); Bresson. (2016:306–38). In general, see M. H. Hansen (2006b). On definitions of "port-of-trade" see Figueira (1984); Möller (2001); Graslin and Maucourant (2005).
92. The classic "taxes and trade" model is that of Hopkins treating the Roman imperial economy (1980); Hopkins (2002).
93. Jursa (2005:180–82).
94. Warburton (2003:47–67).
95. E. Harris, Lewis, and Woolmer (2016) explore market places and market activities in the Greek world.
96. Schoenberger (2008:672).
97. J. Manning (2010:119).
98. Hicks (1969). Various models of early long-distance trade discussed in Aubet (2013:97–113). See Beaujard (2011) on Bronze Age and world systems theory.
99. Warburton (2003:62–63).
100. Cooney (2007); Cooney (2008).
101. Hicks (1969:25).

102. Jursa (2014c); van der Spek (2014).

103. The important Babylonian commodity prices series are available at: http://www.iisg .nl/hpw/babylon.php.

104. Slotsky (1997). An updated overview of work on the Babylonian material in van der Spek, van Leeuwen, and van Zanden (2015).

105. Slotsky and Wallenfalls (2009).

106. Van der Spek, van Leeuwen, and van Zanden (2015:6).

107. Jursa (2010:790).

108. Reger (2003); van der Spek, van Leeuwen, and van Zanden (2015:3). For "price regions," see Shaw (2001:440).

109. Jursa (2005:179), who mentions that the *Chicago Assyrian Dictionary*, the standard reference, translated the word *suqu* as "a commercial technical term, referring to assets outstanding."

110. Bleiberg (1996).

111. Muhs (2016:243–45). On the income of such priests, see Martin (2009:59–66).

112. Hasebroek (1928). D'Arms (1981) and Pleket (1983) for Roman elites. Bresson (2003b); Bresson (2016) for Greece. For the opposite argument, based on very close reading of the evidence, that merchants in Athens were indeed poor but played the crucial role of assuming risk, see Reed (2003).

113. *Ezek.* 26:3–5.

114. Bresson (2003b:162); Woolmer (2016).

115. D. Lewis (2016a:329).

116. Paterson (1998); Bresson (2000); Aubet (2013:127–44), summarizing the Near Eastern evidence for merchants.

117. Crawford (1983:71), citing *P. Mich. Zenon* 28 (256 BCE).

118. *C.Ord.Ptol.* 73 (50 BCE?). Trans. *Select Papyri* II 209. Crawford (1983).

119. Finley (1999:177–79). See also the apt comments by W. Harris (1993:18–20).

120. Based on six price pairs, a "law of one price" obtains, Temin (2013).

121. Hopkins (1980); Hopkins (2002).

122. Erdkamp (2005); see also Erdkamp's (2014) review of Temin.

123. Van Leeuwen, Foldvari, and van Zanden (2015:506–7).

124. Van Leeuwen, Foldvari, and van Zanden (2015:516).

125. Kemp (2006:247–301).

126. *P. Tebt.* 703 (3d century BCE) and *BGU* 1730 (mid-1st century BCE).

127. Catalogued to great effect by Ober (2015a:223–60).

128. Gabrielsen (2005).

129. Jursa (2008).

130. Periodic markets have been well studied for the Roman world. See De Ligt (1993); Shaw (1981) for Roman North Africa. For an updated list of grain prices from across the Mediterranean, see Rathbone and von Reden (2015). A good summary of overall trends by van Leeuwen, Foldvari, and van Zanden (2015).

131. Reger (1994); Reger (2002). On transaction costs, see Silver (1995), and Kehoe, Ratzan, and Yiftach (2015).

132. Reger (1994:271). For prices of goods imported into Delos, see Reger (2002).

133. See the survey of trade in the premodern Mediterranean by Howe (2015). Renfrew and Bahn (1991) distinguish ten forms of trade.

134. W. Harris (2000).

135. Christian (2004:324–25).

136. C. R. Chase-Dunn et al. (2009). For early modern Europe, see Trivellato (2009).
137. Bronze Age trade good recent survey with literature in Broodbank (2013:257–505). On Old Assyrian trade, see Barjamovic (2008). Jursa (2010) for private trading activity in the Neo-Babylonian Empire; Monroe (2009); Monroe (2011) for the late Bronze Age Mediterranean.
138. On food supply Hellenistic Athens, see Oliver (2007); Erdkamp (2005) for Rome. On the control of grain during crises, see above.
139. A good, brief summary of the debate can be found in Morley (2007).
140. Morley (2007:7).
141. On the role of premodern trade in the Indian Ocean, see the excellent treatments by Chaudhuri (1985); Chaudhuri (1990).
142. Wallerstein (1974:39–42); Rostow (1975:14–15). Long-distance trade, "high commerce" they call it, is downplayed by Horden and Purcell (2000).
143. Bentley (1996); Malkin (2011). The decline of the Old Kingdom was marked in part by the loss of prestige goods traded between the Near East and Egypt. On climatic triggers, see above.
144. Raaflaub (2004).
145. Curtin (1984); Chaudhuri (1985).
146. Malkin (2011:9).
147. Goldberg (2012).
148. Bresson (2003b:140–41).
149. Kuhrt (1998); Barjamovic (2008); Barjamovic (2017); M. Larsen (2015).
150. Leidwanger (2013:3302).
151. An alternative view of the Uluburun shipwreck, using a "peer-polity interaction" model, with merchants as agents of royal direction, is given by Van de Mieroop (2007).
152. Warburton (2003). The evidence for trade in ancient Egypt is surveyed by Grimal and Menu (1998).
153. A. Sherratt and Sherratt (1991:366). On monetization and the Uluburun cargo, Pulak (2008); Monroe (2010). On the cargo itself, see Pulak (1996).
154. Frankenstein (1979).
155. Liverani (2014:427–29).
156. Magnusson (1994) on mercantilism. On Smith's usage: *The Wealth of Nations*, book 4, part 2, chapter 2.
157. Frankenstein (1979).
158. Rostovtzeff (1932:16).
159. On "liminality" in this context see Monroe (2011).
160. Frankenstein (1979:266–67); Liverani (2014:423–24). For the story of Wenamun, see Wente (2003); Egberts (1998); Baines (1999).
161. Frankenstein (1979:273).
162. Demand (2011:235).
163. Frankenstein (1979:278).
164. A. Sherratt and Sherratt (1991:366).
165. Broodbank (2013) map 9.1 shows the "emergent" Mediterranean-wide maritime networks in the early Iron Age.
166. Niemeyer (2006:151–54).
167. On Huelva/Helva, see González de Canales, Serrano, and Llompart (2008).
168. Elayi (1981); Aubet (2001); Baslez (1987); Niemeyer (2004); Niemeyer (2006).

169. The traditional "foundation date" is 814 BCE. New material from excavations pushes the date back from the early 8th to the late 9th century BCE. See Docter et al. (2004); Hoyos (2010:6–19) for the foundation stories.
170. There is a very large literature on city-states, going back to Weber. See Stasavage (2011) for later comparative material.
171. Kozuh (2015).
172. Kozuh (2015:90–91).
173. Wiesehöfer (1982).
174. Stolper (1985); Stolper (2005).
175. Morel (2007:493).
176. C. Murray (2017).
177. On Greek trade, I rely here especially on Bresson (2003b); Bresson (2016). The organization of trade in Greek cities is extensively treated in the latter volume.
178. Broodbank (2013:551).
179. On Naukratis, see Möller (2000); Bresson (2005b).
180. E.g., Gabrielsen (2011, esp. 237–38), emphasizing the effects of tax exemption (*ateleia*).
181. Polanyi (1977).
182. On mobility, see Oliver (2011).
183. On the connections between the Black Sea and Egypt, emphasizing especially the presence of Egyptian cults and glassmaking trade, see Archibald (2007) and Reger (2007).
184. Heichelheim (1958:3).
185. On Roman expansion and trade, see Marasco (1988).
186. Hopkins (1983:xxi).
187. Morris (2003).
188. Gabrielsen (2011).
189. Bresson (2005a).
190. A. Wilson (2014). In general, see Lawall (2016).
191. On Rhodian governance, see below.
192. On the data, see, for example, Jongman (2007).
193. For a good example, see Oliver's (2001) study of Rhamnous. On "shifts" and "shocks," I follow Irwin and O'Rourke's (2014) definition.
194. A literature review of key discussion is handily provided in Horden and Purcell (2000:612–15).
195. On the basic problem of connecting pottery, the most basic archaeological remnant of exchange, with trade, see inter alia Gill (1994).
196. On quantification, see Bowman and Wilson (2009).
197. Bringmann (2001); e.g., Antiochus III's gift of timber to Jerusalem mentioned in Josephus, *Ant. Jud.* 12.141.
198. Apollonios's activities are well summarized by Orrieux (1983) in a section notably titled: "Un Commerce sans Commerçants." Cf. the brief discussion below on *P. Cair. Zen.* 59012.
199. D. Thompson (2012:213).
200. J. Manning (2011).
201. *P. Tebt.* 3.2 890 (2d century BCE) perhaps gives a flavor of the small scale, local, private lending practices of a bank in the Herakleopolite nome.
202. On the Geniza merchants, see Goldberg (2012).

203. See Gabrielsen (2011) who emphasizes the complex and intimate relationship between states and private actors with respect to the so-called monopolies.
204. Bresson (2003b).
205. On the relationship between merchants and the state, see also Gabrielsen (2011).
206. Finley (1999:22).
207. De Souza (1999:50–52). On Roman traders, see C. Müller and Hasenohr (2002).
208. J. Ma (2003). Cf. J. Davies (2001:39–40); Shipley (1993:282). On trade diasporas more broadly, see Pomeranz and Topik (2006).
209. Especially as summarized in his great work on Hellenistic economies (Rostovtzeff 1941:1238–58).
210. Reger (2011).
211. The classic study of regional trade is Reger (1994). See also Reger (2011:368).
212. Saller (2005) cautions against seeing strong differences.
213. Sidebotham's work on trade through the Red Sea port at Berenike (2011) concludes that considerable land-based trading via the eastern desert roads in both directions may lead us to think that Rostovtzeff's emphasis on long distance water routes should be reevaluated (Sidebotham 2011:213–14), as it has been for Roman trade.
214. Hopkins (1983:xiv–xvi).
215. D. Robinson and Goddio (2015); Fabre (2011); Pfeiffer (2010).
216. Goddio (2007); Goddio (2010).
217. Pfeiffer (2010:18–19).
218. Briant and Descat (1998).
219. Fabre (2011:13–14).
220. Casson (1954). Erdkamp (2005) for the Roman world.
221. Rathbone (1983).
222. Black Sea: Moreno (2007); Tsetskhladze (2008). For Athens's grain supply: Oliver (2007). For Cyrene, see Bresson (2011), already noting Cyrene's importance to the Greek mainland in the 6th century BCE.
223. Rostovtzeff (1941:1259). Slave trade from the Black Sea region: Avram (2007).
224. Ps. Aristot., *Oik.* II.2.31–34 (=1352 a–b); Dem. 56.7.
225. Möller (2000); Pfeiffer (2010).
226. N. Hudson (2016).
227. Préaux (1939:353–71); Rostovtzeff (1941:226–30); Fraser (1972:132–88).
228. Sijpesteijn (1987:2).
229. Bresson (2012b). On customs duties in Egypt in general, see Sijpesteijn (1987).
230. *P. Cair. Zen.* 59012 (=*SB* III 6779; May–June 259 BCE) is an important text for the Ptolemaic taxation of imports. See further Préaux (1939:372–79); Gabrielsen (1997:181n57); Austin (2006:text 298). Bresson (2012b) offers a reassessment of this important text. A new copy of the Naukratis decree has been found at Thonis (Heracleion), on which see Pfeiffer (2010). On Naukratis itself as a trading port, see Bresson (2000); Möller (2001); Möller (2005). Villing and Schlotzhauer (2006).
231. The papyrus, *TADAE* C.3.7, was published by Porten and Yardeni (1993); and discussed at length by Briant and Descat (1998). Cf. Briant (2002:385–87). On the Persian shift to Thonis, see Briant and Descat (1998:91–92); Pfeiffer (2010:18–19).
232. Bowman (2010:103).
233. The logistics of the ports at Alexandria, and the relationships between these and the older port at Thonis (Heracleion) have now been brilliantly analyzed by Fabre and

Goddio (2010) and Goddio (2011). For Ptolemaic development of eastern desert roads, see most recently Sidebotham (2011:28–31).

234. Goddio and Bernand (2004:153).

235. Mueller (2006). For one milestone marker, which could not have been unique, along the Edfu-Barramiya road leading out to Marsa Nakari on the Red Sea, found at Bir 'Iayyan (*SEG* XLVI 2120, 257 BCE), see Bagnall et al. (1996).

236. Bresson (2012b).

237. Population estimates are notoriously difficult. I rely here on Scheidel (2004).

238. Crawford (1983).

239. On the procession, see D. Thompson (2000) with previous literature cited therein.

240. Fraser (1972).

241. On Roman grain imports from Egypt during the republic, see Casson (1954:184–87).

242. Préaux (1939:353–79).

243. E.g., *P. Lond.* 7 1945; *P. Cair. Zen.* 2 59240.

244. Bresson (2008:222–24). On the commercial structures of Delos, see Karvonis (2008a).

245. Karvonis (2008b); Köse (2005).

246. On Rhodian trade, its navy, and its strong connection to Egypt, see Gabrielsen (1997).

247. Casson (1954:171); Gabrielsen (1997:72–73).

248. Distance: Gabrielsen (1997:71–72). On the winter trade, see, e.g., Dem. 56.30; Gabrielsen (2013).

249. Berthold (1984:49).

250. A letter of Demetrius to Zenon, *P. Lond.* 7 1979 (= P. Lond. Inv. 2092) (Zenon archive, from Alexandria, 252 BC).

251. De Souza (1999:48–53); Gabrielsen (2003:396); Austin (2006:210n1).

252. Polybius 30.31.10. Reger (2003:180–81).

253. On Delos, see Reger (1994).

254. Rauh (1999:166); Gabrielsen (1997:71). Amphorae in Egypt: Marchand and Marangou (2007); Gates-Foster (2011). On Rhodian amphorae at Akoris in Middle Egypt, left out of many accounts, see Kawanishi and Suto (2005).

255. Gibbins (2001:291); Gabrielsen (1997:64–71).

256. Cf. Scheidel (2011b:34n65).

257.

258. On Pytheas, see Roller (2006).

259. On the historiography of Alexander and trade, emphasizing to good effect the connection between Droysen and Wilcken's view of Alexander, see Briant (2009).

260. Briant (2009:183).

261. Wilcken (1967:293–94).

262. See Briant (2009) with literature cited therein.

263. Archibald, Davies, Gabrielsen, and Oliver (2001); Archibald, Davies, and Gabrielsen (2005); Archibald, Davies, and Gabrielsen (2011).

264. Shipley (1993:280). Cf. J. Davies (1984a:270).

265. J. Davies (1984a); Gellner (1983).

266. See, e.g., Briant (2002:387).

267. McCormick (2001:614): "Traders are among the least documented travelers that we have encountered." On Aztec merchants, see Hirth (2016), with an excellent discussion on why merchants are often missing from our sources.

268. Bresson (2003b). I thank Alain Bresson for the reference.
269. E.g., "Traders and merchants" attached to Demetrius's army besieging Rhodes in 305/4 BCE: Diod. Sic XX.82.4–83.1, discussed briefly in De Souza (1999:44–45); Billows (1990:358). On the subjective use of "pirate" see the remarks by Gabrielsen (2003:398–404).
270. Aristot., *Pol.* I; Morley (2007:79–89).
271. Indeed the Egyptian tradition extends back into the New Kingdom. See further, for example, Ryholt (2005:118–19) commenting on a new demotic literary text, "The Avaricious Merchant."
272. Gabrielsen (2007).
273. Rostovtzeff (1941:1269).
274. Rostovtzeff (1941:1274).
275. Indeed of premodern states, or what North, Wallis, and Weingast (2009:38–39) call "natural states."
276. *Eth. Nic.* 8.9.4–6 (1160a); Gabrielsen (2007:192).
277. It is interesting to note that Préaux (1939:364) suggested an evolution between the 3d and 2d centuries in the organization of the eastern trade, pointing in particular to the emergence, apparently, of "intermédiaires" in the aromatics trade.
278. Gabrielsen (1997:123–29); Gabrielsen (2001); Gabrielsen (2011).
279. Gabrielsen (1997:124).
280. On Egyptian associations, see de Cenival (1972); Muhs (2001); Monson (2010).
281. Gabrielsen (2007:195).
282. On the text, see J. Manning (2003).
283. Reger (2003).
284. A useful review of earlier Greek evidence may be found in Reed (2003).
285. Rhodian citizenship for example: *SIG*³ 354.
286. His activity is documented in the largest archive from the Ptolemaic period, the Zenon archive, from Philadelphia in the northeast Fayyum, where one of his large estates was located. On Hellenistic grain trade, See Casson (1954); Rathbone (1983); Athenian grain imports during the Hellenistic period, and the institutional adjustments Athens made is examined by Oliver (2007:228–59).
287. *P. Ryl.* 4 554 (=*SB* V 7637, Philadelphia, 258 BCE) mentions, in a list of shipped goods, Abdemoun of Sidon, a merchant at Rhodes and a close associate ("his brother") of Apollonios: Gabrielsen (1997:74).
288. On the text, see Jansen-Winkeln (1997). Interestingly, and tellingly perhaps, the word used in the text for "merchant" (*mkr*) is a Semitic loan word. The dating is slightly tenuous and is based on the fact that the name of the merchant, Nekhtnebef, i.e., "Nectanebo," would have been a popular personal name bestowed on a male child in and around the reign of Nectanebo II (360–343 BCE). Jansen-Winkeln (1997:115) concludes that the stela should probably be dated to late Dynasty 30 therefore, and not to the Ptolemaic period. I personally do not see any reason, in contrast, to think that the text cannot be situated equally well in the early Ptolemaic period.
289. Bernard, Pinault, and Rougemont (2004). I am grateful to my colleague Andrew Johnston for originally pointing me to this fascinating text.
290. Surveys in: Thapar (2002:174–279); Avari (2007:105–54).
291. *Syll.*³ 495, *SEG* 49.1041 (= Austin [2006:text115]).
292. On Rhodian governance and trade, see the overviews by Berthold (1984), Gabrielsen (1997) and Gabrielsen et al. (1999).

293. Gabrielsen (1997:73).
294. Gabrielsen (1997:80).
295. W. Murray (2012).
296. Trans. Scott-Kilvert (1973).
297. Athen., *Deip.* 5.206d–209b; Casson (1971:185–86); A. Wilson (2011:39).
298. Casson (1971:97–140).
299. *IG* XII Suppl. 348 (= Austin [2006:text 126], 3d century BCE). See A. Wilson (2011) on ship size.
300. A. Wilson (2011a).
301. On the Hellenistic state formation and the Leviathans, see J. Manning (forthcoming).
302. See Kron (forthcoming).
303. Garnsey (1988:107–19).
304. Lawall (2005:189) referring inter alia to de Callataÿ (2005).
305. Bresson (1993).
306. J. Davies (2001:27).
307. See for examples the study of fish amphorae from the Black Sea region by Opait (2007).
308. Lawall (2005:192).
309. Gibbins (2001:288).
310. Gibbins (2001:274).
311. Morley (2007:5); Kron (forthcoming) here on the western Mediterranean bias.
312. Lawall (2005:188), who lays out an important research agenda.
313. Gabrielsen (1997:68–71).
314. Gates-Foster (2011:804).
315. Lawall (2005:194–95). Cf. the remarks of Stolba (2007) with particular emphasis on the wine trade.
316. Scheidel (2011b:21). Cf. Bang (2007). R. Smith (2009:74) stressed "chronic warfare" after the mid-3d century BC that caused a general decline in trade.
317. Scheidel (2011b:23).
318. Menard (1991).
319. Some nuanced disagreement with Scheidel's institutional argument is expressed by A. Wilson (2011b:231–33) in the same volume, arguing for more weight to technological improvements reducing both cost and risk. See also Bang (2007) for a powerful analytical framework of Roman trade, developed further in Bang (2008), which emphasizes market exchange within a tributary mode of production.
320. The increased traffic is also well attested in the Red Sea at the port of Berenike and on the overland land routes in the Egyptian eastern desert. See Sidebotham (2011:125–74).
321. J. Davies (2001:18).
322. Scheidel 2011b:21
323. See above, chapter 5. On timber, see Meiggs (1982); Davies (2001:23–24); and for timber from the Black Sea, see Hannestad (2007).
324. Gabrielsen (2003:395), citing Plutarch, *Pomp.* 24.
325. Scheidel (2011b:34n65).
326. Gabrielsen (1997:66).
327. Polyb. 28.2.17; Casson (1954:182).
328. Well-stressed in Gabrielsen (2003). On war and the Hellenistic economy, see Austin (1986).

329. Gabrielsen (2003:391).
330. Rostovtzeff (1941:196–97); Gabrielsen (2003:395).
331. De Souza (1999:69).
332. For the archaeological survey of this region, see Rauh et al. (2009).
333. Scheidel (2011b:26).
334. Schörle (2010); Sidebotham (2011).
335. See briefly Kitchen (2001:166–70).
336. On the Muziris text, see the important study by Morelli (2011) with previous litera-
     ture cited therein. In the *Periplus* (20) ships should avoid eastern Red Sea coast and
     sail quickly to avoid pirates. Pliny (*N.H.* 6.26.101) tells us that ships had armed
     guards.
337. Oliver (2007).
338. See Oliver (2007:228–59) for an excellent review of the evidence.
339. Gabrielsen (2011).
340. In Egypt: *P. Hib.* 2 198 (=Bagnall and Derow [2004:text 122]; 242 BCE). Bagnall and
     Derow (2004:204n) suggest that internal trade was heavily taxed and such exemp-
     tions "were few in number." I see no way of being certain one way or the other on the
     basis of current evidence.
341. Gibbins (2001:293).
342. Scheidel (2011b:30).

CHAPTER 9. CONCLUSIONS

1. L. Hunt (2014:120).
2. Morris (2005).
3. Wootton (2015:550).
4. Bagnall (2002).
5. Acemoglu and Robinson (2012:3–4).
6. Brooke (2014).
7. See Jenkins (2000) on Weber's use of "disenchantment."
8. *P. Rainer* 19813; trans. Burstein (1985:text 106).
9. See the brief but salient note by J. Davies (2013b:446); Domingo Gygax (2016).
10. Matthews et al. (2012:17).
11. Broodbank (2013:41).
12. P. Brown (2012). On classical Athenian attitudes, see J. Davies (1984b).
13. Cf. W. Harris (2013b:3).

APPENDIX. CLIMATE DATA

1. J. Manning et al. (2017). For a detailed study of these effect during the 3d-century CE
   Roman Empire, see Rossignol and Durost (2007).
2. Cf. the quotation of Chaudhuri in the epigraph to chapter 5.
3. Staubwasser and Weiss (2006).

KEY READINGS

ECONOMIES OF THE ANCIENT NEAR EAST

Jursa, Michael. (2014). "Babylonia in the First Millennium BCE—Economic Growth in Times of Empire," in *The Cambridge History of Capitalism*. 2 vols. Ed. Larry Neal and Jeffrey G. Williamson. Cambridge: Cambridge University Press. Pp. 24–42.

———. (2010). *Aspects of the Economic History of Babylonia in the First Millennium BC: Economic Geography, Economic Mentalities, Agriculture, the Use of Money and the Problem of Economic Growth*. Münster: Ugarit-Verlag.

———. (2005). "Money-Based Exchange and Redistribution: The Transformation of the Institutional Economy in First Millennium Babylonia," in *Autour de Polanyi: Vocabulaires, theories et modalities des échanges, Nanterre, 12–14 Juin 2004*. Ed. P. Clancier, F. Joannès, P. Rouillard, and A. Tenu. Paris: De Boccard. Pp. 171–86.

Liverani, Mario. (2014). *The Ancient Near East: History, Society, and Economy*. London: Routledge.

Silver, Morris. (1995). *Economic Structures of Antiquity*. Westport, CT: Greenwood.

ECONOMIES OF EGYPT

Bleiberg, Edward. (1995). "The Economy of Ancient Egypt," in *Civilizations of the Ancient Near East*. Ed. Jack Sasson. Vol. 3. New York: Charles Scribner's Sons. Pp. 1373–85.

Kemp, Barry J. (2006). "The Birth of Economic Man," in *Ancient Egypt: Anatomy of a Civilization*. London: Routledge. Pp. 302–35.

Moreno García, Juan Carlos. (2014). "Recent Developments in the Social and Economic History of Ancient Egypt," *Journal of Ancient Near Eastern History* 1/2: 231–61.

Muhs, Brian P. (2016). *The Ancient Egyptian Economy, 3000–30 BC*. Cambridge: Cambridge University Press.

Warburton, David. (1997). *State and Temple Economy in Ancient Egypt: Fiscal Vocabulary of the New Kingdom*. Fribourg: University Press.

ECONOMIES OF GREECE

Amemiya, Takeshi. (2007). *Economy and Economics of Ancient Greece*. London: Routledge.

Archibald, Zosia H. (2013). *Ancient Economies of the Northern Aegean: Fifth to First Centuries BC*. Oxford: Oxford University Press.

Bresson, Alain. (2016). *The Making of the Ancient Greek Economy: Institutions, Markets, and Growth in the City-States*. Princeton, NJ: Princeton University Press.

Harris, Edward, David M. Lewis, and Mark Woolmer, eds. (2016). *The Ancient Greek Economy, Markets, Households and City-States*. New York: Cambridge University Press.

Lyttkens, Carl Hampus. (2013). *Economic Analysis of Institutional Change in Ancient Greece: Politics, Taxation and Rational Behavior*. London: Routledge.

Nafissi, Mohammed. (2005). *Ancient Athens and Modern Ideology: Value, Theory, and Evidence in Historical Sciences: Max Weber, Karl Polanyi and Moses Finley*. London: Institute of Classical Studies.

Ober, Josiah. (2015). *The Rise and Fall of Classical Greece*. Princeton, NJ: Princeton University Press.

ECONOMIES OF THE ACHAEMENID EMPIRE

Briant, Pierre. (2002). *From Cyrus to Alexander: A History of the Persian Empire*. Winona Lake: Eisenbrauns. Especially pp. 422–71; 938–47.

Kuhrt, Amélie. (2007). *The Persian Empire: A Corpus of Sources from the Achaemenid Period*. London: Routledge. Pp. 669–729; 763–825.

Wiesehöfer, Joseph. (2009). "The Achaemenid Empire," in *The Dynamics of Ancient Empires: State Power from Assyria to Byzantium*. Ed. Ian Morris and Walter Scheidel. New York: Oxford University Press. Pp. 66–98.

ECONOMIES OF THE HELLENISTIC PERIOD

Aperghis, M. M. (2004). *The Seleukid Royal Economy*. Cambridge: Cambridge University Press.

Austin, M. M. (1986). "Hellenistic Kings, War, and the Economy," *Classical Quarterly* 36/2: 450–66.

Archibald, Zosia H., John K. Davies, and Vincent Gabrielsen, eds. (2011). *The Economies of Hellenistic Societies, Third to First Centuries BC*. Oxford: Oxford University Press.

———. eds. (2005). *Making, Moving, and Managing: The New World of Ancient Economies, 323–31 BC*. Oxford: Oxbow Books.

Archibald, Zosia H., John K. Davies, Vincent Gabrielsen, and G. J. Oliver, eds. (2001). *Hellenistic Economies*. London: Routledge.

Chankowski, Véronique, and Frédérique Duyrat, eds. (2004). *Le Roi et L'Économie: Autonomies locales et structures royales dans l'économie de L'empire séleucide*. Topoi Supplement 6. Lyon: Maison de L'Orient méditerranéen.

Monson, Andrew. (2012). *From the Ptolemies to the Romans: Political and Economic Change in Egypt*. Cambridge: Cambridge University Press.

Reger, Gary. (1994). *Regionalism and Change in the Economy of Independent Delos:* Berkeley: University of California Press.

Rostovtzeff, Michael A. (1941). *The Social and Economic History of the Hellenistic World*. Oxford: Clarendon.

REGIONAL ECONOMIES

Archibald, Zosia H. (2013). *Ancient Economies of the Northern Aegean: Fifth to First Centuries BC*. Oxford: Oxford University Press.

Constantakopoulou, C. (2005). "Proud to Be an Islander: Island Identity in Multi-polis Islands in the Classical and Hellenistic Aegean," *Mediterranean Historical Review* 20: 1–34.

Elton, H., and G. Reger, eds. (2007). *Regionalism in Hellenistic and Roman Asia Minor*. Bordeaux: Ausonius.

Oliver, Graham. (2006). "Hellenistic Economies: Regional Views from the Athenian Polis," in *Approches de l'Économie héllénistique*. Entretiens d'archéologie et d'histoire

7. Saint Bertrand-de-Comminges: Musée archéologique de Saint-Betrand-de-Comminges. Pp. 215–56.

Reger, Gary. (2013). "Economic Regionalism in Theory and Practice," in *Pottery Markets in the Ancient Greek World (8th–1st Centuries B.C.)*. Ed. Athena Tsingarida and Didier Viviers. Brussels: Centre de Recherches en Archéologie et Patrimonie. Pp. 119–31.

———. (1994). *Regionalism and Change in the Economy of Independent Delos:* Berkeley: University of California Press.

ECONOMIES OF THE WESTERN MEDITERRANEAN

Cornell, T. J. (1995). *The Beginnings of Rome: Italy and Rome from the Bronze Age to the Punic Wars (c. 1000–264 BC)*. London: Routledge.

De Angelis, Franco. (2016). *Archaic and Classical Greek Sicily: A Social and Economic History*. Oxford: Oxford University Press.

ECONOMIES OF THE BLACK SEA

Gabrielsen, Vincent, and John Lund, eds. (2007). *The Black Sea in Antiquity: Regional and Interregional Economic Exchanges*. Aarhus: Aarhus University Press.

ECONOMIC THEORY AND ANCIENT ECONOMIES

Bang, Peter F. (2009). "The Ancient Economy and New Institutional Economics," *Journal of Roman Studies* 99: 194–206.

Jones, Donald W. (2014). *Economic Theory and the Ancient Mediterranean*. Malden, MA: Wiley-Blackwell.

Temin, Peter. (2013). *The Roman Market Economy*. Princeton, NJ: Princeton University Press.

Verboven, Koenraad. (2015). "The Knights Who Say NIE. Can Neo-institutional Economics Live Up to Its Expectation in Ancient History Research?," in *Structure and Performance in the Ancient Economy: Models, Methods and Case Studies*. Ed. Paul Erdkamp and Koenraad Verboven. Brussels: Éditions Latomus. Pp. 33–57.

COINAGE, MONEY, AND PRICES

Harris, William V., ed. (2008). *The Monetary Systems of the Greeks and Romans*. Oxford: Oxford University Press.

Howgego, Christopher. (1995). *Ancient History from Coins*. London: Routledge.

Metcalf, William E., ed. (2012). *The Oxford Handbook of Greek and Roman Coinage*. Oxford: Oxford University Press.

Schaps, David M. (2004). *The Invention of Coinage and the Monetization of Ancient Greece*. Ann Arbor: University of Michigan Press.

Thonemann, Peter. (2015). *The Hellenistic World: Using Coins as Sources*. Cambridge: Cambridge University Press.

van der Spek, R. J., Bas van Leeuwen, and Jan Luiten van Zanden, eds. (2015). *A History of Market Performance: From Ancient Babylonia to the Modern World*. London: Routledge.

von Reden, Sitta. (2010). *Money in Classical Antiquity*. Cambridge: Cambridge University Press.

———. (2007). *Money in Ptolemaic Egypt: From the Macedonian Conquest to the End of the Third Century BC*. Cambridge: Cambridge University Press.

ANCIENT TECHNOLOGY

Greene, Kevin. (2008). "Historiography and Theoretical Approaches," in *The Oxford Handbook of Engineering and Technology in the Classical World*. Ed. John Peter Oleson. Oxford: Oxford University Press. Pp. 62–90.
———. (2000). "Technological Innovation and Economic Progress in the Ancient World: M. I. Finley Re-considered," *Economic History Review* 53/1: 29–59.
Nicholson, Paul T., and Ian Shaw, eds. (2000). *Ancient Egyptian Materials and Technology*. Cambridge: Cambridge University Press.
Oleson, John Peter, ed. (2008). *The Oxford Handbook of Engineering and Technology in the Classical World*. Oxford: Oxford University Press.

CLIMATE

Bradley, Raymond S. (2015). *Paleoclimatology: Reconstructing Climates of the Quaternary*. 3d. ed. Oxford: Academic Press.
Brooke, J. L. (2014). *Climate Change and the Course of Global History: A Rough Journey*. Cambridge: Cambridge University Press.
Campbell, Bruce M. S. (2016). *The Great Transition: Climate, Disease and Society in the Late-Medieval World*. Cambridge: Cambridge University Press.
Harper, Kyle. (2017). *The Fate of Rome: Climate, Disease, and the End of an Empire*. Princeton, NJ: Princeton University Press.
Luterbacher, J., et al. (2012). "Review of 2000 Years of Paleoclimatic Evidence in the Mediterranean," in *The Climate of the Mediterranean Region: From the Past to the Future*. Ed. P. Lionello. London: Elsevier. Pp. 87–185.

SOURCES

Bagnall, Roger S. (1995). *Reading Papyri: Writing Ancient History*. London: Routledge.
Bodel, John. (2001). *Epigraphic Evidence: Ancient History from Inscriptions*. London: Routledge.
Davies, John K. (2013). "Mediterranean Economies through the Text of Polybius," in *Polybius and His World: Essays in Memory of F. W. Walbank*. Ed. Bruce Gibson and Thomas Harrison. Oxford: Oxford University Press. Pp. 319–35.
Hall, Jonathan. (2014). *A History of the Archaic Greek World, ca. 1200–479 BCE*. 2d ed. Malden, MA: Wiley-Blackwell. Pp. 16–40.
Howgego, Christopher. (1995). *Ancient History from Coins*. London: Routledge.
Kuhrt, Amélie. (2007). *The Persian Empire: A Corpus of Sources from the Achaemenid Period*. London: Routledge. Pp. 669–729; 763–825.
Pomeroy, Sarah B. (1994). *Xenophon, Oeconomicus: A Social and Historical Commentary*. Oxford: Oxford University Press.
Vandorpe, Katelijn. (2009). "Archives and Dossiers," in *The Oxford Handbook of Papyrology*. Ed. Roger S. Bagnall. Oxford: Oxford University Press. Pp. 216–55.

BIBLIOGRAPHY

Abramitzky, Ran. (2015). "Economics and the Modern Economic Historian," *Journal of Economic History* 75/4: 1240–51.

Abulafia, David. (2011). *The Great Sea: A Human History of the Mediterranean*. Oxford: Oxford University Press.

———. (2005). "Mediterraneans," in *Rethinking the Mediterranean*. Ed. W. V. Harris. Oxford: Oxford University Press. Pp. 64–93.

Abu-Lughod, Janet L. (1995). "The World-System Perspective in the Construction of Economic History," *History and Theory* 34: 86–98.

———. (1989). *Before European Hegemony: The World System AD 1250–1350*. New York.

Acemoglu, Daron. (2008). "Growth and Institutions," in *The New Palgrave Dictionary of Economics Online*. Ed. S. N. Durlauf and L. E. Blume. Basingstoke: Palgrave Macmillan.

Acemoglu, Daron, Simon Johnson, and James A. Robinson. (2001). "The Colonial Origins of Comparative Development: An Empirical Investigation," *American Economic Review* 91/5: 1369–401.

Acemoglu, Daron, and James A. Robinson. (2012). *Why Nations Fail: The Origins of Power, Prosperity, and Poverty*. New York: Crown Business.

Achilli, Alessandro, et al. (2007). "Mitochondrial DNA Variation of Modern Tuscans Supports the Near Eastern Origins of Etruscans," *American Journal of Human Genetics* 80: 759–68.

Adams, Robert McCormick. (2012). "Ancient Mesopotamian Urbanism and Blurred Disciplinary Boundaries," *Annual Review of Anthropology* 41: 1–20.

———. (1981). *Heartland of Cities: Surveys of Ancient Settlement and Land Use on the Central Flood Plain of the Euphrates*. Chicago: University of Chicago Press.

———. (1974). "Anthropological Perspectives on Ancient Trade," *Current Anthropology* 15: 239–49.

———. (1965). *Land behind Baghdad: A History of Settlement on the Diyala Plains*. Chicago: University of Chicago Press.

———. (1960). "Comment," in *Current Anthropology* 1/5–6: 422–23.

Adams, William Y. (1984). "The First Colonial Empire: Egypt in Nubia, 3200–1200 B.C.," *Comparative Studies in Society and History* 26: 36–71.

Aghion, Philippe, and Peter Howitt. (2009). *The Economics of Growth*. Cambridge, MA: MIT Press.

Agut-Labordère, Damien. (2013). "The Saite Period: The Emergence of a Mediterranean Power," in *Ancient Egyptian Administration*. Ed. Juan Carlos Moreno García. Leiden: Brill. Pp. 965–1027.

———. (2011). "Les 'petites citadelles': La sociabilité du tmy 'ville,' 'village' à travers les Sagesses démotiques," in *Espaces et territoires de l'égypte grécoromaine: Actes des journées d'études, 23 juin 2007 et 21 juin 2008*. Ed. Gilles Gorre and Perrine Kosmann. Geneva: Librairie Droz. Pp. 107–20.

Alcock, Susan E. (2007). "The Essential Countryside: The Greek World," in *Classical Archaeology*. Ed. Susan E. Alcock and Robin Osborne. Malden, MA.: Blackwell. Pp. 120–38.

Alcock, Susan E., and John F. Cherry, eds. (2004). *Side-by-Side Survey: Comparative Regional Studies in the Mediterranean World*. Oxford: Oxbow Books.

Alesina, Alberto, and Enrico Spolaore. (2003). *The Size of Nations*. Cambridge, MA: MIT Press.

Alfani, Guido, and Tommy E. Murphy. (2017). "Plague and Lethal Epidemics in the Preindustrial World," *Journal of Economic History* 77/1: 314–43.

Algaze, Guillermo. (2008). *Ancient Mesopotamia at the Dawn of Civilization: The Evolution of an Urban Landscape*. Chicago: University of Chicago Press.

Algazi, Gadi. (2005). "Diversity Rules: Peregrine Horden and Nicholas Purcell's *The Corrupting Sea*," *Mediterranean History Review* 20/2: 227–45.

———. (1993). *The Uruk World System: The Dynamics of Expansion of Early Mesopotamian Civilization*. Chicago: University of Chicago Press.

Allam, Schafik. (2008). "Regarding the *Eisgogeus* at Ptolemaic Law Courts," *Journal of Egyptian History* 1/1justizwesen: 3–19.

Allen, James P. (2002). *The Hekanakht Papyri*. New York: Metropolitan Museum of Art.

Allen, Robert C. (2009). "How Prosperous Were the Romans? Evidence from Diocletian's Price Edict (AD 301)," in *Quantifying the Roman Economy: Methods and Problems*. Ed. Alan K. Bowman and Andrew Wilson. Oxford: Oxford University Press. Pp. 327–45.

———. (2008). "Review of Gregory Clark's 'A Farewell to Alms': A Brief Economic History of the World," *Journal of Economic Literature* 46/4: 946–73.

———. (1997). "Agriculture and the Origins of the State in Ancient Egypt," *Explorations in Economic History* 34: 135–54.

Alley, R. B., D. A. Meese, C. A. Shuman, A. J. Gow, K. C. Taylor, P. M. Grootes, J.W.C. White, M. Ram, E. D. Waddington, P. A. Mayewski, and G. A. Zielinski. (1993). "Abrupt Increase in Snow Accumulation at the End of the Younger Dryas Event," *Nature* 362: 527–29.

Alley, Richard B. (2000). *The Two-Mile Time Machine: Ice Cores, Abrupt Climate Change, and Our Future*. Princeton, NJ: Princeton University Press.

Alston, L. J. (2008). "New Institutional Economics," in *The New Palgrave Dictionary of Economics Online*. 2d ed. Ed. Steven N. Durlauf and Lawrence E. Blume. Basingstoke: Palgrave Macmillan. http://www.dictionaryofeconomics.com/article?id=pde2008_N000170&authstatuscode=202.

Amemiya, Takeshi. (2007). *Economy and Economics of Ancient Greece*. London: Routledge.

Andersen, T. B., C. J. Dalgaard, and P. Selaya. (2016). "Climate and the Emergence of Global Income Differences," *Review of Economic Studies,* 83/4: 1334–63.

Anderson, Greg. (2015). "Retrieving the Lost Worlds of the Past: The Case for an Ontological Turn," *AHR* 120/3: 787–810.

Andreau, Jean. (1995). "Vingt ans d'après *L'Économie antique* de Moses I. Finley," *Annales: Histoire, Sciences Sociales* 50 (1995): 947–60. Reprinted as "Twenty Years After Moses I. Finley's *The Ancient Economy*," in Walter Scheidel and Sitta von Reden, eds., *The Ancient Economy*, New York: Routledge, 2002, pp. 33–49.

———. (1977). "M. I. Finley, la banque antique et l'économie modern," *Annali della Scuola Normale Superiore di Pisa*, 3d ser., 7: 1130–52.

Antonopoulos, John. (1992). "The Tsunami of 426 BC in the Maliakos Gulf, Eastern Greece," *Natural Hazards* 5/1: 83–93.

Aoki, Masahiko. (2001). *Toward a Comparative Institutional Analysis*. Cambridge, MA: MIT Press.

Aperghis, M. M. (2004). *The Seleukid Royal Economy: The Finances and Financial Administration of the Seleukid Empire*. Cambridge: Cambridge University Press.

Archibald, Zosia H. (2013). *Ancient Economies of the Northern Aegean: Fifth to First Centuries BC*. New York: Oxford University Press.

———. (2007). "Contacts between the Ptolemaic Kingdom and the Black Sea in the early Hellenistic Age," in *The Black Sea in Antiquity: Regional and Interregional Economic Exchange*. Ed. Vincent Gabrielsen and John Lund. Aarhus: Aarhus University Press. Pp. 253–71.

———. (2005). "Markets and Exchange: The Structure and Scale of Economic Behavior in the Hellenistic Age," in *Making, Moving, and Managing: The New World of Ancient Economies, 323–31 BC*. Ed. Zosia H. Archibald, John K. Davies, and Vincent Gabrielsen. Oxford: Oxbow Books. Pp. 1–26.

———. (2002). "A River Port and *emporion* in Central Bulgaria: An Interim Report on the British Project at Vetren," *Annual of the British School at Athens* 97: 309–51.

Archibald, Zosia, and John K. Davies. (2011). "Introduction," in *The Economies of Hellenistic Societies, Third to First Centuries BC*. Ed. Zosia H. Archibald, John K. Davies, and Vincent Gabrielsen. Oxford: Oxford University Press. Pp. 1–18.

Archibald, Zosia H., John K. Davies, and Vincent Gabrielsen, eds. (2011). *The Economies of Hellenistic Societies, Third to First Centuries BC*. Oxford: Oxford University Press.

———. eds. (2005). *Making, Moving, and Managing: The New World of Ancient Economies, 323–31 BC*. Oxford: Oxbow Books.

Archibald, Zosia H., John K. Davies, Vincent Gabrielsen, and G. J. Oliver, eds. (2001). *Hellenistic Economies*. London: Routledge.

Arlt, Carolin. (2011). *Deine Seele möge leben für immer und ewig: Die demotischen Mumienschilder im British Museum*. Leuven: Peeters.

Arnold, John H. (2000). *History: A Very Short Introduction*. Oxford: Oxford University Press.

Arruda, Ana Margarida. (2009). "Phoenician Colonization on the Atlantic Coast of the Iberian Peninsula," in *Colonial Encounters in Ancient Iberia: Phoenician, Greek and Indigenous Relations*. Ed. Michael Dietler and Carolina Lopez-Ruiz. Chicago: University of Chicago Press. Pp. 113–30.

Arthur, W. Brian. (2015). *Complexity and the Economy*. Oxford: Oxford University Press.

Aruz, Joan, Sarah B. Graff, and Yelena Rakic, eds. (2014). *Assyria to Iberia at the Dawn of the Classical Age*. New York: Metropolitan Museum of Art.

Aubet, Maria Eugenia. (2013). *Commerce and Colonization in the Ancient Near East*. Trans. Mary Turton. Cambridge: Cambridge University Press. Originally *Comercio y Colonialismo en el Proximo Oriente Antiguo: Los antecedentes coloniales del III y II milenios a. C.* Barcelona: Edicions Bellaterra, 2007.

———. (2001). *The Phoenicians and the West: Politics, Colonies and Trade*. Trans. M. Turton. 2d ed. Cambridge: Cambridge University Press.

Ault, Bradley A., and Lisa C. Nevett, eds. (2005). *Ancient Greek Houses and Households: Chronological, Regional and Social Diversity*. Philadelphia: University of Pennsylvania Press.

Austin, M. M. (2006). *The Hellenistic World from Alexander to the Roman Conquest: A Selection of Ancient Sources in Translation*. 2d ed. Cambridge: Cambridge University Press.

———. (1986). "Hellenistic Kings, War, and the Economy," *Classical Quarterly* 36/2: 450–66.

Austin, M. M., and Paul Vidal-Naquet. (1972). *Économies et societies en Grèce ancienne.* Paris: Librarie Colin. Published in English as *Economic and Social History of Ancient Greece: An Introduction.* 1977. Berkeley: University of California Press.

Avari, Burjor. (2007). *India, the Ancient Past: A History of the Indian Sub-continent from c. 7000 BC to AD 1200.* London: Routledge.

Avram, Alexandru. (2007). "Some Thoughts about the Black Sea and the Slave Trade before Roman Domination (6th–1st Centuries BC)," in *The Black Sea in Antiquity: Regional and Inter-regional Economic Exchanges.* Ed. Vincent Gabrielsen and John Lund. Aarhus: Aarhus University Press. Pp. 239–51.

Babbi, Andrea, Friederike Bubenheimer, Erhart Beatriz Marín-Aguilera, and Simone Mühl, eds. (2015). *The Mediterranean Mirror: Cultural Contacts in the Mediterranean Sea between 1200 and 750 B.C.* Mainz: Verlag des Römisch-Germanischen Zentralmuseums.

Baer, Klaus. (1963). "An Eleventh Dynasty Farmer's Letters to His Family," *Journal of the American Oriental Society* 83/1: 1–19.

Baetens, Geert, and Mark Depauw. (2015). "The Legal Advice of Totoes in the Siut Archive (P. BM. 10591, Verso, Col. I–III)," *Journal of Egyptian Archaeology* 101: 197–215.

Bagnall, Roger S. (2011a). *Everyday Writing in the Graeco-Roman East.* Berkeley: University of California Press.

———. (2011b). "Archaeological Work on Hellenistic and Roman Egypt, 2000–2009," *American Journal of Archaeology* 115/1: 103–57.

———. ed. (2009a). *The Oxford Handbook of Papyrology.* Oxford: Oxford University Press.

———. (2009b). "Response to Alan Bowman," in *Quantifying the Roman Economy: Methods and Problems.* Ed. Alan K. Bowman and Andrew Wilson. Oxford: Oxford University Press. Pp. 205–9.

———. (2005). "Egypt and the Concept of the Mediterranean," in *Rethinking the Mediterranean.* Ed. W. V. Harris. Oxford: Oxford University Press. Pp. 339–47.

———. (2002). "Alexandria: Library of Dreams," in *Proceedings of the American Philosophical Society* 146/4: 348–62.

———. (2001). "Archaeological Work on Hellenistic and Roman Egypt, 1995–2000," *AJA* 105/2: 227–43.

———. (1995). *Reading Papyri: Writing Ancient History.* London: Routledge.

———. (1992). "Landholding in Late Roman Egypt: The Distribution of Wealth," *Journal of Roman Studies* 82: 128–49.

Bagnall, Roger S., and Peter Derow. (2004). *The Hellenistic Period: Historical Sources in Translation.* Malden, MA: Blackwell.

Bagnall, Roger S., and Bruce W. Frier. (1994). *The Demography of Roman Egypt.* Cambridge Studies in Population, Economy and Society in Past Time 23. Cambridge: Cambridge University Press.

Bagnall, Roger, J. G. Manning, Steven Sidebotham, and Roger Zitterkopf. (1996). "A Ptolemaic Inscription from Bir 'Iayyan," *Chronique d'Égypte* 71: 317–30.

Bai, Ying, and James Kai-sing Kung. (2011). "Climate Shocks and Sino-nomadic Conflict," *Review of Economics and Statistics* 93/3: 970–81.

Baines, John R. (1999). "On *Wenamun* as a Literary Text," in *Literatur und Politik im pharaonischen und ptolemäischen Ägypten: Vorträge der Tagung zum Gedenken an*

Georges Posener 5.–10. September 1996 in Leipzig. Ed. Jan Assmann and Elke Blumen-thal. Bibliothèque d'Étude 127. Cairo: Institut français d'archéologie orientale du Caire. Pp. 209–33.

Baker, Alan R. H. (2003). *Geography and History: Bridging the Divide.* Cambridge: Cambridge University Press.

Baker, Heather D. (2014). "House Size and Household Structure: Quantitative Data in the Study of Babylonian Urban Living Conditions," in *Documentary Sources in Ancient Near Eastern and Greco-Roman Economic History: Methodology and Practice.* Ed. Heather D. Baker and Michael Jursa. Oxford: Oxbow. Pp. 7–23.

Balmuth, Miriam S., ed. (2001). *Hacksilber to Coinage: New Insights into the Monetary History of the Near East and Greece.* New York: American Numismatic Society.

Banaji, Jairus. (2007). "Islam, the Mediterranean and the Rise of Capitalism," *Historical Materialism* 15: 47–74.

Bang, Peter F. (2009). "The Ancient Economy and New Institutional Economics," *Journal of Roman Studies* 99: 194–206.

———. (2008). *The Roman Bazaar: A Comparative Study of Trade and Markets in a Tributary Empire.* Cambridge: Cambridge University Press.

———. (2007). "Trade and Empire—in Search of Organizing Concepts for the Roman Economy," *Past and Present* 195: 3–54.

———. (1998). "Antiquity between 'Primitivism' and 'Modernism.'" Center for Cultural Research, University of Aarhus. www.hum.au.dk/ckulturf/pages/publications/pfb /antiquity.htm.

Bang, Peter F., Mamoru Ikeguchi, and Harmut G. Ziche. (2006). *Ancient Economies, Modern Methodologies: Archaeology, Comparative History, Models and Institutions.* Bari: Edipuglia.

Bard, Kathryn A. (2008). *An Introduction to the Archaeology of Ancient Egypt.* Malden, MA: Blackwell.

Barfield, Thomas J. (2001). "The Shadow Empires: Imperial State Formation along the Chinese-Nomad Frontier," in *Empires.* Ed. Susan E. Alcock, Terence N. D'Altroy, Kathleen D. Morrison, and Carla M. Sinopoli. Cambridge: Cambridge University Press. Pp. 10–41.

Barjamovic, Gojko. (2017). "Interlocking Commercial Networks and the Infrastructure of Trade in Western Asia during the Bronze Age," in *Trade and Civilization in the Pre-modern World.* Ed. K. Kristiansen, T. Lindkvist, and J. Myrdal. Cambridge: Cambridge University Press. Pp. 133–67.

———. (2008). "The Geography of Trade: Assyrian Colonies in Anatolia c. 1975–1725 BC and the Study of Early Interregional Networks of Exchange," in *Anatolia and the Jazira during the Old Assyrian Period.* PIHANS 111. Leiden: Netherlands Institute for the Near East. Pp. 87–100.

Barker, Graeme. (2009). *The Agricultural Revolution in Prehistory: Why Did Foragers Become Farmers?* Paperback ed. Oxford: Oxford University Press.

Bar-Matthews, Miryam. (2012). "Environmental Change in the Mediterranean Region," in *The SAGE Handbook of Environmental Change.* Vol. 2. Ed. John A. Matthews et al. London: SAGE. Pp. 163–87.

Baslez, Marie Françoise. (1987). "Le rôle et la place des Phéniciens dans la vie économique des ports de l'Égée," in *Phoenicia and the East Mediterranean in the First Millennium B.C.* Ed. Edward Lipiński. Leuven: Peeters. Pp. 267–85.

Basu, Ratan Lal, and Raj Kumar Sen. (2008). *Ancient Indian Economic Thought: Relevance for Today.* Jaipur: Rawat.

Bates, Robert H., Avner Greif, Margaret Levi, Jean-Laurent Rosenthal, and Barry R. Weingast. (1998). *Analytic Narratives.* Princeton, NJ: Princeton University Press.

Baumard, Nicolas, Alexandre Hyafil, Ian Morris, and Pascal Boyer. (2015). "Increased Affluence Explains the Emergence of Ascetic Wisdoms and Moralizing Religions," *Current Biology* 25/1: 10–15.

Baumer, Christoph. (2012–16). *The History of Central Asia.* 3 vols. London: I. B. Tauris.

Bayly, C. A., and Peter Bang. (2003). "Introduction: Comparing Pre-modern Empires," *Medieval History Journal* 6/2: 169–87.

Baziotopoulou-Valavani, E. A. (2002). "Mass Burial from the Cemetery of Kerameikos," in *Excavating Classical culture: Recent Archaeological Discoveries in Greece: Studies in Classical Archaeology.* Vol. 1. BAR International Series 1031. Ed. M. Stamatopoulou and M. Yeroulanou. Oxford: Archaeopress. Pp. 187–201.

Beaujard, Philippe. (2011). "Evolutions and Temporal Delimitations of Bronze Age World-Systems in Western Asia and the Mediterranean," in *Interweaving Worlds: Systemic Interactions in Eurasia, 7th to the 1st Millennia BC.* Ed. Toby C. Wilkinson, Susan Sherratt, and John Bennet. Oxford: Oxbow. Pp. 7–26.

———. (2010). "From Three Possible Systems to a Single Afro-Eurasian One," *Journal of World History* 21/1: 1–43.

Beinhocker, Eric D. (2006). *The Origin of Wealth: Evolution, Complexity, and the Radical Remaking of Economics.* Boston: Harvard Business School Press.

Bell, Barbara. (1975). "Climate and the History of Egypt: The Middle Kingdom," *American Journal of Archaeology* 79/3: 223–69.

———. (1971). "The Dark Ages in Ancient History. I. The First Dark Age in Egypt," *American Journal of Archaeology* 75/1: 1–26.

Bell, Carol. (2016). "Phoenician Trade: The First 300 Years," in *Dynamics of Production in the Ancient Near East, 1300–500 BC.* Ed. Juan Carlos Moreno García. Oxford: Oxbow. Pp. 91–105.

Bellah, Robert N. (2011). *Religion in Human Evolution: From the Paleolithic to the Axial Age.* Cambridge, MA: Belknap of Harvard University Press.

Beloch, Julius. (1902a). "Zur griechischen Wirtschaftsgeschichte," *Zeitschrift für Socialwissenschaft* 5: 95–13.

———. (1902b). "Zur griechischen Wirtschaftsgeschichte," *Zeitschrift für Socialwissenschaft* 5: 169–79.

———. (1899). "Die Grossindustrie im Altertum," *Zeitschrift für Socialwissenschaft* 2: 18–26.

Bendix, Reinhard. (1960). *Max Weber, an Intellectual Portrait.* Garden City, NJ: Doubleday.

Bennett, J. (2016). "Repeated Demographic-Structural Crises Propel the Spread of Large-Scale Agrarian States throughout the Old World," *Cliodynamics: The Journal of Quantitative History and Cultural Evolution* 7/1:. 1–36.

Bentley, J. H. (1999). "Sea and Ocean Basins as Frameworks of Historical Analysis," *Geographical Review* 89: 215–24.

———. (1996). "Cross-Cultural Interaction and Periodization in World History," *American Historical Review* 101/3: 749–70.

———. (1993). *Old World Encounters: Cross-Cultural Exchanges in Pre-modern Times.* Oxford: Oxford University Press.

Berhane, Fisseha, Benjamin Zaitchik, and Amin Dezfuli. (2014). "Subseasonal Analysis of Precipitation in the Blue Nile River Basin," *Journal of Climate* 27: 325–44.

Bernard, Paul, Georges-Jean Pinault, and Georges Rougemont. (2004). "Deux nouvelles inscriptions grecques de l'Asie central," *Journal des Savants* 2004/2: 227–356.

Berthold, Richard M. (1984). *Rhodes in the Hellenistic Age*. Ithaca, NY: Cornell University Press.

Bintliff, John. (2008). "Considerations on Agricultural Scale—Economies in the Greco-Roman World," in *Feeding the Ancient Greek City*. Ed. Richard Alston and Onno M. van Nijf. Leuven: Peeters. Pp. 17–31.

———. (1991). "The Contribution of an Annaliste/Structural History Approach to Archaeology," in *The Annales School and Archaeology*. Ed. John Bintliff. New York: New York University Press. Pp. 1–33.

Billows, Richard A. (1990). *Antigonos the One-Eyed and the Creation of the Hellenistic State*. Berkeley: University of California Press.

Blanchet, C. L., C. Contoux, and G. Leduc. (2015). "Runoff and Precipitation Dynamics in the Blue and White Nile Catchments during the Mid-Holocene: A Data-Model Comparison," *Quaternary Science Reviews* 130: 222–30.

Blanton, Richard E. and Lane Fargher. (2008). *Collective Action in the Formation of Premodern States*. New York: Springer.

Bleiberg, Edward. (1996). *The Official Gift in Ancient Egypt*. Norman: University of Oklahoma Press.

———. (1995). "The Economy of Ancient Egypt," in *Civilizations of the Ancient Near East*. Ed. Jack Sasson. Vol. 3. New York: Charles Scribner's Sons. Pp. 1373–85.

Block, Fred, and Margaret R. Somers. (2014). *The Power of Market Fundamentalism: Karl Polanyi's Critique*. Cambridge, MA: Harvard University Press.

Blouin, Katherine. (2014). *Triangular Landscapes: Environment, Society, and the State in the Nile Delta under Roman Rule*. Oxford: Oxford University Press.

———. (2013). "The Agricultural Economy of the Mendesian Nome under Roman Rule," in *The Roman Agricultural Economy: Organization, Investment, and Production*. Ed. Alan Bowman and Andrew Wilson. Oxford: Oxford University Press. Pp. 255–72.

Bodel, John. (2001). *Epigraphic Evidence: Ancient History from Inscriptions*. London: Routledge.

Bodenhorn, H., T. W. Guinnane, and T. A Mroz. (2014). "Sample Selection Bias in the Historical Heights Literature," Economic Growth Center Discussion Paper, Yale University.

Boer, Roland. (2015). *The Sacred Economy of Israel*. Louisville, KY: Westminster John Knox Press.

Bogaert, Raymond. (1994). *Trapezitica Aegyptiaca: Recueil de Recherches sur la Banque en Égypte Gréco-Romaine*. Papyrologica Florentina 25. Fireze: Edizioni Gonnelli.

Boiy, T. (2004). *Late Achaemenid and Hellenistic Babylonia*. Orientalia Lovaniensia Analecta 136. Leuven: Peeters.

Boldizzoni, Francesco. (2011). *The Poverty of Clio: Resurrecting Economic History*. Princeton, NJ: Princeton University Press.

Bolle, Hans-Jürgen, ed. (2003). *Mediterranean Climate: Variability and Trends*. Heidelberg: Springer.

Bonneau, Danielle. (1993). *Le Régime administrative de l'eau du Nil dans l'Egypte grecque, romaine et byzantine*. Leiden: Brill.

———. (1971). *Le fisc et le Nil: Incidences des irregularities de la crue du Nil sur la fiscalité dans L'Égypte grecque et romaine*. Paris: Éditions Cujas.

Boserup, Ester. (1965). *The Conditions of Agricultural Growth. The Economics of Agrarian Change under Population Pressure*. Chicago: Aldine.

Bourdieu, Pierre. (2005). "Principles of an Economic Anthropology," in *The Handbook of Economic Sociology*. 2d ed. Ed. Neil J. Smelser and Richard Swedburg. Princeton, NJ: Princeton University Press. Pp. 75–89. Originally published as "Principes d'une anthropologie économique" in *Les structures sociales de l'économie*. Paris: Seuil, 2000.

Bowles, Samuel. (2004). *Microeconomics: Behavior, Institutions, and Evolution*. Princeton, NJ: Princeton University Press.

Bowles, Samuel, and Jyung-Kyoo Choi. (2013). "Coevolution of Farming and Private Property during the Early Holocene," *PNAS* 11/22. www.pnas.org/cgi/doi/10.1073/pnas.1212149110.

Bowles, Samuel, and Herbert Gintis. (2011). *A Cooperative Species: Human Reciprocity and Its Evolution*. Princeton, NJ: Princeton University Press.

Bowman, Alan K. (2013). "Agricultural Production in Egypt," in *The Roman Agricultural Economy: Organization, Investment, and Production*. Ed. Alan Bowman and Andrew Wilson. Oxford: Oxford University Press. Pp. 219–53.

———. (2010). "Trade and the Flag: Alexandria, Egypt and the Imperial House," in *Alexandria and the North-Western Delta*. Ed. Damian Robinson and Andrew Wilson. Oxford: Oxford Centre for Maritime Archaeology. Pp. 103–9.

———. (2009). "Quantifying Egyptian Agriculture," in *Quantifying the Roman Economy: Methods and Problems*. Ed. Alan K. Bowman and Andrew Wilson. Oxford: Oxford University Press. Pp. 177–204.

Bowman, Alan K., and Eugene Rogan, eds. (1999). *Agriculture in Egypt: From Pharaonic to Modern Times*. Oxford: Oxford University Press.

Bowman, Alan K., and Andrew Wilson, eds. (2013). *The Roman Agricultural Economy: Organization, Investment, and Production*. Oxford: Oxford University Press.

———. (2011). *Settlement, Urbanization, and Population*. Oxford: Oxford University Press.

———. (2009). *Quantifying the Roman Economy: Methods and Problems*. Oxford: Oxford University Press.

Bradley, Keith. (1994). *Slavery and Society at Rome*. Cambridge: Cambridge University Press.

Bradley, Keith, and Paul Cartledge, eds. (2011). *The Cambridge World History of Slavery*. Vol. 1, *The Ancient Mediterranean World*. Cambridge: Cambridge University Press.

Bradley, Raymond S. (2015). *Paleoclimatology: Reconstructing Climates of the Quaternary*. 3d. ed. Oxford: Academic Press.

Braidwood, Robert J. (1963). "Summary of Prehistoric Investigations in Kurdistan in Relation to Climatic Change," in *Changes of Climate: Proceedings of the Rome Symposium Organized by UNESCO and WMO*. Paris: UNESCO. Pp. 251–54.

Braudel, Ferdinand. (2001). *The Mediterranean in the Ancient World*. Trans. Sian Reynolds. London: Allen Lane.

———. (1995[1949]). *The Mediterranean and the Mediterranean World in the Age of Philip II*. 2 vols. Berkeley: University of California Press.

———. (1992). *Civilization and Capitalism*. Vol. 3, *The Perspective of the World*. Berkeley: University of California Press.

———. (1979). "Writing the History of the Climate," and "The History of Rain and Fine Weather," in *The Territory of the Historian*. Trans. Ben and Siân Reynolds. Chicago: University of Chicago Press.

———. (1971). *Times of Feast, Times of Famine: A History of Climate since the Year 1000*. New York: Doubleday.

Braund, David. (2011). "The Slave Supply in Classical Greece," in *The Cambridge World History of Slavery*. Vol. 1, *The Ancient Mediterranean World*. Ed. Keith Bradley and Paul Cartledge. Cambridge: Cambridge University Press. Pp. 112–33.

———. (2007). "Black Sea Grain for Athens?," in *The Black Sea in Antiquity: Regional and Inter-regional Economic Exchanges*. Ed. Vincent Gabrielsen and John Lund. Aarhus: Aarhus University Press. Pp. 39–68.

Bresson, Alain. (2016). *The Making of the Ancient Greek Economy: Institutions, Markets, and Growth in the City-States*. Princeton, NJ: Princeton University Press.

———. (2014a). "The Ancient World: A Climatic Challenge," in *Quantifying the Greco-Roman Economy and Beyond*. Ed. François de Callataÿ. Bari: Edipuglia. Pp. 43–62.

———. (2014b). "Capitalism and the Ancient Economy," in *The Cambridge History of Capitalism*. 2 vols. Ed. Larry Neal and Jeffrey G. Williamson. Cambridge: Cambridge University Press, 2014. Pp. 43–74.

———. (2012a). "Greek Epigraphy and Ancient Economics," in *Epigraphy and the Historical Sciences*. Ed. John Davies and John Wilkes. Oxford: Oxford University Press. Pp. 223–47.

———. (2012b). "Wine, Oil, and Delicacies at the Pelousion Customs," in *Das imperial Rom und der hellenistische Osten: Festschrift für Jürgen Deininger zum 75; Geburtstag*. Stuttgart: Steiner. Pp. 69–88.

———. (2011). "Grain for Cyrene," in *The Economies of Hellenistic Societies, Third to First Centuries BC*. Ed. Zosia H. Archibald, John K. Davies, and Vincent Gabrielsen. Oxford: Oxford University Press. Pp. 66–95.

———. (2009). "Electrum Coins, Currency Exchange, and Transaction Costs in Archaic and Classical Greece," *Revue Belge de Numismatique* 140: 71–80.

———. (2008). *L'économie de la Grèce des cités (fin VIe–Ier siècle a. C.)*. Vol. 2, *Les espaces de l'échange*. Paris: A. Colin.

———. (2006). "The Origin of Lydian and Greek Coinage: Cost and Quantity," 3d International Conference of Ancient History, Fudan University, Shanghai, 17–August 21, 2005, *Historical Research* 5: 149–65 [in Chinese]. English-language version provided to me by the author.

———. (2005a). "Ecology and Beyond: The Mediterranean Paradigm," in *Rethinking the Mediterranean*. Ed. W. V. Harris. Oxford: Oxford University Press. Pp. 94–114.

———. (2005b). "Naucratis: De l'emporion a la cite," *Topoi* 12–13: 133–55.

———. (2003a). "Moses Finley," in *Les historiens*. Paris: Armand Colin. Pp. 178–92.

———. (2003b). "Merchants and Politics in Ancient Greece: Social and Economic Aspects," in *Mercanti e politica nel mondo antico*. Ed. Carlo Zaccagnini. Rome: "L'Erma" di Bretschneider. Pp. 139–63.

———. (2002). "Quatre *emporia* antiques: Abul, La Picola, Elizavetovskoie, Naucratis," *Revue des Études Anciennes* 104: 475–505.

———. (2000). *La cité marchande*. Bordeaux: Ausonius.

———. (1993). "La circulation des monnaies rhodiennes jusqu'en 166," *Dialogues d'Histoire Ancienne* 19: 119–69.

Briant, Pierre. (2009). "Alexander and the Persian Empire, between 'Decline' and 'Renovation': History and Historiography," in *Alexander the Great: A New History*. Ed. W. Heckel and L. Trittle. Malden, MA: Blackwell. Pp. 171–88.

———. (2002). *From Cyrus to Alexander: A History of the Persian Empire*. Winona Lake: Eisenbrauns.

———. (1982). *État et pasteurs au Moyen-Orient ancien*. Cambridge: Cambridge University Press.

Briant, Pierre, and Raymond Descat. (1998). "Un register douanier de la satrapie d'Égypte à l'époque achéménide (TAD C3 7)," in *Le Commerce en Égypte ancienne*. Ed. N. Grimal and B. Menu. Cairo: Institute français d'Archéologie orientale. Pp. 59–104.

Bringmann, Klaus. (2001). "Grain, Timber, and Money: Hellenistic Kings, Finance, Buildings and Foundations in Greek Cities," in *Hellenistic Economies*. Ed. Zosia H. Archibald, John K. Davies, Vincent Gabrielsen, and G. J. Oliver. London: Routledge. Pp. 205–14.

Brönnimann, S., and D. Krämer. (2016). "Tambora and the 'Year without a Summer' of 1816: A Perspective on Earth and Human Systems Science," *Geographica Bernensia* G90. doi: 10.4480/GB2016.G90.01.

Broodbank, Cyprian. (2013). *The Making of the Middle Sea: A History of the Mediterranean from the Beginning to the Emergence of the Classical World*. Oxford: Oxford University Press.

———. (2011). "The Mediterranean and the Mediterranean World in the Age of Andrew Sherratt," in *Interweaving Worlds: Systemic Interactions in Eurasia, 7th to the 1st Millennia BC*. Ed. Toby C. Wilkinson, Susan Sherratt, and John Bennet. Oxford: Oxbow. Pp. 27–36. Brooke, J. L. (forthcoming). "The Oscillations of Empire," in *The Oxford Illustrated History of the World*. Ed. Felipe Fernández-Armesto. Oxford: Oxford University Press.

———. (2016). "Malthus and the North Atlantic Oscillation: A Reply to Kyle Harper," *Journal of Interdisciplinary History* 46/4: 563–78.

———. (2014). *Climate Change and the Course of Global History: A Rough Journey*. Cambridge: Cambridge University Press.

Brown, Nathan J. (1994). "Who Abolished Corvee Labour in Egypt and Why?," *Past and Present* 144: 116–37.

Brown, Neville. (2001). *History and Climate Change: A Eurocentric Perspective*. London: Routledge.

Brown, Peter. (2012). *Through the Eye of the Needle: Wealth, the Fall of Rome, and the Making of Christianity in the West, 350–550 AD*. Princeton, NJ: Princeton University Press.

Brunhes, J. (1920). *Human Geography: An Attempt at a Positive Classification, Principles and Examples*. Chicago: Rand, McNally.

Bryson, Reid A., and Christine Padoch. (1981). "On the Climates of History," in *Climate and History: Studies in Interdisciplinary History*. Ed. Robert I. Rotberg and Theodore K. Rabb. Princeton, NJ: Princeton University Press. Pp. 3–17.

Büntgen, Ulf, and Lena Hellmann. (2013). "The Little Ice Age in Scientific Perspective: Cold Spells and Caveats," *Journal of Interdisciplinary History* 44: 353–68.

Büntgen, Ulf, Vladimir S. Myglan, Fredrik Charpentier Ljungqvist, Michael McCormick, Nicola Di Cosmo, Michael Sigl, Johann Jungclaus, Sebastian Wagner, Paul J. Krusic, Jan Esper, Jed O. Kaplan, Michiel A. C. de Vaan, Jürg Luterbacher, Lukas Wacker, Willy Tegel, and Alexander V. Kirdyanov. (2016). "Cooling and Societal

Change during the Late Antique Little Ice Age from 536 to around 660 AD," *Nature Geoscience* 9: 231–36.

Buraselis, Kostas. (2013). "Ptolemaic Grain, Seaways and Power," in *The Ptolemies, the Sea and the Nile: Studies in Waterbourne Power*. Ed. K. Buraselis, M. Stefanou, and D. J. Thompson. Cambridge: Cambridge University Press. Pp. 97–107.

———. (1993). "Ambivalent Roles of Centre and Periphery: Remarks on the Relation of the Cities of Greece with the Ptolemies until the End of Philometor's Age," in *Centre and Periphery in the Hellenistic World*. Ed. Per Bilde, Troels Engberg-Pedersen, Lise Hannestad, Jan Zahle, and Klavs Ransborg. Aarhus: Aarhus University Press. Pp. 251–70.

Burford, Alison. (1993). *Land and Labor in the Greek World*. Baltimore: Johns Hopkins University Press.

Burke, Edmund, III. (2009). "The Big Story: Human History, Energy Regimes, and the Environment," in *The Environment and World History*. Ed. Edmund Burke III and Kenneth Pomeranz. Berkeley: University of California Press. Pp. 33–53.

Burke, Edmund III, and Kenneth Pomeranz, eds. (2009). *The Environment and World History*. Berkeley: University of California Press.

Burke, Peter. (1990). *The French Historical Revolution: The* Annales *School 1929–89*. Stanford, CA: Stanford University Press.

Burstein, Stanley M. (1995). *Graeco-Africana: Studies in the History of Greek Relations with Egypt and Nubia*. New Rochelle, NY: Aristide D. Caratzas.

———. (1985). *The Hellenistic Age from the Battle of Ipsos to the Death of Kleopatra VII*. Cambridge: Cambridge University Press.

Butzer, Karl. (2012). "Collapse, Environment, and Society," *PNAS* 109/10: 3632–39.

———. (2005). "Environmental History in the Mediterranean World: Cross-Disciplinary Investigation of Cause-and-effect Degradation and Soil Erosion," *Journal of Archaeological Science* 32: 1773–800.

———. (2002). "Geoarchaeological Implications of Recent Research in the Nile Delta," in *Egypt and the Levant: Interrelations from the 4th through the Early 3rd Millennium BCE*. Ed. E. Van den Brink and T. E. Levy. London: Leicester University Press. Pp. 83–97.

———. (2001). "Irrigation," in *The Oxford Encyclopedia of Ancient Egypt*. Ed. Donald B. Redford. Vol. 2. Oxford: Oxford University Press. Pp. 183–87.

———. (1999). "Irrigation," in *Encyclopedia of the Archaeology of Ancient Egypt*. Ed. Kathryn A. Bard. London: Routledge. Pp. 381–82.

———. (1997). "Sociopolitical Discontinuity in the Near East c. 2200 BCE: Scenarios from Palestine and Egypt," in *Third Millennium BC Climate Change and Old World Collapse*. Ed. H. Nüzhet Dalfes, George Kukla, and Harvey Weiss. Heidelberg: Springer Verlag. Pp. 245–96.

———. (1996). "Irrigation, Raised Fields, and State Management: Wittfogel Redux?," *Antiquity* 70: 200–4.

———. (1995). "Environmental Change in the Near East and Human Impact on the Land," in *Civilizations of the Ancient Near East*. Ed. Jack M. Sasson. Vol. 1. Peabody, MA: Hendrickson. Pp. 123–51.

———. (1984). "Long-Term Nile Flood Variation and Political Discontinuities in Pharaonic Egypt," in *From Hunters to Farmers: The Causes and Consequences of Food Production in Africa*. Ed. J. Desmond Clark and Steven A. Brandt. Berkeley: University of California Press. Pp. 102–12.

———. (1976). *Early Hydraulic Civilization in Egypt.* Chicago: University of Chicago Press.

———. (1971). *Environment and Archaeology: An Ecological Approach to Prehistory.* 2d ed. Chicago: Aldine-Atherton.

Cahill, Nicholas. (2005). "Household Industry in Greece and Anatolia," in *Ancient Greek Houses and Households: Chronological, Regional and Social Diversity.* Ed. Bradley A. Ault and Lisa C. Nevett. Philadelphia: University of Pennsylvania Press. Pp. 54–66.

———. (2002). *Household and City Organization at Olynthus.* New Haven, CT: Yale University Press.

Calder, William M., III, and Alexander Demandt. (1990). *Eduard Meyer: Leben und Leistung eines Universalhistorikers.* Mnemosyne Supplement 112. Leiden: Brill.

Campbell, Brian, and Lawrence A. Tritle, eds. (2013). *The Oxford Handbook of Warfare in the Classical World.* Oxford: Oxford University Press.

Campbell, Bruce M. S. (2016). *The Great Transition: Climate, Disease and Society in the Late-Medieval World.* Cambridge: Cambridge University Press.

———. (2010). "Nature as Protagonist: Environment and Society in Pre-industrial England," *Economic History Review* 63/2: 281–314.

Capdetrey, Laurent. (2007). *Le pouvoir séleucide: Territoire, administration, finances d'un royaume hellénistique (312–129 avant J.-C.).* Rennes: Presses universitaires de Rennes.

Carlsen, Jesper, Peter Ørsted, and Jens Erik Skydsgaard, eds. (1994). *Land Use in the Roman Empire.* Rome: "L'Erma" di Bretschneider.

Carrard, Philippe. (1992). *Poetics of the New History: French Historical Discourse from Braudel to Chartier.* Baltimore: Johns Hopkins University Press.

Carruthers, Bruce G. (2005). "The sociology of Money and Credit," in *The Handbook of Economic Sociology.* 2d ed. Ed. Neil J. Smelser and Richard Swedburg. Princeton, NJ: Princeton University Press. Pp. 355–78.

Carter, Elizabeth, and Sarah Morris. (2014). "Crisis in the Eastern Mediterranean and Beyond: Survival, Revival, and the Emergence of the Iron Age," *in Assyria to Iberia at the Dawn of the Classical Age.* Ed. Joan Aruz, Sarah B. Graff, and Yalena Rakic. New York: Metropolitan Museum. Pp. 14–23.

Cartledge, Paul. (2011). "The Helots: A Contemporary Review," in *The Cambridge World History of Slavery.* Vol. 1. *The Ancient Mediterranean World.* Ed. Keith Bradley and Paul Cartledge. Cambridge: Cambridge University Press. Pp. 74–90.

———. (2002a). "The Economy (Economies) of Ancient Greece," in *The Ancient Economy: New Approaches.* Ed. Walter Scheidel and Sitta von Reden. New York: Routledge. Pp. 11–32.

———. (2002b). "The Political Economy of Greek slavery," in *Money, Labour and Land: Approaches to the Economies of Ancient Greece.* Ed. Paul Cartledge, Edward E. Cohen, and Lin Foxhall. London: Routledge. Pp. 156–66.

———. (1997). "Introduction," in *Hellenistic Constructs: Essays in Culture, History, and Historiography.* Ed. Paul Cartledge, Peter Garnsey, and Erichy Gruen. Berkeley: University of California Press. Pp. 1–19.

Cartledge, Paul, Edward E. Cohen, and Lin Foxhall, eds. (2002). *Money, Labour and Land: Approaches to the Economies of Ancient Greece.* London: Routledge.

Casson, Lionel, ed. (1989). *The Periplus Maris Erythraei.* Princeton, NJ: Princeton University Press.

———. (1971). *Ships and Seamanship in the Ancient World.* Princeton, NJ: Princeton University Press.

———. (1954). "The Grain Trade of the Hellenistic World," *TAPhA* 85: 168–87.

Chamoux, François. (2003). *Hellenistic Civilization*. Trans. Michel Roussel. Malden, MA: Blackwell.

Champion, Timothy C. (1995). "Introduction," in *Centre and Periphery: Comparative Studies in Archaeology*. Ed. T. C. Champion. London: Routledge. Pp. 1–21.

Chankowski, Véronique, and Frédérique Duyrat, eds. (2004). *Le Roi et L'Économie: Autonomies locales et structures royales dans l'économie de L'empire séleucide*. Topoi Supplement 6. Lyon: Maison de L'Orient méditerranéen.

Chankowski, Véronique, and Pavlos Karvonis, eds. (2012). *Tout vendre, tout acheter: Structures et équipements des marches antiques*. Bordeaux: Ausonius Éditions.

Chase-Dunn, C. R. Niemeyer, A. Alvarez, and H. Inoue. (2009). "Scale Transitions and the Evolution of Global Governance since the Bronze Age," in *Systemic Transitions*. Ed. W. R. Thompson. New York: Palgrave MacMillan. Pp. 261–84.

Chase-Dunn, Christopher, and Thomas D. Hall. (1997). *Rise and Demise: Comparing World-Systems*. Boulder, CO: Westview.

Chaudhuri, K. N. (1990). *Asia before Europe: Economy and Civilisation of the Indian Ocean from the Rise of Islam to 1750*. Cambridge: Cambridge University Press.

———. (1985). *Trade and Civilisation in the Indian Ocean: An Economic History from the Rise of Islam to 1750*. Cambridge: Cambridge University Press.

Chayanov, A. V. (1966). *The Theory of the Peasant Economy*. Ed. Daniel Thorner, Basile Kerblay, and R.E.F. Smith. Homewood, IL: American Economic Association.

Christesen, Paul. (2003). "Economic Rationalism in Fourth-Century B.C.E. Athens," *Greece and Rome* 50/1: 31–56.

Christian, David. (2004). *Maps of Time: An Introduction to Big History*. Berkeley: University of California Press.

Clancier, P., F. Joannès, P. Rouillard, and A. Tenu, eds. (2005). *Autour de Polanyi: Vocabulaires, theories et modalities des échanges, Nanterre, 12–14 Juin 2004*. Paris: De Boccard.

Clark, Gregory. (2009). Review of Angus Maddison, *Contours of the World Economy, 1–2030 AD: Essays in Macro-economic History*, Oxford: Oxford University Press, 2007, *Journal of Economic History* 69/4: 1156–61.

———. (2007). *A Farewell to Alms: A Brief Economic History of the World*. Princeton, NJ: Princeton University Press.

Clarysse, W., and K. Vandorpe. (1995). *Zenon, un Homme d'Affaires grec à l'Ombre des Pyramides*. Leuven: Presses Universitaires.

Clarysse, Willy, and D. J. Thompson. (2006). *Counting the People in Hellenistic Egypt*. 2 vols. Cambridge: Cambridge University Press.

Cline, Eric H. (2014). *1177 B.C.: The Year Civilization Collapsed*. Princeton, NJ: Princeton University Press.

———. (2007). "Rethinking Mycenaean International Trade with Egypt and the Near East," in *Rethinking Mycenaean Palaces II*. Ed. Michael L. Galaty and William A. Parkinson. Los Angeles: Cotsen Institute of Archaeology. Pp. 190–200.

Cocks, R.C.J. (1988). *Sir Henry Maine: A Study in Victorian Jurisprudence*. Cambridge: Cambridge University Press.

Cohen, Edward. (1992). *Athenian Economy and Society: A Banking Perspective*. Princeton, NJ: Princeton University Press.

Cohen, Getzel M. (1983). "Colonization and Population Transfer in the Hellenistic World," in *Egypt and the Hellenistic World: Proceedings of the International Collo-*

quium Leuven 24–26 May 1982. Ed. E. Van 't-Dack, P. van Dessel, and W. van Gucht. Studia Hellenistica 27. Pp. 63–74.

Collingwood, R. G. (1946). *The Idea of History*. Paperback ed. Oxford: Oxford University Press.

Collins, John J., and J. G. Manning, eds. (2016). *Revolt and Resistance in the Ancient Classical World and the Near East: In the Crucible of Empire*. Leiden: Brill.

Colognesi, Luigi Capogrossi. (2004). "'Capitalisme antique' et 'capitalisme médiéval' dans l'ouevre de Weber," in *Sociologie économqiue et économie de l'antiquité: À propos de Max Weber*. Cahiers du Centre de Recherches historiques 34. Paris: École des Hautes Études en Science Sociales. Pp. 21–30.

Commons, John R. (1934). *Institutional Economics*. New York: Macmillan.

Conison. Alex. (2013). "Economic Theory," in *The Encyclopedia of Ancient History*. Ed. Roger S. Bagnall, Kai Brodersen, Craige B. Champion, Andrew Erskine, and Sabine R. Heubner. Malden, MA: Wiley-Blackwell. Pp. 2260–70.

Cook, Scott. (1974). "'Structural Substantivism': A Critical Review of M. Sahlins, *Stone Age Economics*," *Comparative Studies in Society and History* 16/3: 355–79.

———. (1968). "Review of *Primitive, Archaic and Modern Economies: Essays of Karl Polanyi*," *American Anthropologist* 70: 966–69.

Cooney, Kathlyn M. (2010). "Labour in the Egyptian world," in *The Egyptian World*. Ed. Toby Wilkinson. Paperback ed. London: Routledge. Pp. 160–74.

———. (2008). "Profit or Exploitation? The Production of Private Ramesside Tombs within the West Theban Funerary Economy," *Journal of Egyptian History* 1/1: 79–115.

———. (2007). *The Cost of Death: The Social and Economic Value of Ancient Egyptian Funerary Art in the Ramesside Period*. Leiden: Nederlands Instituut voor het Nabije Oosten.

Cooper, Frederick A. (2008). "Greek Engineering and Construction," in *The Oxford Handbook of Engineering and Technology in the Classical World*. Ed. John Peter Oleson. Oxford: Oxford University Press. Pp. 225–55.

Cox, Cheryl Anne. (1998). *Household Interests: Property, Marriage Strategies, and Family Dynamics in Ancient Athens*. Princeton, NJ: Princeton University Press.

Crawford, Dorothy J. (1983). "Nile Grain Transport under the Ptolemies," in *Trade in the Ancient Economy*. Ed. Peter Garnsey, Keith Hopkins, and C. R. Whittaker. Berkeley: University of California Press. Pp. 64–75.

———. (1978). "The Good Official of Ptolemaic Egypt," in *Das ptolemäische Ägypten: Akten d. internat. Symposions, 27.–29. September 1976 in Berlin*. Ed. Herwig Maehler and Volker Michael Strocka. Mainz am Rhein: von Zabern. Pp. 194–202.

———. (1971). *Kerkeosiris: An Egyptian Village in the Ptolemaic Period*. Cambridge: Cambridge University Press.

Critchfield, Richard. (1978). *Shahhat, an Egyptian*. Syracuse, NY: Syracuse University Press.

Cronon, William. (1991). *Nature's Metropolis: Chicago and the Great West*. New York: Norton.

———. (1983). *Changes in the Land: Indians, Colonists, and the Ecology of New England*. New York: Hill and Wang.

Cullen, H. M., P. B. de Menocal, S. Hemming, G. Hemming, F. H. Brown, T. Guilderson, and F. Sirocko. (2000). "Climate Change and the Collapse of the Akkadian Empire: Evidence from the Deep Sea," *Geology* 28/4: 379–82.

Cullen, Heidi M., and Peter B. de Menocal. (2000). "North Atlantic Influence on Tigris-Euphrates Streamflow," *International Journal of Climatology* 20: 853–63.

Cullen, Heidi M., Alexey Kaplan, Phillip A. Arkin, and Peter B. de Menocal. (2002). "Impact of the North Atlantic Oscillation on Middle Eastern Climate and Streamflow," *Climatic Change* 55: 315–38.

Cunliffe, Barry. (1997). *The Ancient Celts*. London: Penguin.

Currie, Thomas E., et al. (2015). "Agricultural Productivity in Past Societies: Toward an Empirically Informed Model for Testing Cultural Evolutionary Hypotheses," *Cliodynamics* 6/1: 24–56.

Curtin, Philip D. (1984). *Cross-Cultural Trade in World History*. Cambridge: Cambridge University Press.

Cuvigny, Hélène. (2009). "The Finds of Papyri: The Archaeology of Papyrology," in *The Oxford Handbook of Papyrology*. Ed. Roger S. Bagnall. New York: Oxford University Press.

Dale, Gareth. (2010). *Karl Polanyi: The Limits of the Market*. Cambridge: Polity.

Dandamaev, M. A. (1984). *Slavery in Babylonia from Nabopolassar to Alexander the Great (626–331 B C)*. DeKalb: Northern Illinois University Press.

Dari-Mattiacci, Giuseppe. (2013). "Slavery and Information," *Journal of Economic History* 73/1: 79–116.

D'Alpoim Guedes, Jade A., et al. (2016). "Twenty-First Century Approaches to Ancient Problems: Climate and Society," *PNAS* 113/51: 14483–91.

D'Arms, John. (1981). *Commerce and Social Standing in Ancient Rome*. Cambridge, MA: Harvard University Press.

———. (1977). "M. I. Rostovtzeff and M. I. Finley: The Status of Traders in the Roman World," in *Ancient and Modern: Essays in Honor of Gerald F. Else*. Ed. John D'Arms and John W. Eadie. Ann Arbor: University of Michigan Press. Pp. 157–79.

Davies, John K. (2013a). "Mediterranean Economies through the Text of Polybius," in *Polybius and His World: Essays in Memory of F. W. Walbank*. Ed. Bruce Gibson and Thomas Harrison. Oxford: Oxford University Press. Pp. 319–35.

———. (2013b). "Ancient Economies," in *A Companion to Ancient History*. Ed. Andrew Erskine. Malden, MA: Wiley-Blackwell. Paperback ed. 2013. Pp. 436–46.

———. (2007). "Classical Greece: Production," in *The Cambridge Economic History of the Greco-Roman World*. Ed. Walter Scheidel, Ian Morris, and Richard Saller. Cambridge: Cambridge University Press. Pp. 333–61.

———. (2005). "Linear and Nonlinear Flow Models for Ancient Economies," in *The Ancient Economy: Evidence and Models*. Ed. J. G. Manning and Ian Morris. Stanford, CA: Stanford University Press. Pp. 127–60.

———. (2004). "Athenian Fiscal Expertise and Its Influence," *Mediterraneo Antico* 7/2: 491–512.

———. (2001). "Hellenistic Economies in the Post-Finley Era," in *Hellenistic Economies*. Ed. Zofia H. Archibald, John Davies, Vincent Gabrielsen, and G. J. Oliver. London: Routlegde. Pp. 11–62.

———. (1998). "Ancient Economies: Models and Muddles," in *Trade, Traders and the Ancient City*. Ed. H. Parkins and C. Smith. London: Routledge. Pp. 225–56.

———. (1992). "Society and Economy," in *The Cambridge Ancient History*. Vol. 5, *The Fifth Century*. Ed. D. M. Lewis, John Boardman, J. K. Davies, and M. Ostwald. Cambridge: Cambridge University Press. Pp. 287–305.

———. (1984a). "Cultural, Social and Economic Features of the Hellenistic World," in *The Cambridge Ancient History* 7/1. 2d ed. Ed. F. W. Walbank, A. E. Astin, M. W Frederiksen, and R. M. Ogilvie. Cambridge: Cambridge University Press. Pp. 257–320.

———. (1984b). *Wealth and the Power of Wealth in Classical Athens*. Salem: Ayer.

———. (1971). *Athenian Propertied Families, 600–300 B.C.* Oxford: Clarendon.

Davies, John K., and John Wilkes, eds. (2012). *Epigraphy and the Historical Sciences.* Proceedings of the British Academy 177. Oxford: Oxford University Press.

Davies, M.I.J. (2009). "Wittfogel's Dilemma: Heterarchy and Ethnographic Approaches to Irrigation Management in Eastern Africa and Mesopotamia," *World Archaeology* 41: 16–35.

Davis, Gil. (2014). "Mining Money in Late Archaic Athens," *Historia* 63/3: 257–77.

Dawkins, Richard. (1976). *The Selfish Gene.* Oxford: Oxford University Press.

De Angelis, Franco. (2016). *Archaic and Classical Greek Sicily: A Social and Economic History.* Oxford: Oxford University Press.

de Callataÿ, François, ed. (2014). *Quantifying the Greco-Roman Economy and Beyond.* Bari: Edipuglia.

———. (2005). "The Graeco-Roman Economy in the Super Long Run: Lead, Copper, and Shipwrecks," *Journal of Roman Archaeology* 18: 361–72.

De Ligt, Luuk. (2012). *Peasants, Citizens and Soldiers: Studies in the Demographic History of Roman Italy 225 BC–AD 100.* Cambridge: Cambridge University Press.

———. (1993). *Fairs and Markets in the Roman Empire: Economic and Social Aspects of Periodic Trade in a Pre-industrial Society.* Amsterdam: Gieben.

Demand, Nancy H. (2011). *The Mediterranean Context of Early Greek History.* Malden, MA: Wiley-Blackwell.

———. (1991). *Urban Relocation in Archaic and Classical Greece.* Norman: University of Oklahoma Press.

De Romanis, Federico, and Marco Maiuro, eds. (2015). *Across the Ocean: Nine Essays on Indo-Mediterranean Trade.* Leiden: Brill.

Descat, Raymond. (2011). "Labour in the Hellenistic Economy: Slavery as a Test Case," in *The Economies of Hellenistic Societies, Third to First Centuries BC.* Ed. Zosia H. Archibald, John K. Davies, and Vincent Gabrielsen. Oxford: Oxford University Press. Pp. 207–15.

De Souza, Philip. (1999). *Piracy in the Greco-Roman World.* Cambridge: Cambridge University Press.

Desprat, S., M.F.S. Goñi, and M.-F. Loutre. (2003). "Revealing Climatic Variability of the Last Three Millennia in Northwestern Iberia Using Pollen Influx Data," *Earth and Planetary Science Letters* 213: 63–78.

DeVries, Jan. (2013). "The Crisis of the Seventeenth Century: The Little Ice Age and the Mystery of the 'Great Divergence,'" *Journal of Interdisciplinary History* 44: 369–77.

———. (1980). "Measuring the Impact of Climate on History: The Search for Appropriate Methodologies," *Journal of Interdisciplinary History* 10/4: 599–630.

DeVries, Jan, and Ad van der Woude. (1997). *The First Modern Economy: Success, Failure, and Perseverance of the Dutch Economy, 1500–1815.* Cambridge: Cambridge University Press.

Dhavalikar, M. K. (1975). "The Beginning of Coinage in India," *World Archaeology* 6/3: 330–38.

Diamond, Alan, ed. (1991). *The Victorian Achievement of Sir Henry Maine: A Centennial Reappraisal*. Cambridge: Cambridge University Press.

Diamond, Jared. (1997). *Guns, Germs and Steel*. New York: W. W. Norton.

Dickinson, Oliver. (2006). *The Aegean from Bronze Age to Iron Age: Continuity and Change between the Twelfth and Eighth Centuries BC*. New York: Routledge.

Dion, R. (1934). *Le val de Loire: Étude de géographie régionale*. Tours: Arrault.

Dixit, Avansah K. (2004). *Lawlessness and Economics: Alternative Modes of Governance*. Princeton, NJ: Princeton University Press.

Docter, R. H. (2002-3). "The Topography of Ancient Carthage: Preliminary Results of Recent Excavations and Some Prospects," *Talanta* 34–35: 113–33.

Docter, R. H. Niemeyer, A. Nijboer, and J. van den Plicht. (2004). "Radiocarbon Dates of Animal Bones in the Earliest Levels of Carthage," *Mediterranean* 1: 557–73.

Dodgshon, Robert A. (1998). *Society in Time and Space: A Geographical Perspective on Change*. Cambridge: Cambridge University Press.

Domingo Gygax, Marc. (2016). *Benefaction and Rewards in the Ancient Greek City: The Origins of Euergetism*. Cambridge: Cambridge University Press.

Donker van Heel, Koen. (2014). *Mrs. Tsenhour: A Female Entrepreneur in Ancient Egypt*. Cairo: American University in Cairo Press.

———. (2012). *Djekhy and Son: Doing Business in Ancient Egypt*. Cairo: American University in Cairo Press.

———. (1995). *Abnormal Hieratic and Early Demotic Texts Collected by the Theban Choachytes in the Reign of Amasis*. Leiden: Self-published.

———. (1994). "The Lost Battle of Peteamonip Son of Petehorresne," in *Acta Demotica: Acts of the Fifth International Conference for Demotists (Pisa, 4th–8th September 1993)*. Ed. E. Bresciani. Egitto e Vicino Oriente 17. Pp. 115–24.

Duistermaat, Kim, and Ilona Regulski, eds. (2011). *Intercultural Contacts in the Ancient Mediterranean: Proceedings of the International Conference at the Netherlands-Flemish Institute in Cairo, 25th to 29th October 2008*. Orientalia Lovaniensia Analecta 202. Leuven: Peeters.

Dull, R., et al. (2012). "Evidence for the Ilopango TBJ Eruption as the Trigger of the AD 536 Event," Association of American Geographers Meeting, New York, February 24, 2012.

Duncan-Jones, R. P. (1982). *The Economy of the Roman Empire: Quantitative Studies*. 2d ed. Cambridge: Cambridge University Press.

Duyrat, Frédérique. (2015). "The Circulation of Coins in Syria and Mesopotamia in the Sixth to First Centuries BC," in *A History of Market Performance: From Ancient Babylonia to the Modern World*. Ed. R. J. van der Spek, Bas van Leeuwen, and Jan Luiten van Zanden. London: Routledge. Pp. 363–95.

Earle, T. K. (1978). *Economic and Social Organization of a Complex Chiefdom: The Halalea District, Kaua'i, Hawaii*. Anthropological Papers 63. Ann Arbor: Museum of Anthropology.

Edgar, Campbell Cowan. (1931). *Zenon Papyri in the University of Michigan Collection*. Ann Arbor: University of Michigan Press.

Egberts, Arno. (1998). "Hard Times: The Chronology of 'The Report of Wenamun' Revised," *Zeitschrift für Ägyptischen Sprache* 125: 93–108.

Eggertsson, Thrainn. (1990). *Economic Behavior and Institutions*. Cambridge: Cambridge University Press.

Ehrenberg, Victor. (1969). *The Greek State*. 2d ed. London: Methuen.

Eisenstadt, S. N. (1993). *The Political Systems of Empires*. New Brunswick, NJ: Transaction.

———. ed. (1986). *The Origins and Diversity of the Axial Age*. Albany: State University of New York Press.

Ekelund, Robert B., and Robert F. Hébert. (2014). *A History of Economic Theory and Method*. Long Grove: Waveland.

Ekholm, K., and J. Friedman. (1979). "'Capital' Imperialism and Exploitation in Ancient World Systems," in *Power and Propaganda: A Symposium on Ancient Empires*. Ed. M. T. Larsen. Copenhagen: Akademisk Vorlag. Pp. 41–58.

Elayi, Josette. (2013). "Achaemenid Persia and the Levant," in *The Oxford Handbook of the Archaeology of the Levant: C. 8000–332 BCE*. Ed. Ann E. Killebrew and Margreet Steiner. Oxford: Oxford University Press. Pp. 107–20.

———. (1981). "The Relations between Tyre and Carthage during the Persian Period," *JANES* 13: 15–29.

Elis, Roy, Stephen Haber, and Jordan Horrillo. (2017). "Climate, Geography, and the Evolution of Economic and Political Systems," unpublished manuscript.

Ellickson, Robert C. (1991). *Order without Law: How Neighbors Settle Disputes*. Cambridge, MA: Harvard University Press.

Eltahir, E.A.B. (1996). "El Niño and the Natural Variability in the Flow of the Nile River," *Water Resources Research* 32/1: 131–37.

Empereur, Jean-Yves. (1982). "Les anses d'amphores timbrées et les amphores: Aspects quantitatifs," *Bulletin de Correspondance hellénique* 106: 219–33.

Erdkamp, Paul. (2016). "Economic Growth in the Roman Mediterranean World: An Early Good-Bye to Malthus?," *Explorations in Economic History* 60: 1–20.

———. (2014). "How Modern Was the Market Economy of the Roman World?," *Oeconomia* 4/2: 225–35. http://oeconomia.revues.org/399.

———. (2005). *The Grain Market in the Roman Empire: A Social, Political and Economic Study*. Cambridge: Cambridge University Press.

———. (2001). "Beyond the Limits of the 'Consumer City': A Model of the Urban and Rural Economy in the Roman World," *Historia* 50/3: 332–56.

Evans, Peter B., Dietrich Rueschemeyer, and Theda Skocpol, eds. (1985). *Bringing the State Back In*. Cambridge: Cambridge University Press.

Eyre, Christopher J. (2014). "The Economy: Pharaonic," in *A Companion to Ancient Egypt*. Ed. Alan B. Lloyd. Malden, MA: Blackwell. Pp. 291–308.

———. (2004). "How Relevant Was Personal Status to the Functioning of the Rural Economy in Pharaonic Egypt?," in *La dépendance rurale dans l'Antiquité égyptienne et proche-orientale*. Ed. Bernadette Menu. Cairo: Institut français d'Archéologie orientale. Pp. 157–86.

———. (2000). "Pouvoir central et pouvoirs locaux: Problèmes historiographiques et méthodologiques," *Méditerranées* 24: 15–39.

———. (1999). "Village Economy in Pharaonic Egypt," in *Agriculture in Egypt: From Pharaonic to Modern Times*. Ed. Alan K. Bowman and Eugene Rogan. Oxford: Oxford University Press. Pp. 33–60.

———. (1995). "The Agricultural Cycle, Farming, and Water Management in the Ancient Near East," in *Civilizations of the Ancient Near East*. Ed. Jack M. Sasson. Vol. 1. Peabody, MA: Hendrickson. Pp. 175–89.

———. (1994). "Feudal Tenure and Absentee Landlords," in *Grund und Boden in Altägypten: (Rechtliche und Sozio-Ökonomische Verhältnisse); Akten des internationalen*

Symposions Tübingen 18.–20. Juni 1990. Ed. Schafik Allam. Tübingen: Selbstverlag des Herausgebers. Pp. 107–33.

———. (1987a). "Work and the Organisation of Work in the Old Kingdom," in *Labor in the Ancient Near East*. Ed. Marvin A. Powell. New Haven: American Oriental Society. Pp. 5–47.

———. (1987b). "Work and the Organisation of Work in the New Kingdom," in *Labor in the Ancient Near East*. Ed. Marvin A. Powell. New Haven: American Oriental Society. Pp. 167–221.

Fabre, David. (2011). "The Shipwrecks of Heracleion-Thonis: A Preliminary Study," in *Maritime Archaeology and Ancient Trade in the Mediterranean*. Ed. Damian Robinson and Andrew Wilson. Oxford: Oxford Centre for Maritime Archaeology. Pp. 13–32.

Fabre, David, and Franck Goddio. (2010). "The Development and Operation of the Portus Magnus in Alexandria: An Overview," in *Alexandria and the North-Western Delta: Joint Conference Proceedings of Alexandria: City and Harbor (Oxford 2004) and Trade and the Topography of Egypt's North-West Delta (Berlin 2006)*. Ed. Damian Robinson and Andrew Wilson. Oxford: Oxford Centre for Maritime Archaeology. Pp. 53–74.

Fales, F. M., and J. N. Postgate. (1995). *Imperial Administrative Records*. Helsinki: Helsinki University Press.

Fantalkin, Alexander. (2006). "Identity in the Making: Greeks in the Eastern Mediterranean during the Iron Age," in *Naukratis: Greek Diversity in Egypt; Studies on East Greek Pottery and Exchange in the Eastern Mediterranean*. Ed. Alexandra Villing and Udo Schlotzhauer. London: British Museum. Pp. 199–208.

Feeney, Denis. (2008). *Caesar's Calendar: Ancient Time and the Beginnings of History*. Berkeley: University of California Press.

Ferguson, Niall. (2012). *Civilization: The West and the Rest*. New York: Penguin.

Figueira, T. J. (1984). "Karl Polanyi and Ancient Greek Trade: The Port of Trade," *Ancient World* 10: 15–30.

Finley, M. I. (1999). *The Ancient Economy*. Updated ed. Berkeley: University of California Press.

———. (1985). *Ancient History: Evidence and Models*. New York: Penguin.

———. ed. (1979). *The Bücher-Meyer Controversy*. New York: Arno.

———. (1975). "Anthropology and the Classics," in *The Use and Abuse of History*. New York: Viking. Pp. 102–19.

———. (1970a). "Aristotle and Economic Analysis," *Past and Present* 47: 3–25.

———. (1970b). *Early Greece: The Bronze and Archaic Ages*. London: Chatto and Windus.

———. (1965a). Review of A. Leo Oppenheim, *Ancient Mesopotamia*, *New York Review of Books* 5/5: 30–32.

———. (1965b). "Technical Innovation and Economic Progress in the Ancient World," *Economic History Review* 18: 29–45.

———. (1951). "Some Problems of Greek Law," *Seminar* 9: 72–91.

Finné, Martin, et al. (2014). "Speleothem Evidence for Late Holocene Climate Variability and Floods in Southern Greece," *Quaternary Research* 81: 213–27.

Fischer-Bovet, Christelle. (2014). *Army and Society in Ptolemaic Egypt*. Cambridge: Cambridge University Press.

Flohr, Pascal, Dominik Fleitmann, Roger Matthews, Wendy Matthews, and Stuart Black. (2016). "Evidence of Resilience to Past Climate Change in Southwest Asia:

Early Farming Communities and the 9.2 And 8.2 ka Events," *Quaternary Science Reviews* 136: 23–39.

Forbes, H. (1992). "The Ethnoarchaeological Approach to Ancient Greek Agriculture: Olive Cultivation as a Case Study," in *Agriculture in Ancient Greece*. Ed. B. Wells. Stockholm: Svenska institutet i Athen. Pp. 87–10.

Forde, C. Daryll. (1934). *Habitat, Economy, and Society*. New York: E. P. Dutton.

Foster, Benjamin R. (1987). "The Late Bronze Age Palace Economy: The View from the East," in *The Function of the Minoan Palaces*. Ed. Robin Hägg and Nanno Marinatos. Stockholm: Svenska institutet i Athen. Pp. 11–16.

Foxhall, Lin. (2007). *Olive Cultivation in Ancient Greece: Seeking the Ancient Economy*. Oxford: Oxford University Press.

———. (2002). Access to Resources in Classical Greece: The Egalitarianism of the Polis in Practice," in *Money, Labor and Land: Approaches to Economies of Ancient Greece*. London: Routledge. Pp. 209–20.

———. (1990). "The Dependent Tenant: Land Leasing and Labour in Italy and Greece," *Journal of Roman Studies* 80: 97–114.

———. (1989). "Household, Gender and Property in Classical Athens," *Classical Quarterly* 39/1: 22–44.

Fraedrich, Klaus, Jianmin Jiang, Friedrich-Wilhelm Gerstengarbe, and Peter C. Werner. (1997). "Multiscale Detection of Abrupt Climate Changes: Application to River Nile Flood Levels," *International Journal of Climatology* 17: 1301–15.

Frank, A. Gunder, and Barry K. Gills, eds. (1996). *The World System: Five Hundred Years or Five Thousand?* Rev. ed. Oxford: Routledge.

Frank, A. Gunder, and William R. Thompson. (2005). "Afro-Eurasian Bronze Age Economic Expansion and Contraction Revisited," *Journal of World History* 16: 115–72.

Frankenstein, Susan. (1979). "The Phoenicians in the Far West: A Function of Neo-Assyrian Imperialism," in *Power and Propaganda: A Symposium on Ancient Empires*. Ed. Mogens Trolle Larsen. Copenhagen: Akademisk Forlag. Pp. 263–94.

Fraser, Peter M. (1972). *Ptolemaic Alexandria*. 3 vols. Oxford: Clarendon.

Frederiksen, M. W. (1975). Review of M. I. Finley, *The Ancient Economy, Journal of Roman Studies* 65: 164–71.

Friedman, Milton. (1953). "The Methodology of Positive Economics," in *Essays in Positive Economics*. Chicago: University of Chicago Press. Pp. 3–43.

Frier, Bruce. (1991). Review of W. Jongman, *The Economy and Society of Pompeii*, Amsterdam: J. C. Gieben, 1988, in *Journal of Roman Archaeology* 4 (1991): 243–47.

———. (1983). "Roman Law and the Wine Trade: The Problem of 'Vinegar Sold as Wine,'" *Zeitschrift der Savigny-Stiftung für Rechtsgeschichte* 100: 257–95.

———. (1982). "Roman Life Expectancy: Ulpian's Evidence," *Harvard Studies in Classical Philology* 86: 213–51.

Frier, Bruce, and Dennis P. Kehoe. (2007). "Law and Economic Institutions," in *The Cambridge Economic History of the Greco-Roman World*. Ed. Walter Scheidel, Ian Morris, and Richard Saller. Cambridge: Cambridge University Press. Pp. 113–43.

Fukuyama, Francis. (2011). *The Origins of Political Order: From Prehuman Times to the French Revolution*. New York: Farrar, Straus, and Giroux.

Funke, P., and M. Haake, eds. (2013). *Greek Federal States and Their Sanctuaries: Identity and Integration*. Stuttgart: Franz Steiner Verlag.

Furobotn, Eirik G. (1997). "The Old and New Institutionalism in Economics," in *Methodology of the Social Sciences, Ethics, and Economics in the Newer Historical School:*

From Max Weber and Rickert to Sombart and Rothacker. Ed. Peter Koslowski. Berlin: Springer Verlag. Pp. 429–63.

Furobotn, Eirik G., and Rudolf Richter. (2005). *Institutions and Economic Theory: The Contribution of the New Institutional Economics.* 2d. ed. Ann Arbor: University of Michigan Press.

Fusaro, Maria. (2010). "After Braudel: A Reassessment of Mediterranean History between the Northern Invasion and the *Caravane Maritime*," in *Trade and Cultural Exchange in the Early Modern Mediterranean: Braudel's Maritime Legacy.* Ed. Maria Fusaro, Mohamed-Salah Omri, and Colin Heywood. London: I. B. Taurus. Pp. 1–22.

Fusfeld, Daniel B. (1957). "Economic Theory Misplaced: Livelihood in Primitive Society," in *Trade and Market in the Early Empires: Economies in History and Theory.* Ed. Karl Polanyi, Conrad M. Arensberg, and Harry W. Pearson. New York: Free Press. Pp. 342–56.

Gabrielsen, Vincent. (2013). "Rhodes and the Ptolemaic Kingdom: The Commercial Infrastructure," in *The Ptolemies, the Sea and the Nile: Studies in Waterborne Power.* Ed. K. Buraselis and M. Stephanou. Cambridge: Cambridge University Press. Pp. 66–81.

———. (2011). "Profitable Partnerships: Monopolies, Traders, Kings and Cities," in *The Economies of Hellenistic Societies, Third to First Centuries BC.* Ed. Zosia H. Archibald, John K. Davies, and Vincent Gabrielsen. Oxford: Oxford University Press. Pp. 216–50.

———. (2007). "Brotherhoods of Faith and Provident Planning: The Non-public Associations of the Greek World," *Mediterranean Historical Review* 22/2: 183–210.

———. (2005). "Banking and Credit Operations in Hellenistic Times," in *Making, Moving, and Managing: The New World of Ancient Economies, 323–31 BC.* Ed. Zofia H. Archibald, John K. Davies, and Vincent Gabrielsen. Oxford: Oxbow Books. Pp. 136–64.

———. (2003). "Piracy and the Slave-Trade," in *A Companion to the Hellenistic World.* Ed. Andrew Erskine. Malden, MA: Blackwell. Pp. 389–404.

———. (2001). "The Rhodian Associations and Economic Activity," in *Hellenistic Economies.* Ed. Zosia H. Archibald, John K. Davies, Vincent Gabrielsen, and G. J. Oliver. London: Routledge. Pp. 215–44.

———. (1997). *The Naval Aristocracy of Hellenistic Rhodes.* Aarhus: Aarhus University Press.

———. (1994). *Financing the Athenian Fleet: Public Taxation and Social Relations.* Baltimore: Johns Hopkins University Press.

Gabrielsen, Vincent, Per Bilde, Troels Engberg-Pedersen, Lisa Hannestadt, and Jan Zahle, eds. (1999). *Hellenistic Rhodes: Politics, Culture, and Society.* Aarhus: Aarhus University Press.

Gagarin, Michael (2005). "The Unity of Greek Law," in *The Cambridge Companion to Ancient Greek Law.* Cambridge: Cambridge University Press. Pp. 29–40.

———. (1995). "The Unity of Greek Law," in *The Cambridge Companion to Greek Law.* Ed. Michael Gagarin and David Cohen. Cambridge: Cambridge University Press. Pp. 29–40.

Gale, N. H., ed. (1991). *Bronze Age Trade in the Mediterranean.* Jonsered: Paul Åströms Förlag.

Galiani, Sebastian, and Itai Sened, eds. (2014). *Institutions, Property Rights, and Economic Growth: The Legacy of Douglass North.* Cambridge: Cambridge University Press.

Galil, Gershon. (2007). *The Lower Stratum Families in the Neo-Assyrian Period*. Leiden: Brill.

Gallant, Thomas. (1991). *Risk and Survival in Ancient Greece*. Stanford, CA: Stanford University Press.

Galor, Oded, and Ömer Özak. (2016). "The Agricultural Origins of Time Preference," *American Economic Review* 106/10: 3064–103.

Gamauf, Richard. (2009). "Slaves Doing Business: The Role of Roman Law in the Economy of a Roman Household," *European Review of History: Revue européenne d'histoire* 16/3: 331–46.

Garlan, Yvon. (1988). *Slavery in Ancient Greece*. Trans. Janet Lloyd. Ithaca, NY: Cornell University Press.

Garland, Robert. (2014). *Wandering Greeks: The Ancient Greek Diaspora from the Age of Homer to the Death of Alexander the Great*. Princeton, NJ: Princeton University Press.

Garnsey, Peter (1998). *Cities, Peasants and Food in Classical Antiquity: Essays in Social and Economic History*. Edited with an addendum by Walter Scheidel. Cambridge: Cambridge University Press.

———. (1988). *Famine and Food Supply in the Graeco-Roman World: Responses to Risk and Crisis*. Cambridge: Cambridge University Press.

Garnsey, Peter, K. Hopkins, and C. R. Whittaker, eds. (1983). *Trade in the Ancient Economy*. Berkeley: University of California Press. Pp. ix–xxv.

Garnsey, Peter, and C. R. Whittaker, eds. (1983). *Trade and Famine in Classical Antiquity*. Cambridge: Cambridge Philological Society.

Gascou, Jean. (2009). "The Papyrology of the Near East," in *The Oxford Handbook of Papyrology*. Ed. Roger S. Bagnall. Oxford: Oxford University Press. Pp. 473–94.

Gates-Foster, Jennifer. (2016). "Finley and Archaeology," in *M. I. Finley: An Ancient Historian and His Impact*. Ed. Daniel Jew, Robin Osborne, and Michael Scott. Cambridge: Cambridge University Press. Pp. 250–69.

———. (2011). "Amphoras in Egypt, 7th c. B.C.–12th c. A.D.," *Journal of Roman Archaeology* 24: 803–7.

Geertz, Clifford. (1978). "The Bazaar Economy: Information and Search in Peasant Marketing," *American Economic Review* 68: 28–32.

Gehrke, Hans-Joachim. (1986). *Jenseits von Athen und Sparta: Das Dritte Griechenland und seine Staatenwelt*. Munich: C. H. Beck.

Gelderblom, Oscar. (2013). *Cities of Commerce: The Institutional Foundations of International Trade in the Low Countries, 1250–1650*. Princeton, NJ: Princeton University Press.

Gellner, Ernest. (1983). *Nations and Nationalism*. Ithaca, NY: Cornell University Press.

Gerring, John. (2012). *Social Science Methodology: A Unified Framework*. Cambridge: Cambridge University Press.

Ghosh, Peter. (2014). *Max Weber and the Protestant Ethic: Twin Histories*. Oxford: Oxford University Press.

Giardino, C. (1992). "Nuragic Sardinia and the Mediterranean: Metallurgy and Maritime Traffic," in *Sardinia in the Mediterranean: A Footprint in the Sea: Studies in Sardinian Archaeology Presented to Miriam S. Balmath*. Ed. R. H. Tykot and Tamsey K. Andrews. Sheffield: Sheffield Academic. Pp. 304–15.

Gibbins, David. (2001). "Shipwrecks and Hellenistic Trade," in *Hellenistic Economies*. Ed. Zosia H. Archibald, John Davies, Vincent Gabrielsen, and G. J. Oliver. London: Routledge. Pp. 273–312.

Giddens, Anthony, and Christopher Pierson. (1998). *Conversations with Anthony Giddens: Making Sense of Modernity*. Stanford, CA: Stanford University Press.

Gill, David W. (1994). "Positivism, Pots, and Long-Distance Trade," in *Classical Greece: Ancient Histories and Modern Ideologies*. Ed. Ian Morris. Cambridge: Cambridge University Press. Pp. 99–107.

Glimcher, Paul W., Colin Camerer, Russell A. Poldrack, and Ernst Fehr. (2008). *Neuroeconomics: Decision Making and the Brain*. Boston: Academic Press.

Goddio, Franck. (2011). "Heracleion-Thonis and Alexandria, Two Ancient Egyptian Emporia," in *Maritime Archaeology and Ancient Trade in the Mediterranean*. Ed. Damian Robinson and Andrew Wilson. Oxford: Oxford Centre for Maritime Archaeology. Pp. 121–37.

———. (2010). "Geophysical Survey in the Submerged Canopic Region," in *Alexandria and the North-Western Delta*. Ed. Damian Robinson and Andrew Wilson. Oxford: Oxford Centre for Maritime Archaeology. Pp. 3–13.

———. (2007). *The Topography and Excavations of Heracleion-Thonis and East Canopus (1996–2006)*. Oxford: Oxford Centre for Maritime Archaeology.

Goddio, Franck, and André Bernand. (2004). *Sunken Egypt: Alexandria*. London: Periplus.

Godelier, Maurice. (1966). *Rationalité et irrationalité en économie*. Paris: F. Maspero.

Goelet, Ogden, Jr. (2015). "Problems of Authority, Compulsion, and Compensation in Ancient Egyptian Labor Practices," in *Labor in the Ancient World*. Ed. Piotr Steinkeller and Michael Hudson. Dresden: ISLET-Verlag. Pp. 523–82.

Goffredo, Stefano, and Zvy Dubinsky, eds. (2014). *The Mediterranean Sea: Its History and Present Challenges*. Dordrecht: Springer Verlag.

Goldberg, Jessica L. (2012). *Trade and Institutions in the Medieval Mediterranean: The Geniza Merchants and Their Business World*. Cambridge: Cambridge University Press.

Goldbrunner, Sara. (2006). *Der verblendete Gelehrte: Der erste Setna-Roman (P. Kairo 30646): Umschrift, Übersetzung und Glossar*. Demotische Studien 13. Sommerhausen: Gisela Zauzich Verlag.

Goldstone, Jack A. (2002). "Efflorescences and Economic Growth in World History," *Journal of World History* 13: 323–89.

González de Canales, Fernando, Leonardo Serrano, and Jorge Llompart. (2008). "The Emporium of Huelva and Phoenician Chronology: Present and Future Possibilities," in *Beyond the Homeland: Markers in Phoenician Chronology*. Ed. Claudia Sagona. Leuven: Peeters. Pp. 631–55.

Goodchild, Helen. (2013). "GIS Models of Roman Agricultural Production," in *The Roman Agricultural Economy: Organization, Investment, and Production*. Ed. Alan Bowman and Andrew Wilson. Oxford: Oxford University Press. Pp. 55–83.

Goody, Jack. (2012). *Metals, Culture and Capitalism: An Essay on the Origins of the Modern World*. Cambridge: Cambridge University Press.

———. (2006). *The Theft of History*. Cambridge: Cambridge University Press.

———. (1990). *The Oriental, the Ancient and the Primitive: Systems of Marriage and the Family in the Pre-industrial Societies of Eurasia*. Cambridge: Cambridge University Press.

———. (1976). *Production and Reproduction: A Comparative Study of the Domestic Domain*. Cambridge: Cambridge University Press.

Gornall, Jemma, Richard Betts, Eleanor Burke, Robin Clark, Joanne Camp, Kate Willett, and Andrew Wiltshire. (2010). "Implications of Climate Change for Agricultural Productivity in the Early Twenty-First Century," *Philosophical Transactions of the Royal Society* 365: 2973–89. doi: 10.1098/rstb.2010.0158.

Gowland, R. L., and P. Garnsey. (2010). "Skeletal Evidence for Health, Nutritional Status and Malaria in Rome and the Empire," in *Roman Diasporas: Archaeological Approaches to Mobility and Diversity in the Roman Empire*. Ed. H. Eckardt. *Journal of Roman Archaeology*. Supplementary series 78. Pp. 131–56.

Gozzoli, Roberto B. (2006). *The Writing of History in Ancient Egypt during the First Millennium BC (ca 1070–180 BC): Trends and Perspectives*. London: Golden House.

Graeber, David. (2011). *Debt: The First 5,000 Years*. Brooklyn, NY: Melville House.

Grafe, Regina. (2012). *Distant Tyranny: Markets, Power, and Backwardness in Spain, 1650–1800*. Princeton, NJ: Princeton University Press.

Grainger, John D. (2010). *The Syrian Wars*. Leiden: Brill.

Granovetter, Mark. (2005). "Comment on Liverani and Bedford," in *The Ancient Economy: Evidence and Models*. Ed. J. G. Manning and Ian Morris. Stanford, CA: Stanford University Press. Pp. 84–88.

———. (2004). "Polanyi Symposium: A Conversation on Embeddedness," *Socio-economic Review* 2: 109–35.

———. (1990). "The Old and the New Economic Sociology: A History and an Agenda," in *Beyond the Marketplace: Rethinking Economy and Society*. Ed. R. Friedland and A. F. Robertson. New York: Aldine. Pp. 89–112.

———. (1985). "Economic Action and Social Structure: The Problem of Embeddedness," *American Journal of Sociology* 91: 481–510.

———. (1978). "Threshold Models of Collective Behavior," *American Journal of Sociology* 83/6: 1420–43.

Grantham, George. (1999). "Contra Ricardo: On the Macroeconomics of Pre-industrial Economies," *European Review of Economic History* 3/2: 199–232.

Gras, Michel. (1995). "La méditerranée occidentale, milieu d'échanges: Un regard historiographique," in *Les Grecs et l'Occident: Actes du Colloque de la Villa 'Kérylos' 1991*. Ed. Georges Vallet. Rome: École françcaise de Rome. Pp. 109–21.

Graslin, L., and J. Maucourant. (2005). "Le port de commerce: Un concept en débat," *Topoi* 12–13: 215–57.

Gravelle, H., and R. Rees. (1992). *Microeconomics*, 2d ed. London: Longman.

Greene, Kevin. (2008). "Historiography and Theoretical Approaches," in *The Oxford Handbook of Engineering and Technology in the Classical World*. Ed. John Peter Oleson. Oxford: Oxford University Press. Pp. 62–90.

———. (2000). "Technological Innovation and Economic Progress in the Ancient World: M. I. Finley Re-considered," *Economic History Review* 53/1: 29–59.

Greene, Molly. (2000). *A Shared World: Christians and Muslims in the Early Modern Mediterranean*. Princeton, NJ: Princeton University Press.

Greif, Avner. (2006). *Institutions and the Path to the Modern Economy: Lessons from Medieval Trade*. Cambridge: Cambridge University Press.

Greif, Avner, and Joel Mokyr. (forthcoming). "Institutions and Economic History: A Critique of Professor McCloskey," *Journal of Institutional Economics*.

Grimal, Nicolas, and Bernadette Menu, eds. (1998). *Le commerce en Égypte ancienne*. Cairo: Institute français d'Archaéologie orientale.

Grove, A. T., and O. Rackham. (2001). *The Nature of Mediterranean Europe: An Ecological History*. New Haven, CT: Yale University Press.

Gschnitzer, Fritz. (1993). "Phoinikisch-karthagisches Verfassungsdenken," *Anfänge politischen Denkens in der Antike*. Ed. K. Rafflaub. Munich: R. Oldenbourg. Pp. 87–198.

———. (1988). "Die Stellung der Polis in der politischen Entwicklung des Altertums," *Oriens Antiquus* 27: 287–302.

Gubel, Eric. (2009). "Héracléopolis et l'interaction culturelle entre l'Égypte et la côte phénicienne pendant la Troisième Période Intermédiaire," in *Elkab and Beyond: Studies in Honour of Luc Limme*. Ed. Wouter Claes, Herman de Meulenaere, and Stan Hendrickx. Leuven: Peeters. Pp. 321–40.

Gunn, J., ed. (2000). *The Years without Summer: Tracing AD 536 and Its Aftermath*. Oxford: Archaeopress.

Gunter, A. C. (2014). "Orientalism and Orientalization in the Iron Age Mediterranean," in *Critical Approaches to Ancient Near Eastern Art*. Ed. Brian A. Brown and Marian H. Feldman. Boston: de Gruyter. Pp. 79–108.

Haber, Stephen. (1999). "Anything Goes: Mexico's 'New' Cultural History," *Hispanic American Historical Review* 79/2: 309–30.

Haldon, J., et al. (2014). "The Climate and Environment of Byzantine Anatolia: Integrating Science, History, and Archaeology," *Journal of Interdisciplinary History* 45/2: 113–61.

Haldon, John. (2015). "Modes of Production, Social Action and Historical Change: Some Questions and Issues," in *Studies on Pre-capitalist Modes of Production*. Ed. Laura da Graca and Andrea Zingarelli. Leiden: Brill. Pp. 204–36.

Hall, Jonathan M. (2014a). *Artifact and Artifice: Classical Archaeology and the Ancient Historian*. Chicago: University of Chicago Press.

———. (2014b). *A History of the Archaic Greek World, ca. 1200–479 BCE*. 2d ed. Malden, MA: Wiley-Blackwell.

Hall, John A., and Ralph Schroeder, eds. (2006). *An Anatomy of Power: The Social Theory of Michael Mann*. Cambridge: Cambridge University Press.

Halstead, Paul. (2014). *Two Oxen Ahead: Pre-mechanized Farming in the Mediterranean*. Cambridge, MA: Wiley-Blackwell.

———. (2011). "Redistribution in Aegean Palatial Polity Societies: Terminology, Scale, and Significance," *American Journal of Archaeology* 115: 229–35.

———. (1987). "Traditional and Ancient Rural Economy in Mediterranean Europe: Plus ça change?," *Journal of Hellenic Studies* 107: 77–87.

Halstead, Paul, and John O'Shea, eds. (1989). *Bad Year Economics: Cultural Responses to Risk and Uncertainty*. Cambridge: Cambridge University Press.

Hannaford, Matthew. (2014). "Climate, Causation and Society: Interdisciplinary Perspectives from the Past to the Future," in *Selected Themes in African Development Studies: Economic Growth, Governance and the Environment*. Ed. Lucky Asuelime, Joseph Yaro, and Suzanne Francis. Cham: Springer Verlag. Pp. 7–25.

Hannah, Robert. (2008). "Timekeeping," in *The Oxford Handbook of Engineering and Technology in the Classical World*. Ed. John Peter Oleson. Oxford: Oxford University Press. Pp. 740–58.

Hannestad, Lise. (2007). "Timber as a Trade Resource of the Black Sea," in *The Black Sea in Antiquity: Regional and Inter-regional Economic Exchanges*. Ed. Vincent Gabrielsen and John Lund. Aarhus: Aarhus University Press. Pp. 85–99.

Hansen, Mogens Herman. (2006a). *The Shotgun Method: The Demography of the Ancient Greek City-State Culture*. Columbia: University of Missouri Press.

———. (2006b). "*Emporion*: A Study of the Use and Meaning of the Term in the Archaic and Classical Periods," in *Greek Colonization: An Account of Greek Colonies and Other Settlements Overseas*. Ed. Gocha R. Tsetskhladze. Vol. 1. Leiden: Brill. Pp. 1–39.

Hansen, Valerie. (1995). *Negotiating Daily Life in Traditional China: How Ordinary People Used Contracts 600–1400*. New Haven, CT: Yale University Press.

Hardy, Gavin, and Laurence Totelin. (2016). *Ancient Botany*. Oxford: Routledge.

Haring, B.J.J. (1997). *Divine Households: Administrative and Economic Aspects of the New Kingdom Royal Memorial Temples in Western Thebes*. Leiden: Nederlands Instituut voor het Nabije Oosten.

Harms, William F. (2004). *Information and Meaning in Evolutionary Processes*. Cambridge: Cambridge University Press.

Harper, Kyle. (2017). *The Fate of Rome: Climate, Disease, and the End of an Empire*. Princeton, NJ: Princeton University Press.

———. (2016). "A Reply to John L. Brooke's 'Malthus and the North Atlantic Oscillation,'" *Journal of Interdisciplinary History* 46/4: 579–84.

———. (2015). "Civilization, Climate, and Malthus: The Rough Course of Global History,'" *Journal of Interdisciplinary History* 45: 549–66.

———. (2011). *Slavery in the Late Roman World, AD 275–425*. Cambridge: Cambridge University Press.

Harris, Edward M. (2016). "The Legal Foundations of Economic Growth in Ancient Greece: The Role of Property Records," in *The Ancient Greek Economy: Markets, Households and City-States*. Ed. Edward M. Harris, David M. Lewis, and Mark Woolmer. Cambridge: Cambridge University Press. Pp. 116–46.

———. (2013). "Finley's Studies in Land and Credit Sixty Years Later," *Dike* 16: 123–46.

———. (2002). "Did Solon Abolish Debt Bondage?," *Classical Quarterly* 52: 415–30.

———. (2001). Review of A. Bresson, *La cité marchande*, Bordeaux: Ausonius, 2000, *Bryn Mawr Classical Review* 2001.09.40.

Harris, Edward M., and David Lewis. (2016). "Introduction," in *The Ancient Greek Economy: Markets, Households and City-States*. Ed. Edward M. Harris, David M. Lewis, and Mark Woolmer. Cambridge: Cambridge University Press. Pp. 1–37.

Harris, Edward M., David Lewis, and Mark Woolmer, eds. (2016). *The Ancient Greek Economy: Markets, Households and City-States*. Cambridge: Cambridge University Press.

Harris, William V., ed. (2013a). *The Ancient Mediterranean Environment between Science and History*. Leiden: Brill.

———. (2013b). "What Kind of Environmental History for Antiquity?," in *The Ancient Mediterranean Environment between Science and History*. Ed. W. V. Harris. Leiden: Brill. Pp. 1–10.

———. (2011a). *Rome's Imperial Economy: Twelve Essays*. Oxford: Oxford University Press.

———. (2011b). "The Roman Economy in the Late Republic, 133–31 BC," in *Rome's Imperial Economy: Twelve Essays*. Oxford: Oxford University Press. Pp. 257–87.

———. (2008). "The Nature of Roman Money," in *The Monetary Systems of the Greeks and Romans*. Ed. W. V. Harris. Oxford: Oxford University Press. Pp. 174–207.

———. (2007). "The Late Republic," in *The Cambridge Economic History of the Greco-Roman World*. Ed. Walter Scheidel, Ian Morris, and Richard Saller. Cambridge: Cambridge University Press. Pp. 511–39.

———. (2006). "A Revisionist View of Roman Money," *Journal of Roman Studies* 96: 1–24.

———. (2005). "The Mediterranean and Ancient History," in *Rethinking the Mediterranean*, ed. W. V. Harris. Oxford: Oxford University Press. Pp. 1–42.

———. (2003). " 'Roman Governments and Commerce, 300 B.C.–A.D. 300," in *Mercanti e politica nel mondo antico*. Ed. Carlo Zaccagnini. Rome: "L'Erma" di Bretschneider. Pp. 275–305.

———. (2000), "Trade 70–192 AD," in *The Cambridge Ancient History*. Vol. 11. 2d ed. Cambridge: Cambridge University Press. Pp. 710–39. Reprinted in *Rome's Imperial Economy: Twelve Essays*, Oxford: Oxford University Press, 2011, pp. 155–87.

———. (1993). "Between Archaic and Modern: Some Current Problems in the History of the Roman Economy," in *The Inscribed Economy: Production and Distribution in the Roman Empire in the Light of Instrumentum Domesticum: The Proceedings of a Conference Held at the American Academy in Rome on 10–11 January, 1992*. Ed. W. V. Harris. Ann Arbor: University of Michigan. *Journal of Roman Archaeology*. Supplementary series 6. Pp. 11–29.

Hasebroek, J. (1928). *Staat und Handel im alten Griechenland*. Tübingen: J.C.B. Mohr. Trans. *Trade and Politics in Ancient Greece*. London: G. Bell and Sons, 1933.

Hassan, Fekri A. (2007). "Extreme Nile Floods and Famines in Medieval Egypt (AD 930–1500) and Their Climatic Implications," *Quaternary International* 173–74: 101–12.

———. (1994). "Population, Ecology and Civilization in Ancient Egypt," in *Historical Ecology: Cultural Knowledge and Changing Landscapes*. Ed. Carole L. Crumley. Santa Fe, NM: School of American Research Press. Pp. 155–81.

———. (1993). "Town and Village in Ancient Egypt: Ecology, Society and Urbanization," in *The Archaeology of Africa: Food, Metals and Towns*. Ed. Thurstan Shaw, Paul Sinclair, Bassey Andah, and Alex Okpoko. London: Routledge. Pp. 551–69.

Haug, Brendan. (2015). "Dependent Labor: The Case of the *Enapographoi Georgoi*," in *Law and Legal Practice in Egypt from Alexander to the Arab Conquest: A Selection of Papyrological Sources in Translation, with Introductions and Commentary*. Ed. James G. Keenan, J. G. Manning, and Uri Yiftach-Firanko. Cambridge: Cambridge University Press. Pp. 430–41.

Hayes, William C. (1955). *A Papyrus of the Late Middle Kingdom in the Brooklyn Museum*. Brooklyn, NY: Brooklyn Museum.

Heichelheim, Fritz M. (1968). *An Ancient Economic History from the Paleolithic Age to the Migrations of the Germanic, Slavic, and Arabic Nations*, revised and complete English ed. Vol. 2. Leiden: A. W. Sijthoff.

———. (1958). *An Ancient Economic History from the Paleolithic Age to the Migrations of the Germanic, Slavic, and Arabic Nations*. Vol. 1. Leiden: A. W. Sijthoff.

———. (1930). *Wirtschaftliche Schwankungen der Zeit von Alexander bis Augustus: Beiträge zur Erforschung der Wirtschaftlichen Wechsellagen*. Aufschwung, Krise, Stockung Bd. 3. Jena: Fischer. Reprint New York: Arno, 1979.

Herrmann-Pillath, Carsten. (2009). "Outline of a Darwinian Theory of Money," Working Paper, Frankfurt School of Finance and Management. http://nbn-resolving.de/urn: nbn: de: 101: 1-20090923136.

Hickey, Todd. (2012). *Wine, Wealth, and the State in Late Antique Egypt: The House of Apion at Oxyrhynchus.* Ann Arbor: University of Michigan Press.

———. (2009). "Writing Histories from the Papyri," in *The Oxford Handbook of Papyrology.* Ed. Roger S. Bagnall. Oxford: Oxford University Press. Pp. 495–520.

Hicks, John. (1969). *A Theory of Economic History.* Oxford: Oxford University Press.

Hind, John. (1995–96). "Traders and Ports-of-Trade (*Emporoi* and *Emporia*) in the Black Sea in Antiquity," *Il Mar Nero* 2: 113–26.

Hirth, Kenneth G. (2016). *The Aztec Economic World: Merchants and Markets in Ancient Mesoamerica.* Cambridge: Cambridge University Press.

Hitchener, R. Bruce. (2005). "The Advantages of Wealth and Luxury": The Case for Economic Growth in the Roman Empire," in *The Ancient Economy: Evidence and Models.* Ed. J. G. Manning and Ian Morris. Stanford, CA: Stanford University Press. Pp. 207–22.

———. (1994). "Image and Reality: The Changing Face of Pastoralism in the Tunisian High Steppe," in *Landuse in the Roman Empire.* Ed. Jesper Carlsen, Peter Ørsted, and Jens Erick Skydsgaard. Rome: "L'Erma" di Bretschneider. Pp. 27–43.

Hodgson, Geoffrey M. (2004). *The Evolution of Institutional Economics: Agency, Structure and Darwinism in American Institutionalism.* London: Routledge.

———. (1993). *Economics and Evolution: Bringing Life Back into Economics.* Ann Arbor: University of Michigan Press.

Hodkinson, Stephen. (2000). *Property and Wealth in Classical Sparta.* London: Duckworth.

Hölbl, Günther. (2001). *A History of the Ptolemaic Empire.* Trans. Tina Saavedra. London: Routledge.

Hoffman, Philip T. (2015). *Why Did Europe Conquer the World?* Princeton, NJ: Princeton University Press.

———. (1996). *Growth in a Traditional Society: The French Countryside 1450–1815.* Princeton, NJ: Princeton University Press.

Hoffmann-Salz, J. (2011). *Die wirtschaftlichen Auswirkungen der römsichen Eroberung: Vergleichende Untersuchungen der Provinzen Syria, Hispania Tarraconensis, Africa Proconsularis und Syria.* Historia Einzelschriften 218. Stuttgart: Franz Steiner.

Höflmayer, Felix, ed. (2017). *The Late Third Millennium in the Ancient Near East: Chronology, C14, and Climate Change.* Chicago: Oriental Institute.

Holleaux, Maurice. (1938). *Études d'épigraphie et d'histoire grecques.* Vol. 1. Paris: de Boccard.

Holmgren, Karin, Alexandra Gogou, Adam Izdebski, Juerg Luterbacher, Marie-Alexandrine Sicre, and Elena Xoplaki. (2016). "Mediterranean Holocene Climate, Environment and Human Societies," *Quaternary Science Reviews* 136: 1–4.

Hong, S., et al. (1994). "Ice Core Evidence of Hemispheric Lead Pollution Two Millennia Ago by Greek and Roman Civilizations," *Science* 265: 1841–43.

Honigman, Sylvie. (2014). *Tales of High Priests and Taxes: The Books of Maccabees and the Judean Rebellion against Antiochus IV.* Berkeley: University of California Press.

Hopkins, Keith. (2002). "Rome, Taxes, Rents and Trade," in *The Ancient Economy.* Ed. W. Scheidel and S. von Reden. New York: Routledge. Pp. 190–230.

———. (1983). "Introduction," in *Trade in the Ancient Economy.* Ed. Peter Garnsey, K. Hopkins, and C. R. Whittaker. Berkeley: University of California Press. Pp. ix–xxv.

———. (1980). "Taxes and Trade in the Roman Empire (200 BC–AD 200)," *Journal of Roman Studies* 70: 101–25.

Horden, Peregrine, and Nicholas Purcell. (2000). *The Corrupting Sea: A Study of Mediterranean History*. Oxford: Blackwell.

Horesh, Niv. (2014). *Chinese Money in Global Context: Historic Junctures between 600 BCE and 2012*. Stanford, CA: Stanford University Press.

Hornborg, Alf, J. R. McNeill, and Joan Martinez-Alier, eds. (2007). *Rethinking Environmental History: World-System History and Global Environmental Change*. Lanham, MD: Altamira.

Hough, Jerry F., and Robin Grier. (2015). *The Long Process of Development: Building Markets and States in Pre-industrial England, Spain, and Their Colonies*. Cambridge: Cambridge University Press.

Howe, Timothy, ed. (2015). *Traders in the Ancient Mediterranean*. Chicago: Ares.

Howgego, Christopher. (1995). *Ancient History from Coins*. London: Routledge.

Hoyer, Dan, and J. G. Manning. (forthcoming). "Empirical Regularities across Time, Space, and Culture: A Critical Review of Comparative Methods in Ancient Historical Research," *Historia*.

Hoyos, Dexter. (2010). *The Carthaginians*. London: Routledge.

Hsiang, Solomon M., and Marshall Burke. (2014). "Climate, Conflict, and Social Stability: What Does the Evidence Say?," *Climatic Change* 123: 39–55.

Hudson, A. M. (2004). "The Archaeology of Money," in *Credit and State Theories of Money*. Ed. L. R. Wray. Cheltenham: Edward Elgar. Pp. 99–127.

Hudson, Michael. (2002). "Restructuring the Origins of Interest-Bearing Debt and the Logic of Clean Slates," in *Debt and Economic Renewal in the Ancient Near East*. Ed. Michael Hudson and Marc van de Mieroop. Bethesda, MD: CDL. Pp. 7–53.

Hudson, Michael, and Baruch A. Levine, eds. (1999). *Urbanization and Land Ownership in the Ancient Near East*. Cambridge, MA: Peabody Museum of Archaeology and Ethnology.

Hudson, Michael, and Marc van de Mieroop, eds. (2002). *Debt and Economic Renewal in the Ancient Near East*. Bethesda, MD: CDL.

Hudson, Nicholas. (2016). "A Hellenistic Household Ceramic Assemblage from Tell el-Timai (Thmuis), Egypt: A Contextual View," *Bulletin of the American Schools of Oriental Research* 376: 199–244.

Huebner, Sabine R., and Geoffrey S. Nathan, eds. (2017). *Mediterranean Families in Antiquity: Households, Extended Families, and Domestic Space*. Chichester: John Wiley and Sons.

Hughes, George R. (1952). *Saite Demotic Land Leases*. Chicago: Oriental Institute.

Hughes, J. Donald. (2007). "Environmental Impacts of the Roman Economy and Social Structure: Augustus to Diocletian," in *Rethinking Environmental History: World-System History and Global Environmental Change*. Ed. Alf Hornborg, J. R. McNeill, and Joan Martinez-Alier. Lanham, MD: Altamira. Pp. 27–40.

———. (2005). *The Mediterranean: An Environmental History*. Santa Barbara, CA: ABC Clio.

———. (1994). *Pan's Travail: Environmental Problems of the Ancient Greeks and Romans*. Baltimore: Johns Hopkins University Press.

Humphreys, Sally. (1969). "History, Economics, and Anthropology: The Work of Karl Polanyi," *History and Theory* 8: 165–212. Reprinted in *Anthropology and the Greeks*. London: Routledge, 1978. Pp. 31–75.

Hunt, Lynn. (2014). *Writing History in the Global Era*. New York: Norton.

Hunt, Peter. (2011). "Slaves in Greek Literary Culture," in the *Cambridge World History of Slavery*. Vol. 1, *The Ancient Mediterranean World*. Ed. Keith Bradley and Paul Cartledge. Cambridge: Cambridge University Press.

Huntington, Ellsworth. (1915). *Civilization and Climate*. New Haven, CT: Yale University Press.

——. (1913). "Changes of Climate and History," *American Historical Review* 19/2: 213–32.

Huß, Werner. (2001). *Ägypten in hellenistischer Zeit: 332–30 v. Chr.* Munich: C. H. Beck.

Ingham, Geoffrey. (2004). *The Nature of Money*. London: Polity.

Inoue, Hiroko, Alexis Álvarez, Eugene N. Anderson, Andrew Owen, Rebecca Álvarez, Kirk Lawrence, and Christopher Chase-Dunn. (2015). "Urban Scale Shifts since the Bronze Age: Upsweeps, Collapses, and Semiperipheral Development," *Social Science History* 39: 175–200.

Irby, Georgia L., ed. (2016). *A Companion to Science, Technology, and Medicine in Ancient Greece and Rome*. Malden, MA: Wiley-Blackwell.

Irwin, Douglas A., and Kevin H. O'Rourke. (2014). "Coping with Shocks and Shifts: The Multilateral Trading System in Historical Perspective," in *Globalization in an Age of Crisis: Multilateral Economic Cooperation in the Twenty-First Century*. Ed. Robert C. Feenstra and Alan M. Taylor. National Bureau of Economic Research Conference Report. Chicago: University of Chicago Press. Pp. 11–42.

Isager, Signe, and Jens Erik Skydsgaard. (1995). *Ancient Greek Agriculture: An Introduction*. Paperback ed. London: Routledge. Originally published 1992, London: Routledge.

Issar, A. A., and M. Zohar. (2010). *Climate Change: Environment and Civilization in the Middle East*. 2d ed. Paperback ed. Berlin: Springer Verlag.

Iyigun, Murat. (2015). *War, Peace, and Prosperity in the Name of God: The Ottoman Role in Europe's Socioeconomic Evolution*. Chicago: University of Chicago Press.

Izdebski, Adam, et al. (2016). "Realising Consilience: How Better Communication between Archaeologists, Historians and Natural Scientists Can Transform the Study of the Past Climate Change in the Mediterranean," *Quaternary Science Review* 136: 5–22.

James, T.G.H. (1962). *The Hekanakhte Papers and Other Early Middle Kingdom Documents*. New York: Metropolitan Museum of Art.

Jameson, Michael J. (2002). "On Paul Cartledge, 'The Political Economy of Greek Slavery," in *Money, Labour and Land: Approaches to the Economies of Ancient Greece*. Ed. Paul Cartledge, Edward Cohen, and Lin Foxhall. London: Routledge. Pp. 167–74.

——. (1994). *A Greek Countryside: The Southern Argolid from Prehistory to the Present Day*. Stanford, CA: Stanford University Press.

——. (1992). "Agriculture in Ancient Greece," in *Proceedings of the Seventh International Symposium at the Swedish Institute at Athens, 16–17 May 1990*. Ed. Berit Wells. Stockholm: Paul Åströms Forlag. Pp. 135–46.

——. (1977–78). "Agriculture and Slavery in Classical Athens," *Classical Journal* 73/2: 122–45.

Jansen-Winkeln, Karl. (1997). "Ein Kaufmann aus Naukratis," *Zeitschrift für ägyptische Spache und Altertumskunde* 124: 105–15.

Janssen, Jac. J. (1979). "The Role of the Temple in the Egyptian Economy during the New Kingdom," in *State and Temple Economy in the Ancient Near East*. Ed. Edward Lipinski. OLA 6. Leuven: Peeters. Pp. 505–15.

———. (1975). "Prolegomenon to the study of Egypt's Economic History during the New Kingdom," *SAK* 3: 127–85.

Jas, R. M., ed. (2000). *Rainfall and Agriculture in Northern Mesopotami*a. Istanbul: Nederlands Historisch-Archaeologisch Instituut.

Jasnow, Richard, and Raymond Westbrook, eds. (2001). *Security for Debt in Ancient Near Eastern Law*. Leiden: Brill.

Jasnow, Richard. (2003). "Middle Kingdom and Second Intermediate Period," "New Kingdom," in *A History of Ancient Near Eastern Law*. Vol. 1. Ed. Raymond Westbrook. Leiden: Brill. Pp. 255–359.

Jaspers, Karl. (1949). *Von Ursprung und Ziel der Geschichte*. Zürich: Artemis-Verlag. Published in English as *The Origin and Goal of History*. Trans. Michael Bullock. I cite from the 2010 Routledge edition.

Jenkins, Richard. (2000). "Disenchantment, Enchantment, and Re-enchantment: Max Weber at the Millennium," *Max Weber Studies* 1: 11–32.

Jew, Daniel, Robin Osborne, and Michael Scott, eds. (2016). *M. I. Finley: An Ancient Historian and His Impact*. Cambridge: Cambridge University Press.

Jia, Ruixue. (2014). "Weather Shocks, Sweet Potatoes and Peasant Revolts in Historical China," *Economic Journal* 124/575: 92–118.

Joannès, Francis. (2002). *La Mésopotamie au 1er millenaire avant J.-C.* 2d ed. Paris: Armand Colin.

Johnson, Janet H. (1998). "Women, Wealth and Work in Egyptian Society of the Ptolemaic Period," in *Egyptian Religion, the Last Thousand Years: Studies Dedicated to the Memory of Jan Quaegebeur*. Ed. Willy Clarysse, Antoon Schoors, and Harco Willems. Orientalia Lovaniensia Analecta 85. Leuven: Peeters. Pp. 1393–421.

Johnston, David. (1999). *Roman Law in Context*. Cambridge: Cambridge University Press.

Jones, A.H.M. (1974). *The Roman Economy: Studies in Ancient Economic and Administrative History*. Oxford: Blackwell.

———. (1948). "Ancient Economic History," Inaugural Lecture, University College London. London: H. K. Lewis.

Jones, Alexander. (2017). *A Portable Cosmos: Revealing the Antikythera Mechanism, Scientific Wonder of the Ancient World*. Oxford: Oxford University Press.

Jones, Donald W. (2014). *Economic Theory and the Ancient Mediterranean*. Malden, MA: Wiley-Blackwell.

Jones, E. L. (1988). *Growth Recurring: Economic Change in World History*. Ann Arbor: University of Michigan Press.

Jones, E. L., and S. J. Woolf, eds. (1969). *Agrarian Change and Economic Development: The Historical Problems*. London: Methuen.

Jongman, Willem M. (2014a). "The New Economic History of the Roman Empire," in *Quantifying the Greco-Roman Economy and Beyond*. Ed. François de Callataÿ. Bari: Edipuglia. Pp. 169–88.

———. (2014b). "Re-constructing the Roman Economy," in *The Cambridge History of Capitalism*. 2 vols. Ed. Larry Neal and Jeffrey G. Williamson. Cambridge: Cambridge University Press. Pp. 75–100.

———. (2013). "Formalism-Substantivism Debate," in *The Encyclopedia of Ancient History*. 1st ed. Ed. Roger S. Bagnall, Kai Brodersen, Craige B. Champion, Andrew Erskine, and Sabine R. Huebner. Oxford: Blackwell. Pp. 2715–18.

————. (2007). "The Early Roman Empire: Consumption," in *The Cambridge Economic History of the Greco-Roman World*. Ed. Walter Scheidel, Ian Morris, and Richard Saller. Cambridge: Cambridge University Press. Pp. 592–618.

————. (1988). *The Economy and Society of Pompeii*. 2d impression 1991. Amsterdam: J. C. Gieben.

Jördens, Andrea. (2015). "Roman and Byzantine Labor Contracts," in *Law and Legal Practice in Egypt from Alexander to the Arab Conquest: A Selection of Papyrological Sources in Translation, with Introductions and Commentary*. Ed. James G. Keenan, J. G. Manning, and Uri Yiftach-Firanko. Cambridge: Cambridge University Press. Pp. 410–30.

————. (1990). *Vertragliche Regelungen von Arbeiten im späten griechischsprachigen Ägypten*. Veröffentlichungen aus der Heidelberger Papyrus-Sammlung 6. Heidelberg: Carl Winter Verlag.

Jouzel, Jean. (2013). "A Brief History of Ice Core Research over the Last 50 Years," *Climate of the Past* 9: 2525–47.

Jursa, Michael. (2015). "Market Performance and Market Integration in Babylonia in the 'Long Sixth Century' BC," in *A History of Market Performance: From Ancient Babylonia to the Modern World*. Ed. R. J. van der Spek, Bas van Leeuwen, and Jan Luiten van Zanden. London: Routledge. Pp. 83–106.

————. (2014a). "Babylonia in the First Millennium BCE—Economic Growth in Times of Empire," in *The Cambridge History of Capitalism*. 2 vols. Ed. Larry Neal and Jeffrey G. Williamson. Cambridge: Cambridge University Press. Pp. 24–42.

————. (2014b). "Factor Markets in Babylonia from the Late Seventh to the Third Century BCE," *Journal of the Economic and Social History of the Orient* 57/2: 173–202.

————. (2014c). "Economic Development in Babylonia from the Late 7th to the Late 4th Century BC: Economic Growth and Economic Crises in Imperial Contexts," in *Documentary Sources in Ancient Near Eastern and Greco-Roman Economic History: Methodology and Practice*. Ed. Heather D. Baker and Michael Jursa. Oxford: Oxbow. Pp. 113–38.

————. (2013). "Agriculture, Ancient Near East," in *The Encyclopedia of Ancient History*. 1st ed. Ed. Roger S. Bagnall, Kai Brodersen, Craige B. Champion, Andrew Erskine, and Sabine R. Huebner. Oxford: Blackwell. Pp. 208–10.

————. (2010). *Aspects of the Economic History of Babylonia in the First Millennium BC: Economic Geography, Economic Mentalities, Agriculture, the Use of Money and the Problem of Economic Growth*. Münster: Ugarit-Verlag.

————. (2009). "The Babylonian Economy in the First Millennium BC," in *The Babylonian World*. Ed. Gwendolyn Leick. Paperback ed. Oxford: Routledge. Pp. 224–35.

————. (2008). "Economic Change and Legal Innovation: On Aspects of Commercial Interaction and Land Tenure in Babylonia in the First Millennium BC," in *Il Diritti del Mondo Cuneiforme: (Mesopotamia e regione adiacenti, ca. 2500–500 a.c.)*. Ed. Mario Liverani and Clelia Mora. Pavia: IUSS. Pp. 601–28.

————. (2005). "Money-Based Exchange and Redistribution: The Transformation of the Institutional Economy in First Millennium Babylonia," in *Autour de Polanyi: Vocabulaires, theories et modalities des échanges, Nanterre, 12–14 Juin 2004*. Ed. P. Clancier, F. Joannès, P. Rouillard, and A. Tenu. Paris: De Boccard. Pp. 171–86.

Kahneman, Daniel. (2003). "Maps of Bounded Rationality: Psychology for Behavioral Economics." *American Economic Review* 93/5: 1449–75.

Kaiser, Brooks A. (2007). "The Athenian Trierarchy: Mechanism Design for the Private Provision of Public Goods," *Journal of Economic History* 67/2: 445–80.

Kakavogianni, O., and M. Anetakis. (2012). "Les agoras commerciales des dèmes antiques de la Mésogée et de la région du Laurion," in *Tout vendre, tout acheter: Structures et équipements des marches antiques.* Ed. Véronique Chankowski and Pavlos Karvonis. Bordeaux: Ausonius Éditions. Pp. 185–99.

Kallet-Marx, Lisa. (1993). *Money, Expense and Naval Power in Thucydides' History 1–5.24.* Oxford: Oxford University Press.

Kaniewski, David, Joël Guiot, and Elsie van Campo. (2015). "Drought and Societal Collapse 3200 Years Ago in the Eastern Mediterranean: A Review," *WIREs Clim Change* 2015. doi: 10.1002/wcc.345.

Kaniewski, David, Elise van Campo, and Harvey Weiss. (2012). "Drought Is a Recurring Challenge in the Middle East," *PNAS* 109/10: 3862–67.

Karvonis, Pavlos. (2008a). "Les Installations commerciales dans la ville de Délos à l'époque hellénistique," *Bulletin de Correspondance Hellénique* 132/1: 153–219.

———. (2008b). "Typologie et evolution des installations commerciales dans les villes grecques du IVe siècle av. J.-C. et de l'époque hellélenistique," *Revue des Études Grecques* 110: 57–81.

Kawanishi, H., and Y. Suto. (2005). *Akoris I: Amphora Stamps.* Kyoto: Akoris Archaeological Project.

Katary, Sally L. D. (2013a). "Agriculture, Pharaonic Egypt," in *The Encyclopedia of Ancient History.* 1st ed. Ed. Roger S. Bagnall, Kai Brodersen, Craig B. Champion, Andrew Erskine, and Sabine R. Huebner. Oxford: Blackwell. Pp. 214–17.

———. (2013b). "The Administration of Institutional Agriculture in the New Kingdom," in *Ancient Egyptian Administration.* Ed. Juan Carlos Moreno García. Leiden: Brill. Pp. 719–83.

———. (2007). "Land Tenure and Taxation," *The Egyptian World.* Ed. Toby Wilkinson. London: Routledge. Pp. 185–201.

Kaye, Noah. (2015). "Defining the Fiscal Role of Hellenistic Monarchy in Shaping Sale," in *Sale and Community Documents from the Ancient World: Individuals' Autonomy and State Interference in the Ancient World.* Legal Documents in Ancient Societies 5. Graeca Tergestina Storia e Civiltà 2. Ed. Éva Jakab. Trieste: EUT Edizioni Università di Trieste. Pp. 81–98.

Keenan, James G. (2000). "The Mediterranean before Modernity," *Classical Bulletin* 76/1: 81–94.

———. (1989). "Pastoralism in Roman Egypt," *Bulletin of the American Society of Papyrologists* 26: 175–200.

———. (1985). "Village Shepherds and Social Tension in Byzantine Egypt," *Yale Classical Studies* 28: 245–59.

Keenan, James G., J. G. Manning, and Uri Yiftach-Firanko, eds. (2014). *Law and Legal Practice in Egypt from Alexander to the Arab Conquest: A Selection of Papyrological Sources in Translation, with Introductions and Commentary.* Cambridge: Cambridge University Press.

Kehoe, Dennis P. (2015). "Poverty, Distribution of Wealth, and Economic Growth in the Roman Empire," in *Structure and Performance in the Roman Economy: Models, Methods and Case Studies.* Ed. Paul Erdkamp and Koenraad Verboven. Brussels: Éditions Latomus. Pp. 183–96.

———. (2007a). "The Early Roman Empire: Production," in *The Cambridge Economic History of the Greco-Roman World.* Ed. Walter Scheidel, Ian Morris, and Richard Saller. Cambridge: Cambridge University Press. Pp. 543–69.

———. (2007b). *Law and Rural Economy in the Roman Empire.* Ann Arbor: University of Michigan Press.

———. (1988). *The Economics of Agriculture on Roman Imperial Estates in North Africa.* Hypomnemata 89. Göttingen: Vandenhoeck & Ruprecht.

Kehoe, Dennis, David M. Ratzan, and Uri Yiftach. (2015). "Introduction," in *Law and Transaction Costs in the Ancient Economy.* Ed. Dennis Kehoe, David M. Ratzan, and Uri Yiftach. Ann Arbor: University of Michigan Press. Pp. 1–35.

Kelly, Morgan, and Cormac Ó Gráda. (2013). "The Waning of the Little Ice Age: Climate Change in Early Modern Europe," *Journal of Interdisciplinary History* 44: 301–25.

Kemp, Barry J. (2006). *Ancient Egypt: Anatomy of a Civilization.* London: Routledge.

Kessler, David, and Peter Temin. (2007). "The Organization of the Grain Trade in the Early Roman Empire," *Economic History Review* 60: 313–32.

Kitchen, Kenneth. (2001). "Economics in Ancient Arabia: From Alexander to the Augustans," in *Hellenistic Economies.* Ed. Zosia H. Archibald, John K. Davies, Vincent Gabrielsen, and G. J. Oliver, eds. London: Routledge. Pp. 157–73.

Kitchen, Kenneth A., and Paul J. N. Lawrence. (2012). *Treaty, Law and Covenant in the Ancient Near East.* 3 vols. Wiesbaden: Harrassowitz.

Klengel, Horst. (1974). "Hungerjahre' in Hatti," *Altorientalische Forschungen* 1: 165–74.

Kloos, Helmut, and Rosalie David. (2002). "The Paleoepidemiology of Schistosomiasis in Ancient Egypt," *Human Ecology Review* 9/1: 14–25.

Knoppers, Gary N., and Paul B. Harvey Jr. (2007). "The Pentateuch in Ancient Mediterranean Context: The Publication of Local Lawcodes," in *The Pentateuch as Torah: New Models for Understanding Its Promulgation and Acceptance.* Ed. Gary N. Knoppers and Bernard M. Levinson. Winona Lake, IN: Eisenbrauns. Pp. 105–41.

Koepke, Nikola, and Joerg Baten. (2005a). "Climate and Its Impact on the Biological Standard of Living in North-East, Centre-West and South Europe during the Last 2000 Years," *History of Meteorology* 2: 147–59.

———. (2005b). "The Biological Standard of Living in Europe during the Last Two Millennia," *European Review of Economic History* 9/1: 61–95.

Komlos, John, and Marieluise Bauer. (2004). "From the Tallest to (One of the) Fattest: The Enigmatic Fate of the American Population in the 20th Century," *Economics and Human Biology* 2: 57–74.

Kondrashov, D., Y. Feliks, and M. Ghil. (2005). "Oscillatory Modes of Extended Nile Records (A.D. 622–1922)," *Geophysical Research Letters* 32:n.p.

Koopman, Siem Jan, and Lennart Hoogerheide. (2015). "Analysis of Historical Times Series with Messy Futures: The Case of the Commodity Prices in Babylonia," in *A History of Market Performance: From Ancient Babylonia to the Modern World.* Ed. R. J. van der Spek, Bas van Leeuwen, and Jan Luiten van Zanden. London: Routledge. Pp. 45–67.

Köse, Veli. (2005). "The Origin and Development of Market-Buildings in Hellenistic and Roman Asia Minor," in *Patterns in the Economy of Roman Asia Minor.* Ed. S. Mitchell and C. Katsari. Swansea: Classical Press of Wales. Pp. 139–66.

Kosmin, Paul J. (2014). *The Land of the Elephant Kings: Space, Territory, and Ideology in the Seleucid Empire.* Cambridge, MA: Harvard University Press.

Kostick, C., and F. Ludlow. (2015). "The Dating of Volcanic Events and Their Impacts upon European Climate and Society, 400–800 CE," *European Journal of Post-classical Archaeologies* 5: 7–30.

Kozuh, Michael. (2015). "A Hand Anything but Hidden: Institutions and Markets in First Millennium BCE Mesopotamia," in *Traders in the Ancient Mediterranean*. Ed. Timothy Howe. Chicago: Ares. Pp. 73–100.

Kraeling, Carl H. (1960). "Preface," in *City Invincible: A Symposium on Urbanization and Cultural Development in the Ancient Near East*. Ed. Carl. H. Kraeling and Robert M. Adams. Chicago: Oriental Institute. Pp. v–viii.

Kraeling, Carl H., and Robert M. Adams, eds. (1960). *City Invincible: A Symposium on Urbanization and Cultural Development in the Ancient Near East*. Chicago: Oriental Institute.

Kraus, Jürgen. (2004). *Die Demographie des alten Ägypten: Eine phänomenologie anhand altägyptisacher Quellen*. PhD diss., Georg-August Universität Göttingen.

Kroll, John H. (2008). "The Monetary Use of Weighed Bullion in Archaic Greece," in *The Monetary Systems of the Greeks and Romans*. Ed. W. V. Harris. Oxford: Oxford University Press. Pp. 12–37.

Kron, Geoffrey. (forthcoming). "Growth and Decline: Forms of Growth; Estimating Growth in the Greek World," in *The Oxford Handbook of Economies in the Classical World*. Ed. E. Lo Cascio, A. Bresson, and F. Vele. Oxford: Oxford University Press.

———. (2016). "Classical Greek Trade in Comparative Perspective," in *The Ancient Greek Economy: Markets, Households, and City-States*. Ed. Edward M. Harris, David M. Lewis, and Mark Woolmer. Cambridge University Press. Pp. 356–80.

———. (2015). "Agriculture," in *A Companion to Food in the Ancient World*. Ed. John Wilkins and Robin Nadeau. Malden, MA: Wiley-Blackwell. Pp. 160–72.

———. (2014). "Comparative Evidence and the Reconstruction of the Ancient Economy: Greco-Roman Housing and the Level and Distribution of Wealth and Income," in *Quantifying the Greco-Roman Economy and Beyond*. Ed. François de Callataÿ. Bari: Edipuglia. Pp. 123–46.

———. (2012). "Nutrition, Hygiene, and Mortality: Setting Parameters for Roman Health and Life Expectancy Consistent with Our Comparative Evidence," in *L'impatto della "Peste Antonina."* Ed. E. Lo Cascio. Bari: Edipuglia. Pp. 193–252.

———. (2008a). "The Much Maligned Peasant: Comparative Perspectives on the Productivity of the Small Farmer in Classical Antiquity," in *People, Land, and Politics: Demographic Developments and the Transformation of Roman Italy 300 BC–AD 14*. Ed. Luuk de Ligt and Simon Northwood. Leiden: Brill. Pp. 71–119.

———. (2008b). "Animal Husbandry, Hunting, Fishing, and Fish Distribution," in *The Oxford Handbook of Engineering and Technology in the Classical World*. Ed. John Peter Oleson. Oxford: Oxford University Press. Pp. 175–222.

———. (2005). "Anthropometry, Physical Anthropology, and the Reconstruction of Ancient Health, Nutrition, and Living Standards," *Historia* 54: 68–83.

———. (2004). "Roman Livestock Farming in Southern Italy: The Case against Environmental Determinism," in *Espaces intégrés et ressources naturelles dans l'empire romain*. Ed. Monique Clavel-Lévêque and Ella Hermon. Besançon: Presses Universitaires de Franch-Comté. Pp. 119–34.

———. (2000). "Roman Ley-Farming," *Journal of Roman Archaeology* 13: 277–87.

Kuhrt, Amélie. (2009). "The Persian Empire," in *The Babylonian World*. Ed. Gwendolyn Leick. Paperback ed. London: Routledge. Pp. 562–76.

———. (2007). *The Persian Empire: A Corpus of Sources from the Achaemenid Period.* London: Routledge.

———. (2000). "The Acheamenid Empire (c. 550–330 BCE): Continuities, Adaptations, Transformations," in *Empires*. Ed. Susan E. Alcock, Terence N. D'Altroy, Kathleen D. Morrison, and Carla M. Sinopoli. Cambridge: Cambridge University Press. Pp. 93–123.

———. (1998). "The Old Assyrian Merchants," in *Trade, Traders and the Ancient City*. Ed. Helen Parkins and Christopher Smith. London: Routledge. Pp. 16–30.

———. (1995). *The Ancient Near East, c. 3000–330 BC*. Oxford: Routledge.

Kurke, Leslie. (1999). *Coins, Bodies, Games, and Gold: The Politics of Meaning in Archaic Greece*. Princeton, NJ: Princeton University Press.

Lamb, Hubert H. (1995). *Climate, History and the Modern World*. 2d ed. London: Routledge.

Lamoreaux, Naomi. (2015). "The Future of Economic History Must Be Interdisciplinary," *Journal of Economic History* 75/4: 1251–57.

Landa, J. T. (1994). *Trust, Ethnicity, and Identity: Beyond the New Institutional Economics of Ethnic Trading Networks, Contract Law, and Gift-Exchange*. Ann Arbor: University of Michigan Press.

Landes, David S. (1998). *The Wealth and Poverty of Nations: Why Some Are So Rich and Some So Poor*. New York: Norton.

Lanni, Adriaan. (2006). *The Law Courts of Democratic Athens*. Cambridge: Cambridge University Press.

Lansing, J. Stephen. (2006). *Perfect Order: Recognizing Complexity in Bali*. Princeton, NJ: Princeton University Press.

Larsen, L. B., B. M. Vinther, K. R. Briffa, T. M. Melvin, H. B. Clausen, P. D. Jones, M.-L. Siggaard-Andersen, C. U. Hammer, et al. (2008). "New Ice Core Evidence for a Volcanic Cause of the A.D. 536 Dust Veil," *Geophysical Research Letters* 35/4: L04708.

Larsen, Mogens Trolle. (2015). *Ancient Kanesh: A Merchant Colony in Bronze Age Anatolia*. Cambridge: Cambridge University Press.

———. ed. (1979). *Power and Propaganda: A Symposium on Ancient Empires*. Copenhagen: Akademisk Forlag.

Lattimore, Owen. (1979). "Geography and the Ancient Empires," in *Power and Propaganda: A Symposium on Ancient Empires*. Ed. Mogens Trolle Larsen. Copenhagen: Akademisk Forlag. Pp. 35–40.

Launaro, Alessandro. (2016). "Finley and the Ancient Economy," in *M. I. Finley: An Ancient Historian and His Impact*. Ed. Daniel Jew, Robin Osborne, and Michael Scott. Cambridge: Cambridge University Press. Pp. 227–49.

Laurence, Ray. (1998). "Land Transport in Roman Italy: Costs, Practice and the Economy," in *Trade, Traders and the Ancient City*. Ed. Helen Parkins and Christopher Smith. London: Routledge. Pp. 129–48.

Lawall, Mark. (2016). "Transport Amphoras, Markets, and Changing Practices in the Economies of Greece, Sixth to First Centuries BCE," in *The Ancient Greek Economy: Markets, Households and City-States*. Ed. Edward M. Harris, David M. Lewis, and Mark Woolmer. Cambridge: Cambridge University Press. Pp. 254–73.

———. (2005). "Amphoras and Hellenistic Economies: Addressing the (Over)-Emphasis on Stamped Amphora Handles," in *Making, Moving, and Managing: The New World of Ancient Economies, 323–31 BC*. Ed. Zosia H. Archibald, John K. Davies, and Vincent Gabrielsen. Oxford: Oxbow Books. Pp. 188–232.

LeGrande, Allegra N., Kevin J. Anchukaitis, Lucien von Gunten, and Leonie Goodwin. (2015). "Volcanoes and Climate," special issue of *Past Global Changes* 23/2.

Lehner, Mark. (2015). "Labor and the Pyramids: The Heit El-Ghurab 'Workers Town' at Giza," in *Labor in the Ancient World*. Ed. Piotr Steinkeller and Michael Hudson. Dresden: ISLET-Verlag. Pp. 397–522.

———. (2000). "Fractal House of Pharaoh: Ancient Egypt as a Complex Adaptive System, a Trial Formulation," in *Dynamics in Human and Primate Societies: Agent-Based Modelling of Social and Spatial Processes*. Ed. Timothy Kohler and George Gumerman. New York: Oxford University Press. Pp. 275–353.

Leichty, Erle. (1975). "A. Leo Oppenheim, 1904–1974," *Journal of the American Oriental Society* 95/3: 369–70.

Leick, Gwendolyn, ed. (2009). *The Babylonian World*. Paperback ed. London: Routledge.

Leidwanger, Justin. (2013). "Modeling Distance with Time in Ancient Mediterranean Seafaring: A GIS Application for the Interpretation of Maritime Connectivity," *Journal of Archaeological Science* 40: 3302–8.

Le Rider, Georges. (2001). *La naissance de la monnaie: Pratiques monétaires de l'Orient ancien*. Paris: Presses universitaires de France.

Le Roy Ladurie, Emmanuel. (1979). "Writing the History of the Climate," in *The Territory of the Historian*. Chicago: University of Chicago Press. Pp. 287–91.

Lewis, David M. (2016a). "The Market for Slaves in the Fifth- and Fourth-Century Aegean," in *The Ancient Greek Economy: Markets, Households and City-States*. Ed. Edward M. Harris, David M. Lewis, and Mark Woolmer. Cambridge: Cambridge University Press. Pp. 316–36.

———. (2016b). "Appendix. Commodities in Classical Athens: The Evidence of Old Comedy," in *The Ancient Greek Economy: Markets, Households and City-States*. Ed. Edward M. Harris, David M. Lewis, and Mark Woolmer. Cambridge: Cambridge University Press. Pp. 381–98.

Lewis, M.J.T. (1997). *Millstone and Hammer: The Origins of Water Power*. Hull: University of Hull Press.

Lindgren, James. (1995). "Measuring the Value of Slaves and Free Persons in Ancient Law," *Chicago-Kent Law Review* 71: 149–215.

Lionello, Piero, ed. (2012). *The Climate of the Mediterranean Region: From the Past to the Future*. London: Elsevier.

Lipartito, Kenneth. (2016). "Reassembling the Economic: New Departures in Historical Materialism," *American Historical Review* 121/1: 101–39.

Lippert, Sandra Luisa. (2004). *Ein demotisches juristisches Lehrbuch: Untersuchungen zu Papyrus Berlin P 23757 ro*. Wiesbaden: Harrassowitz.

Lirb, H. J. (1993). "Partners in Agriculture: The Pooling of Resources in Rural *Societies* in Roman Italy," in *De agricultura: In memoriam Pieter Willem de Neeve*. Ed. H. Sancisi-Weerdenburg, R. J. van der Spek, H. C. Teitler, and H. T. Wallinga. Dutch Monographs on Ancient History and Archaeology 10. Amsterdam: Gieben. Pp. 263–95.

Littman, R. J. (2009). "The Plague of Athens: Epidemiology and Paleopathology," *Mount Sinai Journal of Medicine* 76: 456–67.

Liu, Jianguo, et al. (2007). "Complexity of Coupled Human and Natural Systems," *Science* 317/5844: 1513–16. doi: 10.1126/science.1144004.

Liverani, Mario. (2014). *The Ancient Near East: History, Society, and Economy*. London: Routledge.

————. (2013). *Immaginare Babele: Due secoli di Studi sulla città orientale antica*. Rome: Laterza.

————. (2005). "The Near East: The Bronze Age," in *The Ancient Economy: Evidence and Models*. Ed. J. G. Manning and Ian Morris. Stanford, CA: Stanford University Press. Pp. 47–57.

————. (2003). "The Influence of Political Institutions on Trade in the Ancient Near East (Late Bronze to Early Iron Age)," in *Mercanti e politica nel mondo antico*. Ed. Carlo Zaccagnini. Rome: "L'Erma" di Bretschneider. Pp. 119–37.

————. (2000). "The Libyan Caravan Road in Herodotus IV.181–4," *Journal of the Economic and Social History of the Orient* 43/4: 496–520.

————. (1988). *Antico Oriente: Storia, societa, economia*. Rome: Laterza.

Lo Cascio, Elio. (2009). *Crescita e declino: Studi di Storia dell'economia romana*. Rome: "L'Erma" di Bretschneider.

————. (1994). "The Size of the Roman Population: Beloch and the Meaning of the Republican Census Figures," *Journal of Roman Studies* 84: 23–40.

Lo Cascio, Elio, and Paolo Malanima. (2014). "Ancient and Pre-modern Economies: GDP in Roman Empire and Early Modern Europe," in *Quantifying the Greco-Roman Economy and Beyond*. Ed. François de Callataÿ. Bari: Edipuglia. Pp. 229–51.

Lopez, Robert S. (1976). *The Commercial Revolution of the Middle Ages, 950–1350*. Cambridge: Cambridge University Press.

Love, J. R. (1991). *Antiquity and Capitalism: Max Weber and the Sociological Foundations of Roman Civilization*. London: Routledge.

Lucas, Adam R. (2012). "Technological Change," in *The Encyclopedia of Ancient History*. Malden, MA: Wiley-Blackwell. http://onlinelibrary.wiley.com/doi/10.1002/9781444338386.wbeah06321/full. DOI: 10.1002/9781444338386.wbeah06321.

Ludlow, Francis, and J. G. Manning. (2016). "Revolts under the Ptolemies: A Paleoclimatological Perspective," in *Revolt and Resistance in the Ancient Classical World and the Near East: In the Crucible of Empire*. Ed. John J. Collins and J. G. Manning. Leiden: Brill. Pp. 154–71.

Lukaszewicz, A. (1999). "Le Papyrus Edfou 8 soixante and après," in *Tell-Edfou soixante ans après: Actes du colloque franco-polonais, Le Caire- 15 Octobre 1996*. Cairo: Institut français d'Archéologie orientale. Pp. 29–35.

Luterbacher, J., et al. (2016). "European Summer Temperatures since Roman Times," *Environmental Research Letters* 11/2. doi: 10.1088/1748–9326/11/2/024001.

————. (2012). "Review of 2000 Years of Paleoclimatic Evidence in the Mediterranean," in *The Climate of the Mediterranean Region: From the Past to the Future*. Ed. P. Lionello. London: Elsevier. Pp. 87–185.

Luterbacher, J., and C. Pfister. (2015). "The Year without a Summer," *Nature Geoscience* 8: 246–48.

Lyttkens, Carl Hampus. (2013). *Economic Analysis of Institutional Change in Ancient Greece: Politics, Taxation and Rational Behavior*. London: Routledge.

Ma, Debin. (2011). "Law and Economy in Traditional China, a 'Legal Origin' Perspective on the Great Divergence," in *Law and Long-Term Economic Change: A Eurasian Perspective*. Ed. Debin Ma and Jan Luiten van Zanden. Stanford, CA: Stanford University Press. Pp. 46–67.

Ma, Debin, and Jan Luiten van Zanden. (2011a). "Law and Long-Term Economic Change: An Editorial Introduction," in *Law and Long-Term Economic Change: A Eurasian*

Perspective. Ed. Debin Ma and Jan Luiten van Zanden. Stanford, CA: Stanford University Press. Pp. 1–18.

———. eds. (2011b). *Law and Long-Term Economic Change: A Eurasian Perspective.* Stanford, CA: Stanford University Press.

Ma, John. (2003). "Peer Polity Interaction in the Hellenistic Age," *Past and Present* 180: 9–39.

———. (2000). *Antiochos III and the Cities of Western Asia Minor.* Oxford: Oxford University Press.

Macdowell, Douglas M. (2009). *Demosthenes the Orator.* Oxford: Oxford University Press.

Mackil, Emily. (2013). *Creating a Common Polity: Religion, Economy, and Politics in the Making of the Greek Koinon.* Berkeley: University of California Press.

Macklin, Mark G., et al. (2015). "A New Model of River Dynamics, Hydroclimatic Change and Human Settlement in the Nile Valley Derived from Meta-analysis of the Holocene Fluvial Archive," *Quaternary Science Reviews* 130: 109–23.

Maddison, Angus. (2007). *Contours of the Roman Economy, 1–2020 AD: Essays in Macroeconomic History.* Oxford: Oxford University Press.

Maehler, Herwig. (1983). "Egypt under the Last Ptolemies," *Bulletin of the Institute of Classical Studies* 30: 1–16.

Magnusson, Lars. (1994). *Mercantilism: The Shaping of an Economic Language.* London: Routledge.

Magny, Michel, et al. (2013) "North-South Palaeohydrological Contrasts in the Central Mediterranean during the Holocene: Tentative Synthesis and Working Hypotheses," *Climate of the Past* 9: 2043–71.

Maine, Henry. (1861). *Ancient Law, Its Connection with Early History of Society and Its Relation to Modern Ideas.* London: John Murray.

Mair, Victor H., and Jane Hickman, eds. (2014). *Reconfiguring the Silk Road: New Research on East-West Exchange in Antiquity.* Philadelphia: University of Pennsylvania Press.

Mairs, Rachel. (2014). *The Hellenistic Far East.* Berkeley: University of California Press.

Malanima, Paolo. (2013). "Energy Consumption in the Roman World," in *The Ancient Mediterranean Environment between Science and History.* Ed. W. V. Harris. Leiden: Brill. Pp. 13–36.

Malinine, Michel. (1953). *Choix de Textes juridiques en Hiératique "anormal" et en démotique: Première Partie.* Paris: Librairie Ancienne Honoré Champion.

Malinowsky, Bronislaw. (1922). *Argonauts of the Western Pacific: An Account of Native Enterprise and Adventure in the Archipelagoes of Melanesian New Guinea.* London: Routledge and Kegan Paul.

Malkin, Irad. (2011). *A Small Greek World: Networks in the Ancient Mediterranean.* Oxford: Oxford University Press.

Manassa, Colleen. (2003). *The Great Karnak Inscription of Merneptah: Grand Strategy in the 13th Century BC.* New Haven, CT: Yale Egyptological Seminar.

Mann, Michael. (1986). *The Sources of Social Power.* Vol. 1, *A History of Power from the Beginning to AD 1760.* Cambridge: Cambridge University Press.

Manning, Joseph G. (forthcoming). "Leagues and Kingdoms: Beyond the City-State," in *The Oxford Handbook of Economies in the Classical World.* Ed. Alain Bresson, Elio Lo Cascio, and François Velde. Oxford: Oxford University Press.

———. (2015a). "Hellenistic Trade(rs)," in *Traders in the Ancient Mediterranean.* Ed. Timothy Howe. Chicago: Ares. Pp. 101–39.

———. ed. (2015b). *Writing History in Time of War: Michael Rostovtzeff, Elias Bickerman and the "Hellenization" of Asia*. Stuttgart: Steiner Verlag.

———. (2011). "Networks, Hierarchies, and Markets in the Ptolemaic Economy," in *The Economies of Hellenistic Societies, Third to First Centuries BC*. Ed. Zosia H. Archibald, John K. Davies, and Vincent Gabrielsen. Oxford: Oxford University Press. Pp. 296–323.

———. (2010). *The Last Pharaohs: Egypt under the Ptolemies, 305–30 B.C.* Princeton, NJ: Princeton University Press.

———. (2005). "Texts, Contexts, Subtexts and Interpretative Frameworks: Beyond the Parochial and Toward (Dynamic) Modeling of the Ptolemaic State and the Ptolemaic Economy," *Bulletin of the American Society of Papyrologists* 42: 235–56.

———. (2003). *Land and Power in Ptolemaic Egypt: The Structure of Land Tenure*. Cambridge: Cambridge University Press.

———. (2002–3). "A Ptolemaic Agreement concerning a Donkey with an Unusual Warranty Clause: The Strange Case of P. Dem. Princ. 1 (inv. 7524)," *Enchoria* 28: 46–61.

———. (1999). "The Auction of Pharaoh," in *Gold of Praise: Studies on Ancient Egypt in Honor of Edward F. Wente*. Ed. Emily Teeter and John A. Larson. Chicago: Oriental Institute. Pp. 277–84.

———. (1994). "Land and Status in Ptolemaic Egypt: The Status Designation 'Occupation Title + B3k + Divine Name," in *Grund und Boden in Altägypten: (Rechtliche und Sozio-Ökonomische Verhältnisse); Akten des internationalen Symposions Tübingen 18.–20. Juni 1990*. Ed. Schafik Allam. Tübingen: Selbstverlag des Herausgebers. Pp. 147–75.

Manning, Joseph G., and Ian Morris, eds. (2005). *The Ancient Economy: Evidence and Models*. Stanford, CA: Stanford University Press.

Manning, Joseph G., et al. (2017). "Volcanic Suppression of Nile Summer Flooding Triggers Revolt and Constrains Interstate Conflict in Ancient Egypt," *Nature Communications* 8.

Manning, Sturt W. (2013). "The Roman World and Climate: Context, Relevance of Climate Change, and Some Issues," in *The Ancient Mediterranean Environment between Science and History*. Ed. W. V. Harris. Leiden: Brill. Pp. 103–70.

Marasco, Gabriele. (1988). *Economia, commerce e politica nel Mediterraneo fra il III e il II secolo a. C.* Florence: Dipartimento di Storia.

Marchand, Sylvie, and Antigone Marangou, eds. (2007). *Amphores d'Égypte de la Basse Époque à l'Époque arabe*. Cairo: Institut français d'Archéologie orientale.

Marchant, Jo. (2009). *Decoding the Heavens: Solving the Mystery of the World's First Computer*. Cambridge, MA: Da Capo.

———. (2006). "In Search of Lost Time," *Nature* 444: 534–38 (November 30, 2006). doi: 10.1038/444534a.

Marcus, Joyce. (1998). "The Peaks and Valleys of Ancient States: An Extension of the Dynamic Model," in *Archaic States*. Ed. Gary M. Feinman and Joyce Marcus. Santa Fe: School of American Research Press. Pp. 59–94.

Marek, Christian. (2016). *In the Land of a Thousand Gods: A History of Asia Minor in the Ancient World*. In collaboration with Peter Frei. Trans. Steven Rendall. Princeton, NJ: Princeton University Press.

Maresch, Klaus. (1996). *Bronze und Silber: Papyrologische Beiträge zur Geschichte der Währung im ptolemäischen und römischen Ägypten bis zum 2. Jahrhundert n. Chr.* Papyrologica Coloniensia 25. Opladen: Westdeutscher Verlag.

Margaritis, Evi. (2016). "Agricultural Production and Domestic Activities in Rural Hellenistic Greece," in *The Ancient Greek Economy: Markets, Households and City-States.* Ed. Edward M. Harris, David M. Lewis, and Mark Woolmer. Cambridge: Cambridge University Press. Pp. 187–203.

Marriner, Nick, et al. (2012). "ITCZ and ENSO-Like Pacing of Nile Delta Hydrogeomorphology during the Holocene," *Quaternary Science Reviews* 45: 73–84.

Marshall, Gordon. (1982). *In Search of the Spirit of Capitalism: Max Weber's Protestant Ethic Thesis.* London: Hutchinson.

Marsot, Afaf Lutfi al-Sayyid. (1984). *Egypt in the Reign of Muhammad Ali.* Cambridge: Cambridge University Press.

Martin, Cary J. (2009). *Demotic Papyri from the Memphite Necropolis in the Collections of the National Museum of Antiquities in Leiden, the British Museum and the Hermitage Museum.* Turnhout: Brepols.

Martini, I. Peter, and Ward Chesworth, eds. (2010). *Landscape and Societies: Selected Cases.* Dordrecht: Springer.

Marzano, Annalisa. (2013). "Agricultural Production in the Hinterland of Rome: Wine and Olive Oil," in *The Roman Agricultural Economy: Organization, Investment, and Production.* Ed. Alan Bowman and Andrew Wilson. Oxford: Oxford University Press. Pp. 85–106.

Massa, Charly, Fabrice Monna, Vincent Bichet, Émilie Gauthier, Rémi Losno, and Hervé Richard. (2015). "Inverse Modeling of Past Lead Atmospheric Deposition in South Greenland," *Atmospheric Environment* 105: 121–29.

Mathewson, Kent. (2017). "Obituary: Karl Wilhelm Butzer, 1934–2016," *Journal of Historical Geography* 55: 93–98.

Matthews, John A., et al., eds. (2012). *The Sage Handbook of Environmental Change.* Vol. 1. London: Sage.

Mattingly, David, ed. (2010). *The Archaeology of Fazzan.* Vol. 3, *Excavations of C. M. Daniels.* London: Society for Libyan Studies.

———. (2007). *The Archaeology of Fazzan.* Vol. 2, *Site Gazetteer, Pottery and Other Survey Finds.* London: Society for Libyan Studies.

———. (2003). *The Archaeology of Fazzan.* Vol. 1, *Synthesis.* London: Society for Libyan Studies.

———. (1994). "Regional Variation in Roman Oleoculture: Some Problems of Comparability," in *Landuse in the Roman Empire.* Ed. Jesper Carlsen, Peter Ørsetd, and Jens Erik Skydsgaard. Rome: "L'Erma" di Bretschneider. Pp. 91–106.

Mattingly, David, and R. Bruce Hitchner. (1995). "Roman Africa: An Archaeological Review," *Journal of Roman Studies* 85: 165–213.

Maucourant, J. (2012). "New Institutional Economics and History," *Journal of Economic Issues,* 46/1: 193–208.

Maucourant, J., and S. Plocinaczak. (2013). "The Institution, the Economy and the Market: Karl Polanyi's Institutional Thought for Economists," *Review of Political Economy* 25/3: 512–31.

Mayer, Emanuel. (2012). *The Ancient Middle Classes: Urban Life and Aesthetics in the Roman Empire, 100 BCE–250 CE.* Cambridge, MA: Harvard University Press.

Mayerson, P. (2002). "Three Pharaonic Crops in the Ptolemaic Period: ὄλυρα (Emmer Wheat) and Maslins κριθόπυρον and ὀλυρόκριθον," *Zeitschrift für Papyrologie und Epigraphik* 141: 210–13.

Mayshar, Joram, Omer Moav, and Zvika Neeman. (2014). "Geography, Transparency and Institutions," working paper. http://www2.warwick.ac.uk/fac/soc/economics/staff/omoav/submission_2013398_paper.pdf.

Mazza, Roberta. (2001). *L'archivio degli Apioni: Terra, lavoro e proprieta senatoria nell'Egitto tardo-antico.* Munera 17. Bari: Edipuglia.

McClish, Mark, and Patrick Olivelle. (2012). *The Arthasastra: Selections from the Classic Indian Work on Statecraft.* Indianapolis: Hackett.

McCloskey, Deirdre N. (2015). "Max U vs. Humanomics: A Critique of Neo-institutionalism," *Journal of Institutional Economics.* doi: 10.1017/S1744137415000053.

———. (2010). *Bourgeois Dignity: Why Economics Can't Explain the Modern World.* Chicago: University of Chicago Press.

———. (1996). "The Economics of Choice: Neoclassical Supply and Demand," in *Economics and the Historian.* Ed. T. G. Rawski et al. Berkeley: University of California Press. Pp. 122–58.

———. (1990). *If You're So Smart: The Narrative of Economic Expertise.* Chicago: University of Chicago Press.

McCloskey, Donald N. (1976). "Does the Past Have Useful Economics?," *Journal of Economic Literature* 14/2: 434–61.

McConnell, Joseph R., Gregg W. Lamorey, Steven W. Lambert, and Kendrick C. Taylor. (2002). "Continuous Ice-Core Chemical Analyses Using Inductively Coupled Plasma Mass Spectometry," *Environmental Science and Technology* 36/1: 7–11.

McCormick, Michael. (2001). *Origins of the European Economy: Communications and Commerce AD 300–900.* Cambridge: Cambridge University Press.

McCormick, Michael, et al. (2012). "Climate Change during and after the Roman Empire: Reconstructing the Past from Scientific and Historical Evidence," *Journal of Interdisciplinary History* 43/2: 169–220.

McEvedy, C., and Richard Jones. (1978). *Atlas of World Population History.* New York: Puffin.

McGing, Brian C. (1997). "Revolt Egyptian Style: Internal Opposition to Ptolemaic Rule," *Archiv für Papyrusforschung und verwandte Gebiete* 43/2: 273–314.

McMichael, Anthony J. (2011). "Insights from Past Millennia into Climatic Impacts on Human Health and Survival," *Proceedings of the National Academy of Sciences* 109/13: 4730–37.

McNeill, J. R. (2000). *Something New under the Sun: An Environmental History of the Twentieth-Century World.* New York: W. W. Norton.

———. (1997). "History Upside Down," *New York Review of Books*, May 15, 1997. http://www.nybooks.com/articles/1997/05/15/history-upside-down/.

———. (1992). *The Mountains of the Mediterranean world: An Environmental History.* Cambridge: Cambridge University Press.

McNeill, W. H. (1992). *The Global Condition: Conquerors, Catastrophe and Community.* Princeton, NJ: Princeton University Press.

McNeill, William H. (1976). *Plagues and People.* Garden City, NJ: Anchor.

McPherson, James M. (1988). *Battle Cry of Freedom: The Civil War Era.* New York: Oxford University Press.

Meadows, Andrew, and Kirsty Shipton, eds. (2001). *Money and Its Uses in the Ancient Greek World.* Oxford: Oxford University Press.

Medema, Steven G., and Warren J. Samuels. (2013). *The History of Economic Thought: A Reader.* 2d ed. London: Routledge.

Meiggs, Russell. (1982). *Trees and Timber in the Ancient Mediterranean World*. Oxford: Oxford University Press.

Meikle, Scott. (1995/2002). "Modernism, Economics, and the Ancient Economy," in Walter Scheidel and Sitta von Reden, eds., *The Ancient Economy*, New York: Routledge, 2002, 233–50. Originally published in *Proceedings of the Cambridge Philosophical Society* 41 (1995): 174–91.

———. (1995). *Aristotle's Economic Thought*. Oxford: Clarendon.

Ménard, Claude, and Mary M. Shirley. (2014). "The Contribution of Douglass North to New Institutional Economics," in *Institutions, Property Rights, and Economic Growth: The Legacy of Douglass North*. Ed. Sebastian Galiani and Itai Sened. Cambridge: Cambridge University Press. Pp. 11–29.

———. eds. (2005). *Handbook of New Institutional Economics*. Dordrecht: Springer Verlag.

Menard, R. R. (1991). "Transport Costs and Long-Range Trade, 1300–1800: Was There a European 'Transport Revolution' in the Early Modern Era?" in *The Political Economy of Merchant Empires*. Ed. J. D. Tracy. Cambridge: Cambridge University Press. Pp. 228–75.

Menger, Carl. (1909). "Geld," in *Schriften über Geldtheorie und Währungspolitik*. Ed. F. A. Hayek. Tübingen: Mohr, 1970. Pp. 1–116. English translation in *Carl Menger and the Evolution of Payments Systems: From Barter to Electronic Money*. Ed. M. Latzer and S. Schmitz. Cheltenham: Edward Elgar, 2002. Pp. 25–107.

Menu, Bernadette. (1988). "Les Actes de Vente en Égypte ancienne, particulièrement sous les Rois kouchites et saïtes," *Journal of Egyptian Archaeology* 74: 165–81. Reprinted *in Recherches sur l'Histoire juridique, économique et sociale de l'ancienne Égypte*. Vol. 2. Cairo: Institut français d'Archéolgie orientale, 1998. Pp. 305–23.

Metcalf, William E., ed. (2012). *The Oxford Handbook of Greek and Roman Coinage*. Oxford: Oxford University Press.

Migeotte, Léopold. (2014). *Les finances des cités grecques: Aux périodes classique et hellénistique*. Paris: Les Belles Lettres.

Mikhail, Alan. (2015). "Ottoman Iceland: A Climate History," *Environmental History* 20: 262–84.

Miller, Geoffrey P., ed. (2010). *Economics of Ancient Law*. Cheltenham: Edward Elgar.

Miller, Margaret C. (1997). *Athens and Persia in the Fifth Century BC: A Study in Cultural Receptivity*. Cambridge: Cambridge University Press.

Millett, Paul. (1991). *Lending and Borrowing in Ancient Athens*. Cambridge: Cambridge University Press.

Miron, Ronny. (2012). *Karl Jaspers: From Selfhood to Being*. Amsterdam: Rodopi.

Mitchell, Stephen. (2003). "The Galatians: Representation and Reality," in *A Companion to the Hellenistic World*. Ed. Andrew Erskine. Malden: Blackwell. Pp. 280–93.

Mitchell, Timothy. (2008). "Rethinking Economy," *Geoforum* 39: 1116–21.

———. (2002). *Rule of Experts: Egypt, Techno-Politics, Modernity*. Berkeley: University of California Press.

Modrzejewski, Joseph Mélèze. (2011). *Droit et Justice dans le Monde grec et hellénistique*. *Journal of Juristic Papyrology*. Supplement 10. Warsaw: Warsaw University.

Moeller, Nadine. (2016). *The Archaeology of Urbanism in Ancient Egypt from the Predynastic Period to the End of the Middle Kingdom*. Cambridge: Cambridge University Press.

Mokyr, Joel. (2016). *A Culture of Growth: The Origins of the Modern Economy*. Princeton, NJ: Princeton University Press.

———. (2014). "Culture, Institutions, and Modern Growth," in *Institutions, Property Rights, and Economic Growth: The Legacy of Douglass North*. Ed. Sebastian Galiani and Itai Sened. Cambridge: Cambridge University Press, Pp. 151–91.

———. (2005). "Is There a Theory of Economic History?," in *The Evolutionary Foundations of Economics*. Ed. Kurt Dopfer. Cambridge: Cambridge University Press. Pp. 195–218.

———. (1991). "Evolutionary Biology, Technological Change and Economic History," *Bulletin of Economic Research* 43/2: 127–49.

Mokyr, Joel, and Avner Greif. (forthcoming). "Institutions and Economic History: A Critique of Professor McCloskey," with Avner Greif. *Journal of Institutional Economics*.

Möller, Astride. (2005). "Naukratis as Port-of-Trade Revisited," *Topoi* 12: 183–92.

———. (2001). "Naukratis; or, How to Identify a Port of Trade," in *Prehistory and History: Ethnicity, Class and Political Economy*. Ed. D. W. Tandy. Montreal: Black Rose Books. Pp. 145–58.

———. (2000). *Naukratis: Trade in Archaic Greece*. Oxford: Oxford University Press.

Momigliano, Arnaldo. (1987). "Moses Finley on Slavery: A Personal Note," in *Classical Slavery*. Ed. Moses I. Finley. London: F. Cass. Pp. 1–8.

———. (1953). "In Memoria di Michele Rostovtzeff 1870–1952," *Rivista storica italiana* 66: 67–106.

Monroe, Christopher Mountfort. (2011). "{~?~thispace; also, please correct orientation of single open quote mark.}'From luxuries to anxieties': A Liminal View of the Late Bronze Age World-System," in *Interweaving Worlds: Systemic Interactions in Eurasia, 7th to 1st Millennia BC*. Ed. Toby C. Wilkinson, Susan Sherratt, and John Bennet. Oxford: Oxbow Books. Pp. 87–99.

———. (2010). "Sunk Costs at Late Bronze Age Uluburun," *Bulletin of the American Schools of Oriental Research* 357: 15–29.

———. (2009). *Scales of Fate: Trade, Tradition, and Transformation in the Eastern Mediterranean ca. 1350–1175 BCE*. Münster: Ugarit-Verlag.

Monson, Andrew. (2012). *From the Ptolemies to the Romans: Political and Economic Change in Egypt*. Cambridge: Cambridge University Press.

———. (2010). "Rules of an Egyptian Religious Association from the Early Second Century BCE" (with C. Arlt), in *Honi soit qui mal y pense: Studien zum pharaonischen, griechisch-römischen und spätantiken Ägypten zu Ehren von Heinz-Josef Thissen*. Ed. H. Knuf, C. Leitz, and D. von Recklinghausen. Orientalia Lovaniensia Analecta 194. Leuven: Peeters. Pp. 113–22.

Monson, Andrew, and Walter Scheidel, eds. (2015). *Fiscal Regimes and the Political Economy of Premodern States*. Cambridge: Cambridge University Press.

Morel, Jean-Paul. (2007). "Early Rome and Italy," in *The Cambridge Economic History of the Greco-Roman World*. Ed. Walter Scheidel, Ian Morris, and Richard Saller. Cambridge: Cambridge University Press. Pp. 487–510.

Morelli, Franco. (2011). "Dal Mar Rosso ad Alessandria. Il *verso* (ma anche il *recto*) del 'papiro di Muziris' (SB XVIII 13167)," *Tyche* 26: 199–233.

Moreno, Alfonson. (2007). "Athenian Wheat-Tsars: Black Sea Grain and Elite Culture," in *The Black Sea in Antiquity: Regional and Inter-regional Economic Exchanges*. Ed. Vincent Gabrielsen and John Lund. Aarhus: Aarhus University Press. Pp. 69–84.

Moreno García, Juan Carlos. (2016a). "Economies in Transition: Trade, "Money," Labour and Nomads at the Turn of the 1st Millennium BC," in *Dynamics of Production in the Ancient Near East, 1300–5000 BC*. Oxford: Oxbow. Pp. 1–39.

———. (2016b). "Temples and Agricultural Labor in Egypt, from the Late New Kingdom to the Saite Period," in *Dynamics of Production in the Ancient Near East, 1300–5000 BC*. Ed. Juan Carlos Moreno García. Oxford: Oxbow. Pp. 223–56.

———. (2015). "L'évolution des status de la main-d'œuvre rurale en Égypte de la fin du Nouvel Empire à l'époque Saïte (ca. 1150–525 av. J.-C.)," in *La main d'oeuvre agricole en Méditerranée archaïque*. Ed. J. Zurbach. Bordeaux: Éditions Ausonius. Pp. 15–48.

———. (2014). "Recent Developments in the Social and Economic History of Ancient Egypt," *Journal of Ancient Near Eastern History* 2014/1–2: 231–61.

———. (2012). "Households," in *The UCLA Encyclopedia of Egyptology*. https://escholar ship.org/uc/item/2bn8c9gz.

———. (2009). "From Dracula to Rostovtzeff; or, The Misadventures of Economic History in Early Egyptology," in *Das Ereignis—Geschichtsschreibung zwischen Vorfall und Befund (IBAES, 10)*. Ed. M. Fitzenreiter. London: Golden House. Pp. 175–98.

———. (2007). "The State and the Organization of the Rural Landscape in 3rd Millennium BC Pharaonic Egypt," in *Aridity, Change and Conflict in Africa*. Ed. Michael Bollig, Olaf Bubenzer, Ralf Vogelsang, and Hans-Peter Wotzka. Cologne: Heinrich-Barth-Institut. Pp. 313–30.

Morgan, Mary S. (2003). "Economics," in *The Cambridge History of Science*. Vol. 7, *The Modern Social Sciences*. Ed. Theodore M. Porter and Dorothy Ross. Cambridge: Cambridge University Press. Pp. 275–305.

Morkot, Robert G. (2016). "North-East Africa and Trade at the Crossroads of the Nile Valley, the Mediterranean and the Red Sea," in *Dynamics of Production in the Ancient Near East, 1300–5000 BC*. Ed. Juan Carlos Moreno García. Oxford: Oxbow. Pp. 257–74.

Morley, Neville. (2007). *Trade in Classical Antiquity*. Cambridge: Cambridge University Press.

———. (2004). *Theories, Models and Concepts in Ancient History*. London: Routledge.

———. (2001). "Demography and Development in Classical Antiquity," in *Demography and the Graeco-Roman World: New Insights and Approaches*. Ed. Claire Holleran and April Pudsey. Cambridge: Cambridge University Press. Pp. 14–36.

———. (1999). *Writing Ancient History*. Ithaca, NY: Cornell University Press.

———. (1996). *Metropolis and Hinterland: The City of Rome and the Italian Economy 200 BC–AD 200*. Cambridge: Cambridge University Press.

Morris, Ian. (2014). *War! What Is It Good For? Conflict and the Progress of Civilization from the Primates to the Robots*. New York: Farrar, Straus, Giroux.

———. (2013). *The Measure of Civilization: How Social Development Decides the Fate of Nations*. Princeton, NJ: Princeton University Press.

———. (2010). *Why the West Rules—for Now: The Patterns of History, and What They Reveal about the Future*. New York: Farrar, Straus, Giroux.

———. (2009). "The Greater Athenian State," in *The Dynamics of Ancient Empires: State Power from Assyria to Byzantium*. Ed. I. Morris and W. Scheidel. Oxford: Oxford University Press. Pp. 99–177.

———. (2007). "Early Iron Age Greece," in *The Cambridge Economic History of the Greco-Roman World*. Ed. Walter Scheidel, Ian Morris, and Richard Saller. Cambridge: Cambridge University Press. Pp. 211–41.

———. (2006). "The Growth of Greek Cities in the First Millennium BC," in *Urbanism in the Preindustrial World: Cross-Cultural Approaches*. Ed. Glenn. R. Story. Tuscaloosa: University of Alabama Press. Pp. 27–51.

———. (2005). "Archaeology, Standards of Living, and Greek Economic History," in *The Ancient Economy: Evidence and Models*. Ed. J. G. Manning and Ian Morris. Stanford, CA: Stanford University Press. Pp. 91–126.

———. (2004). "Classical Archaeology," in *A Companion to Archaeology*. Ed. John Bintliff. Malden, MA: Blackwell. Pp. 253–71.

———. (2003). "Mediterraneanization," *Mediterranean Historical Review* 18: 30–55.

———. (2002). "Hard Surfaces," in *Money, Labor and Land: Approaches to Economies of Ancient Greece*. London: Routledge. Pp. 8–43.

———. (2000). *Archaeology as Cultural History: Words and Things in Iron Age Greece*. Malden, MA: Blackwell.

———. (1999). "Foreword," in *The Ancient Economy* by M. I. Finley. 2d ed. Berkeley: University of California Press. Pp. ix–xxxvi.

———. (1994). "The Athenian Economy Twenty Years after *The Ancient Economy*," *Classical Philology* 89/4: 351–66.

———. (1986). "Gift and commodity in archaic Greece." *Man*, n.s., 21: 1–17.

Morris, Ian, and J. G. Manning. (2005a). "The Economic Sociology of the Ancient Mediterranean World," in *The Handbook of Economic Sociology*. 2d ed. Ed. Neil J. Smelser and Richard Swedburg. Princeton, NJ: Princeton University Press. Pp. 131–59.

———. (2005b). "Introduction," in *The Ancient Economy: Evidence and Models*. Stanford, CA: Stanford University Press. Pp. 1–44.

Morris, Ian, Richard P. Saller, and Walter Scheidel. (2007). "Introduction," in *The Cambridge Economic History of the Greco-Roman World*. Ed. Walter Scheidel, Ian Morris, and Richard Saller. Cambridge: Cambridge University Press. Pp. 1–12.

Mouritsen, H. (2011). *The Freedman in the Roman World*. Cambridge: Cambridge University Press.

Mueller, Katja. (2006). *Settlements of the Ptolemies: City Foundations and New Settlement in the Hellenistic World*. Leuven: Peeters.

Muhs, Brian P. (2016). *The Ancient Egyptian Economy 3000–30 BCE*. Cambridge: Cambridge University Press.

———. (2015a). "Transaction Costs and Institutional Change in Egypt, ca. 1070–525 B.C.," in *Law and Transaction Costs in the Ancient Economy*. Ed. Dennis Kehoe, David M. Ratzan, and Uri Yiftach. Ann Arbor: University of Michigan Press. Pp. 80–98.

———. (2015b). "Money, Taxes, and Maritime Trade in Late Period Egypt," in *Thonis-Heracleion in Context*. Ed. Damian Robinson and Franck Goddio. Oxford: Oxford Centre for Maritime Archaeology. Pp. 91–99.

———. (2011). *Receipts, Scribes, and Collectors in Early Ptolemaic Thebes (O. Taxes 2)*. Leuven: Peeters.

———. (2001). "Membership in Private Associations in Ptolemaic Tebtunis," *Journal of the Economic and Social History of the Orient* 44/1: 1–21.

Müller, Christel, and Claire Hasenohr, eds. (2002). *Les Italiens dans le monde grec: IIe siècle av. J.-C.-Ier siècle ap. J.-C. Circulation, activités, integration*. Paris: École Française d'Athènes.

Müller, Gerfrid G. W. (1995–96). "Die Teuerung in Babylon im 6. Jh. v.Chr.," *Archiv für Orientforschung* 42/43: 163–75.

Müller-Wollermann, Renata. (2016). "Temples, Trade and Money in Egypt in the 1st Millennium BC," in *Dynamics of Production in the Ancient Near East, 1300–500 BC*. Ed. Juan Carlos Moreno García. Oxford: Oxbow. Pp. 275–88.

Murray, Sarah C. (2017). *The Collapse of the Mycenaean Economy: Imports, Trade, and Institutions 1300–700 BCE*. Cambridge: Cambridge University Press.

Murray, W. M. (2012). *The Age of Titans: The Rise and Fall of the Great Hellenistic Navies*. Oxford: Oxford University Press.

Muscheler, Raimund, and Erich Fischer. (2012). "Solar and Volcanic Forcing of Decadal-to Millennial-Scale Climatic Variations," in *The Sage Handbook of Environmental Change*. Ed. John A. Matthews et al. Vol. 1. London: Sage. Pp. 444–70.

Nafissi, Mohammed. (2005). *Ancient Athens and Modern Ideology: Value, Theory, and Evidence in Historical Sciences: Max Weber, Karl Polanyi and Moses Finley*. London: Institute of Classical Studies.

———. (2000). "On the Foundations of Athenian Democracy: Marx's Paradox and Weber's Solution," *Max Weber Studies* 1: 56–83.

Naiden, Fred S. (2014). "Finley's War Years," *American Journal of Philology* 135/2: 243–66.

Nakassis, Dimitri. (2013). *Individuals and Society in Mycenaean Pylos*. Leiden: Brill.

Neal, Larry, and Jeffrey G. Williamson, eds. (2014). *The Cambridge History of Capitalism*. 2 vols. Cambridge: Cambridge University Press.

Needham, Joseph, Ling Wang, and Derek J. De Solla Price. (1986). *Heavenly Clockwork: The Great Astronomical Clocks of Medieval China*. 2d. ed. Cambridge: Cambridge University Press.

Nevett, Lisa C. (1999). *House and Society in the Ancient Greek World*. Cambridge: Cambridge University Press.

Nicholson, Paul T., and Ian Shaw, eds. (2000). *Ancient Egyptian Materials and Technology*. Cambridge: Cambridge University Press.

Niemeyer, Hans Georg. (2006). "The Phoenicians in the Mediterranean: Between Expansion and Colonization: A Non-Greek Model of Overseas Settlement and Presence," in *Greek Colonization: An Account of Greek Colonies and Other Settlements Overseas*. Ed. Gocha R. Tsetskhladze. Vol. 1. Leiden: Brill. Pp. 143–68.

———. (2004). "The Phoenicians and the Birth of a Multinational Mediterranean Society," in *Commerce and Monetary Systems in the Ancient World: Means of Transmission and Cultural Interaction*. Ed. Robert Rollinger and Christoph Ulf. Munich: Franz Steiner Verlag. Pp. 245–56.

Nigro, Lorenzo. (2013). "Before the Greeks: The Earliest Phoenician Settlement in Motya—Recent Discoveries by Rome 'La Sapienza' Expedition," *Vicino Oriente* 17: 39–74.

Nishi, Akihiro, et al. (2015). "Inequality and Visibility of Wealth in Experimental Social Networks," *Nature* 526: 426–29. doi:10.1038/nature15392.

North, Douglass. (2005). *Understanding the Process of Economic Change*. Princeton, NJ: Princeton University Press.

———. (1990). *Institutions, Institutional Change and Economic Performance*. Cambridge: Cambridge University Press.

———. (1986). "A Neoclassical Theory of the State," in *Rational Choice*. Ed. Jon Elster. New York: New York University Press. Pp. 248–60.

————. (1981). *Structure and Change in Economic History.* New York: Norton.

North, Douglass C., and Robert Paul Thomas. (1973). *The Rise of the Western World: A New Economic History.* Cambridge: Cambridge University Press.

North, Douglass, John Joseph Wallis, and Barry Weingast. (2009). *Violence and Social Orders: A Conceptual Framework for Interpreting Recorded History.* New York: Cambridge University Press. Paperback with new foreword, 2013.

Novick, Peter. (1988). *That Noble Dream: The "Objectivity Question" and the American Historical Profession.* Cambridge: Cambridge University Press.

Nunn, Nathan, and Diego Puga. (2012). "Ruggedness: The Blessing of Bad Geography in Africa," *Review of Economics and Statistics* 94: 2–36.

Nur, Amos. (2000). "Poseidon's Horses: Plate Tectonics and Earthquake Storms in the Late Bronze Age Aegean and Eastern Mediterranean," *Journal of Archaeological Sciences* 27: 43–63.

Nur, Amos, with Dawn Burgess. (2008). *Apocalypse: Earthquakes, Archaeology, and the Wrath of God.* Princeton, NJ: Princeton University Press. Pp. 224–45.

Ober, Josiah. (2015a). *The Rise and Fall of Classical Greece.* Princeton, NJ: Princeton University Press.

————. (2015b). "Access, Fairness, and Transaction Costs: Nikophon's Law on Silver Coinage (Athens, 375/4 BCE)," in *Law and Transaction Costs in the Ancient Economy.* Ed. Dennis Kehoe, David M. Ratzan, and Uri Yiftach. Ann Arbor: University of Michigan Press. Pp. 51–79.

————. (2014). "Greek Economic Performance, 800–300 BCE: A Comparison Case," in *Quantifying the Greco-Roman Economy and Beyond.* Ed. François de Callataÿ. Bari: Edipuglia. Pp. 103–22.

————. (1993). "Urbanism in Bronze Age Egypt and Northeast Africa," in *The Archaeology of Africa: Food, Metals and Towns.* Ed. Thurstan Shaw, Paul Sinclair, Bassey Andah, and Alex Okpoko. London: Routledge. Pp. 570–86.

O'Connor, David. (1993). "Urbanism in Bronze Age Egypt and Northeast Africa," in *The Archaeology of Africa: Food, Metals and Towns.* Ed. Thurston Shaw, Paul Sinclair, Bassey Andah, and Alex Okpoko. London: Routledge. Pp. 570–86.

O'Connor, David, and David P. Silverman. (1995). *Ancient Egyptian Kingship.* Leiden: Brill.

Oelsner, Joachim, Bruce Wells, and Cornelia Wunsch. (2003). "Neo-Babylonian Period," in *A History of Ancient Near Eastern Law.* Ed. Raymond Westbrook. Vol. 2. Leiden: Brill. Pp. 911–74.

Ogilvie, Sheilagh. (2011). *Institutions and European Trade: Merchant Guilds, 1000–1800.* Cambridge: Cambridge University Press.

O'Leary, Brendan. (1989). *The Asiatic Mode of Production: Oriental Despotism, Historical Materialism and Indian History.* Oxford: Blackwell.

Oleson, John Peter, ed. (2008). *The Oxford Handbook of Engineering and Technology in the Classical World.* Oxford: Oxford University Press.

————. (2000). "Water-Lifting," in *Handbook of Ancient Water Technology.* Ed. Ö. Wikander. Leiden: Brill. Pp. 217–302.

Oliver, Graham J. (2011). "Mobility, Society, and Economy in the Hellenistic Period," in *The Economies of Hellenistic Societies, Third to First Centuries BC.* Ed. Zosia H. Archibald, John K. Davies, and Vincent Gabrielsen. Oxford: Oxford University Press. Pp. 345–67.

———. (2007). *War, Food, and Politics in Early Hellenistic Athens*. Oxford: Oxford University Press.

———. (2001). "Regions and Micro-regions: Grain for Rhamnous," in *Hellenistic Economies*. Ed. Zofia H. Archibald, John K. Davies, Vincent Gabrielsen, and G. J. Oliver. London: Routledge. Pp. 137–55.

Oppenheim, A. Leo. (1964). *Ancient Mesopotamia: Portrait of a Dead Civilization*. Chicago: University of Chicago Press.

———. (1960). "Assyriology—Why and How?," *Current Anthropology* 1/5–6: 409–23.

Orrieux, Claude. (1983). *Les Papyrus de Zenon: L'horizon d'un grec en Égypte au IIIe siècle avant J.C*. Paris: Éditions Macula.

Ortega, Pablo, et al. (2015). "A Model-Tested North Atlantic Oscillation Reconstruction for the Past Millennium," *Nature* 523: 71–74. doi: 10.1038/nature14518.

Osborne, Robin. (1996a). *Greece in the Making, 1200–479 BC*. London: Routledge.

———. (1996b). "Pots, Trade and the Archaic Greek Economy," *Antiquity* 70: 31–44.

———. (1995). "The Economy and Politics of Slavery at Athens," in *The Greek World*, Ed. A. Powell. London: Routledge. Pp. 27–43.

———. (1987). *Classical Landscape with Figures: The Ancient Greek City and Its Countryside*. Dobbs Ferry, NY: Sheridan House.

Papadopoulos, John. (2016). "The Early History of the Greek Alphabet: New Evidence from Eretria and Methone," *Antiquity* 90 (353): 1238–54.

Park, T. (1992). "Early Trends toward Class Stratification: Chaos, Common Property, and Flood Recession Agriculture," *American Anthropologist* 94/1: 90–117. Retrieved from http://www.jstor.org/stable/680039.

Parker, A. J. (1992). *Ancient Shipwrecks of the Mediterranean and the Roman Provinces*. Oxford: BAR.

Parker, Richard. (2013). *Global Crisis: War, Climate Change and Catastrophe in the Seventeenth Century*. New Haven, CT: Yale University Press.

Parkin, Tim G. (1992). *Demography and Roman Society*. Baltimore: Johns Hopkins University Press.

Parkins, Helen. (1998). "Time for a Change? Shaping the Future of the Ancient Economy," in *Trade, Traders and the Ancient City*. Ed. Helen Parkins and Christopher Smith. London: Routledge. Pp. 1–14.

Parpola, Simo, and Kazuko Watanabe (1988). *Neo-Assyrian Treaties and Loyalty Oaths*. State Archives of Assyria, vol. 2. Helsinki: Helsinki University Press.

Paterson, Jeremy. (1998). "Trade and Traders in the Roman World: Scale, Structure, and Organization," in *Trade, Traders and the Ancient City*. Ed. Helen Parkins and Christopher Smith. London: Routledge. Pp. 149–67.

Patterson, Cynthia. (1998). *The Family in Greek History*. Cambridge, MA: Harvard University Press.

Patterson, Orlando. (1982). *Slavery and Social Death: A Comparative Study*. Cambridge, MA: Harvard University Press.

Peacock, Mark S. (2006). "The Origins of Money in Ancient Greece: The Political Economy of Coinage and Exchange," *Cambridge Journal of Economics* 30: 637–50.

Pearce, Laurie. (2014). "Family Structures, Ancient Near East," in *The Oxford Encyclopedia of the Bible and Gender Studies*. Vol. 1. Ed. Julia M. O'Brian. Oxford: Oxford University Press. Pp. 195–99.

Pearson, Harry W., ed. (1977). *The Livelihood of Man*. New York: Academic Press.

———. (1957). "The Secular Debate on Economic Primitivism," in *Trade and Market in the Early Empires: Economies in History and Theory*. Ed. Karl Polanyi, Conrad M. Arensberg, and Harry W. Pearson. New York: Free Press. Pp. 3–11.

Perdu, Olivier. (2014). "Saites and Persians (664–332)," in *A Companion to Ancient Egypt*. Ed. Alan B. Lloyd. Malden, MA: Wiley-Blackwell. Pp. 140–58.

Pestman, P. W. (1993). *The Archive of the Theban Choachytes (Second Century B.C.): A Survey of the Demotic and Greek Papyri Contained in the Archive*. Leuven: Peeters.

———. (1990). *The New Papyrological Primer*. Leiden: Brill.

———. (1981). *A Guide to the Zenon Archive*. Leiden: Brill.

———. (1980). *Greek and Demotic Texts from the Zenon Archive*. Papyrologica Lugduno-Batava, vol. 20. Leiden: Brill.

———. (1961). *Marriage and Matrimonial Property in Ancient Egypt: A Contribution to Establishing the Legal Position of the Woman*. Leiden: E. J. Brill.

Petrie, Cameron A., et al. (2017). "Adaptation to Variable Environments, Resilience to Climate Change: Investigating Land, Water and Settlement in Indus Northwest India," *Current Anthropology* 58/1.

Peyronel, Luca. (2010). "Ancient Near Eastern Economics. The Silver Question between Methodology and Archaeological Data," in *Proceedings of the 6th International Congress on the Archaeology of the Ancient Near East May, 5th–10th 2008, "Sapienza"—Università di Roma*. Vol. 1, *Near Eastern Archaeology in the Past, Present and Future: Heritage and Identity*. Ed. Paolo Matthiae, Frances Pinnock, Lorenzo Nigro, and Nicolò Marchetti. Wiesbaden: Harrassowitz. Pp. 925–48.

Pfeiffer, Stefan. (2010). "Naukratis, Heracleion-Thonis and Alexandria: Remarks on the Presence of Trade Activities of Greeks in the North-West Delta from the Seventh Century B.C. to the End of the Fourth Century B.C.," in *Alexandria and the North-Western Delta*. Ed. Damian Robinson and Andrew Wilson. Oxford: Oxford Centre for Maritime Archaeology. Pp. 15–24.

———. (2004). *Das Dekret von Kanopos (238 v. Chr.): Kommentar und historische Auswertung eines dreisprachigen Synodaldekretes der ägyptischen Priester zu Ehren Ptolemaios' III. und seiner Familie*. München: K. G. Saur.

Phillipson, Nicholas. (2010). *Adam Smith: An Enlightened Life*. New Haven, CT: Yale University Press.

Piketty, Thomas. (2014). *Capital in the Twenty-First Century*. Trans. Arthur Goldhammer. Cambridge, MA: Belknap Press of Harvard University Press.

Pilkington, Nathan. (2013). "Growing Up Roman: Infant Mortality and Reproductive Development," *Journal of Interdisciplinary History* 44: 1–35.

Pleket, H. W. (1990). "Wirtschaft und Gesellschaft des Imperium Romanum: 2. Wirtschaft," in *Handbuch der europäischen Wirtschafts- und Sozialgeschichte*. Vol. 1. Ed. W. Fischer, J. A. van Hooute and H. Kellenbenz. Stuttgart. Pp. 25–160.

———. (1983). "Urban Elites and Businesses in the Greek Part of the Roman Empire," in *Trade in the Ancient Economy*. Ed. P. Garnsey, K. Hopkins, and C. R. Whittaker. Berkeley: University of California Press. Pp. 131–44.

Plender, John. (2015). *Capitalism: Money, Morals and Markets*. London: Biteback.

Poblome, Jeroen. (2015). "The Economy of the Roman World as a Complex Adaptive System: Testing the Case in Second to Fifth Century CE Sagalassos," in *Structure and Performance in the Roman Economy: Models, Methods and Case Studies*. Ed. Paul Erdkamp and Koenraad Verboven. Brussels: Éditions Latomus. Pp. 97–140.

Polanyi, Karl. (1977). *The Livelihood of Man*. Ed. Harry W. Pearson. New York: Academic Press.

———. (1960). "On the Comparative Treatment of Economic Institutions in Antiquity, with Illustrations from Athens, Mycenae, and Alalakh," in *City Invincible: A Symposium on Urbanization and Cultural Development in the Ancient Near East*. Ed. Kraeling and Adams. Chicago: Oriental Institute. Pp. 329–50.

———. (1957a). "Aristotle Discovers the Economy," in *Trade and Market in the Early Empires: Economies in History and Theory*. Ed. Karl Polanyi, Conrad M. Arensberg, and Harry W. Pearson. New York: Free Press. Pp. 64–94.

———. (1957b). "Marketless Trading in Hammurabi's Time," in *Trade and Market in the Early Empires: Economies in History and Theory*. Ed. Karl Polanyi, Conrad M. Arensberg, and Harry W. Pearson. New York: Free. Pp. 12–26.

———. (1957c). "The Economy as Instituted Process," in *Trade and Market in the Early Empires: Economies in History and Theory*. Ed. Karl Polanyi, Conrad M. Arensberg, and Harry W. Pearson. New York: Free Press. Pp. 243–70.

———. (1944). *The Great Transformation*. New York: Farrar and Rinehart.

Polanyi, Karl, Conrad M. Arensberg, and Harry W. Pearson, eds. (1957). *Trade and Market in the Early Empires: Economies in History and Theory*. New York: Free Press.

Polanyi-Levitt, Kari, ed. (1990). *The Life and Work of Karl Polanyi: A Celebration*. Montreal: Black Rose Books.

Pollard, Elizabeth Ann. (2014). "The Mediterranean and Indian Ocean," in *A Companion to Mediterranean History*. Ed. Peregrine Horden and Sharon Kinoshita. Malden, MA: Wiley-Blackwell. Pp. 457–74.

Poloni-Simard, Jacques. (2003). "Fernand Braudel," in *Les historiens*. Paris: Armand Colin. Pp. 137–60.

Pomeranz, Kenneth. (2000). *The Great Divergence: China, Europe, and the Making of the Modern World Economy*. Princeton, NJ: Princeton University Press.

Pomeranz, Kenneth, and Steven Topik, eds. (2006). *The World That Trade Created: Society, Culture, and the World Economy, 1400 to Present*. 2d ed. Armonk, NY: M. E. Sharpe.

Pomeroy, Sarah B. (1997). *Families in Classical and Hellenistic Greece: Representations and Realities*. Oxford: Clarendon.

———. (1994). *Xenophon*, Oeconomicus: *A Social and Historical Commentary*. Oxford: Oxford University Press.

Popham, M. R. (1994). "Precolonization: Early Greek Contact with the East," in *The Archaeology of Greek Colonisation*. Ed. G. R. Tsetskhladze and F. de Angelis. Oxford: Oxford University Committee for Archaeology. Pp. 11–34.

Porten, B., and A. Yardeni. (1993) *Textbook of Aramaic Documents from Ancient Egypt*. Newly copied, edited, and translated into Hebrew and English. Vol. 3, *Literature, Accounts, Lists*. Jerusalem: Department of the History of the Jewish People, Hebrew University.

Posner, Richard A. (1980). "A Theory of Primitive Society, with Special Reference to Law," *Journal of Law and Economics* 23/1: 1–53.

Postgate, J. N. (1979). "The Economic Structure of the Assyrian Empire," in *Power and Propaganda: A Symposium on Ancient Empires*. Ed. Mogens Trolle Larsen. Copenhagen: Akademisk Forlag. Pp. 193–221.

Potts, Daniel T. (1997). *Mesopotamian Civilization: The Material Foundations.* Ithaca, NY: Cornell University Press.

Prag, Jonathan R. W., and Josephine Crawley Quinn, eds. (2013). *The Hellenistic West: Rethinking the Ancient Mediterranean.* Cambridge: Cambridge University Press.

Préaux, Claire. (1978). *Le monde hellénistique, La Grèce et l'Orient (323–146. av. J.-C.).* 2 vols. Paris: Presses universitaires de France.

———. (1939). *L'Économie royale des Lagides.* Brussels: Fondation égyptologique Reine Élisabeth.

Pulak, C. (2008). "The Uluburun Shipwreck and Late Bronze Age Trade," in *Beyond Babylon: Art:, Trade, and Diplomacy in the Second Millennium BC.* Ed. J. Aruz, K. Benzel, and J. M Evans. New York: Metropolitan Museum of Art. Pp. 289–305.

———. (1996). *Analysis of the Weight Assemblages from the Late Bronze Age Shipwrecks at Uluburun and Cape Gelidonya, Turkey.* PhD diss., Texas A&M University.

Purcell, Nicholas. (2012). "Rivers and the Geography of Power," *Pallas* 90: 373–87.

Quack, Joachim Friedrich. (2011). "Das Diktum Tutu über die Eingabe an Numenios," in *Ägypten zwischen innerem Zwist und äußerem Druck: Die Zeit Ptolemaios' VI. bis VIII.* Ed. Andrea Jördens and Joachim Friedrich Quack. Philippika. Marburger altertumskundliche Abhandlungen 45. Wiesbaden: Harrassowitz. Pp. 268–75.

———. (2005). *Einführung in die altägyptische Literaturgeschichte III: Die demotische und gräko-ägyptische Literatur.* Münster: LIT Verlag.

Quinn, Josephine Crawley. (2013). "North Africa," in *A Companion to Ancient History.* Paperback ed. Ed. Andrew Erskine. Malden, MA: Blackwell. Pp. 260–72.

Quirke, Stephen. (1990). *The Administration of Egypt in the Late Middle Kingdom: The Hieratic Documents.* New Malden, UK: Sia.

Raaflaub, Kurt A. (2009). "Learning from the Enemy: Athenian and Persian 'Instruments of Empire,'" in *Interpreting the Athenian Empire.* Ed. John Ma, Nikolas Papazarkadas, and Robert Parker. London: Duckworth. Pp. 89–124.

———. (2004). "Archaic Greek Aristocrats as Carriers of Cultural Interaction," in *Commerce and Monetary Systems in the Ancient World: Means of Transmission and Cultural Interaction.* Ed. Robert Bollinger and Christoph Ulf. Oriens et Occidens 6. Stuttgart: Franz Steiner Verlag. Pp. 197–217.

Raaflaub, Kurt A., and Nathan Rosenstein, eds. (1999). *War and Society in the Ancient and Medieval Worlds: Asia, the Mediterranean, Europe and Mesoamerica.* Washington, DC: Center for Hellenic Studies.

Rabb, Theodore K. (1981). "The Historian and the Climatologist," in *Climate and History: Studies in Interdisciplinary History.* Ed. Robert I. Rotberg and Theodore K. Rabb. Princeton, NJ: Princeton University Press. Pp. 251–52.

Radkau, Joachim. (2009). *Max Weber: A Biography.* Trans. Patrick Camiller. Cambridge: Polity. Original German edition *Max Weber.* Munich: Carl Hanser Verlag, 2005.

———. (2008). *Nature and Power: A Global History of the Environment.* Cambridge: Cambridge University Press.

Radner, Karen. (2015). "Hired Labor in the Neo-Assyrian Empire," in *Labor in the Ancient World.* Ed. P. Steinkeller and M. Hudson. Dresden: ISLET-Verlag. Pp. 329–43.

———. (2011). "The Assur-Nineveh-Arbela Triangle: Central Assyria in the Neo-Assyrian Period," in *Between the Cultures: The Central Tigris Region from the 3rd to the 1st Mil-*

lennium BC. Ed. Peter A. Miglus and Simone Mühl. Heidelberg: Heidelberger Orientverlag. Pp. 321–29.

———. (1999). "Money in the Neo-Assyrian Empire," in *Trade and Finance in Ancient Mesopotamia: Proceedings of the first MOS Symposium (Leiden 1997)*. Ed. J. G. Dercksen. Leiden: Nederlands Instituut voor het Nabije Oosten. Pp. 127–57.

Rahmstorf, Lorenz. (2006). "Zur Ausbreitung vorderasiatischer Innovationen in die frühbronzezeitliche Ägäis," *Prähistorische Zeitschrift* 81: 49–96.

Rainville, Lynn. (2012). "Household Matters: Techniques for Understanding Assyrian Houses," in *New Perspectives on Household Archaeology*. Ed. Bradley J. Parker and Catherine P. Foster. Winona Lake, IN: Eisenbrauns. Pp. 139–64.

Ramsay, John T., and A. Lewis Licht. (1997). *The Comet of 44 BC and Caesar's funeral Games*. Atlanta: Scholars Press.

Rangarajan, L. N. (1992). *Kautilya, the Arthashastra*. Haryana: Penguin Books India.

Rasmussen, Simon, et al. (2015). "Early Divergent Strains of *Yersinia pestis* in Eurasia 5,000 Years Ago," *Cell* 163: 571–82. http://dx.doi.org/10.1016/j.cell.2015.10.009.

Rathbone, Dominic. (2008). "Poor Peasants and Silent Sherds," in *People, Land, and Politics: Demographic Developments and the Transformation of Roman Italy 300 BC–AD 14*. Ed. Luuk de Ligt and Simon Northwood. Leiden: Brill. Pp. 305–32.

———. (2006). "Poverty and Population in Roman Egypt," in *Poverty in the Roman World*. Ed. Margaret Atkins and Robin Osborne. Cambridge: Cambridge University Press. Pp. 100–14.

———. (1994). "Ptolemaic to Roman Egypt: The Death of the Dirigiste State?," in *Production and Public Powers in Antiquity: Proceedings of the Eleventh International Economic History Congress*. Ed. E. Lo Cascio and D. Rathbone. Milan: Università Bocconi. Pp. 29–40. Revised in Cambridge Philological Society. Supplementary vol. 26 (2000): 44–54.

———. (1991). *Economic Rationalism and Rural Society in Third-Century AD Egypt*. Cambridge: Cambridge University Press.

———. (1990). "Villages, Land and Population in Graeco-Roman Egypt," in *Proceedings of the Cambridge Philological Society*, n.s., 36: 103–42.

———. (1983). "The Grain Trade and Grain Shortages in the Hellenistic East," in *Trade and Famine in Classical Antiquity*. Ed. Peter Garnsey and C. R. Whittaker. Cambridge: Cambridge Philological Society. Pp. 45–55.

Rathbone, Dominic, and Sitta von Reden. (2015). "Mediterranean Grain Prices in Classical Antiquity," in *A History of Market Performance: From Ancient Babylonia to the Modern World*. Ed. R. J. van der Spek, Bas van Leeuwen, and Jan Luiten van Zanden. London: Routledge. Pp. 149–235.

Rauh, Nicholas K. (1999). "Rhodes, Rome, and the Eastern Mediterranean Wine Trade, 166–88 BC," in *Hellenistic Rhodes: Politics, Culture, and Society*. Ed. Vincent Gabrielsen, Per Bilde, Troels Engberg-Pedersen, Lise Hannestad, and Jan Zahle. Studies in Hellenistic Civilization 9. Aarhus: Aarhus University Press. Pp. 162–86.

Rauh, N., et al. (2009). "Life in the Truck Lane: Urban Development in Western Rough Cilicia," *Jahreshefte des Österreichischen Archäologischen Institutes in Wien* 78: 253–312.

Rawski, Thomas G., et al. (1996). *Economics and the Historian*. Berkeley: University of California Press.

Ray, John D. (2002). *Reflections of Osiris: Lives from Ancient Egypt.* Oxford: Oxford University Press.

———. (1976). *The Archive of Ḥor.* London: Egypt Exploration Society.

Reale, Oreste, and Paul Dirmeyer. (2000). "Modeling the Effects of Vegetation on Mediterranean Climate during the Roman Classical Period: Part I. Climate History and Model Sensitivity," *Global and Planetary Change* 25: 163–84.

Reale, Oreste, and Jagadish Shukla. (2000). "Modeling the Effects of. Vegetation on Mediterranean Climate during the Roman Classical Period: Part II. Model Simulation," *Global and Planetary Change* 25: 185–214.

Redfield, Robert. (1956). *Peasant Society and Culture: An Anthropological Approach.* Chicago: University of Chicago Press.

Reed, C. M. (2003). *Maritime Traders in the Ancient Greek World.* Cambridge: Cambridge University Press.

Reger, Gary. (2011). "Inter-regional Economies in the Aegean Basin," in *The Economies of Hellenistic Societies, Third to First Centuries BC.* Ed. Zosia H. Archibald, John K. Davies, and Vincent Gabrielsen. Oxford: Oxford University Press. Pp. 368–89.

———. (2007). "Traders and Travelers in the Black and Aegean Seas," in *The Black Sea in Antiquity: Regional and Interregional Economic Exchange.* Ed. Vincent Gabrielsen and John Lund. Aarhus: Aarhus University Press. Pp. 273–85.

———. (2004). "Sympoliteiai in Hellenistic Asia Minor," in *The Greco-Roman East: Politics, Culture, Society.* Ed. Stephen Colvin. Yale Classical Studies 31. Cambridge: Cambridge University Press. Pp. 145–81

———. (2003). "Aspects of the Role of Merchants in the Political Life of the Hellenistic World," in *Mercanti e politica nel mondo antico.* Ed. Carlo Zaccagnini. Rome: "L'Erma" di Bretschneider. Pp. 165–97.

———. (2002). "The Price Histories of Some Imported Goods on Independent Delos," in *The Ancient Economy.* Ed. Walter Scheidel and Sitta von Reden. London: Routledge. Pp. 133–54. Originally published as "The Price Histories of Some Imported Goods on Independent Delos," in *Économie antique: Prix et formation des prix dans les économies antiques.* Ed. J. Andreau, P. Briant, and R. Descat. Saint-Bertrand-de-Comminges: Musée archéologique départemental, 1997. Pp. 53–72.

———. (1994). *Regionalism and Change in the Economy of Independent Delos:* Berkeley: University of California Press.

Reibig, André. (2001). *The Bücher-Meyer Controversy: The Nature of the Ancient Economy in Modern Ideology.* PhD diss., University of Glasgow, accessed online February 3, 2014. http://theses.gla.ac.uk/4321/.

Renfrew, Colin, and Paul Bahn. (1991). *Archaeology: Theories, Methods and Practice.* New York: Thames and Hudson.

Renger, Johannes. (2009). "Economy of Ancient Mesopotamia: A General Outline," in *The Babylonian World.* Ed. Gwendolyn Leick. Paperback ed. London: Routledge. Pp. 187–97.

———. (2005). "K. Polanyi and the Economy of Ancient Mesopotamia," in *Autour de Polanyi: Vocabulaires, theories et modalities des échanges, Nanterre, 12–14 Juin 2004.* Ed. P. F. Clancier, Joannès, P. Rouillard, and A. Tenu. Paris: De Boccard. Pp. 45–65.

———. (2003). "Trade and Market in the Ancient Near East: Theoretical and Factual Implications," in *Mercanti e Politica nel Mondo Antico.* Ed. Carlo Zaccagnini. Rome: "L'Erma" di Bretschneider. Pp. 15–39.

Rheinstein, Max. (1964). *Max Weber on Law in Economy and Society.* New York: Simon and Schuster.

Richerson, Peter J., and Robert Boyd. (2005). *Not by Genes Alone: How Culture Transformed Human Evolution*. Chicago: University of Chicago Press.

Richerson, Peter J., and Morten H. Christiansen, eds. (2013). *Cultural Evolution: Society, Technology, Language, and Religion*. Cambridge, MA: MIT Press.

Ricoeur, Paul. (1988). *Time and Narrative*. Vol. 3. Trans. Kathleen Blamey and David Pellauer. Chicago: University of Chicago Press.

Riehl, Simone, Konstantin E. Pustovoytov, Heike Weippert, Stefan Klett, and Frank Hole. (2014). "Drought Stress Variability in Ancient Near Eastern Agricultural Systems Evidenced by δ13C in Barley Grain," *Proceedings of the National Academy of Sciences* 111/34: 12348–53. doi: 10.1073/pnas.1409516111.

Rihill, T. E. (2011). "Classical Athens," in *The Cambridge World History of Slavery*. Vol. 1, *The Ancient Mediterranean World*. Ed. Keith Bradley and Paul Cartledge. Cambridge: Cambridge University Press. Pp. 48–73.

Ritner, Robert K. (2003). "The Instruction of 'Onchsheshonqy," in *The Literature of Ancient Egypt: An Anthology of Stories, Instructions, Stelae, Autobiographies, and Poetry*. Ed. William K. Simpson. New Haven, CT: Yale University Press. Pp. 497–529.

Roberts, Neil. (2012). "Palaeolimnological Evidence for an East-West Climate See-Saw in the Mediterranean since AD 900," *Global and Planetary Change* 84–85: 23–34.

Roberts, Neil, Warren J. Eastwood, Catherine Kuzucuoglu, Girolamo Fiorentino, and Valentina Caracuta. (2011). "Climatic, Vegetation, and Cultural Change in the Eastern Mediterranean during the Mid-Holocene Environmental Transition," *Holocene* 21: 147–62.

Robinson, Damian, and Franck Goddio, eds. (2015). *Thonis-Heracleion in Context*. Oxford: Oxford Centre for Maritime Archaeology.

Robinson, Eric W. (2011). *Democracy beyond Athens: Popular Government in the Greek Classical Age*. Cambridge: Cambridge University Press.

———. (1997). *The First Democracies: Early Popular Government outside Athens*. Historia Einzelschriften 107. Stuttgart: Franz Steiner Verlag.

Robock, Alan. (2000). "Volcanic Eruptions and Climate," *Review of Geophysics* 38: 191–219.

Rochberg-Halton, F. (1991). "The Babylonian Astronomical Diaries," *Journal of the American Oriental Society* 111/2: 323–32.

Rohling, Eelco J., Angela Hayes, Paul A. Mayewski, and Michal Kucera. (2009). "Holocene Climate Variability in the Eastern Mediterranean and the End of the Bronze Age," in *Forces of Transformation: The End of the Bronze Age in the Mediterranean*. Ed. Christoph Bachhuber and Gareth Roberts. Oxford: Oxbow. Pp. 2–5.

Roland, T. P., C. J. Caseldine, D. J. Charman, C.S.M. Turney, and M. J. Amesbury. (2014). "Was There a '4.2 ka Event' in Great Britain and Ireland? Evidence from the Peatland Record," *Quaternary Science Reviews* 83: 11–27.

Roller, Duane W. (2006). *Through the Pillars of Herakles: Greco-Roman Exploration of the Atlantic*. London: Routledge.

Rosenstein, Nathan. (2012). *Rome and the Mediterranean 290 to 146 BC: The Imperial Republic*. Edinburgh: Edinburgh University Press.

Rossignol, Benoît, and Sébastien Durost. (2007). "Volcanisme global et variations climatiques de courte durée dans l'histoire romaine (Ier s. av. J.-C.-IVème s. ap. J.-C.): Leçons d'une archive glaciaire (GISP2)," *Jahrbuch des römisch-germanischen Zentralmuseums Mainz* 54: 395–438.

Rostovtzeff, Michael I. (1957). *The Social and Economic History of the Roman Empire*. 2d ed., rev. by P. M. Fraser. Oxford: Clarendon.

———. (1941). *The Social and Economic History of the Hellenistic World.* Oxford: Clarendon.

———. (1936). "The Hellenistic World and Its Economic Development," in *American Historical Review* 41/2: 231–52.

———. (1933). "Eduard Meyer (1855–1930)," in *Encyclopaedia of the Social Sciences.* Ed. E.R.A. Seligman and A. Johnson. Pp. 402–3.

———. (1932). *Caravan Cities.* Oxford: Clarendon.

———. (1930). "The Decay of the Ancient World and Its Economic Explanations," *Economic History Review* 2/2: 197–214.

———. (1922). *A Large Estate in Egypt in the Third Century B.C.: A Study in Economic History.* University of Wisconsin Studies in the Social Sciences and History 6. Madison, WI: n.p.

Rostow, W. W. (1975). *How It All Began: Origins of the Modern Economy.* New York: Methuen.

Rotberg, Robert I., and Theodore K. Rabb, eds. (1981). *Climate and History: Studies in Interdisciplinary History.* Princeton, NJ: Princeton University Press.

Roth, Martha T. (1997). *Law Collections from Mesopotamia and Asia Minor.* 2d ed. Atlanta: Scholars Press.

Rothenberg, Winifred Barr. (1992). *From Market-Places to a Market Economy: The Transformation of Rural Massachusetts 1750–1850.* Chicago: University of Chicago Press.

Rothman, M. S., ed. (2001). *Uruk Mesopotamia and Its Neighbors: Cross-Cultural Interactions in the Era of State Formation.* Santa Fe: School of American Research.

Rougemont, G. (2005)."Nouvelles inscriptions grecques de l'asie central," in *Afghanistan, ancien carrefour entre l'Est et l'Ouest.* Ed. O. Bopearachchi and Marie-Françoise Boussac. Turnhout: Brepols. Pp. 127–36.

Rouillard, Pierre. (2009). "Greeks and the Iberian Peninsula: Forms of Exchange and Settlements," in *Colonial Encounters in Ancient Iberia: Phoenician, Greek and Indigenous Relations.* Ed. Michael Dietler and Carolina Lopez-Ruiz. Chicago: University of Chicago Press. Pp. 131–53.

Routledge, Bruce, and Kevin McGeough. (2009). "Just What Collapsed? A Network Perspective on 'Palatial' and 'Private' Trade at Ugarit," in *Forces of Transformation: The End of the Bronze Age in the Mediterranean.* Ed. Christoph Bachhuber and Gareth Roberts. Oxford: Oxbow. Pp. 22–29.

Rowlandson, Jane. (2014). "Administration and Law: Graeco-Roman," in *A Companion to Ancient Egypt.* Ed. Alan B. Lloyd. Malden, MA: Wiley-Blackwell. Pp. 237–54.

———. ed. (1998). *Women and Society in Greek and Roman Egypt: A Sourcebook.* Cambridge: Cambridge University Press.

Russo, Lucio. (2004). *The Forgotten Revolution: How Science Was Born in 300 BC and Why It Had to Be Reborn.* Heidelberg: Springer Verlag.

Rutter, N. K. (2012). "The Coinage of Italy," in *The Oxford Handbook of Greek and Roman Coinage.* Ed. William E. Metcalf. Oxford: Oxford University Press. Pp. 128–41.

Ryholt, Kim. (2005). *The Petese Stories II (P. Petese II): The Carlsberg Papyri 6.* CNI Publications 29. Copenhagen: Museum Tusculanum Press.

Sachs, Jeffrey D. (2012). "Government, Geography and Growth. The True Drivers of Economic Development," *Foreign Affairs.* Accessed August 18, 2015. https://www.foreign affairs.com/reviews/review-essay/government-geography-and-growth.

Sahlins, Marshall. (1976). *Culture and Practical Reason.* Chicago: University of Chicago Press.

———. (1972). *Stone Age Economics*. New York: Aldine de Gruyter.

Said, Rushdi. (1993). *The River Nile: Geology, Hydrology and Utilization*. Oxford: Pergamon.

Salisbury, Richard. (1973). "Economic Anthropology," *Annual Review of Anthropology* 2: 85–94.

Sallares, Robert R. (2014). "Disease," in *A Companion to Mediterranean History*. Ed. Peregrine Horden and Sharon Kinoshita. Malden, MA: Wiley-Blackwell. Pp. 250–62.

———. (2013). "Environmental History," in *A Companion to Ancient History*. Ed. Andrew Erskine. Paperback ed. Malden, MA: Blackwell. Pp. 164–74.

———. (2009). "Environmental History," in *A Companion to Ancient History*, ed. Andrew Erskine. Malden, MA: Wiley-Blackwell. Pp. 164–74.

———. (2007). "Ecology," in *The Cambridge Economic History of the Greco-Roman World*. Ed. W. Scheidel, I. Morris, and R. Saller. Cambridge: Cambridge University Press. Pp. 15–37.

———. (2002). *Malaria and Rome: A History of Malaria in Ancient Italy*. Oxford: Oxford University Press.

———. (1991). *The Ecology of the Ancient Greek World*. Ithaca, NY: Cornell University Press.

Saller, Richard. (2007). "Household and Gender," *The Cambridge Economic History of the Greco-Roman World*. Ed. Walter Scheidel, Ian Morris, and Richard Saller. Cambridge: Cambridge University Press. Pp. 87–112.

———. (2005). "Framing the Debate over Growth in the Ancient Economy," in *The Ancient Economy: Evidence and Models*. Ed. J. G. Manning and Ian Morris. Stanford, CA: Stanford University Press. Pp. 223–38.

Salmeri, Giovanni. (2012). "Epigraphy and the Economy of the Roman Empire," in *Epigraphy and the Historical Sciences*. Ed. John Davies and John Wilkes. Oxford: Oxford University Press. Pp. 249–67.

Sanfey, A. G. (2007). "Social Decision-Making: Insights from Game Theory and Neuroscience," *Science* 318/5850: 598–602.

Santamaria, Ulysses, and Anne M. Bailey. (1984). "A Note on Braudel's Structure as Duration," *History and Theory* 23/1: 78–83.

Sarris, Peter. (2006). *Economy and Society in the Age of Justinian*. Cambridge: Cambridge University Press.

Schaps, David M. (2004). *The Invention of Coinage and the Monetization of Ancient Greece*. Ann Arbor: University of Michigan Press.

Scheidel, Walter. (2017). *The Great Leveler: Violence and the History of Inequality from the Stone Age to the Twenty-First Century*. Princeton, NJ: Princeton University Press.

———. (2015). "The Early Roman Monarchy," in *Fiscal Regimes and the Political Economy of Premodern States*. Ed. Andrew Monson and Walter Scheidel. Cambridge: Cambridge University Press. Pp. 229–57.

———. (2013a). "Population and Demography," in *A Companion to Ancient History*. Ed. Andrew Erskine. Paperback ed. Oxford: Blackwell. Pp. 134–45.

———. (2013b). "Studying the State," in *The Oxford Handbook of the State in the Ancient Near East and Mediterranean*. Ed. Peter Fibiger Bang and Walter Scheidel. Oxford: Oxford University Press. Pp. 5–57.

———. (2012). "Epigraphy and Demography: Birth, Marriage, Family, and Death," in *Epigraphy and the Historical Sciences*. Ed. John Davies and John Wilkes. Oxford: Oxford University Press. Pp. 101–29.

———. (2011a). "The Roman Slave Supply," in *The Cambridge World History of Slavery*. Vol. 1, *The Ancient Mediterranean World*. Ed. Keith Bradley and Paul Cartledge. Cambridge: Cambridge University Press. Pp. 287–310.

———. (2011b). "Comparative Perspective on the Determinants of Scale and Productivity of Roman Maritime Trade in the Mediterranean," in *Maritime Technology in the Ancient Economy: Ship-Design and Navigation*. Ed. W. V. Harris and K. Iara. Portsmouth, RI: Journal of Roman Archaeology. Pp. 21–37.

———. (2008). "Roman Population Size: The Logic of the Debate," in *People, Land and Politics: Demographic Developments and the Transformation of Roman Italy, 300 BC–AD 14*. Ed. L. de Ligt and S. J. Northwood. Leiden: Brill. Pp. 15–70.

———. (2007). "Demography," in *The Cambridge Economic History of the Greco-Roman World*. Ed. Walter Scheidel, Ian Morris, and Richard Saller. Cambridge: Cambridge University Press. Pp. 38–86.

———. (2006). "Stratification, Deprivation and the Quality of Life," in *Poverty in the Roman World*. Ed. Margaret Atkins and Robin Osborne. Cambridge: Cambridge University Press. Pp. 40–59.

———. (2005). "Human Mobility in Roman Italy, II: The Slave Population," *Journal of Roman Studies* 95: 64–79.

———. (2004). "Creating a Metropolis: A Comparative Demographic Perspective," in *Ancient Alexandria between Egypt and Greece*. Ed. W. V. Harris and Giovanni Ruffini. Leiden: Brill. Pp. 1–31.

———. (2003). "The Demographic Expansion: Models and Comparisons," *Journal of Hellenic Studies* 123: 120–40.

———. (2001). *Death on the Nile: Disease and the Demography of Roman Egypt*. Leiden: Brill.

———. (1996). "The Most Silent Women of Greece and Rome: Rural Labor and Women's life in the Ancient World (II)," *Greece and Rome* 43/1: 1–10.

———. (1995). "The Most Silent Women of Greece and Rome: Rural Labor and Women's life in the Ancient World (I)," *Greece and Rome* 42/2: 202–17.

———. (1994). "Grain Cultivation in the Villa Economy of Roman Italy," in *Landuse in the Roman empire*. Ed. Jesper Carlsen, Peter Ørsted and Jens Erick Skydsgaard. Rome: "L'Erma" di Bretschneider. Pp. 159–66.

Scheidel, Walter, and S. J. Friesen (2009). "The Size of the Economy and the Distribution of Income in the Roman Empire," *Journal of Roman Studies* 99: 61–91.

Scheidel, Walter, Ian Morris, and Richard Saller, eds. (2007). *The Cambridge Economic History of the Greco-Roman World*. Cambridge: Cambridge University Press.

Scheidel, Walter, and Sitta von Reden, eds. (2002). *The Ancient Economy*. New York: Routledge.

Schenkel, Wolfgang. (1978). *Die Bewässerungsrevolution im Alten Ägypten*. Mainz: Philipp von Zabern.

Schentuleit, Maren. (2006). *Aus der Buchhaltung swa Weinmagazins im Edfu-Tempel: Der demotische P. Carlsberg 409*. Copenhagen: Museum Tusculanum Press.

Schindler, Daniel E., et al. (2010). "Population Diversity and the Portfolio Effect in an Exploited Species," *Nature* 465: 609–12. doi:10.1038/nature09060.

Schloen, J. David. (2001). *The House of the Father as Fact and Symbol: Patrimonialism in Ugarit and the Ancient Near East*. Winona Lakes, IN: Eisenbrauns.

Schmidt, Anja, Kirsten E. Fristad, and Linda T. Elkins-Tanton, eds. (2015). *Volcanism and Global Environmental Change*. Cambridge: Cambridge University Press.

Schnaiberg, Allan. (2005). "The Economy and the Environment," in *The Handbook of Economic Sociology*. 2d ed. Ed. Neil J. Smelser and Richard Swedburg. Princeton, NJ: Princeton University Press. Pp. 703–25.

Schneider, Adam W., and Selim F. Adah. (2014). "'No Harvest Was Reaped': Demographic and Climatic Factors in the Decline of the Neo-Assyrian Empire," *Climatic Change* 127: 435–46.

Schneider, Helmuth. (2007). "Technology," in *The Cambridge Economic History of the Greco-Roman World*. Ed. Walter Scheidel, Ian Morris, and Richard Saller. Cambridge: Cambridge University Press. Pp. 144–71.

Schoenberger, Erica. (2008). "The Origins of the Market Economy: State Power, Territorial Control, and Modes of War Fighting," *Comparative Studies in Society and History* 50/3: 663–91.

Schörle, Katia. (2010). "From Harbor to Desert: An Integrated Interface on the Red Sea and Its Impact on the Eastern Egyptian Desert," Bolletino di Archeologia online. https://www.researchgate.net/publication/262116511_From_Harbour_to_Desert_An_Integrated_Interface_on_the_Red_Sea_and_its_impact_on_the_Eastern_Desert_of_Egypt.

Scott, James C. (1998). *Seeing Like a State: How Certain Schemes to Improve the Human Condition Have Failed*. New Haven, CT: Yale University Press.

Scott-Kilvert, I. (1973). *Plutarch: The Age of Alexander*. London: Penguin.

Seaford, Richard. (2004). *Money and the Early Greek Mind*. Cambridge: Cambridge University Press.

Searle, John R. (2010). *Making the Social World: The Structure of Human Civilization*. Oxford: Oxford University Press.

Seidlmayer, Stephan Johannes. (2001). *Historische und Modern Nilstände*. Berlin: Achet Verlag.

Seland, Eivind Heldaas. (2010). *Ports and Political Power in the* Periplus: *Complex Societies and Maritime Trade on the Indian Ocean in the First Century AD*. Society for Arabian Studies Monographs 9. Oxford: Archaeopress.

———. (2008). "The Indian Ocean and the Globalization of the Ancient World," *Ancient West and East* 8: 67–79.

———. (2006). "The Indian Ocean in Antiquity: Trade and the Emerging State." PhD diss., University of Bergen.

Sewell, William H., Jr. (2005). *Logics of History: Social Theory and Social Transformation*. Chicago: University of Chicago Press.

Shaw, Brent. (2008). "After Rome. Transformations of the Early Mediterranean World," *New Left Review* 51: 89–114.

———. (2003). "A Peculiar Island: Maghrib and Mediterranean," *Mediterranean Historical Review* 18: 93–125.

———. (2001). "Challenging Braudel: A New Vision of the Mediterranean," *Journal of Roman Archaeology* 14: 419–53.

———. (1995). *Environment and Society in Roman North Africa*. London: Variorum.

———. (1993). "The Early Development of M. I. Finley's Thought: The Heichelheim Dossier," *Athenaeum* 81: 177–99.

———. (1992). "Under Russian Eyes," *Journal of Roman Studies* 82: 216–28.

———. (1984). "Water and Society in the Ancient Maghrib: Technology, Property, and Development," *Antiquités Africaines* 20/1: 121–73.

———. (1981). "Rural Markets in North Africa and the Political Economy of the Roman Empire," *Antiquités Africaines* 17: 37–83.

Shaw, Brent D., and Richard P. Saller. (1981). "Editor's Introduction," in M. I. Finley, *Economy and Society in Ancient Greece*. Harmondsworth: Penguin. Pp. ix–xxvi.

Sherratt, Andrew. (2011). "Global Development," in *Interweaving Worlds: Systemic Interactions in Eurasia, 7th to 1st millennia BC*. Ed. Toby C. Wilkinson, Susan Sherratt, and John Bennet. Oxford: Oxbow Books. Pp. 4–6.

Sherratt, Andrew, and Susan Sherratt. (1993). "The Growth of the Mediterranean Economy in the Early First Millennium BC," *World Archaeology* 24/3: 361–78.

———. (1991). "From Luxuries to Commodities: The Nature of Mediterranean Bronze Age Trading Systems," in *Bronze Age Trade in the Mediterranean*. Ed. N. H. Gale. Jonsered: Paul Åströms Förlag. Pp. 351–86.

Sherratt, Susan. (2010). "Greeks and Phoenicians: Perceptions of Trade and Traders in the Early First Millennium BC," in *Social Archaeologies of Trade and Exchange: Exploring Relationships among People, Places and Things*. Ed. Alexander A. Bauer and Anna S. Agbe-Davies. Walnut Creek, CA: Left Coast. Pp. 119–42.

———. (2003). "The Mediterranean Economy: 'Globalization' at the End of the Second Millennium BCE," in *Symbiosis, Symbolism, and the Power of the Past: Canaan, Ancient Israel, and Their Neighbors from the Late Bronze Age through Roman Palaestina*. Ed. William G. Dever and Seymour Gitin. Winona Lake, IN: Eisenbrauns. Pp. 37–62

———. (2001). "Potemkin Palaces and Route-Based Economies," in *Economy and Politics in the Mycenaean Palace States*. Ed. J. Killen and S. Voutsaki. Cambridge: Cambridge Philosophical Society. Pp. 214–38.

Sherwin-White, Susan. (1987). "Seleucid Babylonia: A Case Study for the Installation and Development of Greek Rule," in *Hellenism in the East: Interactions of Greek and Non-Greek Civilizations from Syria to Central Asia after Alexander*. Ed. Amélie Kuhrt and Susan Sherwin-White. Berkeley: University of California Press. Pp. 1–31.

Shils, Edward. (1991). "Henry Sumner Maine in the Tradition of the Analysis of Society," in *The Victorian Achievement of Sir Henry Maine: A Centennial Reappraisal*. Ed. Alan Diamond. Cambridge: Cambridge University Press. Pp. 143–78.

Shipley, G. (1993). "Distance, Development, Decline? World-Systems Analysis and the 'Hellenistic' World," in *Centre and Periphery in the Hellenistic World*. Ed. P. Bilde et al. Aarhus: Aarhus University Press. Pp. 271–84.

Shipton, Kirsty. (2000). *Leasing and Lending: The Cash Economy in Fourth-Century Athens*. London: Institute of Classical Studies.

Shryock, Andrew, and Daniel Lord Smail, eds. (2011). *Deep History: The Architecture of Past and Present*. Berkeley: University of California Press.

Sidebotham, Steven E. (2011). *Berenike and the Ancient Maritime Spice Route*. Berkeley: University of California Press.

Sigl, M., et al. (2015). "Timing and Climate Forcing of Volcanic Eruptions for the Past 2,500 Years," *Nature* 523: 543–49. doi:10.1038/nature14565.

Sijpesteijn, P. J. (1987). *Customs Duties in Graeco-Roman Egypt*. Zutphen: Terra.

Silver, Morris. (2004). "Modern Ancients," in *Commerce and Monetary Systems in the Ancient World: Means of Transmission and Cultural Interaction*. Ed. Robert Bollinger and Christoph Ulf. Oriens et Occidens 6. Pp. 65–87.

———. (1995). *Economic Structures of Antiquity*. Westport, CT: Greenwood.

———. (1983). "Karl Polanyi and Markets in the Ancient Near East: The Challenge of the Evidence," *Journal of Economic History* 43/4: 795–829.

Simpson, William Kelly, ed. (2003). *The Literature of Ancient Egypt: An Anthology of Stories, Instructions, Stelae, Autobiographies, and Poetry.* New Haven, CT: Yale University Press.

Sirks, Boudewijn. (1991). *Food for Rome: The Legal Structure of the Transportation and Processing of Supplies for the Imperial Distributions in Rome and Constantinople.* Studia Amstelodamensia ad Epigraphicam, Ius Antiquum et Papyrologicam Pertinentia 31. Amsterdam: Gieben.

Skyrms, Brian. (1996). *Evolution of the Social Contract.* Cambridge: Cambridge University Press.

Slingerland, Edward, and Mark Collard, eds. (2011). *Creating Consilience: Integrating the Sciences and the Humanities.* Oxford: Oxford University Press.

Slotsky, Alice L. (1997). *The Bourse of Babylon: Market Quotations in the Astronomical Diaries of Babylonia.* Bethesda, MD: CDL.

Slotsky, Alice, and R. Wallenfalls. (2009). *Tallies and Trends: The Late Babylonian Commodity Prices Lists.* Bethesda, MD: CDL.

Smail, Daniel Lord, and Andrew Shryock. (2013). "History and the 'Pre,'" *American Historical Review* 118/3: 709–37.

Smelser, Neil J., and Richard Swedberg, eds. (2005). *The Handbook of Economic Sociology.* Princeton, NJ: Princeton University Press.

Smil, Vaclav. (1994). *Energy in World History:* Boulder: Westview.

Smith, David C., ed. (1989). *Climate, Agriculture and History.* Washington, DC: Agricultural History Society.

Smith, Richard L. (2009). *Premodern Trade in World History.* London: Routledge.

Smith, Stuart Tyson. (1995). *Askut in Nubia: The Economics and Ideology of Egyptian Imperialism in the Second Millennium B.C.* London: Kegan Paul International.

Snape, Steven. (2014). *The Complete Cities of Ancient Egypt.* London: Thames and Hudson.

Snell, Daniel C. (2011). "Slavery in the Ancient Near East," in *The Cambridge World History of Slavery.* Vol. 1, *The Ancient Mediterranean World.* Ed. Bradley Keith and Paul Cartledge. Cambridge: Cambridge University Press. Pp. 4–21.

Solanki, S. K., et al. (2004). "Unusual Activity of the Sun during Recent Decades Compared to the Previous 11,000 Years," *Nature* 431: 1084–87. doi:10.1038/nature 02995

Soudek, Josef. (1952). "Aristotle's Theory of Exchange: An Inquiry into the Origin of Economic Analysis," *Proceedings of the American Philosophical Society* 96/1: 45–75.

Spolaore, Enrico, and Romain Wacziarg. (2013). "How Deep Are the Roots of Economic Development?," *Journal of Economic Literature* 51/2: 325–69. doi: 10.1257/jel.51.2.325.

Spengler, Robert N., III, Pavel E. Tarasov, and Mayke Wagner. (2016). "Introduction to the Special Issue: 'Introduction and Intensification of Agriculture in Central Eurasia and Adjacent Regions'" *Holocene* 26/10: 1523–26.

Spurr, M. S. (1986). *Arable Cultivation in Roman Italy, c. 200 BC–c. AD 100.* London: Society for the Promotion of Roman Studies.

Stanfield, J. Ron. (1986). *The Economic Thought of Karl Polanyi: Lives and Livelihood.* Houndsmills, UK: Macmillan.

Stanley, Jean-Daniel, et al. (2003). "Short Contribution: Nile Flow Failure at the End of the Old Kingdom, Egypt; Strontium Isotopic and Petrologic Evidence," *Geoarchaeology* 18: 395–402.

Stasavage, David. (2011). *States of Credit: Size, Power, and the Development of European Polities*. Princeton, NJ: Princeton University Press.

Staubwasser, M., and Harvey Weiss. (2006). "Holocene Climate and Cultural Evolution in Late Prehistoric-Early Historic West Asia," *Quaternary Research* 66: 372–87.

Stearns, Peter N. (2010). *Globalization in World History*. London: Routledge.

Steel, Louise. (2010)."Egypt and the Mediterranean World," in *The Egyptian World*. Ed. Toby Wilkinson. London: Routledge. Pp. 459–75.

Stein, Gil. (1994). "The Organizational Dynamics of Complexity in Greater Mesopotamia," in *Chiefdoms, and Early States in the Near East: The Organizational Dynamics of Complexity*. Ed. Gil Stein and Mitchell S. Rothman. Madison: Prehistory Press. Pp. 11–22.

Steinkeller, Piotr. (2015). "Labor in the Early States: An Early Mesopotamian Perspective," in *Labor in the Ancient World*. Ed. P. Steinkeller and M. Hudson. Dresden: ISLET-Verlag. Pp. 1–35.

Steinkeller, Piotr, and Michael Hudson, eds. (2015). *Labor in the Ancient World*. Dresden: ISLET-Verlag.

Steward, Julian H. (1955). "Introduction," and "Some Implications of the Symposium," in *Irrigation Civilizations: A Comparative Study; A Symposium on Method and Result in Cross-Cultural Regularities*. Washington, DC: Pan American Union. Pp. 1–5; 58–78.

Stiglitz, Joseph E. (1993). *Economics*. New York: W. W. Norton.

Stiner, Mary C., Timothy Earle, Daniel Lord Smail, and Andrew Shryock. (2011). "Scale," in *Deep History: The Architecture of Past and Present*. Ed. Andrew Shryock and Daniel Lord Smail. Berkeley: University of California Press. Pp. 242–72.

Stolba, Vladimir F. (2007). "Local Patterns of Trade in Wine and the Chronological Implications of Amphora Stamps," in *The Black Sea in Antiquity: Regional and Interregional Economic Exchange*. Ed. Vincent Gabrielsen and John Lund. Aarhus: Aarhus University Press. Pp. 149–59.

———. (2005). "The Oath of Chersonesos and the Chersonesean Economy in the Early Hellenistic Period," in *Making, Moving, and Managing: The New World of Ancient Economies, 323–31 BC*. Ed. Zosia H. Archibald, John K. Davies, and Vincent Gabrielsen. Oxford: Oxbow Books. Pp. 298–321.

Stolper, Matthew W. (2005). "Farming with the Murašûs and Others: Costs and Returns of Cereal Agriculture in Fifth-Century Babylonian Texts," in *Approaching the Babylonian Economy: Proceedings of the START Project Symposium Held in Vienna, 1–3 July 2004*. Ed. H. D. Baker and M. Jursa. Münster: Ugarit-Verlag. Pp. 323–42.

———. (1985). *Entrepreneurs and Empire: The Murašû Archive, the Murašû Firm, and Persian Rule in Babylonia*. Leiden: Nederlands Instituut voor het Nabije oosten.

Streuver, Stuart, and Felicia Antonelli Holton. (1979). *Koster: Americans in Search of Their Prehistoric Past*. Garden City, NJ: Anchor.

Strobel, Karl. (1996). *Die Galater: Geschichte und Eigenart der keltischen Staatenbildung auf den Boden des hellenistischen Kleinasiens*. Vol. 1, *Untersuchungen zur Geschichte und historischen Geographie des hellenistischen und römischen Kleinasiens*. Berlin: Wiley VCH.

Sutch, Richard. (1996). "Macroeconomics: An Introduction for Historians," in *Economics and the Historian*. Ed. T. G. Rawski et al. Berkeley: University of California Press. Pp. 159–76.

Swedberg, Richard. (1998). *Max Weber and the Idea of Economic Sociology*. Princeton, NJ: Princeton University Press.

Taagepera, Rein. (1979). "Size and Duration of Empires: Growth-Decline Curves, 600 B.C. to 600 A.D.," *Social Science History* 3/3–4: 115–38.

———. (1978). "Size and Duration of Empires: Growth-Decline Curves, 3000 to 600 B.C.," *Social Science Research* 7: 180–96.

Tainter, Joseph A. (1988): *The Collapse of Complex Societies*. Cambridge: Cambridge University Press.

Tandy, David W. (1997). *Warriors into Traders: The Power of the Market in Early Greece*. Berkeley: University of California Press.

Tartaron, Thomas F. (2013). *Maritime Networks in the Mycenaean World*. Cambridge: Cambridge University Press.

Taylor, Claire, and Kostas Vlassopoulos, eds. (2015). *Communities and Networks in the Ancient Greek World*. Oxford: Oxford University Press.

Temin, Peter. (2013). *The Roman Market Economy*. Princeton, NJ: Princeton University Press.

Tenney, Jonathan S. (2012). *Life at the Bottom of Babylonian Society: Servile Laborers at Nippur in the 14th and 13th Centuries B.C.* Leiden: Brill.

Thaler, Richard H. (2015). *Misbehaving: The Making of Behavioral Economics*. New York: W. W. Norton.

Thanawala, Kishor. (1997). "Kautilya's *Arthasastra*: A Neglected Work in the History of Economic Thought," in *Ancient Economic Thought*. Ed. B. B. Price. London: Routledge. Pp. 43–58.

Thapar, Romila. (2002). *Early India: From the Origins to AD 1300*. Berkeley: University of California Press.

Thompson, Dorothy J. (2014). "Kleruchic Land in the Ptolemaic Period," in *Law and Legal Practice in Egypt from Alexander to the Arab Conquest: A Selection of Papyrological Sources in Translation, with Introductions and Commentary*. Ed. James G. Keenan, J. G. Manning, and Uri Yiftach-Firanko. Cambridge: Cambridge University Press. Pp. 363–73.

———. (2012). *Memphis under the Ptolemies*. 2d ed. Princeton, NJ: Princeton University Press.

———. (2011). "Slavery in the Hellenistic world," in *The Cambridge World History of Slavery*. Vol. 1, *The Ancient Mediterranean World*. Ed. Keith Bradley and Paul Cartledge. Cambridge: Cambridge University Press. Pp. 194–213.

———. (2000). "Philadelphus' Procession: Dynastic Power in Mediterranean Context," in *Politics, Administration and Society in the Hellenistic and Roman World*. Proceedings of the International Colloquium, Bertinoro, July 19–24, 1997. Ed. Leon Mooren. Studia Hellenistica 36. Pp. 365–88.

———. (1999a). "Irrigation and Drainage in the Early Ptolemaic Fayyum," in *Agriculture in Egypt: From Pharaonic to Modern Times*. Ed. Alan K. Bowman and Eugene Rogan. Oxford: Oxford University Press. Pp. 107–22.

———. (1999b). "New and Old in the Ptolemaic Fayyum," in *Agriculture in Egypt: From Pharaonic to Modern Times*. Ed. Alan K. Bowman and Eugene Rogan. Oxford: Oxford University Press. Pp. 123–38.

Thompson, M., O. Mørkholm, and C. H. Kraay. (1973). *An Inventory of Greek Coin Hoards*. New York: American Numismatic Society.

Thonemann, Peter. (2015). *The Hellenistic Worl: Using Coins as Sources*. Cambridge: Cambridge University Press.

———. ed. (2013). *Attalid Asia Minor: Money, International Relations, and the State*. Oxford: Oxford University Press.

———. (2011). *The Maeander Valley: A Historical Geography from Antiquity to Byzantium*. Cambridge: Cambridge University Press.

Thür, Gerhard. (2015). "Transaction Costs in Athenian Law," in *Law and Transaction Costs in the Ancient Economy*. Ed. Dennis Kehoe, David M. Ratzan, and Uri Yiftach. Ann Arbor: University of Michigan Press. Pp. 36–50.

Tilly, Charles. (1992). *Coercion, Capital and European States: AD 990–1992*. Cambridge, MA: Blackwell.

———. (1984). *Big Structures, Large Processes, Huge Comparisons*. New York: Russell Sage Foundation.

Todd, Stephen C. (1993). *The Shape of Athenian Law*. Oxford: Clarendon.

Tompkins, Daniel P. (2016). "The Making of Moses Finley," in *M. I. Finley: An Ancient Historian and His Impact*. Ed. Daniel Jew, Robin Osborne, and Michael Scott. Cambridge: Cambridge University Press. Pp. 13–30.

———. (2008). "Weber, Polanyi, and Finley," review of Mohammed Nafissi, *Ancient Athens and Modern Ideology: Value, Theory and Evidence in Historical Sciences: Max Weber, Karl Polanyi and Moses Finley*, London: Institute of Classical Studies, 2005, *History and Theory* 47: 123–36.

Toohey, M., Krüger, K., Sigl, M., et al. (2016). "Climatic and Societal Impacts of a Volcanic Double Event at the Dawn of the Middle Ages," *Climatic Change* 136: 401–12.

Totman, Conrad. (1993). *Early Modern Japan*. Berkeley: University of California Press.

Trampier, Joshua R. (2014). *Landscape Archaeology of the Western Nile Delta*. Atlanta: Lockwood.

Trivellato, Francesca. (2011). "Is There a Future for Italian Microhistory in the Age of Global History?," *California Italian Studies* 2/1. http://escholarship.org/uc/item/0z94n9hq.

———. (2009). *The Familiarity of Strangers: The Sephardic Diaspora, Livorno, and Cross-Cultural Trade in the Early Modern Period*. New Haven, CT: Yale University Press.

Trubek, David. (1972). "Max Weber on Law and the Rise of Capitalism," *Wisconsin Law Review* 720–53. http://digitalcommons.law.yale.edu/fss_papers/4001.

Tsakirgis, Barbara. (2016). "Whole Cloth: Exploring the Question of Self-Sufficiency through the Evidence for Textile Manufacture and Purchase in Greek Houses," in *The Ancient Greek Economy: Markets, Households and City-States*. Ed. Edward M. Harris, David M. Lewis, and Mark Woolmer. Cambridge: Cambridge University Press. Pp. 166–86.

Tsetskhladze, Gocha R. (2008). *Greek Colonisation: An Account of Greek Colonies and Other Settlements Overseas*. Vol. 2. Leiden: Brill.

———. (2006). *Greek Colonisation: An Account of Greek Colonies and Other Settlements Overseas*. Vol. 1. Leiden: Brill.

Turchin, Peter. (2016). *Ages of Discord: A Structural-Demographic Analysis of American History*. Chaplin, CT: Beresta Books.

———. (2015a). *Ultrasociety: How 10,000 Years of War Made Humans the Greatest Cooperators on Earth*. Chaplin, CT: Beresta Books.

———. (2015b). "Seshat: The Global History Databank," *Cliodynamics* 6: 77–107.

———. (2014). "Cultural Evolution and Cliodynamics," *Cliodynamics* 5/1: 1–3.

———. (2013). "The Puzzle of Human Ultrasociality: How Did Large-Scale Complex Societies Evolve?," in *Cultural Evolution: Society, Technology, Language, and Religion*. Ed. Peter J. Richerson and Morten H. Christiansen. Strüngmann Forum Reports 12, Cambridge, MA: MIT Press. Pp. 61–73.

———. (2010). "Warfare and the Evolution of Social Complexity: A Multi-level-Selection Approach," *Structure and Dynamics* 4/3. http://escholarship.org/uc/item/7j11945r.

———. (2009). "A Theory for Formation of Large Empires," *Journal of Global History* 4: 191–217.

———. (2007). *War and Peace and War: The Rise and Fall of Empires.* New York: Plume/Penguin.

———. (2003). *Historical Dynamics: Why States Rise and Fall.* Princeton, NJ: Princeton University Press.

Turchin, Peter, Rob Brennan, Thomas E. Currie, Kevin C. Feeney, Pieter Francois, Daniel Hoyer, J. G. Manning, Arkadiusz Marciniak, Daniel Mullins, Alessio Palmisano, Peter Peregrine, Edward A. L. Turner, and Harvey Whitehouse. (2015). "Seshat: The Global History Databank," *Cliodynamics* 6: 77–107. http://escholarship.org/uc/item/9qx38718.

Turchin, Peter, and Sergey A. Nefedov. (2009). *Secular Cycles.* Princeton, NJ: Princeton University Press.

Turchin, Peter, Harvey Whitehouse, Pieter François, Edward Slingerland, and Mark Collard. (2012). "A Historical Database of Sociocultural Evolution," *Cliodynamics* 3/2: 271–93. http://escholarship.org/uc/item/2v8119hf.

Usokin, I. G., S. K. Solanki, and G. A. Kovaltsov. (2008). "Grand Minima and Maxima of Solar Activity: New Observational Constraints," *Astronomy and Astrophysics* 471: 301–9.

Van Alfen, Peter. (2016). "Aegean-Levantine Trade, 600–300 BCE: Commodities, Consumers, and the Problems of Autarkeia," in *The Ancient Greek Economy: Markets, Households and City-States.* Ed. Edward M. Harris, David M. Lewis, and Mark Woolmer. Cambridge: Cambridge University Press. Pp. 277–98.

Van Bavel, Bas. (2010). *Manor and Markets: Economy and Society in the Low Countries, 500–1600.* Oxford: Oxford University Press.

Van Beek, Bart, and Mark Depauw. (2013). "Quantifying Imprecisely Dated Sources: A Mew Inclusive Method for Charting Diachronic Change in Graeco-Roman Egypt," *Ancient Society* 43: 101–14.

Van de Mieroop, Marc. (2007). *The Eastern Mediterranean in the Age of Ramesses II.* Malden, MA: Blackwell.

———. (2005). "The Invention of Interest: Sumerian Loans," in *The Origins of Value: The Financial Innovations That Created Modern Capital Markets.* Ed. William N. Goetzmann and K. Geert Rouwenhorst. New York: Oxford University Press. Pp. 17–30.

———. (2004). "Economic Theories and the Ancient Near East," in *Commerce and Monetary Systems in the Ancient World: Means of Transmission and Cultural Interaction.* Ed. Robert Bollinger and Christoph Ulf. Oriens et Occidens 6. Stuttgart: Franz Steiner Verlag. Pp. 54–64.

———. (2002). "Credit as a Facilitator of Exchange in Old Babylonian Mesopotamia," in *Debt and Economic Renewal in the Ancient Near East.* Ed. Michael Hudson and Marc van de Mieroop. Bethesda, MD: CDL. Pp. 163–73.

———. (1999). *The Ancient Mesopotamian City.* Oxford: Oxford University Press.

van der Brugge, Caroline, and Kristin Kleber. (2016). "The Empire of Trade and the Empires of Force: Tyre in the Neo-Assyrian and Neo-Babylonian Periods," in *Dynamics of Production in the Ancient Near East, 1300–500 BC.* Ed. Juan Carlos Moreno García. Oxford: Oxbow. Pp. 187–222.

van der Spek, R. J. (2014). "The Volatility of Prices of Barley and Dates in Babylon in the Third and Second Centuries BC," in *Documentary Sources on Ancient Near Eastern and Greco-Roman Economic History: Methodology and Practice*. Ed. Heather D. Baker and Michael Jursa. Oxford: Oxbow. Pp. 234–59.

———. (2011). "The 'Silverization' of the Economy of the Achaemenid and Seleukid Empires and Early Modern China," in *The Economies of Hellenistic Societies, Third to First Centuries BC*. Ed. Zosia H. Archibald, John K. Davies, and Vincent Gabrielsen. Oxford: Oxford University Press. Pp. 402–20.

———. (2008). "Feeding Hellenistic Seleucia on the Tigris and Babylon," in *Feeding the Ancient Greek City*. Ed. R. Alston and O. M. van Nijf. Leuven: Peeters. Pp. 33–45.

———. (2005). "How to Measure Prosperity? The Case of Hellenistic Babylon," in *Approches de l'économie hellénistique*. Ed. R. Descat. St-Bertrand-de-Comminges: Musée archéologique de Saint-Bertrand-de-Comminges. Pp. 287–310.

van der Spek, R. J., and C. A. Mandemakers. (2003). "Sense and Nonsense in the Statistical Approach of Babylonian Prices," *Bibliotheca Orientalis* 60/5–6: 521–37.

van der Spek, R. J., and Bas van Leeuwen. (2014). "Quantifying the Integration of the Babylonian Economy in the Mediterranean World Using a Corpus of Price Data, 400–50 BCE," in *Quantifying the Greco-Roman Economy and Beyond*. Ed. François de Callataÿ. Bari: Edipuglia. Pp. 79–101.

van der Spek, R. J., Bas van Leeuwen, and Jan Luiten van Zanden, eds. (2015). *A History of Market Performance: From Ancient Babylonia to the Modern World*. London: Routledge.

Vandorpe, Katelijn. (2015). "Selling Private Real Estate in a New Monarchical Setting: Sale and Community in Hellenistic Egypt," in *Sale and Community Documents from the Ancient World: Individuals' Autonomy and State Interference in the Ancient World*. Legal Documents in Ancient Societies 5. Graeca Tergestina Storia e Civiltà 2. Ed. Éva Jakab. Trieste: EUT Edizioni Università di Trieste. Pp. 99–115.

———. (2009). "Archives and Dossiers," in *The Oxford Handbook of Papyrology*. Ed. Roger S. Bagnall. Oxford: Oxford University Press. Pp. 216–55.

———. (2002). *The Bilingual Family Archive of Dryton, His Wife Apollonia and Their Daughter Senmouthis*. Collectanea Hellenistica 4. Brussels: Koninklijke Vlaamse Academie van België.

Vandorpe, Katelijn, Willy Clarysse, and Herbert Verreth. (2015). *Graeco-Roman Archives from the Fayum*. Collectanea Hellenistica 6. Leuven: Peeters.

Vandorpe, Katelijn, and Sofie Waebens. (2009). *Reconstructing Pathyris' Archives: A Multicultural Community in Hellenistic Egypt*. Brussels: Koninklijke Vlaamse Academie van België voor Wetenschappen en Kunsten.

van Leeuwen, Bas, Peter Foldvari, and Jan Luiten van Zanden. (2015). "Long-Run Patterns in Market Performance in the Near East, the Mediterranean and Europe from Antiquity to c. AD 1800," in *A History of Market Performance: From Ancient Babylonia to the Modern World*. Ed. R. J. van der Spek, Bas van Leeuwen, and Jan Luiten van Zanden. London: Routledge. Pp. 506–25.

Vargyas, Peter. (2010). "The Alleged Silver Bars of the Temple of Ptah: Traditional Money Use in Achaemenid, Ptolemaic and Roman Egypt," in *From Elephantine to Babylon: Selected Studies of Peter Vargyas on Ancient Near Eastern Economy*. Ed. Zoltan Csabai. Budapest: L'Harmattan. Pp. 165–76. Originally published in *Cultus Deorum: Studia Religionum ad Historiam I; De Oriente Antiquo et Regione Danuvii Praehistorica in Memoriam István Tóth*. Pecs: Szerzök, 2008, pp. 123–38.

———. (2000). "Silver and Money in AChaemedni and Hellenistic Babylonia," in *Assyriologica et Semitica: Festschrift für Joachim Oelsner*. Ed. J. Marzahn and H. Neumann. Münster: Ugarit-Verlag. Pp. 513–21.

———. (1999). "*Kaspu ginnu* and the Monetary Reform of Darius I," *Zeitschrift für Assyriologie und Vorderasiatische Archäologie* 89: 263–84.

Veblen, Thorstein B. (1899). *The Theory of the Leisure Class: An Economic Study in the Evolution of Institutions*. New York: Modern Library.

———. (1898). "Why Is Economics Not an Evolutionary Science?," *Quarterly Journal of Economics*, 12/3: 373–97.

Veïsse, A.-E. (2004). *Les "Revoltes égyptiennes": Recherches sur les troubles intérieurs en Égypte du règne Ptolémée III à la conquete romaine*. Leuven: Peeters

Verboven, Koenraad. (2015a). "The Knights Who Say NIE: Can Neo-institutional Economics Live Up to Its Expectation in Ancient History Research?," in *Structure and Performance in the Ancient Economy: Models, Methods and Case Studies*. Ed. Paul Erdkamp and Koenraad Verboven. Brussels: Éditions Latomus. Pp. 33–57.

———. (2015b). "Models or Muddles? What Are Theories Good for in Ancient Economic History?," in *Structure and Performance in the Ancient Economy: Models, Methods and Case Studies*. Ed. Paul Erdkamp and Koenraad Verboven. Brussels: Éditions Latomus. Pp. 9–14.

Verboven, Koenraad, and J. Poblome, eds. (n.d.). "Complexity: A New Framework to Interpret Ancient Economic Proxy Data," unpublished manuscript.

Verhoogt, Arthur. (1998). *Menches, Komogrammateus of Kerkeosiris: The Doings and Dealings of a Village Scribe in the Late Ptolemaic Period (120–110 BC)*. Leiden: Brill.

Veyne, Paul. (1976). *Le pain et le cirque: Sociologie historique d'un pluralisme politique*. Paris: Seuil. English edition: *Bread and Circuses: Historical Sociology and Political Pluralism*. Trans. Brian Pearce, London, 1990.

Villing, Alexandra, and Udo Schlotzhauer, eds. (2006). *Naukratis: Greek Diversity in Egypt*. London: British Museum.

Vinson, Steve. (2011). "Strictly Tabubue: The Legacy of an Ancient Egyptian Femme Fatale," *KMT: A Modern Journal of Ancient Egypt* 22/3: 46–57.

———. (2008). "Through a Woman's Eyes, and in a Woman's Voice: Ihweret as Focalizor in the *First Tale of Setne Khaemwas*," in *Ptolemy II Philadelphus and His World*. Ed. Paul McKechnie and Philippe Guillaume. Leiden: Brill. Pp. 303–51.

Vlassopoulos, Kostas. (2013). *Greeks and Barbarians*. Cambridge: Cambridge University Press.

———. (2011). "Greek Slavery: From Domination to Property and Back Again," *Journal of Hellenic Studies* 131: 115–30.

———. (2007). *Unthinking the Greek Polis: Ancient Greek History beyond Eurocentrism*. Cambridge: Cambridge University Press.

Vleeming, Sven P. (2011). *Demotic and Greek-Demotic Mummy Labels and Other Short Texts Gathered from Many Publications*. 2 vols. Leuven: Peeters.

———. (1993). *Papyrus Reinhardt: An Egyptian Land List from the Tenth Century B.C.* Berlin: Akademie Verlag.

———. (1991). *The Gooseherds of Hou*. Leuven: Peeters.

von Dassow, Eva. (2011). "Freedom in Ancient Near Eastern Societies," in *The Oxford Handbook of Cuneiform Culture*. Ed. Karen Radner and Eleanor Robson. Oxford: Oxford University Press. Pp. 205–24.

von Reden, Sitta. (2015). *Antike Wirtschaft*. Berlin: De Gruyter.

———. (2010). *Money in Classical Antiquity*. Cambridge: Cambridge University Press.

———. (2007). *Money in Ptolemaic Egypt: From the Macedonian Conquest to the End of the Third Century BC*. Cambridge: Cambridge University Press.

———. (2005). *Exchange in Ancient Greece*. London: Duckworth.

———. (2002). "Money in the Ancient Economy: A Survey of Recent Research," *Klio* 84: 141–74.

Waerzeggers, Caroline. (2014). "Social Network Analysis of Cuneiform Archives—a New Approach," in *Documentary Sources in Ancient Near Eastern and Greco-Roman Economic History: Methodology and Practice*. Ed. Heather D. Baker and Michael Jursa. Oxford: Oxbow. Pp. 207–33.

Walbank, Frank. (2004). "Finley, Sir Moses I. (1912–86)," in *Dictionary of National Biography 1986–2000*. Oxford: Clarendon. Pp. 6720–21.

Waldbaum, J. C. (1978). *From Bronze to Iron: The Transition from the Bronze Age to the Iron Age in the Eastern Mediterranean*. Göteborg: Paul Åströms Förlag.

Wallerstein, Immanuel. (1974). *The Modern World-System I: Capitalist Agriculture and the Origins of the European World-Economy in the Sixteenth Century*. New York: Academic Press.

Wallis, John Joseph. (2014). "Persistence and Change in Institutions: The Evolution of Douglass North," in *Institutions, Property Rights, and Economic Growth: The Legacy of Douglass North*. Ed. Sebastian Galiani and Itai Sened. Cambridge: Cambridge University Press. Pp. 30–49.

Wandsnider, LuAnn. (2004). "Solving the Puzzle of the Archaeological Labyrinth: Time Perspectivism in Mediterranean Surface Archaeology," in *Side-by-Side Survey: Comparative Regional Studies in the Mediterranean World*. Ed. Susan E. Alcock and John F. Cherry. Oxford: Oxbow Books. Pp. 49–62.

Warburton, David A. (2003). *Macroeconomics from the Beginning: The General Theory, Ancient Markets, and the Rate of Interest*. Neuchâtel: Recherches et Publications.

———. (1997) *State and Temple Economy in Ancient Egypt: Fiscal Vocabulary of the New Kingdom*. Fribourg: University Press.

Waterfield, Robin. (1998). *Herodotus: The Histories*. Oxford: Oxford University Press.

Weber, Max. (1998[1909]). *The Agrarian Sociology of Ancient Civilizations*. Trans. R. I. Frank. London: Verso. First published as *Agrarverhältnisse im Altertum*, 1909.

———. (1978). *Economy and Society: An Outline of Interpretive Sociology*. Ed. Guenther Roth and Claus Wittich. 2 vols. Berkeley: University of California Press.

———. (1904). "Objectivity in Social Science and Social Policy," in *The Methodology of the Social Sciences*. New York: Free Press.

Weiss, Harvey. (2016). "Global: Megadrought, Societal Collapse and Resilience at 4.2–3.9 ka BP across the Mediterranean and West Asia," *PAGES* 24/2: 62–63.

———. (2015). "Megadrought, Collapse, and Resilience in Late 3rd Millennium BC Mesopotamia," in *2200 BC- Ein Klimasturz als Ursache für den Zerfall der Alten Welt?* Ed. Harald Meller, Helge Wolfgang Arz, Reinhard Jung, and Roberto Risch. Halle: Landmuseum für Vorgeschichte. Pp. 35–52.

———. ed. (2012). *Seven Generations since the Fall of Akkad*. Wiesbaden: Harrassowitz.

Weiss, Harvey, M.-A. Courty, W. Wetterstrom, F. Guichard, L. Senior, R. Meadow, and A. Curnow. (1993). "The Genesis of Collapse of Third Millennium North Mesopotamia Civilization," *Science* 261: 995–1004.

Wengrow, David. (2006). *The Archaeology of Early Egypt: Social Transformations in North-East Africa, 10,000 to 2650 BC*. Cambridge: Cambridge University Press.

Wente, Edward F. (2003). "The Report of Wenamun," in *The Literature of Ancient Egypt: An Anthology of Stories, Instructions, Stelae, Autobiographies, and Poetry.* Ed. William Kelly Simpson. New Haven, CT: Yale University Press. Pp. 116–24.

Wertime, Theodore A. (1982). "Cypriot Metallurgy against the Backdrop of Mediterranean Pyrotechnology: Energy Reconsidered," in *Early Metallurgy in Cyprus, 4000–500 B.C.* Ed. James D. Muhly, Robert Maddin, and Vassos Karageorghis. Nicosia: Department of Antiquities. Pp. 351–61.

Westbrook, Raymond. (2003a). "The Character of Ancient Near Eastern Law," in *A History of Ancient Near Eastern Law.* Ed. Raymond Westbrook. Vol. 1. Leiden: Brill. Pp. 1–90.

———. ed. (2003b). *A History of Ancient Near Eastern Law.* 2 vols. Leiden: Brill.

———. (2001). "Conclusions," in *Security for Debt in Ancient Near Eastern Law.* Ed. Raymond Westbrook and Richard Jasnow. Leiden: Brill. Pp. 327–40.

Westbrook, Raymond, and Richard Jasnow, eds. (2001). *Security for Debt in Ancient Near Eastern Law.* Leiden: Brill.

White, K. D. (1970). *Roman Farming.* London: Thames and Hudson.

White, Sam. (2013). "The Real Little Ice Age," *Journal of Interdisciplinary History* 44: 327–52.

———. (2011). *The Climate of Rebellion in the Early Modern Ottoman Empire.* New York: Cambridge University Press.

Whitman, James Q. (1995). "At the Origins of Law and the State: Supervision of Violence, Mutilation of Bodies, or Setting of Prices?," *Chicago Kent Law Review* 71/1: 41–84.

Whittow, Mark. (2007). "Beyond the Cultural Turn: Economic History Revived?," *Journal of Roman Archaeology* 20: 697–704.

Wickham, Christopher. (2005). *Framing the Early Middle Ages: Europe and the Mediterranean 400–800.* Oxford: Oxford University Press.

Wiesehöfer, Josef. (2009). "The Achaemenid Empire," in *The Dynamics of Ancient Empires: State Power from Assyria to Byzantium.* Ed. Ian Morris and Walter Scheidel. New York: Oxford University Press. Pp. 66–98.

———. (1982). "Beobachtungen zum Handel des Achämenidenreiches," *Münstersche Beiträge zur Antiken Handelsgeschichte* 1: 5–15.

Wikander, Charlotte. (2008). "Technologies of Calculation," in *The Oxford Handbook of Engineering and Technology in the Classical World.* Ed. Örjan Wikander. Leiden: Brill. Pp. 759–69.

Wikander, Örjan, ed. (2000). *Handbook of Ancient Water Technology.* Leiden: Brill.

Wilcken, Ulrich. (1967). *Alexander the Great.* Trans. G. C. Richards. New York: Norton.

Wilk, Richard R., and Lisa C. Cliggett. (2007). *Economies and Cultures: Foundations of Economic Anthropology.* 2d ed. Cambridge: Westview.

Wilkinson, Endymion. (2000). *Chinese History: A Manual.* Revised and enlarged. Harvard-Yenching Institute Monograph Series 52. Cambridge, MA: Harvard University Asia Center.

Wilkinson, T. J. (2010). "Empire and Environment in the Northern Fertile Crecent," in *Landscape and Societies: Selected Cases.* Ed. I. Peter Martini and Ward Chesworth. Dordrecht: Springer. Pp. 135–51.

———. (2003). *Archaeological Landscapes of the Near East.* Tucson: University of Arizona Press.

Wilkinson, Toby C., ed. (2007). *The Egyptian World.* London: Routledge.

Wilkinson, Toby C., Susan Sherratt, and John Bennet, eds. (2011). *Interweaving Worlds: Systemic Interactions in Eurasia, 7th to 1st Millennia BC*. Oxford: Oxbow Books.

Williams, David F. (2004). "The Eruption of Vesuvius and Its Implications for the Early Roman Amphora Trade with India," in *Transport Amphorae and Trade in the Eastern Mediterranean: Acts of the International Colloquium at the Danish Institute at Athens*. Ed. Jonas Eiring and John Lund. Aarhus: Aarhus University Press. Pp. 441–50.

Williamson, Oliver E. (2002). "The Lens of Contract: Private Ordering," *American Economic Review* 92: 438–43.

———. (2000). "The New Institutional Economics: Taking Stock, Looking Ahead," *Journal of Economic Literature* 38: 595–613.

———. (1975). *Markets and Hierarchies: Analysis and Antitrust Implications*. New York: Free Press.

Wilson, Andrew. (2014). "Quantifying Roman Economic Performance by Means of Proxies: Pitfalls and Potential," in *Long-Term Quantification in Ancient Mediterranean History*. Ed. François de Callataÿ. Bari: Edipuglia. Pp. 147–67.

———. (2013). "Trading across the Syrtes: Euesperides and the Punic World," in *The Hellenistic West: Rethinking the Ancient Mediterranean*. Ed. Jonathan R. W. Prag and Josephine Crawley Quinn. Cambridge: Cambridge University Press. Pp. 120–56.

———. (2011a). "Developments in Mediterranean Shipping and Maritime Trade from the Hellenistic Period to AD 1000," in *Maritime Archaeology and Ancient Trade in the Mediterranean*. Ed. Damian Robinson and Andrew Wilson. Oxford: Oxford Centre for Maritime Archaeology. Pp. 33–59.

———. (2011b). "The Economic Influences of Developments in Maritime Technology in Antiquity," in *Maritime Technology in the Ancient Economy: Ship-Design and Navigation*. Ed. W. V. Harris and K. Iara. Portsmouth, RI: Journal of Roman Archaeology. Pp. 211–33.

———. (2009). "Approaches to Quantifying Roman Trade," in *Quantifying the Roman Economy: Methods and Problems*. Ed. Alan K. Bowman and Andrew Wilson. Oxford: Oxford University Press. Pp. 213–49.

———. (2008). "Machines in Greek and Roman Technology," in *The Oxford Handbook of Engineering and Technology in the Classical World*. Ed. J. P. Oleson. Oxford: Oxford University Press. Pp. 351–52.

———. (2002). "Machines, Power and the Ancient Economy," *Journal of Roman Studies* 92: 1–32.

Wilson, David Sloan. (2006). "Human Groups as Adaptive Units: Toward a Permanent Consensus," in *The Innate Mind*. Vol. 2, *Culture and Cognition*. Ed. P. Carruthers, S. Laurence, and S. Stich. Oxford: Oxford University Press. Pp. 78–90.

———. (2002). *Darwin's Cathedral: Evolution, Religion, and the Nature of Society*. Chicago: University of Chicago Press.

Wilson, Edward O. (1998). *Consilience: The Unity of Knowledge*. New York: Knopf.

Witt, Ulrich. (2008). "Evolutionary Economics," in *The New Palgrave Dictionary of Economics*. 2d ed. Ed. Steven N. Durlauf and Lawrence E. Blume. Palgrave Macmillan. *The New Palgrave Dictionary of Economics Online*. Site imprint Palgrave Macmillan. Accessed August 19, 2016. http://www.dictionaryofeconomics.com/article?id=pde2008_000295. doi: 10.1057/9780230226203.0511.

Wittfogel, Karl A. (1957). *Oriental Despotism: A Comparative Study of Total Power*. New Haven, CT: Yale University Press.

Wolff, Hans-Julius. (1962). *Das Justizwesen der Ptolemäer.* Münchener Beiträge zur Papyrusforschung und antiken Rechtsgeschichte 44. Munich: Beck.

Woodard, Roger D. (1997). *Greek Writing from Knossos to Homer: A Linguistic Interpretation of the Origin of the Greek Alphabet and the Continuity of Ancient Greek Literacy.* Oxford: Oxford University Press.

Woolf, Greg. (1990). "World-Systems Analysis and the Roman Empire," *Journal of Roman Archaeology* 3: 44–58.

Woolmer, Mark. (2016). "Forging Links between Regions," in *The Ancient Greek Economy: Markets, Households and City-States.* Ed. Edward M. Harris, David M. Lewis, and Mark Woolmer. Cambridge: Cambridge University Press. Pp. 66–89.

Wootton, David. (2015). *The Invention of Science: A New History of the Scientific Revolution.* New York: HarperCollins.

Wrightson, Keith. (2011). *Ralph Tailor's Summer: A Scrivener, His City and the Plague.* New Haven, CT: Yale University Press.

Wrigley, E. A. (2010). *Energy and the English Industrial Revolution.* Cambridge: Cambridge University Press.

Wulf, Andrea. (2015). *The Invention of Nature: Alexander von Humboldt's New World.* New York: Knopf.

Wunsch, Cornelia. (2010). "Neo-Babylonian Entrepreneurs," in *The Invention of Enterprise: Entrepreneurship from Ancient Mesopotamia to Modern Times.* Ed. David S. Landes, Joel Mokyr, and William J. Baumol. Princeton, NJ: Princeton University Press. Pp. 40–61.

———. (2009). "The Egibi Family," in *The Babylonian World.* Ed. Gwendolyn Leick. Paperback ed. Oxford: Routledge. Pp. 236–47.

———. (1999). "The Egibi Family's Real Estate in Babylon (6th century BC)," in *Urbanization and Land Ownership in the Ancient Near East.* Ed. Michael Hudson and Baruch A. Levine. Cambridge, MA: Peabody Museum of Archaeology and Ethnology. Pp. 391–413.

Wunsch, Cornelia, and F. Rachel Magdelene. (2014). "Freedom and Dependency: Neo-Babylonian Manumission Documents with Oblation and Service Obligation," in *Extraction and Control: Studies in Honor of Matthew W. Stolper.* Ed. Michael Kozuh, Charles E. Jones, and Christopher Woods. Chicago: Oriental Institute. Pp. 337–46.

Yiftach-Firanko, Uri. (2014). "Evolutions of Forms of Greek Documents of the Ptolemaic, Roman, and Byzantine Periods," in *Law and Legal Practice in Egypt from Alexander to the Arab Conquest: A Selection of Papyrological Sources in Translation, with Introductions and Commentary.* Ed. James G. Keenan, J. G. Manning, and Uri Yiftach-Firanko. Cambridge: Cambridge University Press. Pp. 35–53.

———. (2009). "Law in Graeco-Roman Egypt: Hellenization, Fusion, Romanization," in *The Oxford Handbook of Papyrology.* Ed. Roger S. Bagnall. Oxford: Oxford University Press. Pp. 541–60.

Yoffee, Norman. (2015). *The Cambridge World History* Vol. 3, *Early Cities in Comparative Perspective, 4000 BCE–1200 CE.* Cambridge: Cambridge University Press.

Young, T. Cuyler. (1988). "The Early History of the Medes and the Persians and the Achaemenid Empire to the Death of Cambyses," in *The Cambridge Ancient History.* Vol. 4. 2d ed. Ed. John Boardman, N.G.L. Hammond, D. M. Lewis, and M. Ostwald. Cambridge: Cambridge University Press. Pp. 1–52.

Zeilinga de Boer, Jelle, and Donald Theodore Sanders. (2002). *Volcanoes in Human History: The Far-Reaching Effects of Major Eruptions*. Princeton, NJ: Princeton University Press.

Zettler, R. L. (2003). "Reconstructing the World of Ancient Mesopotamia: Divided Beginnings and Holistic History," *Journal of the Economic and Social History of the Orient* 46: 3–45.

Zurbach, Julien, ed. (2015). *La main-d'oeuvre agricole en Méditerranée archaïque: Statuts et dynamiques économiques; Actes des journées 'Travail de la terre et statuts de la main-d'oeuvre en Grèce et en Méditerranée Archaïques', Athènes, 15 et 16 décembre 2008; Scripta antiqua, 73*. Athens: École française d'Athènes.

———. (2013). "La formation des cités grecques," *Annales: Histoire, Sciences Sociales* 68/4: 957–98.

———. (2009). "Paysanneries de la Grèce archaïque," *Histoire et Sociétés rurales* 31/1: 9–44.

INDEX

Page numbers followed by *f*, *m*, or *t* denote figures, maps, and tables, respectively.